AF804937

The Wiley Handbook of Personality Assessment

The Wiley Handbook of Personality Assessment

Edited by

Updesh Kumar

F 414

PSYCHOLOGISCHES INSTITUT Bibliothek UNIVERSITÄT ZÜRICH

WILEY Blackwell

This edition first published 2016
© 2016 John Wiley & Sons, Ltd.

Registered Office
John Wiley & Sons, Ltd, The Atrium, Southern Gate, Chichester, West Sussex, PO19 8SQ, UK

Editorial Offices
350 Main Street, Malden, MA 02148-5020, USA
9600 Garsington Road, Oxford, OX4 2DQ, UK
The Atrium, Southern Gate, Chichester, West Sussex, PO19 8SQ, UK

For details of our global editorial offices, for customer services, and for information about how to apply for permission to reuse the copyright material in this book please see our website at www.wiley.com/wiley-blackwell.

The right of Updesh Kumar to be identified as the author of the editorial material in this work has been asserted in accordance with the UK Copyright, Designs and Patents Act 1988.

All rights reserved. No part of this publication may be reproduced, stored in a retrieval system, or transmitted, in any form or by any means, electronic, mechanical, photocopying, recording or otherwise, except as permitted by the UK Copyright, Designs and Patents Act 1988, without the prior permission of the publisher.

Wiley also publishes its books in a variety of electronic formats. Some content that appears in print may not be available in electronic books.

Designations used by companies to distinguish their products are often claimed as trademarks. All brand names and product names used in this book are trade names, service marks, trademarks or registered trademarks of their respective owners. The publisher is not associated with any product or vendor mentioned in this book.

Limit of Liability/Disclaimer of Warranty: While the publisher and authors have used their best efforts in preparing this book, they make no representations or warranties with respect to the accuracy or completeness of the contents of this book and specifically disclaim any implied warranties of merchantability or fitness for a particular purpose. It is sold on the understanding that the publisher is not engaged in rendering professional services and neither the publisher nor the author shall be liable for damages arising herefrom. If professional advice or other expert assistance is required, the services of a competent professional should be sought.

Library of Congress Cataloging-in-Publication data applied for

HB ISBN: 9781119173441

A catalogue record for this book is available from the British Library.

Cover image: Zmeel Photography/Getty

Set in 10/12.5pt Galliard by SPi Global, Pondicherry, India
Printed and bound in Malaysia by Vivar Printing Sdn Bhd

1 2016

Dedicated to:
My wife Anju, son Kushal, and daughter Dakshi for their unconditional support and encouragement

Contents

About the Editor

Updesh Kumar, PhD, is Scientist 'G' and Head of the Mental Health Division at Defence Institute of Psychological Research (DIPR), R & D Organization (DRDO), Ministry of Defence, Delhi. Since obtaining his doctorate degree in the area of suicidal behavior from Punjab University, Chandigarh, India, he has more than 24 years of experience as a Scientist in an R&D organization. He specializes in the area of personality assessment, suicidal behavior and test development (personality and intelligence). Dr Kumar has been involved in the selection of officers and Personnel Below Officers' Rank (PBOR) as well as responsible for monitoring the selection system of the Indian Armed Forces for the last 24 years. Dr Kumar has edited seven quality volumes on *Recent Developments of Psychology* (DIPR, 2006), *Counseling: A Practical Approach* (Academic Excellence, 2010), *Suicidal Behaviour: Assessment of People-at-Risk* (SAGE, 2010), *Countering Terrorism: Psychosocial Strategies* (SAGE, 2012), *Understanding Suicide Terrorism: Psychosocial Dynamics* (SAGE, 2014), *Suicidal Behaviour: Underlying Dynamics* (Routledge, 2015), *Positive Psychology: Applications in Work, Health and Well-being* (Pearson Education, 2015), and most recently *The Routledge International Handbook of Psychosocial Resilience* (in press). The books published with SAGE and Routledge have been completed in collaboration with internationally acclaimed academics/researchers from India, the US, the UK, Australia, Singapore, Israel, France, Belarus, Germany, Italy, Hungary, Hong Kong, Norway, Ireland, Ukraine, the Netherlands, and Spain. Dr Kumar has also authored manuals on *Suicide and Fratricide: Dynamics and Management* for defense personnel, *Managing Emotions in Daily Life & at Work Place* for the general population, *Overcoming Obsolescence & Becoming Creative in R&D Environment* for R&D organizations, and *Self-Help Techniques in Military Settings*. He has authored more than 50 other academic publications in the form of research papers, journal articles, and book chapters, and represented his institute at national and international level. Dr Kumar has been a psychological assessor (Psychologist) on various Services Selection Boards for eight years for the selection of officers in the Indian Armed Forces, and also on the selection panel with the prestigious Union Public Service Commission (UPSC), Government of India. He is certified as a psychologist by the British Psychological Society with level 'A' and level 'B' Certificates of Competence in Occupational Testing. He has to his credit many important research projects relating to the Indian Armed Forces. He was conferred with the

DRDO's Best Popular Science Communication Award 2009 by the Hon'ble Defence Minister of India. He has also been the recipient of the DRDO Technology Group Award in 2001 and 2009, Professor Manju Thakur Memorial Award 2009 and 2012 by the Indian Academy of Applied Psychology (IAAP), and the Professor N.N. Sen Best Paper Award for the year 2010 by the Indian Association of Clinical Psychologists (IACP). Recently, he has been conferred with the Laboratory Scientist of the Year Award 2012–2013, and the prestigious DRDO's Scientist of the Year Award 2013 by the Government of India.

About the Contributors

Filippo Aschieri, PhD, is Assistant Professor of Psychology at the Università Cattolica del Sacro Cuore (UCSC) of Milan, Italy. He works at the European Center for Therapeutic Assessment (ECTA) at UCSC as a clinician and supervisor, and serves on the ECTA's Board. He also is a member of the faculty and Executive Committee of the Therapeutic Assessment Institute, a non-profit transnational organization that coordinates training and certification in therapeutic assessment. His current research interests include therapeutic assessment, multicultural assessment, and psychotherapy process and outcome. In 2012 Dr Aschieri was awarded the Martin Mayman Award by the Society for Personality Assessment for distinguished contribution to the personality assessment literature.

Spencer R. Baker, PhD, is an Associate Professor in the Department of Counseling and a Research Scientist with the Behavioral Science Research Center, Hampton University. Dr Baker's primary research interests include adolescent cognitive development, adolescent behavior problems including development of psychopathologies, and the antecedents of adult personality within the context of family and neighborhood. As a methodologist and a psychometrician, he has been actively involved with the Behavioral Science Research Center since 1997. He has authored and co-authored several publications and book chapters and made presentations at international and national conferences on the development of personality and psychopathologies. In these endeavors, Dr. Baker is a co-author of an instrument, the Child Temperament and Personality Questionnaire (CTPQ), that will bridge the gap between measurement of temperament and personality. He is currently using this instrument as a self-report for children aged 10 to 16 years, along with the new NEO Personality Inventory 3 (NEO-PI 3), a more readable version. Currently, he is working on the psychometric properties of both instruments with adolescent and inmate populations.

Reuven Bar-On, PhD, has worked as a psychologist for both public and private organizations since 1972. One of his primary areas of scholarly involvement has been in emotional and social intelligence, and he is acknowledged as one of the leading theorists, researchers and practitioners in this field today. The "Bar-On model of emotional intelligence" is described in the *Encyclopedia of Applied Psychology* as one of the three main approaches to this concept, and the term "EQ" was coined by him in 1985 to describe his approach to assessing it. He began developing the precursor to the *Emotional Quotient Inventory*™ in 1980, which is the first measure of this concept to be published by a psychological test publisher. He developed, co-developed or has acted as a consultant in developing eight other instruments since 1978. The most recent psychometric instrument that Dr Bar-On has developed is the *Multifactor Measure of Performance*™. He has examined the ability of these various instruments to predict different aspects of human behavior and performance. Dr Bar-On has contributed 50 publications in the area of emotional and social intelligence alone, which have been cited more than 7,000 times in articles, books, encyclopedias and doctoral dissertations.

Larry E. Beutler received his PhD from the University of Nebraska and subsequently served on the faculties of Duke University Medical Center, Stephen F. Austin State University, Baylor College of Medicine, the University of Arizona Health Sciences Center, and the University of California at Santa Barbara. He is the Past Director of the National Center for the Psychology of Terrorism and the continuing Director of the Institute for the Study of Equine Assisted Change at Palo Alto University (PAU). He is a Distinguished Professor Emeritus of Psychology, a previous Chair of the Faculty, and Director of Clinical Training at Palo Alto University. He is also Professor Emeritus at the University of California, a diplomate of the American Board of Professional Psychology (ABPP), a fellow of both the American Psychological Association (APA) and Association of Psychological Science (APS), a Past President of Divisions 29 (Psychotherapy) and 12 (Clinical) of APA, and a two-term Past President (international) of the Society for Psychotherapy Research (SPR). Among his citations and achievements, he is a recipient of the Distinguished Career award from SPR, and a Presidential citation for achievement from the APA. He has also been honored for his contributions by the States of Arizona and California. He has published over 40 scholarly articles and chapters and is the author or co-author of 26 books on psychotherapy, assessment, and psychopathology.

Whitney Bliss is a Doctoral Researcher in Clinical Psychology at Palo Alto University. Prior to her graduate school at Brandman University, Whitney worked for the Army as an active duty soldier and then as a civilian specializing in suicide prevention and substance abuse prevention and treatment. Her current research interests include sexual and gender minority service members and veterans, as well as effective ways to educate civilian clinicians in military culture to provide more comprehensive care to military personnel and veterans.

Bruce Bongar, PhD, ABPP, FAPM, is the Calvin Professor of Psychology at Palo Alto University, and Consulting Professor of Psychiatry and the Behavioral Sciences at Stanford University School of Medicine. He is past president of the Section on Clinical Crises and Emergencies of the Division of Clinical Psychology of the American Psychological Association, a diplomat of the American Board of Professional Psychology, and a distinguished fellow of numerous psychological organizations. Professor Bongar has won the Edwin Shneidman Award for outstanding early career contributions to suicide research, the Louis I. Dublin award for lifetime achievement in suicidology research, and the Florence Halpern award for distinguished contributions to the practice of clinical psychology. His research and published work reflect his interest in the wide-ranging complexities of therapeutic interventions with difficult patients in general, and in suicide and life-threatening behaviors in particular.

Andreja Bubić, PhD, is an Assistant Professor at the University of Split in Croatia. She received her PhD at the Max Planck Institute for Human Cognitive and Brain Sciences at the University of Leipzig, where she utilized neuroscientific methods for studying future-oriented cognitive processing. After spending a postdoc in the MGH/HMS Martinos Center for Biomedical Imaging in Boston, USA, she is now in Split where she lectures and does research in the field of cognitive and educational psychology. She has published her research in outlets such as *Current Psychology, Frontiers in Human Neuroscience, Human Brain Mapping, Journal of Cognitive Neuroscience,* and *European Journal of Neuroscience.*

Lindsey L. Bupp is currently a doctoral researcher in clinical and community psychology at Wichita State University. She received her Bachelor's degree in psychology from the University of Arizona in 2009.

James N. Butcher, PhD, is Professor Emeritus of Psychology at the University of Minnesota, serving on its faculty for over 40 years. He received his graduate training at the University of North Carolina. Much of his career focuses on the use of the MMPI, MMPI-2, and MMPI-A across a variety of settings. His achievements include over 250 peer-reviewed articles, 60 books, and 38 years of providing continuing education workshops on the use of the MMPI instruments. Butcher was instrumental in identifying the need for a revision of the original MMPI, which resulted in the MMPI-2 and MMPI-A. He developed a computerized interpretive system, the Minnesota Reports, to assist psychologists in their psychological evaluations with the MMPI-2 and MMPI-A. The Minnesota Reports were originally published in 1981. Currently available Minnesota Reports include the Adult Clinical System-Revised, Reports for Forensic Settings, Revised Personnel System, and Adolescent Interpretive Report (co-authored with Carolyn L. Williams). Several of Professor Butcher's recent books include interpretive recommendations and relevant research for psychologists to aid in their use of the MMPI-2, MMPI-A, and Minnesota Reports. These books include: *A Beginner's Guide to the MMPI-2* (3rd ed.) (2011), *A Beginner's Guide to the MMPI-A* (with Carolyn L. Williams, 2011), *Oxford Handbook of Personality Assessment* (Editor, 2009), *Personality Assessment in Treatment Planning: Use of the MMPI-2 and BTPI* (with Julia Perry, 2008), *Assessing Hispanic Clients Using the MMPI-2 and MMPI-A* (with Jose Cabiya, Emilia Lucio, and Maria Garrido, 2007), and *MMPI/MMPI-2/MMPI-A in Court* (3rd ed.) (with Kenneth Pope and Joyce Seelen, 2006).

Joyce P. Chu, PhD, is an Associate Professor of Clinical Psychology at Palo Alto University (PAU). She co-leads the Multicultural Suicide and Ethnic Minority Mental Health Research Groups at PAU, and is also Director of the Diversity and Community Mental Health emphasis which trains future psychologists to work with underserved populations in the public mental health sector. Dr Chu's work is focused around depression and suicide in ethnic minority adult and geriatric populations, particularly in Asian Americans. Her work is community-collaborative and aims to understand barriers to service use and to develop culturally congruent outreach and service options for Asian Americans and other underserved communities. Dr Chu earned her BA and MA in psychology at Stanford University, her PhD in clinical psychology from the University of Michigan, and did a postdoctoral fellowship at the University of California, San Francisco.

Pietro Cipresso, PhD, is author of more than 100 scientific publications and books like *Modeling Emotions at the Edge of Chaos, Computing Paradigms for Mental Health*, *The Psychology of Social Networking*, and *Virtual Reality: Technologies, Medical Applications and Challenges.* He is Editor at *Central European Journal of Medicine* (Springer), Associate Editor in the Psychology Open Books program (De Gruyter) and of other international peer-reviewed scientific journals and books. Cipresso graduated from Bocconi University of Milan in Economics, and in Statistics and Operational Research. He received his PhD in communication and new technologies, major in Psychology, from IULM University of Milan, and has been a Visiting Researcher at Massachusetts Institute of Technology (MIT). He won the 2012 Clinical Cyber psychology New Investigator Award. He is Principal Investigator or Co-Investigator of several international, European, and national Projects on Emotions, Psychometrics, Psychophysiology, Brain Computer Interface (BCI), and Stress and Virtual Reality.

Patrick D. Converse, PhD, is an Associate Professor in the industrial/organizational psychology program at the Florida Institute of Technology. He received his PhD in industrial/organizational psychology from Michigan State University. His research focuses on personnel selection, work motivation, and individual differences. Professor Converse has published articles and chapters in a variety of journals and books including *Journal of Applied Psychology, Personnel Psychology, Journal of Vocational Behaviour, Human Performance, Personality and Individual Differences, International Journal of Selection and Assessment, A Closer Examination of Applicant Faking Behaviour,* and *New Perspectives on Faking in Personality Assessments.* He serves on the editorial boards for the *Journal of Applied Psychology, Journal of Business and Psychology,* and *International Journal of Selection and Assessment.* He also serves as the committee chair for the Hogan Award for Personality and Work Performance and as an advisory board member for Shadow match USA.

Philip J. Corr's research focuses on individual differences in basic motivational and emotional processes, centered on the reinforcement sensitivity theory (RST) of personality. He has published three books on biological and personality psychology, and has authored numerous papers, using a wide variety of techniques, in such journals as *Journal of Personality and Social Psychology*, *Neuroscience and Bio Behavioral Reviews*, and *Molecular Psychiatry.* Philip's work emphasizes the need for a unified psychology that recognizes the importance of both experimental and differential approaches to understanding the structure and causation of human behaviour. Philip holds editorial posts with several journals, is a Co-Founding President of the British Society for the Psychology of Individual Differences (BSPID); an elected board member of the Society for the Study of Individual Differences (ISSID), from where, in 2001, he won the Early Career Development Award; and President-elect (2013–2015) and President 2015–2017. Philip received his PhD from the University of London and has taught previously at the Institute of Psychiatry and Goldsmith's (both University of London). He has held professorial positions at Swansea University, University of East Anglia, and, now, Professor of Psychology, City University London.

Giulio Costantini is a Doctoral Researcher at the University of Milan-Bicocca, Italy, under the supervision of Professor Marco Perugini. His research is focused especially on the applications of network analysis to personality psychology, on the indirect measurement of personality traits, on replicability issues in psychology, and on power analysis.

Ted B. Cunliffe, PhD, is a psychologist licensed to practice in the State of Florida and Psychological Services Director at Santa Rosa Correctional Institution in Milton, Florida. He received his Master's and Doctoral degrees in clinical psychology from Palo Alto University in Palo Alto, California, pre-doctoral internship from the Medical College of Virginia in Richmond, and post-doctoral training at the Brown University School of Medicine and the Florida Department of Juvenile Justice from 2002–2004. He has worked with forensic populations in a variety of settings including juvenile detention centres, adult prisons, juvenile probation, and outreach programs in the community for over 30 years, and maintains part-time private practices in Miami and Milton, Florida.

C.R. Darolia, PhD, is Professor of Psychology and Chairman of the Department of Psychology and Dean, Social Sciences at Kurukshetra University, Kurukshetra, India. Dr Darolia completed his MPhil and Doctorate degrees from the University of Rajasthan, Jaipur. He specializes in personality, psychometry, and mental abilities, and he has 35 years of teaching experience. During his long teaching and research experience, he has successfully guided 22 PhD and more than 50 MPhil dissertations, the majority of which are in the area of personality and its assessment. He has authored two books in the area of research methodology and statistics, and around 100 research papers in various refereed journals. Dr Darolia is on the editorial board of many journals of repute, and he has presented his research at many national and international platforms.

Christopher J. Edwards is a Doctoral Researcher in Clinical Psychology at Palo Alto University. Chris received his BS in psychology and political science at Roger Williams University before going on to New York University where he obtained a MA in General Psychology. He spent several years working on an in-patient psychiatric unit and has experience working with a housing-first homeless solutions program. His current research interests are focused on improving the treatment of underserved and in-patient populations, including improving the long-term effectiveness of acute in-patient psychotherapy.

Ashley Elefant is a Doctoral Researcher in Clinical Psychology at Palo Alto University. She graduated Magna Cum Laude from the University of the Pacific where she received her BA in English Literature and Spanish Language and Literature. After completing her bachelor's degree, Ashley taught English abroad in Guatemala. When she returned to the United States, Ashley began working at a local crisis center where she was extensively trained in suicide prevention, grief and loss, domestic violence, crisis intervention, and alcohol and drug interventions. She spoke with callers in English and Spanish and provided psychological support through crisis counseling services. Her current research interests include the prevention of adolescent suicide and increasing the accessibility of mental health care to diverse populations, specifically the Latino community.

Stephen E. Finn, PhD, is the founder of the Center for Therapeutic Assessment in Austin, Texas, Clinical Associate Professor of Psychology at the University of Texas at Austin, and a licensed psychologist in Texas. He is the author of *Manual for Using the MMPI-2 as a Therapeutic Intervention* and *In Our Clients' Shoes: Theory and Techniques of Therapeutic Assessment,* as well as numerous journal articles and book chapters in personality assessment. Dr Finn is a fellow of the Society for Personality Assessment (SPA) and the American Psychological Association (APA), and served as SPA president in 2001–2003. He chaired the Psychological Assessment Work Group of the APA's Board of Professional Affairs in 1996–1997, which produced an important and widely cited publication on the utility of assessment. Dr Finn conducts training workshops in therapeutic assessment worldwide.

Rebecca Floyd, PhD, is a Postdoctoral Fellow in Health Psychology within the Medical College of Georgia at Georgia Regents University. She specializes in the provision of services to promote health in patients with MS or HIV. Her internship year was spent within the Bay Pines Veterans Affairs Health Care System in Florida. She completed her doctoral training within the Pacific Graduate School of Psychology at Palo Alto University (PGSP/PAU) in 2014, with specialized training in neuropsychology, forensic psychology, and LGBTQ psychology. Prior to attendance at PGSP/PAU, Becca completed an MA in Theological Studies (2007), a BS in Psychology (2005), and a BA in Religion (2005). Her research interests are in assessment development and program efficacy, with an interest in benefiting underserved populations, and this has led to her active involvement in the Multicultural Suicide Research Center.

Chris D. Fluckinger, PhD, is the Director of the Human Services Program at Bowling Green State University (BGSU), Firelands College, as well as a coordinator of the BGSU Honors College. Dr Fluckinger's primary research interests involve personality measurement issues (e.g., faking, measurement methods, and reactions to personality measures), implications of aging in the workforce (e.g., workforce reduction, fairness/discrimination, and performance issues), and hygiene psychology (e.g., predicting hygiene behaviour, identifying relevant individual differences, and implications for organizational policy). The general theme of these varied lines of research would be to leverage psychological theory and measurement to important organizational and public health issues. His work has appeared in notable journals such as *American Journal of Infection Control*, *Journal of Organizational Behaviour*, and *International Journal of Selection and Assessment*. In addition to his academic accomplishments, Dr Fluckinger has also consulted with a number of regional management, human resource, and industrial and organizational psychology consulting firms.

Carl B. Gacono, PhD, ABAP, is a licensed psychologist who maintains a clinical and forensic private practice in Austin, Texas. Formerly the Assessment Center Director at Atascadero State Hospital and later the Chief Psychologist at the Federal Correctional Institution, Bastrop, Texas, he has over 20 years of correctional and institutional experience. He is the co-author of *The Rorschach Assessment of Aggressive and Psychopathic Personalities*, co-editor of *Contemporary Rorschach Interpretation* and *The Handbook of Forensic Rorschach Assessment*, author of *The Clinical and Forensic Interview Schedule for The Hare Psychopathy Checklist: Revised and Screening Version*, and has authored or co-authored over 80 scientific articles and book chapters. He is the 1994 recipient of the Samuel J. and Anne G. Beck Award for excellence in early career research, and the 2000 Walter G. Klopfer Award. He is a member of the American Board of Assessment Psychology and a Fellow of the Society for Personality Assessment. Dr Gacono is sought as an expert in the area of criminal behavior, psychopathy, treatment of conduct and antisocial personality disorders, and clinical, forensic, and research applications of the Rorschach and Psychopathy Checklists. Clinically, he conducts evaluations and provides psychotherapy to professionals, artists, and the victims of psychopaths.

Zvonimir Galić, PhD, is an Assistant Professor of industrial and organizational psychology at the University of Zagreb, Croatia. His main interests are related to the methods of personality assessment for organizational purposes and the relationship between personality and work behavior. He has published his research in outlets such as *Journal of Vocational Behavior*, *Journal of Personality Assessment*, *International Journal of Selection and Assessment*, *Journal of Personnel Psychology*, *European Journal of Work and Organizational Psychology*, and *Journal of Economic Psychology*. He was a Fulbright Visiting Scholar at Purdue University in the US (academic year 2012/13).

Peter Goldblum, PhD, MPH, is Professor of Psychology and the Co-Director of the Center for LGBTQ Evidence-based Applied Research (CLEAR), the Co-Director of the LGBTQ Emphasis Area at Palo Alto University, and the founder and Director of the Sexual and Gender Identities Clinic at the Gronowski Center in Los Altos, CA. As a pioneer in the development of gay affirmative psychotherapy, he has 35 years experience as a psychotherapist, clinical supervisor, author, teacher, and researcher. He has been instrumental in the development of many community-based programs in the Bay Area, including the Gronowski Center, the Pacific Center, New Leaf (formerly Operation Concern), and was a founder and the first deputy director of the UCSF AIDS Health Project. His publications include two highly acclaimed books, *Strategies for Survival: A Gay Men's Health Manual for the Age of AIDS* (co-authored with Martin Delaney) and *Working with AIDS Bereavement* (co-authored with Sarah Erickson), and many article and book chapters related to sexual and gender minority mental health. More recently his publications have included peer-reviewed articles on gender-based victimization as a predictor of suicide attempts among transgender men and women, a cultural model for explaining suicide among ethnic, sexual, and gender minority individuals, and curriculum development for public psychology programs. He is currently the senior editor for a book on *Youth Suicide and Bullying: Challenges and Strategies for Prevention and Intervention* to be published by Oxford University Press in 2014.

Roger L. Greene, PhD, has focused his interests on the area of self-report measures of personality for a number of years. He is currently working on a number of issues with the Minnesota Multiphasic Personality Inventory (MMPI-2), such as how to match a specific MMPI-2 to prototypic profiles, the assessment of self- and other-deception, the nature of the critical items, the stability of specific profiles, and whether MMPI-2 code types are taxonic or dimensional. He has written a number of books and articles on the MMPI and MMPI-2. Professor Greene received his PhD from Washington State University in 1974. He was a faculty member for 18 years in both the Psychology and Psychiatry Departments at Texas Tech University before coming to Palo Alto University in 1992. Dr Greene has been an active member of the American Psychological Association (APA) and was elected to Fellow status in 1993. He has been a member of the Board of Trustees of the Society for Personality Assessment and the Association of Couples for Marriage Enrichment. He received the Bruno Klopfer award from the Society for Personality Assessment for lifetime contributions to the field of personality assessment. His books on the MMPI-2 have been among the standard references for over two decades.

Richard L. Griffith, PhD, is a Professor in the Industrial Organizational Psychology program at the Florida Institute of Technology, and the Executive Director of the Institute for Cross Cultural Management. He is an expert in testing and personality assessment. He is the Associate Editor of the *European Journal of Psychological Assessment* and has served as an Associate Editor of *Human Performance*, editing the special edition, *Uncovering the Nature of Applicant Faking Behavior: A Presentation of Theoretical Perspectives.* He is the author of over 100 publications, presentations, and chapters in the area of selection, and is co-editor of the book *Closer Examination of Applicant Faking Behavior.* His work has been featured in *Time* magazine and *The Wall Street Journal.*

Corinne M. Henk is currently a doctoral researcher in quantitative psychology at the University of North Carolina at Chapel Hill. She received her Bachelor's degree in psychology from Villanova University in 2012.

Lori Holleran is a Doctoral Researcher in Clinical Psychology at Palo Alto University. She received her undergraduate degree in Psychology and Sociology from Arizona State University, and a Master's degree in Clinical Psychology from Pepperdine University. She has previously collaborated on research considering the relationship between depressive symptoms and Alzheimer's disease at UCLA's Alzheimer's Disease Research Center (ADRC), along with examining individuals' abilities to regulate emotions in response to emotionally charged stimuli with Stanford's Psychophysiology Lab (SPL) affective psychophysiology group. Currently she is involved in research examining factors related to predicting an individual's likelihood of experiencing chronic PTSD at the National Center for PTSD. Clinically, Lori has focused on working with those diagnosed with borderline personality disorder.

Kai T. Horstmann is a Doctoral Researcher in psychological assessment at Humboldt-Universität zu Berlin. Based on his Master's thesis *Putting Lewin's Equation to the Test: The Person-Situation-Interaction assessed with the B5PS,* he now continues to investigate the role of the situation and personality and their interaction for describing and predicting behavior. In his research, he examines how predictive validity of personality assessments can be improved by including the situation perception. Kai Horstmann received his Master's degree in Psychology from Humboldt-Universität zu Berlin. He also works in a personnel consultancy and proceeds with his Master's in Statistics at Humboldt-Universität zu Berlin. Earlier stages of his education included the Georg-August-Universität Göttingen, Cardiff Metropolitan University, and the RWTH Aachen University. During his studies, he worked as a student assistant in cognitive psychology, statistics, and psychological assessment.

Kasie L. Hummel is a Doctoral Researcher in Clinical Psychology at Palo Alto University (PAU) in Palo Alto, California. She earned her BS in psychology and MA in clinical psychology from Minnesota State University in Mankato, MN, where her thesis focused on geriatric psychology. Recently, she was awarded the very competitive Health Professions Scholarship from the United States Air Force and was commissioned as a Second Lieutenant in that service. In addition, Kasie was the recipient of the Otieno Family Assistantship for Clinical Work and a Community Service Award for her exceptional contributions at PAU. Her main research interests include military psychology, trauma, and correctional psychology. Ms Hummel is committed to improving mental health quality and access to those who are underserved, including correctional populations, Native American reservations, and military service members. Her long-term goals are becoming a military psychologist, and conducting trauma research among service members, prison populations, and on the reservations in her home state of South Dakota.

Swati Johar is Scientist 'C' at the Defence Institute of Psychological Research (DIPR), Delhi. She is involved in many major research projects from an interdisciplinary perspective, including research on image and signal processing. She has completed her MTech from BITS, Pilani, India, and the findings of her research work on gestures and speech recognition will be integrated with the New Selection System being developed for the Indian Armed Forces. Emotion recognition and non-verbal behaviour are some of her areas of interest, and she has published scientific articles in peer-reviewed journals. She has been commissioned by Springer to work on the biases of paralanguage and language in emotion, affect and personality to be published as a part of the Springer series Briefs in Speech Technology. She is the author of book chapters dealing with human–computer interaction and technological emergence, and has been an active member of the Institute of Electrical and Electronics Engineers (IEEE) for more than 03 years.

Aaron J. Kivisto, PhD, is a clinical and forensic psychologist and an Assistant Professor in the clinical psychology graduate program at the University of Indianapolis. He obtained his Bachelor's degree in psychology from Augustana College in 2004, and his Master's and Doctoral degrees in clinical psychology from the University of Tennessee in 2008 and 2011, respectively. Following his academic training, Dr Kivisto completed his pre-doctoral internship in the forensic specialty track at NYU School of Medicine/Bellevue Hospital Center, and his post-doctoral fellowship in forensic psychology at Massachusetts General Hospital/Harvard Medical School. Dr Kivisto has published numerous articles on a variety of clinical and forensic matters and maintains a part-time practice of clinical and forensic psychology in Indianapolis.

Maja Parmač Kovačić, PhD, is a postdoctoral researcher in the field of industrial and organizational psychology at the University of Zagreb, Croatia. Her main research interests are related to personality assessment in personnel selection, with the focus on the problem of faking on personality questionnaires. She has published a number of scientific papers on the issue in Croatian and international journals (including *Journal of Personality Assessment* and *International Journal of Selection and Assessment*). Currently she serves on the editorial board of the Croatian journal *Contemporary Psychology*.

Radhika Krishnamurthy, PsyD, ABAP, is Professor of Clinical Psychology at Florida Institute of Technology and a licensed psychologist in Florida. She is (2013–2015) past-president of the Society for Personality Assessment (SPA) and former (2008) president of Section IX, Assessment Psychology, of the American Psychological Association's (APA) Division 12. She is a diplomate of the American Board of Assessment Psychology and a fellow of SPA and APA. Dr Krishnamurthy serves on the editorial boards of the journals *Assessment*, *Journal of Personality Assessment*, and *Psychological Assessment*. She is co-author of two MMPI-A books, *Essentials of MMPI-A Assessment* and *MMPI-A Casebook*, and several book chapters and journal articles on psychological assessment.

John E. Kurtz, PhD, is Professor of Psychology at Villanova University and a licensed clinical psychologist in Pennsylvania. He completed doctoral studies in clinical psychology at Vanderbilt University and received his Bachelor's degree in psychology from the University of California at Berkeley. Dr Kurtz serves on the editorial boards of the *Journal of Personality Assessment* and *Assessment*, and conducts professional training seminars on the Personality Assessment Inventory.

Sumaya Laher, PhD, is a psychologist specializing in the field of psychological assessment. Her doctoral and subsequent research into personality, psychometrics and assessment has been important in pioneering the usage and interpretation of key instruments in South Africa. She recently co-edited a book titled, *Psychological Assessment in South Africa: Research and Applications,* that is fast becoming a seminal text in the area. Aside from psychological assessment, Sumaya contributes actively to research on indigenous knowledge systems with her work on traditional healing systems, particularly those proposed by Islam, Hinduism and African approaches. Her work has been published in leading local and international journals in the field. Sumaya was awarded a youth rating by the South African National Research Foundation in 2013 in recognition of her research outputs. She is an Associate Editor at the *South African Journal of Psychology* and serves as reviewer for a number of local and international journals. Sumaya has presented numerous papers at local and international conferences and has served on the scientific and organizing committees of various conferences. Sumaya serves on the executive of the Psychological Society of South Africa and chairs the research division for the society. She is also a member of the International Test Commission, the International Association for Cross-cultural Psychology, the Society for Personality Assessment, and the World Association for Personality Psychologists.

Brian A. Maruyama is a Doctoral Researcher in Clinical Psychology at Palo Alto University. He is a member of the Ethnic Minority Mental Health Research Group at PAU and has a broad range of interests, including mental health disparities among sexual minorities and culturally competent neuropsychological assessment. Brian graduated from the University of California, Davis, with his BA in psychology and is pursuing his PhD in clinical psychology from PAU.

Robert R. McCrae received a PhD in Personality Psychology from Boston University in 1976. He spent his career at the National Institute of Aging, NIH, from which he retired in 2009. His work has focused on personality structure (particularly the Five-Factor Model), assessment, and development. With Paul T. Costa, Jr., he is author of the NEO Inventories and of *Personality in Adulthood: A Five-Factor Theory Perspective.* With collaborators from around the world, he has conducted cross-cultural research on personality structure, gender differences, and age changes; he has also contributed to studies of stereotypes of personality traits attributed to different genders, age groups, and nations. Five-Factor Theory represents his attempt to integrate research findings on personality traits into a broad account of the nature and functioning of the person.

Michael A. McDaniel received his PhD in Industrial Organizational Psychology from the George Washington University. Prior to joining Virginia Commonwealth University, he was a tenured Associate Professor at the University of Akron. Professor McDaniel has published in *Academy of Management Journal, Journal of Applied Psychology, Personnel Psychology, Intelligence, International Journal of Selection and Assessment,* and *Human Performance.* He is a member of the Academy of Management, and a Fellow of the Society for Industrial, Organizational Psychology, Inc., a Fellow of the American Psychological Association, a Fellow of the Association for Psychological Science, and a member of the Society for Human Resource Management. Professor McDaniel is a member of the doctoral faculty in the management program at Virginia Commonwealth University. His research has spanned several topics in personnel selection, including situational judgment tests, employment interviews, cognitive ability tests, job knowledge tests, the effects of applicant faking on employment decisions, demographic group differences in job performance, and employment tests.

Yumiko Mochinushi is currently pursuing her PhD degree in I/O Psychology at the Florida Institute of Technology. She received her Master of Human Resources and Industrial Relations (MHRIR) from the University of Illinois in 2012, and her MS from the Florida Institute of Technology in 2014. Her research interests range from applicant faking on personality measures, with a focus on faking in cross-cultural contexts, to the development of cross-cultural assessments. She also conducts research on the identification of faking behaviors and has presented papers in several conferences.

Swati Mukherjee is Scientist 'D' at the Defence Institute of Psychological Research (DIPR), Delhi. She is involved in many major research projects of the Institute, including research on suicide in the Armed Forces. She has to her credit a few publications in the form of journal articles and book chapters published by reputable publishers including Taylor & Francis and Sage. She is associate editor of a volume on *Recent Developments in Psychology,* has co-authored a manual on *Suicide and Fratricide: Dynamics and Management* for the Armed Forces personnel, and a manual on *Overcoming Obsolescence & Becoming Creative in R&D Environment for* R&D organizations. Her areas of interest are social psychology, positive mental health practices, and suicidal behaviour. She has been a recipient of the Defence Research & Development Organization (DRDO) Best Performance Award for the year 2008.

Deniz S. Ones (PhD, University of Iowa) is the Hellervik Professor of Industrial Psychology at the University of Minnesota. She is the author of over 150 articles and over 200 international/national conference papers and published abstracts on topics ranging from personality at work, to integrity testing, to performance measurement, to influences of social desirability on psychometric properties of non-cognitive measures, to counterproductive behaviors at work. She has received the best dissertation award as well as the early career distinguished scientific contributions award from the Society for Industrial and Organizational Psychology (SIOP). She is a Fellow of both Divisions 5 (Evaluation, Measurement, and Statistics) and 14 (Industrial and Organizational Psychology) of the American Psychological Association. She has served on the editorial boards of *Personnel Psychology, Journal of Applied Psychology, Journal of Organizational Behavior, Journal of Vocational Behavior, European Journal of Work and Organizational Psychology* and *Zeitschrift für Personalpsychologie (Journal of Personnel Psychology).* She served as the editor-in-chief of the *International Journal of Selection and Assessment* between 2001–2006. She has edited the two-volume *Handbook of Industrial, Work and Organizational Psychology* (with Anderson, Sinangil, and Viswesvaran; SAGE), a special issue of the journal *Human Performance*, on use of cognitive ability tests (with Viswesvaran), and a special issue of the *International Journal of Selection and Assessment* on counterproductive work behaviors. She has also co-edited a SIOP Frontier series book on environmental sustainability.

Vijay Parkash, PhD, is Scientist 'C' at the Defence Institute of Psychological Research (DIPR), Defence R & D Organization (DRDO), Delhi, India. After completing his post-graduate studies as Gold Medalist for the entire social sciences faculty of Kurukshetra University, Kurukshetra, he was awarded a DRDO Research Fellowship and he completed his Doctorate degree in Psychology from Kurukshetra University. Health psychology, personality and psychometrics are his areas of interest, and he has more than ten years of research experience. He has also served as a Psychologist on the Air Force Selection Board for around two years, for the selection of Officers in the Indian Armed Forces. He has been involved in many major research projects related to suicidal behaviour and test constructions for personnel selection in armed and paramilitary forces. He has to his credit two field manuals for soldiers and three edited volumes: *Recent Developments in Psychology*, *Counseling: A Practical Approach*, and *Positive Psychology: Applications in Work, Health and Well-being* (published by Pearson Education). He has published more than 20 other journal articles and book chapters by reputed publishers including Taylor & Francis, Sage Publications, Springer, and Pearson Education. DIPR conferred upon him the laboratory Scientist of the Year Award 2011 for his outstanding contributions.

Marco Perugini, PhD, is a full Professor at the University of Milan-Bicocca, Italy. His broad research interests, resulting in over 100 publications in international journals, include personality psychology, indirect and direct measurement, attitude, evaluative learning, and research methods and analysis. He has been editor of the *European Journal of Personality,* associate editor of the *British Journal of Social Psychology*, and consulting editor of the *International Journal of Psychology*, as well as president of the European Association of Personality Psychology.

K.V. Petrides, PhD, is Director of the London Psychometric Laboratory at UCL and principal author of the family of Trait Emotional Intelligence Questionnaires (TEIQue). He holds a Bachelor's degree in Business Administration with *summa cum laude* honours from PACE University (NYC, USA), a Diploma in Psychology from the University of Nottingham (UK), an MSc in Psychological Research Methods (specialized in psychometrics and behavioral statistics) from the University of Exeter (UK), and a PhD (specialized in individual differences, psychometrics and behavioral statistics) from UCL. He lectures internationally on psychometrics, personality and individual differences, and trait emotional intelligence.

Samantha Pflum, MS, is a fifth year Doctoral Reseacher in Clinical Psychology at Palo Alto University. Her areas of professional interest include suicidology, LGBT issues, bullying, and social support. Clinically, Samantha's work focuses on self-harming adolescents and assessment of youth with developmental disabilities. She is also a lead graduate student in PAU's Transgender Research Consortium.

Aaron L. Pincus, PhD, is a Fellow of the Society for Personality Assessment and a Professor of Psychology at Pennsylvania State University, where he teaches personality assessment and psychotherapy for the doctoral program in clinical psychology. Professor Pincus received his PhD in clinical psychology from the University of

British Columbia where he studied with Jerry S. Wiggins. Professor Pincus has published over 100 articles and chapters, and his research focuses on the development of new assessment measures and methods based on the Interpersonal Circumplex Model, as well as the integration of personality, psychopathology, and psychotherapy using interpersonal theory and assessment. He is the current Editor-in-Chief of the journal *Assessment* and was the recipient of the 2007 American Psychological Association Division 12/American Psychological Foundation Theodore Millon Award for contributions to personality psychology.

Arthur E. Poropat, PhD, is Senior Lecturer in the School of Applied Psychology, Griffith University, Australia. Prior to his academic career, Arthur Poropat had mostly worked in organizational development and workplace learning, prompting his interest in factors contributing to individual learning and performance. Arthur's research on personality and workplace performance led to recognition of parallels with personality and academic performance, while consideration of interpersonal relationships instigated interest in varying the perspective of personality assessments between self and others. His current interests are focused on interpersonal understandings of both personality and various types of performance, with the aim of developing integrated models that can be practically applied in organizational and educational practice.

Giuseppe Riva, PhD, is Director of the Interactive Communication and Ergonomics of New Italy. He is also Professor of General Psychology and Communication Psychology, and a member of the steering committee of the PhD programme in Psychology at the Catholic University of Milan, Italy. According to the scientific databases Web of Science, PubMed/Medline and PsycInfo, Riva is the scholar who authored the highest number of peer-reviewed scientific publications in the field of virtual reality in the world (as of August 2014). These papers range from specialist journals such as *Presence: Teleoperators and Virtual Reality* (MIT Press) to general scientific journals such as *Science* and *Nature.* In its first decade, Riva pioneered many of the applications that enabled the diffusion of Virtual Reality and the internet in the field of healthcare. Specifically, his research work led to the development of a new scientific discipline – cyber psychology – integrating innovative research ranging from usability and ergonomics, clinical psychology and cognitive science, to mobile devices and simulation apparatus. Through the analysis of the cognitive processes involved in simulated realities, he expanded the concept of "presence" the feeling of being there – originally developed by communication and technology scholars.

Michael J. Roche, PhD, is an Assistant Professor of Psychology at Pennsylvania State University, Altoona. He received his PhD in clinical psychology from Pennsylvania State University and completed his pre-doctoral internship at the Massachusetts General Hospital/Harvard Medical School. His research program utilizes intensive repeated measurement designs (e.g., ecological momentary assessment, diary studies) to capture the dynamics of psychopathology, health, and social functioning in daily life.

Mary K. Rothbart, PhD, is Professor Emeritus in the Department of Psychology at the University of Oregon. Dr Rothbart is the recipient of numerous awards recognizing her academic achievements, including the American Psychological Foundation's Gold Medal Award, election into the American Academy of Arts and Sciences, and the Jack Block award for research accomplishments in personality psychology from the Society for Personality and Social Psychology. She is considered to be the world's leading expert on temperament, and recently published her book, *Becoming Who We Are: Temperament and Personality in Development*, with Guilford Press. She is responsible for developing multiple measures of infant, childhood, adolescent, and adult temperament, which are widely used by researchers and practitioners. She received her bachelor's degree from Reed College and her doctorate from Stanford University.

Donald H. Saklofske, PhD, is Professor of Psychology, University of Western Ontario, Canada. He is also Adjunct Professor at the University of Calgary and University of Saskatchewan, Visiting Professor in the School of Psychology at Beijing Normal University and also at BNU in Zhuhai, China, and Research Associate in the Laboratory for Research and Intervention in Positive Psychology and Prevention, University of Florence, Italy. Editorships include the *Journal of Psychoeducational Assessment* and the *Canadian Journal of School Psychology*; Associate Editor for *Personality and Individual Differences* and Editor for the *Human Exceptionality* book series published by Springer. He is a Fellow of the Canadian Psychological Association and the Association for Psychological Science, and serves on the Board of Directors as Past President of the International Society for the Study of Individual Differences and a current member of the Board of the Canadian Psychological Association. His research focuses on personality, intelligence, individual differences and psychological assessment.

Salazar-Schneiderman received her PhD in Clinical Psychology from Palo Alto University and her BA in psychology from the University of California, Berkeley. She is currently employed at El Camino Hospital Psychiatric Emergency Service where she also completed her postdoctoral training. Her research and clinical areas of interest include suicide prevention in the Emergency Department and integration of behavioral medicine in hospital settings.

Alexander B. Siegling is a Doctoral Researcher at the London Psychometric Laboratory (University College, London) focusing on the areas of individual differences and psychometrics. He obtained a BA (Hons) first-class in Psychology from Mount Saint Vincent University (Halifax, Canada) and a MSc in School & Applied Child Psychology from the University of Calgary (Canada).

Matthew Skinta, PhD, ABPP, is a board-certified clinical health psychologist with a private practice in San Francisco's historic Castro neighborhood. He received his PhD, with a focus in health psychology, at Kent State University in Kent, Ohio, followed by a postdoctoral fellowship in HIV Behavioral Medicine at the Harbor-UCLA Medical Center in Torrance, California. Dr Skinta continued his focus on HIV through directing and managing the research program from 2008–2013 at the Alliance Health Project (formerly AIDS Health Project) of the University of California, San Francisco. Currently, he is the clinical supervisor of Palo Alto

University's Sexual and Gender Identities Clinic, while maintaining his private practice alongside consultation and training for area providers. Dr Skinta has published in the area of shame, stigma, and HIV, as well as cultural competency concerns when working with sexual minorities. He has provided graduate-level and postgraduate training in working with sexual minorities, shame, and evidence-based treatment. Dr Skinta is primarily interested in the corresponding functions of shame and self-compassion in the lives of persons affected by HIV/AIDS, as well as the importance of developing effective training that adequately prepares psychologists to speak openly regarding sex and sexuality.

Jason M. Smith, PsyD, graduated from Carlos Albizu University in Miami, Florida, in 2014. He received his Bachelor of Science degree at the University of Miami in Coral Gables in 2007 and his Master of Science degree at Carlos Albizu University in Miami in 2010. He completed his internship with the Kentucky Department of Corrections in LaGrange, Kentucky. His research interests include female psychopathy, the Rorschach, and the Personality Assessment Inventory. He received the 2014 Outstanding Dissertation Award from APA Division 18 Criminal Justice Division for his dissertation entitled *Female Psychopathy: A Rorschach Investigation of Personality Structure*. Presently he is the Staff Psychologist at Federal Correctional Complex (FCC) Hazelton Bruceton Mills, West Virginia, USA

Andrea F. Snell's research focuses on a number of applications of measurement and statistical issues, from longitudinal data analysis to the implementation of personality measures in applied contexts. Her research has been published in a number of respected journals, including *Journal of Applied Psychology*, *Journal of Organizational Behavior*, and *Journal of Applied Social Psychology*. She is also the program chair of the Industrial/Organizational Psychology Program at the University of Akron.

Lacey M. Sommers, MS, is a Doctoral Researcher in Clinical Psychology at Palo Alto University and is currently completing her APA-accredited pre-doctoral internship at the Colorado Mental Health Institute at Pueblo. She graduated from Sonoma State University with a Bachelor's degree in psychology and minors in criminal justice administration and American multicultural studies. Her research interests lie in the application of psychological assessments to diverse patient populations, and how assessments can be used to improve diagnosis and treatment of mental illness. Lacey also co-authored a book chapter with Professor Roger L. Greene, on interpreting the supplementary scales of the MMPI-2 for the newly released 3rd edition of the Psychologists' Desk Reference.

James Sottile is a Doctoral Researcher in Clinical Psychology at Palo Alto University. He received his BA in psychology from Bard College. Before entering graduate school, James worked as a research assistant for the Uniformed Services University of the Health Sciences (USUHS) in Bethesda, MD. While working for USUHS, James assisted with the Army Study to Assess Risk and Resilience in Service Members, the largest epidemiological study of suicide in the military to date. His current research interests include the development of mental health education programs for military service members, as well as effective therapeutic interventions for post-traumatic stress disorder.

Ashton C. Southard received her PhD from the University of Southern Mississippi and is currently a Special Lecturer at Oakland University in Rochester, MI. Her primary research interests are in the area of dark personality features including narcissism, psychopathy, Machiavellianism, and fragile self-esteem.

Danielle Spangler is a Doctoral Researcher in Clinical Psychology at Palo Alto University. She received her masters in Mental Health and Wellness Counseling from New York University, and her BA in psychology from Western Connecticut State University. Danielle has experience working in various community mental health centers with adults and youths with severe mental illnesses. Her current research interests include post-traumatic stress disorder and suicide, as well as identifying resiliency factors to prevent the onset of PTSD following a traumatic event.

Jennifer L. Tackett, PhD, is Associate Professor of Psychology at Northwestern University. Dr Tackett has been recognized by early career awards from the Society for Research in Psychopathology, the Society for Personality Assessment, and the Ontario Ministry of Research and Innovation. She publishes widely on topics including child personality and the development of externalizing psychopathology in children and adolescence. She is the Associate Editor for the *Journal of Personality*, the *Journal of Personality Disorders*, and the *Journal of Research in Personality*, and stands on the editorial board for several more journals. She is currently on the Executive Board for the Society for Research in Psychopathology, and serves as the secretary/treasurer for the Association for Research in Personality. She received her bachelor's degree from Texas A&M University and her doctorate from the University of Minnesota.

Rylan J. Testa, PhD, is visiting faculty at Palo Alto University. He completed his doctoral degree in clinical psychology from Temple University and his pre-doctoral internship at the Department for Veterans Affairs in Palo Alto. His work has focused on prevention and treatment of behavioral patterns related to physical self-harm, including addiction, suicide, medical non-adherence, obesity, and health-related risk-taking. Dr Testa is particularly committed to addressing these issues in underserved communities. Dr Testa has demonstrated early career leadership in the area of transgender psychology, and transgender suicidality. He has authored multiple well-cited articles, conducted large-scale online surveys, and developed new measures in this area of research. He currently serves as Program Manager of the Transgender Research Consortium and the Gender and Youth Program and as Associate Director of LGBTQ Clinical and Translational Research, Education and Training at the new Dorothy and Allen Calvin Center for the Study and Prevention of Suicide.

Caroline S. Tonetti completed her PhD in Clinical Psychology from Palo Alto University in March 2014. Her dissertation was a taxometric analysis of the MMPI-2 scales measuring somatic symptoms. Her previous research on the Depression Obvious and Depression Subtle Scales of the MMPI was published in *Assessment* (1997). Caroline is currently doing her postdoctoral work as a registered Psychological Assistant for Stephanie Brown, PhD, and is specializing in the field of addiction and recovery. Her previous clinical work includes a pre-doctoral fellowship at Stanford University as well as a two years pre-doctoral internship at the Palo Alto Veterans Administration Hospital, Day Hospital.

Burak Tunca, PhD, is Assistant Professor in the School of Business and Law at the University of Agder, Norway, and also a researcher at Agder Research in Norway. His research interests are self-concept based consumer behavior, human and brand personality relationships, and quantitative data analysis.

The late **James B. Victor** was a Professor of Education at Hampton University where he established the Behavior Science Research Center of which he was the Director. Dr Victor was a long-time investigator of child problem behaviors and authored numerous articles and book chapters regarding the education of these children with problem behaviors. These investigations led to the investigation of antecedents of adult personality: childhood temperament. Dr Victor made numerous presentations internationally investigating the development of adult personality from childhood temperament, supported by grants from the National Institutes of Health. He received his bachelor's degree from Utah State University and his doctorate from Syracuse University.

Chockalingam Viswesvaran (PhD, University of Iowa) is Professor of Psychology at Florida International University, Miami. He has served on several editorial boards including those of *Journal of Applied Psychology, Personnel Psychology, Journal of Personnel Psychology,* and *Journal of Organizational Behavior.* He was the associate editor of the *International Journal of Selection and Assessment* from 2001 to 2006 and is currently serving as its Editor. He has received the best dissertation award and the early career distinguished scientific contributions award from the Society for Industrial and Organizational Psychology (SIOP). He is a fellow of SIOP, Divisions 14 (I/O) and 5 (Evaluation, Measurement, and Statistics) of the American Psychological Association, and the Association for Psychological Science (APS). He has co-edited the two-volume *Handbook of Industrial, Work and Organizational Psychology*, a special issue of the *International Journal of Selection and Assessment* on the role of technology in staffing, and a special issue of the journal *Human Performance* on use of cognitive ability tests. He has served on the awards and fellowship committees of SIOP and on the APA Committee on Psychological Tests and Assessments. He has published over 150 journal articles and has made 240 conference presentations.

Deborah L. Whetzel received her PhD in Industrial Organizational Psychology from the George Washington University. She is a manager of the Personnel Selection and Development Program at the Human Resources Research Organization (HumRRO), where her applied work includes managing two large, nationally-administered testing programs. She also develops situational judgment tests, structured interviews, and ratings scales. Her research topics include meta-analyses of the validity of various selection instruments, such as structured interviews and in-baskets, and subgroup differences using situational judgment tests. In addition to publishing in top-tier journals, such as *Journal of Applied Psychology and Personnel Psychology*, she has edited two widely used textbooks: *Applied Measurement Methods* *in Industrial Psychology* and *Applied Measurement: Industrial Psychology in Human Resources Management*. She currently serves as a Division 14 representative on the American Psychological Association Council of Representatives. Dr Whetzel is a Fellow of the Society for Industrial Organizational Psychology, Inc., and a past president of the International Personnel Assessment Council and the Personnel Testing Council of Metropolitan Washington.

Virgil Zeigler-Hill, PhD, is an Associate Professor of Psychology at Oakland University in Rochester, MI. His primary research interests are in three interrelated areas: (1) self-esteem, (2) dark personality features, and (3) interpersonal relationships. His research concerning dark personality features is focused on identifying potentially aversive aspects of personality and examining their connections with important life outcomes (e.g., psychological adjustment). In the area of interpersonal relationships, he examines how personality features as well as beliefs about the self and one's romantic partner influence intimacy, relationship satisfaction, jealousy, infidelity, and longevity in close relationships. He is currently an Associate Editor for *Self and Identity, Journal of Personality Assessment*, and *Evolutionary Psychology*.

Matthias Ziegler, PhD, is a Full Professor of Psychological Assessment at the Humboldt-Universität zu Berlin, Germany. His main research areas are personality and intelligence, and he deals specifically with various assessment approaches, the role of faking, and the interaction between different constructs to predict academic and job performance and knowledge. Dr Ziegler is editor in chief of the *European Journal of Psychological Assessment* and co-editor of the book *New Perspectives on Faking in Personality Assessment*.

Foreword

The history of scientific psychology is usually traced to the establishment of Wilhelm Wundt's Leipzig laboratory in 1879. Shortly thereafter, in 1883, James McKeen Cattell, then a doctoral student at Johns Hopkins University, became an assistant in Wundt's laboratory and was allowed to conduct his dissertation research on individual differences in reaction time. This study of individual differences was a forerunner of personality assessment, and Cattell's early work thus dates the origins of formal personality assessment back to the very beginnings of psychological science.

Personality assessment is notable not only for its long history, but also for the extent to which it captures the basic essence of psychology and for the valuable purposes it serves. Psychology is a behavioral science concerned mainly with how people are disposed to think, feel, and conduct themselves in various situations. These cognitive, affective, and action tendencies of people constitute their personality characteristics, and these characteristics are identified by personality assessment procedures. As for the purposes it serves, personality assessment facilitates decision-making whenever personality characteristics have a bearing on a choice to be made.

Such personality-related choices may involve diagnosing the nature of disorder in a psychologically troubled person, identifying the types of intervention likely to benefit the person, or, should the person's psychological problems have led to hospitalization, suspension of employment, or expulsion from school, whether he or she is ready to return home, to work, or to the classroom. Decisions based in part on personality characteristics may also involve determining whether law-breakers should be held responsible for their illegal conduct, whether individuals are at risk for harming themselves or other people, and whether parents' custodial rights should be modified or terminated. In addition to being helpful in these clinical and forensic applications, assessment of personality characteristics can assist in such personnel decisions as choosing which of several candidates should be hired for a job or promoted to a position of greater responsibility.

The editor and chapter authors of the present volume elaborate the substance and utility of personality assessment in a sweeping overview of the field that is commendable for its scholarship and clinical sophistication. There are chapters that address numerous conceptual, methodological, and ethical issues in personality assessment research and practice; chapters that discuss considerations in using both self-report and performance-based assessment instruments; chapters concerning treatment planning, forensic consultation, and personnel selection; and chapters that discuss the therapeutic benefit of the personality assessment process and the response style of persons being assessed, particularly with respect to efforts at impression management.

A distinctive feature of this volume is an international assemblage of distinguished contributors from 17 countries on five continents. This multinational authorship enhances the content of the book with attention to cross-cultural perspectives and diversity in personality assessment. The quality and coverage of this important book will be a valuable addition to the personality assessment literature and be much appreciated by researchers and practitioners in the field.

Professor Irving B. Weiner, PhD, ABPP
Clinical Professor of Psychiatry and Neurosciences
University of South Florida, USA

Preface

Beginning with the earliest attempts to assess and explain personality by the physiologists like Hippocrates, Canon, Sheldon, and their many predecessors, ranging through the initial psychological descriptions and measurements by Freud, Allport, Cattell, and the contemporary psychologists, the field of personality assessment has evolved and grown enormously to arrive at our present-day comprehensive understanding of varied aspects of personality from different perspectives. Integral to clinical diagnosis and personnel selection, the field of personality assessment today forms a huge and multifarious domain that continues to evolve through a symbiotic relationship between research and practice, and thrives through the dedicated efforts of researchers and advances of techniques facilitated by technological innovations. There is no dearth of literature on personality assessment, ranging from lay psychology tools promising grand results, to theoretically grounded research perspectives in journal articles and comprehensive volumes. However, proceeding further in a structured manner requires an elaborative critical perspective on the research advances and future developments in the concomitant fields. *The Wiley Handbook of Personality Assessment* proposes to address this requirement by systematically delineating the recent advances and the ways forward in the area of personality assessment, along with varied modern theoretical underpinnings and emerging empirical evidences.

Providing a comprehensive perspective on the emerging issues and recent trends in personality assessment, the volume has been divided into two sections, encapsulating "Emerging Conceptual Trends" in the first section, followed by a look into "Emerging Assessment Perspectives and Methodological Issues" in the second. Opening in the first chapter with discussion on "Integrating Trait and Process Approaches to Personality", Robert R. McCrae brings forth the differential utility of trait and process approaches in diagnosis and selection versus interventions. Citing the better relevance of process approach in effective interventions but a relative lack of a unified framework, the author discusses conceptual and empirical work to link processes to traits and further deliberates on some ways in which such research might lead to psychological interventions. Discussing a related issue of "Personality Assessment and Theory", Corr and Poropat throw light on the issue of underlying personality traits impacting the validity of personality assessment. Making a call for application of sophisticated generalizability theory, they delineate the interplay between surface traits and source processes and different sources of variance in personality assessment. Moving further, Horstmann and Ziegler attempt to elaborate on the links of personality with "Situational Perception" in context with Lewin's person–situation interaction formula. Highlighting the role of subjective and individualistic situation perception in one's personality, the authors challenge the perspective of looking at perceptual individual differences and call for inclusion of a pre-operationalized psychological situation for personality assessment.

Victor and his colleagues in the fourth chapter discuss the "Temperamental Components of the Developing Personality". Highlighting the neural networks between genes, temperament, and personality, the authors describe a model conjoining personality as well as temperament scales to locate inherently determined temperament components within a broad personality structure, and they cite certain important empirical findings in the matter of context. Just like temperamental traits, another important dimension of personality is discussed by Viswesvaran and Ones in Chapter 5, wherein they very ably describe "Integrity Tests: A Review of Alternate Conceptualizations and Some Measurement and Practical Issues". Making a call for comprehensive explanations for the construct of integrity as a component of personality, the authors provide a literary synthesis of the nomological net of integrity construct and an existing prominent theoretical model conceptualizing this trait. Further, an attempt has been made to present elaborative theoretical conceptualizations of the integrity construct, review some major measurement issues, summarize some recent controversies, and present some future research directions.

Slowly widening the scope of the volume, Costantini and Perugini put forth "Network Analysis" as a new way to think about personality in Chapter 6. Highlighting the utility of network analysis in conceptualization and measurement of personality, they elaboratively present the fundamental concepts of network analysis and review recent studies conducted by applying the network methodology. They also review the methods and indices used to define different networks and summarize their important properties. Extending the scope of the subject matter further in the next chapter, Petrides, Siegling and Saklofske present "Theory and Measurement of Trait Emotional Intelligence". The authors provide an overview of the operationalization of emotional intelligence as a personality trait; and, covering the key aspects of theory and measurement, they also present a brief critique of popular measures of the construct and highlight varied areas of its application.

Taking the emotional intelligence related discourse to the next step, Reuven Bar-On makes a call for looking "Beyond IQ and EQ" and presents the Bar-On Multifactor Model of Performance to the reader. Along with the introduction of the model, Bar-On also introduces the reader to his proposed assessment tool: the Multifactor Measure of Performance™ (MMP™). Explaining the need for this model, he cites the methodology adopted to develop it, its potential applicability and current limitations, and the ways in which this model can represent a significant paradigm shift in assessment. Progressing further, a similar paradigm shift approach has been described by Southard and Zeigler-Hill wherein they put an emphasis on the significance of "Measuring the Dark Side of Personality". The authors review the existing empirical literature in the area of assessment of dark and aversive personality features, largely concerned with antagonism and manipulation, measurement instruments tapping such features, and the recent attempts made to broaden the conceptualization of dark personality features. "Diversity and Assessment" is the focal point of Chapter 10 authored by Chu and colleagues. Citing the relatively little attention received by cultural and diversity issues in assessment, they accentuate the need for having culturally competent practice of assessment and testing by putting forth a comprehensive literature analysis reviewing the main domains of culture-informed assessment, including culturally-adjusted differential norms, culture-specific validity of the constructs and measures, varied reporting styles, the cultural and technical context of the testing process, and culturally-informed responses to assessment.

Shaping deductively from general to particular, Laher presents "Future Directions for Personality Assessment: An African Perspective". Putting forth the need for cross-cultural validation of the five-factor model of personality, the author discusses African research contributions in the form of development of new assessment tools, based on NEO-Personality Inventory Revised, focused towards informing cross-cultural developments on the understanding of personality structure globally. Some future directions for the five-factor personality theory and assessment have been presented using the findings from the South African projects. As far as in-depth psychopathological personality assessment is concerned, the Minnesota Multiphasic Personality Inventory (MMPI) has been a widely accepted and quite credible instrument and has been revised and improved from time to time. Certain "Advances in the Use and Interpretation of the MMPI-2" have been discussed and called for by Salazar, Tonetti, Sommers, and Greene in Chapter 12. They look into three so-far overlooked topics and analytically examine (a) whether the MMPI-2 code types are actually categories; (b) whether the MMPI-2 somatization scales are categories or dimensions; and (iii) whether it is possible to use item response theory to develop subscales within the MMPI-2 item pool that could be administered independently in computer adaptive testing. The issues have been well addressed by the authors, and crucial future directions have been provided for the MMPI-2 users.

Widening the latitude of coverage and carrying the discussion forward towards applied fields, the second section of the volume delves into "Emerging Assessment Perspectives and Methodological Issues", and incorporates chapters on theoretical and methodological issues involved in various assessment techniques. The section opens with Chapter 13 authored by James N. Butcher, which delineates "Objective Personality Assessment with the MMPI-2". Showing the MMPI-2 as an internationally adaptable measure, the author herein provides a description of test use in clinical, forensic, and personnel evaluations, and addresses the issues of the influence of culture on the personality and mental health problems, the cross-cultural effectiveness of the MMPI-2, the extent of adaptation of the test in international settings, and computer-based personality assessment using the MMPI-2. The utility of MMPI-2 in detecting personality factors influencing job performance in high-risk occupations has been well illustrated by the help of a case study. In the next chapter, Roche and Pincus deliberate about "Precision Assessment: An Individualized and Temporally Dynamic Approach to Understanding Patients in their Daily Lives" by asserting for a person-specific approach to personality assessment by using longitudinal data of daily life. They describe the person-specific paradigm and its potential contribution to the advancement of personality assessment in light of the existing personality theories. They further present concise research evidence on person-specific assessment using an interpersonal framework, and discuss the barriers in the way of its wide entry into the personality assessment domain.

"Are Situational Judgment Tests (SJTs) Better Assessments of Personality than Traditional Personality Tests in High-Stakes Testing?" This question has been raised and aptly addressed by Whetzel and McDaniel in Chapter 15 by highlighting the distinction between self-reports of behavioral tendency and knowledge, and reviewing the importance of this distinction for faking and the construct validity of SJTs. They also review the ways and basis of why SJTs predict job performance and then provide certain recommendations for future research. Moving ahead in discussing assessment methodologies, Galić and colleagues analyze certain limitations of self-report measures and evaluate relatively non-conventional assessment methods of "Conditional Reasoning Problems and Implicit Association Test (IAT) Based Tasks" as alternatives to self-reports for personality assessment. Providing descriptions of both approaches and the general logic behind their use in personality assessment, the authors illustrate their application for measuring trait aggressiveness. In Chapter 17, Krishnamurthy, Finn, and Aschieri talk about "Therapeutic Assessment in Clinical and Counseling Psychology Practice". Emphasizing the unique applicability of therapeutic assessment, the authors provide an overview of its core principles and methods, review the supportive empirical evidence, describe the scope of its applicability, and discuss future directions.

A recent innovation focusing on "Personality Assessment in Ecological Settings by Means of Virtual Reality" is the focal point of Chapter 18, wherein Cipresso and Riva cite the biases associated with questionnaires and self-report measures and propose a protocol of using virtual reality aimed at parsing a structured way to assess the five factors of personality. They present the reader with the "Vpers" test that includes five virtual scenarios to assess each dimension of personality through an interactive environment, thereby assessing personality in a more ecological way and avoiding most of the self-report biases. Taking the volume to more specifics, Gacono and associates explore "The Use of the Hare Psychopathy Checklist (PCL-R) and Rorschach Inkblot Method (RIM) in Forensic Psychological Assessment". Giving consideration to the role of comprehensive multimethod personality assessment in forensic psychology, the authors discuss the distinct role of the forensic psychologist and specific forensic considerations, in addition to traditional clinical considerations of accuracy. The incremental clinical validity of psychological testing has been reviewed, and the authors have called for the integration of the PCL-R and the Rorschach Inkblot Method, demonstrating their joint effectiveness by means of a case study.

Proceeding further from the Rorschach Inkblots, Darolia describes the "Holtzman Inkblot Technique and Personality Assessment" and discusses the distinctive advantages of the Holtzman Inkbolt Technique over the widely accepted RIM. Highlighting the robust psychometric properties, and much more objective administration and computerized scoring system, the author recommends the use of Holtzman Inkblots for more precise and detailed personality assessment. In the next chapter, Edwards, Holleran, and Beutler advocate the use of Systematic Treatment Selection (STS) to match individuals seeking mental health treatment with a particular required therapeutic technique. The authors explicitly describe the STS process and explain its theories and principles along with literary evidences. Further, they assess and analyze the use of integrative assessment and introduce "Innerlife" – a web-based STS measure. Following the ongoing discussions, in Chapter 22 Parkash and I attempt to present a brief meta-analytical synthesis of various "Personality Assessment Paradigms: Issues and Challenges". We attempt to review the relative advantages and disadvantages of different assessment methodologies, and put forth the challenging assessment issues that need to be kept in mind and addressed adequately when starting any kind of personality assessment.

Addressing specific assessment issues in a particular behavioral domain, Hummel, Sottile, Spangler, and Bongar elucidate "The Identification and Assessment of the Correlates of Military Suicide". Citing the latest supportive research evidence from military and veteran populations in the US and from around the world, the authors endeavor to explore various situational, psychological, and personality factors contributing to suicidality in military and veteran populations, and discuss their assessment means. Chapter 24 addresses "Integrative Clinical Assessment of Sexual and Gender Minority Clients", wherein Whitney Bliss and her associates supply an overview of minority stress and its mental health effects, and individual factors that may be associated with discrimination-related stressors. They further present a five-phased model of clinical assessment, and discuss some assessment measures highlighting the Cultural Assessment of Risk of Suicide – Minority Stress Scale (CMSS).

Addressing the basic issues of test construction with a specific approach, Burak Tunca proposes "Using the Johnson-Neyman Procedure to Detect Item Bias in Personality Tests: A Proposed New Method and Practical Guidelines for Data Analysis". Arguing for the need to ensure that the items are not endorsed differently across groups and the statistical results are not confounded, the author provides a review of the existing methods for assessing item bias in personality measures and presents some practical guidelines to the interested researchers for detecting item bias by using the Johnson-Neyman Procedure (e.g., in SPSS and LISREL syntaxes). The volume progresses further with the deliberations of Fluckinger and Snell about "User Reactions to Personality Assessment: Implications for Assessment Credibility, Utility, and Practicality". Mentioning the relative paucity of research on participants' reactions to personality assessment, the authors attempt to address the effects of user reactions as a relatively unexplored dimension of personality assessment, and try to analyze the ways in which consideration of these reactions offers the potential of increased credibility, general interest, utility and practicality.

Highlighting another significant issue of response distortion, Kurtz and colleagues offer "Novel Approaches to Adjusting for Positive Response Distortion (PRD) with the Personality Assessment Inventory (PAI)". They review the existing research efforts to detect and correct for PRD in major personality inventories, and thoroughly explore the Personality Assessment Inventory for its novel approaches of having Positive Impression Management predicted deviation scores and specific scores.

The authors also present their empirical findings showing the utility and limitations of these two novel approaches of PAI to adjust for PRD. Chapter 28 also addresses the related issue of "Applicant Faking Behavior", wherein Griffith and colleagues discuss this phenomenon and provide some insight regarding the findings at different levels of analysis (i.e., scale level, item level, composite level), propose a number of research questions that could be addressed at these levels of analysis, and discuss the implications of this research for the understanding of personality measurement. Towards the end of the volume, Johar and I have tried to make some explorative comments about "Transforming Assessment: New Pedagogies for the Digital Age". We endeavor to explore the technological challenges and try to address the technical advances that can provide newer future directions to psychological assessment. Keeping the utility of varied technological innovations in focus, we attempt to envisage a vision for the diverse applications of newly emerging technologies in the realm of psychological assessment. After discussion of the technological challenges, Mukherjee and I sum up the volume in Chapter 30 with a comprehensive note on "Ethical Issues in Personality Assessment". Ethical concerns always remain at the heart of psychological assessment, and therefore as an ethical editorial duty we discuss the ethical issues involved in personality assessment under various contexts in the light of the ethical guidelines established by different professional associations. Emphasis has been given to the crucial need to progressively evolve and refine the professional and ethical standards of personality assessment, to ensure ideal professional practices and to establish psychological assessment as an accurate and methodical discipline.

The volume includes chapters authored by internationally acclaimed researcher/scholars in their respective fields, and thus attempts to provide a comprehensive, multidirectional perspective on personality assessment. I am privileged to have worked with some of the world's leading researchers/academicians in editing this handbook, which would not have been possible at all without the unconditional support, diligence, commitment, and patience of the contributors. With its focus on the emerging trends and perspectives in personality assessment, the volume builds upon the knowledge base encapsulated by a plethora of existing research in the area, and provides many systematic directions and future possibilities in personality assessment. The volume also breaks new ground by exploring the possibility of using emerging technologies to find ever-expanding applications of personality assessment and enhance its predictive validity. The volume will provide a platform for discussion and a starting point for a fruitful endeavor towards developing a deeper understanding of the multifarious issues involved in personality assessment, and for providing a valuable input for structuring future developments in the area.

Editing a handbook on such a vast area of research like personality assessment is indubitably a gruelling task, and I convey my gratitude to everyone who contributed to this extensive effort and provided me with steady support. I am deeply indebted to the authors for the time and effort they have poured into the project. Their exceptional scholarly work significantly contributed to this eminent and enlightening product. I hope this handbook will create a common platform of interaction for researchers, academics, psychometricians, human resource practitioners, clinical psychologists, forensic psychologists, social workers, and other professionals in the field. It will serve as a pivotal reference point for crucial issues, and will function to generate new ideas for research and the continual advancement of the field of personality assessment.

Updesh Kumar

Section I
Emerging Conceptual Trends

1

Integrating Trait and Process Approaches to Personality: A Sketch of an Agenda

Robert R. McCrae
Gloucester, MA, USA

Since its inception as a separate section of the *Journal of Personality and Social Psychology*, "Personality Processes and Individual Differences" has implicitly defined the field of personality psychology. Great progress has been made in understanding individual differences in personality traits and related characteristics such as interests and values. But despite insightful and fruitful programs of research on such processes as self-regulation (Hoyle, 2010), attachment (Cassidy & Shaver, 2008), and identity formation (McAdams, 2003), there is nothing like a single, coherent account of personality processes *as a whole*. Perhaps this is because there are simply too many different processes at different levels of abstraction (and operating over different timescales) to allow an integration in the foreseeable future. But some commentators might have said the same about personality traits 40 years ago – and yet a reasonable understanding of the scope and hierarchical structure of traits has been achieved (John, Naumann, & Soto, 2008). The same will not happen for personality processes until the challenge is accepted and the task undertaken. Some theorists have begun this project (Fleeson & Jayawickreme, 2015; Hampson, 2012; Hooker & McAdams, 2003; Poropat & Corr, 2015); in this chapter I will sketch out another possible agenda that might structure efforts to understand the full scope and operation of personality processes. It builds on the greatest strength of contemporary personality psychology: our understanding of traits.

Individual Differences: The Five-Factor Model

The hierarchical structure of personality traits

The story of how the welter of trait constructs, labels, and scales was made manageable by the rise of the Five-Factor Model (FFM) of personality has been told many

The Wiley Handbook of Personality Assessment, First Edition. Edited by Updesh Kumar.
© 2016 John Wiley & Sons, Ltd. Published 2016 by John Wiley & Sons, Ltd.

times (Digman, 1990; McCrae & John, 1992). Today most psychologists recognize that, at a minimum, a comprehensive description of personality must include information on five very broad factors: Neuroticism (N), Extraversion (E), Openness to Experience (O), Agreeableness (A), and Conscientiousness (C). Some measure of these five factors is now routinely included in studies of individual difference variables, even if only to show that the variable of chief interest to the researchers offers some incremental validity. It usually does, because there are many important individual differences that are not wholly explained by the topmost level of the FFM. Often, these variables can be construed as narrower traits, or facets. The NEO Personality Inventory-3 (NEO-PI-3: McCrae & Costa, 2010) assesses 30 facets, six for each factor. Facets were chosen to represent the most important constructs in the psychological literature, but they clearly do not exhaust the possibilities – for example, punctuality appears to be a facet of C (Roberts, Bogg, Walton, Chernyshenko, & Stark, 2004) not included in the NEO-PI-3.

Some writers (Goldberg, 1993) have long argued that the trait hierarchy extends below the level of facets, to include distinct ways in which facet-level traits may be expressed. Roughly, these correspond to individual items in a trait scale. McCrae (2015) has called these lower-level traits *nuances*, and argued that they, like higher-level traits, are consensually valid, longitudinally stable, and heritable. Such claims can be examined by analyzing individual items from which the facet-level variance has been statistically removed, leaving only the item-specific variance. Research to date generally supports the hypothesis that nuances form a separate level of the trait hierarchy (Mõttus, McCrae, Allik, & Realo, 2014). What this means is that individuals are characterized over long periods of their lifespan not simply by five broad factors, but by a huge array of distinguishable tendencies. The person brings much more to each encounter with a situation than many of us had imagined.

Considerations for assessment

The hierarchical view of the FFM has three important implications for personality assessment. First, although assessment of the five factors is a useful addition to most research on individual differences – and essential to any understanding of the individual in clinical and other applied contexts – it is ultimately not sufficient. The assessment of facet-level traits (or at least a judicious selection of them) should become routine.

Second, the scales used to assess higher order traits must be sufficiently long to ensure that they assess the trait of interest. Single-item scales suffer not only from low reliability and narrow content that limits their predictive validity (Credé, Harms, Niehorster, & Gaye-Valentine, 2012), but also from a confounding of higher-level variance with facet- and nuance-level variance (McCrae, 2015). A substantial amount of the variance in any single item is specific to that item; the higher-order trait the item is supposed to indicate can be separated from this incidental variance only by aggregating across many items from a longer scale.

Third, researchers need to consider the use of individual items as predictors. On the one hand, they include valid trait variance that may prove particularly useful in understanding a specific criterion; researchers might formulate and test hypotheses about specific items (e.g., Terracciano et al., 2009). On the other hand, individual items are low in reliability, and the sheer number of items in a long inventory means that statistical tests, and thus opportunities for Type 1 errors, are multiplied in exploratory analyses. In addition, single items, unlike the scales they compose, have rarely been examined for construct validity. To understand the association of a particular nuance with some criterion, the researcher must rely on rational interpretation and, ideally, conduct corroborating research to demonstrate that the proposed interpretation is plausible.

Nature and properties of FFM traits

Armed with a comprehensive model and a variety of measures (De Raad & Perugini, 2002), personality psychologists have conducted systematic research and discovered a great deal about the nature of traits. These studies have illuminated the intrinsic nature of personality traits as well as documenting such properties as stability, developmental change, and universality.

Traits have sometimes been construed narrowly as patterns of behavior, suggesting that they are something akin to well-established habits. But a careful consideration of their correlates shows that each of the five factors has motivational (Costa & McCrae, 1988), emotional (Costa & McCrae, 1996), and interpersonal (Costa & McCrae, 2010) manifestations. Traits at all levels of the hierarchy are psychologically deeper than mere habitual behaviors (Costa & McCrae, in press).

They are deeper as well in the sense that they form a kind of core of personality in the broadest sense. FFM traits (Jang, McCrae, Angleitner, Riemann, & Livesley, 1998) and their structure (Yamagata et al., 2006) are heritable; they endure over decades (Terracciano, Costa, & McCrae, 2006) despite the vicissitudes of life experience; and they emerge in strikingly similar form in widely different cultures (McCrae, Terracciano, & 78 Members, 2005). FFM traits are a central part of human nature, and each individual's traits are central parts of his or her identity (McCrae & Costa, 1988a; Sheldon, Ryan, Rawsthorne, & Ilardi, 1997).

The FFM in a framework for personality processes

Cervone (2005) noted that there are two distinct meanings of the term *personality structure*: one refers to the organization of personality variables in a population (for example, the FFM), whereas the other refers to the organization and operation of personality mechanisms within an individual (most famously, Freud's id, ego, and superego). Cervone argued that the FFM cannot refer to both; although it is a useful model of individual differences, it cannot represent the intrapsychic structure of personality. Conceptually, a dimension of individual differences cannot be a mechanism inside an individual's head; emprically, the observed covariation of behaviors or states of any particular person need not, and often does not, mirror the covariation of traits in the population. For example, characteristic levels of cheerfulness and sadness are essentially independent in groups of people, but at any given moment, the degree of cheerfulness in an individual is inversely related to the degree of sadness (Diener & Emmons, 1984).

So far, so good. But Cervone (2005) then concluded that this means that traits of the FFM cannot be causes for, or provide explanations of, the behavior and experience of individuals. This conclusion does not follow, and stems, it appears, from a failure to recognize two distinct meanings of the term *trait*. In one sense, *trait* refers to a characteristic of an individual (e.g., Mary's curly hair or her trustworthiness); in a second sense, *trait* refers to a dimension of individual differences (e.g., curliness of hair or degree of trustworthiness). Tellegen (1991) distinguished the latter by calling it a *trait dimension*, and would say that the FFM is a structural model of personality trait dimensions. Of course, trait dimensions do not cause behavior in individuals, but intrapsychic traits may. Mary's trustworthiness may be a (partial) explanation of why she followed through on her commitment to walk the dog.

For most psychologists (and most laypersons), the idea that there are enduring dispositions within people that help explain their actions is so obvious that it hardly requires a defense. It is also intuitively clear that differences across people help to identify the nature of dispositions within them. We know that the A disposition is not the same as the E disposition because some people are agreeable but not extraverted, and some are extraverted but not agreeable. Readers interested in the arguments that have been offered against this common-sense position and the rebuttals to those arguments can consult McCrae and Costa (2008a; see also McCrae & Costa, 1995). For the present purpose, it suffices to say that it is legitimate to use FFM traits within the person when constructing an account of personality processes.

Intrapsychic Structure and Personality Processes

Needs and the need for traits

Personality processes refer to the ways in which intrapsychic structures interact with each other and the world, so the study of processes or mechanisms must begin by identifying these internal structures – mental contents that account for how people act and feel. The variables that have received the most attention from recent personality process theorists are those that account for the purposeful direction of behavior: needs, motives, goals, strivings. Although important distinctions can be drawn among these constructs (Sheldon, 2011), they share an emphasis on selecting and guiding behavior. Dweck (1996) argued that "our most meaningful affect, cognition, and behavior occur and cohere in relation to our goals" (p. 349), and believed that they formed the most natural level of analysis for personality psychology. Cervone (2005) included goals along with beliefs and standards (or values) as the major intentional mental structures; each has associated appraisal processes. For example, we might evaluate political candidates in terms of our standards of public duty; interpret the results of a political poll as vindication of our belief that the public is ignorant; and decide to contribute to the underdog as a way of furthering our political agenda. *Evaluating*, *interpreting*, and *planning* to achieve our goals are personality processes.

Cervone's (2005) knowledge-and-appraisal personality architecture (KAPA) is based on rather abstract philosophical distinctions about intentional mental contents, and might serve as the basis for a computer simulation of personality. In particular, KAPA does not emphasize the human origin of goals and standards. In contrast, Deci and Ryan's (2000) self-determination theory (SDT) also sees goals as central personality variables, but grounds them in basic human needs for autonomy, competence, and relatedness. Goals themselves are relatively arbitrary – I may aspire to lose weight, or finish reading *War and Peace*, or join a cult – but according to SDT, goal-related pursuits will be rewarding and sustained if and only if they satisfy needs for autonomy, competence, or relatedness.

Intrinsic and extrinsic motivation are central concepts in SDT. Behavior that is performed because individuals "feel free to follow their inner interests" (Deci & Ryan, 2000, p. 234) is intrinsically motivated, and has the potential to satisfy needs for autonomy and competence. If, however, external influences undermine the sense of free behavior (e.g., by imposing a deadline or providing a monetary incentive), the same behavior is no longer as satisfying, and the enjoyment and quality of the performance decline. The mechanism here is a "shift toward a more external perceived locus of causality" (p. 234), a kind of reappraisal that occurs at the level of a specific behavior. Behavior that is performed ultimately because it is required by external forces (e.g., cultural mores) has extrinsic motivation, but the individual can derive some satisfaction of basic needs from these behaviors if he or she internalizes the values embodied in the behavior, ideally integrating them with other values and standards with which the person has identified. Internalization is a process that presumably occurs over a long period of time, and results in a change not simply in behavior, but in the inner nature of the person – one's identity.

In SDT, needs for autonomy, competence, and relatedness are thought to be universal, so the only individual difference variables of interest are measures of the degree to which these needs are satisfied. That, in turn, is thought to be determined by the life experience of the individual, and by the individual's reactions (including defenses) to frustrations of these needs. This emphasis on the environmental determinants of individual differences is understandable, given that much of the research upon which SDT is based was experimental. However, it seems odd for a theory of personality (especially one that values self-determination!) to ignore so completely the contribution of the person. There are at least two reasons why an account of intrapsychic structures should move beyond those universals emphasized by SDT to include innate individual differences, especially personality traits.

First, there is empirical evidence that need satisfaction is related in part to personality traits. Understandably, agreeable extraverts are more satisfied with their relatedness than are antagonistic introverts; adjusted and conscientious extraverts have a greater sense of competence; and open and adjusted extraverts perceive higher levels of autonomy (Sabol, 2005; Weinstein, Pryzbylski, & Ryan, 2012). It is particularly noteworthy that need satisfaction can be thwarted by one's own personality traits. Lamenting his unmet need for relatedness, the defiantly disagreeable Calvin once remarked to Hobbes, "I wish I had more friends, but people are such jerks." (Watterson, 2012). Like SDT, Calvin blames the environment for his condition, although external observers might attribute the problem to his characteristic way of evaluating others.

Second, a consideration of traits could supplement SDT's account of intrinsic motivation. What is it that makes a particular kind of activity interesting for its own sake? There is a substantial literature trying traits to occupational and recreational interests (De Fruyt & Mervielde, 1997; Kandler, Bleidorn, Riemann, Angleitner, & Spinath, 2011). Charitable work may appeal to one high in A3: Altruism; organizing a messy desk may be more engaging to one high in C2: Order. Indeed, the whole concept of intrinsic motivation would seem most applicable to behaviors that are congruent with one's trait profile. Personality processes cannot be fully understood without a consideration of traits as part of the intrapsychic structure. And as Hampson (2012) noted, "studies demonstrate that the addition of personality traits increases the explanatory power of processes involving social-cognitive constructs" (p. 329).

Dynamic processes in Five-Factor Theory

Five-Factor Theory (FFT; McCrae & Costa, 1996, 2008b) is a general theory of personality that was developed to account for the results of research on the FFM. The most striking research finding was that traits seemed to be relatively independent of the particular contexts in which they were expressed. They demonstrated continuity across much of the lifespan (Terracciano et al., 2006), showed little impact of childrearing practices and childhood environments (McCrae & Costa, 1988b), and were found in similar form in the most diverse cultures (McCrae & Costa, 1997). This was odd, because habits and interests certainly change with age; children learn language, religion, and food preferences from their parents; and values and customs vary widely by culture. It appeared to us that there must be a profound difference between personality traits and such things as habits, religion, and customs. FFT described traits as *basic tendencies* (BTs) and distinguishes the other phenomena as *characteristic adaptations* (CAs), because they are the unique adaptations that a particular person makes to specific life circumstances.

Nowadays most personality theories are formulated as systems (Cervone, 2005), and FFT can be summarized in a system diagram. Figure 1.1 shows that the five broad personality factors are classed as BTs, but so are narrower facets and nuances of personality (as well as other characteristics such as intelligence, musical ability, and universal needs for air, food, and perhaps autonomy, competence, and relatedness). All these are postulated to have *biological bases.* However, many of the phenomena that psychologists are interested in (including beliefs, goals, skills, habits, roles, and relationships) are classed as CAs; the *self-concept* is singled out as a particularly important CA.

For the present purposes, the most relevant part of Figure 1.1 is the set of arrows marked *dynamic processes*, which represent the chief causal pathways between components of the system. Across a long time-frame, the crucial paths show the influences (**a**) of personality traits and (**b**) of *external influences* (EIs) on the development of CAs. For example, an individual high in Openness to Aesthetics who is given an opportunity to take piano lessons may develop technical skill and a musical repertoire. Across a short time-frame, Figure 1.1 shows that the individual behaviors that cumulate into the *objective biography* (OB) of the

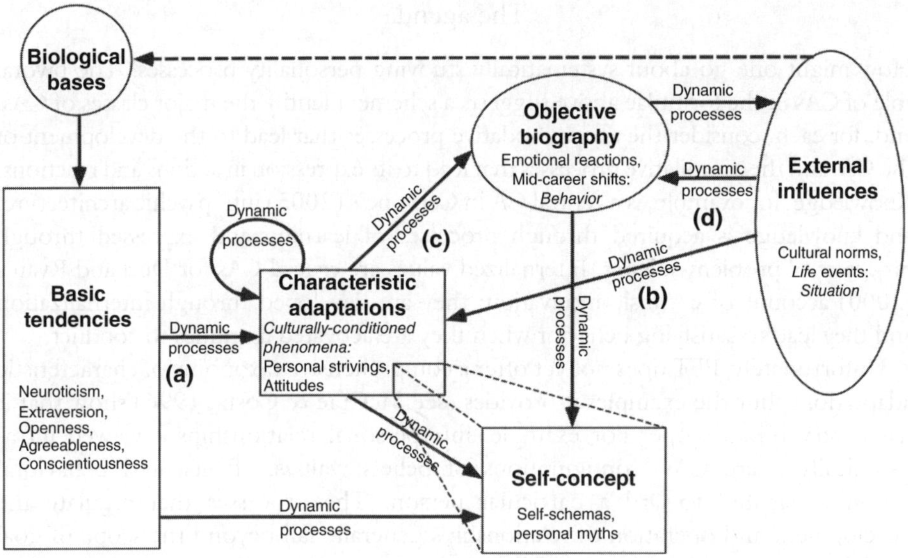

Figure 1.1 A representation of the Five-Factor Theory personality system, with examples of the contents of each component. Intrapsychic components are in rectangles; extrapsychic components are in ellipses. Adapted from McCrae and Costa (2008b).

individual are influenced (**c**) by the habits, beliefs, and so on, of the person and (**d**) by the immediate demands and affordances of the situation. If asked to perform at a party, our pianist may draw on her skills and musical memory to play a popular tune.

Although it is not obvious from the figure, FFT holds that these causal influences work jointly: adaptations are not simply the sum of trait influences plus life experience influences, but mental structures that evolve as individuals with particular traits interact over time with particular life experiences. Similarly, behaviors reflect the response to a given situation by a person with specific CAs.

These two interactive mechanisms might be distinguished by the Piagetian terms *accommodation* (the creation of new mental structures, namely, CAs) and *assimilation* (the generation of acts and reactions consistent with existing CAs in each situation). These can be represented symbolically by the following formulae:

(1) $(BT, EI) \rightarrow CA$ (*accommodation*)

(2) $(CA, EI) \rightarrow OB$ (*assimilation*)

These are the classes of psychological processes of central interest to personality psychologists; other arrows in Figure 1.1 refer to specialized instances of assimilation or accommodation (e.g., modifying the self-concept) or to interactions between the core and periphery of the personality system. The dynamic processes that generate BTs from biological bases are the province of neuroscience; those that account for the influence of the individual's behavior on his or her environment are best studied by social psychologists or sociologists.

The agenda

How might one go about systematically studying personality processes? The pivotal role of CAs in the formulae above suggests a scheme: identify the major classes of CAs, and, for each, consider the accommodative processes that lead to the development of the CA, and the assimilative processes that lead to its expression in actions and reactions. Knowledge, for example, is a central CA in Cervone's (2005) intrapsychic architecture, and knowledge is acquired through processes of learning and expressed through processes of problem-solving. Internalized values are crucial CAs for Deci and Ryan's (2000) account of extrinsic motivation; they are developed through internalization and they lead to satisfying behavior when they are activated as guides to conduct.

Unfortunately, FFT does not yet offer a comprehensive taxonomy of characteristic adaptations, but the examples it provides (see McCrae & Costa, 1996) show that it has a very broad scope. For example, interpersonal relationships – viewed intrapsychically – are CAs: configurations of beliefs, values, affects, and behavioral routines oriented toward a particular person. The processes that regulate the development and operation of relationships generally fall beyond the scope of goal models of personality processes – falling in love or coming to hate one's boss are not usually goal-directed – but they are certainly processes in which personality psychologists (e.g., attachment theorists) have a strong interest. Table 1.1 lists some examples of CAs and their associated processes.

Table 1.1 does not, however, explain *how* BTs, and especially FFM traits, are involved in creating CAs. Postulate 6b of FFT, *Differential dynamics*, states that "some dynamic processes are affected differentially by basic tendencies of the individual, including personality traits" (McCrae & Costa, 1996, p. 75). Take learning, for example. Clearly, the most relevant BT is general intelligence, sometimes defined as the capacity for learning. However, personality traits also affect the learning process, through learning styles or strategies (Bickle, 1996). Costa and Piedmont (2003) described styles of learning based on the two factors of O and C. Open individuals are intrinsically interested in new knowledge, although their interests may not be well focused; conscientious people are diligent scholars who learn well because they apply themselves. Combinations of these two factors (or their lack) lead to different styles of learning. All five factors affect the development of CAs. For example, N predisposes individual to form anxious attachments (Shaver & Brennan, 1992), and E leads people to develop social and enterprising vocational interests (Costa, McCrae, & Holland, 1984).

Note that many of the characteristics that we normally class as correlates of personality traits are acquired through time and experience. No one is born with an innate fondness for skydiving, but almost everyone encounters situations with an element of danger. For some people these are unpleasant encounters, and they learn to avoid them. For others – extraverted excitement-seekers – they provide a special rush that the individual relishes. From peers, movies, and video games, excitement seekers learn the options available in their culture to satisfy the need for thrills, and, given the opportunity, they may try them and find that they greatly enjoy them. Skydiving may become a hobby, the source of a new social circle, and a salient part of the extravert's identity.

Table 1.1 Some examples of personality processes associated with characteristic adaptations

(BT, EI) → CA			*(CA, EI) → OB*
Basic tendency	*Accommodative process*	*Characteristic adaptation*	*Assimilative process*
O[a] →	Implicit learning		
C[b] →	Methodical study	Knowledge	Creativity; Problem-solving
C[c] →	Habit formation		
E[d] →	Acculturation	Daily routines	Role performance; Automaticity
O[e] →	Ego development		
A[f] →	Socialization	Value system	Extrinsic motivation; Prioritization
E[g] →	Mating strategies		
N[h] →	Attachment	Relationships	Jealousy; Communication
N[i] →	Identification		
O[j] →	Identity exploration	Self-concept	Assumed similarity; Self-disclosure

Note: BTs (basic tendencies) interacting with EIs (external influences) lead to the development of CAs (characteristic adaptations) through accommodative processes. The CAs lead to actions and reactions, that is, the OB (objective biography), through assimilative processes. Table notes document associations between traits and accommodative processes. BTs may also affect assimilative processes as moderator variables, although that is not represented in this table.

[a]Kaufman et al. (2010); [b]Bickle (1996); [c]McCrae and Löckenhoff (2010); [d]Ryder, Alden, and Paulhus (2000); [e]Einstein and Lanning (1998); [f]Olver and Mooradian (2003); [g]Nettle (2005); [h]Shaver and Brennan (1992); [i]Johnson and Morgeson (2005); [j]Tesch and Cameron (1987).

McCrae and Costa (1991) distinguished between *temperamental* and *instrumental* links between traits and psychological wellbeing, and Hampson (2012) pointed out that these roughly parallel the distinction between moderator and mediator effects. One might further argue that assimilative processes sometimes show the moderating effects of traits on the expression of CAs, whereas accommodative processes explain how trait manifestation is mediated by CAs. To return to the example of skydiving, a reaction to a first experience of risk-taking is moderated by level of E: everyone may experience some degree of pleasant excitement, but the extravert feels much more than the introvert. We say that such people are temperamentally suited to thrill-seeking. In contrast, becoming a skydiver is a lengthy process that requires training, financial investment, socialization into a subculture, perhaps the development of a new life narrative. All of this is instrumental, with skydiving mediating the satisfaction of the extravert's need for excitement.

Table 1.1 illustrates that multiple processes may be associated with any given CA, and the example of learning shows that different personality factors may affect the same process. In some ideal future, Table 1.1 might be an exhaustive catalog, with all relevant processes listed for each CA, each process classified by the factor (or facet) that affects it. Imagine, then, sorting the rows by personality factor; the result would be a compendium of the ways in which personality traits "get outside the skin" (Hampson, 2012).

McCrae and Löckenhoff (2010) provided a conceptual analysis of how and why individuals high in C come to show high levels of self-control. McCrae (1976) had proposed a number of techniques for self-control, and McCrae and Löckenhoff argued that most of them would be easier for individuals high in C. For example, *balance of interest* is a technique in which people delay or deny gratification by focusing on long-term goals. Because conscientious people have better formulated life goals than undirected people, the balance tips toward self-control more frequently for them. Again, *commitment* is a technique in which people make resolutions and wager their self-esteem on the success with which they keep them; high C individuals have a strong need for achievement which motivates such a wager. Self-control requires the expenditure of effort (Muraven, Tice, & Baumeister, 1998), and conscientious people have more of the purposeful energy that can fuel efforts.

These are, of course, interpretations rather than established facts, but they illustrate how testable hypotheses can be generated by considering the ways in which personality traits affect the processes that produce relevant outcomes. Process research fills in the causal gaps between assessed traits and their established correlates.

Complexities

The tidy organization of Table 1.1 belies the true complexity of understanding processes, and anyone considering work on the proposed agenda needs to be forewarned. Here are a few of the issues that pose complications:

- Personality traits affect some CAs more than others. English speakers growing up in Boston acquire an accent that probably has little or nothing to do with their traits. Not all psychological processes are personality processes.
- Some CAs are more durable than others, and the theoretical status of shortlived phenomena is not always clear. The lifelong goal of becoming a great novelist is surely a CA, but what about the personal project (Little, Lecci, & Watkinson, 1992) of completing an assigned essay by Wednesday? Is that a CA, or better regarded as an outcome, an instance of behavior that is to be explained rather than an intrapsychic structure used to provide explanations?

- Like all causal chains, personality processes are indefinitely divisible into subprocesses. *Achieving a goal* may involve perceiving a situation, appraising it as an opportunity to meet a need, formulating a plan, making an effort, using a skill. In turn, *formulating a plan* may involve remembering learned strategies, weighing the alternatives, coordinating with other planned or ongoing activities, and so on. An exhaustive explanation is impossible; researchers must select a segment of the causal chain that is convenient for research or useful in applications.
- Processes may be multidetermined. Solving a problem may involve divergent thinking moderated by O, repeated efforts requiring high levels of C, and cooperation with others working on the problem (facilitated by A). Different environments can shape or constrain the operation of a psychological process. Further, outcomes often show equifinality, the same result emerging from different processes. The path from traits to behaviors is through personality processes, but there are many alternate routes.

These considerations are not intended to discourage research on personality processes, but they do suggest that no single individual or research team will be able to provide a comprehensive account of them. Perhaps personality psychologists should approach this task like the Human Genome Project, a grand collective effort with enormous potential payoff. (Or perhaps, given the realities of funding in the social sciences, crowd sourcing is a better model.) The researchers cited in the notes to Table 1.1 are pioneers in this project.

Assessing Personality Traits and Processes

An agenda with some similarity to that offered here was proposed by Hooker and McAdams (2003) in what they called the Six-Foci Model. In place of BTs, CAs, and the self-concept, it specifies traits, goals, and life narratives as structures. A class of processes is associated with each structure. In an ambitious study, Hooker, Choun, Mejía, Pham, and Metoyer (2013) assessed the five factors in 99 older adults, and then used internet technology to survey daily stress and progress toward health and social goals over 100 days. Using multilevel analysis, they showed that N hindered, and E and C facilitated, progress toward goals. Sophisticated analyses also revealed interactions between perceived daily stress and traits; in particular, stress interfered with goal progress chiefly among those high in N.

Studies such as this, which trace patterns of action and reaction over time and analyze them in conjunction with enduring traits, will play an important role in research on personality processes. However, many research designs and assessment strategies can advance our understanding of processes without requiring such a commitment of time and participant effort.

The simplest way to build up a body of information about traits and processes is routinely to include measures of traits – at least the five broad factors – in experimental studies. If a given trait facilitates the operation of a process, then those individuals with higher levels of that trait should show more effects in the experimental conditions that activate the process. Historically, these trait moderator effects were called Trait × Treatment interactions, because they were usually concerned with psychotherapy. Clearly, this design has broader applicability. Ideally, specific hypotheses would be tested, but systematic exploratory analyses are also worth reporting. Future meta-analyses could make sense of even small and occasional findings. Social, educational, and clinical psychologists could – and should – contribute to this literature.

One of the advantages of experimental studies is that the participant need not understand which processes are activated; many of them are below the level of awareness. But in some cases, people know full well what is going on in their heads and can report about it if asked. Surely the most widely researched personality processes are ways of coping (Folkman & Lazarus, 1985). McCrae and Costa (1986) asked respondents to recall a particular stressful event and then to indicate which of a series of coping responses they made (and whether it helped them solve the problem or feel better). Carver, Scheier, and Weintraub (1989) created a dispositional coping measure, presumably tapping recurrent coping strategies. Different ways of coping are meaningfully related to basic personality traits (Watson & Hubbard, 1996); in particular, individuals high in N tend to use immature and ineffective mechanisms.

The scope of personality traits is reasonably circumscribed; one can measure most traits of interest with a few hundred items. It does not seem likely that researchers will create comparable omnibus personality process measures, because there are too many discrete processes – McCrae (1982), for example, identified 28 different ways of coping. Instead, assessments of process variables are likely to be specialized and domain-specific; tools that are useful for particular research topics or for educational, clinical, or other applications. Global personality trait assessments will remain useful because they summarize the outcomes of a myriad of internal processes. Regardless of the how or why, extraverts will usually end up acting and reacting like extraverts, neurotics like neurotics. For those trying to understand people, this is very valuable knowledge.

Acknowledgments

I thank Kennon Sheldon, Sarah Hampson, and Corinna Löckenhoff for helpful comments on the manuscript.

Robert R. McCrae receives royalties from the NEO Inventories.

References

Bickle, G. (1996). Personality traits, learning strategies, and performance. *European Journal of Personality, 10* (5), 337–352.

Carver, C.S., Scheier, M.F., & Weintraub, J.K. (1989). Assessing coping strategies: A theoretically based approach. *Journal of Personality and Social Psychology, 56* (2), 267–283.

Cassidy, J., & Shaver, P.R. (Eds.) (2008). *Handbook of Attachment: Theory, Research, and Clinical Applications.* New York: Guilford.

Cervone, D. (2005). Personality architecture: Within-person structures and processes. *Annual Review of Psychology, 56*, 423–452.

Costa, P.T., Jr., & McCrae, R.R. (1988). From catalog to classification: Murray's needs and the Five-Factor Model. *Journal of Personality and Social Psychology, 55* (2), 258–265.

Costa, P.T., Jr., & McCrae, R.R. (1996). Mood and personality in adulthood. In C. Magai & S.H. McFadden (Eds.), *Handbook of Emotion, Adult Development, and Aging* (pp. 369–383). San Diego: Academic Press.

Costa, P.T., Jr., & McCrae, R.R. (2010). The Five-Factor Model, Five-Factor Theory, and interpersonal psychology. In S. Strack & L.M. Horowitz (Eds.), *Handbook of Interpersonal Psychology* (pp. 91–104). New York: Guilford.

Costa, P.T., Jr., & McCrae, R.R. (in press). The NEO Inventories as instruments of psychological theory. In T.A. Widiger (Ed.), *Oxford Handbook of the Five-Factor Model.* Oxford: Oxford University Press.

Costa, P.T., Jr., McCrae, R.R., & Holland, J.L. (1984). Personality and vocational interests in an adult sample. *Journal of Applied Psychology, 69* (3), 390–400.

Costa, P.T., Jr., & Piedmont, R.L. (2003). Multivariate assessment: NEO-PI-R profiles of Madeline G. In J.S. Wiggins (Ed.), *Paradigms of Personality Assessment* (pp. 262–280). New York: Guilford.

Credé, M., Harms, P., Niehorster, S., & Gaye-Valentine, A. (2012). An evaluation of the consequences of using short measures of the Big Five personality traits. *Journal of Personality and Social Psychology, 102* (4), 874–888.

Deci, E.L., & Ryan, R.M. (2000). The "what" and "why" of goal pursuits: Human needs and the self-determination of behavior. *Psychological Inquiry, 11* (4), 227–268.

De Fruyt, F., & Mervielde, I. (1997). The Five-Factor Model of personality and Holland's RIASEC interest types. *Personality and Individual Differences, 23* (1), 87–103.

De Raad, B., & Perugini, M. (2002). *Big Five Assessment.* Gottingen, Germany: Hogrefe & Huber Publishers.

Diener, E., & Emmons, R.A. (1984). The independence of positive and negative affect. *Journal of Personality and Social Psychology, 47* (5), 1105–1117.

Digman, J.M. (1990). Personality structure: Emergence of the Five-Factor Model. *Annual Review of Psychology, 41,* 417–440.

Dweck, C.S. (1996). Capturing the dynamic nature of personality. *Journal of Research in Personality, 30* (3), 348–362.

Einstein, D., & Lanning, K. (1998). Shame, guilt, ego development and the Five-Factor Model of personality. *Journal of Personality, 66* (4), 555–582.

Fleeson, W., & Jayawickreme, E. (2015). Whole trait theory. *Journal of Research in Personality, 56,* 82–92.

Folkman, S., & Lazarus, R.S. (1985). If it changes it must be a process: Study of emotion and coping during three stages of a college examination. *Journal of Personality and Social Psychology, 48* (1), 150–170.

Goldberg, L.R. (1993). The structure of personality traits: Vertical and horizontal aspects. In D.C. Funder, R. Parke, C. Tomlinson-Keasey, & K. Widaman (Eds.), *Studying Lives through Time: Approaches to Personality and Development* (pp. 169–188). Washington, DC: American Psychological Association.

Hampson, S.E. (2012). Personality processes: Mechanisms by which personality traits "get outside the skin". *Annual Review of Psychology, 63,* 315–339.

Hooker, K., Choun, S., Mejía, S., Pham, T., & Metoyer, R. (2013). A microlongitudinal study of the linkages among personality traits, self-regulation, and stress in older adults. *Research in Human Development, 10* (1), 26–46.

Hooker, K., & McAdams, D.P. (2003). Personality reconsidered: A new agenda for aging research. *Journal of Gerontology: Psychological Sciences, 58B* (6), 296–304.

Hoyle, R.H. (Ed.). (2010). *Handbook of Personality and Self-regulation*. Malden, MA: Wiley-Blackwell.

Jang, K.L., McCrae, R.R., Angleitner, A., Riemann, R., & Livesley, W.J. (1998). Heritability of facet-level traits in a cross-cultural twin sample: Support for a hierarchical model of personality. *Journal of Personality and Social Psychology, 74* (6), 1556–1565.

John, O.P., Naumann, L., & Soto, C.J. (2008). Paradigm shift to the integrative Big Five taxonomy: Discovery, measurement, and conceptual issues. In O.P. John, R.W. Robins, & L.A. Pervin (Eds.), *Handbook of Personality: Theory and Research* (3rd ed.) (pp. 114–158). New York: Guilford.

Johnson, M.D., & Morgeson, F.P. (2005). Cognitive and affective identification in organizational settings. *Academy of Management Proceedings, 1* (August), S1–S6.

Kandler, C., Bleidorn, W., Riemann, R., Angleitner, A., & Spinath, F.M. (2011). The genetic links between the Big Five personality traits and general interest domains. *Personality and Social Psychology Bulletin, 37* (12), 1633–1643.

Kaufman, S.B., DeYoung, C.G., Gray, J.R., Jiménez, L., Brown, J., & Mackintosh, N. (2010). Implicit learning as an ability. *Cognition, 116* (3), 321–340.

Little, B.R., Lecci, L., & Watkinson, B. (1992). Personality and personal projects: Linking Big Five and PAC units of analysis. *Journal of Personality, 60* (2), 501–525.

McAdams, D.P. (2003). Identity and the life story. In R. Fivush & C.A. Haden (Eds.), *Autobiographical Memory and the Construction of a Narrative Self: Developmental and Cultural Perspectives* (pp. 187–207). Mahwah, NJ: Erlbaum.

McCrae, R.R. (1976). Self-control: Theories, techniques, and the example of increasing study time. *Dissertation Abstracts International, 37* (3-B), 1410.

McCrae, R.R. (1982). Age differences in the use of coping mechanisms. *Journal of Gerontology, 37* (4), 454–460.

McCrae, R.R. (2015). A more nuanced view of reliability: Specificity in the trait hierarchy. *Personality and Social Psychology Review, 19* (2), 97–112.

McCrae, R.R., & Costa, P.T., Jr. (1986). Personality, coping, and coping effectiveness in an adult sample. *Journal of Personality, 54* (2), 385–405.

McCrae, R.R., & Costa, P.T., Jr. (1988a). Age, personality, and the spontaneous self-concept. *Journal of Gerontology: Social Sciences, 43* (6), S177–S185.

McCrae, R.R., & Costa, P.T., Jr. (1988b). Do parental influences matter? A reply to Halverson. *Journal of Personality, 56* (2), 445–449.

McCrae, R.R., & Costa, P.T., Jr. (1991). Adding *Liebe und Arbeit:* The full Five-Factor Model and well-being. *Personality and Social Psychology Bulletin, 17* (2), 227–232.

McCrae, R.R., & Costa, P.T., Jr. (1995). Trait explanations in personality psychology. *European Journal of Personality, 9* (4), 231–252.

McCrae, R.R., & Costa, P.T., Jr. (1996). Toward a new generation of personality theories: Theoretical contexts for the Five-Factor Model. In J.S. Wiggins (Ed.), *The Five-Factor Model of Personality: Theoretical Perspectives* (pp. 51–87). New York: Guilford.

McCrae, R.R., & Costa, P.T., Jr. (1997). Personality trait structure as a human universal. *American Psychologist, 52* (5), 509–516.

McCrae, R.R., & Costa, P.T., Jr. (2008a). Empirical and theoretical status of the Five-Factor Model of personality traits. In G. Boyle, G. Matthews, & D. Saklofske (Eds.), Sage *Handbook of Personality Theory and Assessment* (Vol. *1*, pp. 273–294). Los Angeles: Sage.

McCrae, R.R., & Costa, P.T., Jr. (2008b). The Five-Factor Theory of personality. In O.P. John, R.W. Robins, & L.A. Pervin (Eds.), *Handbook of Personality: Theory and Research* (3rd ed.) (pp. 159–181). New York: Guilford.

McCrae, R.R., & Costa, P.T., Jr. (2010). *NEO Inventories Professional Manual.* Odessa, FL: Psychological Assessment Resources.

McCrae, R.R., & John, O.P. (1992). An introduction to the Five-Factor Model and its applications. *Journal of Personality, 60* (2), 175–215.

McCrae, R.R., & Löckenhoff, C.E. (2010). Self-regulation and the Five-Factor Model of personality traits. In R.H. Hoyle (Ed.), *The Handbook of Self-regulation and Personality* (pp. 145–168). Oxford: Blackwell Publishing.

McCrae, R.R., Terracciano, A., & 78 Members of the Personality Profiles of Cultures Project. (2005). Universal features of personality traits from the observer's perspective: Data from 50 cultures. *Journal of Personality and Social Psychology, 88* (3), 547–561.

Mõttus, R., McCrae, R.R., Allik, J., & Realo, A. (2014). Cross-rater agreement on common and specific variance of personality scales and items. *Journal of Research in Personality, 52*, 47–54.

Muraven, M., Tice, D.M., & Baumeister, R.F. (1998). Self-control as a limited resource: Regulatory depletion patterns. *Journal of Personality and Social Psychology, 74* (3), 774–789.

Nettle, D. (2005). An evolutionary approach to the extraversion continuum. *Evolution and Human Behavior, 26*, 363–373.

Olver, J.M., & Mooradian, T.A. (2003). Personality traits and personal values: A conceptual and empirical integration. *Personality and Individual Differences, 35* (1), 109–125.

Poropat, A.E., & Corr, P. (2015). Thinking bigger: The Cronbachian paradigm and personality theory. *Journal of Research in Personality, 56*, 59–69.

Roberts, B., Bogg, T., Walton, K.E., Chernyshenko, O.S., & Stark, S.E. (2004). A lexical investigation of the lower-order structure of Conscientiousness. *Journal of Research in Personality, 38* (2), 164–178.

Ryder, A.G., Alden, L.E., & Paulhus, D.L. (2000). Is acculturation unidimensional or bidimensional? A head-to-head comparison in the prediction of personality, self-identity, and adjustment. *Journal of Personality and Social Psychology, 79* (1), 49–65.

Sabol, J. (2005). *Personality traits and basic psychological needs as predictors of life satisfaction.* Unpublished thesis, University of Zagreb, Zagreb.

Shaver, P.R., & Brennan, K.A. (1992). Attachment styles and the "Big Five" personality traits: Their connection with each other and with romantic relationship outcomes. *Personality and Social Psychology Bulletin, 18* (5), 536–545.

Sheldon, K.M. (2011). Integrating behavioral-motive and experiential-requirement perspectives on psychological needs: A two process model. *Psychological Review, 118* (4), 552–569.

Sheldon, K.M., Ryan, R.M., Rawsthorne, L.J., & Ilardi, B. (1997). Trait self and true self: Cross-role variation in the Big Five personality traits and its relations with psychological authenticity and subjective well-being. *Journal of Personality and Social Psychology, 73* (6), 1380–1393.

Tellegen, A. (1991). Personality traits: Issues of definition, evidence and assessment. In W. Grove & D. Cicchetti (Eds.), *Thinking Clearly about Psychology: Essays in honor of Paul Everett Meehl* (Vol. *2*, pp. 10–35). Minneapolis: University of Minnesota Press.

Terracciano, A., Costa, P.T., Jr., & McCrae, R.R. (2006). Personality plasticity after age 30. *Personality and Social Psychology Bulletin, 32* (8), 999–1009.

Terracciano, A., Sutin, A.R., McCrae, R.R., Deiana, B., Ferrucci, L., Schlessinger, D., et al. (2009). Facets of personality linked to underweight and overweight. *Psychosomatic Medicine, 71* (6), 682–689.

Tesch, S.A., & Cameron, K.A. (1987). Openness to experience and the development of adult identity. *Journal of Personality, 55* (4), 615–630.

Watson, D., & Hubbard, B. (1996). Adaptational style and dispositional structure: Coping in the context of the Five-Factor Model. *Journal of Personality, 64* (4), 737–774.

Watterson, B. (2012). *The Complete Calvin and Hobbes.* Kansas City, MO: Andrews McMeel.

Weinstein, N., Pryzbylski, A.K., & Ryan, R.M. (2012). The index of autonomous functioning: Development of a scale of human autonomy. *Journal of Research in Personality, 46* (4), 397–413.

Yamagata, S., Suzuki, A., Ando, J., Ono, Y., Kijima, N., Yoshimura, K., et al. (2006). Is the genetic structure of human personality universal? A cross-cultural twin study from North America, Europe, and Asia. *Journal of Personality and Social Psychology, 90* (6), 987–998.

2

Personality Assessment and Theory

Philip J. Corr
City University, London, UK

Arthur E. Poropat
Griffith University, Australia

The purpose of personality assessment is to provide descriptive (operational) measures of underlying (latent) constructs that account for systematic differences between people in affect, cognition, and behavior, sampled over time and across situations, and usually related to a specific outcome (e.g., occupational performance or everyday prediction of others' future behavior). Related to this main aim of assessment is a second more theoretical one, namely to uncover the causal roots of observed individual differences, in neurological, psychological or social terms. From a scientific perspective, this second aim is just as important as the first one; however, in much of personality psychology that focuses on testing and assessment, it is seen as either unimportant or, at least, subsidiary to the main task at hand.

This chapter argues that, not only are both aims essential, but neglect of the causal question undermines the validity of personality assessment in general. To our scientific minds, the way forward in personality assessment is to acknowledge this fact, appreciate its implications, and to adopt new procedures to address it directly.

An obvious, but highly important, first point to make when considering the nature of personality assessment is that the operational *something* to be assessed is valid only in terms of underlying latent factors. Only by understanding the true nature of these underlying constructs, and their separate influences on variance components, can we begin to have a chance of understanding the true nature of measured factors. Although far from easy in application, the bridging of this gulf is a major challenge facing personality assessment in particular, and personality psychology more generally.

To repeat a crucial point, this is not merely a conceptual matter. Even in applied areas of assessment (e.g., personnel selection), we need to know the nature of *why* personality measures correlate with real-world outcomes (e.g., occupational success). Included among the answer to this *why* question will be consideration of both person and environmental factors, and their interactions, and the influence of multiple sources of variance.

The Wiley Handbook of Personality Assessment, First Edition. Edited by Updesh Kumar.
© 2016 John Wiley & Sons, Ltd. Published 2016 by John Wiley & Sons, Ltd.

In this chapter, we discuss the importance of the theoretical bases of personality assessment, especially as it relates to 'construct validity' and the importance of a rigorous methodological model of assessment that takes into account different sources of variance that have theoretical meaning and should not be assigned to the residual term of "method variance," and certainly not "error". We conclude with specific recommendations for different forms of assessment that not only provide reliable measurement but also a deeper conceptual understanding and, thus, construct validity and generalization of results.

Firstly, we discuss the important distinction between two major levels of explanation: surface traits and source processes. Subsequently, we relate these levels to different sources of variance in trait ratings. In doing so, we base our discussion around the "Big Five" descriptive model of personality.

Surface Traits and Causal Sources

The lexical terms that make up everyday conversation are highly descriptive of personality differences, and the lexical hypothesis provides a rationale for this fact. We use such terms not only to describe but also to understand and predict future behavior.

As is well known, the lexical hypothesis originated with the English Victorian polymath, Sir Francis Galton, and was later developed by Allport and Odbert (1936), Tupes and Christal (1958), Norman (1963), and Goldberg (1981). It is defined by descriptive markers (Goldberg, 1992) and was developed by empirically identifying factors within common-language descriptors of persons (Goldberg, 1993; Saucier & Goldberg, 2001). Exploratory factor analyses of English adjectives in the middle of the twentieth century converged on five factors: Extraversion, Neuroticism, Agreeableness, Conscientiousness, and Openness to Experience/Intellect. In one form or another, these factors are represented in all models of personality, even those not originally intended to measure them (Markon, Krueger, & Watson, 2005). These factors are not merely descriptive, but have predictive importance as shown by robust correlations with outcomes as such: mortality, divorce, occupational level (Roberts Kuncel, Shiner, Caspi, & Goldberg, 2007), work performance (Hurtz & Donovan, 2000), academic performance (Poropat, 2009, 2014a, 2014b), and psychiatric diagnosis (Gore & Widiger, 2013).

As a description of variation at this surface population level, the Big Five does an excellent job, but it should be obvious that a statistical account at this high level of abstraction is bound to be influenced by a broad range of factors, ranging from biological (DNA) to societal. In other words, there are likely to be many sources of influence on factor scores. It may be for this very reason that the "catch-all" Big Five factors are ubiquitous in personality research and have such wide-scale validity.

But, what this five-centric descriptive model singly fails to provide is information regarding the specific causal "sources" of these surface traits. The lexical hypothesis claims that such natural language descriptive terms encode important social relations and, even assuming the validity of this claim, it does not add very much to our understanding of causal processes.

Scientific explanation looks for *reasons* for the existence of observed phenomena: for *causes*. In the case of personality traits, what we are observing at this surface level is the end product of a chain of (possibly highly complex) interacting processes. Thus, to understand exactly what personality assessment is yielding, we need to acknowledge this fact.

Bridging the Operational–Latent Gap

As discussed in detail elsewhere (Poropat & Corr, 2015) there have been notable attempts to bridge the gap between descriptive and causal models of personality, and it would be fair to say that these attempts have been less successful than initial hope suggested. Why should this be so? As Poropat and Corr (2015) noted, attempts to integrate models have been impaired by their different theoretical-epistemological starting points (Popple & Levi, 2000). Specifically, descriptive models have adopted a *between*-subjects, individual differences perspective that focuses on population-wide, higher-level differences between people – this perspective is associated with the tradition of Sir Francis Galton. In (often stark) contrast, causal models have pursued a *within*-subjects perspective that examines the patterning of effects over time and across situations – this perspective is associated with the experimental tradition of Wilhelm Wundt. The result of these traditions has been the production of models that are not readily commensurable.

Consider the Big Five personality model in a little more detail. Recall that this model has been developed on the basis of factor analyses (Saucier, 2009) and this has been taken as confirmation of its reality, which has been further supported by the efficacy of its various measurement inventories for the prediction of criterion variables (Roberts et al., 2007). In contrast, causal models of personality (e.g., the reinforcement sensitivity theory (RST) of personality; Gray & McNaughton, 2000) start from an analysis of behavioral reactions to different situations; and only then is the attempt made to map systems identified with population-wide personality traits, for example behavioral inhibition and behavioral approach (Carver & White, 1994).

Before discussing these matters further, we note that the issues we discuss are long-standing, and have been well rehearsed over the years by some notable psychologists – however, they have not yet been adequately addressed. For example, the late, great Hans Eysenck (1997) stated in his last journal article:

> It is suggested that the scientific status of psychology is put in danger by the lack of paradigms in many of its fields, and by the failure to achieve unification; psychology is breaking up into many different disciplines. One important cause was suggested by Lee Cronbach (…): the continuing failure of the two scientific disciplines of psychology – the experimental and the correlational – to come together and mutually support each other.

Well, what is the relevance of these considerations for personality assessment? Firstly, these issues have tended to be overlooked in the theoretical development of personality models, and especially in the building of different forms of personality assessment, which, too often, are seen to stand apart from these more abstract theoretical issues. To repeat, operational measure is *about* latent constructs. Depending on theoretical-epistemological starting points, assessment will have different construct meanings: this is our key point in this chapter.

These conceptual issues are clearly important in interpreting the products of personality assessment. They are the grand theoretical backdrop to the next, more methodologically-focused issue we discuss: the role played by different sources of variance.

The Multifacted Nature of Assessment

Personality psychology is challenged by the fact that both as a phenomenon (Andersen & Chen, 2002) and in assessment (Kenny & West, 2008), traits are essentially social – even when they are known to have a strong biological component. Important in this respect is the recognition that personality assessment yields measures that reflect both (a) raters, and (b) targets of their assessments. How can we use this knowledge to advance understanding of personality assessment?

Of significance is *generalizability theory* (Cronbach, 1957; Cronbach, Gleser, Nanda, & Rajaratnam, 1972; Cronbach, Rajaratnam, & Gleser, 1963), which offers an integrative framework for personality assessment. As suggested by Poropat and Corr (2015), the resolution to the Galtonian and Wundtian perspectives, discussed above, may come from this Cronbachian paradigm. In addition, this perspective addresses the different sources of ratings variance integral to personality assessment.

Generalisability theory provides a means of modeling the full range of influences in psychological assessment, which include sources related to: traits, targets, raters, contexts, measurement tools, and temporal factors. This approach is more than interactionism (see Reynolds et al., 2010, for a recent consideration of this approach): it draws attention to the importance of personality *judgement* as much as the expression of personality in the target.

Everyday observation of other people's personality entails raters, or judges.[1] Outside formal testing situations, this is the most pervasive form of personality assessment. Empirical research confirms that, in their own right, such ratings have substantial validity in the prediction of criterion variables (Connelly & Ones, 2010; Poropat, 2014a, 2014b). Oftentimes, the variance attributed to judges is assigned to method "error" or "bias" (Podsakoff, MacKenzie, Lee, & Podsakoff, 2003; Podsakoff, MacKenzie, & Podsakoff, 2012); however, it is known that these aspects of assessment can predict criterion-linked effects of greater magnitude than those associated with the purported traits being measured (Lance, Dawson, Birkelbach, & Hoffman, 2010) – this is perhaps to be expected because judges have their own, often unique, perspective on target personalities.

[1] Many writers on psychological measurement prefer the term "raters" (e.g., Lance, Dawson, Birkelbach, & Hoffman, 2010). We prefer to use "judges" for the person who provides the rating, and "targets" for the person whose personality is being rated, in order to be consistent with Funder (2001).

The Cronbachian Perspective

Now, in contrast to both the Galtonian and Wundtian perspectives, the Cronbachian paradigm assumes that *both* psychological phenomena and measurement types reflect multiple causal factors, and it is necessary to model these factors in order to provide a comprehensive personality model (Cronbach et al., 1963; Cronbach et al., 1972). This approach can be contrasted with the assumptions of classical test theory (CTT) which permeate many personality models – CTT assumes that observed scores (X) reflect some underlying true score (T) and a random error component (E), as summarized by the well-known equation:

$$X = T + E \tag{2.1}$$

However, it is known that systematic variance is related to the specific form of assessment. In recognition of this fact, attempts have been made to account for these influences. In relation to CTT, the ***normative accuracy model*** (Lance, Baranik, Lau, & Scharlau, 2009) includes a systematic measurement bias term (SB), as shown by:

$$X = T + SB + E \tag{2.2}$$

As the name implies, *bias* is assumed to be *invalid*; however, as some researchers have noted, this "bias" is often a valid reflection of the target (Hoffman & Woehr, 2009; Lance et al., 2010): It reflects "valid differences in perception" (Borman, 1974, p. 107).

Indeed, the size of these judge or target effects can be substantial, accounting for as much as three-quarters of non-random variance in multitrait–multirater studies (Lance et al., 2009). For example, Connelly and Ones (2010) compared self- and other ratings of personality, and found that the average self–other agreement across Big Five dimensions varied depending on the source of ratings, with self-raters agreeing much more strongly with other raters from within their family (mean $R^2 = 0.18$ uncorrected; 0.72 corrected) than with other raters from work (mean $R^2 = 0.04$ uncorrected; 0.42 corrected), demonstrating the substantial consequences of varying the source of personality ratings. Despite the relatively low self–other agreement at work, Connelly and Ones (2010) found that other-rated personality was as good as or substantially better than self-rated personality for predicting work performance, indicating that it provides independent validity.

In order to address these systematic and valid sources of assessment, generalizability theory provides a framework for their integration. Specifically, it allows for the decomposition of measures, such as those typically used in personality research, into a set of factors. An example of a generalizability theory model, in which components of ratings are identified on the basis of who has been the object or the provider of the relevant rating, is outlined in Equation 3.3.

$$rating_{ij} = Target_i + Judge_j + Target_i \times Judge_j + residual_{ij} \tag{2.3}$$

From this perspective, the systematic bias of Equation 2.2 is composed of valid variance, not mere error. So, in the model represented in Equation 2.3, ratings are a function of not only persistent variance between targets, but also variance between judges and the interaction between these factors. In this more general model, targets present a phenotype (i.e., they provide opportunities to be observed) that judges use or fail to use in ways that reflect judges' own individual differences (Funder, 2001).

Returning to the Big Five model of personality, this analysis implies that factor analyses of personality ratings contain, and conflate, variance attributed to the presence of effects related to targets, judges, and interactions between targets and judges. In support of this claim, Funder, Kolar, and Blackman (1995) provided an example of these separate effects: they reported that judges can validly assess personality even when their ratings are only modestly correlated (mean $r = 0.25$) with those of judges who have observed targets in different contexts. These judge–target relationships clearly complicate models of personality assessment; yet, at the same time, they make it more accurate and comprehensive.

In addition to these considerations, the intra-individual processes that lead to observable inter-individual differences always occur within situations and are always linked with outcomes (Van Egeren, 2009); for this reason, the target term in Equation 2.3 may be decomposed further, as shown in Equation 2.4:

$$\begin{aligned} Target_i = {} & Process_m + Situation_n + Outcome_o + Process_m \times Situation_n \\ & + Process_m \times Outcome_o + Situation_n \times Outcome_o \\ & + Process_m \times Situation_n \times Outcome_o + residual_{mno} \end{aligned} \tag{2.4}$$

With respect to Equation 2.4, for example, the consequences of individual differences in sensitivity to aversive stimuli (RST) will depend on the situation (e.g., presence or absence of events or stimuli) and outcomes (consequences that will accrue to the individual), plus their various interactions.

Just as the target effects in Equation 2.3 can be decomposed, so too can the judge effects, and in a comparable manner because a judge's rating is, in itself, a behavior, determined in part by the judge's own processes. It has long been accepted that judges' ratings are affected by the outcome they are pursuing when producing a rating (Vazire, 2010), but they are also affected by the specific target behaviors observed and the situation in which these are observed (Kammrath, Mendoza-Denton, & Mischel, 2005; Reynolds & Karraker, 2009; Saucier, Bel-Bahar, & Fernandez, 2007).

Indeed, such is the relevance of situations for judges, when they are not provided with sufficient information about them, then either they infer or actively create situations to enable them to construct ratings (Wiemers & Poropat, 2013). So for judges, their "situation" can be decomposed by considering the targets' observed behaviors and observed situations. These points lead to Equation 2.5, which has been simplified for presentation but which can be readily expanded:

$$\begin{aligned} Judge_j = {} & Process_p + Observed\ Behavior_q + Observed\ Situation_r + Outcome_s \\ & + 2\text{-}way\ interactions + 3\text{-}way\ interactions + 4\text{-}way\ interactions \\ & + residual_{mno} \end{aligned} \tag{2.5}$$

The final step in this analysis would be the integration of equations 2.3, 2.4 and 2.5, which for the sake of simplicity is not attempted here.

Temporal effects, such as those analysed by Fleeson and Gallagher (2009), are not explicitly incorporated within this analysis, but they are implicit within the various effects associated with situations and outcomes, which vary substantially with time. In a similar manner, cultural and linguistic effects are subsumed within components such as situations, outcomes, and interactions between processes and these factors. It should also be noted that this analysis implicitly accounts for the finding that factor analyses of intra-individual (Wundtian) variations produce different factors to more traditional factor analyses of inter-individual (Galtonian) variations (Molenaar & Campbell, 2009), because they combine different variance components.

Implications for Real World Personality Assessment

The above discussion highlights a number of implications for personality assessment, some of which at first may appear rather daunting. But we believe that closer attention to them may point to important ways forward to improve the reliability and validity of all forms of assessment. Yet, implementing these solutions is not going to be easy. To begin with, there remains a strong emphasis on correlations between ratings and exploratory factor analyses in personality research. However, these systematically omit (or otherwise obscure) large portions of the variance and associated causal factors, as discussed above. Worse still, partialling of variance into target and judge components does not adequately address this issue, because knowing the amount of variance associated with targets and judges does not explain what produces it. In order to cast new light on this specific issue, it would be necessary to deconstruct these variance components further.

Given these considerations, the personality models that exist, as epitomized by the Big Five, cut across these complicating factors to yield very broad factors of general relevance. This is an important achievement and goes a long way to confirming the general nature of personality at *this* specific level of description. However, it sidesteps the more fine-grained analysis of personality that is crucial in many applied contexts.

The inescapable problem that faces the personality psychologist is the sheer complexity of the object of study – it is for this understandable reason that most psychologists do not include individual differences measures in their research work. Therefore, for reasons all too easy to comprehend, typical forms of personality assessment have not risen to these challenges. How would it be possible to rise adequately to meet them?

The Way Forward?

The requirement to achieve the potential of a fully-fledged Cronbachian paradigm in personality assessment would entail much larger and more comprehensive databases than are currently available. At a minimum, such a database would include sets of factors corresponding to targets crossed with judges crossed with situations crossed with intra-individual (neurobiological) processes. As noted by Poropat and Corr (2015), although it remains useful to nibble at the edges of a problem, it is time to start thinking bigger. It needs to be recognised that the magnitude of this enterprise would be comparable to the shift in physics from table-top experiments of Newton and Faraday to multinational collaborations involving very large research teams. The vogue for "big data" in the internet age now has a parallel in the field of personality psychology and, perhaps, the technology afforded by the internet will enable the realization of this vastly expanded personality research program. It is far from being impractical, but it does require an industrial revolution for psychology, transmorphing from cottage industry to factory-scale production.

However, lest it be implied that we must wait for this distant research utopia to materialize, our analysis suggests that we can move steadily towards this goal by more modest and incremental means, namely by increasingly including components of the generalizability theory in ongoing research – there is evidence that this has already started to happen (e.g., Kandler, Riemann, Spinath, & Angleitner, 2010; Riemann & Kandler, 2010). As a specific suggestion, immediate research efforts could be directed at examining how both targets and judges are affected by intra-individual processes and situational factors, and their interactions.

This research program may begin to show just how different forms of personality assessment models are maximally useful in specific contexts and for specific outcomes. For example, ratings by family, friends, and colleagues, across different situations and outcomes, should be expected to yield valuable information concerning the true nature of personality, including the common variance to the target and the unique contributions from raters, situations, and outcomes.

This general form of research holds considerable potential for differentiating underlying intra-individual (biological) processes from more social processes, and importantly how these factors relate to each other. Unfortunately, this approach is rarely seen in biologically oriented models of personality (e.g., RST), yet it is highly applicable.

What is needed is a new role of "personality analyst," comparable to "analysts" in econometrics. The unifying skills of this new role could then be called upon to assist in the more sophisticated analysis of specific personality research questions (e.g., how sensitivity to gain and loss relate to various forms of occupational performance, which comprise subjective performance and subjective reputation).

There may also be more specific merits of placing emphasis on different processes. For example, a Wundtian-based approach may be best at predicting and explaining intra-individual factors, such as psychosocial development and cognitive processes – the implication is that temperament/personality theories (e.g., RST), when validly assessed, may provide a more effective account of within-individual cognitive development and decision-making. In contrast, but not in contradistinction, a Galtonian-based approach may be maximally useful for predicting socially valued outcomes, such as career success, and work and academic performance, since it is at this level where population-level differences between people are most marked. Of course, integrating intra- and inter-individual differences would remain important, but only where this is required. The Cronbachian perspective discussed above shows just how this aim may be achieved.

Concluding Thoughts

The goal of any scientific endeavor is to produce a fully integrated *causal* model of nature: causes cannot be inferred from effects, therefore a principled theoretical approach, armed with methodological tools, is needed. Couched in terms of a Cronbachian perspective and generalizability theory, in relation to personality assessment and the underlying causal processes it operationalizes, a comprehensive approach requires consideration of a more complete range of variance factors, which combines target, judge, situation, and outcome.

The counsel of caution issued by our approach is that the nature of personality factors and processes warrants more than the simple assumption that personality (operational) assessment reflects, in some simple and straightforward matter, underlying (latent) theoretical constructs, and all else that is measured is nuisance "method variance." The true dynamic action of personality processes may well be in the interaction of these factors and not in their separate main effects.

Although adopting a Cronbachian paradigm poses many challenges, the scientific payoff would be considerable if it afforded the opportunity to unravel the multifaceted true nature of personality. This approach should even help to tease out the causal processes as examined in such areas such as functional neuroimaging, which no less requires the matching of judge, situation, and outcome effects to explain the personality of the target subject. The full potential of the synthesis of the theoretical, statistical, and technological can now be glimpsed on the personality psychology horizon.

References

Allport, G.W., & Odbert, H.S. (1936). Trait names: A psycho-lexical study. *Psychological Monographs, 47*(1), 1–171.

Andersen, S.M., & Chen, S. (2002). The relational self: An interpersonal social-cognitive theory. *Psychological Review, 109*(4), 619–645.

Borman, W.C. (1974). The rating of individuals in organizations: An alternative approach. *Organizational Behavior and Human Performance, 12,* 105–124.

Carver, C.S., & White, T.L. (1994). Behavioral inhibition, behavioral activation, and affective responses to impending reward and punishment: The BIS/BAS scales. *Journal of Personality and Social Psychology, 67*(2), 319–333.

Connelly, B.S., & Ones, D.S. (2010). An other perspective on personality: Meta-analytic integration of observers' accuracy & predictive validity. *Psychological Bulletin, 136* (6), 1092–1122.

Cronbach, L.J. (1957). The two disciplines of scientific psychology. *American Psychologist, 12* (11), 671–684.

Cronbach, L.J., Gleser, G.C., Nanda, H., & Rajaratnam, N. (1972). *The Dependability of Behavioral Measurements: Theory of Generalizability for Scores and Profiles.* New York: Wiley.

Cronbach, L.J., Rajaratnam, N., & Gleser, G.C. (1963). Theory of generalizability: A liberalization of reliability theory. *British Journal of Statistical Psychology, 16* (2), 137–163.

Eysenck, H.J. (1997). Personality and experimental psychology: The unification of psychology and the possibility of a paradigm. *Journal of Personality and Social Psychology, 73* (6), 1224–1237.

Fleeson, W., & Gallagher, P. (2009). The implications of big five standing for the distribution of trait manifestation in behavior: Fifteen experience-sampling studies and a meta-analysis. *Journal of Personality & Social Psychology, 97* (6), 1097–1114.

Funder, D.C. (2001). Accuracy in personality judgement: Research and theory concerning an obvious question. In B.W. Roberts, & R.T. Hogan (Eds.), *Personality Psychology in the Workplace* (pp. 121–140). Washington, DC: American Psychological Association.

Funder, D.C., Kolar, D.C., & Blackman, M.C. (1995). Agreement among judges of personality: Interpersonal relations, similarity, and acquaintanceship. *Journal of Personality and Social Psychology, 69* (4), 656–672.

Goldberg, L.R. (1981). Language and individual differences: The search for universals in personality lexicons. In L. Wheeler (Ed.), *Review of Personality and Social Psychology* (Vol. 2) (pp. 141–165). Beverley Hills, CA: Sage.

Goldberg, L.R. (1992). The development of markers for the Big-Five factor structure. *Psychological Assessment, 4* (1), 26–42.

Goldberg, L.R. (1993). The structure of phenotypic personality traits. *American Psychologist, 48* (1), 26–34.

Gore, W.L., & Widiger, T.A. (2013). The DSM-5 dimensional trait model and five-factor models of general personality. *Journal of Abnormal Psychology, 122* (3), 816–821.

Gray, J.A., & McNaughton, N. (2000). *The Neuropsychology of Anxiety: An Enquiry into the Functions of the Septo-hippocampal System.* Oxford: Oxford University Press.

Hoffman, B.J., & Woehr, D.J. (2009). Disentangling the meaning of multisource performance rating source and dimension factors. *Personnel Psychology, 62* (4), 735–765.

Hurtz, G.M., & Donovan, J.J. (2000). Personality and job performance: The Big Five revisited. *Journal of Applied Psychology, 85* (6), 869–879.

Kammrath, L.K., Mendoza-Denton, R., & Mischel, W. (2005). Incorporating if/then personality signatures in person perception: Beyond the person-situation dichotomy. *Journal of Personality and social Psychology, 88* (4), 605–618.

Kandler, C., Riemann, R., Spinath, F.M., & Angleitner, A. (2010). Sources of variance in personality facets: A multiple-rater twin study of self-peer, peer-peer, and self-self (dis) sgreement. *Journal of Personality, 78* (5), 1565–1594.

Kenny, D.A., & West, T.V. (2008). Self-perception as interpersonal perception. In J.V. Wood, A. Tesser, & J.G. Holmes (Eds.), *The Self and Social Relationships* (pp. 119–138). New York: Psychology Press.

Lance, C.E., Baranik, L.E., Lau, A.R., & Scharlau, E.A. (2009). If it ain't trait it must be method. In C.E. Lance & R.J. Vandenberg (Eds.), *Statistical and Methodological Myths and Urban Legends: Doctrine, Verity and Fable in the Organizational and Social Sciences* (pp. 337–360). New York: Routledge.

Lance, C.E., Dawson, B., Birkelbach, D., & Hoffman, B.J. (2010). Method effects, measurement error, and substantive conclusions. *Organizational Research Methods, 13* (3), 435–455.

Markon, K.E., Krueger, R.F., & Watson, D. (2005). Delineating the structure of normal and abnormal personality: An integrative hierarchical approach. *Journal of Personality and Social Psychology, 88* (1), 139–157.

Molenaar, P.C.M., & Campbell, C.G. (2009). The new person-specific paradigm in psychology. *Current Directions in Psychological Science, 18* (2), 112–117.

Norman, W.T. (1963). Toward an adequate taxonomy of personality attributes: Replicated factor structure in peer nomination personality ratings. *Journal of Abnormal and Social Psychology, 66* (6), 574–583.

Podsakoff, P.M., MacKenzie, S.B., Lee, J.-Y., & Podsakoff, N.P. (2003). Common method biases in behavioral research: A critical review of the literature and recommended remedies. *Journal of Applied Psychology, 88* (5), 879–903.

Podsakoff, P.M., MacKenzie, S.B., & Podsakoff, N.P. (2012). Sources of method bias in social science research and recommendations on how to control it. *Annual Review of Psychology, 63*, 539–569.

Popple, A., & Levi, D.M. (2000). Wundt versus Galton – two approaches to gathering psychophysical measurements. *Perception, 29* (4), 379–381.

Poropat, A.E. (2009). A meta-analysis of the five-factor model of personality and academic performance. *Psychological Bulletin, 135* (2), 322–338.

Poropat, A.E. (2014a). A meta-analysis of adult-rated child personality and academic performance in primary education. *British Journal of Educational Psychology, 84* (Pt. 2), 239–252.

Poropat, A.E. (2014b). A meta-analysis of other-rated personality and academic performance. *Learning and Individual Differences, 34*, 24–32.

Poropat, A., & Corr, P.J. (2015). Thinking bigger: The Cronbachian paradigm and personality theory integration. *Journal of Research in Personality, 56*, 59–69.

Reynolds, B., & Karraker, K. (2009). A big five model of disposition and situation interaction: Why a "helpful" person may not always behave helpfully. *New Ideas on Psychology, 21* (1), 1–13.

Reynolds, K.J., Turner, J.C., Branscombe, N.R., Mavor, K.I., Bizumic, B., & Subasic, E. (2010). Interactionism in personality and social psychology: An integrated approach to understanding the mind and behaviour. *European Journal of Personality, 24* (5), 458–482.

Riemann, R., & Kandler, C. (2010). Construct validation using multitrait-multimethod-twin data: The case of a general factor of personality. *European Journal of Personality, 24* (3), 258–277.

Roberts, B.W., Kuncel, N.R., Shiner, R.L., Caspi, A., & Goldberg, L.R. (2007). The power of personality: The comparative validity of personality traits, socioeconomic status, and cognitive ability for predicting important life outcomes. *Psychological Science, 2* (4), 313–345.

Saucier, G. (2009). Recurrent personality dimensions in inclusive lexical studies: Indications for a Big Six structure. *Journal of Personality, 77* (5), 1577–1614.

Saucier, G., Bel-Bahar, T., & Fernandez, C. (2007). What modifies the expression of personality tendencies? Defining basic domains of situation variables. *Journal of Personality, 75* (3), 479–503.

Saucier, G., & Goldberg, L.R. (2001). Lexical studies of indigenous personality factors: Premises, products and prospects. *Journal of Personality, 69* (6), 847–879.

Tupes, E.C., & Christal, R.E. (1958). Stability of personality trait rating factors obtained under diverse conditions. *USAF Wright Air Development Center Technical Note, 16*, 58–61.

Van Egeren, L.F. (2009). A cybernetic model of global personality traits. *Personality and Social Psychology Review, 13* (2), 92–108.

Vazire, S. (2010). Who knows what about a person? The self-other knowledge asymmetry (SOKA) model. *Journal of Personality and Social Psychology, 98* (2), 281–300.

Wiemers, M., & Poropat, A.E. (2013). *Detection and use of information in personality perception: A think-aloud methodology.* Paper presented at the Australian Conference on Personality and Individual Differences, Brisbane, Australia.

3

Situational Perception: Its Theoretical Foundation, Assessment, and Links to Personality

Kai T. Horstmann and Matthias Ziegler

Institute for Psychology, Humboldt-Universität zu Berlin, Germany

In an experiment conducted in 2008 it was shown that getting handed a warm or a cold cup of coffee influenced whether another person was judged as more or less interpersonally warm. This finding was published in *Science* (Williams & Bargh, 2008). A small change in the situation the subjects were in thus had major consequences – irrespective of the subjects' personality. Other famous experiments have also demonstrated that situations can have strong effects on behavior, from Zimbardo's prison experiment to Milgrim's obedience research (cf. Krueger, 2009).

By 1936 Kurt Lewin had highlighted the importance of both the environment and the person as potentially important determinants of behavior, which resulted in the famous equation $B = f(P,E)$ (Lewin, 1936, p. 12). Yet, when it comes to the prediction of behavior, researchers as well as practitioners mostly still keep to the sole assessment of the person aspect within the equation and disregard the situation. How is that possible?

Starting with Lewin's equation, we will provide answers to this question and discuss both concepts relevant to the prediction of behavior according to Lewin, highlighting their interrelatedness. The lack of an existing situational taxonomy has often been criticized and is seen as one of the main reasons for the lack of situational assessment. We will present two recent taxonomies closing this gap. Finally, research ideas will be outlined to give guidance and starting points to other researchers who seek to improve the prediction of human behavior using assessments of both personality and situation.

The Wiley Handbook of Personality Assessment, First Edition. Edited by Updesh Kumar.
© 2016 John Wiley & Sons, Ltd. Published 2016 by John Wiley & Sons, Ltd.

Lewin's Equation and the Person–Situation Debate

To understand the person and situation effects on behavior, all components of Lewin's equation (i.e., behavior, person, and environment) need to be clarified. It is important to note that none of these factors can be explained independently of the other.

Behavior

Behavior refers to any activity a person performs, an action, a thought, a decision, movement or answer in a questionnaire (Baumeister, Vohs, & Funder, 2007). Fleeson and Noftle (2008) even went a step further and differentiated between the content of behavior (i.e., the reason for an action) and the behavior enactment (i.e., what the person does). The same behavior enactment, for example drinking a cup of coffee, can have different behavior contents, for example joining a friend and socializing, or drinking coffee to stay awake. A precise definition of behavior is thus crucial before it can be predicted based on person and situation.

The person

The person is usually characterized by "qualities that are relatively invariant across situations and over time" (Shoda & Mischel, 2000, p. 407). Time or situations are thus an essential part of the definition of personality, which is the assessment approach to operationalize person.

Fleeson and Noftle (2008) also separated time and situations from the person by defining personality as individual differences that either affect or describe a person's behavior. Note that in this definition, time and situations are not necessarily directly related to the definition of personality. Nevertheless, Lewin's concepts remain interrelated, and personality is not independently conceptualized without the other two (Funder, 2006; Lewin, 1936).

It is furthermore the assumed stability of the personality traits that allows predictions and explanations of behavior (Edwards & Templeton, 2005; Epstein, 1983). Two questions directly arise from this assumption: (a) is personality stable; and (b) is it possible to predict behavior with personality? The answer for the second question obviously depends on the first question – if something *randomly* varies, it is not possible to predict anything with it. In *Personality Assessment*, Walter Mischel focused on the instability of personality and claimed that it is nearly impossible to predict behavior with personality (Mischel, 1968, 2009). This led to the person–situation debate, a controversy in psychology that sought to answer the question of whether behavior depended more on the subject's personality or the situation (or both)[1] and has received considerable research attention (Webster, 2009). Two solutions presented themselves from the beginning. The first was to aggregate multiple measurements of personality and behavior and regard deviations from the

[1] Behavior can actually be influenced by the person, the situation, and their interaction, and any combination of these three effects (Krueger, 2009).

average score as measurement errors (Epstein, 1979). The average score is thus treated as the true value of a parameter. This resulted in low yet non-zero as well as meaningful correlations of personality with behavior (Funder, Guillaume, Kumagai, Kawamoto, & Sato, 2012; Mischel & Shoda, 1995). The other way forward was to identify stable patterns of personality and behavior across different measurement occasions or situations, leading eventually to the term cross-situational consistency (e.g., Bem & Allen, 1974). Variation in behavior may thus occur, yet it may not vary randomly but *systematically*.

Behavior as an expression of personality is, for example, rank-order consistent across situations when someone is more talkative at a funeral than others, and more talkative at a party than others, even though his or her overall level of talkativeness has changed from one occasion to another. Behavior thus varies, but dependent on the occasion. This idea acknowledges two issues Lewin had already stated in 1936 and a lot of researchers have now agreed upon. First, behavior is influenced by the situation (e.g., Bem & Allen, 1974; Deinzer et al., 1995; Edwards & Templeton, 2005; Endler & Magnusson, 1976; Fleeson, 2004; Furr & Funder, 2004; Mischel, 1968, 2004; Mischel & Peake, 1982; Rauthmann et al., 2014; Reis, 2008; Shoda, Mischel, & Wright, 1994; Wagerman & Funder, 2009; Ziegler, Ehrlenspiel, & Brand, 2009). Secondly, to quantify this influence and thus re-establish consistency of personality, a theory for the assessment of situations has to be developed (cf. Lewin, 1936, p. 13).

The situation

The definition of a situation is far less examined and validated than theories and assessment methods of personality (Rauthmann, 2015). Small changes between two settings (e.g., holding a warm vs. a cold cup of coffee) may be everything that makes a salient difference between two situations.

Fleeson and Noftle (2008) referred to single observations of behavior as *occasions*, instead of situations. An occasion may either be different points in time, different behavioral content, or different situational content. Different points in time may just be two different measurement occasions without any further specification of the occasion, as it is for example considered in the latent-state-trait theory (Steyer, Schmitt, & Eid, 1999). Behavioral content refers to the quality of the action taken, as already explained above. The same motion, for example, may have a different meaning, depending on the behavioral content. The classic person–situation debate, however, did mostly refer to situational content, and this is what most researchers (and probably laypersons) do initially think of when comparing the diverging influence of two occasions, for example a party vs. a funeral (Fleeson & Noftle, 2008).

Any of these different types of occasions must be specified when considered in a study or in the definition of consistency. Yet for the prediction of behavior in the context of the person–situation debate, the most useful and promising approach is that of situational content. Situational content has thus to be classified or described; in other words, a taxonomy has to be developed (Rauthmann, Sherman, & Funder, 2015). Without a descriptive system, predictions of behavior based on the assessment of situational information will be nearly impossible.

The Objective and Subjective Approaches

Two broad approaches can be identified for the description of situations:[2] an objective one that is independent of the person in that situation, and a subjective one (Furr & Funder, 2004).

Objective approach

An objectively described situation is what Lewin referred to as the environment. For a more consistent use of terminology, Rauthmann and colleagues (2015) define three different and hierarchically ordered "kinds of situational information" (p. 4): cues, characteristics and classes. Cues are what Lewin would refer to as parts of the environment (e.g., a chair, a keyboard, or a coffee cup). They can be considered objective features, as they exist independently of the perceiver. A complete and *objective* description of a situation would require sampling all cues of a situation. Such an approach to assessing situations obviously quickly runs into practical limitations. Lewin acknowledged that there are psychologically important features (i.e., cues) of a situation that may be different for each person, and that these cues may be less relevant. He thus referred to the combination of a person in a particular environment as a situation: "Even when from a standpoint of the physicist the environment is identical or nearly identical for a child and for an adult, the psychological situation can be fundamentally different" (Lewin, 1936, p. 24). It may furthermore be very tiresome and even impossible to define (a) an exhaustive list of objective situation characteristics and (b) an exhaustive list of situations that could occur (Edwards & Templeton, 2005; Hogan, 2009; Rauthmann et al., 2014; Saucier, Bel-Bahar, & Fernandez, 2007). Finally, for the prediction of behavior, one would need to know in which exact situation the behavior is likely to occur, which is also close to impossible. The objective approach, however, can be useful when particular aspects of a situation are to be examined, as in the case of the coffee cup (Furr & Funder, 2004).

Subjective approach

For these reasons, instead of the sampling of all situational cues, one can move on and define situations in terms of their "psychologically important meanings" (Rauthmann et al., 2015), which the authors refer to as situational *characteristics.* Since psychologically important meanings are construed by the perceiver, characteristics are thus a subjective approach to situational taxonomization. Furthermore, different people could perceive relevant features of the same situation in a similar way but to a different extent (e.g., Asendorpf, 2009; Funder, 2006; Wagerman & Funder, 2009). Situations may thus have characteristics in the same way that persons have traits, independently of the perceiver (see Edwards & Templeton, 2005, p. 707). Every party will be, to some extent, fun, and even though your best friend's party

[2]From now on, we will use the terms situation and situational content interchangeably. That does not mean that the other two types of occasions are not equally important in their own right.

may be more fun than your neighbor's party, both will be more fun (hopefully!) than a funeral. The more similar two situations are, the more similar should be the perception of the situation by a specific individual. Consequently, the more similar (and thus consistent) should also be the behavior of this person in the situations.

Finally, situational characteristics could be aggregated to situational classes (e.g., parties in general to funerals in general, or funny compared with sad situations). However, by using such a classification scheme, much of the information about the specific situation would be lost (Rauthmann et al., 2015).

There are now two ways in which situational characteristics may be relevant: they may either be perceived *for one situation by several persons* or *different situations may be characterized by one person*, measuring the general tendency of this one person to perceive different situations in the same way (Rauthmann, 2015). The following two taxonomies both adopt the view that inter-individual differences in people's interpretation of a situation can be explained by underlying dimensions. Thus, both taxonomies operationalize Lewin's situation idea as situational perception, and thus a within-person variable (see also Rauthmann et al., 2015).

Two Situational Taxonomies

Two recently suggested taxonomies will be presented that follow these ideas: the DIAMONDS taxonomy (Rauthmann et al., 2014) and the Situation 5 (Ziegler, 2014). Whereas the DIAMONDS taxonomy is based on the analyses of an existing assessment tool used to describe situations, the Situation 5 are grounded in the lexical approach.

The Situational Eight DIAMONDS

The Situational Eight DIAMONDS taxonomy was proposed by Rauthmann and colleagues in 2014. It is based on the Riverside Situational Q-Sort (Sherman, Nave, & Funder, 2010, 2012, 2013; RSQ, Wagerman & Funder, 2009), a tool for describing any situation. Participants were required to rate randomly selected and self-experienced situations on 89 different items, for example, "someone needs help." The relevance of the item for the situation is coded on a nine-point scale, ranging from "highly characteristic" to "highly uncharacteristic."[3]

Factor analyses of ratings from 1,589 participants revealed eight underlying dimensions of situational perceptions (the capital letters constituting the acronym, DIAMONDS): *Duty* (e.g., something needs to be done, the situation contains work), *Intellect* (e.g., the situation contains intellectual engagement or cognitive demands), *Adversity* (e.g., situation contains threats, problems), *Mating* (e.g., situation is conductive to sex, love, romance), *pOsitivity* (e.g., situation is enjoyable and pleasant), *Negativity* (e.g., situation may elicit any type of negative feeling), *Deception* (e.g., situation contains mistrust or hostility), and *Sociality* (e.g., situation contains socializing,

[3]A 9-binned Q-Sort as well as 9- and 4-point Likert scales were used in different samples. Data were *z*-transformed to control for the different response types of each sample.

interpersonal warmth). In a set of five studies, the authors provide evidence for the validity and usefulness of the Situational Eight DIAMONDS scores. One study did show that the DIAMONDS scores are "meaningfully associated" (Rauthmann et al., 2014, p. 21) with self-reported behavior, which was assessed with the Riverside Behavioral Q-Sort (Funder, Furr, & Colvin, 2000). For example, the Duty score correlated with the item "concentrating, working hard at task" (r = 0.64) in one sample. A subsequent study showed the relatedness to the Big Five personality domain scores and their combined ability to predict behavior. Even though the DIAMONDS scores were correlated to some domains, they also predicted variance in behavior that was not predicted by the Big Five personality domain scores.

Other advantages the authors of the DIAMONDS see are a uniform communication of situational perception and their effects, compatibility to other personality domains and a simultaneous use of person and situation measures. It furthermore offers a way of describing, comparing and classifying situations as well as the description of situational change, such as when does one situation end and another one begin (Rauthmann et al., 2014, pp. 34–35).

To measure the DIAMONDS, short and long questionnaire versions exist. The long version, called the S8* (Rauthmann & Sherman, 2015a), consists of 24 items with three items per DIAMONDS dimension (e.g., item for Adversity: "I am being criticized"). Cronbach's α of the DIAMONDS scores range from 0.61 (Mating) to 0.90 (Duty). For the short version, the number of items was even further reduced and the authors recommend using one or two item scales per dimension (Rauthmann & Sherman, 2015b).

Overall, evidence is presented that the Situational Eight DIAMONDS constitute a useful taxonomy for situations and can predict self-reported behavior. Yet they assess situation-specific content, which might prove to be irrelevant for the prediction of future behavior without knowledge about future situations.

The Situation 5

The Big Five Inventory of Personality in Occupational Situations (B5PS; Ziegler, 2014) is a measurement tool that assesses the Big Five personality domains and facets in hypothetical work situations. Alongside the Big Five, five dimensions of situational perception (Situation 5) can be assessed.

The lexical approach is mostly known with reference to the Big Five (e.g., John & Srivastava, 1999). It is based on the assumption that important and relevant features of objects will find their way into human language (Allport & Odbert, 1936; Deary, 2009). Collecting all possible descriptors of, for example, persons, and by extraction of an underlying structure from ratings of these descriptors, models for the underlying dimensions of human personality can be extracted. Yet, this may not only apply to features of persons but also to descriptions of different situations (e.g., Edwards & Templeton, 2005; Yang, Read, & Miller, 2006). Note that, since only those characteristics that are perceived to be relevant are transferred to human language, this approach is also a subjective approach to situational taxonomization aiming at situational perception.

For the development of the Situation 5, Ziegler (2014) extracted roughly 15,000 adjectives from a German spelling dictionary. These were then condensed to 3,000 by exclusion of such adjectives that were not suitable for the description of situations. They were even further reduced to about 300 by dropping such words that were rarely used, possibly unknown or duplicates; 521 participants were then required to rate self-experienced situations from the previous day with 75 of these adjectives, such as monotonous, professional, or full of potential. By means of factor analysis, seven factors were initially extracted from these ratings: *mental and physical load*, *cognitive load*, *monotony*, *expectation of results*, *vitality*, *valence*, and *situational environmental conditions*. As the construction aimed at developing a test useful in work settings, the last factor was dropped in further development stages.

The factor structure was replicated in a representative sample ($N = 387$) of the German-speaking countries: Austria, Germany and Switzerland. The calculations revealed that the valence factor highly correlated with all other factors and was thus split into two higher-order factors: *strain* and *vigor*. Five factors of situational perception were thus ultimately retained. Under the higher-order factor *strain*, these were *mental and physical load* (e.g., burdening, stressful and physically demanding), *cognitive load* (e.g., cognitively demanding, taxing, complex or unclear), and *monotony* (e.g., boring, uninteresting, dull). Under the higher-order factor *vigor*, these were *expectation of results* (e.g., potentially rewarding, positive outcome is expected) and *vitality* (e.g., lively, dynamic, turbulent and vivid); 59 adjectives were selected for the description of these situational perceptions.

To measure the Situation 5 in combination with the Big Five, a unique approach was taken. Based on the assumption that personality and situational perception interact, hypothetical behavior as an indicator for the Big Five is measured along with the perception of the situation. A hypothetical situation (called a vignette) is presented to the participant on a computer screen, such as "You have been sleeping badly for days and would like to offload one of your tasks onto someone else. Right now you are in a team meeting."[4] After reading the situation, the participant has to rate it on one of the Situation 5 dimensions; in this case "I perceive the situation as burdensome" (*mental and physical load*). After rating this item on a six-point Likert scale (1 = strong agreement, 6 = strong disagreement), a new statement appears on the screen and subjects can rate a possible hypothetical behavior, here "I ask for help" (*agreeableness*). Applying this technique, the Situation 5 and Big Five are assessed with a total of 211 vignettes. Construct reliabilities (and Cronbach's α) for the Situation 5 range from 0.85 (cognitive load) to 0.95 (mental and physical load).

It could further be shown that the Situation 5 explained variance in work engagement (Dedication, Vigor, Absorption) beyond the variance that was explained by the Big Five.

DIAMONDS and S5

The construction process for the Situation 5 resembles that of DIAMONDS. Both tests rely for their construction process on the ratings of self-experienced and self-reported situations. Moreover, both tests share another very central aspect which

[4] All situations are taken from an occupational setting.

sets both taxonomies apart from prior theories. Whilst Wagerman and Funder (2009; cf. Asendorpf, 2009) explicitly state that situational characteristics must be independent of the perceiver, the Situation 5 and the DIAMONDS are located within the perceiver and can be interpreted as *general tendencies to perceive a situation* in a certain way. A close inspection of both taxonomies suggests that some of the dimensions at least share variance. Thus, an integration of both models seems feasible from a theoretical point of view.

Yet, a decisive difference between the two taxonomies that makes any integration difficult lies within the assessment approach taken. Whereas the DIAMONDS measurement tools can be used to capture situational perceptions of any situation, the Situation 5 are currently bound to the 211 vignettes. The analyses underlying the DIAMONDS thus find the common variance underlying self-ratings of different persons and *different situations*. The Situation 5, however, are based on the correlations of self-ratings of different persons for the *same situations*. This might explain the larger number of dimensions in the DIAMONDS model.

One could say that, whereas the DIAMONDS tools measure the participant's perception of one *specific* situation, the Situation 5 measure captures the perception of (work) situations in *general*. Having an assessment for general situational perceptions is potentially extremely useful for predicting future behavior. Hogan (2009) criticized that the assessment of situations can only lead to predictions of behavior at distinct points in time (or in situations). This is true, and especially when the future situations are unknown, it will not allow better predictions. Assessing situational perceptions that reside within persons allows estimation of how a person will generally see future situations. The situation can thereby be incorporated into any prediction formulae for behavior.

Theories of Person–Situation Interaction

Even though some taxonomies exist (for an overview, see Rauthmann et al., 2014; Yang et al., 2006), theories of person–situation interaction remain imprecise and basically do not allow concrete derivations of empirically testable hypotheses. Does, for example, the perception of a situation as monotonous lead to more or less conscientious behavior? Or, in more general terms, what is the effect of a straining situation – now that we think we can define it – on personality and its expression?

With respect to occupational settings, the trait activation theory (TAT; Tett & Burnett, 2003; Tett & Guterman, 2000) postulates that a trait will only be expressed in a situation that is relevant to this trait. This implies that a higher predictive validity of scores from personality measures can be achieved when the assessment situation resembles that of the working context (cf. Hunthausen, Truxillo, Bauer, & Hammer, 2003; Mussel & Spengler, 2015; Shaffer & Postlethwaite, 2012; Ziegler et al., 2014). Comparing different situations (i.e., working context to assessment situations) requires the use of a situational taxonomy, though. The existence of taxonomies like the DIAMONDS or Situation 5 now allows such comparisons to be performed. Moreover, it is now possible to assess how typical work situations are perceived (by incumbents). This in turn could help to specify concrete hypotheses regarding the impact of personality test scores on future job performance. Assessments of situational perceptions should also allow the prediction of future performance, especially in settings where situational influences are thought to be important or varying situational circumstances are likely to occur. However, such promising applications, which are ultimately based on Lewin's equation, need to be tested first. As pointed out above, there is some empirical evidence supporting these ideas.

In a more general approach, the cognitive-affective system theory (CAPS; Mischel & Shoda, 1995) postulates *if…then* contingencies to behavior: if certain situational stimuli are perceived, then a specific behavioral response is given. These contingencies vary from person to person, yet they are, within a person, supposed to be stable. With reference to this theory, Eaton, South, and Krueger (2009), for example, highlighted the worth of situational taxonomies for the understanding and description of personality disorders. They proposed research designs that would greatly benefit from situational taxonomies. Understanding which situation (*if*…) might lead to the expression (…*then*) of a personality disorder, and in which one the person might function adequately could, for example, facilitate therapy.

Such theories (e.g., TAT, CAPS) outline possible mechanisms of the person–situation interaction. The next step will be the inclusion of scientifically valid and generalizable situational taxonomies into these theories to generate testable hypotheses. By stating more explicitly the expected effects of this long-debated interaction, the field will be able to move beyond general statements such as "situational forces affect behavior" (Furr & Funder, 2004, p. 442) and arrive at testable hypothesis such as "a person that expects results from a situation tends to exhibit more conscientious behavior than is predicted by his or her trait level of conscientiousness alone".

The Way Forward

Summarizing the developments of the last five years, the field has mostly agreed that behavior is influenced by the person and the situation the person is in. Recent developments focus on situational perceptions within persons as the means to quantify situational influences. Different situational taxonomies and measurement tools for the assessment of situations and situational perception are now available (Rauthmann et al., 2014; Wagerman & Funder, 2009; Ziegler, 2014). Whereas Hogan in 2009 argued that the person–situation debate was over due to a lack of possibilities to describe situations, we think that due to the recent progress made, it was never easier to answer some of the pertinent questions within the debate.

So, how can personality assessment profit from these advances? What is needed to further improve the ultimate goal, the prediction of human behavior?

Development and integration of taxonomies

First of all, even though situational taxonomies have been developed, there is still plenty of space for further taxonomies and their validation. Rauthmann et al. (2014) presents six steps to consider when developing a taxonomy. Depending on

(1) the underlying theories (their background, e.g., personality psychology or social psychology), (2) the situational information sampled (i.e., the level of analysis), (3) the structuring of the information (i.e., within situation as in DIAMONDS, or across situations as in Situation 5), (4) the generation of the situational information (e.g., lexical approach or generated by laypersons), (5) the presentation of situational information (e.g., real situations or hypothetical situations), and finally (6) the structuring of the situational information (e.g., factor analysis or cluster analysis), a vast universe of possible situation taxonomies unfolds itself. Each of these taxonomies may have a value in its own right. Nevertheless, finding their common core should remain the overarching goal. Science is not helped by a plethora of different taxonomies, each emphasizing some specific aspect of situations.

Integration of situation and personality

Then, the underlying theories have to be developed and improved. The main task will be linking situational taxonomies explicitly to personality measures as well as behavioral outcomes. For personality assessment to profit from situational taxonomies, Ziegler and Horstmann (2015) pointed out that it is crucial to explicitly link situational taxonomies to personality theories and examine their combined ability to predict behavior. The variance that is due to the person, the situation (as perceived), as well as their interaction, has to be teased apart (Ziegler & Ziegler, 2015). With respect to the behavioral outcome, the authors point out that the right criterion has to be chosen. Personality assessment often seeks to predict outcomes such as career success or wellbeing. Personality traits might only be predictive of these outcomes when both the predictor and the criterion are assessed under comparable circumstances. The predictive validity of personality assessments will surely profit from a precise definition of these circumstances (Ziegler & Horstmann, 2015).

It is therefore essential that a variety of studies are conducted that use comparable and well-integrated concepts of personality and situation (perception) and can thus generate, in the long and cumulative sense, a better understanding of the person–situation interaction.

Conclusion

Personality assessment can profit from new situational taxonomies, guidelines for the examination of consistency and the development of further taxonomies. Theories, which help to understand the interaction of a person with a situation, eventually have to be formulated to pave the way for more precise predictions of behavior than are currently possible. Step by step, we may reach a point where the different behavioral implications that a warm or a cold cup of coffee can have will surprise fewer people than it did in 2008.

References

Allport, G.W., & Odbert, H.S. (1936). Trait-names: A psycho-lexical study. *Psychological Monographs, 47* (1), 1–171.

Asendorpf, J. (2009). Personality: Traits and situations. In G. Matthews & P.J. Corr (Eds.), *The Cambridge Handbook of Personality Psychology* (pp. 43–53). New York: Cambridge University Press.

Baumeister, R.F., Vohs, K.D., & Funder, D.C. (2007). Psychology as the science of self-reports and finger movements: Whatever happened to actual behavior? *Perspectives on Psychological Science, 2* (4), 396–403.

Bem, D., & Allen, A. (1974). On predicting some of the people some of the time. *Psychological Review, 81* (6), 506–520.

Deary, I. (2009). The trait approach to personality. In G. Matthews & P.J. Corr (Eds.), *The Cambridge Handbook of Personality Psychology* (pp. 89–109). Cambridge: Cambridge University Press.

Deinzer, R., Steyer, R., Eid, M., Notz, P., Schwenkmezger, P., Ostendorf, F., & Neubauer, A. (1995). Situational effects in trait assessment: The FPI, NEOFFI, and EPI questionnaires. *European Journal of Personality, 9* (1), 1–23.

Eaton, N.R., South, S.C., & Krueger, R.F. (2009). The Cognitive–Affective Processing System (CAPS) approach to personality and the concept of personality disorder: Integrating clinical and social-cognitive research. *Journal of Research in Personality, 43* (2), 208–217.

Edwards, J., & Templeton, A. (2005). The structure of perceived qualities of situations. *European Journal of Social Psychology, 723* (35), 705–723.

Endler, N.S., & Magnusson, D. (1976). Toward an interactional psychology of personality. *Psychological Bulletin, 83* (5), 956–974.

Epstein, S. (1979). The stability of behavior: On predicting most of the people much of the time. *Journal of Personality and Social Psychology, 37* (7), 1097–1126.

Epstein, S. (1983). Aggregation and beyond: Some basic issues on the prediction of behavior. *Journal of Personality, 51* (3), 360–392.

Fleeson, W. (2004). Moving personality beyond the person-situation debate. The challenge and the opportunity of within-person variability. *Current Directions in Psychological Science, 13* (2), 83–87.

Fleeson, W., & Noftle, E.E. (2008). Where does personality have its influence? A supermatrix of consistency concepts. *Journal of Personality, 76* (6), 1355–1386.

Funder, D.C. (2006). Towards a resolution of the personality triad: Persons, situations, and behaviors. *Journal of Research in Personality, 40* (1), 21–34.

Funder, D.C., Furr, R.M., & Colvin, C.R. (2000). The Riverside Behavioral Q-sort: A Tool for the Description of Social Behavior. *Journal of Personality, 68* (3), 451–489.

Funder, D.C., Guillaume, E., Kumagai, S., Kawamoto, S., & Sato, T. (2012). The person-situation debate and the assessment of situations. *Japanese Journal of Personality, 21* (1), 1–11.

Furr, R.M., & Funder, D.C. (2004). Situational similarity and behavioral consistency: Subjective, objective, variable-centered, and person-centered approaches. *Journal of Research in Personality, 38* (5), 421–447.

Hogan, R. (2009). Much ado about nothing: The person–situation debate. *Journal of Research in Personality, 43* (2), 249.

Hunthausen, J.M., Truxillo, D.M., Bauer, T.N., & Hammer, L.B. (2003). A field study of frame-of-reference effects on personality test validity. *Journal of Applied Psychology, 88* (3), 545–551.

John, O., & Srivastava, S. (1999). The Big-Five trait taxonomy: History, measurement, and theoretical perspectives. In L.A. Pervin & O.P. John (Eds.), *Handbook of Personality: Theory and Research (Vol. 2)* (pp. 102–138). New York: Guilford Press.

Krueger, J.I. (2009). A componential model of situation effects, person effects, and situation-by-person interaction effects on social behavior. *Journal of Research in Personality, 43* (2), 127–136.

Lewin, K. (1936). *Principles of Topological Psychology. New York-London.* New York: McGraw Hill.

Mischel, W. (1968). *Personality and Assessment.* New York: Wiley.

Mischel, W. (2004). Toward an integrative science of the person. *Annual Review of Psychology, 55*, 1–22.

Mischel, W. (2009). From Personality and Assessment (1968) to Personality Science, 2009. *Journal of Research in Personality, 43* (2), 282–290.

Mischel, W., & Peake, P.K. (1982). Beyond déjà vu in the search for cross-situational consistency. *Psychological Review, 89* (6), 730–755.

Mischel, W., & Shoda, Y. (1995). A cognitive-affective system theory of personality: Reconceptualizing situations, dispositions, dynamics, and invariance in personality structure. *Psychological Review, 102* (2), 246–268.

Mussel, P., & Spengler, M. (2015). Investigating intellect from a trait activation perspective: Identification of situational moderators for the correlation with work-related criteria. *Journal of Research in Personality, 55*, 51–60.

Rauthmann, J. (2015). Structuring situational information: A road map of the multiple pathways to different situational taxonomies. *European Psychologist, 20* (3), 176–189.

Rauthmann, J., Gallardo-Pujol, D., Guillaume, E.M., Todd, E., Nave, C.S., Sherman, R.A., … Funder, D.C. (2014). The situational eight DIAMONDS: A taxonomy of major dimensions of situation characteristics. *Journal of Personality and Social Psychology, 107* (4), 677–718.

Rauthmann, J., & Sherman, R.A. (2015a). Measuring the Situational Eight DIAMONDS characteristics of situations. *European Journal of Psychological Assessment.* Advance online publication. doi:10.1027/1015-5759/a000246

Rauthmann, J., & Sherman, R.A. (2015b). Ultra-brief measures for the situational Eight DIAMONDS domains. *European Journal of Psychological Assessment.* Advance online publication. doi:10.1027/1015-5759/a000245

Rauthmann, J., Sherman, R.A., & Funder, D.C. (2015). Principles of situation research: Towards a better understanding of psychological situations. *European Journal of Personality, 29* (3), 363–381.

Reis, H.T. (2008). Reinvigorating the concept of situation in social psychology. *Personality and Social Psychology Review, 12* (4), 311–329.

Saucier, G., Bel-Bahar, T., & Fernandez, C. (2007). What modifies the expression of personality tendencies? Defining basic domains of situation variables. *Journal of Personality, 75* (3), 479–503.

Shaffer, J., & Postlethwaite, B. (2012). A matter of context: A meta-analytic investigation of the relative validity of contextualized and noncontextualized personality measures. *Personnel Psychology, 65* (3), 445–494.

Sherman, R.A., Nave, C.S., & Funder, D.C. (2010). Situational similarity and personality predict behavioral consistency. *Journal of Personality and Social Psychology, 99* (2), 330–343.

Sherman, R.A., Nave, C.S., & Funder, D.C. (2012). Properties of persons and situations related to overall and distinctive personality-behavior congruence. *Journal of Research in Personality, 46* (1), 87–101.

Sherman, R.A., Nave, C.S., & Funder, D.C. (2013). Situational construal is related to personality and gender. *Journal of Research in Personality, 47* (1), 1–14.

Shoda, Y., & Mischel, W. (2000). Reconciling contextualism with the core assumptions of personality psychology. *European Journal of Personality, 14* (5), 407–428.

Shoda, Y., Mischel, W., & Wright, J.C. (1994). Intraindividual stability in the organization and patterning of behavior: Incorporating psychological situations into the idiographic analysis of personality. *Journal of Personality and Social Psychology, 67* (4), 674–687.

Steyer, R., Schmitt, M., & Eid, M. (1999). Latent state–trait theory and research in personality and individual differences. *European Journal of Personality, 13* (5), 389–408.

Tett, R.P., & Burnett, D.D. (2003). A personality trait-based interactionist model of job performance. *Journal of Applied Psychology, 88* (3), 500–517.

Tett, R.P., & Guterman, H.A. (2000). Situation trait relevance, trait expression, and cross-situational consistency: Testing a principle of trait activation. *Journal of Research in Personality, 34* (4), 397–423.

Wagerman, S., & Funder, D. (2009). Personality psychology of situations. In P.J. Corr & G. Matthews (Eds.), *The Cambridge Handbook of Personality Psychology* (pp. 27–42). New York: Cambridge University Press.

Webster, G.D. (2009). The person–situation interaction is increasingly outpacing the person–situation debate in the scientific literature: A 30-year analysis of publication trends, 1978–2007. *Journal of Research in Personality, 43* (2), 278–279.

Williams, L.E., & Bargh, J.A. (2008). Experiencing physical warmth promotes interpersonal warmth. *Science, 322* (5901), 606–607.

Yang, Y., Read, S.J., & Miller, L.C. (2006). A taxonomy of situations from Chinese idioms. *Journal of Research in Personality, 40* (5), 750–778.

Ziegler, M. (2014). *B5PS. Big Five Inventory of Personality in Occupational Situations.* Mödling, Austria: Schuhfried GmbH.

Ziegler, M., Bensch, D., Maaß, U., Schult, V., Vogel, M., & Bühner, M. (2014). Big Five facets as predictor of job training performance: The role of specific job demands. *Learning and Individual Differences, 29*, 1–7.

Ziegler, M., Ehrlenspiel, F., & Brand, R. (2009). Latent state–trait theory: An application in sport psychology. *Psychology of Sport and Exercise, 10* (3), 344–349.

Ziegler, M., & Horstmann, K. (2015). Discovering the second side of the coin: Integrating situational perception into psychological assessment. *European Journal of Psychological Assessment, 3* (2), 69–74.

Ziegler, M., & Ziegler, J. (2015). A better understanding of psychological situations: Chances and challenges for psychological assessment. *European Journal of Personality, 29* (3), 418–419.

4

Temperamental Components of the Developing Personality

James B. Victor†
Hampton University, Virginia, USA

Mary K. Rothbart
University of Oregon, USA

Spencer R. Baker
Hampton University, Virginia, USA

Jennifer L. Tackett
Northwestern University, USA

Until recent years the field of personality psychology has largely been interested in differences among adults, whereas temperament has most often been studied in infants and young children (Rothbart & Bates, 2006; but see Caspi & Shiner, 2006). In addition, traits underlying individual differences in temperament and personality have been thought to be relatively stable. However, rapid progress in genetics and the view that genes are differentially expressed with development and experience has largely undermined this idea. Instead, temperament and personality, in common with much of psychology, may prove to be based on common neural networks that underlie both human capacities and individual differences in their employment and efficiency (Posner & Rothbart, 2007).

Understanding how infant temperament influences the development of childhood and adult personality is thus of basic importance to the study of individual differences. Moreover, the joint study of temperament and personality provides an important step towards analysis of how genes and experience shape underlying neural networks. In this chapter, we use a model employing both personality and temperament scales to locate temperament components within a broad personality structure, creating a greater possibility for empirically informed longitudinal studies of personality development.

† Deceased

The Wiley Handbook of Personality Assessment, First Edition. Edited by Updesh Kumar.
© 2016 John Wiley & Sons, Ltd. Published 2016 by John Wiley & Sons, Ltd.

In the lexical tradition of adult personality research, trait descriptive adjectives originally taken from the dictionary are administered in self- and other-rating scales (Digman, 1990; Goldberg, 1990). Broad support for the extraction of five (plus or minus two) factors has been reported, with the factors typically identified using principal components and/or factor analytic techniques (Digman, 1990; Goldberg, 1990). The Big Five resulting factors have been labeled Extraversion, Neuroticism, Agreeableness, Conscientiousness, and Openness to Experience/Intellect. Lower-level scales have also been defined and investigated, although their content varies more substantially across measures (Saucier & Ostendorf, 1999).

Early work extending the five-factor approach to children was reported by Digman and his colleagues (Digman & Inouye, 1986; Digman & Takemoto-Chock, 1981). Using a trait-descriptive adjective scale based on five-factor content, the original five factors from adult research were extracted from teachers' ratings. These findings have been subsequently replicated (e.g., Goldberg, 2001; Graziano & Ward, 1992; Halverson et al., 2003; Tackett et al., 2012; Victor, 1994), providing strong support for an analogous (although typically not identical) five-factor structure of child individual differences. Researchers have also replicated a five-factor structure for pre-adolescent and adolescent students using the adult NEO PI-R five-factor questionnaires (De Fruyt, Mervielde, Hoekstra, & Rolland, 2000) and the Hierarchical Personality Inventory for Children (Mervielde & De Fruyt, 1999). Researchers using the California Q-Set (Block, 1961) for children aged 3–17 with a variety of informants have also provided evidence for emergent Five-Factor Model (FFM) traits using this approach, although typically those traits are embedded among additional traits not measured by the FFM (Robins, John, & Caspi, 1994; Van Lieshout & Haselager, 1994).

Shiner (1998), however, has raised three fundamental concerns regarding use of the Big Five/Five Factor approach in childhood. First, without a strong theoretical analysis, it offers little or no conceptual framework for making decisions about lower-order traits. Second, contributions of lower-order component traits may be obscured when only higher-order traits are studied. Finally, measuring reliable and valid lower-level traits may yield evidence for different higher-order dimensions than those identified to date. Shiner's concerns suggest the need to (a) broaden the trait descriptors selected; (b) focus on the conceptual basis of each trait; and (c) begin at the subscale or lower trait level. Specifically, the study of temperamental traits originated from a rich theoretical approach to child development, one not typically attended to by researchers of adult personality. This chapter attempts to merge the strengths of these two approaches, allowing the theoretically rich literature on early temperament to empirically guide research on personality development.

Three phases of research were used to investigate early temperament association with later personality development (see Halverson et al., 2003); however, only the latter two phases are described in this chapter. Not considered here is Phase I, which describes the organization of items from parent descriptions of their children into homogeneous lower-level scales. These lower-level scales were modeled after the adult FFM constructs and facets (NEO PI-R; Costa & McCrae, 1992) into the Hampton Scales of Child Personality. This chapter begins with Phase II. In Phase II, scales of child temperament (the Children's Behavior Questionnaire (CBQ);

Rothbart, Ahadi, Hershey & Fisher, 2001) are added to the Hampton Scales. Phase III adds further CBQ temperament scales and items, analyzing data for 30 child temperament and personality scales for internal consistency, factor structure and replication. Mother/father correlations, test–retest correlations, and stability of parent rating scales over two years are also examined.

Phase II: Adding Temperament CBQ Content to the Hampton Child Personality Scales

Rothbart and Derryberry (1981) defined temperament as individual differences in reactivity and self-regulation, assumed to have a constitutional basis. Reactivity refers to the excitability, responsivity or arousability of emotion, action and attention systems, whereas self-regulation refers to the neural and behavioral processes, including orienting and executive attention (effortful control), that modulate reactivity (Rothbart & Derryberry, 1981). This broad framework (Rothbart, 1989; Rothbart & Derryberry, 1981), based on evolutionarily conserved systems of emotion, activation, motivation, and attention, allows for the study of positive emotional reactions (including sociability) and approach tendencies, irritable negative emotionality (anger/frustration), fear (including behavioral inhibition), and self-regulatory mechanisms of attention (inhibitory control, attentional focusing, perceptual sensitivity, and soothability). These dimensions are assessed in the Children's Behavior Questionnaire (CBQ; Rothbart et al., 2001), and contribute to our research in Phases II and III.

After comparing the content of the Hampton Scales and the Children's Behavior Questionnaire (CBQ; Rothbart et al., 2001), it was clear to us that a number of the Hampton Scales were already tapping aspects of temperament, including emotional reactivity and distractibility. On the other hand, the CBQ temperament measure contained a broad construct of effortful control (EC), including scales assessing attentional focusing, inhibitory control, and perceptual sensitivity, none of which was represented in the Hampton Scales. By designating several of the Hampton scales as surrogates for temperament scales, and by adding the three scales assessing EC, we attempted to strengthen the congruence of the Conscientiousness (0.69) and Openness (0.59) factors. In Phase II of this study, we designated several of the Hampton Scales as temperament surrogates (anger hostility, fearful/anxious, self-consciousness/shy withdrawn, distractibility, and sociability), and added three effortful control scales from the CBQ. We first addressed whether adding the three EC temperament scales would strengthen the Hampton Scale structure. The Children's Behavior Questionnaire (CBQ; Rothbart et al., 2001) and the CBQ Short Form (Putnam & Rothbart, 2006) are the instruments from which temperament scales were drawn for Phase II.

Phase II samples

Sample 1 ($N = 739$) and Sample 2 ($N = 237$) were gathered following the procedures in Phase I. Questionnaires were collected from preschools, private schools, churches, dance classes, and health organizations in North Carolina and Virginia, by trained and paid data collectors. Parents were paid a small fee or participated in a fundraiser for their child's organization. Data collected were based on a signed site agreement and a signed individual consent form to participate. Additional data were collected from parents for class credit, by students trained in data collection procedures. These samples were used to test whether three EC scales (attentional focusing, inhibitory control, and perceptual sensitivity) enhanced the factor structure of the Hampton 22 scales, particularly the dimensions of Conscientiousness and Openness to Experience. Using Procrustes rotations and Comprehensive Exploratory Factor Analyses (CEFA), we investigated the structure.

CEFA with oblique, targeted rotations of the raw data provides a test of fit for factor solutions. These procedures are very similar to using structural equation modeling (SEM) to perform confirmatory factor analyses. Browne, Cudeck, Tateneni, and Mels (1998) developed the CEFA to provide fit indexes of the root mean square error of approximation (RMSEA) and the Expected Cross Validation Index (ECVI; Browne & Cudeck, 1993) to estimate asymptotic standard errors of rotated factor loading and factor intercorrelations. Using the estimated standard errors, one can then estimate statistical significance of the factor loadings. Our choice of using both Procrustes and CEFA targeted rotations in combination provides several useful indices. Procrustes rotations allow computation of factor and scale coefficients of congruence, and CEFA provides fit indices as well as factor intercorrelations.

Results and discussion

For the Hampton/CBQ analysis, we used Procrustes rotation, allowing computation of both a factor congruence coefficient and scale or variable congruence coefficients. We used the two Hampton and CBQ samples for the analysis. The CBQ short form items (Putnam & Rothbart, 2006) were assessed at the scale level, similar to the scales developed in the NEO PI-R guided approach. However, the CBQ items had been developed for children aged 3 to 7 years (Rothbart et al., 2001) and were applied here to children aged 3 to 12 years. The CBQ also consisted of longer item statements than the parent descriptors used in the Hampton 22 scales.

Using Procrustes rotations, we compared the factor loadings from Sample 1 ($N = 739$) with those from Sample 2 ($N = 237$). As predicted, including the three CBQ scales increased congruence coefficients for both Openness (from 0.59 to 0.74) and Conscientiousness (from 0.69 to 0.77). In addition, in the comparison analysis, the congruence coefficients for both factors and the remaining scales were all above 0.90. This gave substantial support to the idea that the EC scales would add strength to the broad dimensions of Openness and Conscientiousness, and these results were replicated for both factors and scales across factors. Each scale contributed as expected to the factors. This work strongly suggests that adding temperament content to the personality measure can allow us to address important theoretical questions. In Phase III, we further extended the measure by strengthening current scales, writing new ones, and adding further temperament scales from the CBQ.

Phase III: A Combined Measure of Child Temperament and Personality – The CTPQ

To construct the Child Temperament and Personality Questionnaire (CTPQ), we developed new scales that included adaptations of parent descriptors, CBQ Short Form items, and items developed in the Hampton laboratory for assessing depression/sadness, openness to actions, and diligence. Other weak four-item parent description scales were also strengthened by adapting CBQ Short Form items and/or writing new items. These included scales for assertiveness and excitement-seeking; distractibility was combined with CBQ distractibility items. The eight scales thus added to the Hampton 22 scales included three NEO-PI related scales: depression/sadness, openness to actions, and diligence. An impulsivity scale was also adapted from our earlier work (Victor, Halverson, & Montague, 1985). Finally, four scales – soothability, attentional focusing, inhibitory control, and perceptual sensitivity – were modified from the CBQ short form to be included in the CTPQ. Although soothability was not used in Phase II, it represents an important self-regulatory variable that is not captured in the content of the Hampton scales.

A baseline sample (Sample 3, $N = 566$) and a comparison sample (Sample 4, $N = 366$) of children aged 3 to 13, with data gathered similarly to Phases I and II, provided data on children's temperament and personality. These data provided the measurement model for the factor structure of the combined scales and allowed computation of Cronbach alphas. Based on the similarity of factor loadings described below, the two samples were merged and a CEFA was performed. The merged sample consisted of 932 children from rural and urban settings in 11 states, fairly evenly divided across age (47.6% boys, 52.4% girls) and race/ethnicity (53.1% European American, 32.4% African American, 6.9% multiracial, 3.3% Hispanic, 1.3% Asian/Pacific Islander, and 2.7% other or not specified). Children's parents represented a wide range of socioeconomic indicators of occupation, education level, work status, and housing status (rent or own).

Results and discussion

For the Cronbach alpha analyses, 17 children outside of the age range of the questionnaire were removed, for a combined sample of 915 children 3–12 years old. Alpha reliabilities for the CTPQ scales were similar and substantial across the total sample (915), the two age groups (older = 518, younger = 397), socioeconomic groups (higher = 389, lower = 526), child gender (boys = 439, girls = 476), and race/ethnicity groups (white = 487, black = 298). There were also 130 children from other ethnicities with sample sizes too small to analyze. Very similar patterns were shown across these groups, with Cronbach alphas ranging from 0.60 to 0.89 (detailed analyses available upon request). Mother/father correlations, two-week test–retest correlations, and two-year stability correlations are presented in Table 4.1. Cross-parent agreement (mother to father) was obtained for 44 children. These correlations were modest to substantial, ranging from 0.23 for openness to ideas, to 0.74 for anger/irritability, with a median of 0.53, consistent with other studies (Tackett, 2011). Test–retest correlations for 90 children across a two-week period

Table 4.1 Mother/father correlations, test–retest correlations, and two-year stability correlations

CTPQ Scale (number of items)	*Mother/ father*	*Test– retest*	*Two- year*		*Mother/ father*	*Test– retest*	*Two- year*
Internalizing negative affectivity				Sociable extraversion			
Fear/worry (5)	0.69	0.80	0.26	Positive emotions (7)	0.62	0.76	0.46
Dependency (6)	0.37	0.73	0.30	Gregariousness (5)	0.55	0.80	0.49
Depression/sadness (7)	0.53	0.78	0.36	Warmth (5)	0.64	0.78	0.54
Social shyness (6)	0.50	0.83	0.45	Soothability (4)	0.48	0.67	0.10
Distractibility (5)	0.36	0.76	0.43	Cooperativeness (6)	0.53	0.78	0.36
				Considerate of others (5)	0.58	0.90	0.46
Externalizing negative affectivity/stimulation seeking							
Assertiveness (6)	0.54	0.87	0.21	Anger/irritability (6)	0.74	0.80	0.28
Excitement seeking (6)	0.40	0.78	0.37	Impulsivity (6)	0.64	0.74	0.31
Self-centered (6)	0.65	0.87	0.33	Manipulativeness (4)	0.59	0.86	0.45
Non-compliance (6)	0.66	0.79	0.38	Activity (6)	0.53	0.86	0.41
Conscientiousness				Openness to experience			
Order (5)	0.63	0.85	0.24	Openness to ideas (7)	0.23	0.82	0.44
Diligence (5)	0.55	0.82	0.22	Aesthetics/ creativity (6)	0.62	0.84	0.45
Self-discipline (5)	0.38	0.85	0.45	Intellect/quick to learn (7)	0.54	0.89	0.43
Competence (6)	0.49	0.87	0.28	Openness to actions (6)	0.46	0.85	0.34
Inhibitory control (7)	0.33	0.85	0.31	Perceptual sensitivity (6)	0.40	0.87	0.33
Attentional focusing (7)	0.40	0.90	0.19				

Note: Mother/father correlations $N = 44$; test–retest after two weeks $N = 90$; two-year stability $N = 122$.

were even more substantial, ranging from 0.69 to 0.90, with a median of 0.84. The sample size for two-year stability was 122. The across-age stability correlations varied by scale. The two lowest were soothability (0.10) and attentional focusing (0.19). The two highest were warmth (0.54) and gregariousness (0.49).

The 30 scales also provided a measurement model for studies addressing the factor structure of the combined scales. Both principal component analyses with orthogonal rotations and maximum likelihood analyses with oblique rotations consistently illustrated a four-factor solution for younger children and a five-factor solution for older children. However, CEFA with targeted oblique rotations on the baseline sample (n = 566) illustrated that a five-factor solution was the best fit for both age groups. Several scales displayed loadings across three or more factors, indicating some redundancy among the original 30 scales. A regression analysis was therefore performed using each scale in turn as the dependent variable. Four scales (cooperativeness, considerate of others, openness to actions, and competence) showed multiple loadings and could be accounted for in large part by the remaining variables (approximately 70% of the variance). Although future work will include these scales for additional study, the data presented here is based upon the remaining 26 subscales (the structure was very similar to the 30-scale structure).

The same Procrustes targeted rotation procedures were repeated for a baseline sample and a comparison sample for the scales of the CTPQ (171 items). The baseline Sample 3 consisted of 566 children, aged 3–12, and the comparison Sample 4 consisted of 366 children, aged 3–12, rated by their parents. Congruence coefficients for the 26 scales ranged from 0.71 to 0.96 and factor congruence coefficients from 0.79 to 0.89, with an overall congruence coefficient of 0.85. The scale and factor congruence coefficients comparing the factor loadings of data from 366 children to the baseline sample of 566 were all larger than 0.93 and the overall congruence coefficient was 0.97.

A comprehensive exploratory factor analysis (CEFA) with targeted oblique rotations was performed on the total sample (N = 915), younger children (7 years and younger) and older children (8 years and older), and a five-factor solution was the best fit for all three analyses. Table 4.2 shows the factor structure for the total sample, reflecting a five-factor solution, and accounting for 70% of the variance.

The first factor, which we have labeled *Externalizing negative affect/Sensation-seeking* (ENA) is made up of three of the original Hampton Agreeableness scales (self-centered, non-compliance/aggression, and manipulative), along with excitement-seeking, assertiveness, anger/irritability, impulsivity and activity. The second factor, which we have labeled *Sociable extraversion* (SE), is made up of gregariousness/sociability, warmth, positive emotion, the CBQ scale of soothability, and activity. It is notable that activity double-loads on *Unsocialized stimulation seeking* (USS) and on SE. If activity can be taken as a sign of general extraversion/surgency (Rothbart & Bates, 2006), extraversion may be differentiated over time into two forms – one less and one more socialized. A second double-loading scale is inhibitory control, which loads negatively on ENA and positively on Conscientiousness.

The third factor, labeled *Internalizing negative affectivity* (INA), is similar to the Hampton scale Neuroticism factor minus anger/irritability (i.e., fear/worry, self-consciousness, shyness, dependency, and distractibility). Anger/irritability now loads primarily on the *Externalizing negative affect/Sensation-seeking* (ENA) factor, so that two forms of negative affect are identified. One includes anger and aggression, the other, the more internalizing emotions of anxiety, depression, and self-consciousness. These dimensions are congruent with those proposed by Shiner (1998) and consistent with other studies (Tackett et al., 2012). The self-regulation scale that is negatively related to the ENA factor is inhibitory control, that is, the capacity to inhibit action. The INA scales, on the other hand, are related positively to distractibility and negatively to attentional focusing. These findings suggest that ENA is more highly regulated by the inhibition of action; INA by the regulation of

Table 4.2 Comprehensive exploratory factor analysis (CEFA) for 26 scales – full sample ($N = 915$)

	ENA	*SE*	*INA*	*C*	*O*
Assertiveness	**0.76**	0.02	−0.15	0.08	0.25
Excitement seeking	**0.72**	0.13	0.03	−0.06	−0.06
Self-centered	**0.73**	−0.20	0.13	0.01	0.06
Non-compliance/aggression	**0.72**	−0.28	0.10	−0.02	−0.08
Anger hostility	**0.62**	−0.31	0.21	−0.03	0.05
Impulsivity	**0.60**	0.06	0.24	−0.20	−0.04
Manipulative	**0.60**	−0.10	0.20	−0.08	−0.04
Activity	**0.55**	**0.40**	−0.10	0.00	−0.05
Positive emotion	0.12	**0.80**	−0.00	0.04	0.19
Gregariousness	0.13	**0.73**	−0.12	0.08	0.14
Warmth	−0.26	**0.62**	0.18	−0.02	0.28
Soothability	−0.15	**0.51**	0.11	0.00	−0.09
Fear/worry	0.00	−0.10	**0.71**	0.08	−0.00
Dependency	−0.07	0.15	**0.68**	−0.07	−0.13
Depression/sadness	0.18	−0.22	**0.65**	0.05	0.09
Social shyness	−0.07	−0.36	**0.64**	0.06	0.03
Distractibility	0.15	−0.12	**0.52**	**−0.41**	0.02
Order	0.16	0.02	0.10	**0.81**	−0.08
Diligence	−0.11	−0.00	−0.20	**0.64**	0.16
Self-discipline	−0.11	−0.22	0.13	**0.66**	0.17
Inhibitory control	**−0.36**	0.03	0.01	**0.46**	0.20
Attention focusing	−0.10	−0.16	−0.30	**0.36**	**0.45**
Openness to ideas	0.04	0.21	0.01	−0.06	**0.80**
Aesthetics/creativity	−0.05	0.03	0.12	−0.12	**0.75**
Intellect/quick to learn	0.10	0.04	−0.18	0.14	**0.67**
Perceptual sensitivity	0.11	0.14	0.08	0.11	**0.44**

Note: INA, Internalizing negative affectivity; SE, Sociable extraversion; O, Openness to experience; ENA, Externalizing negative affectivity; C, Conscientiousness.

thoughts. In ENA, many action-related behaviors such as impulsivity and aggression are included. In INA, most of the scales are emotion or attention-related ones.

The fourth factor, labeled *Conscientiousness*, is composed of subscales of order, diligence, inhibitory control, self-discipline, attentional focusing, and distractibility. The temperament effortful control (EC) scales of inhibitory control and attention focusing load on Conscientiousness, as was found in the earlier Hampton/CBQ studies. With distractibility combined with items from the CBQ scale of attention shifting, it also double-loads on *Internalizing negative affectivity*. The fifth factor is *Openness to experience*, composed of four scales: aesthetics/creativity, openness to ideas, intellect/quick to learn, and temperamental perceptual sensitivity from the CBQ. In adult studies we have also found direct links between perceptual sensitivity scales and Big Five Openness (Evans & Rothbart, 2007), whereas a perceptual sensitivity scale loaded on the Extraversion/surgency factor in infancy (Gartstein & Rothbart, 2003). The structure of this domain is also consistent with recent work (Herzhoff & Tackett, 2012).

Overarching Discussion

The current model, with combined parent descriptor traits and temperament scales, demonstrates a fairly different structure from the usual Big Five or FFM factors. The original scales of Extraversion, for example, have split into Sociable Extraversion and Externalizing Negative Affectivity/Stimulation-Seeking. The Externalizing Negative Affectivity/Stimulation-Seeking (ENA) factor resembles Zuckerman's (1994) Impulsive Unsocialized Sensation Seeking (ImpUSS) dimension. Unlike Zuckerman's model, however, anger/irritability and aggression are also components of our ENA factor. In addition, the Agreeableness scales have not contributed to a single Agreeableness factor. Instead, scales at the positive pole of Agreeableness are part of the Sociable Extraversion factor, whereas the scales at the negative pole are part of the Externalizing Negative Affectivity factor. Thus the five-factor structure here includes differentiated negative affect factors, representing internalizing and externalizing, along with factors for sociable extraversion, conscientiousness, and openness.

The two negative affectivity factors illustrate, as Shiner (1998) proposed, a differentiation between combined fear, worry, and guilt and anger/irritability. Shiner also speculated about the existence of a dimension of dependency, and a scale for dependency emerged from this research, contributing to INA. A dependency scale has also been found in the Dutch version of the California Q-set (Van Lieshout & Haselager, 1994). However, the Van Lieshout and Haselager factor contains items relating to children's clinging to adults, whereas in the current INA factor, dependency describes children who need help doing things, give in to others, and so on.

The model shows both similarities to and differences from the Hampton Child Personality Scale structure. For example, Internalizing Negative Affectivity performs similarly to Neuroticism in the Hampton scales, but anger-hostility, part of the Neuroticism factor in the Hampton scales, now loads more heavily on Externalizing Negative Affectivity/Sensation-Seeking. The self-consciousness/social shyness scale remains the same as in the Hampton scale analysis. It is conceptually close to the adult NEO PI-R scale of social shyness, in that it includes "is shy with people," but it also includes "lacks confidence." Finally, a depression/sadness scale combining adapted CBQ and NEO guided items further contributes to a differentiated set of scales assessing Internalizing Negative Affectivity. Distractibility shows consistent double-loadings on Internalizing Negative Affectivity and Conscientiousness.

The Conscientiousness factor has been greatly strengthened by combining three parent descriptor dimensions with three temperament dimensions (inhibitory control, attention focusing, and distractibility). Openness to experience is also now a much stronger dimension with four subscales, including openness to ideas, aesthetics/creativity, and intellect/quick to learn, as well as the temperamental effortful control scale of perceptual sensitivity. The CTPQ offers a number of scales proposed by Shiner (1998), as can be seen in Table 4.3. Only dimensions of mastery motivation and wellbeing in Shiner's list are not assessed in the CTPQ. The CTPQ also offers a considerably broader and more differentiated group of traits that go beyond Shiner's list, including scales of depression/sadness, positive emotion, warmth, cooperativeness, considerate of others, self-centered, non-compliance,

Table 4.3 NEO PI-R Facets, Hampton Child Personality and CTPQ scales compared with Shiner's (1998) proposed child personality traits

Facets of the NEO PI-R	*Hampton (CBQ and CTPQ)*	*Shiner's proposed traits*
Neuroticism		
N1 anxiety	Fear/worry	Fear/worry
N2 angry hostility	Anger/irritability	Anger/irritability
N3 depression	(Scale did not form, later CTPQ depression/sadness)	(Not mentioned in review)
N4 self-consciousness	Social shyness	Social inhibition
N5 impulsiveness*	(Scale did not form, later CTPQ impulsivity)	Inhibitory control-impulsivity
N6 vulnerability**	(Scale did not form, later CTPQ dependency)	Dependency
(Not part of the NEO PI-R)	Distractibility (later with CBQ attentional shifting, CTPQ)	(Not mentioned in review)
Extraversion		
E1 warmth	Warmth	(Not mentioned in review)
E2 gregariousness	Gregariousness	Sociability
E3 assertiveness	Assertiveness	Dominance
E4 activity	Activity	Activity
E5 excitement seeking	Excitement seeking	Excitement seeking
E6 positive emotion	Positive emotion	(Related to wellbeing)
(Not part of the NEO PI-R)	(CBQ soothability)	(Not mentioned in review)
Openness to experience		
O1 fantasy	(Scale did not form)	(No openness scales in review)
O2 aesthetics	Aesthetics/creative	(Not mentioned in review)
O3 feelings	(Scale did not form)	(Not mentioned in review)
O4 actions	(Scale did not form)	(Not mentioned in review)
O5 ideas	Openness to ideas	(Not mentioned in review)
O6 values	(Scale did not form)	(Not mentioned in review)
(Not part of NEO PI-R)	Intellect/quick to learn	(Not mentioned in review)
(Not part of NEO PI-R)	(CBQ perceptual sensitivity)	(Not mentioned in review)
Agreeableness		
A1 trust	Cooperativeness	Undifferentiated prosocial disposition
A2 straightforwardness	Manipulative	Low undifferentiated prosocial disposition
A3 altruism	Considerate of others	Undifferentiated prosocial disposition
A4 compliance	Non-compliance/aggression	Aggressiveness
A5 modesty	Self-centered	Low undifferentiated prosocial disposition
A6 tender-mindedness	(Combined with other scales)	(Not mentioned in review)
Conscientiousness		
C1 competence	Competence	Mastery motivation
C2 order	Order	Persistence

(*Continued*)

Table 4.3 (Continued)

Facets of the NEO PI-R	*Hampton (CBQ and CTPQ)*	*Shiner's proposed traits*
C3 dutifulness	(Combined with other scales)	(Not mentioned in review)
C4 achievement striving	(Combined with other scales)	Mastery motivation
C5 self-discipline	Self-discipline	Persistence (effortful control)
C6 deliberation	(Scale did not form)	(Not mentioned in review)
(Not part of NEO PI-R)	Diligence	Mastery motivation
(Not part of NEO PI-R)	CBQ attentional focusing	(Not mentioned in review)
(Not part of NEO PI-R)	CBQ inhibitory control	Inhibitory control-impulsivity

* Impulsiveness in the NEO PI-R refers to controlling one's urges and does not reflect the typical definitions of impulsive behavior in children.

** Facet variable vulnerability to stress in the NEO PI-R did not form a scale from parent descriptions. The scale dependency from parent descriptions may not represent vulnerability to stress.

impulsivity, manipulativeness, order, self-discipline, competence, attentional focusing, distractibility, openness to ideas, and aesthetics and perceptual sensitivity.

We now consider these findings in terms of the two goals of these studies: identifying specific temperament components of personality, and placing these components in a developmental context. Within Extraversion, the two broad factors that have emerged, with activity loading on both, suggest that the extraversion/surgency found in infancy (Gartstein & Rothbart, 2003) may branch into two trajectories. In the first, Externalizing Negative Affectivity/Sensation-Seeking (ENA), children demonstrate temperamental excitement-seeking, assertiveness, anger/irritability, impulsivity, and activity, along with three of the former Agreeableness scales (self-centered, non-compliance/aggression, and manipulative). In the second, Sociable Extraversion (SE), children demonstrate temperamental gregariousness/sociability, warmth, positive emotion, soothability, and activity.

Extracting a major factor that is heavily defined by the antagonistic aspects of Agreeableness is consistent with other studies of child personality (De Pauw, Mervielde, & Van Leeuwen, 2009; Tackett et al., 2012), although it is unclear whether the lack of a coherent Agreeableness factor in childhood (consisting of both high and low Agreeableness items) reflects a developmental process or a methodological challenge. De Pauw and colleagues (2009) included multiple measures from both temperament and personality models and did find agreeableness scales reflecting both ends of the dimension to load together, although the factor was still largely weighted by low-agreeableness facets and thus labeled by the authors as "Disagreeableness". It is also important to note that the De Pauw et al. (2009) study extracted an additional factor reflecting only activity facets in a sample of 4–5 year old children. As the activity dimension is a key aspect of temperament models which is largely absent from adult personality models, this may reflect the developmental salience of this individual difference domain, which becomes more integrated into other aspects of personality across development.

Internalizing Negative Affectivity (INA) includes loadings from all the negative affect scales except anger/irritability, which loads on the ENA factor. Based on previous longitudinal research (Rothbart, Derryberry, & Hershey, 2000), we would expect temperamental infant fear to predict the INA factor positively and the ENA factor negatively (Rothbart & Bates, 2006). We would also expect different outcomes for children based in part on the balance between fear and anger/irritability and in part on the effectiveness of socialization. Here, gene X environment analyses may prove particularly illuminating.

Equally important findings emerge in connection with personality Conscientiousness, Internalizing Negative Affectivity and Externalizing Affectivity, and the temperamental characteristics of inhibitory control, attentional focusing, and distractibility. These qualities develop early in life, with inhibitory control and attentional focusing as aspects of EC strongly developing between 2 and 7 years of age. The EC temperament factor has been linked to performance indicative of the efficiency of the brain's executive attention system (Posner & Rothbart, 2007; Rothbart & Rueda, 2005). We are now examining possible precursors of the executive attention system in infancy (Sheese, Rothbart, Posner, White, & Fraundorf, 2008) based on previous temperament research.

Factors drawn from personality studies that are similar to Conscientiousness have been given many other labels, including Orderliness, Self-Control, Constraint, Achievement, Superego Strength, and Will to Achieve (Digman, 1989). Each construct carries different and quite complex connotations. By linking this factor to its temperament components, which in turn are linked to executive attention, we are getting closer to one set of processes that may underlie these complex constructs. It is also likely that children's motivation to succeed in these areas will contribute to the development of conscientiousness.

The link between temperamental perceptual sensitivity and personality Openness is another exciting finding. A recent study by Herzhoff and Tackett (2012) examined combined items from temperamental scales of fantasy/openness, low intensity pleasure, and perceptual sensitivity with personality scales of intellect and openness in a sample of 9–10 year old children. This work found perceptual sensitivity to represent a key component of the broader openness construct, but with content that is not typically covered by measure of child personality. In adult research, we have found strong correlations between a broader measure of orienting sensitivity and openness (Evans & Rothbart, 2007). In infant temperament research, perceptual sensitivity contributes to Extraversion/surgency factor, but in childhood, it is part of Effortful Control. These findings suggest that the complex factor of openness in the adult may be related to the infant and young child's sensitivity to stimulus change. We can also hypothesize that openness changes over development in relation to other aspects of personality structure. One possibility, for example, is that children prone to negative affect may become less open as a self-protective strategy. Research also supports evidence for stronger covariation between openness and conscientiousness in childhood (Goldberg, 2001; Tackett et al., 2012) compared with the high covariation found between openness and extraversion in adulthood. Better understanding of the development of openness across development represents an exciting avenue for future research.

We believe that these findings, emerging from psychometric work involving an extensive and demographically diverse group of subjects and combining temperament and personality measures, yield advances toward our two goals and lead to more theory-guided research. At the same time, the integrated temperament and personality measure developed here will allow researchers access to both broad and differentiated measures of individual differences that are applicable to a very wide range of children.

Acknowledgments

This research was partially supported by a National Institute of Mental Health grant MH53272 to James B. Victor, and the conceptualization and planning for integrating child temperament and personality was supported by a collaborative National Science Foundation planning grant NSF 0127711 to James B. Victor and Mary K. Rothbart, and by NIH Grants to Mary K. Rothbart.

We are appreciative of early conversations with Paul Costa that helped to conceptualize Phase I of this project, and with Robert McCrae for his ideas regarding scale development. We thank research team members Simone Barr, Christina Felton, Wanda Gill, Dana Davis Griffin, Brittany Myatt, Holly Ramsawh, and Allison Scott, for their work on this project.

Portions of this work were presented at the 11th European Conference on Developmental Psychology, Uppsala, Sweden; the Eleventh European Conference on Personality held in Groningen, the Netherlands; and the Society for Research in Child Development.

References

Block, J. (1961). *The Q-sort Method in Personality Assessment and Psychiatric Research.* Springfield, IL: Charles C. Thomas.

Browne, M.W., & Cudeck, R. (1993). Alternative ways of assessing model fit. In K.A. Bollen & J.S. Long (Eds.), *Testing Structural Equation Models* (pp. 136–161). Newbury Park, CA: Sage.

Browne, M.W., Cudeck, R., Tateneni, K., & Mels, G. (1998). *Comprehensive exploratory factor analysis.* Retrieved from http://quantrm2.psy.ohio-state.edu/browne/

Caspi, A., & Shiner, R.L. (2006). Personality development. In W. Damon, R. Lerner, & N. Eisenberg (Eds.), *Handbook of Child Psychology, Vol. 3: Social, Emotional, and Personality Development* (6th ed.) (pp. 300–365). New York: John Wiley & Sons, Ltd.

Costa, P.T., & McCrae, R.R. (1992). *Revised NEO Personality Inventory (NEO-PI-R) and NEO Five-Factor Inventory (NEO-FFI) Manual.* Odessa, FL: Psychological Assessment Resources.

De Fruyt, F., Mervielde, I., Hoekstra, H.A., & Rolland, J.P. (2000). Assessing adolescents' personality with the NEO PI-R. *Assessment, 7* (4), 329–346.

De Pauw, S.S.W., Mervielde, I., & Van Leeuwen, K.G. (2009). How are traits related to problem behavior in preschoolers? Similarities and contrasts between temperament and personality. *Journal of Abnormal Child Psychology, 37* (3), 309–325.

Digman, J.M. (1989). Five robust trait dimensions: Development, stability, and utility. *Journal of Personality, 57* (2), 195–215.

Digman, J.M. (1990). Personality structure: Emergence of the five factor model. *Annual Review of Psychology, 41*, 417–440.

Digman, J.M., & Inouye, J. (1986). Further specification of the five robust factors of personality. *Journal of Personality and Social Psychology, 50* (1), 116–123.

Digman, J.M., & Takemoto-Chock, N.K. (1981). Factors in the natural language of personality: Re-analysis, comparison, and interpretation of six major studies. *Multivariate Behavioral Research, 16* (2), 149–170.

Evans, D., & Rothbart, M.K. (2007). Developing a model for adult temperament. *Journal of Research in Personality, 41* (4), 868–888.

Gartstein, M.A., & Rothbart, M.K. (2003). Studying infant temperament via the Revised Infant Behavior Questionnaire. *Infant Behavior and Development, 26* (1), 64–86.

Goldberg, L.R. (1990). An alternative "description of personality": The Big-Five Factor structure. *Journal of Personality and Social Psychology, 59* (6), 1216–1229.

Goldberg, L.R. (2001). Analyses of Digman's child-personality data: Derivation of Big Five factor scores from each of six samples. *Journal of Personality, 69* (5), 709–744.

Grazlano, W.G., & Ward, D. (1992). Probing the big five in adolescence: Personality and adjustment during a developmental transition. *Journal of Personality, 60* (2), 425–439.

Halverson, C.F., Havill, V.L., Deal, J., Baker, S.R., Victor, J.B., Pavlopoulos, V., ...Wen, L. (2003). Personality structure as derived from parental ratings of free descriptions of children: The inventory of child individual differences. *Journal of Personality, 71* (6), 995–1026.

Herzhoff, K., & Tackett, J.L. (2012). Establishing construct validity for Openness-to-Experience in middle childhood: Contributions from personality and temperament. *Journal of Research in Personality, 46* (3), 286–294.

Mervielde, I., & De Fruyt, F. (1999). Construction of the Hierarchical Personality Inventory for Children (HIPIC). In I. Mervielde, I. Dreary, F. De Fruyt, & F. Ostendorf (Eds.), *Personality Psychology in Europe. Proceedings of the Eighth European Conference on Personality Psychology* (pp. 107–127). Tilburg, Netherlands: Tilburg University Press.

Posner, M.I., & Rothbart, M.K. (2007). Research on attention networks as a model for the integration of psychological science. *Annual Review of Psychology, 58*, 1–23.

Putnam, S.P., & Rothbart, M.K. (2006). Development of Short and Very Short Forms of the Children's Behavior Questionnaire. *Journal of Personality Assessment, 87* (1), 102–112.

Robins, R.W., John, O.P., & Caspi, A. (1994). Major dimensions of personality in early adolescence: The Big Five and beyond. In C.F. Halverson, G.A. Kohnstamm, & R.P. Martin (Eds.), *The Developing Structure of Temperament and Personality from Infancy to Adulthood* (pp. 267–292). Hillsdale, NJ: Erlbaum.

Rothbart, M.K. (1989). Temperament and development. In G.A. Kohnstamm, J.E. Bates, & M.K. Rothbart (Eds.), *Temperament in Childhood* (pp. 187–247). Chichester: John Wiley & Sons, Ltd.

Rothbart, M.K., Ahadi, S.A., Hershey, K.L., & Fisher, P. (2001). Investigations of temperament at three to seven years: The Children's Behavior Questionnaire. *Child Development, 72* (5), 1394–1408.

Rothbart, M.K., & Bates, J.E. (2006). Temperament. In W. Damon, R. Lerner, & N. Eisenberg (Eds.), *Handbook of Child Psychology, Vol. 3: Social, Emotional, and Personality Development* (6th ed.) (pp. 96–196). New York: John Wiley & Sons, Ltd.

Rothbart, M.K., & Derryberry, D. (1981). Development of individual differences in temperament. In M.E. Lamb, & A.L. Brown (Eds.), *Advances in Developmental Psychology (Vol. I)* (pp. 37–86). Hillsdale, NJ: Erlbaum.

Rothbart, M.K., Derryberry, D., & Hershey, K. (2000). Stability of temperament in childhood: Laboratory infant assessment to parent report at seven years. In V.J. Molfese, & D.L. Molfese (Eds.), *Temperament and Personality Development Across the Life Span* (pp. 85–119). Hillsdale, NJ: Erlbaum.

Rothbart, M.K., & Rueda, M.R. (2005). The development of effortful control. In U. Mayr, E. Awh, & S. W. Keele (Eds.), *Developing Individuality in the Human Brain: A Festschrift Honoring Michael I. Posner – May 2003* (pp. 167–188). Washington, DC: American Psychological Association.

Saucier, G., & Ostendorf, F. (1999). Hierarchical subcomponents of the Big Five personality factors: A cross-language replication. *Journal of Personality and Social Psychology, 76* (4), 613–627.

Sheese, B.E., Rothbart, M.K., Posner, M.I., White, L.K., & Fraundorf, S.H. (2008). Executive attention and self-regulation in infancy. *Infant Behaviour and Development, 31* (3), 501–510.

Shiner, R.L. (1998). How shall we speak of children's personalities in middle childhood? A preliminary taxonomy. *Psychological Bulletin, 124* (3), 308–332.

Tackett, J.L. (2011). Parent informants for child personality: Agreement, discrepancies, and clinical utility. *Journal of Personality Assessment, 93* (6), 539–544.

Tackett, J.L., Slodobodskaya, H.R., Mar, R.A., Deal, J., Halverson, C.F., Jr., Baker, S.R., et al. (2012). The hierarchical structure of childhood personality in five countries: Continuity from early childhood to early adolescence. *Journal of Personality, 80* (4), 847–879.

Van Lieshout, C.F.M., & Haselager, G.J.T. (1994). The Big Five personality factors in Q-sort descriptions of children and adolescents. In C.F. Halverson, G.A. Kohnstamm, & R.P. Martin (Eds.), *The Developing Structure of Temperament and Personality from Infancy to Adulthood* (pp. 293–318). Hillsdale, NJ: Erlbaum.

Victor, J.B. (1994). The five-factor model applied to individual differences in school behavior. In C.F. Halverson, Jr., G.A. Kohnstamm, & R.P. Martin (Eds.), *The Developing Structure of Temperament and Personality from Infancy to Adulthood* (pp. 355–366). Hillsdale, NJ: Erlbaum.

Victor, J.B., Halverson, C.F., Jr., & Montague, R.B. (1985). Relations between reflection-impulsivity and behavioral impulsivity in preschool children. *Developmental Psychology, 21* (1), 141–148.

Zuckerman, M. (1994). An alternative five factor model for personality. In C.F. Halverson, G.A. Kohnstamm, & R.P. Martin (Eds.), *The Developing Structure of Temperament and Personality from Infancy to Adulthood* (pp. 53–68). Hillsdale, NJ: Erlbaum.

5

Integrity Tests: A Review of Alternate Conceptualizations and Some Measurement and Practical Issues

Chockalingam Viswesvaran
Florida International University, Miami, United States

Deniz S. Ones
University of Minnesota, United States

Individual differences in trustworthiness of individuals has been a source of fascination for observers of human nature and behavior. The core of the Aristotelian conceptualization of ethos is the moral character or trustworthiness of the individual. Those with a moral character are viewed as honest, ethical, and benevolent. In organizational studies, integrity and ethicality has been a central concept (cf. Ones, 1993; Ones, Viswesvaran, & Schmidt, 1993; Sackett & Wanek, 1996) as it has consequences not only for individual employee behaviors from the lowest to the highest ranks, but also for organizational level outcomes (e.g., corporate responsibility).

Supporting empirical research has linked integrity to important individual and organizational outcomes (cf. Berry, Sackett, & Weimann, 2007; Fine, 2010; Goldberg, Grenier, Guion, Sechrest, & Wing, 1991; Mikulay & Goffin, 1998; Nicol & Paunonen, 2002; Sackett, Burris, & Callahan, 1989; Vangent, 2010). Individual differences in integrity as assessed by integrity tests have been linked to several important criteria like absenteeism (Ones, Viswesvaran, & Schmidt, 2003), drug use (Schmidt, Viswesvaran & Ones, 1997), externalizing behaviors (Blonigen et al., 2011), academic performance (Crede & Niehorster, 2009), and organizational training performance (Ones & Viswesvaran, 1998), among others. Figure 5.1 summarizes the meta-analytic findings on the validity of integrity tests for a variety of work behaviors and outcomes.

Integrity tests predict counterproductive behaviors (CWB) well (Ones et al., 2012). Refraining from counterproductive work behaviors (or exercising personal discipline) is one of the primary factors of job performance, along with task performance and citizenship behaviors (Viswesvaran & Ones, 2000). In addition,

The Wiley Handbook of Personality Assessment, First Edition. Edited by Updesh Kumar.
© 2016 John Wiley & Sons, Ltd. Published 2016 by John Wiley & Sons, Ltd.

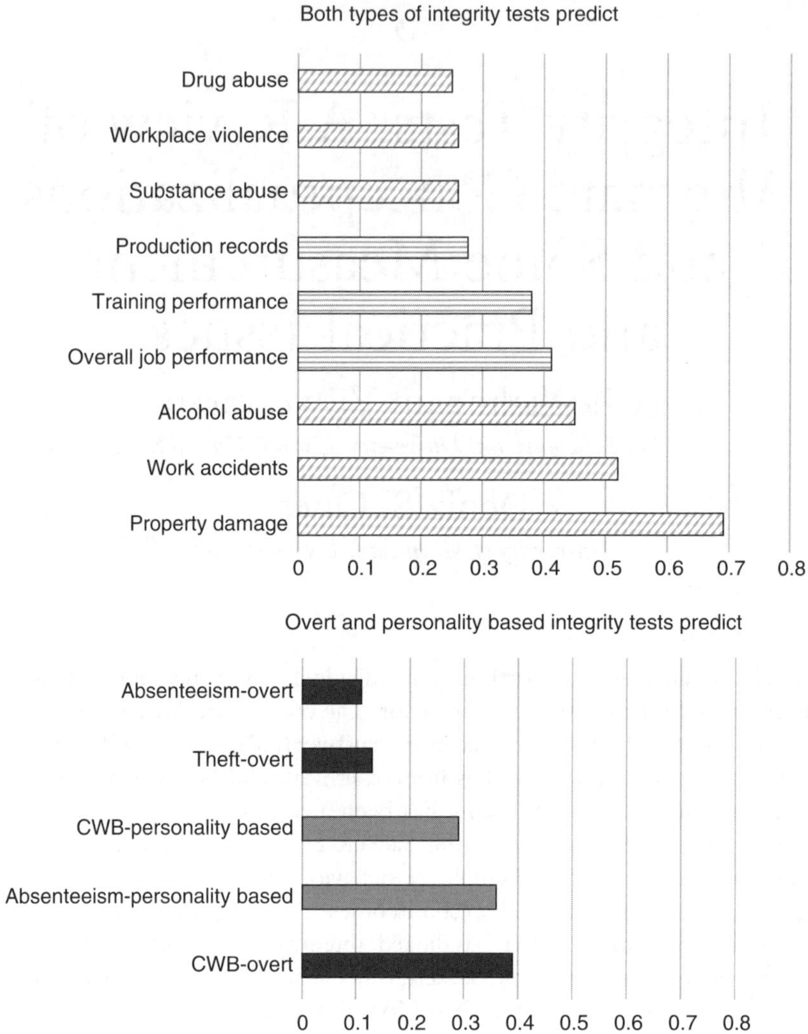

Figure 5.1 The level of criterion-related, operational validities are indicated on the *x* axes. Horizontal stripes shading indicates validities for positive criteria; dark gray shading indicates validities for overt tests; light gray shading indicates validities for personality-based tests.

integrity tests predict overall job performance well (Ones et al., 2012). In fact, integrity tests have been shown to have the highest incremental validity over cognitive ability, arguably the single best individual differences predictor of job performance (cf. Ones et al., 1993; Schmidt & Hunter, 1998). Thus, integrity is a critically important determinant of overall job performance. In turn, individual job performance forms the basis for team and organizational performance (Campbell & Wiernik, 2015). Thus, integrity is central to understanding all organizational behavior, at all organizational levels of analysis.

Given this centrality, it is imperative to understand what the construct of integrity entails. Some researchers (e.g., Becker, 1998) have attempted to define integrity based on justice principles and different ethical frameworks. Becker (1998) employed the philosophy of objectivism (Piekoff, 1991) to define integrity as loyalty to rational principles and values. Other ethical frameworks like deontology, utilitarianism, relativism, and so on, have been employed to study how morality and integrity can be defined (Donaldson & Dunfee, 1994; Trevino, 1986).

While an understanding of the theoretical roots of integrity are important, integrity tests have been developed and used in organizational sciences, by now, for over 70 years (Sackett et al., 1989). These tests were developed independently to address an important need in employee selection as several organizations have stressed the importance of honesty and integrity in their employees. Counterproductive work behaviors from employees have cost organizations billions of dollars worldwide (Ones, 2002), and such behaviors include theft, white-collar crime, sexual harassment, and violence on the job. As noted earlier and displayed in Figure 5.1, integrity tests have demonstrated substantial validity for predicting such counterproductive behaviors.

Different terms have been used to denote these tests (Sackett & Wanek, 1996, detail how the terms have changed over the years) but all these measures are based on assessing individual differences in personality. Ones and Viswesvaran (2001) noted that: (1) the integrity tests have items similar to those found in traditional personality scales; (2) integrity tests were developed to assess personality constructs of relevance for work environments; (3) they were designed to be used with job applicants as reflected in their normative data; and (4) most importantly, they were designed to predict workplace behaviors. In fact, Ones and Viswesvaran (2001) stated that integrity tests can be called criterion-focused occupational personality scales (COPS). The question then becomes how integrity tests relate to the different personality constructs, and in this chapter we present four different conceptualizations that have been advanced over the years. Following this, we present some measurement and methodological issues that have been raised concerning the empirical data available on integrity tests.

Mapping Integrity Test Scores in the Personality Trait Space

Ones, Viswesvaran, and Dilchert (2005) described personality as:

> A spectrum of individual attributes that consistently distinguish people from one another in terms of their basic tendencies to think, feel, and act in certain ways. The enduring nature and consistency of personality characteristics are manifested in predictable tendencies of individuals to behave in similar ways across situations and settings. (p. 390)

Assessments of personality constructs in organizational settings have focused on attributes or traits organized into different frameworks. The Five-Factor approach to personality structure and its assessment (Goldberg, 1992; Costa & McCrae, 1992) suggests that the different personality traits can be grouped into five factors: Neuroticism (vs. Emotional Stability), Extraversion, Openness, Agreeableness, and

Conscientiousness. Others have argued for more (Hough, 1992) or less (Eysenck, 1991) than five factors as the optimal number of factors to describe the most important or useful individual variations in personality. Regardless of the exact number of factors, all researchers agree that human personality can be described in a hierarchy of personality attributes ranging from broad to increasingly more specific factors (Dilchert, Ones, & Krueger, 2014; Markon, Krueger, & Watson, 2005; Ones et al., 2005).

At the apex of the personality continuum is the general factor of personality (DeYoung, Quilty, & Peterson, 2007). At the next level of the hierarchy are meta-traits (DeYoung, Peterson, & Higgins, 2002): Stability/Socialization (referred to as Factor Alpha by Digman (1997), describing a latent higher-order factor of personality defined by the co-variation between Conscientiousness, Agreeableness and Emotional Stability), and Plasticity (referred to as Factor Beta by Digman (1997), describing a latent higher order factor of personality defined by the co-variation between Extraversion and Openness). At the next level are the Big Five factors.

The hierarchy continues under each of the Big Five. There is evidence for two aspects of each of the Big Five (DeYoung et al., 2007). The aspects of the Big Five are: Withdrawal and Volatility for Neuroticism, Assertiveness and Enthusiasm for Extraversion, Intellect and Experiencing for Openness, Compassion and Politeness for Agreeableness, and Industriousness and Orderliness for Conscientiousness. Facets of the Big Five are more specific constructs than aspects (e.g., Depression and Anxiety each are more specific than Withdrawal for Neuroticism). The precise number of empirically justifiable facets of each of the Big Five is an active research area (see Connelly, Ones, Davies, & Birkland, 2014, for Openness). A distinction can be made about pure and compound facets. Pure facets sample behaviors, cognitions, feelings, and tendencies from only one Big Five domain (e.g., Activity facet of Extraversion). Compound facets, on the other hand, sample behaviors, cognitions, feelings, and tendencies from multiple Big Five domains (e.g., Warmth captures variance from Extraversion and Agreeableness). Compound traits can blend traits at and from multiple levels of the personality hierarchy (Wilmot, Ones, & DeYoung, 2015). Although main personality scaffolding follows the above-described structure, given that many different compound traits have been proposed, it is difficult to identify a simple structure.

In the past two decades, industrial, work and organizational psychologists have mainly relied on the Big Five taxonomy of personality traits to cumulate the empirical literature (cf. Barrick & Mount, 1991; Salgado, 1997). In fact, the Five-Factor model (cf. Ones et al., 2005) of personality is the most widely employed framework in discussing personality traits (Salgado & De Fruyt, 2005). Thus, the mapping of integrity test scores into the personality domain starts with a focus on the Big Five factors of personality. We discuss four different ways in which integrity test scores have been postulated to relate to personality traits.

Before presenting these, we need to reference the literature which shows that different integrity tests relate to one another, and although different dimensions have been presented, there is a common underlying latent dimension of integrity across the different tests and dimensions (Ones, 1993). Sackett et al. (1989) introduced the distinction between overt and personality-based integrity tests. Overt tests contain transparent items that clearly indicate to the test-taker that their integrity is being assessed, whereas the personality-based tests (also referred to as disguised purpose tests) attempt to assess integrity by relying on typical personality items. Ones (1993), using both meta-analytic data and a large primary data-set that correlated scores across seven different tests, demonstrated the presence of a general underlying dimension of integrity. Other factor-analytic studies of individual integrity tests (e.g., Collins & Schmidt, 1993; Cunningham & Ash, 1988; Hakstian, Farrell, & Tweed, 2002; Harris & Sackett, 1987; Hunt, Hansen & Paajanen, 1997) have also supported the latent construct of integrity. Wanek, Sackett, and Ones (2003) presented a detailed content analysis of several integrity tests, identifying homogeneous item clusters that contribute to the measurement of integrity. Here our focus is on the mapping of this underlying construct of integrity across personality traits.

Integrity as conscientiousness

One of the conceptualizations of integrity in terms of personality traits was to equate it to the Big Five factor of conscientiousness. In our initial work on integrity tests between 1990 and 1993, we also hypothesized that integrity tests primarily assessed conscientiousness. Indeed, individuals high on conscientiousness have been described as being dependable, reliable, prudent, and methodical (Hogan & Ones, 1997). Murphy and Lee (1994) correctly pointed out that the descriptors of individuals high on integrity and those high on conscientiousness are strikingly similar. Both types of *individuals* are described as dependable, careful, and responsible, and low on proclivities to engage in risky behavior. Several researchers have pointed out that *items* used to measure conscientiousness are similar to those used to measure integrity (Hogan & Hogan, 1989; O'Bannon, Goldinger & Appleby, 1989; Wanek, 1995; Wanek et al., 2003). However, there are certain item contents unique to integrity tests (e.g., punitiveness towards wrongdoers) and some descriptors associated with integrity do not only indicate conscientiousness. In addition, some descriptors of conscientiousness, like achievement striving, do not necessarily apply to integrity.

Empirical research has shown the two – integrity and conscientiousness – to be as highly correlated as alternate measures of conscientiousness (Hogan & Hogan, 1989; Jones & Terris, 1983; Ones, 1993; Woolley & Hakstian, 1992). Yet we should point out that meta-analyses indicate that the corrected correlations between specific integrity tests and conscientiousness scales do not typically exceed 0.60. Thus, there appears to be evidence that the two constructs are not isomorphic, and retain their distinctiveness in their respective measurements.

An obvious hypothesis that has been advanced is that integrity could be a facet of conscientiousness. Roberts, Chernyshenko, Stark, and Goldberg (2005) suggested that "virtue," defined as the "propensity to be honest and tell the truth," is a facet of conscientiousness. However, this is a finding that has not replicated well across measures (currently conscientiousness is recognized to have at least four replicable relatively pure facets: achievement orientation, order, dependability, and cautiousness).

There are several compound facets incorporating conscientiousness that have been examined as the source trait for integrity. Compound facets refer to subdimensions of each of the Big Five that capture variance from multiple Big Five domains. Compound facets function as specific indicators of a given Big Five factor when composited with other pure facets of the same factor. Most prominently, self-control has been posited as a key determinant of counterproductive work behaviors (CWB), with speculation that it may constitute the source of integrity variability. Self-control is a compound trait representing variance from both conscientiousness and emotional stability. We believe that it is relevant but not sufficient to understanding the construct of integrity (see the fourth conceptualization described below).

In all this, a key question in postulating integrity as a conscientiousness-based trait (factor, aspect, pure or compound facet) is to test whether the correlation of integrity to behavioral outcomes (e.g., job performance) can be accounted for by conscientiousness. In a direct test of this hypothesis, Murphy and Lee (1994) found that partialling out conscientiousness scores from integrity had little effect on the predictive validity of integrity scores. However, Ones (1993) showed that partialling out integrity substantially reduced the validity of conscientiousness, suggesting that the relationship between conscientiousness and integrity is not one of identity, but conscientiousness (or some facets of conscientiousness that are predictive of job performance) is a component of integrity. These findings lead to the third and fourth conceptualizations of integrity that we present below – integrity as a super factor of personality spanning across three of the Big Five factors, and integrity as a distinct factor comprising traits from different Big Five dimensions. Before getting into those two conceptualizations, we present another view of integrity as a personality dimension on par with the Big Five factors of personality, but distinct from them.

Integrity as the sixth factor of personality

Ashton and colleagues (2004) have argued that the personality domain is better described by six and not five factors. That is, in addition to the usual five factors of personality (emotional stability, extraversion, openness, agreeableness, and conscientiousness), Ashton et al. (2004) argue for the presence of an honesty–humility (H–H) factor that they conceptualize as at the same level of the personality hierarchy as the Big Five. They note the pervasiveness and cross-cultural applicability of this factor as well.

Lee, Ashton, and Shin (2005) have suggested subsequently that the honesty–humility factor is similar to the integrity construct and has stronger correlates with counterproductive behaviors than other personality variables such as the Big Five. Marcus, Lee, and Ashton (2007) have gone on to postulate that the H–H factor will correlate more strongly with overt integrity tests, but the other personality dimensions are likely to correlate with personality-based integrity tests.

We do not doubt the existence of honesty and humility as measurable personality constructs. However, we have serious doubts about (1) whether this personality variable is best understood at the same level of personality hierarchy (i.e., same level of generality and breadth) as the Big Five; and (2) whether the construct space covered by the only current operationalization of the variable is isomorphic to personality traits tapped in integrity tests: overt and personality-based.

Currently, there is only one measure of the H–H factor which is embedded in the HEXACO personality inventory. That is, notwithstanding IPIP parallel items; there are no independently developed alternate measures of the factor. This lack of independent triangulation is concerning. The conceptualization of the honesty–humility construct in the HEXACO includes the following facets: sincerity (unwillingness to be manipulative and dishonest in dealing with others), fairness (unwillingness to take advantage of others and cheat to get ahead), greed avoidance (being less concerned with wealth and status), and modesty (being humble). It is evident that these facets are all interpersonally oriented. In fact, Agreeableness is highly correlated with the honesty–humility scale. Further bolstering its Agreeableness roots, the Dark Triad are also correlated with the honesty–humility measure (Lee & Ashton, 2004), and recent meta-analytic evidence establishes the overlap across Dark Triad traits (Machiavellianism, Narcissism, and Psychopathy) and Agreeableness (Moore & Ones, 2015; O'Boyle, Forsyth, & Woo, 2015).

Thus, it is very likely that the H–H factor as assessed in the HEXACO is a bloated specific factor arising from individual differences in Agreeableness. The fact that the H–H factor has been shown to relate to counterproductive work behaviors (Lee, Ashton, & de Vries, 2005) suggests that agreeableness is an important personality variable that must be represented in the best predictors of the CWB domain. The correct conceptualization of integrity tests must take agreeableness into account along with conscientiousness. The fact that the honesty–humility scale lacks a conscientiousness element makes it a severely deficient indicator of integrity.

Integrity as a composite of facets from different Big Five dimensions

Marcus, Höft, and Riediger (2006) advanced the thesis that integrity is defined by a combination of several narrow facets from multiple dimensions of the Big Five. For example, Hough and Schneider (1996) found (although in a relatively small sample) that several facet scales of NEO PI-R correlated with the Hogan Reliability scale, a personality-based integrity test. Hakstian et al. (2002) also reported facets from different dimensions of the Big Five correlated with integrity scores. Based on the findings that integrity tests displayed sizeable relationships with several personality facets from different Big Five dimensions, Marcus et al. (2006) suggested that there is a general factor of integrity in overt integrity tests, but there is no such underlying factor for personality-based integrity tests. For personality-based integrity tests, Marcus et al. (2006) argued that the general integrity represented a formative construct drawing from several facets from multiple Big Five dimensions, but not an underlying latent construct.

However, Marcus et al.'s (2006) results are in direct conflict with other researchers' findings, including Hogan and Brinkmeyer (1997) and Ones (1993). By their own admission, Marcus and colleagues' research was prone to sampling error as its sample size was less than one tenth that for Hogan and Brinkmeyer's investigation. Furthermore, the integrity test examined was a newly created instrument designed specifically for the German culture (i.e., its convergence with other landmark integrity measures is unknown). In contrast, Ones' (1993) work relied on several overt and personality-based tests and used both primary and meta-analytic data confirming a latent integrity construct spanning across both overt and personality-based integrity tests.

There is also a theoretical problem with Marcus and colleagues' argument. Marcus et al. (2006), based on reported correlations from test manuals and item descriptions, chose ten facets from the conscientiousness, agreeableness and emotional stability dimensions of the NEO PI-R as the traits forming, in their view, a composite variable of integrity. However, finding that 10 of the 15 facets correlate with a personality-based integrity test does not negate the view that the three Big Five dimensions form a latent super factor based on their shared variance across these very facets. A more parsimonious conceptualization is to construe Integrity as reflecting a super factor comprising three of the Big Five dimensions. We turn to this conceptualization now.

Integrity as a higher-order factor of personality

This fourth conceptualization of integrity views it as reflecting a latent factor whose lower-level primary factors include conscientiousness, agreeableness, and emotional stability. Early primary and meta-analytic investigations established that integrity tests are correlated with conscientiousness, agreeableness, and emotional stability, in that order (Ones, 1993; Ones & Viswesvaran, 2001). Although the Big Five dimensions of personality were developed to be orthogonal, they are not (Ones et al., 2005). Unreliability-corrected meta-analytic correlations among them tend to be above 0.20 (see values reported in Davies, Connelly, Ones, & Birkland, 2015; Markon et al., 2005; Ones, Viswesvaran, & Reiss, 1996). These non-zero correlations indicate the possible presence of psychologically meaningful higher-order factors. Focusing on the overlap among the Big Five, Digman (1997) analyzed multiple data-sets and found that there are two higher-order factors to the Big Five: Factors Alpha and Beta. Using both self- and other ratings of personality, Digman (1997) reported that conscientiousness, agreeableness, and emotional stability can be grouped together in what he termed as Factor Alpha. Digman (1997) likened this factor to the normal personality development of individuals. Barrick and colleagues (cf. Barrick & Ryan, 2003) have referred to this as the assessment of functional personality. This is a meta-trait reflecting a higher order construct of socialization. It involves abiding by society's rules, norms, and conventions, and reflects other-directed psychosocial maturity. More recently, Factor Alpha has been termed "Stability" (DeYoung et al., 2002). Factor Beta involves extraversion and openness and constitutes a higher-order factor of "personal growth", more recently referred to as "Plasticity" (DeYoung et al., 2002). Both primary (DeYoung, 2006) and meta-analytic investigations (Markon et al., 2005) have confirmed the existence of these two higher-order factors in the personality hierarchy.

Integrity tests appear to tap into the latent factor represented by Factor Alpha. In addition to integrity tests, several COPS such as stress tolerance scales, substance abuse scales, and customer service scales correlated substantially with conscientiousness, emotional stability, and agreeableness, but not with extraversion or openness. Consistent with this view, Ones and Viswesvaran (2001) found that several criterion-focused personality scales correlated with these three dimensions, *although the relative importance varied across the three dimensions.* For example, integrity tests correlate best with conscientiousness, followed by high correlations with emotional stability and agreeableness. On the other hand, customer service scales correlate best with agreeableness, followed by emotional stability and conscientiousness. Overall, evidence from multiple streams of research (e.g., substance abuse, stress tolerance, customer service) suggests that integrity is an underlying latent construct spanning across three of the five factors of personality.

There is another theoretical reason for expecting that integrity tests are a good indicator for meta-trait Alpha. Research on personality determinants of counterproductive work behaviors (CWB) has clearly identified conscientiousness, agreeableness, and emotional stability as the Big Five dimensions strongly related to CWB (Berry, Ones, & Sackett, 2007). In constructing scales, overt and personality-based, to predict CWB, it is entirely expected that empirical test construction methodologies would have identified and used items that tap into socialization, psychosocial maturity, and abiding by society's rules and norms. Such a scale would be a good marker for the higher-order personality Factor Alpha. Thus, theoretical and empirical evidence align very closely. Both large-scale primary and meta-analytic studies support the same conclusion: integrity is best conceptualized as a higher-order latent meta-trait.

Assessing the Empirical Evidence for Integrity Tests: Some Measurement and Practical Issues

In this section we discuss measurement of integrity in applied versus lab settings, cross-cultural applications, and the role of test publisher research.

Integrity measurement in lab versus applied settings

Integrity tests were developed to address an important concern in organizations. The tests were developed and commercially employed to assess workplace deviance (Sackett et al., 1989), and different labels like honesty and dependability were used to describe these tests. Integrity test was later used as a label, and the research to assess and define this construct of integrity was undertaken. This underscores an important point: to understand and make inferences about the construct of integrity tests, we need to obtain empirical data using these commercial instruments and with working employee populations (preferably in high-stakes testing situations like personnel selection). Empirical research that uses student samples or non-organizational criteria is not as informative or relevant here, and can easily lead to erroneous conclusions. Most commercial integrity tests have demonstrated their usefulness in selection settings with applicant samples. Voluminous data from these settings cannot be put aside in favor of lab studies conducted with student samples and extraordinarily narrow (and often contrived) criteria.

Cross-cultural applications

The psychometric evidence on integrity has come primarily from paper and pencil tests developed and researched in the US. However, integrity tests are used in several dozen countries (e.g., Australia, Israel, Italy, Germany, Mexico, Russia, Sweden, South Africa, Turkey, among others). Given the increased globalization of organizations, cultural differences in integrity assessments have been investigated, and both etic as well as emic approaches have been employed. For example, Fortmann, Leslie, and Cunningham (2002) examined the cross-cultural equivalence of a popular integrity test – Reid Report – in Latin America and South Africa. On the other hand, Fine (2010) described the development of an integrity test for international comparisons, whereas Peng (2012) described a scale to assess integrity in Chinese contexts. Future research is likely to shed light on cross-cultural differences in the meaning of integrity. As integrity tests are increasingly used internationally, we call on our international colleagues to continue building an evidentiary basis for the use of such tests in various cultural contexts.

Role of test publisher research

In the past few years, there have been questions raised about test publisher research on integrity tests. Van Iddekinge, Roth, Raymark, and Odle-Dusseau (2012) have argued that integrity test publisher research is positively biased and therefore should be discounted.

These critics have presented two main arguments for mistrusting test publisher data on integrity test validities. First, they suggest that there should be concerns that such data are not made freely available to all researchers to evaluate the claims, and secondly, that financial incentives are present to distort the validity data in a positive manner. All data come with a cost, and commercial tests developed for use with job applicants have a large development cost. As such, it is not reasonable to expect that these data will be made freely available to all researchers. Harris et al. (2012) and the Association of Test Publishers (2010) have provided guidelines about non-disclosure agreements. It is important to note that this is not unique to integrity test publishers but to all areas where real-world organizational data are presented, be it evaluation of organizational diversity training programs, or multi-source feedback, or the validity of high-fidelity multimedia simulations using avatars. For example, realistic tests of multitasking ability that are used in personnel selection are developed by consulting companies, and questioning their construct validity because all that we have is an unpublished technical manual for that commercial test is unwarranted. These commercial tests are developed by teams of professional psychometricians who happen to work for consulting firms. Thus, if there are any validity differences reported between the studies done by the test publishers and others, such differences could very well reflect the care taken by the test publishers in administering the tests in high-stakes testing situations. The concern of financial stakes is also multifaceted in that even researchers with no affiliations to test publishers may have a financial stake in their findings (e.g., may have authored papers favoring other forms of selection such as interviews, or appeared as an expert witness for job candidates challenging tests). Ones et al. (2012) have presented arguments identifying the fallacies in Van Iddekinge et al.'s (2012) opinions, and pointing out the relevance and trustworthiness of test publisher data, especially if such data include reports from applied settings.

We wholly reject the notion that applied practitioners who develop and market integrity tests are not to be trusted in their research. Test developers and publishers should be conducting and presenting research on the integrity tests that they market. Our professional standards (e.g., Standards for Psychological Testing) require test developers to present data in support of their assessments. If all data that test publishers bring to bear on their tests are discounted, this would be a Catch-22 situation. Industrial and organizational psychology cannot be an applied science without applied data from those in the trenches.

Conclusions

In this chapter, we presented four conceptualizations of how integrity tests might map into the personality domain. Both empirical and theoretical evidence suggest that integrity is a super factor that is hierarchically superordinate to three of the Big Five dimensions – Conscientiousness, Agreeableness and Emotional Stability. These three of the Big Five dimensions relate to many criteria-focused occupational scales (Ones & Viswesvaran, 2001), albeit with different levels of importance. For integrity, Conscientiousness has the highest correlation, followed by Emotional Stability and Agreeableness. We also addressed some measurement and practical issues. Integrity is a crucial individual differences variable. Its assessment via self-report integrity tests is a major contribution to our field. A scientific basis for integrity testing is strong. We stay tuned for more exciting research in this area in the years to come.

References

Ashton, M.C., Lee, K., Perugini, M., Szarota, P., De Vries, R.E., Di Bias, L., … Boele, D.R. (2004). A six-factor structure of personality-descriptive adjectives: Solutions from psycholexical studies in seven languages. *Journal of Personality and Social Psychology, 86* (2), 356–366.

Association of Test Publishers. (2010). *Model Guidelines for Preemployment Integrity Testing* (3rd ed.). Washington, DC: Association of Test Publishers.

Barrick, M.R., & Mount, M.K. (1991). The Big Five personality dimensions and job performance: A meta-analysis. *Personnel Psychology, 44* (1), 1–26.

Barrick, M.R., & Ryan, A.M. (2003). *Personality and Work: Reconsidering the Role of Personality in Organizations.* San Francisco: Jossey Bass.

Becker, T.E. (1998). Integrity in organizations: Beyond honesty and conscientiousness. *Academy of Management Review, 23* (1), 154–161.

Berry, C.M., Ones, D.S., & Sackett, P.R. (2007a). Interpersonal deviance, organizational deviance and their common correlates: A review and meta-analysis. *Journal of Applied Psychology, 92* (2), 410–424.

Berry, C.M., Sackett, P.R., & Weimann, S. (2007b). A review of recent developments in integrity test research. *Personnel Psychology, 60* (2), 271–301.

Blonigen, D.M., Patrick, C.J., Gasperi, M., Steffen, B., Ones, D.S., Arvey, R.D., … Nascimento, E. (2011). Delineating the construct network of the Personnel Reaction Blank: Associations with externalizing tendencies and normal personality. *Psychological Assessment, 23* (1), 18–30.

Campbell, J.P., & Wiernik, B.M. (2015). The modeling and assessment of work performance. *Annual Review of Organizational Psychology and Organizational Behavior, 2*, 47–74.

Collins, J.M., & Schmidt, F.L. (1993). Personality, integrity, and white collar crime: A construct validity study. *Personnel Psychology, 46* (2), 295–311.

Connelly, B., Ones, D.S., Davies, S., & Birkland, A. (2014). Opening up openness: A theoretical sort following critical incidents methodology and a meta-analytic investigation of the trait family measures. *Journal of Personality Assessment, 96* (1), 17–28.

Costa, P.T., Jr., & McCrae, R.R. (1992). Four ways five factors are basic. *Personality and Individual Differences, 13* (6), 653–665.

Crede, M., & Niehorster, S. (2009). Individual difference influences on self-focused and other-focused counterproductive behaviors. *Personality & Individual Differences, 47* (7), 769–776.

Cunningham, M.R., & Ash, P. (1988). The structure of honesty: Factor analysis of the Reid Report. *Journal of Business and Psychology, 3* (1), 54–66.

Davies, S., Connelly, B., Ones, D.S., & Birkland, A. (2015). The General Factor of Personality: The “Big One,” a self-evaluative trait, or a methodological gnat that won’t go away? *Personality and Individual Differences, 81*, 13–22.

DeYoung, C.G. (2006). Higher order factors of the Big Five in a multi-informant sample. *Journal of Personality and Social Psychology, 91* (6), 1138–1151.

DeYoung, C.G., Peterson, J.B., & Higgins, D.M. (2002). Higher-order factors of the Big Five predict conformity: Are there neuroses of health? *Personality and Individual Differences, 33* (4), 533–552.

DeYoung, C.G., Quilty, L.C., & Peterson, J.B. (2007). Between facets and domains: 10 aspects of the Big Five. *Journal of Personality and Social Psychology, 93* (5), 880–896.

Digman, J.M. (1997). Higher-order factors of the big five. *Journal of Personality and Social Psychology, 73* (6), 1246–1256.

Dilchert, S., Ones, D.S., & Krueger, R.F. (2014). Maladaptive personality constructs, measures and work behaviors. *Industrial and Organizational Psychology, 7* (1), 98–110.

Donaldson, T., & Dunfee, T.W. (1994). Toward a unified conception of business ethics: Integrative social contracts theory. *Academy of Management Review, 19* (2), 252–284.

Eysenck, H.J. (1991). Dimensions of personality: 16, 5 or 3 criteria for a taxonomic paradigm. *Personality and Individual Differences, 12* (8), 773–790.

Fine, S. (2010). Cross-cultural integrity testing as a marker of regional corruption rates. *International Journal of Selection and Assessment, 18* (3), 251–259.

Fortmann, K., Leslie, C., & Cunningham, M. (2002). Cross-cultural comparisons of the Reid Integrity scale in Latin America and South Africa. *International Journal of Selection and Assessment, 10* (1-2), 98–108.

Goldberg, L.R. (1992). The development of markers for the Big-Five factor structure. *Psychological Assessment, 4* (2), 26–42.

Goldberg, L.R., Grenier, J.R., Guion, R.M., Sechrest, L.B., & Wing, H. (1991). *Questionnaires used in the prediction of trustworthiness in pre-employment selection decisions.* Washington, DC: American Psychological Association.

Hakstian, A.R., Farrell, S., & Tweed, R.G. (2002). The assessment of counterproductive tendencies by means of the California Psychological Inventory. *International Journal of Selection and Assessment, 10* (1–2), 58–86.

Harris, M.M., & Sackett, P.R. (1987). A factor analysis and item response theory analysis of an employee honesty test. *Journal of Business and Psychology, 2* (2), 122–135.

Harris, W.G., Jones, J.W., Klion, R., Arnold, D.W., Camara, W., & Cunningham, M.R. (2012). Test publishers' perspective on "An updated meta-analysis": Comment on Van Iddikinge, Roth, Raymark and Odle-Dusseau (2012). *Journal of Applied Psychology, 97* (3), 531–536.

Hogan, J., & Brinkmeyer, K. (1997). Bridging the gap between overt and personality-based integrity tests. *Personnel Psychology, 50* (3), 587–599.

Hogan, J., & Hogan, R.T. (1989). How to measure employee reliability. *Journal of Applied Psychology, 74* (2), 273–279.

Hogan, J., & Ones, D.S. (1997). Conscientiousness and integrity at work. In R. Hogan, J.A. Johnson & S. Briggs (Eds.), *Handbook of Personality Psychology* (pp. 849–870). New York: Academic Press.

Hough, L.M. (1992). The "big five" personality variables – construct confusion: Description versus prediction. *Human Performance, 5* (1–2), 139–155.

Hough, L.M., & Schneider, R.J. (1996). Personality traits, taxonomies, and applications in organizations. In K.R. Murphy (Ed.), *Individual Differences and Behavior in Organizations* (pp. 31–88). San Francisco, CA: Jossey-Bass.

Hunt, S.T., Hansen, T.L., & Paajanen, G.E. (1997). *The empirical structure and construct validity of a widely used, personality-based integrity test.* Paper presented at the annual conference of the Society for Industrial and Organizational Psychology, St. Louis, Missouri.

Jones, J.W., & Terris, W. (1983). Predicting employee theft in home improvement centers. *Psychological Reports, 52,* 187–201.

Lee, K., & Ashton, M.C. (2004). Psychometric proporties of the HEXACO Personality Inventory. *Multivariate Behavioral Research, 39* (2), 329–358.

Lee, K., Ashton, M.C., & Shin, K.H. (2005a). Personality correlates of workplace anti-social behavior. *Applied Psychology: An International Review, 54* (1), 81–98.

Lee, K., Ashton, M.C., & de Vries, R.E. (2005b). Predicting workplace delinquency and integrity with the HEXACO and five-factor models of personality structure. *Human Performance, 18* (2), 179–197.

Marcus, B., Höft, S., & Riediger, M. (2006). Integrity tests and the five-factor model of personality: A review and empirical test of two alternative positions. *International Journal of Selection and Assessment, 14* (2), 113–130.

Marcus, B., Lee, K., & Ashton, M.C. (2007). Personality dimensions explaining relationships between integrity tests and counterproductive behavior: Big five, or one in addition? *Personnel Psychology, 60* (1), 1–34.

Markon, K.E., Krueger, R.F., & Watson, D. (2005). Delineating the structure of normal and abnormal personality: An integrative hierarchical approach. *Journal of Personality and Social Psychology, 88* (1), 139–157.

Mikulay, S.M., & Goffin, R.D. (1998). Measuring and predicting counter productivity in the laboratory using integrity and personality testing. *Educational and Psychological Measurement, 58* (6), 768–790.

Moore, M., & Ones, D.S. (2015). *Incremental validity of the dark triad traits.* Poster presented at the 30th Annual Conference of the Society for Industrial and Organizational Psychologists, Philadelphia, PA.

Murphy, K.R., & Lee, S.L. (1994). Does conscientiousness explain the relationship between integrity and job performance? *International Journal of Selection and Assessment, 2* (4), 226–233.

Nicol, A.M., & Paunonen, S.V. (2002). Validity evidence for the different item styles of overt honesty measures. *Journal of Business and Psychology, 16* (3), 431–445.

O'Bannon, M.R., Goldinger, L.A., & Appleby, G.S. (1989). *Honesty and Integrity Testing: A Practical Guide.* Atlanta, GA: Applied Information Resources.

O'Boyle, E., Forsyth, D., & Woo, S.E. (2015). *Dark triad and socially aversive personality traits in the workplace.* Seminar presented at the 30th Annual Conference of the Society for Industrial and Organizational Psychologists, Philadelphia, PA.

Ones, D.S. (1993). *The construct validity of integrity tests* (unpublished doctoral dissertation). University of Iowa, Iowa City.

Ones, D.S. (2002). Introduction to special issue on counterproductive behaviors at work. *International Journal of Selection and Assessment, 10* (1–2), 1–4.

Ones, D.S., & Viswesvaran, C. (1998). Integrity testing in organizations. In R.W. Griffin, A. O'Leary, & J.M. Collins (Eds.), *Dysfunctional Behavior in Organizations* (Vol. 2). Greenwich, CT: JAI Press.

Ones, D.S., & Viswesvaran, C. (2001). Integrity tests and other COPS used in personnel selection. *International Journal of Selection and Assessment, 9* (1–2), 31–39.

Ones, D.S., Viswesvaran, C., & Dilchert, S. (2005). Personality at work: Raising awareness and correcting misconceptions. *Human Performance, 18* (4), 389–404.

Ones, D.S., Viswesvaran, C., & Reiss, A.D. (1996). Role of social desirability in personality testing for personnel selection: The red herring. *Journal of Applied Psychology, 78* (4), 679–703.

Ones, D.S., Viswesvaran, C., & Schmidt, F.L. (1993). Comprehensive meta-analysis of integrity test validities: Findings and implications for personnel selection and theories of job performance. *Journal of Applied Psychology, 78* (4), 679–703.

Ones, D.S., Viswesvaran, C., & Schmidt, F.L. (2003). Personality and absenteeism: A meta-analysis of integrity tests. *European Journal of Personality, 17* (S1), S19–S38.

Ones, D.S., Viswesvaran, C., & Schmidt, F.L. (2012). Integrity tests predict counterproductive work behaviors and job performance well: A comment on Van Iddekinge, Roth, Raymark, and Odle-Dusseau (2012). *Journal of Applied Psychology, 97* (3), 537–542.

Peikoff, L. (1991). *Objectivism: The Philosophy of Ayn Rand.* New York: Meridian.

Peng, H. (2012). Counterproductive work behaviors among Chinese Knowledge workers. *International Journal of Selection and Assessment, 20* (2), 119–138.

Roberts, B.W., Chernyshenko, O.S., Stark, S., & Goldberg, L.R. (2005). The structure of Conscientiousness: An empirical investigation based on seven major personality questionnaires. *Personnel Psychology, 55* (1), 103–139.

Sackett, P.R., Burris, L.R., & Callahan, C. (1989). Integrity testing for personnel selection: An update. *Personnel Psychology, 42* (3) 491–529.

Sackett, P.R., & Wanek, J.E. (1996). New developments in the use of measures of honesty, integrity, conscientiousness, dependability, trustworthiness, and reliability for personnel selection. *Personnel Psychology, 49* (4), 787–829.

Salgado, J.F. (1997). The Five Factor Model of personality and job performance in the European Community. *Journal of Applied Psychology, 82* (1), 30–43.

Salgado, J.F., & De Fruyt, F. (2005). Personality in personnel selection. In A. Evers, N. Anderson, & O. Voskuijl (Eds.), *The Blackwell Handbook of Personnel Selection* (pp. 174–198). Oxford: Blackwell.

Schmidt, F.L., & Hunter, J.E. (1998). The validity and utility of selection methods in personnel psychology: Practical and theoretical implications of 85 years of research findings. *Psychological Bulletin, 124* (2), 262–274.

Schmidt, F.L., Viswesvaran, C., & Ones, D.S. (1997). Validity of integrity tests for predicting drug and alcohol abuse: A meta-analysis. In W.J. Bukoski (Ed.), *Meta-analysis of drug Abuse Prevention Programs* (pp. 69–95). Rockville, MD: NIDA Press.

Trevino, L.K. (1986). Ethical decision making in organizations: A person-situation interactionist model. *Academy of Management Review, 11* (3), 601–617.

Vangent, Inc. (2010). Manual for the Reid Report Risk assessment. Chicago, IL: Vangent, Inc.

Van Iddekinge, C.H., Roth, P.L., Raymark, P.H., & Odle-Dusseau, H.N. (2012). The criterion related validity of integrity tests: An updated meta-analysis. *Journal of Applied Psychology, 97* (3), 499–530.

Viswesvaran, C., & Ones, D.S. (2000). Perspectives on models of job performance. *International Journal of Selection and Assessment, 8*, 216–227.

Wanek, J.E. (1995). *The construct of integrity: Item level factor analysis of the dimensions underlying honesty testing and big-five measures of personality.* (Unpublished doctoral dissertation). Retrieved from Dissertation Abstracts International Section A: Humanities and Social Sciences (618990043).

Wanek, J.E., Sackett, P.R., & Ones, D.S. (2003). Towards and understanding of integrity test similarities and differences: An item-level analysis of seven tests. *Personnel Psychology, 56* (4), 873–894.

Wilmot, M.P., Ones, D.S., & DeYoung, C.G. (2015). Reliability generalization and meta-analysis of the Big Five Aspects scale. Poster presented at the 30th Annual Conference of the Society for Industrial and Organizational Psychologists, Philadelphia, PA.

Woolley, R.M., & Hakstian, A.R. (1992). A comparative study of integrity tests: The criterion-related validity of personality-based and overt measures of integrity. *International Journal of Selection and Assessment, 1* (1), 27–40.

6

Network Analysis: A New Way to Think about Personality

Giulio Costantini and Marco Perugini
University of Milan-Bicocca, Milan, Italy

A network is a simple and abstract representation of a group of entities and of their relationships as a set of *nodes* and a set of *edges* that connect the nodes. This kind of representation, as simple as it might seem, has important merits. Networks can be used for representing systems that would appear completely unrelated otherwise. A network is all of what is common among phenomena as different as scientists that collaborate (Newman, 2001), web pages that link to each other (Albert, Jeong, & Barabási, 1999), airports (Guimerà, Mossa, Turtschi, & Amaral, 2005), and the expression of genes (Zhang & Horvath, 2005), to name just a few examples. This is possible because networks allow to abstract from the properties that make these systems so different and to focus on what they have in common: elements (e.g., scientists, pages, airports, genes) with pairwise connections (papers, web links, flights, similarity of expression). As a consequence, networks allow the examination of the properties shared by such systems: without networks it would be difficult even to ask whether, for instance, the World Wide Web and metabolism react in a similar or in a different manner to targeted attacks and random failures (Albert, Jeong, & Barabási, 2000). Recently also personality and psychopathology have been modeled as networks (Costantini et al., 2015; Cramer, Waldorp, Van der Maas, & Borsboom, 2010; Cramer et al., 2012b; Schmittmann et al., 2013). When a new system is modeled as a network, one can investigate whether it enjoys relevant properties that have been discovered in other systems. Recent findings showed, for instance, that similar dynamics may affect systems as different as the climate, financial markets (Scheffer et al., 2012), and depression (van de Leemput et al., 2014).

This chapter is divided into three sections. The first section provides a general introduction to network analysis, focusing in particular on the main types of networks and on the most important network indices. The second section is a review of the most important applications of network analysis in personality psychology. The final section provides an example of how network analysis can be applied to gather insights about the structure of personality.

The Wiley Handbook of Personality Assessment, First Edition. Edited by Updesh Kumar.
© 2016 John Wiley & Sons, Ltd. Published 2016 by John Wiley & Sons, Ltd.

Introduction to Network Analysis

There are several types of network, each one characterized by the kind of relationships that are allowed among nodes. When applying network analysis, the first decision to make is which kind of network provides the best model of a specific phenomenon. Once a network has been defined, one can compute indices that reflect characteristics of the whole network or of specific nodes. In this section, we introduce concepts that we consider most important for network analysis in personality.[1] We chose to omit formulae and computational details, since most indices can be easily computed with R (R Core Team, 2015) and its packages (for a tutorial of network analysis in personality using R, see Costantini et al., 2015).

Types of networks: weights, signs, and directions

A network is said to be *unweighted* if the edges can be either absent or present, but no information is coded about the intensity of the relationship; otherwise, if some kind of information about the intensity is coded, the network is said to be *weighted*. For instance, weights in transportation networks can distinguish an important airline route from a less important one, and in scientific collaboration networks they allow the distinction of an important collaboration from an occasional one (Barrat, Barthélemy, Pastor-Satorras, & Vespignani, 2004).

A network is said to be *unsigned* if only positive relationships are allowed (e.g., "A likes B"). Some relationships, however, are naturally represented by including both positive and negative edges (e.g., "A likes B, B dislikes C"). If both positive and negative edges are present, the network is said to be *signed*. Negative edges are relevant when it is necessary to represent both friendly and hostile relationships (Kunegis, Lommatzsch, & Bauckhage, 2009; Leskovec, Huttenlocher, & Kleinberg, 2010), but also when it is necessary to distinguish between positive and negative associations among variables (Costantini & Perugini, 2014).

A network is said to be *undirected* if the relationships among its nodes are symmetrical; conversely, if the represented relationships are not symmetrical, the network is said to be *directed*. For instance, the World Wide Web can be represented as a directed network in which nodes represent web pages and an arrow goes from node A to node B if web page A includes a hyperlink to web page B (Albert et al., 1999). This kind of relationship is not symmetrical, since it is possible that web page A links to another web page B without B linking to A.

Network indices

Networks can be represented graphically by means of energy-based algorithms, which consider the edges as if they were forces in two-dimensional space and attempt to minimize the total energy of the system by iteratively improving the position of

[1]For comprehensive introductions to network analysis, see for instance de Nooy, Mrvar, and Batagelj (2011); Kolaczyk (2009); and Newman (2010).

the nodes (Fruchterman & Reingold, 1991). Graphical representations allow the immediate visualization of important information on the network, but network analysis provides several indices to formally describe characteristics of the whole network and of specific nodes. These indices allow us to answer important questions, such as the possibility for the nodes to influence each other (Humphries & Gurney, 2008; Watts & Strogatz, 1998), the robustness of a network (Albert et al., 2000), or the importance of specific nodes (Freeman, 1978).

Properties of specific nodes

The importance of specific nodes in a network is reflected by the concept of *centrality* (Freeman, 1978). There are several definitions of centrality. *Degree centrality* is the number of edges that connect a node with the rest of the network: all else being equal, a node with many connections has a stronger influence on the network than a node with fewer connections. *Strength centrality* is a generalization of degree centrality that also takes into account the edge weights (Barrat et al., 2004).

Degree and strength consider only the direct influence of a node (i.e., non-mediated by other nodes); however, even if two nodes have the same number of connections (degree), one can be in a more favorable position than the other for interacting with the rest of the network. The *distance* between two nodes is the length of the shortest path that connects those nodes, where the shortest path can be a direct edge connecting the nodes or a path that traverses other nodes. *Closeness centrality* (Freeman, 1978) is defined as the inverse of the sum of the distances of the focal node from all the other nodes in the network. A node is high in closeness centrality if the shortest paths that lead to other nodes in the network are generally small. The implication is that a high closeness central node can quickly influence (or be influenced by) any other node in the network, directly or indirectly by means of other nodes.

Betweenness centrality measures how much a node is important for other nodes to influence each other: a node is high in betweenness centrality if many of the shortest paths that connect the remaining nodes pass through that node (Freeman, 1978). For instance, in the worldwide air transportation network, Amsterdam is connected with the rest of the network by many more flights than Anchorage (Amsterdam has a higher degree centrality). Nevertheless, Anchorage is more betweenness central than Amsterdam, since many of the shortest connections between cities in Alaska and the rest of the world pass through Anchorage (Guimerà et al., 2005). Removing a betweenness central node generally increases the distance between other nodes: If the Anchorage airport were to be removed from the network, flying between cities in Alaska and other places in the world would require more stopovers.

Nodes can also be described by their *clustering coefficient*, which is the number of connections among the neighbors of a node over the maximum possible number of such connections (Watts & Strogatz, 1998). If a node has a high clustering coefficient, its neighbors are connected with each other, therefore that node is not necessary for its neighbors to reach or to influence each other and can be considered as redundant (Costantini & Perugini, 2014; Latora, Nicosia, & Panzarasa, 2013; Newman, 2010). The clustering coefficient has been initially developed for unweighted networks, but it has been extended to consider also edge weights (Saramäki, Kivelä, Onnela, Kaski, & Kertész, 2007) and signs (Costantini & Perugini, 2014).

Large-scale structures

The large-scale organization of a network, namely its *topology*, can provide deeper understanding of the properties of the network and of its generating processes. Consider, for instance, the simple network structure in Figure 6.1A, a *regular ring lattice* (Watts & Strogatz, 1998), in which each node has the same number of neighbors, and all of the neighbors are close to each other. This structure implies that if an individual wanted to contact another randomly selected individual using a chain of mutual acquaintances, the required chain would be very long.[2] Could this be considered a reasonable model of the global social network? In a popular experiment, Milgram showed that when individuals were asked to generate a similar chain of acquaintances, a chain of six individuals was generally enough to reach a target (Travers & Milgram, 1969). This is known as the *small-world* phenomenon, and was later investigated by Watts and Strogatz (1998), who showed that it is sufficient to randomly rewire a small proportion of the connections in a regular lattice for the network to become a small-world. The necessary proportion of connections to rewire is so small that the local structure of the network, as reflected in the clustering coefficient, is not substantially altered by this process. Figure 6.1B shows the same network in Figure 6.1A after rewiring only 14 out of 200 edges. This small portion of rewires is enough to reduce the average length of the chain from around 13 to around 5 individuals. For real-world social networks this means that a few individuals that have a friend far away are sufficient to shorten the average distance between two individuals by a large amount, even assuming that most of one's acquaintances live close by. Watts and Strogatz (1998) also showed that non-social networks (e.g., neural networks, power-grid networks, collaboration networks) can have the small-world property. Recently, Humphries and Gurney (2008) proposed a small-worldness index: a network with a value of the index greater than 1 has stronger small-worldness than corresponding randomized networks, and a network with a value greater than 3 can be considered as a small-world.

Erdős and Rényi (1959, 1960) examined the behavior of random graphs, defined only by a certain number of nodes and a certain probability that an edge between any two nodes is present, each edge being therefore equiprobable (Figure 6.1C). They proved that the probability of a *component* (a group of nodes directly or indirectly connected to each other) that includes most nodes in a random network does not increase gradually with the number of edges, but shows a *phase transition*: When the number of edges is less than a certain threshold (half the number of the nodes), such a component is almost certainly absent, but if the probability of an edge becomes higher than the threshold, the component is almost certainly present. Similar phase transitions were proved to occur for other properties of the network (Erdős & Rényi, 1960).

[2] In the network in Figure 6.1A the average chain would require around 13 individuals, if the shortest possible path was always selected.

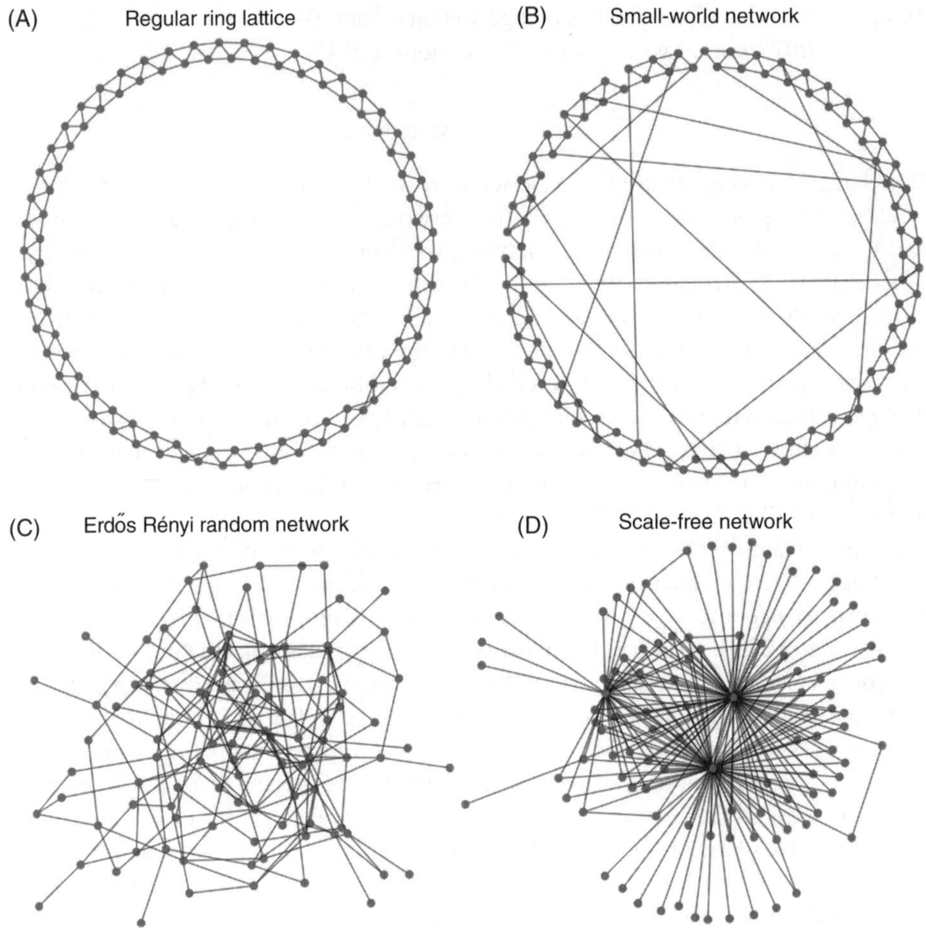

Figure 6.1 Four networks with 100 nodes and 200 edges. (A) Regular ring lattice: each node is connected with the four closest nodes. (B) The same network as A, after rewiring 14 edges, shows the small-world property. (C) Erdős-Rényi random network: the edges are placed randomly among nodes. (D) A network simulated using the preferential attachment procedure (Barabási & Albert, 1999). The networks were simulated with the R package *igraph* (Csárdi & Nepusz, 2006) and the plots were obtained with package *network* (Butts, Handcock, & Hunter, 2014).

Random processes could in principle give rise to any possible network; however, in random networks it is very unlikely to have nodes with many more connections than the rest of the nodes. Consider, for instance, the World Wide Web, in which each website administrator does not have access to the global structure of the Web, but decides from a local standpoint which hyperlinks to include in her page. One may think that the unsupervised behavior of many independent website administrators could give rise to a random structure similar to those described by Erdős and Rényi. However, Albert et al. (1999) showed that in the real World Wide Web network some web pages have a number of links (degree centrality) that is disproportionately larger than that of the typical node. This kind of topology, defined by the fact that degree centrality follows a power-law distribution, has been found to characterize several real-world networks and has been called *scale-free topology* (Barabási & Albert, 1999; Barabási & Bonabeau, 2003). A scale-free topology can be generated by a process of *preferential attachment* (Barabási & Albert, 1999), in which any new node (e.g., a new web page) is more likely to send a connection to another node that is already very degree central (e.g., a very important website) than to a peripheral node. An example of a network generated by this process is presented in Figure 6.1D. Scale-free networks are dominated by a few very central nodes, called *hubs* (Barabási & Bonabeau, 2003), and although they are resistant to random failures (e.g., the deletion of a random node), attacks that specifically target hubs can quickly disconnect the network (Albert et al., 2000). Knowing the topology of a network, therefore, has important implications for intervention (e.g., targeting metabolic networks by developing drugs; Hopkins, 2008) or for protection (e.g., protecting infrastructures from terrorist attacks; Latora & Marchiori, 2005).

Networks in Personality Psychology

In the study of personality and psychopathology, networks have been recently proposed as alternative models to latent variables (Cramer et al., 2012b; Schmittmann et al., 2013). According to a realist interpretation of latent variables (e.g., McCrae & Costa, 2008), individuals have different levels of unobservable variables, such as *extraversion* and *depression*, which can be inferred from specific observable manifestations, such as *going to parties* and *liking people* for extraversion (Cramer et al., 2012b), or *worrying*, *fatigue*, and *insomnia* for depression (Borsboom & Cramer, 2013). Such manifestations are usually assessed by means of items (or by aggregates of items, such as facets) in self-report questionnaires. An estimate of an individual's level on the latent variable can be computed with factor analysis, as a weighted sum score of the item scores. In this perspective, these observable manifestations are considered as exchangeable indicators of the latent variable (Borsboom, Mellenbergh, & van Heerden, 2003), while their causal role (e.g., the fact that insomnia can cause fatigue) is typically disregarded. In alternative conceptualizations of latent variables, personality factors have been conceived of as summaries of behavioral patterns that are useful for simplification, assessment, or prediction, without necessarily claiming their reality or their causal role (Ashton & Lee, 2005; Funder, 2001; Lee, 2012). However, in this view of personality, direct interactions among lower-level variables, such as those assessed by personality items or facets, are usually not considered.

The network perspective shifts the focus of investigation towards the direct interactions between those behaviors, cognitions, emotions, and symptoms that in the latent variable perspective are only considered as indicators. For instance, liking people makes it more likely to accept invitations to parties, and going to parties and interacting with new people makes the person more talkative, and so on (Cramer et al., 2012b). Similarly, in a depressed individual, worrying may increase insomnia, which in turn increases fatigue, and so on (Borsboom & Cramer, 2013). These direct interactions are more accurately modeled as networks than as the effects of latent variables. In this view, personality traits and psychopathological diseases are conceived of as properties that emerge from the complex organization of such networks. This focus can provide a better view on the cognitive, motivational, and functional dynamics that characterize the personality system, therefore favoring empirical investigations of such mechanisms (Perugini, Costantini, Hughes, & De Houwer, 2015; Wood, Gardner, & Harms, 2015).

When networks are used to model personality or psychopathology, nodes represent items, facets, or symptoms, while edges represent their pairwise associations (Borsboom & Cramer, 2013; Costantini et al., 2015; Cramer et al., 2012b). In such networks it is important to distinguish large from small associations and positive from negative associations, therefore personality networks are typically both weighted and signed. The simplest strategy to estimate a personality network is to draw an edge between any two nodes if the variables that they represent are correlated, the weight and sign of the edge corresponding to the correlation coefficient (Cramer et al., 2012b; Epskamp, Cramer, Waldorp, Schmittmann, & Borsboom, 2012). When dealing with binary data, such as reflecting a yes/no response format or the presence versus absence of a symptom, one can compute similar networks by using tetrachoric correlations[3] (Cramer, Borsboom, Aggen, & Kendler, 2012a). Such *correlation networks* are useful for visualizing complex pattern of relationships. For instance, Cramer and colleagues (Cramer et al., 2012b) showed that the topology of the correlation network computed from the NEO PI-R (Costa & McCrae, 1992) was different from the one that would have arisen had the network being generated by the Five-Factor Model (McCrae & Costa, 2008). Correlation networks have also been used to show that life events can have a different impact on the connections between specific depressive symptoms, therefore suggesting the inadequacy of the latent variable model to describe depression (Cramer et al., 2012a). Correlation networks are also useful to address theoretical confusions due to the presence of scales that assess the same construct with different names, and of scales that assess different constructs under the same name. Such cases can be visually detected in a network, under the assumption that scales that are supposed to assess the same construct should have similar positions in the network (i.e., a similar pattern of connections), while scales assessing different constructs should occupy different positions (Schlegel, Grandjean, & Scherer, 2013; Ziegler, Booth, & Bensch, 2013).

The simplicity and ease of interpretation makes correlation networks appealing in many situations; however their main limitation is that they cannot disentangle the associations due to a genuine link between two variables and spurious relationships that are due to other variables in the network. When one is interested in the net association between two nodes, one can compute *partial correlation networks*, in which an edge between any two variables is drawn if they correlate after the variance that they share with all other nodes in the network is removed, the weight and the

[3]A similar strategy to handle binary data is to consider the log odds ratio instead of the tetrachoric correlations (Cramer, Waldorp, Van der Maas, & Borsboom, 2010).

sign of the edge corresponding to the partial correlation (Costantini et al., 2015; Epskamp et al., 2012). Partial correlation networks have been used, for instance, to investigate the relationships among post-traumatic stress disorder symptoms and to identify central symptoms that could constitute targets for intervention (McNally et al., 2014).

Correlation and partial correlation networks model the whole correlation matrix. Regularized partial correlation networks instead force some of the connections to be exactly zeros, while keeping a good fit with the data. Penalties such as the lasso or the adaptive lasso (Krämer, Schäfer, & Boulesteix, 2009) can be used to compute more parsimonious personality and psychopathology networks from continuous data (Costantini et al., 2015) and from binary data (van Borkulo et al., 2014). Such networks have been used, for instance, to explore the structure of a network computed from the questionnaire HEXACO-60 (Ashton & Lee, 2009; Costantini et al., 2015), and to investigate the differential impact of spousal loss on distinct depressive symptoms (Fried et al., 2015).

Undirected correlation, partial correlation, and regularized partial correlation networks can be computed from cross-sectional data. Such networks are useful under the hypothesis that most relations in the network are symmetrical (Costantini et al., 2015). However, when asymmetric relationships have an important role, intensive longitudinal data (Fleeson, 2001; Hamaker, Ceulemans, Grasman, & Tuerlinckx, 2015) can be used to compute directed networks. Although these methods typically do not allow the breadth of content that can be obtained with cross-sectional studies, they allow us to investigate how personality and psychopathology dynamics unfold in time. Data collected with experience sampling methods can be used for assessing the network dynamics of a single individual over time using vector autoregressive methods (Wild et al., 2010). An R package has been recently developed that can help psychologists and therapists in this endeavor (Epskamp, 2015). Multilevel extensions of such methods have also been proposed that allow estimating such networks in a population (Bringmann, Lemmens, Huibers, Borsboom, & Tuerlinckx, 2015; Bringmann et al., 2013). For instance, van de Leemput and colleagues (2014) showed that the transition between a normal and a depressed state both in patients and in the general population is preceded by an increase in the links in a temporal multilevel mood network.

A few recent studies computed personality networks from questionnaire data (e.g., Costantini et al., 2015; Cramer et al., 2012b; Epskamp et al., 2012). Questionnaire items are selected to conform to a precise structure, such as with five (Costa & McCrae, 1992) or six factors (Lee & Ashton, 2004). Although network analysis can give important information about the structure of a questionnaire, it is hard to disentangle whether the results reflect the structure of personality or the features of that questionnaire. A more systematic approach is possible according to the psycholexical hypothesis, which states that the most important personality characteristics are encoded in the lexicon (e.g., Ashton & Lee, 2005). The lexicon provides a set of personality items that have been selected as being important descriptors of personality, rather than according to factorial simplicity as it happens with items of factors conforming to a precise factorial structure. Despite this important property, to the best of our knowledge, network analysis has never been applied before to psycholexical data for investigating the structure of personality. In the next section we will do so.

Network Analysis of a Lexical Data-set

The aims of this analysis were to analyze a network computed from psycholexical data and to inspect whether the topology of a personality network can be affected by selecting items to conform to a simple factor structure, such as the Big Five (e.g., John & Srivastava, 1999), as is typically done when constructing a questionnaire. We considered two data-sets, from which we computed three networks. The first data-set included 274 participants, who self-rated on 492 personality descriptive adjectives representative of the Italian lexicon.The data-set has been previously analyzed by Caprara and Perugini (1994). The second data-set included 577 participants, who self-rated on 285 adjectives, most of which were selected from the set of 492 adjectives according to their communalities with a circumplex Big Five solution (Caprara & Perugini, 1994). The second dataset has been previously analyzed by Perugini and Leone (1996) in the development of the *Short Adjective Checklist to measure Big Five* (SACBIF), a 50-items adjective measure of the Big Five.[4] We computed: (1) a network including the 50 SACBIF adjectives (Figure 6.2A); (2) a network including 285 adjectives (Figure 6.2B); and (3) a network including 492 adjectives (Figure 6.2C). All networks were computed with the adaptive lasso method (Costantini et al., 2015; Krämer et al., 2009). The first two networks were computed on the second data-set, while the third network was computed on the first data-set.

The nodes representing the SACBIF items in the first two networks are shaded according to the corresponding Big Five factor, while the other nodes are shaded according to the highest correlation with the SACBIF scale scores.[5] If the highest correlation of an item with a scale score was less than 0.30 in absolute value, the corresponding node was not shaded. In the first network (Figure 6.2A), four clusters corresponding to extraversion, agreeableness, conscientiousness, and emotional stability were clearly visible, while openness seemed to be less cohesive. In the second network (Figure 6.2B) a tendency to cluster according to the Big Five was still visible, but with many more exceptions than for the reduced network. In the third network (Figure 6.2C), clustering according to the Big Five was even less clear.

We computed centralities and clustering coefficients[6] of each node in the second network, which was computed on a larger sample size and had a larger number of

[4]For the analysis of the second data-set, we considered only self-report and not peer-report data. Additional details on the two data-sets can be found in Caprara and Perugini (1994) and Perugini and Leone (1996).

[5]In the first data-set not all SACBIF markers were available, therefore the scale scores were computed by averaging the available markers (45 out of 50).

[6]We report the Zhang's signed index of clustering coefficient (Costantini & Perugini, 2014), which produced the most reliable index in a previous simulation (Costantini et al., 2015).

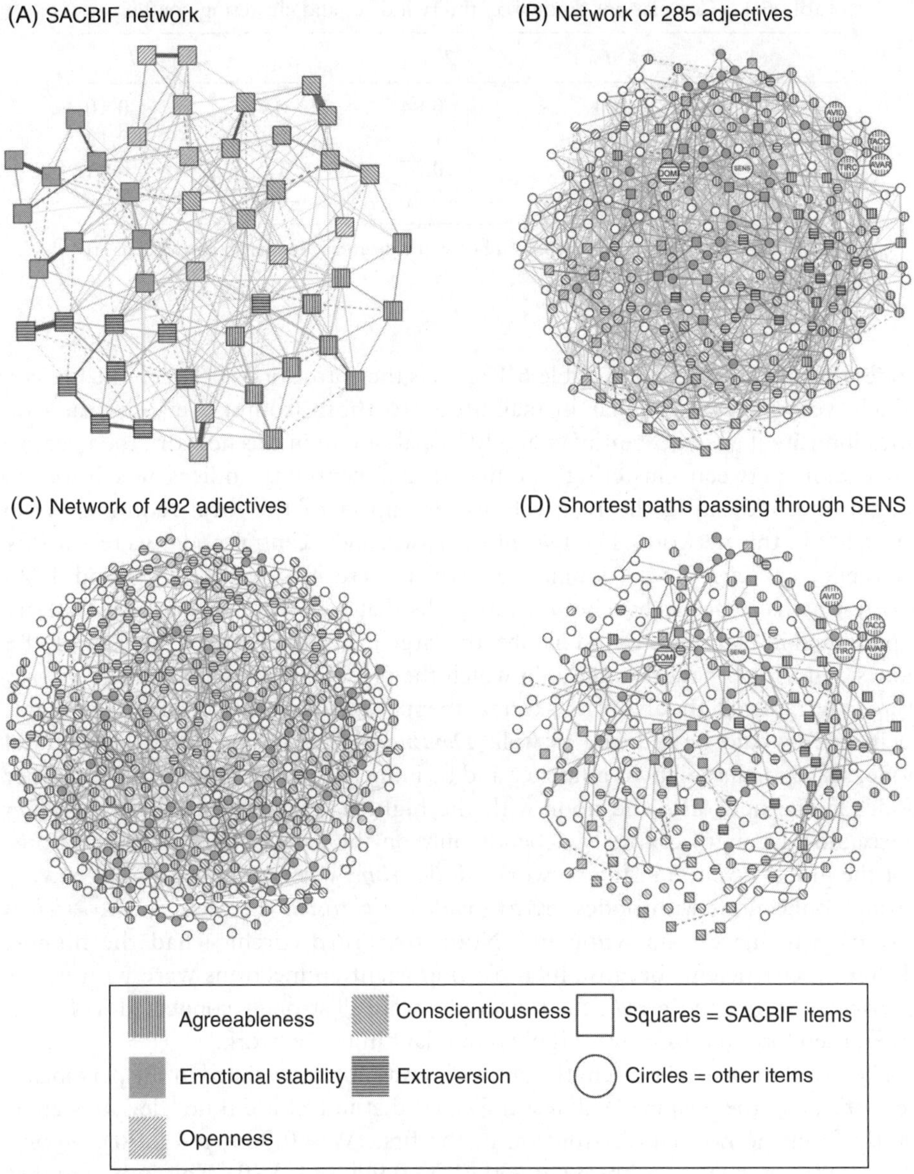

Figure 6.2 Network analysis on a psycholexical data-set. (A) Network of the 50 adjectives included in the SACBIF. (B) Network of the 285 adjectives in sample 2; SACBIF items are represented as squares. (C) Network of the 492 adjectives in sample 1. (D) Same as B, but only the shortest paths that pass through SENS are represented. SENS = sensibile (*sensitive*); DOMI = dominante (*dominant*); TACC = taccagno (*tightfisted*); AVAR = avaro (*avaricious*); TIRC = tirchio (*stingy*); AVID = avido (*greedy*). Positive lines are full and negative lines are dashed. Networks were computed with the package *parcor* (Krämer et al., 2009) and plotted with *qgraph* (Epskamp et al., 2012, 2015).

Table 6.1 Correlations among centrality indices and clustering coefficient

	1	*2*	*3*	*4*
Betweenness	1	0.84	0.73	–0.10
Closeness	0.84	1	0.63	–0.12
Strength	0.71	0.67	1	0.04
Clustering	–0.20	–0.20	–0.06	1

Note: Pearson correlations are reported below the diagonal, Spearman correlations are reported above the diagonal.

nodes than the first network. Table 6.1 reports the correlations between the indices, which were generally similar in magnitude to those from a previous study on questionnaire items (Costantini et al., 2015), although in this network the negative correlation between clustering coefficient and centrality indices was lower in magnitude, indicating the relatively lower impact of the local redundancy on centrality in this network. The two most betweenness-central nodes were *sensitive* (sensibile) and *dominant* (dominante), which were involved in 1770 and 1520 shortest paths respectively. The shortest paths that pass through node *sensitive* are represented in Figure 6.2D and involve the large majority of nodes (221 out of 285 nodes). In a hypothetical scenario in which the possibility for node *sensitive* to vary were to be reduced, the ability for several other personality characteristics to influence each other would be reduced as well. *Dominant* was the most closeness-central node, reflecting its ability to influence and be influenced quickly by changes in other nodes in the network. The node with the highest strength-centrality was *stingy* (taccagno). Strength-centrality depends only on the local pattern of connections, not the global position in the network. Node *stingy* was central because of its very strong connections with nodes *greedy* (avido), *tightfisted* (tirchio), and *avaricious* (avaro), which were its synonyms. Node *tightfisted* (tirchio) had the highest clustering coefficient, because its most important connections were with nodes *avaricious*, *stingy*, and *greedy*; the four nodes were all strongly connected with each other, therefore *tightfisted* was highly redundant in the network.

The distribution of the strength centralities was not heavy tailed in the personality networks, and the Shapiro-Wilk test indicated that in fact it did not deviate significantly from the normal distribution in the first ($W = 0.984$, $p = 0.90$), second ($W = 0.997$, $p = 0.91$), or third network ($W = 0.996$, $p = 0.30$). This indicated that the personality network does not have the scale-free property (e.g., Barrat et al., 2004). We inspected the small-world property in the three networks. The small-worldness index (Humphries & Gurney, 2008) of the complete network (Figure 6.2C) was 3.02, slightly above the threshold of 3, indicating that the complete personality network has the small-world property. However, in the second network (Figure 6.2B), in which the nodes were selected according to a circumplex Big Five structure, the small-worldness was 2.04, and in the first network (Figure 6.2A), in which the items were selected according to a simple factor structure, the small-worldness was 1.11. Interestingly, the small-worldness index of the first network (Figure 6.2A) was in line with the small-worldness of 1.01 obtained by a previous study based on questionnaire data (Costantini et al., 2015). These results might suggest that the small-world property of personality structure can be masked by selecting items to conform to a specific factor structure: the simpler the factorial structure, the stronger the masking. The small-world property of the personality network is in line with the small-world topology of the psychopathological network that emerged from an analysis of DSM symptoms (Borsboom, Cramer, Schmittmann, Epskamp, & Waldorp, 2011). Although the DSM network was computed using a different method, the DSM network considered a very large set of symptoms, without selecting them to conform to a simple structure. However, one cannot exclude the possibility that the small-worldness index is also sensitive to the number of nodes: future studies will be needed to clarify this issue.

Conclusions

In this chapter, we presented the basic concepts of network analysis and discussed recent developments in the application of network analysis in the context of personality psychology and psychopathology. Using a psycholexical data-set, we showed how centrality indices can be used to identify nodes whose manipulation might have the largest impact on the network, and how clustering coefficients can be used to identify redundant nodes, whose removal should not have a detectable impact on the network. Additionally, we discussed how the topology of the personality network could be altered if the nodes are previously selected to conform to a precise structure. The application of network analysis in psychology, including personality, is in its very infancy. Drawing a parallel with other scientific fields (e.g., physics, genetics, computer science, sociology) where network analysis is more established, we think that this approach has a strong potential to establish itself in the psychological field and contribute to advances in empirical and theoretical knowledge.

Acknowledgments

This work was supported by Fondazione Cariplo Research Grant Number 2010-1432, "Dottorato ad altaformazione in Psicologia Sperimentale e Neuroscienze Cognitive" (Advanced Education Doctorate in Experimental Psychology and Cognitive Neurosciences), awarded to Giulio Costantini.

References

Albert, R., Jeong, H., & Barabási, A.L. (1999). Diameter of the world-wide web. *Nature, 401* (6749), 130–131.

Albert, R., Jeong, H., & Barabási, A.L. (2000). Error and attack tolerance of complex networks. *Nature, 406* (6794), 378–382.

Ashton, M.C., & Lee, K. (2005). A defence of the lexical approach to the study of personality structure. *European Journal of Personality, 19* (1), 5–24.
Ashton, M.C., & Lee, K. (2009). The HEXACO-60: a short measure of the major dimensions of personality. *Journal of Personality Assessment, 91* (4), 340–345.
Barabási, A.L., & Albert, R. (1999). Emergence of scaling in random networks. *Science, 286* (5439), 509–512.
Barabási, A.L., & Bonabeau, E. (2003). Scale-free networks. *Scientific American, 288* (5), 60–69.
Barrat, A., Barthélemy, M., Pastor-Satorras, R., & Vespignani, A. (2004). The architecture of complex weighted networks. *PNAS, 101* (11), 3747–3752.
Borsboom, D., & Cramer, A.O.J. (2013). Network analysis: an integrative approach to the structure of psychopathology. *Annual Review of Clinical Psychology, 9* (1), 91–121.
Borsboom, D., Cramer, A.O.J., Schmittmann, V.D., Epskamp, S., & Waldorp, L.J. (2011). The small world of psychopathology. *PLoS One, 6* (11), e27407.
Borsboom, D., Mellenbergh, G.J., & van Heerden, J. (2003). The theoretical status of latent variables. *Psychological Review, 110* (2), 203–219.
Bringmann, L.F., Lemmens, L.H.J.M., Huibers, M.J.H., Borsboom, D., & Tuerlinckx, F. (2015). Revealing the dynamic network structure of the Beck Depression Inventory-II. *Psychological Medicine, 45* (4), 747–757.
Bringmann, L.F., Vissers, N., Wichers, M., Geschwind, N., Kuppens, P., Peeters, F., ... Tuerlinckx, F. (2013). A network approach to psychopathology: new insights into clinical longitudinal data. *PLoS One, 8* (4), e60188.
Butts, C.T., Handcock, M.S., & Hunter, D.R. (2014). Network: classes for relational data. *R package version, 1*.11.3.
Caprara, G.V., & Perugini, M. (1994). Personality described by adjectives: The generalizability of the Big Five to the Italian lexical context. *European Journal of Personality, 8* (5), 357–369.
Costa, P.T., & McCrae, R.R. (1992). *Revised NEO Personality Inventory (NEO PI-R) and NEO Five-Factor Inventory (NEO FFI): Professional Manual.* Odessa, FL: Psychological Assessment Resources.
Costantini, G., Epskamp, S., Borsboom, D., Perugini, M., Mõttus, R., Waldorp, L.J., & Cramer, A.O.J. (2015). State of the art personality research: A tutorial on network analysis of personality data in R. *Journal of Research in Personality, 54*, 13–29.
Costantini, G., & Perugini, M. (2014). Generalization of clustering coefficients to signed correlation networks. *PLoS One, 9* (2), e88669.
Cramer, A.O.J., Borsboom, D., Aggen, S.H., & Kendler, K.S. (2012a). The pathoplasticity of dysphoric episodes: differential impact of stressful life events on the pattern of depressive symptom inter-correlations. *Psychological Medicine, 42* (5), 957–965.
Cramer, A.O.J., van der Sluis, S., Noordhof, A., Wichers, M., Geschwind, N., Aggen, S.H., ... Borsboom, D. (2012b). Dimensions of normal personality as networks in search of equilibrium: you can't like parties if you don't like people. *European Journal of Personality, 26* (4), 414–431.
Cramer, A.O.J., Waldorp, L.J., Van der Maas, H.L.J., & Borsboom, D. (2010). Comorbidity: a network perspective. *Behavioral and Brain Sciences, 33* (2–3), 137–150.
Csárdi, G., & Nepusz, T. (2006). The igraph software package for complex network research. *InterJournal Complex Systems*, 3443126.
De Nooy, W., Mrvar, A., & Batagelj, V. (2011). *Exploratory Social Network Analysis With Pajek* (2nd ed.). Cambridge: Cambridge University Press.

Epskamp, S. (2015). *graphicalVAR: Graphical VAR for experience sampling data* [computer software manual]. Retrieved from http://cran.r-project.org/package=graphicalVAR (R package version 0.1.2).

Epskamp, S., Costantini, G., Cramer, A.O.J., Waldorp, L.J., Schmittmann, V.D., & Borsboom, D. (2015). *qgraph: Graph plotting methods, psychometric data visualization and graphical model estimation* [computer software manual]. Retrieved from http://cran.r-project.org/package=qgraph (R package version 1.3.1).

Epskamp, S., Cramer, A.O.J., Waldorp, L.J., Schmittmann, V.D., & Borsboom, D. (2012). qgraph: Network visualizations of relationships in psychometric data. *Journal of Statistical Software, 48* (4), 1–18.

Erdős, P., & Rényi, A. (1959). On random graphs I. *Publicationes Mathematicae, 6*, 290–297.

Erdős, P., & Rényi, A. (1960). On the evolution of random graphs. *Publ. Math. Inst. Hungar. Acad. Sci, 5*, 17–61.

Fleeson, W. (2001). Toward a structure- and process-integrated view of personality: Traits as density distributions of states. *Journal of Personality and Social Psychology, 80* (6), 1011–1027.

Freeman, L.C. (1978). Centrality in social networks conceptual clarification. *Social Networks, 1* (3), 215–239.

Fried, E.I., Bockting, C., Arjadi, R., Borsboom, D., Amshoff, M., Cramer, A.O.J., … Stroebe, M. (2015). From loss to loneliness: The relationship between bereavement and depressive symptoms. *Journal of Abnormal and Social Psychology, 124* (2), 256–265.

Fruchterman, T.M.J., & Reingold, E.M. (1991). Graph drawing by force-directed placement. *Software: Practice and Experience, 21* (11), 1129–1164.

Funder, D.C. (2001). Personality. *Annual Review of Psychology, 52*, 197–221.

Guimerà, R., Mossa, S., Turtschi, A., & Amaral, L.A.N. (2005). The worldwide air transportation network: Anomalous centrality, community structure, and cities' global roles. *PNAS, 102* (22), 7794–7799.

Hamaker, E.L., Ceulemans, E., Grasman, R.P.P.P., & Tuerlinckx, F. (2015). Modeling affect dynamics: State-of-the-art and future challenges. *Emotion Review*. Advance online publication. doi:10.1177/1754073915590619

Hopkins, A.L. (2008). Network pharmacology: the next paradigm in drug discovery. *Nature Chemical Biology, 4* (11), 682–690.

Humphries, M.D., & Gurney, K. (2008). Network "small-world-ness": A quantitative method for determining canonical network equivalence. *PLoS One, 3* (4), e0002051.

John, O.P., & Srivastava, S. (1999). The Big Five trait taxonomy: history, measurement, and theoretical perspectives. In L.Pervin, & O.P. John (Eds.), *Handbook of Personality, Theory and Research* (2nd ed.) (pp. 102–138). New York: Guilford Press.

Kolaczyk, E.D. (2009). *Statistical Analysis of Network Data: Methods and Models*. New York: Springer.

Krämer, N., Schäfer, J., & Boulesteix, A.L. (2009). Regularized estimation of large-scale gene association networks using graphical Gaussian models. *BMC Bioinformatics, 10* (384), 1–24.

Kunegis, J., Lommatzsch, A., & Bauckhage, C. (2009). The Slashdot Zoo: mining a social network with negative edges. In *Proceedings of the 18th International Conference on World Wide Web* (pp. 741–750).

Latora, V., & Marchiori, M. (2005). Vulnerability and protection of infrastructure networks. *Physical Review E, 71* (1), 015103-4.

Latora, V., Nicosia, V., & Panzarasa, P. (2013). Social cohesion, structural holes, and a tale of two measures. *Journal of Statistical Physics, 151* (3–4), 745–764.

Lee, J.J. (2012). Common factors and causal networks. *European Journal of Personality, 26* (4), 441–442.

Lee, K., & Ashton, M.C. (2004). Psychometric properties of the HEXACO personality inventory. *Multivariate Behavioral Research, 39* (2), 329–358.

Leskovec, J., Huttenlocher, D., & Kleinberg, J. (2010). Signed networks in social media. *Proceedings of the SIGCHI Conference on Human Factors in Computing Systems*, 1361–1370.

McCrae, R.R., & Costa, P.T. (2008). Empirical and theoretical status of the five-factor model of personality traits. In G. Boyle, G. Matthews, & D. Saklofske (Eds.), *Sage Handbook of Personality Theory and Assessment* (pp. 273–294). London: SAGE Publications.

McNally, R.J., Robinaugh, D.J., Wu, G.W.Y., Wang, L., Deserno, M.K., & Borsboom, D. (2014). Mental disorders as causal systems: A network approach to posttraumatic stress disorder. *Clinical Psychological Science.* Advance online publication. doi:10.1177/2167702614553230

Newman, M.E.J. (2001). The structure of scientific collaboration networks. *PNAS, 98* (2), 404–409.

Newman, M.E.J. (2010). *Networks: An Introduction.* New York: Oxford University Press.

Perugini, M., Costantini, G., Hughes, S., & De Houwer, J. (2015). A functional perspective on personality. *International Journal of Psychology.* Advance online publication. doi:10.1002/ijop.12175

Perugini, M., & Leone, L. (1996). Construction and validation of a short adjectives checklist to measure Big Five (SACBIF). *European Journal of Psychological Assessment, 12* (1), 33–42.

R Core Team. (2015). *R: A Language and Environment for Statistical Computing.* Wien, Austria.

Saramäki, J., Kivelä, M., Onnela, J.P., Kaski, K., & Kertész, J. (2007). Generalizations of the clustering coefficient to weighted complex networks. *Physical Review E, 75* (2), 027105.

Scheffer, M., Carpenter, S.R., Lenton, T.M., Bascompte, J., Brock, W., Dakos, V., … Vandermeer, J. (2012). Anticipating critical transitions. *Science, 338* (6105), 344–348.

Schlegel, K., Grandjean, D., & Scherer, K.R. (2013). Constructs of social and emotional effectiveness: Different labels, same content? *Journal of Research in Personality, 47* (4), 249–253.

Schmittmann, V.D., Cramer, A.O.J., Waldorp, L.J., Epskamp, S., Kievit, R.A., & Borsboom, D. (2013). Deconstructing the construct: A network perspective on psychological phenomena. *New Ideas in Psychology, 31* (1), 43–53.

Travers, J., & Milgram, S. (1969). An experimental study of the small world problem. *Sociometry, 32* (4), 425–443.

van Borkulo, C.D., Borsboom, D., Epskamp, S., Blanken, T.F., Boschloo, L., Schoevers, R.A., & Waldorp, L.J. (2014). A new method for constructing networks from binary data. *Scientific Reports, 4* (5918).

Van de Leemput, I.A., Wichers, M., Cramer, A.O.J., Borsboom, D., Tuerlinckx, F., Kuppens, P., … Scheffer, M. (2014). Critical slowing down as early warning for the onset and termination of depression. *PNAS, 111* (1), 87–92.

Watts, D.J., & Strogatz, S.H. (1998). Collective dynamics of "small-world" networks. *Nature, 393* (6684), 440–442.

Wild, B., Eichler, M., Friederich, H.C., Hartmann, M., Zipfel, S., & Herzog, W. (2010). A graphical vector autoregressive modelling approach to the analysis of electronic diary data. *BMC Medical Research Methodology, 10* (28), 1–13.

Wood, D., Gardner, M.H., & Harms, P.D. (2015). How functionalist and process approaches to behavior can explain trait covariation. *Psychological Review, 122* (1), 84–111.

Zhang, B., & Horvath, S. (2005). A general framework for weighted gene co-expression network analysis. *Statistical Applications in Genetics and Molecular Biology, 4* (1), 1–37.

Ziegler, M., Booth, T., & Bensch, D. (2013). Getting entangled in the nomological net. *European Journal of Psychological Assessment, 29* (3), 157–161.

7

Theory and Measurement of Trait Emotional Intelligence

K.V. Petrides and Alexander B. Siegling
University College, London, UK

Donald H. Saklofske
University of Western Ontario, Canada

Trait emotional intelligence (trait EI or trait emotional self-efficacy) emerged as a psychological construct from the distinction between trait EI and ability EI (Petrides & Furnham, 2000). This distinction intended to reflect the fundamental psychometric distinction between measures of typical and maximum performance (Cronbach, 1949) within the context of the burgeoning literature on EI. Petrides and Furnham (2000) noted that different measurement approaches would almost certainly produce different results, even if the underlying EI model being operationalized is one and the same. It has since been demonstrated in numerous studies that the various methodologies used in the measurement of EI do not converge (e.g., Di Fabio & Saklofske, 2014a, 2014b; Davis & Humphrey, 2012; Warwick & Nettelbeck, 2004), and that it is imperative to differentiate between typical and maximum performance measurement in the field of EI (e.g., Freudenthaler & Neubauer, 2007; Martins, Ramalho, & Morin, 2010).

The trait EI and ability EI labels are not mere substitutes for self-report (typical) and maximum-performance measurement, but denote the underlying nature of the constructs that arise through the application of these methodologies. Specifically in relation to trait EI, the label does not simply refer to any old variance captured by a self-report questionnaire whose authors claim assesses "emotional intelligence." Rather, it explicitly refers to a comprehensive conceptualization of the affective variance in the realm of personality, as expressed in the construct's sampling domain shown in Table 7.1. This point has crucial implications for meta-analyses, which tend to group studies on purely semantic and, consequently, highly dubious grounds (Pace & Brannick, 2010).

As far as ability EI is concerned, it has become clear, following a string of self-report questionnaires purporting to operationalize this construct (e.g., Bar-On, 1997; Salovey,

The Wiley Handbook of Personality Assessment, First Edition. Edited by Updesh Kumar.
© 2016 John Wiley & Sons, Ltd. Published 2016 by John Wiley & Sons, Ltd.

Table 7.1 The sampling domain of trait emotional intelligence in adults

	High scorers perceive themselves as ...
Wellbeing	
Self-esteem	... successful and self-confident.
Trait happiness	... cheerful and satisfied with their lives.
Trait optimism	... confident and likely to "look on the bright side" of life.
Self-control	
Emotion control	... capable of controlling their emotions.
Stress management	... capable of withstanding pressure and regulating stress.
Impulsiveness (low)	... reflective and less likely to give into their urges.
Emotionality	
Emotion perception (self and others)	... clear about their own and other people's feelings.
Emotion expression	... capable of communicating their feelings to others.
Relationships	... capable of having fulfilling personal relationships.
Trait empathy	... capable of taking someone else's perspective
Sociability	
Social awareness	... accomplished networkers with excellent social skills.
Emotion management (others)	... capable of influencing other people's feelings.
Assertiveness	... forthright, frank, and willing to stand up for their rights.
Independent facets*	
Adaptability	... flexible and willing to adapt to new conditions.
Self-motivation	... driven and unlikely to give up in the face of adversity.

*These two facets feed directly into the global trait emotional intelligence score without going through any factor.

Mayer, Goldman, Turvey, & Palfai, 1995; Schutte et al., 1998; Wong & Law, 2002), that maximum-performance procedures ought to be employed instead. However, the intrinsically subjective nature of emotional experience undermines the quest for items that can be scored according to truly veridical criteria on which the development of maximum-performance tests squarely depends (Matthews, Zeidner, & Roberts, 2007).

The practice of applying non-standard scoring procedures, such as "consensus" and "expert" scoring, in order to contrive correct responses among a number of equally logical alternatives leads to conceptual and psychometric problems that have been extensively discussed in the literature (Brody, 2004; Fiori et al., 2014; Maul, 2012; Roberts, Zeidner, & Matthews, 2001). These procedures yield scores that are not only foreign to cognitive ability, but also psychologically unintelligible, as it is unclear whether they reflect confounding with vocabulary size (Wilhelm, 2005), conformity to social norms (Matthews, Emo, Roberts, & Zeidner, 2006), theoretical knowledge about emotions (Austin, 2010), stereotypical judgments (O'Sullivan, 2007), or some unknown combination of these factors. There are numerous other challenges facing the construct of ability EI (Follesdal & Hagtvet, 2009), which is perhaps one reason why most research in the field is conducted on the construct of trait EI.

What is Trait Emotional Intelligence?

Trait EI is defined as a constellation of emotional perceptions located at the lower levels of personality hierarchies (Petrides, Pita, & Kokkinaki, 2007b). The construct essentially concerns people's perceptions of their emotional abilities, hence "trait emotional self-efficacy" as an alternative label for it.

Conceptually, trait EI integrates the affective aspects of personality. Personality is an enormous domain that comprises characteristics like motives, interests, values, emotional traits, social traits, and many others (Funder, 2012). Traditionally, the affective aspects of personality had been scattered across the Big Five factors and, consequently, it was difficult to study them in a coherent fashion. With the introduction of trait EI, these aspects were incorporated into a unified and comprehensive model comprising 15 distinct facets. Factor analytic research (Petrides, 2009) has shown that these 15 facets form four broad factors (Wellbeing, Self-Control, Emotionality, and Sociability), which in turn give rise to global trait EI at the apex of the hierarchy of emotion-related personality traits (see Figure 7.1).

Table 7.1 shows the sampling domain of trait EI (i.e., its constituent elements or facets). The sampling domain was derived from a content analysis of early models of EI and cognate constructs, such as alexithymia, affective communication, emotional expression, and empathy (Petrides, 2009). The rationale was to include core elements common to more than one model, but exclude peripheral elements appearing in only a single conceptualization. This is analogous to procedures used in classical psychometric scale development, whereby the commonalities (shared core) of the various items in a scale are carried over into a total (internally consistent) score, with their random or unique components (noise) being cancelled out in the process.

Below is a brief summary of the 15 trait EI facets. These descriptions form part of the foundation for the correct interpretation of trait EI profiles. In the interests of clarity, we do not constantly reiterate in these paragraphs that the descriptions

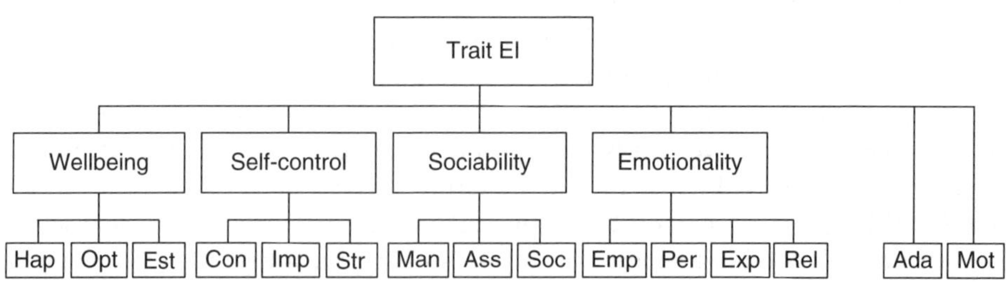

Figure 7.1 The 15 facets of the TEIQue positioned with reference to their corresponding factor. A brief description of the facets is given in Table 7.1. EI, emotional intelligence; Ada, adaptability; Ass, assertiveness; Con, emotion control (regulation); Emp, empathy; Est, self-esteem; Exp, emotion expression; Hap, happiness; Imp, low impulsivity; Man, emotion management; Mot, self-motivation; Opt, optimism; Per, emotion perception; Rel, relationships; Soc, social awareness; Str, stress management. © K.V. Petrides, London Psychometric Laboratory, 2001. All rights reserved.

concern self-perceptions – how respondents view their own self or, in the case of observer-ratings (e.g., Gugliandolo, Costa, Cuzzocrea, Larcan, & Petrides, 2015), how raters view the ratees.

Adaptability. High scorers are flexible in their approach to work and life. They are willing and able to adapt to new environments and conditions – in fact, they may even enjoy novelty and regular change. Low scorers are change-resistant and find it difficult to modify their work- and lifestyle. They are generally inflexible and have fixed ideas and views.

Assertiveness. Individuals with high scores on this facet are forthright and frank. They know how to ask for things, give and receive compliments, and confront others when necessary. They have leadership qualities and can stand up for their rights and beliefs. Low scorers tend to back down, even if they know they are right and have difficulty saying "no," even when they feel they must. As a result, they often end up doing things they do not want to do. In most cases, they prefer to be part of a team rather than to lead it.

Emotion expression. High scores on this facet suggest fluency in communicating emotions to others. Those high on emotion expression know what the best words are for expressing their feelings accurately and unambiguously. Low scores on this facet indicate a difficulty in communicating emotion-related thoughts, even in situations when this is necessary. People with low scores find it difficult to let others know how they feel. Inability to express emotions may be indicative of a more generalized problem of lack of self-confidence and social assertiveness.

Emotion management (in others). This facet concerns one's perceived ability to manage other people's emotional states. High scorers on the emotion management facet can influence other people's feelings (e.g., calm them down, console them, and motivate them). They know how to make others feel better when they need it. Low scorers can neither influence nor manage others' feelings. They become overwhelmed when they have to deal with other people's emotional outbursts and are less likely to enjoy socializing and networking.

Emotion perception. This facet measures emotion perception in oneself and in others. High scorers on this facet are clear about what they feel and able to decode other people's emotional expressions. In contrast, people with low scores are often confused about their feelings and do not pay much attention to the emotional signals that others send out.

Emotion regulation. This facet measures short-, medium-, and long-term control of one's own feelings and emotional states. High scorers have control over their emotions and can change unpleasant moods or prolong pleasant moods through personal insight and effort. They are psychologically stable and know how to pick themselves up after emotional setbacks. Low scorers are subject to emotional seizures and periods of prolonged anxiety or depression. They find it difficult to deal with their feelings and are often moody and irritable.

Low impulsiveness (impulse control). This facet measures mainly dysfunctional (unhealthy), rather than functional (healthy) impulsivity. Low impulsiveness involves thinking before acting and reflecting carefully before making decisions. High scorers on this facet weigh all the information before they make up their mind. Low scorers tend to be impetuous and to give in to their urges. Much like children, they desire immediate gratification and have low self-control. They often speak without having thought things through and they change their mind frequently.

Relationships. This facet mainly concerns one's personal relationships, including close friends, partners, and family. It is about starting and maintaining emotional bonds with others. High scorers usually have fulfilling personal relationships that positively affect their productivity and emotional wellbeing. They know how to listen and be responsive to the people close to them. Low scorers find it difficult to bond well with others and tend to undervalue their personal relationships. They often behave in ways that hurt those close to them.

Self-esteem. This facet measures one's overall evaluation of oneself. Along with *happiness* and *optimism*, it reflects one's general wellbeing. High scorers have a positive view of themselves and their achievements. They are confident, positive, and satisfied with most aspects of their life. Low scorers tend to lack self-respect and not value themselves very highly. Low self-esteem scores are often the result of challenges in one or more of the other trait EI facets.

Self-motivation. People with high scores on this facet are driven by a need to produce high-quality work. They tend to be determined and persevering. They do not need to be externally rewarded for their efforts because they have a strong sense of achievement and are motivated from within. Low scorers tend to require a lot of incentives and encouragement in order to get things done. They expect constant rewards to keep going and they are more likely to give up in the face of adversity. They also tend to have reduced levels of drive and persistence.

Social awareness. High scorers believe they have excellent social skills and are socially sensitive, adaptable, and perceptive. They are good at negotiating, brokering deals, and influencing others. In addition, they tend to have control over their emotions and the manner in which they express them, which enables them to function confidently in diverse social contexts, like parties or networking events. Low scorers believe they have limited social skills and often feel anxious in unfamiliar settings because they are unsure about how to behave. They find it difficult to express themselves clearly and have a small circle of acquaintances.

Stress management. High scorers on this facet can handle pressure calmly and effectively because they have developed successful coping mechanisms. More often than not, they are good at regulating their emotions, which helps them to tackle stress. Low scorers are less likely to have evolved stress-coping strategies and may prefer to altogether avoid situations that are potentially hectic. Their vulnerability to stress can become problematic, if it leads them to reject important, but time-demanding, projects.

Trait empathy. This facet concerns the "perspective-taking" aspect of empathy: seeing the world from someone else's point of view. In other words, it has to do with whether one can understand other people's needs and desires. People with high scores on this facet tend to be skillful in conversations and negotiations because they take into account the viewpoints of those they are dealing with. They can put themselves "in somebody else's shoes" and appreciate how things seem to them. Low scorers have difficulty adopting other people's perspectives. They tend to be opinionated and argumentative and may often seem self-centered.

Trait happiness. This facet concerns pleasant emotional states, primarily directed towards the present, rather than the past (which is more to do with life satisfaction) or the future (which is more to do with optimism). High scorers are cheerful and feel good about themselves. Low scorers often feel blue and can be overly negative about things. More generally, people with low scores on this facet tend to be disappointed with their life as it is at present.

Trait optimism. Like *happiness*, this facet is linked to wellbeing, albeit in a forward-looking way. High scorers look on the bright side and expect positive things to happen in their life. Low scorers are pessimistic and view things from a negative perspective. They are less likely to identify and pursue new opportunities and tend to be risk-averse.

Location of Trait EI in Personality Factor Space

Locating trait EI in personality space is important for integrating the construct within the mainstream personality literature. Petrides et al. (2007b) performed factor location studies that suggested that trait EI is a *distinct* (because it can be isolated in personality space) and *compound* (because it is correlated with several personality dimensions) construct that lies at the *lower levels* of personality hierarchies (because the trait EI factor is oblique, rather than orthogonal to the Giant Three and the Big Five). This conclusion enables us to connect the personality conceptualization of EI to the established literature on differential psychology, which is a key conceptual advantage.

Trait EI theory is also relevant to the emerging literature on the General Factor of Personality (GFP; Rushton et al., 2009). The factor location findings mentioned above were recently replicated by Pérez-González and Sanchez-Ruiz (2014), who further reported that the trait EI factor is positively correlated with the "Big Two" personality super-factors (Alpha/Stability and Beta/Plasticity; DeYoung, 2006; Digman, 1997) as well as with the GFP.

The fact that a GFP can be extracted from combined personality–trait EI data-sets (e.g., Veselka et al., 2009) corroborates the view that trait EI ought to be fully integrated into multilevel personality hierarchies, somewhere between the highly specific traits at their base and the broad general factors at their apex. Indeed, in a large meta-analytic study ($K = 142$; $N = 36{,}268$), Van der Linden et al. (submitted) has estimated that the overlap between trait EI and the GFP ($r \approx 0.85$) is sufficiently high to suggest that the former could be used as a proxy for the latter.

Measures of Trait Emotional Intelligence

While measures related to or tapping facets of EI, including coping, stress management, mood, adaptability, and emotion, have been a feature of individual differences and personality psychology for many decades, the earliest measures of EI *per se* first appeared in the 1990s. The two major models and methods of measurement described as ability and trait EI have given rise to a number of scales and instruments that vary in their breadth and depth of coverage of the construct. There are also extensive variations in terms of their psychometric properties and nomological networks. More broadly, an important limitation in the field of EI measurement concerns the variation in definitions and sampling domains, which hinders the integration of findings from different measures and the systematic accumulation of knowledge. Further research on the properties of existing sampling domains may eventually yield a consensual definition around which all trait EI research can profitably be centered (Siegling, Petrides, & Martskvishvili, 2015).

Trait EI measures generally use a self-report format, adopting the perspective that it is the personal and subjective aspects of one's emotional life, experiences and interactions that are central to an understanding of EI. While simple to administer and score, it is important to ensure that the respondent is providing accurate responses to questions and not "faking" or distorting in order to achieve other goals. Various methods can be applied to guard against this potential threat, including the incorporation of validity indices and algorithms that are standard features among the most sophisticated of trait EI measures (Petrides, 2009).

A comprehensive and detailed review of the leading trait EI measures and their key psychometric characteristics is presented in Siegling, Saklofske, and Petrides (2015). Several general as well as four domain-specific trait EI measures are worth reviewing in brief. The former include the Trait Emotional Intelligence Questionnaire (TEIQue; Petrides, 2009), the Emotional Quotient Inventory (EQ-i; Bar-On, 1997), the Assessing Emotions Scale (AES; Schutte et al., 1998), and the largely outdated Trait-Meta-Mood Scale (TMMS; Salovey, Mayer, Goldman, Turvey, & Palfai, 1995). Domain-specific trait EI measures concern the workplace and include the Wong and Law Emotional Intelligence Scale (WLEIS; Wong & Law, 2002), the Workgroup Emotional Intelligence Profile (WEIP; Jordan, Ashkanasy, Härtel, & Hooper, 2002), the Multidimensional Emotional Intelligence Assessment (MEIA; Tett, Fox, & Wang, 2005), and the GENOS Emotional Intelligence Inventory (Gignac, 2010).

Which scale is most appropriate for a particular application must be determined with reference to a number of criteria, such as: the context (clinical, educational, occupational, etc.), the profile of the respondent (age, gender, cultural background, etc.), and the depth of information required (global, factor, or facet scores). While several trait EI instruments show reasonable psychometric properties, there exist extensive differences in their nomological networks and construct validity. These are evident in specific types of construct validity, but perhaps none more so than in incremental validity, which may be defined as the degree to which a measure explains or predicts a phenomenon of interest, relative to other measures (Haynes & Lench, 2003).

Incremental Validity of Trait Emotional Intelligence

One of the most debated and critical psychometric issues of a "fuzzy" and popularized concept, such as EI, is that of incremental validity. As demonstrated in several published meta-analyses, the information obtained from trait EI measures contributes significantly to predictions beyond cognitive ability, personality traits, and other relevant constructs (e.g., Andrei, Siegling, Aloe, Baldaro, & Petrides, in press; O'Boyle, Humphrey, Pollack, Hawver, & Story, 2011). For a most accurate estimate, the incremental validity and value of a construct ought to be inferred from its best measures: those that have been used relatively often and excelled psychometrically on other aspects of construct validity. Below we present a summary of findings with the TEIQue, EQ-i, AES, WLEIS, and GENOS. We have omitted reference to the TMMS due to its multidimensional structure and lack of a global trait EI score, and to the WEIP and MEIA, which are newer measures that have not yet been used extensively in the scientific literature.

TEIQue

Many studies have examined the incremental validity of the TEIQue above higher-order personality dimensions and other relevant predictors in various criterion domains. The evidence was recently integrated in a review and meta-analysis (Andrei et al., in press), which revealed significant incremental effects in 80% of 114 analyses reported across 24 peer-reviewed articles. A statistically significant meta-analytic effect was reported ($\Delta R^2 = 0.06$, SE = 0.0116; 95% CI: 0.03–0.08). The number of covariates controlled, the form of the TEIQue (full vs. short), and the focus on higher-order personality dimensions versus other individual-difference constructs as covariates did not impact on the size of the effects.

Moreover, studies, including meta-analyses (Martins et al., 2010) that have directly compared multiple measures of trait EI in terms of incremental validity, have consistently found the TEIQue to explain the largest amount of unique variance over and above various baseline constructs and criteria (Di Fabio & Saklofske, 2014a, 2014b; Freudenthaler, Neubauer, Gabler, Scherl, & Rindermann, 2008; Gardner & Qualter, 2010). It is worth noting that many impressive findings pertaining to incremental validity have actually been established with the short form of the TEIQue, which obviously provides more limited coverage of the construct than the full form.

EQ-i

A substantial range of studies has examined the incremental validity of the EQ-i. Concerning criteria of mental health and psychological wellbeing, EQ-i scores predicted alcohol use, albeit weakly at $r = -0.10$, after controlling for personality (Big Five) and verbal ability (SAT) scores (Brackett & Mayer, 2003). In contrast, they did not predict drug use, smoking, social deviance, high-school rank (i.e., a ranking of the student relative to peers), and college grade-point average (GPA). More consistent predictive effects on criteria were reported in Di Fabio and Saklofske (2014a), where the EQ-i accounted for unique variance over and above fluid intelligence, the Big Five, and ability EI in core self-evaluations, resilience, and life satisfaction. Also controlling for Big Five effects, another study showed unique EQ-i effects on life satisfaction, rumination, and three different coping style variables (rational, detached, and emotional; Petrides, Pérez-González, & Furnham, 2007a). Lastly, Parker, Keefer, and Wood (2011) found two of the four EQ-i: Short factors to be uniquely related to ADHD symptomatology, controlling for the Big Five; the stress management factor was a unique predictor of inattention, hyperactivity–impulsivity, and ADHD combined, whereas the intrapersonal factor predicted inattention and ADHD combined, but not hyperactivity–impulsivity on its own.

Another set of studies has examined the incremental validity of the EQ-i in work settings. Di Fabio and Saklofske (2014b) demonstrated incremental effects on three occupational criteria (decision-making self-efficacy, career indecision, and indecisiveness), controlling for fluid intelligence, the Big Five, and ability EI, while Ono, Sachau, Deal, Englert, and Taylor (2011) demonstrated incremental effects on the job performance of US federal criminal investigators, controlling for cognitive ability and the Big Five. Finally, Livingstone and Day (2005) reported significant contributions of the EQ-i to job and life satisfaction, after accounting for the Big Five. However, this analysis was conducted at the factor level of the instrument, with only one of its five factors (Mood) attaining significance in the two regression equations.

AES

In an early investigation of incremental validity, Saklofske, Austin, and Minski (2003) reported that the AES predicted life satisfaction, social and emotional loneliness, and depression over and above the Big Five. Gardner and Qualter (2010) showed that the AES predicted unique variance in a range of criteria (hostility, social loneliness, family loneliness, romantic loneliness, happiness, and life satisfaction) after controlling for the Big Five, gender, and age. In contrast, it did not show significant incremental effects in relation to physical and verbal aggression, anger, eating disorders, and alcohol use.

Less promising results were reported by Brackett and Mayer (2003), who found the AES to be uniquely, yet inversely, related to high-school rank ($r = -0.16$) and unrelated to drug use, alcohol use, cigarette smoking, social deviance, and college GPA. Their analyses controlled for the effects of the Big Five and SAT scores. In another study that used multiple criteria of wellbeing and adjustment, the EQ-i explained incremental variance in social network size after controlling for the Big Five (Austin, Saklofske, & Egan, 2005). In contrast, no incremental effects were observed for the criteria of social network satisfaction (i.e., whether participants were satisfied with their social networks), life satisfaction, alcohol consumption, health, and visits to the family doctor.

WLEIS

A relatively small number of studies have examined the incremental validity of the WLEIS. For a sample of hospitality service employees, Kim and Agrusa (2011) found that the WLEIS predicted task and avoidance, but not emotion, coping, after controlling for industry category, sociodemographic variables, extraversion, and neuroticism. Kong, Zhao, and You (2012) found the effects of WLEIS on mental distress to be partially mediated by negative and positive affect, although WLEIS scores still accounted for unique variance in this model. In contrast, in a study with a similar research design (Kong & Zhao, 2013), WLEIS effects on life satisfaction were fully mediated by positive and negative affect.

GENOS

Although the GENOS can be counted among the more widely used work-oriented measures, few studies have examined its incremental validity (Palmer, Stough, Harmer, & Gignac, 2009). The technical manual reports that the scale showed incremental validity in predicting sales performance, controlling for work-related behaviors, such as days on territory and length of calls, and also in predicting recruitment consultants' annual revenue generation, controlling for the effects of the Big Five, intelligence, and socially desirable responding (Gignac, 2010).

Summary

The aforementioned measures of trait EI have demonstrated incremental validity on manifold criteria, controlling for manifold baseline predictors. Of these measures, the TEIQue seems to make the most consistent and strongest incremental contributions, followed by the EQ-i. The AES has shown considerable variability in terms of yielding statistically significant incremental effects across criteria and studies, whereas the incremental validity of the workplace-oriented measures (WLEIS and GENOS) has not been thoroughly established yet, due to the fairly small number of relevant research designs in the scientific literature. Another complicating factor in the body of research work concerning the AES, WLEIS, and GENOS is the variation in the constructs that have been used as baseline predictors in the various investigations of their incremental validity.

Conclusion

Trait EI is a scientific theory (Petrides, 2010) in the sense that it is *testable* (i.e., it is possible to conduct research studies to test its main premises), *falsifiable* (i.e., it is possible to be proven false), and *general* (i.e., it is not tied to a single instrument). In addition to these three properties, which are crucial from a scientific perspective, trait EI theory enjoys at least another three advantages relative to other EI models.

First, trait EI theory fully acknowledges the subjective nature of emotional experience, thus resolving multiple problems plaguing models that view emotions as something abstract, detached, and severed from the individual who experiences them. Second, trait EI theory integrates the construct into mainstream theories of psychology instead of treating it as a novel entity dissociated from accumulated scientific knowledge. Third, trait EI theory is readily extendable into related areas (e.g., social intelligence), rather than restricted to a single idiosyncratic model (Petrides, Mason, & Sevdalis, 2011).

With respect to incremental validity, there can be little doubt that trait EI improves on criterion prediction over and above a multitude of other constructs, including collectively the Big Five personality dimensions. Nevertheless, it is important to distinguish between explanation and prediction, and acknowledge that the former is at least as important as the latter, if not more so (Scriven, 1959). A preoccupation with incremental predictive validity in the literature may prove unproductive, especially because of the well-documented difficulties of personality psychology on the explanation front (Uher, 2013). It is on its explanatory power that the full promise of trait EI theory rests, rather than on its amply demonstrated incremental predictive validity.

References

Andrei, F., Siegling, A.B., Aloe, A.M., Baldaro, B., & Petrides, K.V. (in press). The incremental validity of the Trait Emotional Intelligence Questionnaire (TEIQue): A systematic review and meta-analysis. *Journal of Personality Assessment.*

Austin, E.J. (2010). Measurement of ability emotional intelligence: Results for two new tests. *British Journal of Psychology, 101* (Pt 3), 563–578.

Austin, E.J., Saklofske, D.H., & Egan, V. (2005). Personality, well-being and health correlates of trait emotional intelligence. *Personality and Individual Differences, 38* (3), 547–558.

Bar-On, R. (1997). *BarOn Emotional Quotient Inventory: Technical Manual.* Toronto: Multi-Health Systems Inc.

Brackett, M.A., & Mayer, J.D. (2003). Convergent, discriminant, and incremental validity of competing measures of emotional intelligence. *Personality and Social Psychology Bulletin, 29* (9), 1147–1158.

Brody, N. (2004). What cognitive intelligence is and what emotional intelligence is not. *Psychological Inquiry, 15* (3), 234–238.

Cronbach, L.J. (1949). *Essentials of Psychological Testing.* New York: Harper and Row.

Davis, S.K., & Humphrey, N. (2012). The influence of emotional intelligence (EI) on coping and mental health in adolescence: Divergent roles for trait and ability EI. *Journal of Adolescence, 35* (5), 1369–1379.

DeYoung, C.G. (2006). Higher-order factors of the Big Five in a multi-informant sample. *Journal of Personality and Social Psychology, 91* (6), 1138–1151.

Di Fabio, A., & Saklofske, D.H. (2014a). Promoting individual resources: The challenge of trait emotional intelligence. *Personality and Individual Differences, 65*, 19–23.

Di Fabio, A., & Saklofske, D.H. (2014b). Comparing ability and self-report trait emotional intelligence, fluid intelligence, and personality traits in career decision. *Personality and Individual Differences, 64*, 174–178.

Digman, J.M. (1997). Higher-order factors of the Big Five. *Journal of Personality and Social Psychology, 73* (6), 1246–1256.

Fiori, M., Antonietti, J.P., Mikolajczak, M., Luminet, O., Hansenne, M., & Rossier, J. (2014). What is the ability emotional intelligence test (MSCEIT) good for? An evaluation using Item Response Theory. *PloS One, 9* (6), e98827.

Follesdal, H., & Hagtvet, K.A. (2009). Emotional intelligence: The MSCEIT from the perspective of generalizability theory. *Intelligence, 37*(1), 94–105.

Freudenthaler, H.H., & Neubauer, A.C. (2007). Measuring emotional management abilities: Further evidence of the importance to distinguish between typical and maximum performance. *Personality and Individual Differences, 42* (8), 1561–1572.

Freudenthaler, H.H., Neubauer, A.C., Gabler, P., Scherl, W.G., & Rindermann, H. (2008). Testing and validating the Trait Emotional Intelligence Questionnaire (TEIQue) in a German-speaking sample. *Personality and Individual Differences, 45* (7), 673–678.

Funder, D.C. (2012). *The Personality Puzzle* (6th ed.). New York: W.W. Norton & Co.

Gardner, K.J., & Qualter, P. (2010). Concurrent and incremental validity of three trait emotional intelligence measures. *Australian Journal of Psychology, 62* (1), 5–13.

Gignac, G.E. (2010). *Genos Emotional Intelligence Inventory Technical Manual* (2nd ed.). Sydney: Genos Pty Ltd.

Gugliandolo, M.C., Costa, S., Cuzzocrea, F., Larcan, R., & Petrides, K.V. (2015). Trait emotional intelligence and behavioral problems among adolescents: A cross-informant design. *Personality and Individual Differences, 74*, 16–21.

Haynes, S.N., & Lench, H.C. (2003). Incremental validity of new clinical assessment measures. *Psychological Assessment, 15* (4), 456–466.

Jordan, P.J., Ashkanasy, N.M., Härtel, C.E.J., & Hooper, G. (2002). Workgroup emotional intelligence: Scale development and relationship to team process effectiveness and goal focus. *Human Resource Management Review, 12* (2), 195–214.

Kim, H.J., & Agrusa, J. (2011). Hospitality service employees' coping styles: The role of emotional intelligence, two basic personality traits, and socio-demographic factors. *International Journal of Hospitality Management, 30* (3), 588–598.

Kong, F., & Zhao, J. (2013). Affective mediators of the relationship between trait emotional intelligence and life satisfaction in young adults. *Personality and Individual Differences, 54* (2), 197–201.

Kong, F., Zhao, J., & You, X. (2012). Trait emotional intelligence and mental distress: The mediating role of positive and negative affect. *International Journal of Psychology, 47* (6), 1–7.

Livingstone, H.A., & Day, A.L. (2005). Comparing the construct and criterion-related validity of ability-based and mixed-model measures of emotional intelligence. *Educational and Psychological Measurement, 65* (5), 757–779.

Martins, A., Ramalho, N., & Morin, E. (2010). A comprehensive meta-analysis of the relationship between emotional intelligence and health. *Personality and Individual Differences, 49* (6), 554–564.

Matthews, G., Emo, A., Roberts, R.D., & Zeidner, M. (2006). What is this thing called emotional intelligence? In K.R. Murphy (Ed.), *A Critique of Emotional Intelligence: What are the Problems and How Can They be Fixed?* (pp. 3–36). Mahwah, NJ: Erlbaum.

Matthews, G., Zeidner, M., & Roberts, R.D. (2007). Emotional intelligence: Consensus, controversies, and questions. In G. Matthews, M. Zeidner, & R.D. Roberts (Eds.), *The Science of Emotional Intelligence: Known and Unknowns* (pp. 3–46). Oxford: Oxford University Press.

Maul, A. (2012). The validity of the Mayer–Salovey–Caruso Emotional Intelligence Test (MSCEIT) as a measure of emotional intelligence. *Emotion Review, 4* (4), 394–402.

O'Boyle, E.H., Humphrey, R.H., Pollack, J.M., Hawver, T.H., & Story, P.A. (2011). The relation between emotional intelligence and job performance: A meta-analysis. *Journal of Organizational Behavior, 32* (5), 788–818.

Ono, M., Sachau, D.A., Deal, W.P., Englert, D.R., & Taylor, M.D. (2011). Cognitive ability, emotional intelligence, and the Big Five personality dimensions as predictors of criminal investigator performance. *Criminal Justice and Behavior, 38* (5), 471–491.

O'Sullivan, M. (2007). Trolling for trout, trawling for tuna: The methodological morass in measuring emotional intelligence. In G. Matthews, M. Zeidner, & R. Roberts (Eds.), *Emotional Intelligence: Knowns and Unknowns* (pp. 258–287). Oxford: Oxford University Press.

Pace, V.L., & Brannick, M.T. (2010). How similar are personality scales of the "same" construct? A meta-analytic investigation. *Personality and Individual Differences, 49* (7), 669–676.

Palmer, B.R., Stough, C., Harmer, R., & Gignac, G.E. (2009). The Genos Emotional Intelligence Inventory: A measure designed specifically for workplace applications. In J.D.A. Parker, C. Stough, & D.H. Saklofske (Eds.), *Assessing Emotional Intelligence: Theory, Research, and Applications* (pp. 103–117). New York: Springer.

Parker, J.D.A., Keefer, K.V, & Wood, L.M. (2011). Toward a brief multidimensional assessment of emotional intelligence: Psychometric properties of the Emotional Quotient Inventory-Short Form. *Psychological Assessment, 23* (3), 762–777.

Pérez-González, J.C., & Sanchez-Ruiz, M.J. (2014). Trait emotional intelligence anchored within the big five, big two and big one frameworks. *Personality and Individual Differences, 65*, 53–58.

Petrides, K.V. (2009). *Technical Manual for the Trait Emotional Intelligence Questionnaires (TEIQue)*. London: London Psychometric Laboratory.

Petrides, K.V. (2010). Trait emotional intelligence theory. *Industrial and Organizational Psychology, 3* (2), 136–139.

Petrides, K.V., & Furnham, A. (2000). On the dimensional structure of emotional intelligence. *Personality and Individual Differences, 29* (2), 313–320.

Petrides, K.V., Mason, M., & Sevdalis, N. (2011). Preliminary validation of the construct of trait social intelligence. *Personality and Individual Differences, 50* (6), 874–877.

Petrides, K.V., Pérez-González, J.C., & Furnham, A. (2007a). On the criterion and incremental validity of trait emotional intelligence. *Cognition & Emotion, 21* (1), 26–55.

Petrides, K.V., Pita, R., & Kokkinaki, F. (2007b). The location of trait emotional intelligence in personality factor space. *British Journal of Psychology, 98* (Pt 2), 273–289.

Roberts, R.D., Zeidner, M., & Matthews, G. (2001). Does emotional intelligence meet traditional standards for an intelligence? Some new data and conclusions. *Emotion, 1* (3), 196–231.

Rushton, J.P., Bons, T.A., Ando, J., Hur, Y.M., Irwing, P., Vernon, P.A., Petrides, K.V., & Barbaranelli, C. (2009). A general factor of personality from multitrait–multimethod data and cross–national twins. *Twin Research and Human Genetics, 12* (4), 356–365.

Saklofske, D.H., Austin, E.J., & Minski, P.S. (2003). Factor structure and validity of a trait emotional intelligence measure. *Personality and Individual Differences, 34* (4), 707–721.

Salovey, P., Mayer, J.D., Goldman, S., Turvey, C., & Palfai, T. (1995). Emotional attention, clarity, and repair: Exploring emotional intelligence using the Trait Meta-Mood scale. In J.W. Pennebaker (Ed.), *Emotion, Disclosure, and Health* (pp. 125–154). Washington, DC: American Psychological Association.

Schutte, N.S., Malouff, J.M., Hall, L.E., Haggerty, D.J., Cooper, J.T., Golden, C.J., & Dornheim, L. (1998). Development and validation of a measure of emotional intelligence. *Personality and Individual Differences, 25* (2), 167–177.

Scriven, M. (1959). Explanation and prediction in evolutionary theory. *Science, 130* (3374), 477–482.

Siegling, A.B., Petrides, K.V., & Martskvishvili, K. (2015a). An examination of a new psychometric method for optimizing multi-faceted assessment instruments in the context of trait emotional intelligence. *European Journal of Personality, 29* (1), 42–54.

Siegling, A.B., Saklofske, D.H., & Petrides, K.V. (2015b). Measures of ability and trait emotional intelligence. In G.J. Boyle, G. Matthews, & D.H. Saklofske (Eds.), *Measures of Personality and Social Psychological Constructs* (pp. 381–414). San Diego: Academic Press.

Tett, R.P., Fox, K.E., & Wang, A. (2005). Development and validation of a self-report measure of emotional intelligence as a multidimensional trait domain. *Personality and Social Psychology Bulletin, 31* (7), 859–888.

Uher, J. (2013). Personality psychology: Lexical approaches, assessment methods, and trait concepts reveal only half of the story – Why it is time for a paradigm shift. *Integrative Psychological and Behavioral Science, 47* (1), 1–55.

Van der Linden, D., Pekaar, K., Bakker, A.B., Aitken Schermer, J., Vernon, P.A., & Petrides, K.V. (submitted). Overlap between the General Factor of Personality and emotional intelligence: A meta-analysis and a genetic correlation study.

Veselka, L., Schermer, J.A., Petrides, K.V., Cherkas, L.F., Spector, T.D., & Vernon, P.A. (2009). A General Factor of Personality: Evidence from the HEXACO model and a measure of trait emotional intelligence. *Twin Research and Human Genetics, 12* (5), 420–424.

Warwick, J., & Nettelbeck, T. (2004). Emotional intelligence is…? *Personality and Individual Differences, 37* (5), 1091–1100.

Wilhelm, O. (2005). Measures of emotional intelligence: practice and standards. In R. Schulze, & R.D. Roberts (Eds.), *International Handbook of Emotional Intelligence* (pp. 131–154). Seattle, WA: Hogrefe & Huber.

Wong, C.S., & Law, K.S. (2002). The effects of leader and follower emotional intelligence on performance and attitude: An exploratory study. *Leadership Quarterly, 13* (3), 243–274.

8

Beyond IQ and EQ: The Bar-On Multifactor Model of Performance

Reuven Bar-On

The Bar-On Multifactor Model of Performance is a conceptual model that is designed to comprehensively examine, understand and enhance key factors thought to contribute to and predict performance. Moreover, it is an operational framework designed to help understand why some people perform better than others, and to determine which contributing factors need to be strengthened in order to enhance performance in individuals who are underperforming.

The Multifactor Model of Performance (MMP) comprises 28 factors, thought to be the key contributors to and predictors of performance. These 28 factors are clustered into the following five meta-factors considered below: (1) Health and Stamina; (2) Cognitive Functioning; (3) Intra-Personal Strength; (4) Inter-Personal Compatibility; and (5) Trans-Personal Development. The *Multifactor Measure of Performance*™ (*MMP*™), which is described in the next section, was created to assess these factors. Multivariate statistics will be applied to examine data generated by the ongoing norming of this psychometric instrument, and the findings will then be used to evaluate the *a priori* theoretical structure described below.

Fitness and Stamina: One's overall level of physical fitness and stamina. This proposed meta-factor comprises the following two factors thought to contribute to performance, representing the "body" in the familiar "body, mind and soul" adage.

- (1) *Physical Fitness*: Striving to obtain and maintain good physical fitness, which contributes to performance, stamina, and productivity. This, in turn, impacts one's overall wellbeing as well.
- (2) *Discomfort Tolerance*: Temporarily suspending everyday physical needs and comforts, from time to time, in order to complete a task or project on time.

Cognitive Functioning: One's overall level of cognitive and adaptive functioning, which is a proposed meta-factor comprising the following eight factors thought to contribute to performance. This represents the "mind" in the "body, mind and soul" adage.

The Wiley Handbook of Personality Assessment, First Edition. Edited by Updesh Kumar.
© 2016 John Wiley & Sons, Ltd. Published 2016 by John Wiley & Sons, Ltd.

- (3) *General Cognitive Competence*: Effectively learning new information and applying learned knowledge, logic and reasoning for the purpose of understanding and solving problems in order to survive, adapt and better navigate through life.
- (4) *Situational Awareness*: Evaluating the immediate situation, paying attention to detail as well as understanding, clarifying and closing gaps between the subjective perception of reality and objective reality.
- (5) *Applying Experience*: Appropriately and effectively applying past experience, in order to facilitate current problem analysis, problem-solving and decision-making.
- (6) *Flexibility*: Effectively coping with and adapting to change, as well as dealing with unexpected, unpredictable and confusing situations. Being flexible also helps to cope with setbacks, failures, and crises, as well as to resiliently recover from them.
- (7) *Resourcefulness*: Being innovative and considering different ways of coping with problematic situations, especially when previous approaches have failed.
- (8) *Decision-Making*: Generating potentially effective solutions to problems, weighing the pros and cons of each possibility, deciding on the best solution and implementing it.
- (9) *Action-Planning*: Planning and initiating goal-oriented activity designed to deal with challenges or problematic situations.
- (10) *Immediate Implementation*: Rapidly implementing some form of goal-oriented action designed to cope with a situation that needs to be dealt with immediately. This requires accurately and quickly sizing up the immediate situation, deciding on the best plan of action to address the problem, and implementing it as promptly as possible.

Intra-Personal Strength: One's overall level of intra-personal strength is a proposed meta-factor comprising the following 12 factors thought to contribute to performance and overall wellbeing. This can be viewed as the "soul" – or the "intra-personal soul" – in the "body, mind and soul" adage.

- (11) *Self-Awareness*: Accurately looking inward at oneself in order to better understand and accept oneself, including one's weaknesses as well as strengths.
- (12) *Self-Image Accuracy*: The degree of accuracy, sincerity and honesty one displays in presenting one's self-image to others.
- (13) *Self-Image Consistency*: The degree of consistency one displays in presenting one's self-image to others and showing them how one really is most of the time.
- (14) *Decisiveness*: Expressing oneself openly, clearly and boldly, which includes being able to convey feelings, beliefs and ideas in a non-aggressive manner. This depends on one's sense of inner strength and self-confidence.
- (15) *Self-Reliance*: Being independent from others and being able to think things out alone, make decisions and act independently when needed.
- (16) *Courage*: Willing to fearlessly confront a situation that could endanger oneself, such as standing up for one's convictions or rights, defending someone who

is being ridiculed or attacked for some reason, or intervening when someone's life is in immediate danger.

- (17) *Self-Control*: Controlling one's emotions and maintaining self-composure, which is essentially having our emotions "work for us and not against us."
- (18) *Endurance and Coping*: Managing one's feelings in stressful situations, which helps one function effectively while remaining relatively calm.
- (19) *Self-Motivation*: Being positive, optimistic and energized in doing what one does.
- (20) *Engagement*: Being fully committed to one's work, which builds on feeling passionate about what one enjoys doing.
- (21) *Determination*: Being committed to decisions that are made and goals that are set, and determined to follow through with them.
- (22) *Perseverance*: Persevering and following through with a task until it is completed.

Inter-Personal Compatibility: One's overall level of inter-personal compatibility, which is a proposed meta-factor comprising the following four factors thought to contribute to performance and overall wellbeing. This can be viewed as the "soul" – or the "inter-personal soul" – in the "body, mind and soul" adage.

- (23) *Humility*: Inspiring others without boasting about one's position, achievements or self, typically characterized by a pattern of unpretentious rather than egocentric or arrogant behavior. Humble people receive criticism without becoming defensive or offended. They remain teachable, most of their life, by being open to learn from others.
- (24) *Social-Awareness*: Being aware of others, their feelings and concerns, which helps one interact with people and become a more cooperative, constructive and contributing team player.
- (25) *Connectedness*: Being able to connect with other people and to establish and maintain mutually satisfying interpersonal relationships.
- (26) *Social Responsibility*: Living according to a set of principles, values and beliefs, which guide one's decisions and ability to do the right thing.

Trans-Personal Development: One's overall level of trans-personal development, which is a proposed meta-factor comprising the following two factors thought to contribute to performance and a sense of fulfillment in life. This requires the ability to go beyond oneself, and one's personal needs and goals. It can be viewed as the "soul" – or the "trans-personal soul" – in the familiar "body, mind and soul" adage.

- (27) *Meaningfulness*: Finding meaning in what one does as well as being passionately involved in meaningful pursuits that benefit others in addition to oneself. This leads to a more fulfilling life and an overall sense of fulfillment.
- (28) *Overall Well-Being*: Feeling content and satisfied with who one is and with one's life in general, including one's health, relationships, work, and the meaningfulness of what one has accomplished and how it might contribute to others, the community and society.

Based on the way the above factors are structured and described, the theoretical meta-structure of this model can be viewed as an expanded version of the "*body, mind and soul*" explanation of human behavior and performance. In light of the fact that this is a *theory* of performance, which emerged from what the author considers to be the key contributors to performance, based on years of professional experience and the way he reviewed the literature, the extent to which it exists in reality needs to be empirically examined; and this will be done by factor analyzing the 28 factors which are assessed by the *MMP*™ as it continues to be normed.

The *Multifactor Measure of Performance*™

The *Multifactor Measure of Performance*™ (*MMP*™) is a psychometric instrument that was developed by the author to assess the 28 factors of his Multifactor Model of Performance (MMP). The *MMP*™ was originally designed as a research tool to be used in studying various aspects of performance as well as the MMP itself. It was also thought that the *MMP*™ could eventually be applied to determine systematically and relatively quickly which MMP factors need to be strengthened in individuals in order to help them perform at a higher level.

It is important to emphasize that the *MMP*™ is not a measure of personality or of cognitive, emotional or social intelligence, although personal traits and abilities might indeed impact the key predictors of the author's model of performance, and performance in general. The *MMP*™ was not designed to assess the *ability* to perform, but rather performance itself. Moreover, the items were phrased in such a way to encourage respondents to describe the way they typically *behave* in various situations, and not their ability to behave in those situations.

The beta version of the *MMP*™ is web-based and accessible at www.ReuvenBarOn.org. The beta version contains 216 items, in the form of brief sentences, and takes an average of 50 minutes to complete. Respondents are asked to respond "as openly and accurately as possible." Following each item, they are presented with the following five response options: (1) *doesn't describe me at all*; (2) *describes me rarely*; (3) *describes me sometimes*; (4) *describes me often*; (5) *describes me perfectly*.

The software developed for scoring this questionnaire first sums the responses to each item – ranging from 1 to 5 – in order to create scale scores, which is done by dividing the total sum of the responses for each scale by the number of items in the scale. This process creates scale scores ranging from a minimum of 1.0 to a maximum of 5.0. These scores are then presented using the familiar 5 Star Rating System. This rating system was used because it avoids the need to provide complicated explanations of what "standard scores" are and mean.

In that score interpretation is more accurate and meaningful when standard scores are used, because they resolve potential demographic differences within and between national norms (Anastasi, 1988), *MMP*™ scores will be based on standard scores as this instrument is more extensively normed across cultures. Although scoring will eventually be based on norm-based assessment, "ipsative assessment" (Baron, 1996) using the 5 Star Rating System will be used in the meantime.

The beta version of the *MMP*™ has been programmed on an interactive assessment-development platform. The software that drives the platform first assesses how well respondents are currently functioning, based on the degree of adeptness they display in the 28 predictors of performance measured by the *MMP*™. It provides an in-depth analysis that maps their strengths as well as areas that can be further strengthened in order to enhance overall performance. The development component of this interactive program then provides a number of straightforward suggestions for strengthening the weaker factors, which are automatically generated by significantly low scale scores.

The average individual report that is provided contains approximately 25 pages, depending upon the number of suggestions generated by low scores, and it is divided into the following four sections: (a) a numeric summary of the scores and what they mean; (b) a graphic overview of the results; (c) a textual summary of the results in full-text; and (d) suggestions for enhancing overall performance. These summaries focus on the *MMP*™'s scale scales, which assess the predictors of performance described in the previous section. In addition to the 28 scale scores and 5 global scale scores that assess the MMP factors and meta-factors respectively, the beta version of the *MMP*™ also assesses the respondent's overall level of performance, how well they think they are currently performing at work, their general level of motivation, how satisfied they are with their work, as well as self-perceived work-related risk and stress factors.

The following is the framework used in interpreting each *MMP*™ scale score:

- 1 Star (1.0–1.4) = It very rarely describes the respondent.
- 2 Stars (1.5–2.4) = It rarely describes the respondent.
- 3 Stars (2.5–3.4) = It describes the respondent.
- 4 Stars (3.5–4.4) = It often describes the respondent.
- 5 Stars (4.5–5.0) = It very often describes the respondent.

Why Create this Conceptual and Psychometric Model of Performance?

The primary reason for creating the author's multifactor model of performance emerged from his desire to learn more about what contributes to human behavior, performance and wellbeing, which has continued to interest him throughout most of his professional career. After completing a master's degree, the experience of working as a clinical psychologist eventually led him back to graduate school to conduct research on "the development of a concept of psychological well-being" (Bar-On, 1988). From 1978 to the present time, the author has developed or co-developed 12 psychometric instruments designed to assess a variety of different factors that contribute to performance and wellbeing, in one way or another, including measures of: (1) physical health; (2) psychological health; (3) wellbeing; (4) neurocognitive functioning; (5) emotional and social intelligence; (6) moral competence; (7) leadership; and (8) meaningfulness. The development of the multifactor model and measure of performance, described in this chapter, is a continuation and expansion of his earlier work.

The original reason for developing the *MMP*™ was to create a research tool that could be used to study various aspects of human behavior, performance and wellbeing, as well as his multifactor model of performance. Additionally, it was also thought that the *MMP*™ could eventually be used as an assessment instrument to help determine which specific factors need to be strengthened in order to enhance performance and overall wellbeing.

In light of the fact that nearly all models that have attempted to describe, assess and/or enhance predictors of performance have focused on a very limited number of factors, the author felt a need to comprehensively address as many key factors as possible.

An additional reason for developing *MMP*™ was to explore the feasibility of creating a *single* instrument that could be used to assess a wide range of factors that contribute to human behavior, performance, and wellbeing, rather than relying on a *number* of different instruments (referred to as the "assessment battery" by psychodiagnosticians). Essentially, the model described here is an attempt to *replace* the traditional battery of tests with a single instrument that could assess an even wider range of factors. It is hoped that this approach will significantly reduce the expense and time involved in administering and scoring a number of different assessment instruments and summarizing their generated findings. It was also reasoned that such an approach could be used *at least* as a screener to more accurately, cost-effectively and quickly direct the attention of practitioners to where to expand the assessment process and where to avoid further examination.

The Method Applied in Developing the Bar-On Model

The development of the author's multifactor model of performance (MMP) and the psychometric model to assess it (*MMP*™) are inseparable. More succinctly, each contributes to the development of the other. The development of the *MMP*™ began by (a) first conceptualizing the MMP, which (b) necessitated finding or constructing a research tool to determine the extent to which this concept exists in reality and the degree to which it is reliable, valid, and applicable; and (c) the empirical examination of the *MMP*™ will continue to shape the conceptual model.

The author's approach in developing the *MMP*™ was similar to the one he applied in developing the Bar-On EQ-i and other psychometric instruments (Bar-On, 1988, 1997, 2004, 2006a). Specifically regarding the development of the *MMP*™, he followed the following procedure: (1) identifying factors in the literature thought to predict performance; (2) selecting and defining 28 predictors of performance; (3) creating and selecting scale items for the beta version of the *MMP*™; (4) editing the 216 scale items; and, eventually, (5) applying statistics to shorten and psychometrically strengthen the *MMP*™. These five stages of test and concept development are described below.

(1) Identifying potentially relevant factors in the literature thought to predict performance

The first step in conceptualizing the model of performance presented here was to review the literature that focuses on various aspects of performance including: (a) how it has been described and assessed; (b) what contributes to it; and (c) proposed methods of enhancing it.

In reviewing the literature, what became abundantly clear from the beginning was the frequent acknowledgment that predictors of human behavior, performance and wellbeing are multifactorial in nature and very complex. In spite of this acknowledgment, or perhaps because of it, many if not most theories of performance focus only on very few predictors, as was previously mentioned.

Listed below are a number of the more relevant references thought to support the factorial components of the Bar-On model. An attempt was made to reference publications that have summarized empirical research or conducted meta-analyses of studies.

Fitness and stamina. Based on a number of studies summarized in the literature, physical health, fitness and stamina have a significant impact on performance and productivity (e.g., Boles, Pelletier, & Lynch, 2004; Conn, Hafdahl, Cooper, Brown, & Lusk, 2009; Fritz & Sonnentag, 2005; Pronk & Kottke, 2009). Based on the findings reviewed, healthier individuals perform on a higher level and are more productive than those who are less healthy.

Cognitive functioning. Research in this area has generated a large number of findings demonstrating that cognitive and adaptive competence contributes significantly to performance and productivity as well. In addition to general cognitive competence as well as adeptness in problem-solving and decision-making (e.g., Bartel, 1995; Cote & Miners, 2006; Hsu, 2008; Weitz, Sujan, & Sujan, 1986), research has also examined the importance of intellectual flexibility (e.g., Bar-On, 2006b; Thomas & Feldman, 2008; Weitz et al., 1986), resourcefulness (e.g., Hsu, 2008; Kuncel, Hezlett, & Ones, 2004; Thomas & Feldman, 2008), action-planning and goal-setting (e.g., Janssen & Van Yperen, 2004; Locke & Latham, 2002; Locke, Shaw, Saari, & Latham, 1981; Mento, Steel, & Karren, 1987) as key contributors to performance and productivity.

Intra-personal strength. There is a plethora of research studies found in the literature that have examined various aspects of intra-personal strength, indicating its significant impact on occupational as well as academic performance. Many of the studies conducted to date have examined the impact of self-awareness, self-efficacy and self-esteem on performance (e.g., Cote & Miners, 2006; Judge, Jackson, Shaw, Scott, & Rich, 2007; Rich, Lepine, & Crawford, 2010). Even more studies have examined the ability to cope with stress (e.g., Matteson & Ivancevich, 1987; Motowidlo, Packard, & Manning, 1986; Sullivan & Bhagat, 1992), self-motivation (e.g., Cheng & Fox, 2007; Rich et al., 2010; Weitz et al., 1986) and commitment to one's work (e.g., Becker, Billings, Eveleth & Gilbert, 1996; Halbesleben & Wheeler, 2008; Markos & Sridevi, 2010; Rich et al., 2010) as important contributors to individual and organizational performance and productivity. A more recent interest appears to be in studying the relationship between "courageous leadership" and organizational performance. What is surprising, however, is the dearth of studies that have examine the impact of determination and perseverance on performance.

Inter-personal compatibility. The idea that "social intelligence" is an important factor in inter-personal compatibility has been proposed for nearly a century (Thorndike, 1920). The vast majority of studies that have examined the impact of this contributor to performance and wellbeing have concentrated primarily on empathy, the ability to establish and maintain relationships with others and doing the morally right thing in relating with them (e.g., Lennick & Kiel, 2007; Schwepker & Ingram, 1996; Van Scotter & Motowidlo, 1996). The importance of "humility" in leadership and its impact on organizational performance has only recently begun to interest researchers (e.g., Baker & O'Malley, 2008; Collins, 2001; Martinuzzi, 2009).

Trans-personal development. While satisfaction with one's work and a general sense of wellbeing contribute to performance and productivity (e.g., Altman, 2001; Petty, McGee & Cavender, 1984; Yousef, 2000), the importance of finding meaning in what one does has also been attracting a great deal of research interest over the past two decades (e.g., Ashar & Lane-Maher, 2004; Galinsky-Zamor, 2003; Giacalone & Jurkiewicz, 2003; Karakas, 2010).

(2) Selecting and defining the *a priori* key predictors of performance

After reviewing the literature to gain a better understanding of what appear to be significant contributors to performance, the next step involved determining which of these factors are more frequently studied and are the most important. Summarizing what appeared to be the most important factors suggested that there are between 20 and 30 key predictors of performance. The author included a few additional factors that he thought were potentially important predictors, even though they had initiated very little research activity to date. Additionally, a few factors were divided into subfactors even though empirical evidence was not found in the literature to support this decision. This process suggested the existence of 28 key factors, whose inclusion in the proposed model would eventually need to be empirically examined in order to be justified.

The next phase in developing this model involved defining the 28 *a priori* predictors of performance that were selected. The approach was similar to the one applied in defining the factors of emotional and social intelligence measured by the EQ-i™ (Bar-On, 1997).

First, the author attempted to define the factors as clearly as possible. The definitions that emerged were then reviewed by a number of colleagues and lay people (five psychologists and an equal number of laypeople), whose feedback helped to increase the clarity and enhance the overall quality of the definitions. This was done to strengthen the instrument's content and face validity, which increases the possibility of obtaining more robust construct validity in the end (Anastasi, 1988; Jackson, 1970).

(3) Creating and selecting scale items for the beta version of the *MMP*™

The next step in developing the beta version of the *MMP*™ involved creating hundreds of items for the scales, based on the definitions, by first *brainstorming* as many potential items as possible. Additionally, the above-mentioned colleagues and laypeople were requested to suggest a number of "questions they might ask to determine whether one is competent in the 28 factors based on the definitions."

The above approach created an item pool of approximately 800 items. Eight items were then selected for 27 of the 28 scales of the beta version of the questionnaire. The reason for selecting items for 27 of the 28*MMP*™ scales and not for all 28 scales was that one of the scales, Self-Image Consistency, is scored by averaging "absolute differences" between what are thought to be the most similar items within eight randomly selected scales. In order to avoid creating a lengthy questionnaire, which would be too demanding for many respondents and thus run the risk of "test sabotaging" (Anastasi, 1988; Bar-On, 1988, 1997; Jackson, 1970), eight items were selected for the remaining 27 scales, thus creating a questionnaire of 216 items. In that 5–7 items per scale is adequate for most psychometric instruments whose development is guided by applying multivariate statistics (Bar-On, 1997; Cattell & Burdsal, 1975; Tabachnick & Fidell, 2001), eight items per scale were selected in the beta version (a) taking into consideration potential cross-cultural difficulties in understanding the meaning of some of the items, and (b) to increase the possibility of a sufficient number of items loading on the same factor in order to statistically determine its nature and factorial strength (Bar-On, 1997; Cattell & Burdsal, 1975).

In selecting the items for each of the scales, an effort was made to capture all aspects of the definition of the factors they were designed to assess. In addition to avoiding item redundancy, which would artificially increase the instrument's reliability (internal consistency), at attempt was also made to select brief rather than lengthy sentences, as well as to avoid those with complex syntax. Additionally, the author avoided selecting compound sentences and items with potentially conflicting content, which make responding problematic if not impossible.

As was previously mentioned, nearly all of the items selected were worded in such a way to tap behavior and not the potential for behaving in a particular way.

The author also avoided items with religious, political, and sexual content, in order to reduce the risk of "test sabotaging"in some respondents (Bar-On, 1988, 1997).

(4) Editing the 216 scale items

The same psychologists and laypeople who were asked to comment on the definitions of the factors and create items for the 28 *MMP*™ scales were also requested to review the 216 items that were selected and "provide suggestions for improving them." To do this, they were asked to complete the questionnaire. Their feedback was used to further edit a number of the items.

(5) Applying statistics to shorten and statistically strengthen the *MMP*™

Applying statistics to shorten and strengthen the *MMP*™ represents the last phase in developing the final version of the questionnaire. As norming expands across cultures and provides increasingly more data, multivariate statistics will be applied to identify the psychometrically stronger scales and items that will be included in the final version of the *MMP*™. Based on past experience in applying this approach in test development (e.g., Bar-On, 1997), the final version of this questionnaire will most probably comprise fewer scales and considerably fewer items.

The beta version of the *MMP*™ is currently being normed and validated. An example of one of the largest such studies is being directed by Robert Morris in the US, who contacted approximately 40,000 potential participants to date. An additional example of an extensive norming project is also being carried out by Anu Sebastian in India, who is reaching out to a large number of participants. These two studies involve participants working primarily in public safety and security representing a wide variety of professions and occupations; and both of these projects are designed to examine the ability of the *MMP*™ to predict occupational performance rated by supervisors.

In addition to applying the above approach to concomitantly shorten and statistically strengthen the *MMP*™, additional statistical procedures will be carried out to examine the psychometric properties and strengths of the final version of this questionnaire. This will include procedures designed to examine mean values and standard deviations of scale scores as well as differences in scores based on gender, age, and other demographic factors, within and between normative samples. Additionally, scale reliability including internal consistency and stability, intercorrelations between scales as well as the nature of the questionnaire's overall factorial structure will also be examined. In addition to factorial validity, the questionnaire's construct, predictive and incremental validity will also be examined over time.

The Potential Applicability and Importance of this Model

The importance of the model presented in the present chapter will depend on the extent to which it will be applied and the degree to which it will be capable of enhancing performance in the end. If this model can be effectively applied in the following areas, for example, and provide significant results, this will demonstrate both its importance and its value as a model of performance: (1) parenting; (2) education; (3) career counseling; (4) human resource management; (5) healthcare delivery; and (6) research designed to improve performance. These potential applications are briefly explored below.

(1) Parenting. If the factors identified here prove to be significant predictors of performance and wellbeing, it would be important to apply this model as a *guide* to help parents raise children who are better prepared for life. Parents could be taught how best to strengthen these factors in raising their children. It would also

be helpful to empirically examine which of these factors are the strongest predictors of effective parenting and child development. Educational programs in parenting could be developed for parents to learn techniques designed to strengthen these specific factors.

(2) Education. As with parenting and as the natural extension of child-rearing, this model could also be applied in education for the same reasons. It could help enhance cooperative and constructive behavior in addition to improving academic performance. As with parenting, moreover, it will be important to examine which of the model's factors better predict the ability of teachers to be effective educators. In addition to the content that is traditionally taught in school (the *what*), it is no less important for youth to learn better ways of behaving and interacting with others as well as to enhance their performance in a variety of different areas (the *how*). As with parents, educational programs could be developed to teach educators what is important to know about successful teaching as well as successful learning.

(3) Career counseling. Career counseling is an extension of education and positioned between the school and the workplace; and here, too, it is thought that career counselors could also benefit from applying this multifactor model of performance. The author is interested in creating a *library* of occupational profiles, by applying statistics to determine which constellation of *MMP*™ scales best predicts successful performance in a number of different occupations. People requesting career counseling in the future might be asked to complete the *MMP*™; and based on their results, they could receive a list of potential occupations they are more suited for and in which they have the best chance to succeed. This could help them to make more accurate and cost-effective decisions regarding the occupation they choose to pursue.

(4) Human resource management. In addition to career counselors, it would be helpful if HR consultants could have access to a library of occupational profiles highlighting which *MMP*™ scales best predict high performance in specific occupations. This would help them make better selection decisions in hiring and promoting candidates to various positions. Such profiles could also facilitate the development of training programs for candidates selected for a certain position (i.e., to teach them what they need to know to be successful in that specific position, in addition to what they are typically taught). By using such an approach, HR consultants could increase the chances of selecting and developing high performers, thereby increasing overall organizational performance and productivity.

(5) Healthcare. If the factors that the author has identified are found to effectively predict health and wellbeing, as well as performance, the *MMP*™ could eventually be applied in healthcare. Healthcare providers might eventually use a brief and modified version of the *MMP*™ as a screener to provide a quick indication of the individual's current health and wellbeing, as well as to determine whether they are at high risk for developing health issues in the future. Once again, this particular application would depend on extensive research aimed at determining the degree to which the *MMP*™

is capable of predicting one's overall level of health as well as certain types of physical and emotional conditions, based on ICD-10 categories for example (World Health Organization, 2009). It might also prove valuable to examine which factors are capable of predicting medical compliance, as well as prognostic estimates and average recovery times from various disorders. Knowing more about the doctor–patient relationship might also be helpful in enhancing the therapeutic nature of this relationship to potentially improve medical compliance, prognosis, and recovery time in certain medical conditions. Such an application would, once again, depend on cautiously analyzing the findings from extensive research in this area.

(6) Research. In light of the fact that the author originally developed the *MMP*™ for the purpose of studying his proposed model of performance as well as performance in general, it is hoped that this instrument will be applied as a research tool to empirically study performance – what contributes to it, what improves it, and how it develops over time.

Concluding Comments

The present chapter described the author's 28-factor concept and measure of performance, as well as why and how it was developed. The importance of it being a multifactorial model, with an expanded assessment potential, was emphasized. This instrument's uniqueness is also seen in enabling a multifactorial assessment in *one* sitting and by completing a *single* psychometric instrument that takes less than an hour to complete. Additionally, it is web-based, easily accessible, and provides immediate results together with suggestions to improve performance and overall wellbeing. The possibility of psychologists using *one* psychometric instrument rather than *several* different instruments will significantly reduce assessment time as well as the cost of assessment.

Taking the above features into account, this unique approach could prove to be a valuable contribution to psychological assessment and perhaps represent a paradigm shift in this field.

The feasibility of applying the *MMP*™ in parenting, education, career counseling, human resource management, and healthcare delivery was discussed. It was cautioned, however, that the applicability and thus the value of this model in these and in other areas will depend on the extent to which its construct and predictive validity can be demonstrated.

The way in which this conceptual and psychometric model was developed suggests the possibility of a basic limitation. More succinctly, the development of the Bar-On Multifactor Model of Performance was based on the way Bar-On reviewed the literature and how he selected what he thought were the key contributors to and predictors of performance. It is very well possible that other researchers would have reviewed the literature differently, selected other predictors, and/or defined them in a different manner. Additionally, others might have decided to combine what were perceived to be similar factors and/or divide other factors into two or more separate factors.

Other possible limitations can be seen in not including more experts in the field of performance to provide feedback on the key predictors that were selected, the way they were defined, and the items that were selected to assess them.

A rather obvious limitation regarding the current presentation of this model is that it is still a *work in progress*, meaning that findings have not yet been analyzed and presented that examine the factorial structure of the proposed conceptual model (the MMP) and the ability of the measure of this model (the *MMP*™) to predict objectively rated performance. However, the norming and validation of the *MMP*™ has only recently begun as the final draft of this chapter was submitted to the editor. Although norming and validation is a lengthy process that continues for many years in test development, this represents the essential next steps that need to be taken in order to examine and further develop this conceptual and psychometric model.

Findings will be analyzed and published when sufficient results are available. In this regard, the author is most interested in studying the extent to which the *MMP*™ can predict academic and occupational performance as well as overall health and wellbeing. Those who are interested in using the *MMP*™ for research purposes and contributing to the norming and validation of this instrument are encouraged to do so.

In concluding this chapter, the author hopes that sharing his approach to concept-building and test development will be helpful for some readers. It is his desire that some will benefit from this and improve the process even further.

References

Altman, M. (2001). *Worker Satisfaction and Economic Performance.* Armonk, NY: M.E. Sharp.

Anastasi, A. (1988). *Psychological Testing* (6th ed.). New York: Macmillan Publishing.

Ashar, H., & Lane-Maher, M. (2004). Success and spirituality in the new business paradigm. *Journal of Management Inquiry, 13* (3), 249–260.

Baker, W.F., & O'Malley, M. (2008). *Leading with Kindness: How Good People Consistently get Superior Results.* New York: AMACOM.

Baron, H. (1996). Strengths and limitations of ipsative measurement. *Journal of Occupational and Organizational Psychology, 69* (1), 49–56.

Bar-On, R. (1988). *The development of a concept of psychological well-being.* (Unpublished doctoral dissertation.) Rhodes University, Grahamstown, South Africa.

Bar-On, R. (1997). *The Bar-On Emotional Quotient Inventory (EQ-i): Technical Manual.* Toronto, Canada: Multi-Health Systems.

Bar-On, R. (2004). The Bar-On Emotional Quotient Inventory (EQ-i): Rationale, description, and summary of psychometric properties. In G. Geher (Ed.), *Measuring Emotional Intelligence: Common Ground and Controversy* (pp. 111–142). Hauppauge, NY: Nova Science Publishers.

Bar-On, R. (2006a). The Bar-On model of emotional-social intelligence. *Psicothema, 18*, 13–25.

Bar-On, R. (2006b). *The EQ-i Leadership User's Guide.* Toronto, Canada: Multi-Health Systems.

Bartel, A.P. (1995). Training, wage growth and job performance: Evidence from a company database. *Journal of Labor Economics, 13* (3), 401–425.

Becker, T.E., Billings, R.S., Eveleth, D.M., & Gilbert, N.L. (1996). Foci and bases of employee commitment: Implications for job performance. *Academy of Management Journal, 39* (2), 464–482.

Boles, M., Pelletier, B., & Lynch, W. (2004). The relationship between health risks and work productivity. *Journal of Occupational & Environmental Medicine, 46* (7), 737–745.

Cattell, R.B., & Burdsal, C.A. (1975). The radial parcel double factoring design: A solution to the item-versus-parcel controversy. *Multivariate Behavioral Research, 10* (2), 165–179.

Cheng, E., Li, H., & Fox, P. (2007). Job performance dimensions for improving final project outcomes. *Journal of Constructive Engineering and Management, 133* (8), 592–599.

Collins, J. (2001). *Good to Great: Why Some Companies Make the Leap... and Others Don't.* New York: Random House.

Conn, V.S., Hafdahl, A.R., Cooper, P.S., Brown, L.M., & Lusk, S.L. (2009). Meta-analysis of workplace physical activity interventions. *American Journal of Preventive Medicine, 37* (4), 330–339.

Cote, S., & Miners, C.T.H. (2006). Emotional intelligence, cognitive intelligences, and job performance. *Administrative Science Quarterly, 51* (1), 1–28.

Fritz, C., & Sonnentag, S. (2005). Recovery, health, and job performance: Effects of weekend experiences. *Journal of Occupational Health Psychology, 10* (3), 187–199.

Galinsky-Zamor, J. (2003). Workplace spirituality and organizational performance. *Public Administration Review, 63* (3), 355–363.

Giacalone, R.A., & Jurkiewicz, C.L. (2003). *Handbook of Workplace Spirituality and Organizational Performance.* Armonk, NY: M.E. Sharpe.

Halbesleben, J.R.B., & Wheeler, A.R. (2008). The relative roles of engagement and embeddedness in predicting job performance and intention to leave. *Work & Stress: An International Journal of Work, Health & Organizations, 22* (3), 242–256.

Hsu, I.C. (2008). Knowledge sharing practices as a facilitating factor for improving organizational performance through human capital: A preliminary test. *Expert Systems with Applications, 35* (3), 1316–1326.

Jackson, D.N. (1970). A sequential system for personality scale development. In C.D. Spielberger (Ed.), *Current Topics in Clinical and Community Psychology* (pp. 61–96). New York: Academic Press.

Janssen, O., & Van Yperen, N.W. (2004). Employees' goal orientations, the quality of leader-member exchange and the outcomes of job performance and job satisfaction. *Academy of Management Journal, 47* (3), 368–384.

Judge, T.A., Jackson, C.L., Shaw, J.C., Scott, A., & Rich, B.L. (2007). Self-efficacy and work-related performance: The integral role of individual differences. *Journal of Applied Psychology, 92* (1), 107–127.

Karakas, F. (2010). Spirituality and performance in organizations: A literature review. *Journal of Business Ethics, 94* (1), 89–106.

Kuncel, N.R., Hezlett, S.A., & Ones, D.S. (2004). Academic performance, career potential, creativity, and job performance: Can one construct predict them all? *Journal of Personality and Social Psychology, 86* (1), 148–161.

Lennick, D., & Kiel, F. (2007). *Moral Intelligence: Enhancing Business Performance and Leadership Success.* Upper Saddle River, NJ: Wharton School Publishing.

Locke, E.A., & Latham, G.P. (2002). Building a practically useful theory of goal setting and task motivation: A 35-year odyssey. *American Psychologist, 57* (9), 705–717.

Locke, E.A., Shaw, K.N., Saari, L.M., & Latham, G.P. (1981). Goal setting and task performance: 1969–1980. *Psychological Bulletin, 90* (1), 125–152.

Markos, S., & Sridevi, M.S. (2010). Employee engagement: The key to improving performance. *International Journal of Business and Management, 5* (12), 89–96.

Martinuzzi, B. (2009). *The Leader as a Mensch: Become the Kind of Person Others Want to Follow.* San Francisco, CA: Six Seconds Emotional Intelligence Press.

Matteson, M.T., & Ivancevich, J.M. (1987). *Controlling Work Stress: Effective Human Resource and Management Strategies.* San Francisco, CA: Jossey-Bass.

Mento, A.J., Steel, R.P., & Karren, R.J. (1987). A meta-analytic study of the effects of goal setting on task performance: 1966–1984. *Organizational Behavior and Human Decision Processes, 39* (1), 52–83.

Motowidlo, S.J., Packard, J.S., & Manning, M.R. (1986). Occupational stress: Its causes and consequences for job performance. *Journal of Applied Psychology, 71* (4), 618–629.

Petty, M.M., McGee, G.W., & Cavender, J.W. (1984). A meta-analysis of the relationships between individual job satisfaction and individual performance. *Academy of Management Review, 9* (4), 712–721.

Pronk, N.P., & Kottke, T.E. (2009). Physical activity promotion as a strategic corporate priority to improve worker health and business performance. *Preventive Medicine, 49* (4), 316–321.

Rich, B.L., Lepine, J.A., & Crawford, E.R. (2010). Job engagement: Antecedents and effects on job performance. *Academy of Management Journal, 53* (3), 617–635.

Schwepker, C.H., & Ingram, T.N. (1996). Improving sales performance through ethics: The relationship between salesperson moral judgment and job performance. *Journal of Business Ethics, 15* (11), 1151–1160.

Sullivan, S.E., & Bhagat, R.S. (1992). Organizational stress, job satisfaction and job performance: Where do we go from here? *Journal of Management, 18* (2), 353–374.

Tabachnick, B.G., & Fidell, L.S. (2001). *Using Multivariate Statistics* (4th ed.). Needham Heights, MA: Allyn & Bacon.

Thomas, W.H., & Feldman, D.C. (2008). The relationship of age to ten dimensions of job performance. *Journal of Applied Psychology, 93* (2), 392–423.

Thorndike, E.L. (1920). Intelligence and its uses. *Harper's Magazine, 140*, 227–235.

Van Scotter, J.R., & Motowidlo, S.J. (1996). Interpersonal facilitation and job dedication as separate facets of contextual performance. *Journal of Applied Psychology, 81* (5), 525–531.

Weitz, B.A., Sujan, H., & Sujan, M. (1986). Knowledge, motivation, and adaptive behavior: A framework for improving selling effectiveness. *Journal of Marketing, 50* (4), 174–191.

World Health Organization. (2009). *International Statistical Classification of Diseases and Related Health Problems* (10th ed.). Geneva: World Health Organization.

Yousef, D.A. (2000). Organizational commitment: A mediator of the relationships of leadership behavior with job satisfaction and performance in a non-western country. *Journal of Managerial Psychology, 15* (1), 6–24.

9

Measuring the Dark Side of Personality

Ashton C. Southard and Virgil Zeigler-Hill
Oakland University, Rochester, MI, USA

There are certainly many personality features that are considered by both psychologists and the general public to be socially desirable and beneficial to harmonious relationships (e.g., agreeableness, extraversion). However, there is also a "dark" side of human personality that has garnered much empirical attention over the past decade. Dark personality features are broadly considered to be those that are found to be socially aversive and often reflect tendencies such as interpersonal manipulation, exploitation, and a general lack of concern for others (Zeigler-Hill & Marcus, in press). In this chapter, we will first focus on the conceptualization and measurement of a well-studied constellation of dark personality traits that are known as the Dark Triad (i.e., narcissism, psychopathy, and Machiavellianism; Paulhus & Williams, 2002). Second, we will briefly review empirical findings concerning these dark personality features. Third, we will turn our attention to recent attempts to expand the conceptualization of dark personality features. It is important to note that we will explicitly focus on *subclinical* levels of dark personality features in the general population, rather than focusing on personality disorders within clinical populations.

The Dark Triad of Personality

Paulhus and Williams (2002) introduced the Dark Triad of personality, which includes the personality features of narcissism, psychopathy, and Machiavellianism. Although there are similarities between these personality features (e.g., interpersonal manipulation is a common characteristic shared between narcissism, psychopathy, and Machiavellianism; Paulhus & Williams, 2002), they are considered to represent empirically distinct constructs because there are also important differences. For example, narcissism has been found to be strongly related to self-enhancement tendencies,

The Wiley Handbook of Personality Assessment, First Edition. Edited by Updesh Kumar.
© 2016 John Wiley & Sons, Ltd. Published 2016 by John Wiley & Sons, Ltd.

psychopathy is only weakly associated with self-enhancement, and Machiavellianism is unrelated to self-enhancement (Paulhus & Williams, 2002).

Narcissism

The personality construct of narcissism is derived from the Greek myth of Narcissus who tragically fell in love with his own reflection. Currently, extreme levels of narcissism are classified by psychiatrists and clinical psychologists as narcissistic personality disorder (NPD) in the *Diagnostic and Statistical Manual of Mental Disorders* (DSM-5; American Psychiatric Association, 2013). Although the construct of narcissism was originally conceptualized in the clinical literature (Furnham & Crump, 2005), social and personality psychologists typically consider narcissism to be a normal personality trait with adaptive and maladaptive features (see Cain, Pincus, & Ansell, 2008; Miller & Campbell, 2008; Pincus & Lukowitsky, 2010, for reviews of the distinctions between clinical and non-clinical conceptualizations of narcissism). In the studies that have focused on the Dark Triad, narcissism is generally characterized as exaggerated feelings of grandiosity, vanity, self-absorption, and entitlement (e.g., Morf & Rhodewalt, 2001).

There are a variety of contemporary measures of narcissism (see Campbell & Miller, 2011, for a review), but the most frequently used measure of narcissism in the general population is the Narcissistic Personality Inventory (NPI; Raskin & Hall, 1979, 1981). The NPI consists of 40 items that are presented in a forced-choice format such that respondents must choose between a narcissistic and a non-narcissistic statement to best describe themselves (e.g., “I am a special person” or “I am no better or no worse than most people”). The NPI is well validated and it is often considered to be the standard measure of narcissism in the general population (e.g., Paulhus & Williams, 2002). It is important to note that narcissism is generally considered to be a multidimensional construct and several researchers have proposed different underlying factor solutions for the NPI. Emmons (1984, 1987) proposed a four-factor solution consisting of Exploitativeness/Entitlement (characterized by interpersonal manipulation and exploitation of others), Leadership/Authority (characterized by enjoying leadership roles and having authority over others), Superiority/Arrogance (characterized by grandiose self-views, arrogance, and exaggerated feelings of self-importance), and Self-absorption/Self-admiration (characterized by obsession with personal appearance and uniqueness). Raskin and Terry (1988) proposed a seven-factor solution consisting of Authority, Self-sufficiency, Superiority, Exhibitionism, Exploitativeness, Vanity, and Entitlement. More recently, Ackerman et al. (2011) proposed a three-factor solution consisting of Leadership/Authority, Grandiose Exhibitionism, and Entitlement/Exploitativeness that has gained considerable popularity over the past few years.

In addition to the structural ambiguity of the NPI, its subscales tend to have relatively poor internal consistencies across the various factor structures that have been proposed (see Tamborski & Brown, 2011, for a review). This issue seems to be especially problematic for the subscales of the NPI that capture feelings of entitlement and a willingness to exploit others. Researchers often decide to use the total

NPI score rather than its subscale scores because of their poor internal consistencies. However, the use of the total NPI score has its own set of accompanying problems since it combines subscales that often have very different patterns of association with outcomes. For example, NPI subscales capturing entitlement and exploitation tend to be associated with outcomes that are indicative of poor psychological adjustment, whereas subscales that capture leadership and authority tend to be associated with indicators of psychological health (e.g., Brown, Budzek, & Tamborski, 2009).

Recent research using the NPI has examined whether narcissism is related to a wide array of outcomes. Narcissism has been found to be associated with increased prejudice and perceptions of immigrant threat (Hodson, Hogg, & MacInnis, 2009), use of self-enhancement tactics (e.g., Paulhus & Williams, 2002), and aggression following threats to self-esteem or status (e.g., Jones & Paulhus, 2010; Twenge & Campbell, 2003). Individuals with high levels of narcissism have also been found to view themselves as good leaders (Furtner, Rauthmann, & Sachse, 2011; Zuroff, Fournier, Patall, & Leybman, 2010) and believe they are higher in emotional intelligence than other individuals (Petrides, Vernon, Schermer, & Veselka, 2011). Additionally, higher levels of narcissism have not only been linked to larger financial losses in gambling (Jones, 2013), but also to unethical behaviors among CEOs (Amernic & Craig, 2010). Overall, research paints a view of narcissistic individuals as possessing an inflated self-image, being very defensive and protective of their self-image, believing they are superior to others, and behaving in ways that are sometimes unethical.

Another way of conceptualizing narcissism focuses on its pathological manifestations and distinguishes between grandiose and vulnerable forms of pathological narcissism (e.g., Miller et al., 2011; Pincus et al., 2009). Grandiose and vulnerable forms of pathological narcissism are usually measured via the Pathological Narcissism Inventory (PNI; Pincus et al., 2009), which consists of 52 items, and responses are provided on Likert-type scales. Grandiose narcissism (e.g., "I often fantasize about being admired and respected") is characterized by dominance, grandiosity, arrogance, interpersonal exploitation, and feelings of entitlement. Vulnerable narcissism (e.g., "It's hard to feel good about myself unless I know other people admire me") is characterized by introversion, negative emotionality, coldness, the need for self-affirmation from others, and internal grandiose fantasies.

Recent research has investigated similarities and differences in the way that grandiose and vulnerable forms of pathological narcissism relate to a number of intrapersonal processes and interpersonal behaviors (see Dowgwillo, Dawood, & Pincus, in press, for an extended review of these findings). For example, Lamkin, Clifton, Campbell, and Miller (2014) examined the relationships that grandiose and vulnerable forms of narcissism had with individuals' perceptions of their social networks. Their findings indicated that both forms of pathological narcissism were related to viewing one's close friends and family members more negatively, but that grandiose pathological narcissism was also associated with perceiving one's social network of close others as relatively unimportant. This is interesting in light of research indicating that individuals with high levels of grandiose narcissism are typically liked more by others in the early stages of relationships (e.g., Back, Schmukle, & Egloff, 2010), whereas individuals with high levels of vulnerable narcissism are not (Miller et al., 2011). However, the favorable impressions that others tend to form for grandiose narcissists tend to fade over time as they get to know the narcissistic individuals better and realize that they are disagreeable and emotionally unstable (Paulhus, 1998).

Psychopathy

Psychopathy is a personality feature that is characterized by callousness, impulsivity, reckless behavior, and criminality (e.g., Jones & Paulhus, 2011). Psychopathy has traditionally been viewed as consisting of two general domains (e.g., Harpur, Hare, & Hakstian, 1989): primary psychopathy (characterized by personality factors such as lack of guilt/empathy, shallow affect, and interpersonal exploitation), and secondary psychopathy (characterized by behavioral tendencies such as early conduct problems, promiscuous sexuality, criminal tendencies, and a generally unstable, antisocial lifestyle). Similar to narcissism, psychopathy originated in the clinical literature (see Furnham & Crump, 2005, for a review) and was initially studied almost exclusively in forensic and clinical populations (e.g., Cleckley, 1941/1988). The Psychopathy Checklist (PCL; Hare, 1980) and the Psychopathy Checklist - Revised (PCL-R; Hare, 1991, 2003) were developed to measure psychopathy in clinical and forensic populations, with the PCL-R often being considered as the "gold standard" of psychopathy measures (e.g., Acheson, 2005; Cooke & Michie, 2001). The PCL-R conforms to the traditional two-factor structure and consists of 20 criteria with scores that are computed by combining clinical interviews along with accumulated psychiatric data files (Hare, 1991, 2003). The PCL-R has allowed researchers to gain a better understanding of the nature of psychopathy as well as the behavioral tendencies that are linked with particular aspects of psychopathy (e.g., Book, Clark, Forth, & Hare, 2006; Gacono, 2000; Hare, 2003; Hervé & Yuille, 2007; Patrick, 2006).

Social and personality psychologists have suggested that there is a possibility that some individuals with psychopathic tendencies may be able to navigate the social environment of the general population and avoid involvement in the criminal justice system (e.g., Williams, Paulhus, & Hare, 2007). Williams et al. (2007) argue that measuring psychopathy in the general population using the PCL-R is difficult because it requires clinical interviews and reviews of individuals' past behavior. As a result, several authors have developed self-report measures of psychopathic tendencies that are intended for use in non-clinical/non-forensic samples (e.g., Levenson, Kiehl, & Fitzpatrick, 1995; Lilienfeld & Andrews, 1996; Williams et al., 2007). Because the PCL-R is considered to be the "gold standard" for the measurement of psychopathy (e.g., Acheson, 2005; Cooke & Michie, 2001), self-report measures of psychopathy have often been compared to the PCL-R in order to determine how well they converge with its underlying two-factor structure (e.g., Williams & Paulhus, 2004). One of the first self-report measures of psychopathy was the Self-Report Psychopathy (SRP) scale that was developed by Hare (1985). The SRP was followed by the Self-Report Psychopathy Scale - II (SRP-II; Hare, Harpur, & Hemphill, 1989). Research has been somewhat limited using the SRP-II because its items were never published.

Although the SRP-II was validated by Hare and his colleagues (e.g., Hare, 1991; Widiger et al., 1996) in forensic and clinical samples, Williams and Paulhus (2004) found that the underlying structure of the SRP-II obtained in a community sample did not correspond to that of the PCL-R.

Following the SRP-II, other authors developed self-report measures of psychopathy for use in the general population. Two of the most notable of these measures have been the Levenson Self-Report Psychopathy Scale (LSRP; Levenson et al., 1995) and the Psychopathic Personality Inventory (PPI; Lilienfeld & Andrews, 1996). The LSRP – similar to the SRP-II – was designed to measure the two factors of psychopathy suggested by the PCL-R in non-clinical populations (Levenson et al., 1995). The LSRP consists of 24 items (16 items that measure primary psychopathy and 10 items that measure secondary psychopathy), and responses are made on 4-point scales ranging from "strongly disagree" to "strongly agree." In contrast to the SRP-II and the LSRP which were constructed using the traditional two-factor model of psychopathy, the PPI was designed to be a more comprehensive measure of psychopathy and includes eight underlying subfacets (Lilienfeld & Andrews, 1996): Machiavellian Egocentricity (characterized by placing self-interests above the interests of others), Social Potency (characterized by social charm and effective manipulation tactics), Cold Heartedness (characterized by callousness and lack of guilt), Carefree Nonplanfulness (characterized by a casual lack of concern over forethought, or planning), Fearlessness (characterized by a lack of anxiety or fear regarding harm or injury and fervent risk-taking), Blame Externalization (characterized by consistently blaming others for personal misfortunes and rationalization of wrong-doing), Impulsive Nonconformity (reckless disregard for social morality or social norms), and Stress Immunity (characterized by lack of anxiety in response to stressful situations).

Recently, three-factor and four-factor models of psychopathy have been proposed as even the underlying factor structure of the PCL-R has become a somewhat contested issue (e.g., Cooke & Michie, 2001; Hare, 2003; Hare & Neumann, 2006). A three-factor model was proposed by Cooke and colleagues (Cooke & Michie, 2001; Cooke, Michie, & Skeem, 2007) who suggest that items on the PCL-R measuring antisocial tendencies should be excluded because they are not a core feature of the psychopathy construct. A factor analysis performed on the PCL-R that excluded antisocial items produced a hierarchical three-factor solution such that a higher-order superordinate factor of psychopathy was composed of three lower-order factors representing interpersonal tendencies, affective tendencies, and lifestyle characteristics (Cooke & Michie, 2001). However, several researchers (e.g., Hare, 2003; Neumann, Hare, & Newman, 2007) have criticized the procedures used by Cooke and Michie (2001), including their exclusion of antisocial items, because it is argued that antisocial behavior is an inherent aspect of psychopathy.

Four-factor models of psychopathy – as measured by the PCL-R – have also been advanced in recent years (e.g. Hare, 2003; Hare & Neumann, 2006, 2008; Vitacco, Neumann, & Jackson, 2005). These four factors include interpersonal (e.g., lack of honesty and trustworthiness in relationships with others), affective (e.g., lack of guilt and empathy for others), impulsive (e.g., lack of financial responsibility and disregard for safety), and antisocial lifestyle (e.g., criminality) tendencies (e.g., Neumann et al., 2007). Notably, these four-factor models include PCL-R items that measure antisociality, and this factor structure has been replicated using a short version of the PCL-R known as the Psychopathy Checklist-Short Version (PCL-SV; Hart, Cox, & Hare, 1995) which relies less on mental health records and can be used in samples drawn from the general population (e.g., Vitacco et al., 2005). A similar four-factor structure has emerged for the Psychopathy Checklist: Youth Version (PCL:YV; Forth, Kosson, & Hare, 2003) in samples of adolescent offenders (e.g., Neuman, Kosson, Forth, & Hare, 2006).

The factor structures of self-report measures of psychopathy have also recently been questioned (e.g., Williams et al., 2007). Accordingly, Williams et al. (2007) revised the SRP to create the Self-Report Psychopathy Scale-III (SRP-III), which includes more items that measure antisocial behavior and trimmed three items that measured anxiety. In two studies using samples of undergraduates, the authors found that the SRP-III is best represented by four underlying factors that resemble the four factors of the PCL-R in forensic samples. The four factors of the SRP-III include Interpersonal Manipulation (pathological lying, which maps onto the PCL-R interpersonal factor), Criminal Tendencies (criminal activity and versatility, which maps onto the PCL-R antisocial lifestyle factor), Erratic Lifestyle (recklessness and unpredictability, which maps onto the PCL-R impulsivity factor), and Callous Affect (lack of remorse and empathy, which maps onto the PCL-R affect factor). The four-factor structure of the SRP-III has also been replicated in community samples (e.g., Mahmut, Menictas, Stevenson, & Homewood, 2011).

Recent research has examined how the four factors of psychopathy relate to a variety of unethical and antisocial tendencies. For example, Hodson et al. (2009) examined how the facets of psychopathy – in conjunction with the other members of the Dark Triad – related to prejudice and intergroup threat. Findings indicated that the Callous Affect and Interpersonal Manipulation factors were both related to higher levels of prejudice as well as stronger perceptions of threat from immigrants, whereas the Erratic Lifestyle and Criminal Tendencies factors were not significantly related to either. Williams et al. (2007) examined relationships between the four factors of psychopathy and preferences for antisocial (e.g., enjoyment of playing violent, first-person shooter video games and watching horror movies) and prosocial entertainment (e.g., enjoyment of playing card games and watching figure skating), as well as engagement in a number of types of misconduct including crime (e.g., assault), bullying (e.g., physical intimidation), anti-authority behaviors (e.g., verbally assaulting parents or other authority figures), drug abuse (e.g., public drunkenness, misuse of heroin, cocaine, or other drugs), and driving misconduct (e.g., street racing, speeding). Results revealed that the Erratic Lifestyle, Interpersonal Manipulation, and Callous Affect factors were positively related to preference for antisocial entertainment, and that the Interpersonal Manipulation and Callous Affect factors were negatively associated with preference for prosocial entertainment. All four factors were positively related to bullying and anti-authority behaviors. Callous affect was the only factor unrelated to crime and drug misuse, whereas both Callous Affect and Criminal Tendencies were unrelated to driving misconduct. Overall, these results indicate that each of the four factors of psychopathy are related to antisocial and unethical behaviors, but these relationships are not identical.

Machiavellianism

Machiavellianism is a personality feature designed to capture dispositional agreement with the teachings of Niccolò Machiavelli (1513/1981), who was a philosopher and political advisor to the Medici family in Florence in the early sixteenth century. His advice for political leaders was published in his book *The Prince*, which suggested that leaders should be cold, strategic, manipulative, pragmatic, and immoral so that they could maintain control over large populations. The construct of Machiavellianism was introduced by Christie and Geis (1970), and it is characterized by strategic manipulation of others, extreme self-centeredness, cynical world views, and an intense focus on agentic goals.

Machiavellianism – in contrast to narcissism and psychopathy – has traditionally been considered to be a unidimensional construct and is most commonly measured using the Mach-IV scale developed by Christie and Geis (1970). The Mach-IV is considered the "gold standard" for the measurement of Machiavellianism (e.g., Rauthmann & Will, 2011) and consists of 20 statements (e.g., "The best way to handle people is to tell them what they want to hear," "Never tell anyone the real reason you did something unless it is useful to do so") with responses provided using scales that range from 1 (*strongly disagree*) to 5 (*strongly agree*). Although Christie and Geis (1970) developed a subsequent Mach-V scale that was intended to improve the measurement of Machiavellianism, the forced-choice format of the Mach-V proved to be problematic and it is rarely used (Wrightsman, 1991).

Although the Mach-IV is generally considered to be reliable and valid (e.g., Jones & Paulhus, 2009), and is the most widely used measure of Machiavellianism, it has not been revised for more than 40 years and several researchers have suggested that some of its items are outdated and that substantial revisions are needed (e.g., Jones & Paulhus, 2009; Rauthmann & Will, 2011). Rauthmann (2013) recently employed item response theory to develop a short-form of the Mach-IV that he referred to as the MACH*. In his analyses, Rauthmann found that many of the items on the Mach-IV had a relatively low likelihood of being endorsed and provided little information. As a result, he concluded that five items provided most of the information regarding an individual's level of Machiavellianism. The five items that constitute the MACH* reflect cynicism and misanthropy (e.g., "Anyone who completely trusts anyone is asking for trouble"). Rauthmann reports that the MACH* scale demonstrates adequate psychometric properties including good internal consistency ($\alpha = 0.77$).

Researchers have yet to make use of Rauthmann's (2013) MACH* scale, with the vast majority of recent studies continuing to use the Mach-IV. For example, the Mach-IV has been found to be associated with a number of other constructs including a negative association with emotional intelligence (i.e., one's perceived ability to understand and influence the emotions of others; e.g., Austin, Farrelly, Black, & Moore, 2007; Barlow, Qualter, & Stylianou, 2010). O'Connor and Athota (2013) found that agreeableness moderated the negative association between Machiavellianism and emotional intelligence such that it only emerged for individuals with low levels of agreeableness. This suggests that the link between Machiavellianism and emotional intelligence may not be as simple and direct as once believed because other factors such as agreeableness may also play a role.

Comprehensive Dark Triad Measurement

Researchers have stressed that the three components of the Dark Triad should be assessed in conjunction in order to determine the unique contributions of each personality feature (Paulhus & Williams, 2002). However, research assessing all three members of the Dark Triad has been relatively difficult because the instruments designed to measure each construct are relatively lengthy (e.g., Jones, in press). In order to address this issue, several authors have constructed relatively concise instruments that measure each Dark Triad construct. The first to emerge was the *Dirty Dozen* developed by Jonason and Webster (2010). The Dirty Dozen attempts to measure the Dark Triad traits with only four items each for narcissism (e.g., "I tend to want others to admire me"), psychopathy (e.g., "I tend to lack remorse"), and Machiavellianism (e.g., "I have used deceit or lied to get my way"; Jonason & Webster, 2010). Although several authors have cautioned against treating the constructs of the Dark Triad as interchangeable (e.g., Furnham, Richards, & Paulhus, 2013; Jones & Paulhus, 2011; Paulhus & Williams, 2002), Jonason and Webster have sometimes collapsed the three constructs into a single composite variable (e.g., Jonason, Li, Webster, & Schmitt, 2009). Soon after the publication of the Dirty Dozen, researchers began to examine whether or not the brevity of the measure sacrificed construct validity, and findings have indicated that this may indeed be the case (e.g., Miller et al., 2012). Unfortunately, the Dirty Dozen has been considered as a "cautionary tale" in the development of measures that attempt to briefly measure complex personality constructs (Jones, in press; Miller et al., 2012).

The Short Dark Triad (SD3; Jones & Paulhus, 2014) is another brief measure of the Dark Triad that has recently been developed. The SD3 attempts to measure the Dark Triad constructs with nine items each for narcissism (e.g., "People see me as a natural leader"), psychopathy (e.g., "I like to get revenge on authorities"), and Machiavellianism (e.g., "It's not wise to tell your secrets"; Jones & Paulhus, 2014). Researchers have compared the utility of the SD3 and the Dirty Dozen with regard to their convergent, discriminant, incremental, and criterion validity (Lee et al., 2013; Maples, Lamkin, & Miller, 2014). Findings have indicated that the subscales of the SD3 are more closely related to longer measures of the Dark Triad traits, and the SD3 is often considered to be the preferred brief measure of the Dark Triad.

Current and Future Directions

Research concerning dark personality features has increased substantially since Paulhus and Williams (2002) introduced the Dark Triad. This body of research has examined how the constructs of the Dark Triad relate to a wide array of outcomes (see Furnham et al., 2013, for an extended overview of these results). It is important to note, however, that researchers have acknowledged that narcissism, psychopathy, and Machiavellianism are certainly not the only personality features that should be considered "dark," as these constructs only capture a relatively limited range of aversive personality characteristics that are largely concerned with antagonism and manipulation (e.g., Zeigler-Hill & Marcus, in press). For example, Buckels, Jones, and Paulhus (2013) recently proposed that the construct of sadism (i.e., the humiliation of others, patterns of cruelty and demeaning behavior, as well as harming others physically, sexually, or psychologically for personal enjoyment) should be considered in conjunction with the Dark Triad, extending this model into the "Dark Tetrad."

One promising attempt to broaden the view of dark personality features has been to consider the model of personality pathology developed for the DSM-5 (American Psychiatric Association, 2013), which resulted in the development of the Personality Inventory for the DSM-5 (PID-5; Krueger, Derringer, Markon, Watson, & Skodol, 2012). The PID-5 assesses 25 specific facets of personality as well as five broad pathological personality dimensions, including negative affect (i.e., the tendency to experience various negative emotions and intense emotional reactions), detachment (i.e., avoidance of close relationships, social isolation, and anhedonia), antagonism (i.e., interpersonal manipulation, deceitfulness, and grandiosity), disinhibition (i.e., impulsivity, irresponsibility, and attention problems), and psychoticism (i.e., feelings of disconnection from reality, illogical thought patterns, and perceptual dysregulation). The dimensions of the PID-5 represent the maladaptive extremes of the Big Five personality dimensions such that negative affect aligns with neuroticism, detachment aligns with introversion, antagonism aligns with disagreeableness, disinhibition aligns with low conscientiousness, and psychoticism aligns with low openness (e.g., Gore & Widiger, 2013; but see Krueger et al., 2011, for different results concerning the similarity between psychoticism and openness). This is an important development in the measurement of dark personality features because it has been suggested that the existing measures of the Big Five personality dimensions typically capture moderate levels of these dimensions and fail to assess extreme or abnormal levels (e.g., Samuel, Simms, Clark, Livesley, & Widiger, 2010). Research utilizing the PID-5 is still in its initial stages, but the existing literature has provided support for links between the PID-5 dimensions and various maladaptive outcomes (e.g., Hopwood, Schade, Krueger, Wright, & Markon, 2013; Noser et al., 2015; Strickland, Drislane, Lucy, Krueger, & Patrick, 2013), suggesting that this instrument has considerable potential to increase our understanding of the darker aspects of personality.

Another recent attempt to broaden our view of dark personality features has been to focus on particular features that have traditionally received relatively little empirical attention in psychology. For example, Marcus, Zeigler-Hill, Mercer, and Norris (2014) developed the Spitefulness Scale, which was intended to capture individual differences in the willingness of individuals to incur costs to themselves in order to inflict costs on others. This view of spitefulness is largely consistent with its use in evolutionary biology (e.g., Hamilton, 1970) and behavioral economics (e.g., Fehr & Fischbacher, 2005). Marcus and his colleagues (2014) found spitefulness to be positively associated with the Dark Triad. Results have also found spitefulness to be associated with a hostile interpersonal style (Southard, Noser, Pollock, Mercer, & Zeigler-Hill, 2015), low levels of guilt (Marcus et al., 2014), a limited ability to interpret the mental and emotional states of others, and little concern for avoiding harm to others when making moral decisions (Ewing, Zeigler-Hill, & Vonk, 2015; Zeigler-Hill, Noser, Roof, Vonk, & Marcus, 2015). In summary, these findings provide preliminary insight into the nature of spitefulness, suggesting that individuals with high levels of spitefulness have a relatively difficult time interpreting the mental states and emotions of others, behave in an aggressive or antagonistic fashion, and feel little remorse for their actions.

Conclusion

It is our belief that research regarding dark personality features is indeed valuable and will continue to increase our understanding of human behavior in the future. Although research on the Dark Triad has greatly contributed to this understanding, we hope that advancements in the conceptualization and measurement of dark personality features will lead to many valuable expansions in our understanding of socially aversive behavior. There are a number of promising innovations in this field, so we look forward to the interesting avenues of research on the horizon for the study of dark personality features.

References

Acheson, S.K. (2005). Review of the Hare Psychopathy Checklist-Revised, 2nd edition. In R.A. Spies, & B.S. Plake (Eds.), *The Sixteenth Mental Measurements Yearbook* (pp. 429–431). Lincoln, NE: Buros Institute of Mental Measurements.

Ackerman, R.A., Witt, E.A., Donnellan, M.B., Trzesniewski, K.H., Robins, R.W., & Kashy, D.A. (2011). What does the narcissistic personality inventory really measure? *Assessment, 18* (1), 67–87.

American Psychiatric Association. (2013). *Diagnostic and Statistical Manual of Mental Disorders* (5th ed.). Washington, DC: American Psychiatric Publishing.

Amernic, J.H., & Craig, R.J. (2010). Accounting as a facilitator of extreme narcissism. *Journal of Business Ethics, 96* (1), 79–93.

Austin, E.J., Farrelly, D., Black, C., & Moore, H. (2007). Emotional intelligence, Machiavellianism and emotional manipulation: Does EI have a dark side? *Personality and Individual Differences, 43* (1), 179–189.

Back, M.D., Schmukle, S.C., & Egloff, B. (2010). Why are narcissists so charming at first sight? Decoding the narcissism-popularity link at zero acquaintance. *Journal of Personality and Social Psychology, 98* (1), 132–145.

Barlow, A., Qualter, P., & Stylianou, M. (2010). Relationship between Machiavellianism, emotional intelligence and theory of mind in children. *Personality and Individual Differences, 48* (1), 78–82.

Book, A.S., Clark, H.J., Forth, A.E., & Hare, R.D. (2006). The PCL-R and PCL:YV: Forensic applications and limitations. In R.P. Archer (Ed.), *Clinical Assessment Instruments in Forensic Settings: Uses and Limitations* (pp. 147–179). Mahwah, NJ: Erlbaum.

Brown, R.P., Budzek, K., & Tamborski, M. (2009). On the meaning and measure of narcissism. *Personality and Social Psychology Bulletin, 35* (7), 951–964.

Buckels, E.E., Jones, D.N., & Paulhus, D.L. (2013). Behavioural confirmation of everyday sadism. *Psychological Science, 24* (11), 2201–2209.

Cain, N.M., Pincus, A.L., & Ansell, E.B. (2008). Narcissism at the crossroads: Phenotypic description of pathological narcissism across clinical theory, social/personality psychology, and psychiatric diagnosis. *Clinical Psychology Review, 28* (4), 638–656.

Campbell, W.K., & Miller, J.D. (2011). *The Handbook of Narcissism and Narcissistic Personality Disorder: Theoretical Approaches, Empirical Findings, and Treatments.* Hoboken, NJ: John Wiley & Sons, Ltd.

Christie, R., & Geis, F. (1970). *Studies in Machiavellianism.* New York: Academic Press.

Cleckley, H. (1941/1988). *The Mask of Sanity.* St. Louis, MO: Mosby.

Cooke, D.J., & Michie, C. (2001). Refining the construct of psychopathy: Towards a hierarchical model. *Psychological Assessment, 13* (2), 171–188.

Cooke, D.J., Michie, C., & Skeem, J. (2007). Understanding the structure of the Psychopathy Checklist-Revised: An exploration of the methodological confusion. *British Journal of Psychiatry, 190* (49), s39–s50.

Dowgwillo, E.A., Dawood, S., & Pincus, A. (in press). The dark side of narcissism. In V. Zeigler-Hill, & D.K. Marcus (Eds.), *The Dark Side of Personality.* Washington, DC: American Psychological Association.

Emmons, R.A. (1984). Factor analysis and construct validity of the Narcissistic Personality Inventory. *Journal of Personality Assessment, 48* (3), 291–300.

Emmons, R.A. (1987). Narcissism: Theory and measurement. *Journal of Personality and Social Psychology, 52* (1), 11–17.

Ewing, D., Zeigler-Hill, V., & Vonk, J. (2015). Spitefulness and deficits in the social-perceptual and social-cognitive components of theory of mind. Unpublished manuscript.

Fehr, E., & Fischbacher, U. (2005). The economics of strong reciprocity. In H. Gintis, S. Bowles, R. Boyd, & E. Fehr (Eds.), *Moral Sentiments and Material Interests: The Foundations of Cooperation in Economic Life* (Vol. *6*) (pp. 151–191). Cambridge, MA: MIT Press.

Forth, A.E., Kosson, D.S., & Hare, R.D. (2003). *The Psychopathy Checklist: Youth Version.* Toronto, Canada: Multi-Health Systems.

Furnham, A., & Crump, J. (2005). Personality traits, types and disorders. *European Journal of Personality, 19* (3), 167–184.

Furnham, A., Richards, S.C., & Paulhus, D.L. (2013). The Dark Triad of personality: A 10 year review. *Social and Personality Psychology Compass, 7* (3), 199–216.

Furtner, M.R., Rauthmann, J.F., & Sachse, P. (2011). The self-loving self-leader: An examination of the relationship between self-leadership and the Dark Triad. *Social Behavior and Personality, 39* (3), 369–380.

Gacono, C.B. (2000). *The Clinical and Forensic Assessment of Psychopathy: A Practioners' Guide.* Mahwah, NJ: Erlbaum.

Gore, W.L., & Widiger, T.A. (2013). The *DSM-5* dimensional trait model and five-factor models of general personality. *Journal of Abnormal Psychology, 122* (3), 816–821.

Hamilton, W.D. (1970). Selfish and spiteful behaviour in an evolutionary model. *Nature, 228* (5277), 1218–1220.

Hare, R.D. (1980). A research scale for the assessment of psychopathy in criminal populations. *Personality and Individual Differences, 1* (2), 111–117.

Hare, R.D. (1985). Comparison of procedures for the assessment of psychopathy. *Journal of Consulting and Clinical Psychology, 53* (1), 7–16.

Hare, R.D. (1991). *The Hare Psychopathy Checklist - Revised.* Toronto, Canada: Multi-Health Systems.

Hare, R.D. (2003). *The Hare Psychopathy Checklist - Revised* (2nd ed.). Toronto, Canada: Multi-Health Systems.

Hare, R.D., Harpur, T.J., & Hemphill, J.D. (1989). *Scoring Pamphlet for the Self-Report Psychopathy Scale: SRP-II.* Unpublished manuscript, Simon Fraser University, Vancouver, British Columbia, Canada.

Hare, R.D., & Neumann, C.S. (2006). The PCL-R assessment of psychopathy: Development, structural properties, and new directions. In C.J. Patrick (Ed.), *Handbook of Psychopathy* (pp. 58–88). New York: Guilford.

Hare, R.D., & Neumann, C.S. (2008). Psychopathy as a clinical and empirical construct. *Annual Review of Clinical Psychology, 4* (1), 217–246.

Harpur, T.J., Hare, R.D., & Hakstian, R.A. (1989). Two-factor conceptualization of psychopathy: Construct validity and assessment implications. *Psychological Assessment, 1* (1), 6–17.

Hart, S.D., Cox, D.N., & Hare, R.D. (1995). *Manual for the Psychopathy Checklist: Screening Version (PCL: SV).* Toronto, Canada: Multi-Health Systems.

Hervé, H., & Yuille, J. (2007). *The Psychopath: Theory, Research, and Practice.* Mahwah, NJ: Erlbaum.

Hodson, G., Hogg, S.M., & MacInnis, C.C. (2009). The role of "dark personalities" (narcissism, Machiavellianism, psychopathy), Big Five personality factors, and ideology in explaining prejudice. *Journal of Research in Personality, 43* (4), 686–690.

Hopwood, C.J., Schade, N., Krueger, R.F., Wright, A.G.C., & Markon, K.E. (2013). Connecting DSM-5 personality traits and pathological beliefs: Toward a unifying model. *Journal of Psychopathology and Behavioral Assessment, 35* (2), 162–172.

Jonason, P.K., Li, N.P., Webster, G.W., & Schmitt, D.P. (2009). The Dark Triad: Facilitating short-term mating in men. *European Journal of Personality, 23* (1), 5–18.

Jonason, P.K., & Webster, G.D. (2010). The Dirty Dozen: A concise measure of the Dark Triad. *Psychological Assessment, 22* (2), 420–432.

Jones, D.N. (2013). What's mine is mine and what's yours is mine. *Journal of Research in Personality, 47* (5), 563–571.

Jones, D.N. (in press). The nature of Machiavellianism: Distinct patterns of misbehavior. In V. Zeigler-Hill, & D.K. Marcus (Eds.), *The Dark Side of Personality.* Washington, DC: American Psychological Association.

Jones, D.N., & Paulhus, D.L. (2009). Machiavellianism. In M.R. Leary, & R.H. Hoyle (Eds.), *Handbook of Individual Differences in Social Behavior* (pp. 93–108). New York: Guilford.

Jones, D.N., & Paulhus, D.L. (2010). Different provocations trigger aggression in narcissists and psychopaths. *Social Psychological and Personality Science, 1* (1), 12–18.

Jones, D.N., & Paulhus, D.L. (2011). Differentiating the Dark Triad within the interpersonal circumplex. In L.M. Horowitz, & S. Strack (Eds.), *Handbook of Interpersonal Psychology: Theory, Research, Assessment, and Therapeutic Interventions* (pp. 249–269). New York: John Wiley & Sons, Ltd.

Jones, D.N., & Paulhus, D.L. (2014). Introducing the Short Dark Triad (SD3): A brief measure of dark personality traits. *Assessment, 21* (1), 28–40.

Krueger, R.F., Derringer, J., Markon, K.E., Watson, D., & Skodol, A.E. (2012). Initial construction of a maladaptive personality trait model and inventory for DSM-5. *Psychological Medicine, 42* (9), 1879–1890.

Krueger, R.F., Eaton, N.R., Clark, L.A., Watson, D., Markon, K.E., Derringer, J., ... Livesley, W.J. (2011). Deriving an empirical structure of personality pathology for DSM-5. *Journal of Personality Disorders, 25* (2), 170–191.

Lamkin, J., Clifton, A., Campbell, W.K., & Miller, J.D. (2014). An examination of the perceptions of social network characteristics associated with grandiose and vulnerable narcissism. *Personality Disorders: Theory, Research, and Treatment, 5* (2), 137–145.

Lee, K., Ashton, M.C., Wiltshire, J., Bourdage, J.S., Visser, B.A., & Gallucci, A. (2013). Sex, power, and money: Prediction from the Dark Triad and Honesty-Humility. *European Journal of Personality, 27* (2), 169–184.

Levenson, M.R., Kiehl, K.A., & Fitzpatrick, C.M. (1995). Assessing psychopathic attributes in a noninstitutionalized population. *Journal of Personality and Social Psychology, 68* (1), 151–158.

Lilienfeld, S.O., & Andrews, B.P. (1996). Development and preliminary validation of a self-report measure of psychopathic personality traits in noncriminal populations. *Journal of Personality Assessment, 66* (3), 488–524.

Machiavelli, N. (1981). *The Prince.* New York: Bantam Classics. (Original work published in 1513.)

Mahmut, M.K., Menictas, C., Stevenson, R.J., & Homewood, J. (2011). Validating the factor structure of the Self-Report Psychopathy Scale in a community sample. *Psychological Assessment, 23* (3), 670–678.

Maples, J.L., Lamkin, J., & Miller, J.D. (2014). A test of two brief measures of the Dark Triad: The Dirty Dozen and the Short Dark Triad. *Psychological Assessment, 26* (1), 326–331.

Marcus, D.K., Zeigler-Hill, V., Mercer, S.H., & Norris, A.L. (2014). The psychology of spite and the measurement of spitefulness. *Psychological Assessment, 26* (2), 563–574.

Miller, J.D., & Campbell, W.K. (2008). Comparing clinical and social-personality conceptualizations of narcissism. *Journal of Personality, 76* (3), 449–476.

Miller, J.D., Few, L.R., Seibert, A., Watts, A., Zeichner, A., & Lynam, D.R. (2012). An examination of the Dirty Dozen measure of psychopathy: A cautionary tale about the costs of brief measures. *Psychological Assessment, 24* (4), 1048–1053.

Miller, J.D., Hoffman, B.J., Gaughan, E.T., Gentile, B., Maples, J., & Campbell, W.K. (2011). Grandiose and vulnerable narcissism: A nomological network analysis. *Journal of Personality, 79* (5), 1013–1042.

Morf, C.C., & Rhodewalt, F. (2001). Expanding the dynamic self-regulatory processing model of narcissism: Research directions for the future. *Psychological Inquiry, 12* (4), 243–251.

Neumann, C.S., Hare, R.D., & Newman, J.P. (2007). The super-ordinate nature of the Psychopathy Checklist-Revised. *Journal of Personality Disorders, 21* (2), 102–117.

Neumann, C.S., Kosson, D.S., Forth, A.E., & Hare, R.D. (2006). Factor structure of the Hare Psychopathy Checklist: Youth Version (PCL: YV) in incarcerated adolescents. *Psychological Assessment, 18* (2), 142–154.

Noser, A.E., Zeigler-Hill, V., Vrabel, J.K., Besser, A., Ewing, T.D., & Southard, A.C. (2015). Dark and immoral: The links between pathological personality features and moral values. *Personality and Individual Differences, 75*, 30–35.

O'Connor, P.J., & Athota, V.S. (2013). The intervening role of agreeableness in the relationship between trait emotional intelligence and Machiavellianism: Reassessing the potential dark side of EI. *Personality and Individual Differences, 55* (7), 750–754.

Patrick, C.J. (2006). *Handbook of Psychopathy.* New York: Guilford.

Paulhus, D.L. (1998). Interpersonal and intra psychic adaptiveness of trait self-enhancement: A mixed blessing? *Journal of Personality and Social Psychology, 74* (5), 1197–1208.

Paulhus, D.L., & Williams, K.M. (2002). The Dark Triad of personality: Narcissism, Machiavellianism, and psychopathy. *Journal of Research in Personality, 36* (6), 556–563.

Petrides, K.V., Vernon, P.A., Schermer, J.A., & Veselka, L. (2011). Trait emotional intelligence and the Dark Triad of personality. *Twin Research and Human Genetics, 14* (1), 35–41.

Pincus, A.L., Ansell, E.B., Pimentel, C.A., Cain, N.M., Wright, A., & Levy, K.N. (2009). Initial construction and validation of the Pathological Narcissism Inventory. *Psychological Assessment, 21* (3), 365–379.

Pincus, A.L., & Lukowitsky, M.R. (2010). Pathological narcissism and narcissistic personality disorder. *Annual Review of Clinical Psychology, 6*, 421–446.

Raskin, R., & Hall, C.S. (1979). *A Narcissistic Personality Inventory. Psychological Reports, 45*, 590.

Raskin, R., & Hall, C.S. (1981). The narcissistic personality inventory: Alternate form reliability and further evidence of construct validity. *Journal of Personality Assessment, 45* (2), 159–162.

Raskin, R., & Terry, H. (1988). A principal-components analysis of the Narcissistic Personality Inventory and further evidence of its construct validity. *Journal of Personality and Social Psychology, 54* (5), 890–902.

Rauthmann, J.F. (2013). Investigating the MACH-IV with item response theory and proposing the trimmed MACH*. *Journal of Personality Assessment, 95* (4), 388–397.

Rauthmann, J.F., & Will, R. (2011). Proposing a multidimensional Machiavellianism conceptualization. *Social Behavior and Personality, 39* (3), 391–404.

Samuel, D.B., Simms, L.J., Clark, L.A., Livesley, W.J., & Widiger, T.A. (2010). An item response theory integration of normal and abnormal personality scales. *Personality Disorders: Theory, Research, and Treatment, 1* (1), 5–21.

Southard, A.C., Noser, A.E., Pollock, N.C., Mercer, S.H., & Zeigler-Hill, V. (2015). The interpersonal nature of dark personality features. *Journal of Social and Clinical Psychology, 34* (7), 555–586.

Strickland, C.M., Drislane, L.E., Lucy, M., Krueger, R.F., & Patrick, C.J. (2013). Characterizing psychopathy using DSM-5 personality traits. *Assessment, 20* (3), 327–338.

Tamborski, M., & Brown, R.P. (2011). The measurement of trait narcissism in social-personality research. In W.K. Campbell, & J.D. Miller (Eds.), *Handbook of Narcissism and Narcissistic Personality Disorder: Theoretical Approaches, Empirical Findings, and Treatment* (pp. 133–140). New York: Guilford.

Twenge, J.M., & Campbell, W.K. (2003). "Isn't it fun to get the respect that we are going to deserve?" Narcissism, social rejection, and aggression. *Personality and Social Psychology Bulletin, 29* (2), 261–272.

Vitacco, M.J., Neumann, C.S., & Jackson, R.L. (2005). Testing of a four-factor model of psychopathy and its association with gender, ethnicity, intelligence and violence. *Journal of Consulting and Clinical Psychology, 73* (3), 466–476.

Widiger, T.A., Cadoret, R., Hare, R.D., Robins, L., Rutherford, M., Zanarini, M., … Frances, A. (1996). DSM-IV antisocial personality disorder field trial. *Journal of Abnormal Psychology, 105* (1), 3–16.

Williams, K.M., Paulhus, D.L. (2004). Factor structure of the Self-Report Psychopathy Scale (SRP-II) in non-forensic samples. *Personality and Individual Differences, 37* (4), 765–778.

Williams, K.M., Paulhus, D.L., & Hare, R.D. (2007). Capturing the four-factor structure of psychopathy in college students via self-report. *Journal of Personality Assessment, 88* (2), 205–219.

Wrightsman, L.S. (1991). Interpersonal trust and attitudes towards human nature. In J.P. Robinson, P.R. Shaver, & L.S. Wrightsman (Eds.), *Measures of Personality and Social Psychological Attitudes* (pp. 373–412). San Diego, CA: Academic Press.

Zeigler-Hill, V., & Marcus, D.K. (in press). *The Dark Side of Personality.* Washington, DC: American Psychological Association.

Zeigler-Hill, V., Noser, A.E., Roof, C., Vonk, J., & Marcus, D.K. (2015). Spitefulness and moral values. *Personality and Individual Differences, 77,* 86–90.

Zuroff, D.C., Fournier, M.A., Patall, E.A., & Leybman, M.J. (2010). Steps toward an evolutionary personality psychology: Individual differences in the social rank domain. *Canadian Psychology, 51* (1), 58–66.

10

Diversity and Assessment

Joyce P. Chu, Brian A. Maruyama, Ashley Elefant, and Bruce Bongar

Palo Alto University, California, USA

Background and History of Multicultural Personality Assessment

Multicultural research in psychology has increased dramatically in recent years, with growing evidence that cultural factors impact many aspects of psychology including symptom presentation, diagnosis, treatment, and assessment (Dana, 2000; Church, 2001; Leong, Leung, & Cheung, 2010). Within this cultural research, studies on culturally competent assessment have been less developed than other areas such as diagnosis and treatment (Dana, 2000). It has been recognized for some time that standard personality assessments carry some cultural bias and are affected by cultural influence. Yet, only recently has research begun to examine systematically the effects of culture to incorporate culturally competent assessment into standard personality assessment (Dana, 2000; Flaugher, 1978).

The need for culturally competent psychological and personality assessment is evident when examining the changing demographics of the United States. In 2010, 36.3% of the US population identified as part of an ethnic minority group (Center for Disease Control and Prevention, 2014a), and this percentage is expected to grow significantly in the coming years. The Latino population alone, for example, is estimated to comprise 31% of the US population by 2060 (Center for Disease Control and Prevention, 2014b). These changing demographics demonstrate the clear importance of developing culturally competent personality assessments.

Historically, culture has been neglected in the development of personality assessments (Dana, 2000; Hall, Bansal, & Lopez, 1999; Laher, 2007). One key example of this lack of integration of culture into personality assessment is evident with the Minnesota Multiphasic Personality Inventory (MMPI). The MMPI was first introduced in the 1940s by Hathaway and McKinley to evaluate personality, and it quickly became one of the most used clinical instruments for the assessment of personality (Butcher, 2004; Hall et al., 1999; Hill, Pace, & Robbins, 2010). However, this measure used a standardization sample that did not include ethnic minorities, and

The Wiley Handbook of Personality Assessment, First Edition. Edited by Updesh Kumar.
© 2016 John Wiley & Sons, Ltd. Published 2016 by John Wiley & Sons, Ltd.

was criticized by many researchers for being racially biased (Butcher, 2005; Dana, 2000; Pritchard & Rosenblatt, 1980). Subsequently, the instrument was redeveloped in 1989 (the MMPI-2) with the goals of revising test items that may have contained racial bias, and restandardizing population norms of the testing instrument to be more representative of ethnic minorities in the population (Hall et al., 1999). The MMPI-2 was also translated into several different languages, such as Spanish and Chinese (Butcher, 2004, 2005). These attempts to make the MMPI-2 more culturally appropriate represented important advances with regards to the development of culturally competent personality assessments.

Although multicultural personality assessment has witnessed important improvements over the past several decades, its development is still nascent with several challenges to the creation of reliable and valid personality assessments for diverse populations (Church, 2001; Dana, 2000). One source of these difficulties lies in a lack of diversity and assessment research, with limited generativity and dissemination. Second, the cultural assessment literature has been marked by a constricted focus on culturally adjusted norms and language translation as a means of developing culturally competent multicultural personality assessments. Although culturally adjusted norms and language translation represent an important part of the process, this narrow focus ignores other important cultural factors related to administration, interpretation, and validity of personality assessment instruments (Dana, 2000; Leong et al., 2010). Finally, there has been little theoretical guidance about the main ways or domains in which culture can affect assessment, and how assessment instruments should be developed, administered, and interpreted to account for such domains of cultural influence.

The purpose of this chapter is to conduct a literature review of current research on multicultural personality assessment, to establish the five main domains or ways in which culture informs assessment. Together, these domains constitute a solid foundation for culturally competent assessment to guide future advances in the research and practice of personality assessment with diverse populations. These five domains of culturally competent assessment include: (1) a need for differential norms that represent diverse populations; (2) assessment tools should represent culturally valid representations of the construct; (3) assessment scales should be constructed and interpreted to account for cultural idioms of distress and reporting style; (4) consideration of the cultural and technical context of the testing process; and (5) assessment feedback should be modified to account for culturally informed responses and expectations.

Differential Norms

Differential norms can play an important role in the interpretation of personality assessment results. Normative data provide a wealth of information by allowing researchers to compare an individual's raw scores to a population of similar individuals. Raw scores for assessment measures derive their meaning from standardization or normative samples with which they are developed and tested (Geisinger, 1994).

Without a sufficient degree of congruence between the standardization sample and the individual being tested, raw scores become meaningless. Thus, when using an assessment measure on a particular population, it is important to ensure the measure was normed on a population similar to that being tested.

Church (2001) described sample bias as occurring when normative samples of an assessment tool do not match respondent characteristics. These characteristics can include a range of cultural identities such as region of origin, ethnicity, language, and sexual orientation. Yet many factors and characteristics are involved in ensuring an adequate match between the test subject and the normative sample. With numbers of diverse groups in the US growing rapidly, it is critical for psychologists to appreciate the complex nature of culture. It is unfeasible to assume that two individuals from the same ethnic background will adhere to the same cultural standards, as differences within cultural groups are often greater than differences between cultural groups.

Acculturation has received particular research attention as a demographic characteristic that can affect outcomes of personality assessment and the validity of assessment norms (Vijver & Phalet, 2004). Research suggests that acculturation can affect basic personality characteristics such as extraversion, emotional stability, social desirability, or acquiescence (e.g., Grimm & Church, 1999; Ward & Kennedy, 1993). Thus, while many researchers simply gloss over issues of acculturation in assessment, Vijver and Phalet (2004) assert that the concurrent use of an acculturation measure can strengthen the validity of multicultural assessment through the use of differential cutoff scores, criterion data, or even statistical manipulation. Using acculturation scores as a covariate in regression models may also help to account for the role of acculturation in multicultural personality assessment (Vijver & Phalet, 2004). The use of acculturative information could prove invaluable in providing culturally competent personality assessment services.

When it is determined that the target population differs from the normative sample in critical areas or demographic characteristics (whether due to acculturation, age, gender, education, or others), a different set of norms may be necessary before the assessment results can be interpreted meaningfully. Indeed, research has highlighted the need for different norms with numerous well-known personality assessment measures. For example, on the MMPI, some cultural minority groups consistently demonstrate elevated scores on scales 2, 8, and 9 relative to the normative sample, indicative of the need for shifted norms rather than true elevations in pathology (Butcher, 1996). Because of notable differences between adolescent and adult populations, the Minnesota Multiphasic Personality Inventory (MMPI) – Adolescent was developed specifically for use with adolescent populations (Geisinger, 1994). The TEMAS version of the Tell-Me-A-Story projective personality assessment was developed as a specialized Thematic Apperception Test (TAT) for urban minority children (Constantino & Malgady, 2000). The developers found that tailoring the TEMAS to situations applicable to the target population yielded more accurate and significant results. More accurate results, however, does not imply that cultural differences were fully accounted for. Ambiguity and inconsistent interpretations of projective tests of personality make it difficult to discern the appropriateness of these tests for use with diverse populations.

Several challenges inherent to the creation of differential norms preclude its role as a universal or comprehensive solution to the need for culturally competent personality assessment. First, the empirical task of creating separate norms for different cultural identity groups can be a time-consuming and resource-heavy endeavor. Financial and practical constraints make it unlikely that specialized norms or versions of test instruments can be developed for multitudes of cultural subgroups. Second, because within-group variability is often greater than between-group variability, differential norms often represent an oversimplified solution inapplicable to the various response styles present within any one cultural group. Finally, norms based on a small subset of demographic characteristics become untenable as mixed race and multiple intersecting identities become increasingly common (e.g., which gender, age, or ethnic norms would one choose for a 68-year-old African-American transgender individual?). Despite these challenges, creation of differential norms has provided important advancements in accounting for cultural variations in assessment responses across diverse groups.

Cultural Validity of the Construct

Cultural variations in personality construct validity

A second domain in which culture affects personality assessment relates to construct validity – whether the assessment actually measures what it is supposed to measure (Geisinger, 1994). Construct bias is a term used to describe incongruence in conceptualization of a construct between cultural groups (Vijver & Phalet, 2004). A similar term, conceptual equivalence, refers to whether or not a construct assessed by an assessment instrument has the same meaning in different cultures (Dana, 2000; Leong et al., 2010).

Indeed, research suggests that validity of personality constructs can be inconsistent depending on one's cultural identity or group membership. For example, assessing personality based on trait-level differences may not be ideal in cross-cultural assessment, as collectivist cultures tend to be less familiar with Western practices of introspection and self-assessment (Church, 2001). These essential differences can lead to a host of issues that may serve to invalidate the results of personality assessments. When assessing an individual from a collectivist background, measures may require adaptations in wording to reflect a more relationally oriented version of personality, since individuals from collectivist cultures are more likely to act based on social roles rather than individual trait characteristics (Church, 2001). For example, in Western cultures, an individual may attribute his or her actions of caring for elderly parents to personality constructs such as conscientiousness, whereas in collectivist cultures, caring for one's elderly parents is an expected social role for children.

The most popular and well-researched model of personality – the extroversion, agreeableness, conscientiousness, openness to experience, and neuroticism factors of the Five-Factor Model of personality (McCrae & Costa, 1987) – has itself been questioned for its validity across cultures. Factor analysis research comparing Western measures of personality with measurements in non-Western cultures has revealed a potential sixth personality factor, interpersonal relatedness, suggesting that theories of personality may not be equally applicable or stable across cultures (Cheung, Cheung, Leung, Ward & Leong, 2003). Additionally, personality may be mercurial in nature, changing across the life span as a function of life experience.

A need for measures that assess culturally valid representations of personality constructs

Given the culturally variant nature of personality constructs, assessment tools should be evaluated and/or modified to ensure that they embody culturally valid representations of the constructs they assess. As establishing conceptual equivalence has proven to be a complex task, researchers have proffered different ways to evaluate construct validity in assessment. Factor analysis has commonly been used to ensure construct validity across cultures (Church, 2001). Factor-analytic techniques allow researchers to not only assess the validity of constructs between differing cultural groups, but also provide information on how some constructs may present differently in other cultures by looking at specific factor loadings (Geisinger, 1994). Alternatively, Geisinger (1994) suggested the use of an editorial board to assess and make necessary changes to establish conceptual equivalence.

Several personality assessment tools have been criticized for potential difficulties with conceptual non-equivalence. Projective measures of personality like the Rorschach and the Thematic Apperception Test (TAT) have been discussed as being based in culturally insensitive interpretations of personality. Although versions of these widely used projective tests have been standardized and normed with various cultures, it remains uncertain whether the Western psychoanalytic theories that the TAT and Rorschach are based on can apply to other cultures (Church, 2001). Geisinger (1994) observed that a personality assessment, such as the MMPI-A, that asks questions about going to a school dance or the movies may not make any sense to someone from a developing country. Although these questions may represent one construct in the US, this construct may not be the same across all cultures, and adaptations must be made to accurately examine conceptual equivalence.

In some cases when constructs are determined to be strongly culturally variant, entirely new "indigenous" measures have been created to fit the cultural needs of a population. Pursuant to a factor analysis showing a non-Western personality factor of interpersonal relatedness, the Cross-Cultural Personality Inventory-2 (CPAI-2) was developed indigenously for use in non-Western cultures (Cheung et al., 2003). With increasing diversity across the globe, however, there are practical limitations to developing indigenous or specific measures of personality that will apply to every cultural group. The growing number of individuals with intersecting identities confers additional challenges; straddling multiple cultural identities can lead to a variety of presentations that would require increasingly specialized levels of analysis. As a compromise, researchers in cross-cultural personality assessment have begun to find utility in integrating both universally endorsed personality constructs and culture-specific personality constructs to develop a more encompassing personality assessment for diverse groups (Leong et al., 2010).

Cultural Idioms of Distress and Reporting and Response Style

The third domain of intersection of culture with personality assessment states that assessment scales should be constructed and interpreted to account for cultural idioms of distress and reporting and response style. Idioms of distress refer to the various ways in which members of different cultural groups express distress and psychological symptoms (Nichter, 1981). These idioms of distress affect how people from cultural groups present their symptoms, what symptoms people feel, and how they report these symptoms to mental healthcare providers.

For example, individuals from non-Western cultures are more likely to experience mental health problems somatically rather than psychologically (Mak & Zane, 2004; Ryder et al., 2008). This idiom of distress can be seen throughout non-Western cultures, but is particularly salient for those from traditional Asian cultures. Assessment instruments have been modified to incorporate these cultural idioms of distress; somatic symptoms are added as one of three main factors screened in the Vietnamese Depression Scale (VDS; Dinh, Yamada, & Yee, 2009). An understanding of idioms of distress and the successful incorporation of these cultural differences into psychological tests is crucial for culturally competent assessment.

When considering the development of culturally competent personality assessment, cultural variations in reporting style should also be taken into consideration (Laher, 2007). Reporting style refers to how an individual reports his or her symptoms and how much an individual reports (e.g., over- or under-reporting) (Heiervang, Goodman, & Goodman, 2008), and response style refers to the way an individual responds to survey questions regardless of the content of the questions (Van Vaerenbergh & Thomas, 2013).

Culture can impact the validity of test results in many ways due to cultural differences in reporting and response style. Those from Western cultures (e.g., the US) are more likely to engage in self-enhancement behaviors than individuals from Eastern cultures (e.g., Japan), which can impact reporting style (Norasakkunkit & Kalick, 2002). Questionnaires may show those from Eastern cultures as having more severe symptoms, based on their lack of comparable engagement in self-enhancement behaviors, than their Western peers. This difference in assessment scores would be indicative of a difference in reporting style rather than a true difference in severity of symptoms (Norasakkunkit & Kalick, 2002; Leong et al., 2010).

Hamamura, Heine, and Paulhus (2008) also noted that Asian-Americans have a central tendency bias to report more moderate symptoms, regardless of the severity of the actual symptoms, than their Caucasian peers. Asian-Americans may therefore under-report the severity of their symptoms based on differences in cultural values alone. Finally, forced-choice responses – those that require either a "true" or "false" response – potentially limit the cultural validity of measurement. Having to choose between a "true" or "false" response may misrepresent responses from some cultures by not allowing for contextual, situational, and cultural factors to be addressed in the response (Laher, 2007). Laher (2007) suggested that in order to obtain the most accurate and culturally competent assessment of personality, a battery of tests combined with client interview would be most prudent for examination of all of the responses within the client's cultural context.

Overall, cultural variations in idioms of distress and reporting and response styles can result in an over- or under-estimation of true scores on an assessment instrument. It will be important for assessment practitioners to assess and note such cultural factors, and adjust score interpretation accordingly. Utilization of multiple modes of assessment can help to detect cultural differences due to reporting or response style, and all assessment results should be understood within the cultural context of the clients' lives.

Cultural and Technical Context of the Testing Process

In creating a culturally competent personality assessment administration, literature suggests that one must consider the cultural and technical context of the testing process. It is a common assumption that assessment measures yield consistent responses from the same respondent regardless of the type of room, examiner, or method of administration. However, one important factor in considering equivalence of assessments is the cultural and technical context in which the assessment is given (Flaugher, 1978), as people from different cultural backgrounds react differentially to several aspects of the testing environment.

First, the language (e.g., wording choice of the instrument, as well as test administration in an individual's preferred language) in which assessments are given can affect the validity of one's test responses. Linguistic equivalence, also known as translational equivalence, is focused on the accuracy of translation of test items. Many potential problems arise as the result of translating personality assessments from one language to another, such as differences in the meaning of words, differences in connotation, and masculine bias of wording. Furthermore, regional differences in word usage make it difficult to create linguistically equivalent personality assessments. Brislin (1993) recommended a translation followed by back-translation procedure (i.e., translating back to the original language and examining for parity with the original version) to help ameliorate non-equivalence issues. Geisinger (1994) recommended taking this process one step further, through the use of an editorial board who would back-translate the document as a group in order to discuss any possible differences in opinion or concerns about the translation. When working with more than one linguistically equivalent version of an assessment tool, one must be aware that issues of metric equivalence can still exist. Lopez and Romero (1988), for example, found that although there are many similarities between the English and Spanish versions of the Wechsler Adult Intelligence Scale (WAIS), there are important psychometric differences that preclude direct comparison between English WAIS and Spanish WAIS scores.

Second, characteristics or behaviors of the examiner or environment can elicit different responses that reflect cultural influence rather than the true construct in question. Stereotype threat, for instance, occurs when the tester or testing environment activates a negative stereotype about one's cultural identity group; research shows that stereotype threat can negatively affect one's test performance (e.g., Steele & Aronson, 1995). Stereotypes can be activated by minute aspects of the testing environment or materials (Thames et al., 2013). For example, discomfort by the examinee with the tester (i.e., because of previous negative experiences with others of a similar gender or race, or because of the tester's interpersonal mannerisms) may discourage versus facilitate open, introspective, and/or honest responses on assessment instruments (Thames et al., 2013).

Third, the method of test administration – termed technical equivalence – can also affect one's assessment responses. Ryder et al. (2008), for example, found that the same respondents reported different severity levels of symptomatology depending on method of test administration via spontaneous report, self-report questionnaire, versus in-person clinical interview. Specifically, Chinese participants reported more somatic symptoms than their Euro-Canadian counterparts when queried directly via clinical interview or spontaneous report. These group differences in somatization were not apparent when assessed via self-report questionnaire. Morrison and Downey (2000) found similarly that ethnic minority clients at a counseling center were less likely than non-minority peers to disclose suicidal ideation on self-report; a greater level of ideation became evident only after direct suicide risk assessment by a provider.

The mediating reasons why different methods of test administration or testing environment yield different responses in ethnic minority individuals is still largely unknown, though a cadre of cultural factors may account for such effects. Social desirability, cultural mistrust of healthcare professionals, cultural practices of expressivity versus inhibition, stigma about psychology, and so on, may represent cultural variables that could affect testing response and are deserving of further study. Clearly, research is needed to further quantify the effects of the cultural and technical context of the testing environment on personality assessment responses, and to identify the cultural factors that mediate differential testing responses.

When conducting assessment, it is essential to remember that many factors beyond the assessment items themselves, such as the cultural and technical context of the testing process, may affect the equivalence and validity of results (Dana, 2000). Although some factors may be out of the control of the test administrator, efforts should be directed towards minimizing extraneous factors, adapting the test environment to maximize open responding depending on the client's cultural background, and contextualizing one's interpretation of test responses within salient cultural influences in the testing environment.

Culturally Informed Responses to Feedback

Providing feedback about test results to clients is an integral part of the assessment process, with the field of psychology moving towards a more comprehensive model of feedback provision (Finn & Tonsager, 1992). In fact, research indicates that providing assessment feedback to clients in a professional and compassionate manner can, in and of itself, serve as a clinical intervention. A series of experimental studies found a number of positive consequences of providing empathetic feedback to college students after completing the MMPI-2 (Finn & Tonsager, 1992; Newman & Greenway, 1997). Compared with control participants who only received examiner attention, participants in the feedback condition demonstrated a significant decrease in symptomatology that persisted at follow-up two weeks later. Additionally, participants in the experimental condition evidenced greater levels of hopefulness and self-esteem compared with the control group immediately and two weeks following feedback.

Although few dispute the importance of giving assessment feedback to clients, there is a dearth of research investigating the effects of different approaches to client feedback, and even fewer investigations of feedback as influenced by issues of cultural diversity. There is a need for psychologists to understand potential issues that culture can present when providing feedback to clients.

For instance, some of the individual difference characteristics responsible for the effectiveness of assessment feedback may be culturally variant. In Finn and Tonsager's (1992) study, authors found that participants who were more self-reflective at intake were generally more likely to show positive reactions to MMPI-2 feedback. Self-reflection varies depending on cultural identity such as age (e.g., Haga, Kraft, & Corby, 2009), highlighting that one must account for cultural variation in self-reflection or other emotion regulation tendencies when tailoring one's approach towards assessment feedback.

Client response to the *mode* of assessment feedback may also be culturally determined. Feedback may be delivered by the provider via several modes: in person versus in a written report. Some providers may even decide it is prudent not to provide feedback at all. Most models of feedback provision have been based on person-to-person provision of feedback, emphasizing a humanistic component that engages the client and allows them to feel more involved (Finn & Tonsager, 1992). Yet, just as the technical context or mode of assessment administration can elicit different responses from different cultural individuals, mode of feedback can also elicit difference responses. For example, providing a written report of assessment results to a cultural minority client with a limited familiarity with or understanding of psychological and medical jargon may serve to alienate the client or decrease effectiveness of the assessment feedback.

A last example of cultural influence on assessment feedback involves expectations of involvement by the client, the assessor, and the client's therapist in the feedback process. According to Kreilkamp (1989) active participation by the client is a basic and important component of providing assessment feedback that motivates clients to take ownership of their results. The recommendation may be less applicable for clients from collectivistic cultures who may prefer not to collaborate as an active participant or advocate in the process of feedback provision. Cultures that value respect for authority figures may view client participation in the feedback provision as disrespectful or unwanted.

Providing feedback to clients about their personality assessment results can be a challenging, yet rewarding experience. The challenges become increasingly more complicated with the need for incorporation of diversity and cultural considerations. Clearly, flexibility and careful consideration of cultural aspects will be an integral part of competently providing feedback to clients. Additional research is needed to investigate recommended models of feedback provision with diverse populations.

Conclusion

The literature to date concerning multicultural personality assessment is rich with recommendations for practice and further research. As the field of personality assessment moves forward, it is essential that findings from the literature be incorporated into practice. Without awareness and knowledge of cultural differences, personality assessment can be misleading or inaccurate. Competence in personality assessment, as with psychological assessment in general, requires administrators to be knowledgeable about the appropriateness and limits of the test they are using, including cultural variables that can impact the testing process and test performance.

The current literature analysis indicated that development, administration, interpretation, and client feedback of results from assessment measures should incorporate cultural influences in five main domains: differential norms, incorporation of culturally valid representations of the construct, cultural idioms of distress and reporting and response style, the cultural and technical context of the testing process, and culturally informed responses to assessment feedback. By accounting for these cultural domains, personality assessment will have a better chance at creating a testing process with utility in a variety of contexts and diverse populations.

The future of personality assessment is ripe with potential. With accumulating research on personality across cultures, assessment is becoming more advanced. Further research investigating personality differences between cultural groups, within cultural groups, and across cultures is needed to enhance the validity of existing personality constructs and theories. Studies are needed to further identify cultural variables that may interfere with the substantive validity of true assessment results, to examine the ideal testing environment and assessment feedback conditions depending on cultural background, and to provide guidelines for incorporating idioms of distress and reporting and response style into culturally competent interpretation of test results. Research is also needed to investigate solutions to appropriately assess personality constructs in diverse groups without creating individualized assessments for the infinite numbers of cultural identity subgroups. The field of diversity and personality assessment is in a nascent stage with considerable potential for advancement. The five domains in this paper provide a basis to conceptualize the effects of culture on assessment, and provide guidelines for practice and future research in diversity and assessment.

References

Brislin, R.W. (1993). *Understanding Culture's Influence on Behavior.* New York: Harcourt Brace.

Butcher, J.N. (1996). *International Adaptations of the MMPI-2: Research and Clinical Applications.* Minneapolis: University of Minnesota Press.

Butcher, J.N. (2004). Personality assessment without borders: Adaptation of the MMPI-2 across cultures. *Journal of Personality Assessment, 83* (2), 90–104.

Butcher, J.N. (2005). *MMPI-2: A Practitioner's Guide.* Washington, DC: American Psychiatric Association.

Center for Disease Control and Prevention. (2014a). *Racial & ethnic minority populations.* Retrieved from http://www.cdc.gov/minorityhealth/populations/remp.html

Center for Disease Control and Prevention. (2014b). *Hispanic or Latino Populations.* Retrieved from http://www.cdc.gov/minorityhealth/populations/REMP/hispanic.html

Cheung, F.M., Cheung, S.F., Leung, K., Ward, C., & Leong, F. (2003). The English version of the Chinese Personality Assessment Inventory. *Journal of Cross-Cultural Psychology, 34* (4), 433–452.

Church, A. (2001). Personality measurement in cross-cultural perspective. *Journal of Personality, 69* (6), 979–1006.

Constantino, G., & Malgady, R.G. (2000). Multicultural and cross-cultural utility of the TEMAS (Tell-Me-A-Story) test. In R.H. Dana (Ed.), *Handbook of Cross-cultural and Multicultural Personality Assessment* (pp. 481–513). Mahwah, NJ: Lawrence Erlbaum Associates.

Dana, R.H. (Ed.). (2000). *Handbook of Cross-cultural and Multicultural Personality Assessment.* Mahwah, NJ: Lawrence Erlbaum Associates.

Dinh, T.Q., Yamada, A.M., & Yee, B.W.K. (2009). A culturally relevant conceptualization of depression: an empirical examination of the factorial structure of the Vietnamese Depression Scale. *International Journal of Social Psychiatry, 55* (6), 496–505.

Finn, S.E., & Tonsager, M.E. (1992). Therapeutic effects of providing MMPI-2 test feedback to college students awaiting therapy. *Psychological Assessment, 4* (3), 278–287.

Flaugher, R.L. (1978). The many definitions of test bias. *American Psychologist, 33* (7), 671–679.

Geisinger, K.F. (1994). Cross-cultural normative assessment: Translation and adaptation issues influencing the normative interpretation of assessment instruments. *Psychological Assessment, 6* (4), 304–312.

Grimm, S.D., & Church, A.T. (1999). A cross-cultural study of response biases in personality measures. *Journal of Research in Personality, 33* (4), 415–441.

Haga, S.M., Kraft, P., & Corby, E.K. (2009). Emotion regulation: Antecedents and well-being outcomes of cognitive reappraisal and expressive suppression in cross-cultural samples. *Journal of Happiness Studies, 10* (3), 271–291.

Hall, G.C.N., Bansal, A., & Lopez, I.R. (1999). Ethnicity and psychopathology: A meta-analytic review of 31 years of comparative MMPI/MMPI-2 Research. *Journal of Psychological Assessment, 11* (2), 186–197.

Hamamura, T., Heine, S.J., & Paulhus, D.L. (2008). Cultural differences in response styles: The role of dialectical thinking. *Personality and Individual Differences, 44* (4), 932–942.

Heiervang, E., Goodman, A., & Goodman, R. (2008). The Nordic advantage in child mental health: separating health differences from reporting style in a cross-cultural comparison of psychopathology. *Journal of Child Psychology and Psychiatry, 49* (6), 678–685.

Hill, J.S., Pace, T.M., & Robbins, R.R. (2010). Decolonizing personality assessment and honoring indigenous voices: A critical examination of the MMPI-2. *Cultural Diversity and Ethnic Minority Psychology, 16* (1), 16–25.

Kreilkamp, T. (1989). *Time-limited, Intermittent Therapy with Children and Families.* New York: Brunner/Mazel.

Laher, S. (2007). Personality re-conceptualized: A millonian approach. *South African Journal of Psychology, 37* (1), 82–95.

Leong, F.L., Leung, K., & Cheung, F.M. (2010). Integrating cross-cultural psychology research methods into ethnic minority psychology. *Cultural Diversity and Ethnic Minority Psychology, 16* (4), 590–597.

Lopez, S., & Romero, A. (1988). Assessing the intellectual functioning of Spanish-speaking adults: Comparison of the EIWA and the WAIS. *Journal of Processional Psychology: Research and Practice, 19* (3), 263–270.

Mak, W.W., & Zane, N.W. (2004). The phenomenon of somatization among community Chinese Americans. *Social Psychiatry and Psychiatric Epidemiology, 39* (12), 967–974.

McCrae, R.R., & Costa, P.T. (1987). Validation of the five-factor model of personality across instruments and observers. *Journal of Personality and Social Psychology, 52* (1), 81–90.

Morrison, L.L., & Downey, D.L. (2000). Racial differences in self-disclosure of suicidal ideation and reasons for living: implications for training. *Cultural Diversity and Ethnic Minority Psychology, 6* (4), 374.

Newman, M.L., & Greenway, P. (1997). Therapeutic effects of providing MMPI-2 test feedback to clients at a university counseling service: A collaborative approach. *Psychological Assessment, 9* (2), 122–131.

Nichter, M. (1981). Idioms of distress: Alternatives in the expression of psychosocial distress: A case study from South India. *Culture, Medicine and Psychiatry, 5* (4), 379–408.

Norasakkunkit, V., & Kalick, S.M. (2002). Culture, ethnicity, and emotional distress measures: The role of self-construal and self-enhancement. *Journal of Cross-Cultural Psychology, 33* (1), 56–70.

Pritchard, D.A., & Rosenblatt, A. (1980). Racial bias in the MMPI: A methodological review. *Journal of Consulting and Clinical Psychology, 48* (2), 263–267.

Ryder, A.G., Yang, J., Zhu, X., Yao, S., Yi, J., Heine, S.J., & Bagby, M. (2008). The cultural shaping of depression: Somatic symptoms in China, psychological symptoms in North America. *Journal of Abnormal Psychology, 117* (2), 300–313.

Steele, C.M., & Aronson, J. (1995). Stereotype threat and the intellectual test performance of African Americans. *Journal of Personality and Social Psychology, 69* (5), 797–811.

Thames, A.D., Hinkin, C.H., Byrd, D.A., Bilder, R.M., Duff, K.J., Mindt, M.R., & … Streiff, V. (2013). Effects of stereotype threat, perceived discrimination, and examiner race on neuropsychological performance: Simple as Black and White? *Journal of the International Neuropsychological Society, 19* (5), 583–593.

Van Vaerenbergh, Y., & Thomas, T.D. (2013). Response styles in survey research: A literature review of antecedents, consequences, and remedies. *International Journal of Public Opinion Research, 25* (2), 195–217.

Vijver, F., & Phalet, K. (2004). Assessment in multicultural groups: The role of acculturation. *Applied Psychology: An International Review, 53* (2), 215–236.

Ward, C., & Kennedy, A. (1993). Where's the 'culture' in cross-cultural transition? Comparative studies of sojourner adjustment. *Journal of Cross-Cultural Psychology, 24* (2), 221–249.

11

Future Directions for Personality Assessment: An African Perspective

Sumaya Laher
University of the Witwatersrand, South Africa

An examination of personality research on the Five-Factor Model (FFM) globally will reveal much research being conducted in Europe, North America and to a lesser extent in Asia (see McCrae, Terracciano and 79 Members of the Personality Profiles of Cultures Project, 2005). The implication of this has been the development of five-factor personality theory and assessment instruments that conform to the cultural milieu of these regions. However, in the last 10 to 15 years there has been increased recognition that the Five-Factor Theory and the Five-Factor Model need to become more cross-culturally valid and applicable in order to support the claims of psychic unity and universality (Laher, 2013). The work of Fanny Cheung and colleagues in the Chinese context was instrumental in highlighting this need, and has ensured that Asian research into personality has informed changes in the ways in which the structure of personality is understood globally (Cheung et al., 2008).

Researchers in South Africa specifically also recognized the need for African contributions to personality theory and assessment (Heuchert, Parker, Stumpf, & Myburgh, 2000; Laher, 2013; Valchev et al., 2014). A recent South African text entitled *Psychological Assessment in South Africa: Research and Applications* (Laher & Cockcroft, 2013) demonstrates the breadth of research being conducted in personality assessment in South Africa. Ongoing research is undertaken on the 16PF, the OPQ, the OPP, and the MBTI. However research on these instruments is conducted largely within corporate environments and results are primarily used to meet the requirements of South African legislation. Section 8 of the South African Employment Equity Act (No. 55 of 1998; amended in 2014) stipulates that psychological testing and other similar assessments are prohibited unless the test or assessment being used is classified by the Health Professions Council of South Africa and is empirically demonstrated to be valid and reliable, not biased against employee or group, and can be applied fairly across groups (Employment Equity Act (Act No. 55) 2014).

The Wiley Handbook of Personality Assessment, First Edition. Edited by Updesh Kumar.
© 2016 John Wiley & Sons, Ltd. Published 2016 by John Wiley & Sons, Ltd.

This legislation promulagated in 1998 was primarily in response to the misuse of psychological assessment by South Africa's apartheid government. Psychological assessment was used to justify job reservation and Bantu education for a number of years in South Africa, leading to sanctions against South Africa. This meant that South Africa had no access to international tests until sanctions were lifted in the early 1990s (see Laher & Cockcroft, 2014). This legislation induced a conscientization amongst South African researchers and practitioners, and research into psychological assessment across the fields in psychology began to emerge. As indicated, in the field of personality assessment, research was primarily conducted on international or etic tests imported by assessment companies primarily for corporate needs to meet legislative requirements.

Within this climate there were groups of researchers who chose to focus on the debates within personality psychology. More specifically the focus was on etic versus emic instruments, as well as the universal applicability of the FFM of personality. Two emic instruments have been developed (the Basic Traits Inventory and the South African Personality Inventory), and research projects using the NEO PI-R and the CPAI-2 have been informing the debates on personality theory and assessment in African contexts. These projects are outlined in this chapter, together with a critical discussion on the contributions of the key projects mentioned above towards informing developments on the understanding of personality structure globally. The chapter will conclude with recommendations for the way forward for five-factor personality theory and assessment using the findings from the South African projects.

Research on the NEO PI-R in African and South African Contexts

Much of the research on the FFM in the African and South African context has utilized the NEO PI-R. Evidence for the universality of the FFM comes from the study by McCrae et al. (2005) conducted across 50 cultures using the NEO PI-R. The lowest reliability coefficients in this study were from the African countries. Burkina Faso and Botswana exhibited coefficients that closely resembled those found in Asian cultures, but Nigeria, Ethiopia, Uganda and Morocco were visibly lower (McCrae et al., 2005). Also evident from McCrae et al. (2005) was the differential replicability of the Openness to Experience domain. Openness did not replicate well in Asian and African countries, with Thailand, Indonesia, India, Malaysia, Botswana, Nigeria, Ethiopia, Uganda, and Morocco demonstrating congruence coefficients of 0.84 or less.

Research in an African context found similar results. Piedmont, Bain, McCrae and Costa (2002) reported alpha coefficients exceeding 0.81 for the NEO PI-R domains using a Shona translation of the NEO PI-R in a sample of 314 Zimbabweans. However, only 14 of the 30 facet scales exhibited alpha coefficients between 0.50 and 0.65. The remainder of the facet scales exhibited coefficients below 0.50. Piedmont et al. (2002) also found that although the five-factor structure was obtained,

Extraversion and Agreeableness did not replicate as well as Neuroticism, and Conscientiousness and Openness to Experience replicated poorly.

Rossier, Dahourou and McCrae (2005) reported alpha coefficients for the five domains of between 0.71 to 0.85, with a median alpha coefficient of 0.79 in a sample of 470 French-speaking individuals in Burkina Faso. Facet scale coefficients ranged from 0.16 to 0.68, with a median alpha coefficient of 0.52 (Rossier et al., 2005).

Mohammed, Unher, and Sugawara (2009) used the English version of the NEO Five Factor Inventory (NEO-FFI) in a sample of 50 Japanese students as well as 50 Egyptian students. Cronbach alpha coefficients for the domains in the Japanese sample exceeded 0.83 for the five factors. In the Egyptian sample, Neuroticism had an alpha coefficient of 0.63, Extraversion had a coefficient of 0.76, Openness to Experience 0.75, Agreeableness 0.70 and Conscientiousness 0.73 (Mohammed et al., 2009).

Teferi and Laher (2013) reported alpha coefficients of 0.79 for Neuroticism, 0.50 for Extraversion, 0.45 for Openness to Experience, 0.73 for Agreeableness and 0.82 for Conscientiousness using a Tigrignan translation of the NEO PI-R in a sample of 410 Eritrean individuals. Only five facet scales (Depression, Positive Emotions, Aesthetics, Dutifulness and Deliberation) exhibited alpha coefficients in the range of 0.51 to 0.61; all other facet scales were below this. Teferi and Laher (2013) found a five-factor solution but it was only Conscientiousness that replicated as expected. Openness to Experience replicated poorly, and Extraversion did not replicate as a factor at all, with Extraversion facets loading across all five factors (Teferi & Laher, 2013).

In a South African context, results have been more variable. Heaven and Pretorius (1998) found support for the five factors with an Afrikaans-speaking South African sample, but found that the five factors did not replicate well for a Sotho-speaking South African sample. A study by Heuchert et al. (2000) indicated support for the Five-Factor Model on a sample of 408 South African university students.

Zhang and Akande (2002) explored the reliability of the NEO-FFI in a sample of 368 students from four universities in South Africa. Coefficients below 0.5 were found for the Neuroticism and Openness to Experience domains. Seventeen items with poor item-total correlations were deleted as follows: four from Neuroticism, three from Extraversion, five from Openness to Experience, three from Agreeableness, and two from Conscientiousness. Following item deletion, a 0.78 alpha coefficient was found for Neuroticism, 0.75 for Extraversion, 0.56 for Openness to Experience, 0.63 for Agreeableness, and 0.79 for Conscientiousness. Zhang and Akande (2002) reported that a five-factor structure could be obtained in a South African sample, but this replicability was weak and differed as a function of gender, race, educational level, and socioeconomic status.

Rothman and Coetzer (2003) reported Cronbach's alpha coefficients exceeding 0.76 for the five factors in a sample of 159 South African employees in a pharmaceutical organization. Facet-scale alpha coefficients ranged between 0.55 and 0.83 for all facets, with the exception of Values (0.48) and Tender Mindedness (0.34) (Rothman & Coetzer, 2003). Similarly, Storm and Rothman (2003), using a sample of 131 South African employees in a corporate pharmaceutical group, reported Cronbach's alpha coefficients exceeding 0.74 for the five factors, but no information was given on the facet scales in this study.

Also in the South African context, Laher and Quy (2009) reported reliability coefficients ranging from 0.89 to 0.92 on the domain scales and coefficients ranging from 0.52 to 0.82 for the facet scales, using a sample of 94 psychology undergraduate students at a university in Johannesburg. However, the facet scales of Activity (0.45), Actions (0.49), and Tender-Mindedness (0.48) had alpha coefficients less than 0.5 (Laher & Quy, 2009).

The most recent evidence for the reliability of the five factors comes from Laher (2010) who considered the applicability of the NEO PI-R in a sample of 425 students at a university in Johannesburg, South Africa. Reliability coefficients exceeded 0.87 for all five factors. Facet-scale reliability coefficients ranged between 0.50 and 0.81, but with the exception of Tender-Mindedness (0.50) and Actions (0.55), all other facets had reliability coefficients at or exceeding 0.60.

From the literature presented above, it is evident that internal consistency reliability is poorer in African countries. Reliability coefficients were particularly poor in African countries that used translated versions, adding weight to the argument around the poorer data quality of translated versions (see McCrae et al., 2005; Piedmont et al., 2002). Alternately, Piedmont et al. (2002) suggested the possibility that African languages like the Shona language may lack equivalent terms for the English language items. This concurs with findings by Teferi and Laher (2013) with the Eritrean translation, as well as with those from an unpublished thesis which examined a Xhosa translation of the NEO PI-R (Horn, 2000).

The questionnaire format might also have been foreign to these cultures, resulting in artefactual results. Piedmont et al. (2002) also alluded to the possibility that differences may occur in response styles and response biases in African samples. Allik and McCrae (2004) argued that acquiescent response biases as well as a tendency to avoid extreme responses are more prominent in collectivistic cultures, but this case of metric equivalence has yet to be fully explored in an African context. In a South African context, Laher (2010) found evidence for method bias across home language that contradicts the findings of Allik and McCrae (2004) that English second language speakers are more likely to endorse extreme responses.

Reliability coefficients were better with studies using the English version of the NEO PI-R particularly in the South African context, but with the exception of Laher's (2010) and Laher and Quy's (2009) study, they were still lower than the coefficients for other countries reported in McCrae et al. (2005). Thus, in all the studies cited above, language proficiency in English is cited as playing a role in the observed differences. These studies do not, however, underestimate the role of true cultural differences. The possibility exists that there may be some underlying elemental differences based on cultural experience that have yet to be discovered and explored. McCrae et al. (2005) argued that it is possible that Africans may have certain emic dimensions of personality that set them apart from non-Africans. This concurs with Piedmont et al. (2002) who posited the possibility that some of the constructs measured by the NEO PI-R may have no counterpart in Shona culture, especially at the facet level. They cite the example of Excitement Seeking (an essentially self-centered motivation), which is foreign in collectivistic cultures. Teferi and Laher (2013) also found Excitement Seeking problematic in the Tigrignan translation both in terms of translation as well as replication.

McCrae et al. (2005) also argued that these results may be due to the fact that the NEO PI-R was developed within a Western tradition, and completing it may be a more meaningful task for Westerners than for non-Westerners. Allik and McCrae (2004) suggested the possibility that traits like Extraversion and Openness to Experience are more valued and therefore more readily endorsed in Western cultures, whereas cooperation and tradition are more valued in non-Western cultures.

Furthermore, African cultures according to McCrae et al. (2005) share certain features such as close bonds within the family and a traumatic history of European colonialism that might have led to similarities in personality structure. When the African cultures were combined (N = 940), better congruence coefficients were obtained. A congruence coefficient of 0.96 was found for Neuroticism, 0.91 for Extraversion, 0.88 for Openness to Experience, 0.95 for Agreeableness and 0.96 for Conscientiousness (McCrae et al., 2005).

Piedmont et al. (2002) also discussed the weak replicability of Openness to Experience, suggesting that this is a heritable trait but that its development may be primarily in relation to urbanization and industrialization, and would therefore not feature in non-industrialized, agrarian cultures.

Whilst this may be a possibility for certain parts of Africa, it is certainly not the case for a large part of the continent, and particularly in South Africa where the studies cited were conducted with relatively urbanized and industrialized individuals. In 1999, Okeke, Draguns, Sheku and Allen argued in support of this, despite the presentation of African cultures as "slowly changing, rural, and small cultural groups untouched by the worldwide social, political, economic, and technological transformations of the 20th century. Yet, the typical contemporary African is more likely to be resident of the urban conglomerates in and around Accra, Dakar, Johannesburg, Kinshasa, Lagos and Nairobi" (p. 140).

This argument may assist in explaining in Laher and Quy's (2009) and Laher's (2010) results. Contrary to the literature, which suggested that alpha coefficients would be lower in African samples, Laher's (2010) study suggested that the internal consistency reliability of the NEO PI-R is equivalent to that found in the US and other Western and some Eastern countries (e.g., Japan, South Korea, Hong Kong, Turkey) (see McCrae et al., 2005). According to Laher (2010), sufficient agreement with the normative sample was found to support evidence for the applicability of the NEO PI-R and by extension the FFM in a sample of South African university students. This variation in results may be linked to the samples used in the studies. Laher (2010) used university students who are generally described as more individualistic as well as more acculturated to Western culture (Van Dyk & De Kock, 2004). Hence the NEO PI-R and by extension the FFM appears to replicate better in individualistic samples.

However, one does need to examine in line with McCrae et al. (2005) and Piedmont et al. (2002) whether there are emic expressions of personality in African cultures. Two projects in South Africa sought to do this. The first project developed the Basic Traits Inventory which used the FFM as a starting point to create an instrument that would measure personality in a South African context (Taylor & De Bruin, 2013). The second project used a bottom-up approach similar to that of

Cheung et al. (2008). South African individuals from all cultural groups in South Africa were interviewed, and these data were used to develop the South African Personality Inventory (SAPI).

The Basic Traits Inventory (BTI)

The BTI measures the five factors of Neuroticism, Extraversion, Openness to Experience, Agreeableness, and Conscientiousness. Neuroticism consists of four facets, whilst the other four factors have five facets each (see Taylor & de Bruin, 2013). The nomenclature and flavour of some of the facets are similar to those of the NEO PI-R but others have a slightly different focus. For example, Extraversion on the BTI consists of Gregariousness, Positive Affectivity, Ascendance, Excitement-Seeking, and Liveliness (Taylor & De Bruin, 2006).

The Basic Traits Inventory (BTI) is a self-report instrument consisting of 193 items and requires approximately 30–45 minutes to complete. It is suitable for individuals from the age of 16 years with a minimum educational level of grade ten. BTI items are answered on a 5-point scale ranging from strongly agree (1) to strongly disagree (5). The test was standardized on a group of 5,352 South Africans, the majority of whom were students, while others worked in a call centre or in the police service. Internal consistency reliability coefficients exceeded 0.79 for the factors across several studies (see Taylor & de Bruin, 2013). The factor analysis, for determining the construct validity of the BTI, demonstrated a satisfactory fit with the FFM of personality (Taylor & de Bruin, 2013). These results provide evidence for the replicability of the FFM using an emic instrument. However, all the samples mentioned in Taylor and de Bruin (2013) are from urban settings with participants who are fluent in English and who have at least a Grade 12 education. Taylor (2008) found evidence for response bias in that indigenous African language speaking groups hardly ever used the "disagree" and "agree" options, usually opting for more extreme responding.

The South African Personality Inventory Project (SAPI)

The South African Personality Inventory (SAPI) project aims at developing a single, unified personality inventory for South Africa that incorporates both universal (etic) and unique (emic) personality factors found across the diversity of cultures in this country. In the first stage of this project, structured interviews were conducted with 1,308 South Africans from the 11 language groups to gather information about personality-descriptive terms. This resulted in 50,000 personality-descriptive terms, which were reduced to 190 personality dimensions via the use of cluster analysis. The 190 dimensions were further clustered and finally resulted in nine clusters, namely Extraversion, Soft-Heartedness, Conscientiousness, Emotional Stability, Intellect, Openness, Integrity, Relationship Harmony, and Facilitating (Nel et al., 2012). The quantitative phase of this project is currently under way. Hill et al. (2013) administered 2,573 items on a convenience sample of 6,735 participants. They found that 2,268 items were valid and reliable representations of the SAPI facets, and are currently working on further refining the items to develop the SAPI.

Valchev et al. (2011, 2013) analysed the data of Nel et al. (2012) further and found support for the distinction between two broad clusters in the SAPI, with one cluster representing primarily agentic or personal-growth elements (Conscientiousness, Extraversion, Intellect, Openness, Emotional Stability, and Integrity) and a second cluster representing a more communal or social-relational cluster (Facilitating, Relationship Harmony, and Soft-Heartedness). In South Africa, the population is split (primarily due to apartheid separatist development policies) into a Black group (consisting of indigenous South African ethnic groups, people of Indian or South Asian descent, and people of mixed race ancestry) and a White group (consisting of people of European descent). The White group tends to display more individualistic tendencies whilst the Black group shows more collectivistic tendencies (Valchev et al., 2011; Laher, 2015). Valchev et al. (2013) found that the personal-growth factor was more prevalent in the White grouping and the social-relational cluster was more prevalent in the Black grouping. This finding speaks to Wiggins and Trapnell (1996), who suggested that Agency and Communion were the two most important personality factors in their dyadic interactional model of personality. It also brings to the fore the arguments discussed earlier as to the replicability of the FFM in African contexts. Within the Individualism–Collectivism framework (Triandis, 2001), Africans also generally score more towards Collectivism (see Hofstede, 2014). Hence the variability in replicability of the FFM may be linked to the cultural distinctions on the Individualism–Collectivism continuum. Valchev et al. (2011) reported that Black individuals described personality more along situational and contextual referents rather than using traited terms, whilst White individuals used more trait descriptions. Valchev et al. (2011) cite the example of Openness and Intellect, which are largely identified as being amongst the least replicable factor in collectivistic cultures like the African cultures, but which was found in their study with a more communal flavour. Openness amongst Black indigenous South African groups was expressed not as being intelligent but as being socially intelligent and clever in practical situations, and not only being knowledgeable but also as sharing knowledge. Evidence for the social-relational aspect of personality was also obtained using the CPAI-2 in the South African context.

Research on the Cross-Cultural Personality Assessment Inventory-2 (CPAI-2)

As indicated earlier in this chapter, Cheung et al. (2008) argued that while the FFM was recoverable using the NEO PI-R in a Chinese setting, it did not provide a comprehensive description of personality. Most notably, what was lacking were the interdependent aspects of Chinese culture and by extension Chinese personality. Thus Cheung and colleagues began work on developing an indigenous personality inventory, the culmination of which is the current Cross-Cultural Personality Assessment Inventory-2 (CPAI-2).

The CPAI-2 (English version) is a self-report instrument consisting of 341 items, which are answered in a dichotomous (true/false) response format. It takes approximately 90 minutes to complete and is suitable for individuals in the age range of 18 to 70 with at least a Grade 6 level of education (Cheung et al., 2008). The CPAI-2 has 28 personality scales, which group into four factors, namely Social Potency/Expansiveness (8 scales), Dependability (9 scales), Accommodation (5 scales), and Interpersonal Relatedness (6 scales). Evidence in support of this four-factor model, which includes both personal and social relational elements, was found in Asian, American, Dutch, and Romanian contexts (see Laher, 2015).

Branco e Silva and Laher (2012) explored the CPAI-2 Interpersonal Relatedness factor in relation to the SAPI social relational cluster in a sample of 489 South African students using a joint factor analysis. Results revealed four factors. The first factor had loadings on the Integrity, and Relationship Harmony clusters of the SAPI, and Social Sensitivity from the CPAI-2 Interpersonal Relatedness factor. Factor 2 had loadings from the Harmony cluster of the SAPI and the Harmony subscale from the CPAI-2 Interpersonal Relatedness factor. The third factor had loadings from Traditionalism vs Modernity, Discipline, Thrift vs Extravagance, and Ren Qing from the CPAI-2 Interpersonal Relatedness factor. The final factor represented the validity and social desirability scales. Mean differences across language and ethnic groupings were also explored. Second-language English speakers and Blacks scored significantly higher than White English first-language speakers on Interpersonal Relatedness, Traditionalism vs Modernity, and Facilitating, but significantly lower on Integrity. Laher (2015) administered the CPAI-2 and NEO PI-R to 425 South African university students. Laher (2015) found support for the FFM from both instruments, but the results also indicated empirical support for a social relational aspect of personality as evident from the CPAI-2 factors and scales. Valchev et al. (2014) administered a combination of the SAPI social-relational scales and either the BTI (Taylor & De Bruin, 2006) or the CPAI's Interpersonal Relatedness scales to a sample of 1,043 Black and 440 White students. They found that the SAPI social-relational scales were more strongly related to the relational than the tradition-focused aspects of the CPAI-2 Interpersonal Relatedness dimension. The social-relational scales were also structurally equivalent for Black and White individuals, providing further evidence for the relevance of social-relational aspects to individualist contexts.

Implications for the FFM

From the discussion it is evident that the psychic unity of the FFM is supported. However, particularly in African contexts with populations that can be described as more collectivist, the FFM does not replicate clearly. Several reasons for this were postulated by McCrae et al. (2005), Piedmont et al. (2002) and Allik and McCrae (2004). Empirical research on the NEO PI-R, the BTI, the SAPI, and the CPAI-2 have allowed for further exploration of the variability of these results, and support the argument that the FFM replicates more clearly in samples that are more individualist. Evidence from the SAPI and CPAI-2 studies indicate that a social-relational cluster is definitely supported in the South African and Asian contexts. The Interpersonal Relatedness component from the CPAI-2 was found to replicate in American, Dutch, and Romanian samples (see Laher, 2015). Hence it is clear that the FFM is currently lacking a social-relational component.

Valchev et al. (2011) demonstrated a further difference in which personality is expressed across individualist and collectivist cultures, with individuals in collectivist cultures using more situational and context-based terms to describe personality. This evidence suggests that exploring the replicability of the FFM using an instrument like the NEO PI-R in more collectivist African cultures will result in poor replicability as the traitedness of the personality descriptions in the items in such an inventory will not be congruent with the ways in which personality is expressed in these contexts. Aside from the item-level, there is likely to be incongruence at the level of construct conceptualization as indicated in the Openness example from Valchev et al. (2011). Teferi and Laher (2013) found a similar scenario with the expression of Extraversion in Eritrean culture where it was thought that the trait did exist but replicated poorly only because of the way in which it was conceptualized and operationalized in the NEO PI-R. As it is measured in the NEO PI-R, Extraversion is conceptualized as an outgoing, gregarious, and excitement-seeking construct that did not fit in with the Eritrean understanding of Extraversion, as Eritreans are generally described as a whole as being less quiet and not as gregarious. Valchev et al. (2014) make reference to the differential expression of Agreeableness in individualist and collectivist cultures. Thus it is necessary for the FFM to acknowledge that a social-relational element exists within personality, and it is not necessarily the case that this needs to exist as a separate factor as argued by some researchers (Cheung et al., 2008; Laher, 2013). It is possible that current conceptualizations can be changed so as to incorporate a more communal element, such that the agentic and communal are balanced to obtain a more holistic understanding of the expression of the five factors.

In accordance with FFT, the replicability of the five factors in whatever form presently suggests that the assumption that the five factors are Basic Tendencies is supported. However, the differences in the ways in which the five factors present across cultures suggests that the assumption that what is being measured are characteristic adaptations also holds. The evidence in this chapter suggests that currently, at the level of characteristic adaptations, it is only expressions of personal growth and agency that are being measured. It is necessary to incorporate social-relational expressions in order to achieve true psychic unity in the FFM.

Conclusion

In terms of the way forward, it is recommended that research be conducted at the level of items as well as construct and model conceptualization. Valchev et al. (2011) suggests that questionnaire items need to be framed in more concrete and contextualized terms to be more relevant in the South African context. These items, however need to be administered across diverse samples from diverse cultures along with traditional items to get a better sense of the items that are more meaningful across individualist and collectivist cultures. Given the findings of response bias in collectivist cultures, it is also necessary to incorporate this into studies in this sphere. It is necessary to employ emic instruments like the SAPI and the CPAI-2 along with etic instruments like the NEO PI-R to better inform the nature of the five factors that constitute personality.

The Extraversion example from Teferi and Laher (2013) suggests cultural norms in the expression of Extraversion. Valchev et al. (2013) found that personality descriptions amongst Black participants often made reference to norms in behaviour which could be grouped into social-relational norms: norms of tradition, progress and moral integrity. This is not unique to South Africa as Cheung et al. (2008) also make reference to these in their four-factor model, with concepts of face-saving, family orientation, and other social-relational norms. The role of norms in establishing a universal model would need further exploration. Presently cultural norms are incorporated into FFT under External Influences (McCrae & Costa, 2008), but even in FFT the role of cultural norms is unclear.

Laher (2013) also suggests that further research be undertaken with regards to the South African concept of *Ubuntu*, which originates from an African aphorism, "umuntungumuntungabantu" (isiZulu version) or "mothokemothokabatho" (Sesotho version), which translates as, "a person is a person through other persons" (p. 214). This is based on the premise that the traits associated with *Ubuntu* (generous, hospitable, friendly, caring, compassionate, open and available to others, affirming of others, does not feel threatened that others are able and good) can be subsumed within the Extraversion and Agreeableness factors in the FFM. However, no formal research has yet been conducted to determine whether *Ubuntu* has a role to play in understanding the social-relational aspects of personality in South Africa and in other cultures (Nel et al., 2012). It may very well be that *Ubuntu* represents a more tradition-focused dimension like face-saving in the CPAI-2 than a social-relational dimension (and similarly with the SAPI Facilitating dimension). To date this scale has not been adequately described in any of the personality models (Valchev et al., 2014). Facilitating by definition is about conveying knowledge, giving guidance, and empowering others within a social context. Thus it is perceived as having the function of transmitting wisdom, which is of special importance in the Black group in South Africa (Valchev et al., 2014). As with *Ubuntu*, it remains to be seen whether this dimension will be more tradition-focused or have a broader social-relational relevance. Further research also needs to be undertaken with regards to the Integrity dimension found in the SAPI. Valchev et al. (2014) argue that Integrity has a strong conceptual similarity with the Honesty-Humility dimension from the HEXACO model (see Ashton & Lee, 2007).

In conclusion, it is evident from the African (and particularly the South African) context that the FFM needs to be expanded to include a more social-relational element so as to increase the applicability and psychic unity of the model.

References

Allik, J., & McCrae, R.R. (2004). Toward a geography of personality traits: Patterns of profiles across 36 cultures. *Journal of Cross-Cultural Psychology, 35* (1), 13–28.

Ashton, M.C., & Lee, K. (2007). Empirical, theoretical, and practical advantages of the HEXACO model of personality structure. *Personality and Social Psychology Review, 11* (2), 150–166.

Branco e Silva, L., & Laher, S. (2012). *Exploring the collective dimension of personality using the SAPI and the CPAI-2.* Paper presented at the 30th International Congress of Psychology, 22–27 July, CTICC, Cape Town, South Africa.

Cheung, F.M., Cheung, S., Zhang, J., Leung, K., Leong, F., & Yeh, K.H. (2008). Relevance of Openness as a personality dimension in Chinese culture: Aspects of its cultural relevance. *Journal of Cross-Cultural Psychology, 39* (1), 81–108.

Employment Equity Act (Act No. 55). (2014). *Government Gazette, 583* (37238), 16 January 2014. Retrieved from http://www.labour.gov.za/DOL/downloads/legislation/acts/employment-equity/eea_amend2014.pdf

Heaven, P.C., & Pretorius, A. (1998). Personality structure among Black and White South Africans. *Journal of Social Psychology, 138* (5), 664–666.

Heuchert, J.W.P., Parker, W.D., Stumpf, H., & Myburgh, C.P.H. (2000). The Five-Factor Model of personality in South African college students. *American Behavioral Scientist, 44* (1), 112–125.

Hofstede, G. (2014). *Cultural Tools: Country Comparison – South Africa.* Retrieved from http://geert-hofstede.com/south-africa.html

Horn, B.S. (2000). *A Xhosa translation of the revised Neo Personality Inventory: A pilot study.* (Unpublished master's dissertation). University of Port Elizabeth, South Africa.

Hill, C., Nel, J., Van de Vijver, F., Meiring, D., Valchev, V., Adams, B., & De Bruin, G. (2013). Developing and testing items for the South African Personality Inventory (SAPI). *South African Journal of Industrial Psychology, 39* (1), 1–13.

Laher, S. (2010). *Exploring the applicability of the NEO-PI-R and the CPAI-2 in the South African context.* (Unpublished PhD dissertation). University of the Witwatersrand, South Africa.

Laher, S. (2013). Understanding the Five Factor Model and Five Factor Theory through a South African cultural lens. *South African Journal of Psychology, 43* (2), 208–221.

Laher, S. (2015). Exploring the utility of the CPAI-2 in a South African sample: Implications for the FFM. *Personality and Individual Differences, 81*, 61–75.

Laher, S., & Cockcroft, K. (2013). *Psychological Assessment in South Africa: Research and Applications.* Wits University Press: Johannesburg.

Laher, S., & Cockcroft, K. (2014). Psychological assessment in post-apartheid South Africa: the way forward. *South African Journal of Psychology, 44* (3), 303–314.

Laher, S., & Quy, G. (2009). Exploring the role of spirituality in the context of the Five Factor Model of Personality in a South African sample. *Journal of Psychology in Africa, 19* (4), 513–521.

McCrae, R.R., & Costa, P.T., Jr. (2008). The Five Factor Theory of personality. In O.P. John, R.W. Robins, & L.A. Pervin (Eds.), *Handbook of Personality: Theory and Research* (3rd ed.) (pp. 157–180). New York: Guilford Press.

McCrae, R.R., Terracciano, A., & 79 members of the Personality Profiles of Cultures Project. (2005). Universal features of personality traits from the observer's perspective: Data from 50 cultures. *Journal of Personality and Social Psychology, 88* (3), 547–561.

Mohammed, E.F., Unher, M., & Sugawara, M. (2009). Big Five personality factors: Cross-cultural comparison between Japanese and Egyptian students. *Acta Psychologica Sinica, 8*, 135–141.

Nel, J.A., Valchev, V.H., Rothmann, S., van de Vijver, F.J.R., Meiring, D., & De Bruin, G.P. (2012). Exploring the personality structure in the 11 languages of South Africa. *Journal of Personality, 80* (4), 915–948.

Okeke, B.I., Draguns, J.G., Sheku, B., & Allen, W. (1999). Culture, self and personality in Africa. In Y.T. Lee, C.R. McCauley, & J.G. Draguns (Eds.). *Personality and Person Perception across Cultures* (pp. 139–162). Mahwah, NJ: Lawrence Erlbaum Associates.

Piedmont, R.L., Bain, E., McCrae, R.R., & Costa, P.T., Jr. (2002). The applicability of the Five Factor Model in a sub-Saharan culture: The NEO-PI-R in Shona. In R.R. McCrae, & J. Allik (Eds.), *The Five-Factor Model of Personality across Cultures* (pp. 155–174). New York: Kluwer Academic.

Rossier, J., Dahourou, D., & McCrae, R.R. (2005). Structural and mean level analyses of the Five-Factor Model and Locus of Control: Further evidence from Africa. *Journal of Cross-Cultural Psychology, 36* (2), 227–246.

Rothman, S., & Coetzer, E.P. (2003).The Big Five personality dimensions and job performance. *South African Journal of Industrial Psychology, 29* (1), 68–74.

Storm, K., & Rothman, S. (2003). The relationship between burnout, personality traits and coping strategies in a corporate pharmaceutical group. *South African Journal of Industrial Psychology, 29* (4), 35–42.

Taylor, N. (2008). *Construct, item, and response bias across cultures in personality measurement.* (Unpublished doctoral thesis). Johannesburg: University of Johannesburg.

Taylor, N., & De Bruin, G.P. (2006). *BTI: Manual of the Basic Traits Inventory.* Johannesburg: Jopie van Rooyen.

Taylor, N., & De Bruin, G.P. (2013). The Basic Traits Inventory. In S. Laher, & K. Cockroft (Eds.), *Psychological Assessment in South Africa: Research and Applications* (pp. 409–423). Johannesburg: Wits University Press.

Teferi, T.B., & Laher, S. (2013). Exploring the reliability and validity of a Tigrignan translation of the NEO-PI-R in an Eritrean sample. *IFE Psychologia, 21* (1), 164–181.

Triandis, H.C. (2001). Individualism-Collectivism and personality. *Journal of Personality, 69* (6), 907–924.

Valchev, V.V., Nel, J.A., van de Vijver, F., Meiring, D., De Bruin, G.P., & Rothmann, S. (2013). Similarities and differences in implicit personality concepts across ethnocultural groups in South Africa. *Journal of Cross-Cultural Psychology, 44* (3), 365–388.

Valchev, V.H., Van de Vijver, F.J.R., Meiring, D., Nel, J.A., Laher, S., Hill, C., & Adams, B.G. (2014). Beyond agreeableness: Social-relational personality concepts from an indigenous and cross-cultural perspective. *Journal of Research in Personality, 48* (1), 17–32.

Valchev, V., Van de Vijver, F., Nel, A., Rothmann, S., Meiring, D., & De Bruin, G.P. (2011). Implicit personality conceptions of the Nguni-cultural linguistic groups of South Africa. *Cross-Cultural Research, 45* (3), 235–266.

Van Dyk, G.A.J., & De Kock, F.S. (2004). The relevance of the Individualism-Collectivism (IC) factor for the management of diversity in the South African National Defence Force. *South African Journal of Industrial Psychology, 30* (2), 90–95.

Wiggins, J.S., & Trapnell, P.D. (1996). A dyadic-interactional perspective on the Five-Factor Model. In J.S. Wiggins (Ed.), *The Five Factor Model of Personality: Theoretical Perspectives* (pp. 88–162). New York: Guilford Press.

Zhang, L.-F., & Akande, A. (2002). What relates to the Big Five among South African university students? *IFE PsychologIA: An International Journal, 10* (2), 49–74.

12

Advances in the Use and Interpretation of the MMPI-2[1]

Salazar-Schneiderman, Caroline S. Tonetti, Lacey M. Sommers, and Roger L. Greene

Palo Alto University, Palo Alto CA, USA

The Minnesota Multiphasic Personality Inventory-2 (Butcher, Dahlstrom, Graham, Tellegen, & Kaemmer, 1989) has a long and venerable history as the most frequently used self-report measure of psychopathology. Although the MMPI-2 is used and researched constantly, most of this research has focused on refining the extant instrument rather than actual innovations. The present chapter will look at three distinct topics, none of which has been reported before. The first topic is whether MMPI-2 codetypes, the core of the interpretive system, are actually categories as they have been conceptualized. If codetypes are not categories, the process for interpreting the MMPI-2 would need to be revised. The second topic is whether the MMPI-2 scales assessing somatic symptoms, which underline the 1-3/3-1 codetype, are categories or dimensions. Again, the strategy for interpreting MMPI-2 scales assessing somatic symptoms would need to reflect whether they are a category or a dimension. The third topic examines whether it is possible to use item response theory (IRT) to develop scales within the MMPI-2 item pool that could be administered in a computer adaptive testing (CAT) format so that the examinee need not respond to all of the items within a scale if they are not relevant for the person. These three topics illustrate some of the future direction(s) that can be pursued in MMPI-2 research.

Are MMPI-2 Codetypes Categories or Dimensions?

The MMPI was originally intended to be used as a discrete collection of individual scales for the assessment of psychopathology in which an elevation on a specific scale was expected to be related to a specific diagnosis. However, it was quickly evident

[1] The authors appreciate the comments of David S. Nichols on an earlier draft of this chapter.

The Wiley Handbook of Personality Assessment, First Edition. Edited by Updesh Kumar.
© 2016 John Wiley & Sons, Ltd. Published 2016 by John Wiley & Sons, Ltd.

that the MMPI clinical scales were correlated and patients with specific disorders exhibited elevations on more than one scale, demonstrating that an individual scale did not correspond uniquely to a specific disorder. This finding led to the strategy of using codetypes, the two highest clinical scales at a T score of 70 or higher, as the basis for the interpretation of the MMPI (Dahlstrom & Welsh, 1960) and the development of MMPI references summarizing the information for each codetype (cf. Greene, 2011b, Chapter 5). Despite the general use of codetypes for the interpretation of the MMPI and MMPI-2 for over 50 years, no published study has investigated whether codetypes are actual categories.

Salazar (2011) was among the first to evaluate whether specific MMPI-2 codetypes functioned as categories or dimensions with her study of 1-3/3-1 codetypes. She used taxometric analyses developed by Meehl and colleagues (Meehl & Yonce, 1994; Waller & Meehl, 1998) to determine whether 1-3/3-1 codetypes were taxonic or dimensional. Taxometric techniques are useful in identifying whether a set of indicators relate to one another in a manner that is consistent with the presence of a meaningful identified type or category (taxon) (Widiger, 2001). Taxometrics can be used to evaluate taxonic and dimensional models as competing alternative hypotheses (Ruscio, Haslam, & Ruscio, 2006). This distinction holds important implications for the development and use of assessment instruments (Ruscio & Ruscio, 2002). For example, the goal when assessing a taxonic construct is to assign individuals to groups, whereas the goal when assessing dimensional constructs is to locate the individual's position along these dimensions. In the former case, the individual either is or is not a member of the group, while in the latter case, the individual is classified as having more or less of the dimension in question.

Salazar (2011) created three separate packets of items from the items with the codetype 1-3/3-1; items that were common to both Scales 1 and 3 were used only one time. These packets of items were used as the indicator variables in the taxometric analyses. The subset packets assumed that the inherent construct within the 1-3/3-1 codetype was distributed equally among all of the items. Accordingly, the 92 unique items with the 1-3/3-1 codetype were combined into a single scale and then each item was correlated with the total score for these 92 items. The item with the highest correlation with the total score on the combined set of items was put in the first packet; the second highest correlated item was put in the second packet; and the third highest correlated item was put in the third packet. This procedure was followed until there were no more items with a correlation greater than ±0.30 with the total score. There were a total of 14 items in each of the three subset packets.

The factor and rational packets relied on empirical and clinical methods for identifying groupings of items within these same 92 items, respectively. The factor packets were created by using principal-components factor analysis of the 92 items. The three-, four-, and five-factor solutions were evaluated to determine the number of items with a factor loading greater than ±0.30 to be used in the taxometric analyses. The four- and five-factor solutions resulted in one or two additional factors with insufficient numbers of items that could be used in the analysis, so a three-factor solution was used. The three factor packets had 41, 9, and 14 items.

The rational packets were developed by asking seven judges, who were experienced in the use and interpretation of the MMPI-2, to sort the same 92 items into a self-titled category that best described the grouping of items. The judges' categories were then reviewed and common themes were identified across the judges. Those items having a common theme among at least four judges were used in the final analysis. Salazar's (2011) labels for these four rational packets of items were: specific physical symptoms (30 items), interpersonal relations (19 items), general distress (9 items), and depressive physical symptoms (8 items).

Two statistically independent procedures, MAMBAC (Mean Above Minus [mean] Below A Cut; Meehl & Yonce, 1994) and MAXEIG (Maximum Eigen value; Waller & Meehl, 1998), were used for each packet of items. The MAMBAC analyses were performed within each set of packets of items by using one packet as the input indicator and the other packets as the output indicators. These analyses were conducted for all possible combinations of packets as input and output indicators. The MAXEIG analyses were performed in a similar manner within each set of packets of items, with one packet as the input indicator and the remaining packets as the output indicator. The MAXEIG procedure provided a consistency check for the MAMBAC procedure. Ruscio, Haslam and Ruscio (2006) developed programs for R statistical software, which were used for the analyses and to create simulated taxonic and dimensional data-sets. The actual distributions were used to compare the results of the MAMBAC and MAXEIG procedures with the simulated data.

Salazar (2011) selected a random sample of 1,000 patients drawn from a larger set of psychiatric in-patients and out-patients ($N = 154{,}710$) in the Caldwell MMPI-2 clinical data-set (Caldwell, 2007) screened for excessive item omissions (>30) and inconsistent item endorsement (VRIN > 14). This sample was used to develop each packet of items. The three sets of 1-3/3-1 codetype indicator packets (subset, factor, and rational) were analyzed using MAMBAC and MAXEIG. Table 12.1 provides the averaged base rates for each set of packets of items for both MAMBAC and MAXEIG. The base rates were somewhat consistent between MAMBAC and MAXEIG in all three sets of item packets, with the base rates ranging from 0.28 to 0.64. However, the base rates that Salazar found in her sample are much higher than the frequency of occurrence of 1-3/3-1 codetypes, which ranges from 2.51–21.95% across a range of samples of patients (Greene, 2011b, p. 161). The frequency of occurrence of 1-3/3-1 codetypes in the Caldwell MMPI-2 (2007) clinical data-set that was used in Salazar's study was 10.85%. If Salazar was able to identify a category within this general sample of patients, it appears to be something different from a 1-3/3-1 codetype *per se*.

Table 12.1 also includes the comparison curve fit index (CCFI: Ruscio, Ruscio, & Meron, 2007), which provides another consistency check for taxometric procedures. The CCFI is based on the comparison of an averaged curve of the obtained data with both a simulated categorical and a simulated dimensional curve. CCFI values can range from 0 (dimensional) to 1 (categorical). The more a CCFI value deviates from 0.50, the stronger the results.When the results are between 0.40 and 0.60 they are considered to be ambiguous and should be interpreted with caution.The CCFIs for all of these packets of items were either in the Ambiguous or Dimensional range,

Table 12.1 Summary of taxometric analyses for specific MMPI-2 codetypes

	MAMBAC				*MAXEIG*			
Packet	*M*	*SD*	*CFFI*	*Outcome*	*M*	*SD*	*CFFI*	*Outcome*
1-3/3-1 (Salazar, 2011)								
Rational	0.49	0.11	0.53	Ambiguous	0.64	0.24	0.58	Ambiguous
Factor	0.55	0.08	0.57	Ambiguous	0.54	0.13	0.22	Dimensional
Subset	0.34	0.01	0.58	Ambiguous	0.28	0.09	0.31	Dimensional
4-7/7-4 (Cooper, 2013)								
Rational	0.28	0.13	0.72	Taxonic	0.27	0.06	0.32	Dimensional
Factor	0.43	0.04	0.45	Ambiguous	0.26	0.15	0.22	Dimensional
Subset	0.33	0.01	0.57	Ambiguous	0.28	0.05	0.35	Dimensional
4-8/8-4 (Moseman, 2013)								
Rational	0.26	0.06	0.73	Taxonic	0.21	0.04	0.34	Dimensional
Factor	0.29	0.09	0.63	Taxonic	0.22	0.05	0.30	Dimensional
Subset	0.24	0.06	0.60	Ambiguous	0.16	0.03	0.22	Dimensional
4-9/9-4 (Henderson, 2014)								
Rational	0.32	0.09	0.76	Taxonic	0.34	0.07	0.27	Dimensional
Factor	0.40	0.04	0.58	Ambiguous	0.26	0.05	0.13	Dimensional
Subset	0.31	0.02	0.51	Ambiguous	0.17	0.02	0.22	Dimensional
6-8/8-6 (Cepeda, 2014)								
Rational	0.25	0.04	0.40	Ambiguous	0.19	0.05	0.13	Dimensional
Factor	0.29	0.02	0.31	Dimensional	0.22	0.06	0.25	Dimensional
Subset	0.24	0.02	0.42	Ambiguous	0.14	0.01	0.23	Dimensional
6-9/9-6 (Baretto, 2012)								
Rational	0.48	0.12	0.19	Dimensional	0.54	0.20	0.45	Ambiguous
Factor	0.69	0.12	0.46	Ambiguous	0.33	0.17	0.53	Ambiguous
Subset	0.31	0.01	0.47	Ambiguous	0.15	0.01	0.22	Dimensional

Note: MAMBAC, Mean Above Minus (Mean) Below A Cut; MAXEIG, Maximum Eigenvalue; CCFI, Comparison Curve Fit Index.

suggesting that a category or taxon is not being identified. Thus, Salazar's (2011) findings did not support the existence of 1-3/3-1 codetypes being a category within a general sample of clinical patients.

A series of similar studies were performed using taxometric analyses within other MMPI-2 codetypes (4-7/7-4 [Cooper, 2013]; 4-8/8-4 [Moseman, 2013]; 4-9/9-4 [Henderson, 2014]; 6-8/8-6 [Cepeda, 2014]; 6-9/9-6 [Baretto, 2012]). These results are also summarized in Table 12.1. The results of these studies are very similar to those reported by Salazar (2011) in that the base rates were relatively consistent between MAMBAC and MAXEIG within each codetype, and the base rates were substantially higher than would be expected for the frequency of occurrence of the specific codetype within a general clinical sample. The CCFI for these codetypes generally were indicative of a dimensional construct or was ambiguous as to the classification. For all 18 comparisons of the six codetypes represented in Table 12.1

that used MAMBAC, four were classified as taxonic, 12 were classified as ambiguous, and two were classified as dimensional. For MAXEIG, none were classified as taxonic, four were classified as ambiguous, and 14 were classified as dimensional. If there is a category being identified within these MMPI-2 codetypes, which does not appear to be case, it is not specific to the codetype. Instead it would appear to represent a variable(s) whose base rate is around 0.25 across all of them. Further evidence that a category is not being found within each codetype is that the sum of the base rates across these six codetypes is substantially over 1.00 (which would be the sum of all of the codetypes within a given sample).

Given that it does not appear that MMPI-2 codetypes are categories as they have been conceptualized for over 50 years, the next issue would seem to be whether the common groupings of items such as the clinical, content, or factor within the MMPI-2 are categorical or dimensional. The next section will evaluate whether MMPI-2 scales assessing physical symptoms are categorical or dimensional.

Are MMPI-2 Somatization Scales Categories or Dimensions?

There are a number of MMPI/MMPI-2 scales that assess somatic symptoms: Scale 1 (Hypochondriasis [Hs]), Scale 3 (Hysteria [Hy]) and the Wiener (Wiener, 1948) subscale for Scale 3, Hysteria, Obvious (Hy,0); two MMPI content scales (Wiggins, 1966): Poor Health (HEA) and Organic Symptoms (ORG); one MMPI-2 content scale (Butcher et al., 1989), Health Concerns (HEA), with three Content Component Subscales (Ben-Porath & Sherwood (1993): Gastrointestinal Symptoms (HEA_1), Neurological Symptoms (HEA_2), and General Health Concerns (HEA_3)). There is also the Lachar and Wrobel (1979) Critical Items Set, Somatic Symptoms (LWSoma). The MMPI-2 Restructured Form (Ben-Porath & Tellegen, 2008) has one restructured clinical scale that assesses somatic symptoms (RC1) with three subscales: Gastrointestinal Complaints (GIC), Head Pain Complaints (HPC), and Neurological Complaints (NUC).

There is a high degree of item overlap among all of these scales measuring somatic symptoms, and consequently high correlations among them. For example, Scale 1 (Hs), Health Concerns (HEA), and Somatic Complaints (RC1) share 20 to 23 items and their correlation ranges from 0.96 to 0.97. Additionally, the Lachar and Wrobel (1979) Somatic Symptoms critical items list shares 9 of its 23 items with Hy,O and 20 items with HEA, resulting in correlations of 0.92 and 0.97, respectively. These four scales are considered psychometrically redundant and do not contribute incremental information about the test taker (Greene, 2011b, p. 401). Scale 1 (Hs), Health Concerns (HEA), and Restructured Clinical Scale 1 (RC1) share 17 items, and 12 more items are common to at least two of these scales, leaving 20 unique items across the three. It appears that each scale is tapping a slightly different pool of somatic symptoms. While the critical item list (LWSoma) and the content scales were derived independently, nevertheless they have considerable overlap and high correlation (0.89–0.97).

One issue that needs to be addressed with the scales that assess somatic symptoms on the MMPI-2 is whether these scales are assessing a category or a dimension of somatic symptoms. As discussed above, a 1-3/3-3 codetype was assumed to be a category that reflected the somatic symptoms being reported by the individual, but it does not appear that the 1-3/3-1 codetype is a category *per se*. It is still possible that somatic symptoms form a category that is not being assessed adequately by the 1-3/3-1 codetype, which was explored by Tonetti (2013). She selected a large sample of MMPI-2 profiles in a general clinical sample and used taxometric procedures to evaluate whether the scales that measure somatic symptoms are a category or a dimension.

Tonetti (2013) used a sample of 500 men and 500 women drawn randomly from a larger set of psychiatric in-patients and out-patients ($N = 154{,}710$) in the Caldwell MMPI-2 clinical data-set (Caldwell, 2007) screened for excessive item omissions (>30) and inconsistent item endorsement (VRIN > 14). Due to the gender effects in the frequency of reporting physical symptoms, she conducted the analyses separately for men and women.

The MMPI/MMPI-2 scales that assess somatic symptoms served as the indicator variables and are sufficient in number to ensure the reliability of the taxonic results (Ruscio, Ruscio, & Keane, 2004; Ruscio et al., 2007). These scales were: Scale 1 (Hs) and Scale 3 (Hy); Wiggins' (1966) Poor Health (HEA) and Organic Symptoms (ORGcontent) scales; Butcher et al's. (1989) Health Concerns (HEA) content scale; the Lachar and Wrobel (1979) critical items (LWSoma); and Harris and Lingoes' (1955) subscales for Scale 8 (Sc_6) and Scale 3 (Hy_3 and Hy_4). The MMPI-2 Restructured Form (MMPI-2-RF; Ben-Porath & Tellegen, 2008) restructured clinical scale, Somatic Complaints (RC1; Tellegen et al., 2003) was also used.

The two statistically independent MAMBAC and MAXEIG procedures were used with these 10 MMPI/MMPI-2 somatic symptoms scales. The MAXEIG procedure provided a consistency check for the MAMBAC procedure. Each of the 10 scales were used as indicator variables and analyzed with these two taxometric procedures.

Table 12.2 shows the mean base rates for men and women on each somatization scale for both the MAMBAC and MAXEIG analyses. The mean base rates for the MAMBAC and MAXEIG procedures were higher for women than men as would be expected, although the base rates were quite different between the two procedures within men and women. The MAMBAC base rate was 0.34 (SD = 0.02) and MAXEIG base rate was 0.17 (SD = 0.04) for women, while the MAMBAC base rate was 0.26 (SD = 0.01) and MAXEIG was 0.11 (SD = 0.02) for men.

Table 12.2 also includes the comparison curve fit index (CCFI: Ruscio et al., 2007) which provides another consistency check. The CCFI values for the MAXEIG procedure were clearly in the dimensional direction for both men and women, while these values for the MAMBAC procedure were either ambiguous (men) or possibly categorical (women).

Tonetti's (2013) results suggest that somatic symptoms as measured by MMPI/MMPI-2 scales are more likely to be dimensional than categorical. Consequently, scores on these scales should be used to describe whether the person is reporting more or less of these somatic symptoms. Once it appears that these scales are measuring a dimension, it becomes important to assess whether there is one general dimension, several specific dimensions, or some combination of both underlying these somatic symptoms.

Table 12.2 Base rates for MAMBAC and MAXEIG analyses by gender and scale

Scale	*Abbreviation*	*MAMBAC*	*MAXEIG*
Men			
Hypochondriasis	Hs	0.26	0.08
Hysteria, Obvious	Hy-O	0.26	0.09
Health Concerns	HEA	0.27	0.09
Somatic Complaints	RC1	0.25	0.10
Poor Health	W-HEA	0.26	0.13
Organic Complaints	W-ORG	0.26	0.10
L&W Somatic Symptoms	LWSOMA	0.26	0.10
Lassitude-Malaise	Hy_3	0.28	0.13
Somatic Complaints	Hy_4	0.25	0.11
Bizarre Sensory Experiences	Sc_6	0.23	0.15
Mean		0.26	0.11
SD		0.01	0.02
CCFI		0.54 Ambiguous	0.27 Dimensional
Women			
Hypochondriasis	Hs	0.34	0.11
Hysteria, Obvious	Hy-O	0.34	0.11
Health Concerns	HEA	0.34	0.14
Somatic Complaints	RC1	0.33	0.14
Poor Health	W-HEA	0.35	0.19
Organic Complaints	W-ORG	0.35	0.16
L&W Somatic Symptoms	LWSOMA	0.33	0.15
Lassitude-Malaise	Hy_3	0.39	0.22
Somatic Complaints	Hy_4	0.34	0.17
Bizarre Sensory Experiences	Sc_6	0.31	0.25
Mean		0.34	0.17
SD		0.02	0.04
CCFI		0.66 Categorical	0.25 Dimensional

If MMPI-2 scales are assessing dimensions rather than categories, it also becomes feasible to evaluate whether these scales can be administered in a computer adaptive manner which requires that a construct be a single dimension rather than a category. This issue will be explored in the next section.

Computer Adaptive Testing

The stagnant state of the field in psychological assessment in recent decades may be, in part, due to the belief that many of the assumptions required for developing a computer adaptive administration cannot be met by the most popular self-report inventories of psychopathology. For example, the MMPI-2 clinical and validity scales do not meet the unidimensionality assumption of item response theory (IRT), and previous attempts to fit this type of model to MMPI/MMPI-2 scales have been largely unsuccessful (e.g., Carter & Wilkinson, 1984; Childs, Dahlstrom, Kemp, & Panter, 2000; Panter, Swygert, Dahlstrom, & Tanka, 1997).

Numerous factor analytic studies conducted on the MMPI/MMPI-2 have identified a negative affect dimension. Welsh (1956) labeled this factor Anxiety (A) and described it as a measure of general anxiety and maladjustment (Greene, 2011b). Welsh Anxiety (A) comprises a number of items that reflect general subjective distress and negative affect, and, at both the scale- and item-level, is a marker for the first and major source of variance on the MMPI-2 (Nichols, 2006). More recently, Tellegen et al. (2003) constructed a Demoralization (RCd) scale for the MMPI-2 Restructured Form (MMPI-2-RF; Ben-Porath & Tellegen, 2008) to represent Watson and Tellegen's (1985) theoretical model of affect. According to Tellegen et al. (2006), "Demoralization is characterized by unhappy, dysphoric mood, a sense of helplessness and inability to cope with one's current circumstances, and general dissatisfaction with one's condition" (p. 157). This scale has yielded similar results to those reported for Welsh Anxiety (A), meaning this scale also is a measure of general distress and negative affect. Greene (2011a) has estimated that there are approximately 75 items that inquire about negative affect within the MMPI-2 item pool.

The influence of demographic variables on MMPI-2 scales has been evaluated almost exclusively within the context of classical test theory, in which the focus is on the scale as a total set of items rather than the individual items within the scale (Greene, 2011b). Research has shown that sociodemographic factors have negligible effects on MMPI-2 scales (cf. Greene, 2011b, Chapter 11). This outcome is believed to be the result of "a cancelling-out process" wherein a subset of items are biased against one group (e.g., Asians) and a different subset of items are biased against another group (e.g., Caucasians) (Waller, Thompson, & Wenk, 2000). The reader who is interested in the influence of demographic variables on most MMPI-2 scales can consult Greene (2011b, Chapter 11).

Assessments derived from the methods of classical test theory do not need to account for the influence of sociodemographic variables at the item level. However, studies using IRT analyses have shown that sociodemographic factors contribute to differential item functioning, and that more needs to be done by researchers to develop psychological assessments free of item bias. Items without bias are even more important in computer adaptive administration to decrease the number of items that need to be available in the pool of items for a specific dimension. If the items for a specific dimension are biased by gender, age, education, and ethnicity, the number of needed items increases geometrically.

Ruano, Sommers, Williams, and Greene (2012) used IRT to investigate the impact of demographic variables at the item level on the restructured clinical (RC) scales. Their analyses revealed that age, gender, and education bias were prevalent for a number of items on the RC scales, with Low Positive Emotions (RC2), Antisocial Behavior (RC4), and Hypomanic Activation (RC9) having the greatest number of items with differential item functioning greater than $|\pm 0.3|$.

A negative affect or internalized distress dimension has consistently emerged in the self-report assessment literature, and research suggests that this construct is unipolar, that is, the high end of this dimension reflects the presence of negative affect, whereas the low end reflects its absence. Given that this construct is strongly supported in the research on self-rated mood and its prevalence in the MMPI-2 item pool, Sommers (2014) used IRT with the MMPI-2 item pool to examine whether a unidimensional scale of internalized distress free from bias could be created that would be able to be administered in a computer adaptive manner.

Sommers (2014) used a sample of 250 participants selected randomly from the Caldwell clinical data-set (Caldwell, 2007) for each combination of the demographic variables of age, education, and gender. Age was classified into three ranges: 20–39; 40–59; and 60–79. Education was classified into three ranges: 9–12; 13–16; and 17–20. Table 12.3 provides the descriptive data for these groupings of demographic variables.

Factor analytic methods were used to develop the Internalized Distress (ID) scale with items from the MMPI-2 item pool. The Welsh Anxiety (A) and Demoralization (RCd) scales were selected as model scales for Internalized Distress (ID). [These MMPI-2 scales were selected because they are reliable and valid measures of general subjective distress and both scales are unidimensional.]

Table 12.3 Demographic characteristics of the participants

			Education (years)					
			9–12		*13–16*		*17–20*	
Age (years)	*M*	*SD*	*M*	*SD*	*M*	*SD*	*M*	*SD*
Men								
20–39	30.66	5.50	11.66	0.77				
	30.46	5.19			14.74	1.14		
	32.57	5.07					18.20	1.11
40–59	46.45	5.14	11.66	0.78				
	47.02	5.05			14.71	1.14		
	47.48	5.11					18.61	1.05
60–79	64.46	4.26	11.50	0.94				
	64.68	4.62			14.96	1.11		
	64.26	4.12					18.55	1.12
Women								
20–39	30.66	5.25	11.71	0.69				
	31.23	5.23			14.78	1.27		
	31.26	4.94					17.86	0.92
40–59	47.48	5.21	11.63	0.85				
	47.06	5.05			14.75	1.19		
	47.54	5.29					18.24	0.98
60–79	65.08	4.96	11.68	0.79				
	64.46	4.42			14.82	1.24		
	64.88	4.77					18.25	0.95

The development of the Internalized Distress (ID) scale began with an item-total correlation of all 567 MMPI-2 items to identify those items with the highest correlations with the Welsh Anxiety (A) and Demoralization (RCd) scales. The 39 items with the highest correlation coefficients were selected to make up the Internalized Distress (ID) scale. The length of the Internalized Distress scale was matched with the Welsh Anxiety scale so that all three scales could be compared as to their potential item biases. The component structure of the 39-item Internalized Distress scale was also examined using principal component analysis to ensure that the scale represented a single dimension. The factor loadings for all items on all three scales were |±0.40| except for a single item (428) on the Welsh Anxiety scale.

A two-factor item response theory (IRT) model was applied to the data using BILOG-MG (du Toit, 2003) to evaluate the items for differential item functioning (DIF), which is a measure of item bias. A DIF of |±0.3| was used as the criterion for bias. These analyses were used to investigate for age, gender, and education bias for all of the items on the Internalized Distress (ID), Demoralization (RCd), and Welsh Anxiety (A) scales.

Table 12.4 shows the number of items with differential item functioning by age for men on Internalized Distress. [Sommers (2014) can be consulted for similar

Table 12.4 Frequency of differential item functioning by age for men on Internalized Distress (ID)

	Years of education								
	9–12			*13–16*			*17–20*		
Range of DIF	*20–39*	*20–39*	*40–59*	*20–39*	*20–39*	*40–59*	*20–39*	*20–39*	*40–59*
0.91+									
0.81–0.90									
0.71–0.80									
0.61–0.70									
0.51–0.60									
0.41–0.50									
0.31–0.40		3	1		1	1		3	2
0.21–0.30	3	5	3	2	7		2	2	
0.11–0.20	8	2	5	10	5	6	9	5	5
0.00–0.10	9	9	12	8	7	13	11	10	18
-0.01–-0.1	6	10	9	11	9	11	9	8	2
-0.11–-0.2	11	5	5	5	4	6	4	5	8
-0.21–-0.3	2	2	3	2	4	2	2	5	4
-0.31–-0.4		1	1	1	1		2		
-0.41–-0.5		2						1	
-0.51–-0.6									
-0.61–-0.7					1				
-0.71–-0.8									
-0.81–-0.9									
-0.91–									
	40–59	60–79	60–79	40–59	60–79	60–79	40–59	60–79	60–79
Threshold adjustment	-0.53	-0.47	0.06	-0.36	-0.34	0.02	0.11	-0.11	-0.22

information on all three scales and for all combinations of the demographic variables evaluated.] For example, the range adjustment for this scale when men aged 20–39 with 9–12 years of education are compared with men ages 60–79 with the same level of education was −0.47; the scores for the younger men were about half a standard deviation lower than for the older men. The younger men were reporting less internalized distress than the older men. After this range adjustment was made for all of the items in comparing these two groups, there were six items with DIF greater than |±0.3|. Specifically, there are three items in the range of 0.31 to 0.40, indicating that these items relate to internalized distress more strongly in younger men, and there are two items with differential item functioning in the range of −0.41 to −0.50 and one item in the range of −0.31 to −0.40, indicating that these items relate to internalized distress more strongly in older men. Overall, the greatest number of items with differential item functioning by age was found when men between the ages of 20 to 39 with 9–12 years of education were compared to men aged 60 to 79 with a similar level of education.

Overall, there were 22 items that were relatively unbiased for each combination of demographic variables. Internalized Distress (ID) had the greatest number of unbiased items across the various combinations of demographic variables, with 19 items showing relatively no bias. These findings indicate that it is possible to develop a computer adaptive assessment to measure internalizing symptoms in a clinical sample with enough items that are free from bias for age, education, and gender.

Table 12.5 illustrates the characteristics of the 22 items that were relatively unbiased for each combination of demographic variables. Threshold is a standard score (M = 0; SD = 1) that is a measure of how much distress is being reported by these clinical patients. Item 130 with a threshold of 0.021 is at the mean of scores for these 22 items; that is, half of the patients would be expected to endorse this item. The strategy in computer adaptive testing is to begin testing on a dimension of items with an item that is at a threshold of approximately 0.00. If the person endorses this item in the deviant direction, an item about half a standard deviation higher is administered (e.g., item 299 or 277). If the person did not endorse this second item, a third item about half a standard deviation lower is administered (e.g., item 196). Slope is a measure of how well an item discriminates among patients at a given threshold. Items with a higher slope are more discriminating among patients at the threshold. If an item with a threshold around 0.800 needed to be administered, item 554 with a slope of 1.712 would be selected over items 485 and 482. Using this computer adaptive strategy, it is feasible to classify clients accurately into one of four categories (no internalized distress; mild internalized distress; moderate internalized distress; and severe internalized distress) using from two to five items. If more precise placement is desired, a few additional items could be administered.

Sommers (2014) has demonstrated that it is possible to develop a set of items to measure internalized distress that are relatively free of demographic bias and that are capable of being administered in a computer adaptive manner. Unbiased items are extremely important in computer adaptive testing because of the limited number of items that are administered to any single individual. If unbiased items are not available to assess a given dimension, additional items will need to be available in the item pool

Table 12.5 Characteristics of items unbiased by age, education, and gender

Item	*T/F*	*Slope*	*Threshold*
196	T	1.438	−0.530
388	F	1.368	−0.171
56	T	1.385	−0.100
377	T	1.872	−0.024
130	T	1.363	0.021
95	F	2.004	0.260
325	T	1.223	0.280
301	T	1.322	0.300
273	T	1.828	0.347
299	T	1.454	0.402
277	T	1.469	0.585
65	T	2.105	0.607
91	F	0.828	0.790
485	T	0.932	0.803
554	T	1.712	0.816
482	T	1.130	0.824
338	T	0.735	0.846
170	T	1.125	0.858
463	T	1.616	0.934
454	T	1.759	1.001
505	T	1.444	1.049
94	T	1.478	1.329

so that a specific patient can be administered an unbiased item. It should be apparent that a computer adaptive scale would result in significant item reductions, time saving, and a more convenient and therapeutic assessment process for patients.

Summary

This chapter has demonstrated that MMPI-2 codetypes, the core of any MMPI-2 interpretive system, probably are not categories, but are more likely to be dimensions. Thus, patients will need to be described as having more or less of the characteristics of any given codetype rather than as being members of that category. It was also determined that the MMPI-2 scales measuring somatic symptoms are dimensional, and this may be part of the reason that 1-3/3-1 codetypes are dimensional rather than categorical. Finally, it was illustrated how a set of items measuring internalized distress could be identified within the MMPI-2 item pool that are relatively free of demographic bias and capable of being administered in a computer adaptive manner. It is time for self-report measures of psychopathology to adopt a computer adaptive strategy for assessing the dimensions of psychopathology to increase the efficiency of the assessment process.

References

Baretto, J. (2012). *A taxometric analysis of MMPI-2 6-9/9-6 codetypes.*) Unpublished Doctoral Dissertation.) Palo Alto University, Palo Alto CA, USA.

Ben-Porath, Y.S., & Sherwood, N.E. (1993). *The MMPI-2 Content Component Scales: Development, Psychometric Characteristics, and Clinical Application.* Minneapolis: University of Minnesota Press.

Ben-Porath, Y.S., & Tellegen, A. (2008). *MMPI-2 Restructured Form: Manual for Administration, Scoring, and Interpretation.* Minneapolis: University of Minnesota Press.

Butcher, J., Dahlstrom, G.W., Graham, J.R., Tellegen, A., & Kaemmer, B. (1989). *Minnesota Multiphasic Personality Inventory (MMPI-2). Manual for Administration and Scoring.* Minneapolis: University of Minnesota Press.

Caldwell, A. (2007). MMPI-2 data research field for clinical patients. Unpublished raw data.

Carter, E., & Wilkinson, L. (1984). A latent trait analysis of the MMPI. *Multivariate Behavioral Research, 19* (4), 385–407.

Cepeda, E. (2014). *A taxometric analysis of the MMPI-2 6-8/8-6 codetype to determine the presence of taxonic or dimensional constructs.* (Unpublished Doctoral Dissertation.) Palo Alto University, Palo Alto CA, USA.

Childs, R.A., Dahlstrom, W.G., Kemp, S.M., & Panter, A.T. (2000). Item response theory in personality assessment: A demonstration using the MMPI-2 Depression scale. *Assessment, 7* (1), 37–54.

Cooper, R.A. (2013). *A taxometric analysis of the MMPI-2 4-7/7-4 codetype: Taxonic or dimensional?* (Unpublished Doctoral Dissertation.) Palo Alto University, Palo Alto CA, USA.

Dahlstrom, W.G., & Welsh, G.S. (1960). *An MMPI Handbook.* Minneapolis: University of Minnesota Press.

duToit, M. (2003). *IRT from SSI: BILOG-MG MULTILOG PARSCALE TESTFACT.* Lincolnwood, IL: Scientific Software International.

Greene, R.L. (2011a). Some considerations for enhancing psychological assessment. *Journal of Personality Assessment, 93* (3), 198–203.

Greene, R.L. (2011b). *The MMPI-2: An Interpretive Manual* (3rd ed.). Needham Heights, MA: Allyn & Bacon.

Harris, R.E., & Lingoes, J.C. (1955). *Subscales for the MMPI: An Aid to Profile Interpretation.* Unpublished manuscript, University of California.

Henderson, B. (2014). *An examination of whether MMPI-2 4-9/9-4 codetypes are categorical or dimensional.* (Unpublished Doctoral Dissertation.) Palo Alto University, Palo Alto CA, USA.

Lachar, D., & Wrobel, T.A. (1979). Validating clinicians' hunches: Construction of a new MMPI critical item set. *Journal of Consulting and Clinical Psychology, 47* (2), 277–284.

Meehl, P.E., & Yonce, L.J. (1994). Taxomeric analysis: I. Detecting taxonicity with two quantitative indicators using means above and below a sliding cut (MAMBAC procedure). *Psychological Reports, 74* (3, Pt 2), 1059–1274.

Moseman, S. (2013). *A taxometric analysis of the MMPI-2 4-8/8-4 codetype.* (Unpublished Doctoral Dissertation.) Palo Alto University, Palo Alto CA, USA.

Nichols, D.S. (2006). The trials of separating bath water from baby: A review and critique of the MMPI-2 restructured clinical scales. *Journal of Personality Assessment, 87* (2), 121–138.

Panter, A., Swygert, K., Dahlstrom, W., & Tanaka, J. (1997). Factor analytic approaches to personality item-level data. *Journal of Personality Assessment, 68* (3), 561–589.

Ruano, S., Sommers, L.M., Williams, S., & Greene, R.L. (2012, March). *The importance of demographic variables in the computer adaptive assessment of psychopathology.* Paper presented at the midwinter meeting of the Society for Personality Assessment, Chicago.

Ruscio, J., Haslam, N., & Ruscio, A. (2006). *Introduction to the taxometric method: A practical guide.* Mahwah, NJ : Erlbaum.

Ruscio, A.M., & Ruscio, J. (2002). The latent structure of analogue depression: Should the Beck Depression Inventory be used to classify groups? *Psychological Assessment, 14* (2), 135–145.

Ruscio, J., Ruscio, A.M., & Keane, T.M. (2004). Using taxometric analysis to distinguish a small latent taxon from a latent dimension with positively skewed indicators: The case of Involuntary Defeat Syndrome. *Journal of Abnormal Psychology, 113* (1), 145–154.

Ruscio, J., Ruscio, A., & Meron, M. (2007). Applying the bootstrap to taxonic analysis: Generating empirical sampling distributions to help interpret results. *Multivariate Behavioral Research, 42* (2), 349–386.

Salazar, J.J. (2011). *A taxometric analysis of MMPI-2 codetype 1-3/3-1.* (Unpublished Doctoral Dissertation.) Palo Alto University, Palo Alto CA, USA.

Sommers, L.M. (2014). *Using item response theory to evaluate a scale of internalized distress for computer adaptive administration.* (Unpublished Doctoral Dissertation.) Palo Alto University, Palo Alto CA, USA.

Tellegen, A., Ben-Porath, Y.S., McNulty, J.L., Arbisi, P.A., Graham, J.R., & Kaemmer, B. (2003). *MMPI–2 Restructured Clinical (RC) scales: Development, Validation, and Interpretation.* Minneapolis: University of Minnesota Press.

Tellegen, A., Ben-Porath, Y.S., Sellbom, M., Arbisi, P.A., McNulty, J.L., & Graham, J.R. (2006). Further evidence on the validity of the MMPI-2 Restructured Clinical (RC) Scales: Addressing questions raised by Rogers et al. and Nichols. *Journal of Personality Assessment, 87* (2), 148–171.

Tonetti, C.S. (2013). *A taxometric analysis of somatization as it is defined and assessed by the MMPI-2.* (Unpublished Doctoral Dissertation.) Palo Alto University, Palo Alto CA, USA.

Waller, N.G., & Meehl, P.E. (1998). *Multivariate Taxometric Procedures: Distinguishing Types from Continua.* Thousand Oaks, CA: Sage.

Waller, N.G., Thompson, J.S., & Wenk, E. (2000). Using IRT to separate measurement bias from true group differences on homogeneous and heterogeneous scales: An illustration with the MMPI. *Psychological Methods, 5* (1), 125–146.

Watson, D., & Tellegen, A. (1985). Toward a consensual structure of mood. *Psychological Bulletin, 98* (2), 219–235.

Welsh, G.S. (1956). Factor dimensions A and R. In G.S. Welsh, & W.G. Dahlstrom (Eds.), *Basic Readings on the MMPI in Psychology and Medicine* (pp. 264–281). Minneapolis: University of Minnesota Press.

Widiger, T.A. (2001). What can be learned from taxometric analyses? *Clinical Psychology: Science and Practice, 8* (4), 528–533.

Wiener, D.N. (1948). Subtle and obvious keys for the MMPI. *Journal of Consulting Psychology, 12* (3), 164–170.

Wiggins, J.S. (1966). Substantive dimensions of self-report in the MMPI item pool. *Psychological Monographs, 80* (Whole N. 630).

Section II

Emerging Assessment Perspectives and Methodological Issues

13

Objective Personality Assessment with the MMPI-2: An Internationally Adaptable Measure

James N. Butcher

University of Minnesota, Minneapolis, USA

The Minnesota Multiphasic Personality Inventory (MMPI-2) is the most widely researched and used clinical personality inventory in contemporary assessment psychology. The MMPI was originally published by the psychologist Starke Hathaway and psychiatrist J.C. McKinley in the 1940s as a means of obtaining a client's perspective on their personality characteristics and mental health problems in psychiatric and medical settings through a self-report questionnaire. This true–false personality inventory rapidly became a standard personality instrument during the Second World War, and came to be used in a variety of applications such as mental health evaluations, personnel screening, and forensic evaluations. The extent of use of the MMPI resulted from its user-friendly self-report administration format and because of the symptom measures that have well established validity in assessing clinical symptoms and syndromes (Butcher, 2011; Friedman, Bolinskey, Levak & Nichols, 2015). The original MMPI was revised in the 1980s and published in two separate forms – an adult version, the MMPI-2 (Butcher, Dahlstrom, Graham, Tellegen, & Kaemmer, 1989), and an adolescent form, MMPI-A (Butcher et al., 1992). The MMPI-2 questionnaire, described below, is a 567-item inventory comprising symptoms, beliefs, and attitudes in adults above age 18.

Assessing Test Validity

One of the most important features of the MMPI-2 in addressing a client's personality responses is that there are measures that provide information as to how openly and honestly the individual cooperated in sharing symptoms and attitudes. The measures

The Wiley Handbook of Personality Assessment, First Edition. Edited by Updesh Kumar.
© 2016 John Wiley & Sons, Ltd. Published 2016 by John Wiley & Sons, Ltd.

on the MMPI-2 to address response attitudes are referred to as *validity scales*. The validity measures contribute substantially to the assessment of clients because many people being evaluated are motivated to present themselves in ways that do not disclose accurate information. For example, people being evaluated in pretrial criminal evaluations might exaggerate their symptoms in order to appear more psychologically disturbed than they are. And, applicants being evaluated for positions as airline pilots or police officers who are given the MMPI-2 tend to present themselves as highly virtuous and having no mental health or personality symptoms. Thus it is important in MMPI-2 interpretation to determine whether the client has cooperated sufficiently with the testing to provide valid results (Baer, Wetter, Nichols, Greene, & Berry, 1995; Bagby, Buis, & Nicholson, 1995). The basic validity scales for the MMPI-2 are described below.

The Cannot Say Index (?)

One important validity measure, though not considered a "scale", is the *Cannot Say* Score. This index is the total number of items omitted in the inventory. High numbers of omitted items (*Cannot Say* scores greater than 30) can indicate that the client is uncooperative with the assessment and can invalidate the protocol.

TRIN and VRIN Scales

Some clients approach the items on the MMPI-2 by responding in an inconsistent manner – a characteristic that could be found among some individuals who seek to manipulate the test results. Two inconsistency scales have been developed for the MMPI-2. These scales are based on the analysis of the individual's response to the items in a consistent or inconsistent manner. The scales comprise item pairs that involve responses that are semantically inconsistent; for example, a pair of items that contain content that cannot logically be answered in the same direction if the subject is responding consistently to the content. The VRIN scale is a valuable measure of random responding. The TRIN scale assesses a client's tendency to endorse a significant percentage of the MMPI-2 items in either an "all True" or "all False" manner (Butcher et al., 2001).

The L (Lie) Scale

The L scale, developed for the original MMPI, is a measure of the client's willingness to acknowledge faults or problems (Hathaway & McKinley, 1942). Individuals who score high on this scale are presenting an overly favorable picture of their personality attributes and adjustment. People who score high on the L scale tend to be claiming virtue that is not found among people in general. The L scale is particularly valuable in providing response information in situations such as personnel screening or family custody cases, because many people in these situations attempt to show only positive aspects of themselves and present themselves as "better" adjusted than they actually are.

The *K* (Defensiveness) Scale

The *K* scale is a measure of test defensiveness that was originally developed by Meehl (see Meehl and Hathaway, 1946) to assess whether a client is responding in an overly defensive way or showing a tendency to minimize problems. The *K* scale, in addition to serving as an index of defensiveness, serves also as a correction factor to compensate for the tendency of some people to deny problems. If a client shows high defensiveness on the MMPI-2 items, a portion of the *K* scale score (*Hs.* + 0.5K; *Pd* + 0.4K; *Pt* + 1K; *Sc* + 1K; and *Ma* + 0.2K) is added to five clinical scales as a means of detecting certain symptoms that the client likely avoided endorsing due to defensiveness. The *K* scale has been shown to be a valuable measure of test defensiveness (see Baer et al., 1995); however, the use of the *K* score to correct for defensiveness has not proven to make a differential contribution much beyond what the scale scores do separately. They are used today primarily because so much of the research included them.

The S (Superlative Self Presentation) Scale

The S scale was developed through a refined empirical scale construction approach. First, items that empirically discriminated between a sample of airline pilot job applicants and the MMPI-2 normative sample were obtained. Next, the items on the S scale were further refined by excluding items that reduced the scale homogeneity (Butcher et al., 2001). Finally, the 50 items on the S scale were factor-analyzed in order to develop subscales that allowed for further understanding of test defensiveness by examining the item content the client endorsed. The five subscales for the S scale are: *Beliefs in Human Goodness* (S1); Serenity (S2); *Contentment with Life* (S3); *Patience and Denial of Irritability and Anger* (S4); and *Denial of Moral Flaws* (S5) (Butcher & Han, 1995). The S scale is highly correlated with the *K* scale (0.81), confirming the assessment of test defensiveness. However, the S scale contains more extensive item content and allows the practitioner to obtain a perspective on the types of defensive item contents the subject is endorsing.

The Infrequency Scales

There are three infrequency scales on MMPI-2 that have been developed to assess infrequent or exaggerated responding to the items: the F or Infrequency Scale, the F(B) or Back F Scale, and the F(p) or Infrequency Psychopathology Scale. They address unusual responding by highlighting the client's endorsement of extreme or rarely endorsed items. The original F scale for the MMPI was developed to evaluate the tendency of some clients to exaggerate their problems on the test by over-responding to extreme items. The items on this measure are very unusual or bizarre symptoms that are rarely endorsed by test-takers. People who endorse a number of these items tend to exaggerate symptoms on the MMPI-2, perhaps as a way of trying to convince professionals that they need psychological services. This test-taking strategy is also found among clients in personal injury cases who feel a need to claim problems in order to influence the decision-makers in the case that they are severely impaired. The F scale can be elevated for several possible reasons. The profile could be invalid because the client became confused or disoriented or responded in a random manner. High F scores are also found among clients who are malingering or producing exaggerated responses in order to falsely claim mental illness (Bagby et al., 1995). The F(B) scale focuses upon rarely endorsed items that appear towards the end of the MMPI-2 test booklet, and the F(p) scale is a measure of rarely endorsed items within a general psychiatric sample.

The Lees-Haley Fake Bad Scale (FBS), or Symptom Validity Scale

Although the controversial Fake Bad Scale or FBS published by Lees-Haley, English and Glenn (1991) has been widely criticized for its potential for mislabeling people with legitimate disability claims as "faking," it was included as a validity measure on the MMPI-2 in 2007 by the test publisher. A number of researchers have reported problems with the FBS (e.g., Butcher, Gass, Cumella, Kally & Williams, 2008; Butcher, Hass, Greene & Nelson, 2015; Friedman et al., 2015; Gass, Williams, Cumella, Butcher, & Kally, 2010). Moreover, the FBS has been excluded from a number of court cases because it is considered biased against people with genuine symptoms and is biased against women. The scale provides results that are viewed as biased and potentially damaging to clients because it falsely labels clients as malingering (see discussions by Butcher et al., 2015; Friedman et al., 2015). Therefore, this scale is not recommended for use in psychological assessment.

Assessing Clinical Symptom Patterns

The assessment of clinical problems with the MMPI-2 is addressed through several ways of summarizing self-reported symptoms and behaviors. We will examine three types of scales that comprise the MMPI-2's problem measures: the traditional, empirically-based clinical scales and profile codes, the MMPI-2 content scales, and the supplemental scales that address specific problem areas. A scale is a group of items from the MMPI-2 item pool that have been shown to measure certain symptom patterns or personality traits. Each item cluster or scale is compared to a reference group or "normed" on a population of individuals without mental health problems. This normative group serves as the reference base for comparing all profiles.

The MMPI-2 clinical scales

Hathaway and McKinley (1940) developed the eight clinical scales to empirically differentiate patients with specific symptoms into clinical problem types. For example, they developed several mental health problem scales: Scale 1, *Hypochondriasis* (the *Hs* scale); Scale 2, *Depression* (the *D* scale); Scale 3, *Hysteria* (the *Hy* scale); Scale 4, *Psychopathic Deviate* (the *Pd* scale); Scale 6, *Paranoia* (the

Pa scale); Scale 7, *Psychastenia* (the *Pt* scale); Scale 8, *Schizophrenia* (the *Sc* scale); and Scale 9, *Mania* (the *Ma* scale). In addition, they published two other scales on the clinical profile to address problems of sex role identification (the *Mf* scale or Scale 5) and *Social Introversion and Extraversion* (the *Si* or Scale 10). If a scale elevation, for example on the *Depression* scale, is obtained in a particular profile, the empirically-based correlations for that scale are used in the scale summary. The MMPI-2 clinical scales are briefly summarized as follows:

1. *Hs* (Hypochondriasis). Clients who score high on *Hs* tend to present numerous vague physical problems and may be unhappy, self-centered, whiny, complaining, and attention-demanding. They also report feeling dissatisfied with life and cynical toward others.
2. *D* (Depression). People who score high on the *D* scale report feeling depressed, having low self-esteem, and feelings of inadequacy. Scale elevations reflect great discomfort and a need for change or symptomatic relief. High scorers are pessimistic and unhappy, feel useless, and are indecisive and socially withdrawn.
3. *Hy* (Hysteria). High scorers may rely on defenses such as denial and repression to deal with stress. They tend to be dependent and naïve. They show little insight into problems. High levels of stress may be channeled through the development of physical symptoms.
4. *Pd* (Psychopathic Deviate). Elevations measure acting-out behaviors – antisocial attitudes, rebelliousness, disrupted family relations, lying, impulsiveness, school or legal difficulties. Alcohol or drug problems may be present.
5. *Mf* (Masculinity-Femininity). High-scoring males are described as having an unusual pattern of stereotypically feminine interests. Because the direction of scoring is reversed, high-scoring women are seen as having masculine or "macho" interests.
6. *Pa* (Paranoia). Elevations on this scale are often associated with being suspicious, aloof, shrewd, guarded, worrying, and overly sensitive. High scorers may be hostile and argumentative. Problems in relationships are common.
7. *Pt* (Psychasthenia). High scorers on this measure tend to be quite anxious and report being tense, overly preoccupied with details, obsessional, and rigid. High scorers tend to have low self-confidence.
8. *Sc* (Schizophrenia). High scorers may have an unconventional or schizoid lifestyle. They can be withdrawn, shy, and moody, and they may feel inadequate, tense, and confused. They may have unusual or strange thoughts, poor judgment, and erratic moods. Career problems and low personal achievement are probable. Very high scores on Sc are associated with schizoid thinking and schizophrenia.
9. *Ma* (Mania). High scorers may be impulsive and overly energetic. Acting-out behaviors and life problems occur among high-scoring clients.
10. *Si* (Social Introversion–Extroversion). High scorers are introverted, shy, withdrawn, socially reserved, submissive, over-controlled, lethargic, conventional, tense, inflexible, and guilt-prone. Low scorers are extroverted, outgoing, gregarious, expressive, and talkative.

MMPI-2 codetypes

If more than one of the clinical scales is elevated in the clinical range (above a T score of 65), the scale patterns or configurations of scores (referred to as profile or code types) are interpreted. Code types result from clients endorsing two or more of the clinical scales. For example, if the Psychopathic Deviate Scale (*Pd*) and the Hysteria Scale (*Hy*) are elevated, the codetype (4-3/3-4), the interpretation is based upon the empirically established codetype correlates for the 4-3/3-4 profile type. This codetype reflects clients with probable acting-out personality disorders. Symptoms reflecting anger control, impulsivity, poor judgment, and aggressive behavior may be present. Clients with this pattern may engage in impulsive and aggressive behavior. They are described as being immature, impulsive, egocentric, and selfish. Family problems and other relationship difficulties are common. These clients are usually not motivated for psychotherapy and not amenable to change (see Butcher, 2011; Greene, 2011, for further information about codetype correlates).

Content-based scales

The MMPI-2 contains 15 scales that assess the content themes that an individual endorses in the item pool. The content scales are homogeneous item clusters that address particular themes (for example, depression, anxiety, obsessive thinking) representing clear communication about the client's admitted problems to the practitioner. The content scales summarize different symptom areas and mental health problems: examples include Antisocial Practices (*ASP*), Bizarre Mentation (*BIZ*), and Family Problems (*FAM*).

Supplementary scales

Several supplementary scales have been developed to assess specific problems, such as the potential to develop problems of substance misuse or addiction, whether or not the individual acknowledges having problems with drugs or alcohol: the MacAndrew Addiction Scale (*MAC-R*), the Addiction Potential Scale (*APS*), and the Addiction Acknowledgment Scale (*AAS*). The Marital Distress Scale or *MDS* assesses clients' attitudes toward their marital relationship. The *Pk* Scale is a PTSD measure of a client's past experience of trauma. These special scales allow the practitioner to assess specific problems that are not as clearly addressed in the clinical or content scales.

Use of the MMPI-2 in International Applications

There is a long-term and well-established interest in the adaptation of psychological measures developed in one culture to assess personality characteristics and mental health problems that people experience. For example, the Rorschach Inkblot

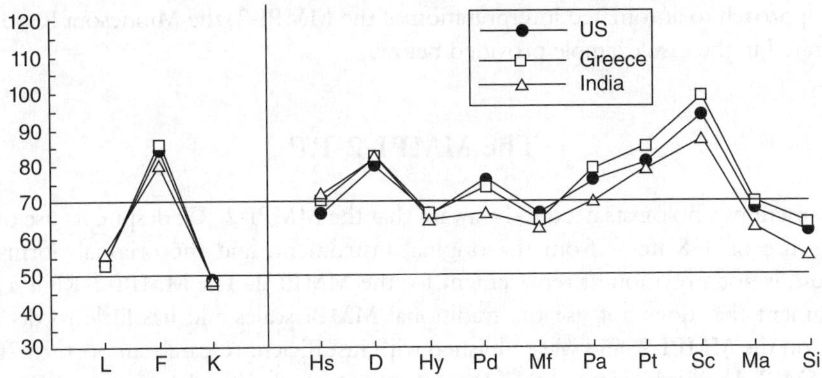

Figure 13.1 MMPI profiles for clients diagnosed with schizophrenia in India, Greece, and the US. *Source*: Minnesota Multiphasic Personality Inventory profile form. © 1942, 1943, 1948, 1970, 1948, 1976, 1982 by the Regents of the University of Minnesota. All rights reserved. Reprinted by permission of the University of Minnesota Press.

Test, developed in Switzerland by Hermann Rorschach in 1921 (see Rorschach, 1942), was widely accepted by psychologists in other countries for assessing personality and mental health symptoms. Shortly after the MMPI was published in 1940, psychologists in other countries began to translate and adapt the test for clinical use, for example, by Reda (1948) in Italy; Sundberg (1956) in Germany; and Abe (1955) in Japan (see discussions in Butcher & Pancheri, 1976). Numerous studies have demonstrated the applicability of the MMPI cross-culturally. For example, Thatte, Manos and Butcher (1987) conducted a study evaluating the assessment of schizophrenic patients on the MMPI in the US, India, and Greece. As shown in the profile similarity in Figure 13.1, the patients from all three countries responded in a highly similar manner, producing comparable MMPI profiles.

After the MMPI-2 was published in 1989, extensive efforts were conducted to adapt the revised instrument in many countries (Butcher, 1996). There have been over 33 translations and adaptations of the MMPI-2 for use in other countries. The items and scales have shown remarkable effectiveness when used in other languages and cultures (Butcher, 1996; Butcher, Tsai, Coelho, & Nezami, 2006).

Computer-Based Interpretation of the MMPI-2

Over 50 years ago, computer-based scoring and interpretation of the MMPI became an important development in personality assessment and in the use of the objective symptom measures for assisting practitioners in making clinical decisions about clients (Fowler, 1967). The substantial research base of the MMPI and the objective nature of its interpretation procedures for interpreting clinical scale scores and codetypes (patterns of scale elevations) made it possible for psychologists to develop computer programs that summarize profile scale elevations or code types (Butcher, 2011).

One approach to automated interpretation of the MMPI-2, the Minnesota Report, is illustrated in the case example provided below.

The MMPI-2-RF

Assessment psychologists need to be aware that the MMPI-2-RF, despite its use of the name, use of 338 items from the original instrument, and the original norms for the test, is not a revision or replacement for the MMPI-2. The MMPI-2-RF is a new instrument that does not use the traditional MMPI scales and has little to do with those on the MMPI-2, and was published with insufficient research support. In 2008, the MMPI-2 publisher introduced the new version called the Restructured Form of the MMPI-2 or MMPI-2-RF. It comprises only 60% of the MMPI-2 items and the scales that were included were constructed differently from the empirical scales in the original instrument. The Restructured Scales were constructed following a theory-based approach rather than the empirically-derived test method developed by Hathaway and McKinley and revised by Butcher et al. in 1989 (see discussion by Ranson, Nichols, Rouse, & Harrington, 2009). The MMPI-2-RF does not address the same constructs as the MMPI-2; for example, in the construction of the Restructured Scales, the authors of MMPI-2-RF dropped all of the *Hy* items from the traditional Hysteria Scale of MMPI-2, except 5, and actually reversed the scoring direction of the remaining items. Therefore, the scale bears no resemblance to the original MMPI *Hy* scale but actually measures cynicism – a concept that is well covered in the current MMPI-2 Cynicism Content Scale. The test manual for the MMPI-2-RF points out that the RC3 scale is negatively correlated with the *Hy* scale from which it was "restructured." Many of these MMPI-2-RF scales are controversial and have been heavily criticized in the assessment literature (see discussion by Rouse, Greene, Butcher, Nichols, & Williams, 2008). Most of the MMPI-2-RF scales were completely new and have not been sufficiently researched to support clinical and forensic decisions (Greene, Rouse, Butcher, Nichols & Williams, 2009; Rouse et al., 2008). Six recent MMPI-2 textbooks have recommended against using the MMPI-2-RF to make important decisions such as in forensic evaluations (Butcher, 2011; Butcher et al., 2015; Friedman et al., 2015; Graham, 2012; Greene, 2011; and Nichols, 2011).

Application of the MMPI-2 in Personnel Selection

The MMPI and MMPI-2 have been widely researched and validated in personnel screening settings (for a listing of personnel assessment references with the MMPI/MMPI-2 and historic highlights on using the MMPI/MMPI-2 in personnel screening, see www.umn.edu/mmpi).

The MMPI-2 is primarily used in evaluating the mental health status of applicants in positions of public responsibility or high-risk occupations such as airline pilot applicants, air traffic controllers, police and fire department personnel, or nuclear power plant employees (Butcher, Gucker, & Hellervik, 2009). For example, in the US, the

Federal Aviation Administration recommends that applicants being considered for positions as airline pilots or air traffic control tower operators undergo a psychological evaluation to ensure that people employed in these responsible positions are qualified and do not experience psychological problems that could negatively impact public safety (Federal Aviation Administration, 2013). The MMPI-2 is recommended.

The following case description illustrates the use of the MMPI-2 in airline pilot screening.

Case Illustration

Applicant's background

The applicant, William B., is 37-year-old pilot who currently flies part-time for the US Navy Reserves. He grew up in a small Midwestern city where he attended high school. He and his two brothers lived with their father and mother who operated a local gasoline service station. During high school he was active in sports and played baseball and hockey for his high school team. After he graduated from high school, he attended a junior college for two years, then completed his BA degree in aviation management at a Midwestern State university. Upon graduation from college, he entered the US Navy and completed flight school. During most of his career he served as a basic flight instructor and was not assigned to a flight squadron or overseas duty. He served in the military for 15 years and decided to leave the Navy after he was not promoted to the rank of O-5.

Mr B. has been married twice and has no children. He was recently divorced from his second wife after 18 months of marriage. His first marriage also ended in divorce after three years. Mr B. has experienced a number of driving problems over the past 10 years; he received five speeding tickets and one ticket for failure to stop at a red light. He was convicted of Driving Under the Influence (DUI) and had his driver's license suspended for one year in 2005.

Interview information

Mr B. was neatly dressed in business attire for the interview. He was somewhat awkward at the beginning of the interview but became more comfortable as the interview progressed. He was generally open in the interview to questions that were asked. For example, he reported that he had been disappointed not to be promoted in the military and indicated that he believed that he had some "so-so" performance reviews when he first entered the military. He also acknowledged that he was not hired by another airline two years ago because he was defensively invalid on two MMPI-2 administrations.

In addition to the assessment interview that was conducted with Mr B., he was also administered the MMPI-2 (see the MMPI-2 validity scale profile in Figure 13.2 and his clinical scale profile in Figure 13.3). His MMPI-2 profile was extremely unusual for an airline pilot applicant, as noted in the computer-based Minnesota Report narrative in Exhibit 13.1.

MMPI®-2 Airline Pilots Interpretive Report
08/22/2014, Page 2 **ID: 082214**

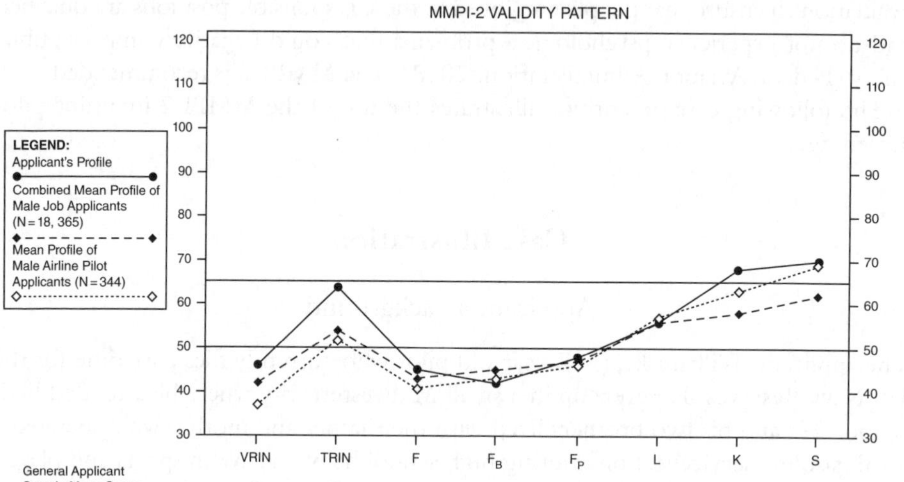

	VRIN	TRIN	F	F_B	F_P	L	K	S
General Applicant Sample Mean Score:	42	54	43	45	47	56	58	62
Airline Pilot Sample Mean Score:	37	52	41	43	46	57	63	69
Applicant's Raw Score:	**4**	**7**	**3**	**0**	**1**	**5**	**24**	**42**
Applicant's T Score:	**46**	**64F**	**45**	**42**	**48**	**56**	**68**	**70**
Non-Gendered T Score:	46	65F	46	42	49	57	69	70
Response %:	100	100	100	100	100	100	100	100

Cannot Say (Raw):	0
Percent True:	29
Percent False:	71

	Raw Score	T score	Resp. %
S_1-Beliefs in Human Goodness	15	70	100
S_2-Serenity	9	61	100
S_3-Contentment with Life	5	55	100
S_4-Patience/Denial of Irritability	8	68	100
S_5-Denial of Moral Flaws	4	58	100

Figure 13.2 MMPI-2 Validity Scale Profile for Mr B. *Source*: *The Minnesota Report™: Revised Personnel System* (3rd ed.) by James N. Butcher. © 1989, 1991, 1994, 1995, 2001, 2003 by the Regents of the University of Minnesota. Portions excerpted from *MMPI®-2 (Minnesota Multiphasic Personality Inventory®-2) Manual for Administration, Scoring, and Interpretation*, Revised Edition by Butcher et al. (2001). © 2001 by the Regents of the University of Minnesota. Reproduced by permission of the University of Minnesota Press. All rights reserved. "MMPI®" and "Minnesota Multiphasic Personality Inventory®" are registered trademarks and "MMPI-2," "Minnesota Multiphasic Personality Inventory-2" and "The Minnesota Report" are trademarks of the University of Minnesota.

Recommendation

Mr B. was not recommended for employment. His performance on the MMPI-2, suggesting likely long-term personality problems that could impact work relationships including suspicion and mistrust of authority, anger control, and difficulties in interpersonal relationships, were considered problematic for participating in the cooperative environment of commercial aviation. His difficulties in working with others and his problematic impulsive behavior, as noted by the MMPI-2, were confirmed in his background information, interview data, and his work history.

MMPI®-2 Airline Pilots Interpretive Report **ID: 082214**
08/22/2014, Page 3

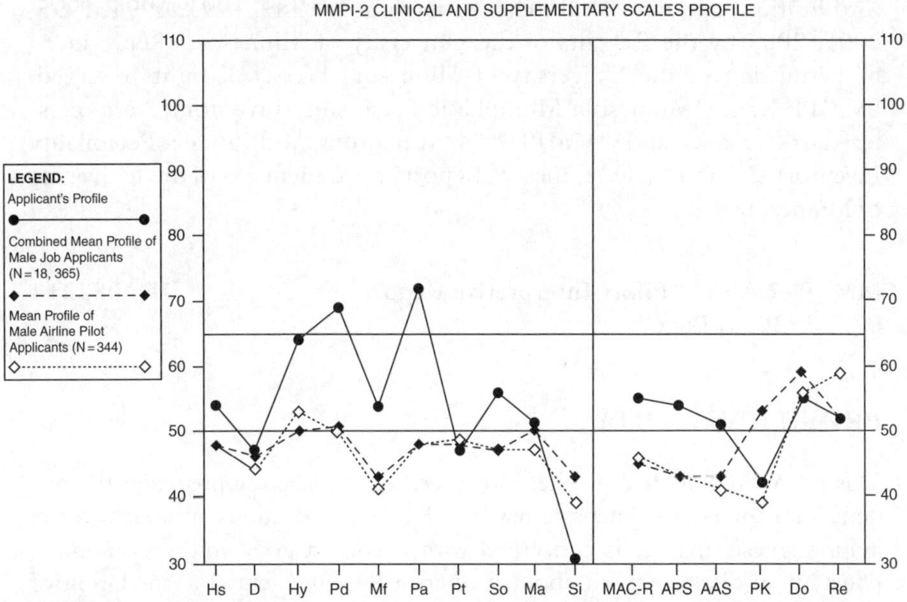

	Hs	D	Hy	Pd	Mf	Pa	Pt	So	Ma	Si	MAC-R	APS	AAS	PK	Do	Re
General Applicant Sample Mean Score:	48	46	50	51	43	48	48	47	50	43	45	43	43	53	59	52
Airline Pilot Sample Mean Score:	48	44	53	50	41	48	49	47	47	39	46	43	41	39	56	59
Applicant's Raw Score:..	**2**	**17**	**27**	**21**	**28**	**16**	**1**	**6**	**16**	**7**	**23**	**25**	**3**	**3**	**18**	**21**
K Correction Score:	12			10			24	24	5							
Applicant's T Score:	**54**	**47**	**64**	**69**	**54**	**72**	**47**	**56**	**51**	**30**	**55**	**54**	**51**	**42**	**55**	**52**
Non-Gendered T Score:	53	45	62	70		71	46	57	52	30	58	55	53	42	55	51
Response %:	100	100	100	100	100	100	100	100	100	100	100	100	100	100	100	100

Welsh Code: 6′4 + 3 − 8159/27:0# K + − L/F:
Profile Elevation: 57.5

Figure 13.3 MMPI-2 Clinical Scale Profile for Mr B. *Source*: Excerpted from *The Minnesota Report™: Revised Personnel System* (3rd ed.) by James N. Butcher. © 1989, 1991, 1994, 1995, 2001, 2003 by the Regents of the University of Minnesota. Portions excerpted from *MMPI®-2 (Minnesota Multiphasic Personality Inventory®-2) Manual for Administration, Scoring, and Interpretation*, Revised Edition by Butcher et al. (2001). © 2001 by the Regents of the University of Minnesota. Reproduced by permission of the University of Minnesota Press. All rights reserved. "MMPI®" and "Minnesota Multiphasic Personality Inventory®" are registered trademarks and "MMPI-2," "Minnesota Multiphasic Personality Inventory-2" and "The Minnesota Report" are trademarks of the University of Minnesota.

Exhibit 13.1 MMPI-2 Minnesota Report Narrative Printout for Mr B. Excerpted from *The Minnesota Report™: Revised Personnel System* (3rd Edition) by James N. Butcher. Copyright © 1989, 1991, 1994, 1995, 2001, 2003 by the Regents of the University of Minnesota. Reproduced by permission of the University of Minnesota Press. All rights reserved. "MMPI®" and "Minnesota Multiphasic Personality Inventory®" are registered trademarks and "MMPI-2," "Minnesota Multiphasic Personality Inventory-2," and "The Minnesota Report" are trademarks of the University of Minnesota.

MMPI®-2 Airline Pilots Interpretive Report **ID: 082214**
08/22/2014, Page 5

PROFILE VALIDITY

This is a valid MMPI-2 profile. However, the applicant approached the test items in a somewhat defensive manner. His overly cautious approach to the items suggests that he is concerned with making a good impression and is reluctant to disclose much about his personal adjustment. Interpretation of the clinical profile should allow for the possibility that he minimized his problems.

PERSONAL ADJUSTMENT

The applicant, in his attempt to portray himself in an overly positive manner, has probably influenced his scores on the other scales of the MMPI-2. Although interpretations are provided in this report for the clinical and content scales, it should be kept in mind that the applicant has not cooperated sufficiently with the evaluation. The following interpretations should be considered provisional until the applicant's generally defensive test responding can be further evaluated. The applicant appears to be overly sensitive and easily hurt by others. His approach to life is somewhat rigid, moralistic, and self-righteous. He tends to remain aloof and detached, and he is cautious around other people, fearing they will take advantage of him. He is somewhat touchy and may be argumentative at times. He tends to blame other people for his own failings.

In addition, the following description is suggested by the content of this applicant's responses. He may avoid confrontation and ignore problems to avoid alienating other people. He may be somewhat native in the way he deals with people. He seems to have had a great deal of conflict with authority in the past and is quite resentful of societal and parental standards of conduct. He reported having some antisocial beliefs and attitudes.

INTERPERSONAL RELATIONS

He is somewhat rigid and aloof and does not fully trust anyone. He may be difficult to deal with owing to his rigid, opinionated, and rather argumentative style.

The content of this applicant's MMPI-2 responses suggests the following additional information concerning his interpersonal relations. His tendencies toward spontaneity, impulsiveness, and exhibitionism make him appear fun-loving, perhaps serving as the "life of the party" at times.

PROFILE FREQUENCY

Profile interpretation can be greatly facilitated by examining the relative frequency of clinical scale patterns in various settings. An elevated score on the Pa scale occurred in 9.6% of the MMPI-2 normative sample of men (N = 1,138). Only 3.16% of the normative sample of men obtained clinical scale spikes on Pa above a T score of 65. This elevated MMPI-2 profile configuration (4-6/6-4) is very rare in samples of normals. It occurred in less than 1% of the MMPI-2 normative sample of men. This profile pattern and scale elevation were obtained by only 0.5% of the prototypal sample of airline pilots (Butcher, 1994). In the Pearson Assessments Archival Database (1944), an elevated Pa high point in this range occurred in 1.68% of the males.

CONTEMPORARY PERSONNEL BASE RATE INFORMATION

Additional contemporary base rate data are available to serve as a basis for interpreting airline pilot applicants' profiles. The relative frequency of this profile in various personnel settings is useful information for clinical interpretation because highly elevated Pa patterns can suggest possible negative interpersonal factors in airline pilot applicants. The relative frequency of this MMPI-2 high-point Pa score is 8% for applicants in the large Pearson Assessments (Butcher et al., 2000) applicant sample (N = 18,365 males) without regard to elevation. Moreover, 4.7% of the male applicants have this high-point scale spike at or above a T score of 65 with well-defined Pa scores. In a specific airline pilot sample (N = 344 males), male applicants produced a Pa high-point score with a frequency of 7.6%. Moreover, 3.5% of male applicants had well-defined high-point Pa spikes at or above a T score of 65. It should be kept in mind that extremely elevated scores (at or above a T of 65) are rare and should be given special consideration in the interpretation. This elevated MMPI-2 two-point profile configuration (4-6/6-4) occurs in 4.7% of the men in the Pearson Assessments (Butcher et al., 2000) combined personnel sample (N = 18,365 males) without regard to elevation and in 1.3% of cases with well-defined scores at or above a T score of 65. In addition, 4.1% of men in the airline pilot applicant sample (N = 344 males) produced this codetype at any level of elevation. However, only 0.3% had this profile pair elevated at or above a T score of 65.

PROFILE STABILITY

The relative elevation of his highest clinical scale scores suggests some lack of clarity in profile definition. Although his most elevated clinical scales are likely to be present in his profile pattern if he is retested at a later date, there could be some shifting of these elevations in the profile code. The difference between the profile type used to develop the present report and the next highest scale in the profile code was 3 points. So, for example, if the client is tested at a later date, his profile might involve more behavioral elements related to elevations on Pd. If so, then on retesting, acting-out, aggressive, and irresponsible behavior might become more prominent. The applicant's personality pattern is not likely to change significantly. He may appear somewhat intractable and is typically rigid, detached, and somewhat suspicious. He may have periods in which hostility, increased mistrust, and anger are salient features of personal relationships.

POSSIBLE EMPLOYMENT PROBLEMS

His psychological adjustment problems may result in difficulties for him. His capacity to work closely with others in a crew environment requires further evaluation. He may have some problems with supervision because he is not very open to suggestions. The applicant's rigid and mistrustful behavior may produce stress in working relationships. He may be docile and cooperative with superiors but aggressive and demanding toward subordinates. He may be hostile to other employees.

CONTENT THEMES

MMPI-2 content themes may serve as a source of hypotheses for further investigation. These content themes summarize similar item responses that appear with greater frequency with this applicant than with most people.

His intolerance of others' opinions may limit his work relationships.
He may be rigid and inflexible in his thinking.
He may harbor resentment or hostility toward others.
He may have irresponsible attitudes.
He may sometimes disregard rules when it suits him.
He may have problems with authority and may at times break rules.
He may tend to question supervisory decisions.
He may be unusually sensitive to criticism.

Summary

The MMPI-2 is one of the most widely used self-report personality questionnaires around the world today. This personality inventory, originally published in 1940 by Hathaway and McKinley (1940) and revised in 1989 by Butcher and colleagues, is an empirically derived measure that provides the practitioner with scores on a number of scales that address mental health symptoms or personality attributes. These personality scales summarize the client's response attitudes, mental health symptoms, personality characteristics, and special problems that the client might be experiencing. The MMPI-2 was developed according to the empirical scale construction strategy – that is, the items for the scales were chosen because they empirically differentiated the client from known clinical groups and normal populations. The measures on the MMPI-2 have been widely validated across a broad range of clinical, personnel, and criminal settings.

Topics addressed in this chapter include: the influence of culture on the personality and mental health problems people experience, the effectiveness of the MMPI-2 in assessing clients from different cultural backgrounds, and the use of the test in international settings. Computer-based personality assessment using the MMPI-2 was also described. The MMPI-2 can provide valuable personality information about clients in a variety of settings. This chapter includes a case study from a personnel evaluation setting to illustrate the utility of the MMPI-2 in detecting potential mental health or personality factors that could influence job performance in high-risk occupations.

References

Abe, M. (1955). On the personality inventory. *Bulletin of Tohoku Institute of Correctional Science, 1*, 161–162.

Baer, R.A., Wetter, M.W., Nichols, D., Greene, R., & Berry, D.T. (1995). Sensitivity of MMPI-2 validity scales to underreporting of symptoms. *Psychological Assessment, 7* (4), 419–423.

Bagby, R.M., Buis, T., & Nicholson, R.A. (1995). Relative effectiveness of the standard validity scales in detecting fake-bad and fake-good responding: Replication and extension. *Psychological Assessment, 7* (1), 84–92.

Butcher, J.N. (1996). *International Adaptations of the MMPI-2*. Minneapolis: University of Minnesota Press.

Butcher, J.N. (2011). *The MMPI-2: A Beginner's Guide* (3rd ed.). Washington, DC: American Psychological Association.

Butcher, J.N., Dahlstrom, W.G., Graham, J.R., Tellegen, A.M., & Kaemmer, B. (1989). *Minnesota Multiphasic Personality Inventory-2 (MMPI-2): Manual for Administration and Scoring*. Minneapolis, MN: University of Minnesota Press.

Butcher, J.N., Gass, C.S., Cumella, E., Kally, Z., & Williams, C.L. (2008). Potential for bias in MMPI-2 assessments using the Fake Bad Scale (FBS). *Psychological Injury and the Law, 1* (3), 191–209.

Butcher, J.N., Graham, J.R., Ben-Porath, Y.S., Tellegen, A., Dahlstrom, W.G., & Kaemmer, B. (2001). *Minnesota Multiphasic Personality Inventory-2: Manual for Administration and Scoring* (Revised edition). Minneapolis, MN: University of Minnesota Press.

Butcher, J.N., Gucker, D.K., & Hellervik, L.W. (2009). Clinical personality assessment in the employment context. In J.N. Butcher (Ed.), *Oxford Handbook of Personality Assessment* (pp. 582–598). New York: Oxford University Press.

Butcher, J.N., & Han, K. (1995). Development of an MMPI-2 scale to assess the presentation of self in a superlative manner: The S Scale. In J.N. Butcher, & C.D. Spielberger (Eds.), *Advances in Personality Assessment, Vol. 10* (pp. 25–50). Hillsdale, NJ: LEA Press.

Butcher, J.N., Hass, G.A., Greene, R.L., & Nelson, L.D. (2015). *Using the MMPI-2 in Forensic Assessment.* Washington, DC: American Psychological Association.

Butcher, J.N., & Pancheri, P. (1976). *Handbook of Cross-National MMPI Research.* Minneapolis, MN: University of Minnesota Press.

Butcher, J.N., Tsai, J., Coelho, S., & Nezami, E. (2006). Cross cultural applications of the MMPI-2. In J.N. Butcher (Ed.), *MMPI-2: The Practioner's Handbook* (pp. 505–537). Washington, DC: American Psychological Association.

Butcher, J.N., Williams, C.L., Graham, J.R., Tellegen, A., Ben-Porath, Y.S., Archer, R.P., & Kaemmer, B. (1992). *Manual for Administration, Scoring, and Interpretation of the Minnesota Multiphasic Personality Inventory for Adolescents: MMPI-A.* Minneapolis, MN: University of Minnesota Press.

Federal Aviation Administration. (2013). *Guide for Aviation Medical Examiners: Decision Considerations, Disease Protocols, Psychiatric and Psychological Evaluations.* Washington DC: Federal Aviation Administration. Retrieved from http://www.faa.gov/about/office_org/headquarters_offices/avs/offices/aam/ame/guide/dec_cons/disease_prot/ppevals/

Fowler, R.D. (1967). Computer interpretation of personality tests: The automated psychologist. *Comprehensive Psychiatry, 8* (6), 455–467.

Friedman, A.F., Bolinskey, P.K., Levak, R., & Nichols, D.S. (2015). *Psychological Assessment with the MMPI-2/RF* (3rd ed.). New York: Routledge/Taylor & Francis.

Gass, C.S., Williams, C.L., Cumella, E., Butcher, J.N., & Kally, Z. (2010). Ambiguous measures of unknown constructs: The MMPI-2 Fake Bad Scale (aka Symptom Validity Scale, FBS, FBS-r). *Psychological Injury and the Law, 3* (1), 81–85.

Graham, J.R. (2012). *MMPI-2: Assessing Personality and Psychopathology* (5th ed.). New York: Oxford University Press.

Greene, R.L. (2011). *MMPI-2/MMPI-2-RF: An Interpretive Manual* (3rd ed.). Boston: Allyn & Bacon.

Greene, R.L., Rouse, S.V., Butcher, J.N., Nichols, D.S., & Williams, C.L. (2009). The MMPI-2 Restructured Clinical (RC) Scales and Redundancy: Response to Tellegen, Ben-Porath, and Sellbom. *Journal of Personality Assessment, 91* (3), 1–5.

Hathaway, S.R., & McKinley, J.C. (1940). A multiphasic personality schedule (Minnesota): 1. Construction of the schedule. *Journal of Psychology, 10* (2), 249–254.

Hathaway, S.R., & McKinley, J.C. (1942). *The Minnesota Multiphasic Personality Schedule.* Minneapolis, MN: University of Minnesota Press.

Lees-Haley, P.R., English, L.T., & Glenn, W.J. (1991). A Fake Bad Scale on the MMPI-2 for personal injury claimants. *Psychological Reports, 68* (1), 203–210.

Meehl, P., & Hathaway, S.R. (1946). The K factor as a suppressor variable in the MMPI. *Journal of Applied Psychology, 30* (5), 525–564.

Nichols, D.S. (2011). *Essentials of MMPI-2 Assessment* (2nd ed.). New York: John Wiley & Sons Ltd.

Ranson, M., Nichols, D.S., Rouse, S.V., & Harrington, J. (2009). Changing or replacing an established personality assessment standard: Issues, goals, and problems, with special reference to recent developments in the MMPI-2. In J.N. Butcher (Ed.), *Handbook of Personality Assessment* (pp. 112–139). New York: Oxford University Press.

Rouse, S.V., Greene, R.L., Butcher, J.N., Nichols, D.S., & Williams, C.L. (2008). What do the MMPI-2 Restructured Clinical Scales reliably measure? Answers from multiple research settings. *Journal of Personality Assessment, 90* (5), 435–442.

Rorschach, H. (1942). *Psychodiagnostics: A Diagnostic Test Based on Perception.* Bern, Switzerland: Hans Huber (originally published in 1921).

Sundberg, N.D. (1956). The use of the MMPI for cross-cultural personality study: A preliminary report on the German translation. *Journal of Abnormal and Social Psychology, 52* (2), 281–283.

Thatte, S., Manos, N., & Butcher, J.N. (1987). *Cross-cultural study of abnormal personality in three countries: United States, India, and Greece.* Paper given at the 10th Annual Conference on Personality Assessment, Brussels, Belgium.

14

Precision Assessment: An Individualized and Temporally Dynamic Approach to Understanding Patients in their Daily Lives

Michael J. Roche
Penn State – Altoona, USA

Aaron L. Pincus
Pennsylvania State University, USA

We believe the way forward in psychological assessment is accomplished through an assessment approach that recognizes temporal dynamics, context-driven expressions of personality and psychopathology, and the integration of idiographic and nomothetic patterns (e.g., Hopwood, Zimmermann, Pincus, & Krueger, 2015; Pincus et al., 2014). All of this can be accomplished through precision assessment. Precision assessment refers both to the increased precision available by collecting data over time in the patient's daily life (i.e., a personalized quantitative diary), and the increased precision in data analysis by making use of person-specific methods of analysis. Such an approach provides an opportunity to capture the dynamics underlying many theories of psychopathology. In the present chapter, we describe the rationale for precision assessment, review literature on nomothetic, temporally dynamic patterns, provide an example of precision assessment, and discuss the contribution of precision assessment to the field of psychological assessment more broadly.

Temporal Dynamics in Psychopathology

The DSM-5 increasingly recognizes the role of temporal dynamics in the description of psychopathology. Length of symptom expression is an important characteristic for accurate diagnosis of bipolar disorder (rapid cycling specifier), borderline personality

The Wiley Handbook of Personality Assessment, First Edition. Edited by Updesh Kumar.
© 2016 John Wiley & Sons, Ltd. Published 2016 by John Wiley & Sons, Ltd.

disorder (affective instability), trauma-related disorders (acute stress disorder vs. post-traumatic stress disorder), depression (major depression vs. dysthymia), and many others (American Psychiatric Association, 2013). There is also increased recognition that diagnoses within a cluster can change over time (e.g., anorexia, bulimia, binge-eating disorder; Eddy et al., 2008), and there is even evidence that once-thought stable personality disorder symptoms can change across years (Lenzenweger, 2006; Skodol et al., 2005). This emphasis accords with personality research which has long recognized the importance of considering dynamic and changing presentations of how personality manifests (e.g., Allport, 1937; Block, 1995; Borkenau & Ostendorf, 1998; Cattell, 1952; Cervone, 2005; Church et al., 2013; Fleeson, 2001), and the importance of identifying contexts that exacerbate the expression of symptoms (Eaton, South, & Krueger, 2009; Mischel, 1968; Mischel & Shoda, 1995; Pincus & Wright, 2011).

Yet, clinical diagnosis and psychological assessment (including personality assessment) is commonly conducted during a single occasion, which does not permit the exploration of temporally dynamic processes as they unfold. Approaching diagnosis and assessment this way limits the potential of what assessment can provide for the clinician. We present an approach to enhance traditional psychological assessment that incorporates the dimension of time.

Temporally Dynamic Data

Longitudinal data is ideal to capture the temporal dynamics and contexts inherent in the expressions of psychopathology. Longitudinal data can be collected using longer timescales (years or months) and/or shorter timescales (weeks, days, or hours). This chapter focuses specifically on the shorter timescales captured by asking individuals to report on experiences unfolding in their daily life. A common approach to this data collection is to ask a patient to self-report on experiences they have throughout their day for a period of time (ranging from a few days to a few weeks), often with a mobile application created to run on their smart phone (Gunthert & Wenze, 2012). Importantly, the data are collected in the contexts of their daily life, maximizing external validity. There are variations on the timing of data collection (e.g., random prompting, event-contingent prompting, and end-of-day records) depending on the needs of the researcher/clinician. This approach has many names, including experiencing sampling methodology (ESM), ecological momentary assessment (EMA), intensive-repeated-measures in naturalistic-settings (IRM-NS), and diary study, to name a few. Regardless of the name, these data collection designs are a robust and growing trend in researching psychopathology because they can capture clinical phenomena on the timescale in which they occur. Moreover, such methods can reduce imprecision caused by retrospective biases, such as memory bias (e.g., mood-state congruent recall), memory heuristics (e.g., availability heuristic) and errors related to semantic knowledge (belief of how events should have unfolded; Reis, 2012; Schwartz, 2007).

Temporally Dynamic Theories

Longitudinal data also map directly onto theories that articulate temporal dynamics. For instance, Fleeson and Jayawickreme (2015) developed "whole trait theory," which is a conceptual framework to understand the dynamics of personality and psychopathology. They suggest that personality is best captured as a density distribution of behavioral states the individual employs repeatedly in daily life, and propose temporally dynamic social-cognitive mechanisms that give rise to these distributions.

The Cognitive Affective Processing System (CAPS; Mischel & Shoda, 1995) is another framework that suggests that personality is defined by if–then contingencies that developed from repeatedly experiencing a particular context (*if*) which tends to elicit a predictable pattern of behaving (*then*). For instance, describing a person as aggressive is oversimplified. Instead, this framework would note the contexts (*ifs*) that intensify aggressive behavior (*then*), which appear to have developed into a relatively enduring if–then pattern. CAPS continues to gain prominence in the field of personality as well as clinical psychology as an organizational framework (Rhadigan & Huprich, 2012). However, this framework lacks specificity in identifying a taxonomy of contexts (*ifs*) and behaviors (*thens*) deemed important to assess (but see Rauthmann et al., 2014), and does not provide a theoretical framework to guide predictions among these variables.

Contemporary interpersonal theory is a temporally dynamic and interdisciplinary framework that can overlay onto the CAPS model, and provide specific variables and associations among those variables (Hopwood, Pincus, & Wright, in press; Pincus & Ansell, 2013). Interpersonal theory identifies two fundamental dimensions to organize interpersonal phenomena. Agency is the condition of mastery, assertion, and control, often expressed behaviorally as dominance (vs. submission). Communion is the condition of connection, solidarity, and affiliation, often expressed behaviorally through friendliness (vs. unfriendliness). Interpersonal theory provides specificity regarding which contexts (*ifs*) to consider (i.e., agentic and communal perceptions of others) and behaviors (*thens*) to understand (i.e., agentic and communal behaviors). It further articulates specific if–then normative patterns along the dimension of agency (i.e., a negative association whereby perceiving more dominance in others invites one to become more submissive, and vice versa) and communion (i.e., a positive association whereby perceiving more friendliness in others invites one to become more friendly as well, and vice versa). Such patterns emerged from clinical theory (Carson, 1969; Kiesler, 1983), and research supports these normative patterns in laboratory-based social interactions (Thomas, Hopwood, Woody, Ethier, & Sadler, 2014) and in social interactions occurring naturally in the daily lives of students (Erickson, Newman, & Pincus, 2009), patients (Sadikaj, Moskowitz, Russell, Zuroff, & Paris, 2013), and community populations (Côté, Moskowitz, & Zuroff, 2012).

Temporally Dynamic Analyses

Experiencing sampling methodology (ESM)/longitudinal data allow us to assess and research psychopathology at several different levels and units of analysis. For the purpose of this chapter we highlight the domain of interpersonal research because interpersonal theory provides a nomological net for the study of personality assessment, psychopathology, and psychotherapy (Pincus, 2010), and it includes a theoretical framework to tether data analyses to theory (Pincus et al., 2014). ESM data have been employed to explore a vast number of topics including mood/affect (Aan het Rot, Hogenelst, & Schoevers, 2012), eating disorder symptoms (Ambwani, Roche, Minnick, & Pincus, 2015), substance misuse (Ansell, Laws, Roche, & Sinha, 2015; Zheng, Cleveland, Molenaar, & Harris, 2015), and many others, but reviews of these domains are beyond the scope of this chapter.

Between-person analyses of dynamic processes

Between-person analyses are traditionally employed with data collected at a single time point. The extension of this into longitudinal data is to calculate a summary score (density distribution) of the data collected over time (e.g., calculating a within-person mean, within-person standard deviation, and other calculations of variability – see Ram, Conroy, Pincus, Hyde, & Molloy, 2012) and similarly correlate the variables. For instance, Roche (2014) found that across a 14-day nightly diary design, student participants with higher average interpersonal distress (density distribution calculated as a within-person mean) tended to report higher levels of anger, anxiety, and depression, and no satisfaction with life. Notably, this density distribution of interpersonal distress incremented a baseline measure of interpersonal distress for these outcomes, suggesting that the longitudinal approach enhances traditional single-occasion assessment.

The more commonly calculated density distribution in the interpersonal literature is a standard deviation. A within-person standard deviation on the agency dimension is referred to as agentic "flux," and similarly for communion described as communal "flux." The circular standard deviation for agency and communion is known as "spin," which quantifies diversity of interpersonal behaviors enacted or perceived over time (Moskowitz & Zuroff, 2004). In a sample of community adults completing social interaction records for 20 days, higher agentic flux was associated with higher levels of neuroticism, higher communal flux was associated with higher levels of disagreeableness, and higher spin was associated with higher neuroticism, disagreeableness, and introversion (Moskowitz & Zuroff, 2004). In a 21-day study of community participants, within-person means of agency and communion were related to both anxiety and depression, but flux scores were uniquely predictive of anxiety (Rappaport, Moskowitz, & D'Antono, 2014). In a 20-day study of females with and without borderline personality disorder, the borderline group demonstrated higher variability in communal (friendly and unfriendly) and agentic (dominant) behaviors (Russell, Moskowitz, Zuroff, Sookman, & Paris, 2007) reflecting greater lability. In a set of studies in the workplace, higher spin was associated with feeling more distant from co-workers, and co-workers reported more avoidance of people who had higher spin scores (Côté et al., 2012). Higher spin was also linked to lower levels of serotonergic activity in the brain (Moskowitz, Zuroff, Aan het Rot, & Young, 2011).

Within-person analysis of dynamic processes

A within-person analysis examines, for the typical patient, the association between two temporally dynamic variables. These form an if–then pattern of association that can map onto the CAPS and interpersonal frameworks. For instance, perceiving others' agency and communion (*ifs*) can be associated with one's own agentic and communal behavior (*thens*). Agentic complementarity would reflect a negative within-person association between agentic perceptions and behaviors, while communal complementarity would reflect a positive within-person association between communal perceptions and behaviors. In a 20-day study of community-dwelling adults, complementarity of agency and communion were found (Fournier, Moskowitz, & Zuroff, 2008), and in a separate sample in the workplace, individuals were more likely to exhibit communal complementarity when not at work, and when at work in a high-status role, while agentic complementarity in this sample was only found in work settings, and was strengthened when the individual was in a high-status role (Moskowitz, Ringo Ho, & Turcotte-Tremblay, 2007). Personality also moderates the strength of complementarity, where agentic complementarity is weaker for individuals higher in pathological narcissism (Roche et al., 2013), communal complementarity is weaker for individuals higher in agreeableness (Yao & Moskowitz, 2015), and communal complementarity in the direction of mutual unfriendliness is stronger for individuals higher in borderline traits (Sadikaj et al., 2013).

Within-that-person analyses of dynamic processes

To this point we have described nomothetic patterns in research, but the power of this kind of data for clinical assessment is that we can also examine within-person patterns of a single individual (i.e., precision assessment). A within-that-person analysis applies within-person statistics to a signal individual, recognizing that the patterns of a "typical" patient may not apply to any one patient (Molenaar & Campbell, 2009). At the same time, drawing from a theoretical framework with normative if–then processes already identified (i.e., complementarity) can provide guidance on which if–then processes to explore (Hopwood et al., 2015).

Roche, Pincus, Conroy, Hyde, and Ram (2014) asked a male clinical patient (and his wife) to take part in a 21-day social interaction diary study. He completed 136 social interactions in the study, 85 of which were with his wife, and both husband and wife reported on their mutual interactions. Using this data, we were able to examine interpersonal complementarity, contexts disrupting complementarity, how disruptions to complementarity impacted the patient's functioning, and agreement among husband and wife on their interpersonal exchanges.

We found that this patient exhibited agentic and communal complementarity across social interactions in his daily life. However, his agentic complementarity only manifested when he saw himself in the more dominant role. Departures from agentic complementarity lowered his self-esteem, but did not impact his mood. Finally, he and his wife agreed on how his interpersonal behaviors were enacted, but they disagreed on her interpersonal behavior.

Specifically, the husband perceived her dominance as unfriendly, which was unlike how he perceived all others. The wife disagreed, reporting her dominant behaviors (during the interactions they shared) were not unfriendly. Note how such data can uncover unique contexts, associations, and discrepancies within the patient's daily life that can facilitate identification of the patient's core conflicts and treatment planning.

Within-that-person analysis (also referred to as a person-specific/idiographic approach) to capture complexity in human functioning is gaining traction in psychiatry (van Os, Delespaul, Wigman, Myin-Germeys, & Wichers, 2013), human development (Ram et al., 2012), and many other fields. There is already a growing literature on how to use such methods for treatment evaluation (i.e., single case research designs; see Smith, 2012), routine outcome monitoring of ongoing therapy cases (van Os, Delespaul, Barge, & Bakker, 2014), and mobile intervention methods (Newman Szkodny, Llera, & Przeworski, 2011). This emerging literature ranges from simple to complex analyses such as unified SEM (Zheng et al., 2015), state-space models (Boswell, Anderson, & Barlow, 2014), network analysis (Wichers, 2014), and several others. Precision assessment is an emerging approach that can personalize patient care and provide the clinician with nuanced descriptions of patient problems as experienced in daily life.

Precision Assessment: Putting it All Together

The use of ESM/longitudinal diary data can significantly enhance the enterprise of psychological assessment. Cattell's data box (1952) identified persons, variables, and occasions of time as dimensions to consider when designing a research study. We propose considering the design of a psychological assessment battery along these same dimensions of persons (self-report, informant report), variables (content of what is captured, nature of variables as attitudinal descriptions, performance-based, or ability-based), and crucially now the differences uncovered by timescale in which the process is captured (Ram et al., 2012).

Different analytic approaches to longitudinal data can present the clinician with different information. Consider the example of a positive association between depression and suicidality. For this example, assume a sample of 50 patients reporting levels of depression and suicidality each night for 7 nights.

The between-person analysis would first transform the data into a single score of depression and a single score of suicidality for each patient, and then correlate depression and suicidality for the sample. A positive association would mean a patient higher in depression tends also to be a patient who is more suicidal (a between-person finding). Clinically, this represents a *baseline risk factor*, in that the clinician knows *who* may be at higher risk for suicidality if they know their patient's level of depression. It does not speak to whether reducing this patient's depression would lead to decreased suicidality. This is because a between-person analysis cannot identify a within-person pattern, except in rare instances where ergodicity principles are met (Molenaar & Campbell, 2009).

The within-person analysis would examine how daily scores of depression and suicidality are related, using some strong statistical assumptions to produce a single score for the sample meant to reflect the "typical patient." A positive association would mean, for the typical patient, experiencing higher depression that day tends to be associated with reporting higher suicidality that day. Clinically, this represents a *modifiable risk factor*, in that the clinician knows *when* a patient could be at higher risk for suicidality if they know the patient's level of depression that day. Yet, what is true of the "typical patient" may not be true for any given patient.

A within-that-person analysis conducted on a single patient would deliver a within-person association that allows the clinician to observe directly whether depression is associated with suicidality for that patient. Clinically, this constitutes a *patient-specific modifiable risk factor*, in that the clinician knows *when a specific patient* will be more prone to suicidality given their reported pattern. This is akin to asking a doctor to x-ray *your* arm if you think it is broken, rather than requesting the within-person association between a typical patient that falls and a typical diagnosis of broken arm, or a baseline risk factor for a broken arm based on your demographic characteristics.

When evaluating suicidality risk (and we would argue psychological assessment more broadly), the clinician likely wants to know all three levels of analysis. The clinician would like to know the baseline factors that may predispose the patient to be "riskier" than the other patients the clinician sees. They would also want to be familiar with typical modifiable risks for suicidality so that they can check with the patient about these risks. Yet the clinician also wants to know the specific patterns that are true for the presenting patient to maximize their care. Attending to risk at each level of analysis builds an empirically informed (between-person, within-person) yet personally tailored (within-that-person) plan of intervention.

Consider these three levels applied to the precision assessment case described earlier (i.e., the husband and his wife). At the between-person level, research suggests knowing his diagnosis of narcissism, borderline personality disorder or agreeable traits could inform us about an expected pattern (baseline risk for not engaging in complementarity). At the within-person level, research findings indicated that status is a normative modifiable risk factor, and indeed we found that his dominance status influenced his agentic complementarity. Yet we also uncovered unexpected and unique within-that-person associations (patient-specific modifiable risk factors) including how complementarity related to self-esteem and identifying a specific individual in his life where unique and troubling interpersonal exchanges occur. Thus, his precision assessment revealed a mix of normative and idiographic patterns that could be targeted through intervention.

Benefits of precision assessment

There are several benefits of using precision assessment to increment typical psychological assessment approaches. First and foremost, it can capture patient-specific dynamics and contexts that exacerbate their symptoms, on the timescale they occur, and in the ecologically valid contexts of daily life. This alone adds an important nuance to traditional assessment approaches. As clinicians, we are trained to observe patterns. This is true irrespective of modality: the CBT therapist may use thought records to observe patterns between feelings and facts, the DBT therapist may utilize chain analysis to notice where skills and distress tolerance are and are not used, the eating disorder therapist uses food logs to observe patterns between contexts/feelings/meal times and eating disorder symptoms, and dynamic therapists may use their relationship in the room and careful observation of other relationships the patient describes to infer patterns of self–other-affect relationships. Precision assessment offers a more systematic way for any therapist to observe these patterns, which may alert clinicians to processes and topics they do not routinely consider to be crucial to understanding the exacerbation of symptoms (but which may be very important for a particular patient). Also, statistical analyses of data may identify small but important patterns that the clinician may find hard to detect in the course of therapy. Thus, systematic precision assessments may alert the therapist to an uncommon or subtle pattern that may have taken longer to identify otherwise.

If an assessment is performed at the onset of treatment and again at a later time, the clinician can observe differences that would reflect ecologically valid markers of treatment progress. This type of daily life assessment moves beyond what a patient reports that they understand in the consultation room, and attempts to capture how their functioning has actually improved in daily life. Moreover, precision assessment can capture more nuanced mechanisms of change useful for the clinician or researcher of treatment comparison studies (i.e., not just that depression was reduced, but whether the association between depression and suicidality weakened, or whether the pattern particularly weakened on days that the patient also reported using DBT/CBT skills).

Limitations of precision assessment

The limitations of precision assessment can be grouped into those inherent in ESM data in general, and those specific to precision assessment. ESM data do provide an arguably more accurate snapshot of current behavioral states and instability compared with retrospective self-reports. However, the findings may not generalize into the future if the patient is sampled at an atypical time in their life (e.g., just lost a family member, just promoted, etc.). It is likely most generalizable to the time period in their life just following the assessment, therefore employing an assessment such as this just before the beginning of treatment would maximize its relevance. The data collected are commonly self-report data (although see Mehl & Conner, 2012, for a review of passive data collection methods) and have the typical limitations inherent in self-report data. The timescale in which the data are collected can also profoundly impact the process observed. This is especially true for lagged time analyses (e.g., depression scores today predicting suicidality scores tomorrow), where carryover effects that may be reasonable on the order of minutes or hours may not be reasonable on the order of days and weeks.

Precision assessment takes an idiographic framework that is not ideal for testing nomothetic theories. In terms of psychological assessment, precision assessment can tell you what the pattern is, but not how unique it is compared with others. Perhaps that doesn't matter if the association (although normative) is still disruptive for the patient. This limitation could be addressed by developing a normative sample that clinicians could use to determine how unique vs. normative their patient patterns are. Finally, precision assessment requires multiple reports over time from patients, which may not be feasible for certain patients.

Implementation

Providing a detailed explanation of implementation is beyond the scope of this chapter (see Roche et al., 2014; Trull & Ebner-Priemer, 2009, for details). The central difficulty in implementation is that there is no standard assessment presently. Unlike other personality assessments which have a standard set of items, administration protocol, scoring protocol, and clinician feedback, precision assessment is still evolving and requires more work for the clinician to implement. The authors are in the process of developing a standard precision assessment instrument with norms for use in clinical assessment, but until that time, clinicians would need to design their own precision assessment battery.

To do this, the clinician should consider whether their patient can self-report accurately. Patients have been able to successfully complete protocols; in fact, several research studies already cited have utilized patient samples for research. The content of items will depend on the referral question, but may be informed through theory (e.g., interpersonal theory), presenting symptoms (e.g., depression, suicidality), and/or topics identified in collaboration with the patient. The three most common timescales are 6–8 random prompts throughout the day, event-contingent prompts throughout the day (e.g., every social interaction, every urge to binge-eat), and a nightly diary. The optimal time for assessment is probably at the onset of treatment to inform treatment goals, or periodically to coincide with treatment plan updates to evaluate how treatment has impacted patient functioning in daily life. Patients can complete the records on a paper survey they turn into the clinician, or by accessing a website hosting the survey (this is easily implemented using several online data collection platforms, or even through Google forms). Research suggests that the data yielded by a paper or online approach are equivalent, but monitoring patient compliance with the assessment protocol is easier when the participants submit the surveys online (Bolger, Davis, & Rafaeli, 2003).

Analyzing the data can become difficult if aspiring towards the more complex analyses (e.g., multilevel models, dynamic factor analysis, network analysis). Roche and colleagues (2014) demonstrated a more simple method relying mainly on correlations and t-tests, and developed a scoring program (available by request from the first author) to calculate all the statistics and deliver the scores in a patient-friendly handout complete with figures and text.

Summary

Precision assessment is an ecologically valid, temporally dynamic, empirically informed, and individualized approach to patient care. It is at the forefront of research advancements by bringing together several emerging trends including longitudinal research, cutting-edge statistical methods, and technological capabilities. It also brings clinicians a completely new way to capture their patient's experiences, and provides a foundation for testing temporally dynamic theories of psychopathology. To be sure, this approach has several limitations that must be addressed before it can flourish. Yet, at present, precision assessment represents, for researchers and clinicians alike, an innovative and promising approach to move the field of psychological assessment forward.

References

Aan het Rot, M., Hogenelst, K., & Schoevers, R.A. (2012). Mood disorders in everyday life: A systematic review of experience sampling and ecological momentary assessment studies. *Clinical Psychology Review, 32* (6), 510–523.

Allport, G.W. (1937). *Personality: A Psychological Interpretation.* Oxford: Henry Holt.

Ambwani, S., Roche, M.J., Minnick, A.M., & Pincus, A.L. (2015). Negative affect, interpersonal perception, and binge eating behavior: An experience sampling study. *International Journal of Eating Disorders, 48,* 715–726.

American Psychiatric Association. (2013). *Diagnostic and Statistical Manual of Mental Disorders: DSM-5.* Arlington, VA: American Psychiatric Association.

Ansell, E.B., Laws, H.B., Roche, M.J., & Sinha, R. (2015). Effects of recreational marijuana use on impulsivity and hostility: A within-person daily diary study. *Drug and Alcohol Dependence, 148,* 136–142.

Block, J. (1995). A contrarian view of the five-factor approach to personality description. *Psychological Bulletin, 117* (2), 187–215.

Bolger, N., Davis, A., & Rafaeli, E. (2003). Diary methods: Capturing life as it is lived. *Annual Review of Psychology, 54,* 579–616.

Borkenau, P., & Ostendorf, F. (1998). The Big Five as states: How useful is the five-factor model to describe intra individual variations over time? *Journal of Research in Personality, 32* (2), 202–221.

Boswell, J.F., Anderson, L.M., & Barlow, D.H. (2014). An idiographic analysis of change processes in the unified trans-diagnostic treatment of depression. *Journal of Counseling and Clinical Psychology, 82* (6), 1060–1071.

Carson, R.C. (1969). *Interaction Concepts of Personality.* Chicago, IL: Aldine Publishing Company.

Cattell, R.B. (1952). The three basic factor-analytic designs: Their interrelations and derivatives. *Psychological Bulletin, 49* (5), 499–520.

Cervone, D. (2005). Personality architecture: Within-person structures and processes. *Annual Review of Psychology, 56,* 423–452.

Church, A.T., Katigbak, M.S., Ching, C.M., Zhang, H., Shen, J., Arias, R.M., & Alverez, J.M. (2013). Within-individual variability in self-concepts and personality states: Applying density distribution and situation-behavior approaches across cultures. *Journal of Research in Personality, 47* (6), 922–935.

Côté, S., Moskowitz, D.S., & Zuroff, D.C. (2012). Social relationships and intra individual variability in interpersonal behavior: Correlates of interpersonal spin. *Journal of Personality and Social Psychology, 102* (3), 646–659.

Eaton, N.R., South, S.C., & Krueger, R.F. (2009). The Cognitive–Affective Processing System (CAPS) approach to personality and the concept of personality disorder: Integrating clinical and social-cognitive research. *Journal of Research in Personality, 43* (2), 208–217.

Eddy, K.T., Dorer, D.J., Franko, D.L., Tahilani, K., Thompson-Brenner, H., & Herzog, D.B. (2008). Diagnostic crossover in anorexia nervosa and bulimia nervosa: Implications for DSM-V. *American Journal of Psychiatry, 165* (2), 245–250.

Erickson, T.M., Newman, M.G., & Pincus, A.L. (2009). Predicting unpredictability: Do measures of interpersonal rigidity/flexibility and distress predict intra individual variability in social perceptions and behavior? *Journal of Personality and Social Psychology, 97* (5), 893–912.

Fleeson, W. (2001). Toward a structure- and process-integrated view of personality: Traits as density distributions of states. *Journal of Personality and Social Psychology, 80* (6), 1011–1027.

Fleeson, W., & Jayawickreme, E. (2015). Whole trait theory. *Journal of Research in Personality, 56*, 82–92.

Fournier, M.A., Moskowitz, D.S., & Zuroff, D.C. (2008). Integrating dispositions, signatures, and the interpersonal domain. *Journal of Personality and Social Psychology, 94* (3), 531–545.

Gunthert, K.C., & Wenze, S.J. (2012). Daily diary methods. In M.R. Mehl, & T.S. Conner (Eds.), *Handbook of Research Methods for Studying Daily Life* (pp. 144–160). New York: Guilford Press.

Hopwood, C.J., Pincus, A.L., & Wright, A.G.C. (in press). The interpersonal situation: Integrating personality assessment, case formulation, and intervention. In D. Samuel, & D. Lynam (Eds.), *Purdue Symposium on Psychological Science*. New York: Oxford.

Hopwood, C.J., Zimmermann, J., Pincus, A.L., & Krueger, R.F. (2015). Connecting personality structure and dynamics: Towards a more evidence based and clinically useful diagnostic scheme. *Journal of Personality Disorders, 29* (4), 431–448.

Kiesler, D.J. (1983). The 1982 interpersonal circle: A taxonomy for complementarity in human transactions. *Psychological Review, 90* (3), 185–214.

Lenzenweger, M.F. (2006). The Longitudinal Study of Personality Disorders: History, design considerations, and initial findings. *Journal of Personality Disorders, 20* (6), 645–670.

Mehl, M.R., & Connor, T.S. (2012). *Handbook of Research Methods for Studying Daily Life*. New York: Guilford.

Mischel, W. (1968). *Personality and Assessment*. New York: John Wiley & Sons, Ltd.

Mischel, W., & Shoda, Y. (1995). A cognitive-affective system theory of personality: Reconceptualizing situations, dispositions, dynamics, and invariance in personality structure. *Psychological Review, 102* (2), 246–268.

Molenaar, P.C.M., & Campbell, C.G. (2009). The new person-specific paradigm in psychology. *Current Directions in Psychological Science, 18* (2), 112–117.

Moskowitz, D.S., Ringo Ho, M., & Turcotte-Tremblay, A. (2007). Contextual influences on interpersonal complementarity. *Personality and Social Psychology Bulletin, 33* (8), 1051–1063.

Moskowitz, D.S., & Zuroff, D.C. (2004). Flux, pulse, and spin: Dynamic additions to the personality lexicon. *Journal of Personality and Social Psychology, 86* (6), 880–893.

Moskowitz, D.S., Zuroff, D.C., Aan het Rot, M., & Young, S.N. (2011). Tryptophan and interpersonal spin. *Journal of Research in Personality, 45* (6), 692–696.

Newman, M.G., Szkodny, L.E., Llera, S.J., & Przeworski, A. (2011). A review of technology-assisted self-help and minimal contact therapies for anxiety and depression: Is human contact necessary for therapeutic efficacy? *Clinical Psychology Review, 31* (1), 89–103.

Pincus, A.L. (2010). Introduction to the Special Series on integrating personality, psychopathology, and psychotherapy using interpersonal assessment. *Journal of Personality Assessment, 92* (6), 467–470.

Pincus, A.L., & Ansell, E.B. (2013). Interpersonal theory of personality. In J. Suls, & Tennen (Eds.), *Handbook of Psychology, Vol. 5: Personality and Social Psychology* (2nd ed.) (pp. 141–159) Hoboken, NJ: John Wiley & Sons, Ltd.

Pincus, A.L., Sadler, P., Woody, E., Roche, M.J., Thomas, K.M., & Wright, A.G.C. (2014). Multimethod assessment of interpersonal dynamics. In C.J. Hopwood, & R.F. Bornstein (Eds.), *Multimethod Clinical Assessment* (pp. 51–91). New York: Guilford.

Pincus, A.L., & Wright, A.G.C. (2011). Interpersonal diagnosis of psychopathology. In L.M. Horowitz, & S. Strack (Eds.), *Handbook of Interpersonal Psychology: Theory, Research, Assessment, and Therapeutic Interventions* (pp. 359–381), Hoboken, NJ: John Wiley & Sons, Ltd.

Ram, N., Conroy, D.E., Pincus, A.L., Hyde, A.L., & Molloy, L. (2012). Tethering theory to method: Using measures of intra individual variability to operationalize individuals' dynamic characteristics. In G. Hancock, & J. Harring (Eds.), *Advances in Longitudinal Modeling in the Social and Behavioral Sciences* (pp. 81–110). Charlotte, NC: Information Age Publishing.

Rappaport, L.M., Moskowitz, D.S., & D'Antono, B. (2014). Naturalistic interpersonal behavior patterns differentiate depression and anxiety symptoms in the community. *Journal of Counseling Psychology, 61* (2), 253–263.

Rauthmann, J.F., Gallardo-Pujol, D., Guillaume, E.M., Todd, E., Nave, C.S., Sherman, R.A., ... Funder, D.C. (2014). The situational eight DIAMONDS: A taxonomy of major dimensions of situation characteristics. *Journal of Personality and Social Psychology, 107* (4), 677–718.

Reis, H.T. (2012). Why researchers should think "Real-World": A conceptual rationale. In M.R. Mehl, & T.S. Conner (Eds.), *Handbook of Research Methods for Studying Daily Life* (pp. 3–21). New York: Guilford Press.

Rhadigan, C., & Huprich, S.K. (2012). The utility of the cognitive–affective processing system in the diagnosis of personality disorders: Some preliminary evidence. *Journal of Personality Disorders, 26* (2), 162–178.

Roche, M.J. (2014). *Using the Inventory of Interpersonal Problems as a daily measure of personality dysfunction.* Paper presented at the Society for Interpersonal Theory and Research, New Haven, CT.

Roche, M.J., Pincus, A.L., Conroy, D.E., Hyde, A.L., & Ram, N. (2013). Pathological narcissism and interpersonal behavior in daily life. *Personality Disorders: Theory, Research, and Treatment, 4* (4), 315–323.

Roche, M.J., Pincus, A.L., Conroy, D.E., Hyde, A.L., & Ram, N. (2014). Enriching psychological assessment using a person-specific analysis of interpersonal processes in daily life. *Assessment, 21* (5), 515–528.

Russell, J.J., Moskowitz, D.S., Zuroff, D.C., Sookman, D., & Paris, J. (2007). Stability and variability of affective experience and interpersonal behavior in borderline personality disorder. *Journal of Abnormal Psychology, 116* (3), 578–588.

Sadikaj, G., Moskowitz, D.S., Russell, J.J., Zuroff, D.C., & Paris, J. (2013). Quarrelsome behavior in borderline personality disorder: Influence of behavioral and affective reactivity to perceptions of others. *Journal of Abnormal Psychology, 122* (1), 195–207.

Schwartz, N. (2007). Retrospective and concurrent self-reports: The rationale for real-time data capture. In A.S. Stone, S. Shiffman, A.A. Atienza, & L. Nebeling (Eds.), *The Science of Real Time Data Capture* (pp. 11–26). New York: Oxford University Press.

Skodol, A.E., Gunderson, J.G., Shea, M.T., McGlashan, T.H., Morey, L.C., Sanislow, C.A., et al. (2005). The collaborative longitudinal personality disorders study (CLPS): Overview and implications. *Journal of Personality Disorders, 19* (5), 487–504.

Smith, J.D. (2012). Single-case experimental designs: A systematic review of published research and current standards. *Psychological Methods, 17* (4), 510–550.

Thomas, K.M., Hopwood, C.J., Woody, E., Ethier, N., & Sadler, P. (2014). Momentary assessment of interpersonal process in psychotherapy. *Journal of Counseling Psychology, 61* (1), 1–14.

Trull, T.J., & Ebner-Priemer, U. (2009). The role of ambulatory assessment in psychological science. *Current Directions in Psychological Science, 23* (6), 466–470.

Wichers, M. (2014). The dynamic nature of depression: a new micro-level perspective on mental disorders that meets current challenges. *Psychological Medicine, 44* (7), 1349–1360.

van Os, J., Delespaul, P., Barge, D., & Bakker, R.P. (2014). Testing a Health Momentary Assessment Routine Outcome monitoring application: A focus on restoration of daily life positive mood states. *PLoS ONE, 9* (12), e115254.

van Os, J., Delespaul, P., Wigman, J., Myin-Germeys, I., & Wichers, M. (2013). Beyond DSM and ICD: introducing "precision diagnosis" for psychiatry using momentary assessment technology. *World Psychiatry, 12* (2), 113–117.

Yao, Q., & Moskowitz, D.S. (2015). Trait agreeableness and social status moderate behavioral responsiveness to communal behavior. *Journal of Personality, 83* (2), 191–201.

Zheng, Y., Cleveland, H.H., Molenaar, P.C.M., & Harris, K.S. (2015). An alternative framework to investigating and understanding intraindividual processes in substance abuse recovery: An idiographic approach and demonstration. *Evaluation Review, 39* (2), 229–254.

15

Are Situational Judgment Tests Better Assessments of Personality than Traditional Personality Tests in High-Stakes Testing?

Deborah L. Whetzel
Human Resources Research Organization, USA

Michael A. McDaniel
Virginia Commonwealth University, USA

Personality, Situational Judgment Tests, and Faking

Traditional personality assessments, such as the International Personality Item Pool (Goldberg, 1999), provide respondents with a list of behaviors (e.g., work hard, feel comfortable around people) and they are asked to rate the accuracy with which each statement describes their behavior. In high-stakes testing situations in which decisions are made based on test results (e.g., admissions decisions in the case of educational tests, and employment decisions in the case of personnel selection testing), applicants are likely to be motivated to respond to achieve a favorable score. For example, using a traditional personality assessment, people applying for a sales job may present themselves as more extroverted and sociable than they really are. Faking has been studied extensively in non-cognitive self-report measures, such as personality inventories, biodata inventories, and integrity tests (e.g., Alliger & Dwight, 2000; Becker & Colquitt, 1992; Douglas, McDaniel, & Snell, 1996; Graham, McDaniel, Douglas, & Snell, 2002; Ones, Viswesvaran, & Reiss, 1996). Research makes it clear that personality tests can be faked.

Two major research streams have addressed situational judgment tests (SJTs) and faking. One research stream addresses the maximum limits of faking using lab studies where students are instructed to fake (Juraska & Drasgow, 2001; Nguyen, Biderman, & McDaniel, 2005). Nguyen et al. found that when instructed to fake using behavioral tendency questions, the faking effect ranged from *d* of 0.15 to 0.34. The authors concluded that, "… in practice, SJT scores obtained under the knowledge

The Wiley Handbook of Personality Assessment, First Edition. Edited by Updesh Kumar.
© 2016 John Wiley & Sons, Ltd. Published 2016 by John Wiley & Sons, Ltd.

response format could be treated as being relatively immune from faking. Essentially, the scores on the SJT knowledge response format will be as high as the applicant can make them regardless of the inclination to fake" (p. 257).

The other research stream focuses on typical levels of faking in real-world settings, often comparing students, applicants, and incumbents (Peeters & Lievens, 2005; Ployhart, Weekley, Holtz, & Kemp, 2003). In a comparison between applicants' and incumbents' responses to a paper-based personality measure and a paper-based SJT, Ployhart et al. (2003) found that differences were significantly greater for personality measures of conscientiousness and emotional stability than for SJT items. Peeters and Lievens (2005) investigated the use of SJTs to supplement student admission procedures. Using a sample of 293 psychology students, they found that scores of students who were instructed to fake were significantly higher than those of students in the honest condition. Lievens, Peeters, and Schollaert (2008) concluded that faking has less impact on SJTs than on personality inventories.

Hooper, Cullen, and Sackett (2006) reviewed existing literature on faking and SJT mean scores, and drew three important conclusions. First, SJTs might be prone to faking with effect sizes ranging from 0.08 to 0.89. Second, this large variability could be explained by several moderating variables: (a) when SJTs had a stronger cognitive loading, they were less fakable; (b) more transparent items were more fakable; and (c) behavioral tendency response instructions led to greater levels of fakability than knowledge instructions used (Nguyen et al., 2005). Third, they concluded that SJTs are less fakable than personality inventories. In sums, research shows that faking has less impact on SJTs than on personality inventories (Lievens, Peeters, & Schollaert, 2008).

In their study comparing mean SJT scores of applicants and incumbents, MacKenzie, Ployhart, Weekley, and Ehlers (2010) found that, in contrast to most non-cognitive predictors, applicants obtained lower scores on SJTs than incumbents in all six organizations studied. A practical implication of this finding is that SJTs will more effectively distinguish among applicants than alternative non-cognitive predictors, such as personality.

Depending on how the SJT is designed, people may respond to item alternatives in several ways. They may indicate which actions they would most and least likely perform; they may select which responses are the best and worst actions; or they may rate the effectiveness of each response. The response approaches to SJT items fall into two categories (McDaniel, Hartman, Whetzel, & Grubb, 2007). Respondents can be asked to describe their behavioral tendencies (e.g., which of these responses would I likely do?) or they can be asked to display their knowledge (e.g., which of these responses is the best thing to do?). We offer that knowledge instructions are faking-resistant because both the faking and honest respondents have the same goal, that is, to use their knowledge to select the best answer. This assertion is supported by Nguyen et al. (2005). Although some research suggests that faking might improve SJT scores somewhat (Hooper et al., 2006), we assert that SJTs with behavioral tendency instructions and personality tests can be easily faked, but SJTs with knowledge instructions are substantially faking-resistant. Thus, in high-stakes situations, in which applicants are motivated to fake, we suggest that SJTs with knowledge instructions will yield less faking-distorted assessments than traditional personality measures.

Do SJTs Measure Personality?

McDaniel et al. (2007) reported the relationship between the two types of SJT response instructions with cognitive ability and personality. They found that SJTs correlate in varying degrees with the Big Five personality traits (Digman, 1990), and that the magnitude of these correlations is moderated by the SJT response instructions. SJTs with behavioral tendency instructions tend to be more correlated with personality and less correlated with cognitive ability than SJTs with knowledge instructions. Further evidence of the SJT as a measure of personality is provided by Arthur, Glaze, Jarrett, White, Schurig, and Taylor (2014). Using a knowledge-based set of instructions, they found that the SJT correlated 0.31 with Agreeableness, 0.34 with Conscientiousness, and 0.24 with Emotional Stability. In summary, in situations in which there is little motivation to fake, SJTs with behavioral tendency instructions would capture the most personality variance. However, in high-stakes testing situations, we assert that SJTs with knowledge instructions will yield more accurate assessments of personality due to their faking resistance.

We note that the assessment of personality using SJTs comes with some drawbacks. Factor analyses of SJT items often yield solutions that are difficult to interpret (McDaniel & Whetzel, 2005; Schmitt & Chan, 2006), and many attempts to develop SJTs that measure particular constructs have had only limited success (e.g., Oswald, Schmitt, Kim, Ramsay, & Gillespie, 2004). One problem is that a single SJT item can assess multiple constructs (McDaniel & Whetzel, 2005). This situation makes forming homogeneous scales from SJT items unlikely. Thus, if the goal is to create homogeneous scales of personality traits, personality tests are preferred. If the goal is to measure personality in high-stakes testing situations, we assert that SJTs are preferred.

Although homogeneous scales are rare in SJT applications, there have been attempts to construct taxonomies for SJTs. Based on the work of Huffcutt, Conway, Roth, and Stone (2001), Christian, Edwards, and Bradley (2010) used a taxonomy of criterion constructs (contextual, task, and managerial performance) and identified a taxonomy of SJT content (leadership, interpersonal, and managerial skills). They found that SJTs measuring interpersonal, teamwork, and leadership skills had higher validity than a heterogeneous composite (SJTs that could not be classified by construct). They also found that SJTs measuring leadership and interpersonal skills were more valid for measuring managerial performance. In sum, there is ample research evidence showing that SJTs are correlated with personality and are faking-resistant when knowledge instructions are used. However, few explanations have been provided about why SJTs predict job performance.

SJTs as a Measures of Procedural Job Knowledge

One plausible explanation for the relationships among SJTs and personality variables is that SJTs can be used to assess personality indirectly through procedural job knowledge. Campbell (1990) and Campbell, McCloy, Oppler, and Sager (1992) provided a model of job performance in which performance is a function of declarative knowledge

Table 15.1 Sample SJT item measuring procedural knowledge

You are working as the leader of a team charged with performing a task for a client. The client just called you and needs to move the deadline to be earlier than the original schedule.

A. Discuss the new deadline with your team and have them help determine methods for meeting it.
B. Develop a set of intermediate deadlines and present them to the team.
C. Tell the client that the team will not be able to meet the deadline.
D. Do not mention the new deadline to the team, but encourage them to hurry up.

(knowledge of facts, rules, principles, and procedures), procedural knowledge and skill (knowing what to do), and motivation (the choices to expend effort, the level of effort to expend, and persist in the expenditure of effort). Individual differences in stable traits, such as personality, are indirectly related to job performance through their effects on these direct determinants. As such, personality affects procedural knowledge (e.g., agreeable people are likely to understand how to negotiate with others), and procedural knowledge affects job performance (e.g., knowledge of how to negotiate with others affects job performance). As another example, someone who has learned that expressions of emotional stability are more effective than expressions of neuroticism in situations that involve interactions with clients has more knowledge about how to act effectively in a consulting job, assuming that a calm demeanor toward clients is more effective than a nervous disposition in that job. An SJT item that measures procedural knowledge of team management is shown in Table 15.1.

Those who have procedural knowledge of team management may understand that goals set jointly among members of a team are more likely to be accepted by the team and that accepted goals are more likely to be met. Those who are agreeable may have this knowledge and may be more likely to select option A. Thus, people who are more agreeable are more likely to have procedural knowledge of how to manage a team, and successful management of a team may be required to perform a particular job. These examples describe how SJTs measure personality indirectly through procedural job knowledge.

Consistent with this model, SJTs have been developed to measure diverse procedural knowledge domains such as teamwork knowledge (McClough & Rogelberg, 2003; Morgeson, Reider, & Campion, 2005; Mumford, Van Iddekinge, Morgeson, & Campion, 2008; Stevens & Campion, 1999), aviation pilot judgment (Hunter, 2003), employee integrity (Becker, 2005), call-center performance (Konradt, Hertel, & Joder, 2003), academic performance (Oswald et al., 2004), personal initiative (Bledow & Frese, 2009), conflict resolution (Olson-Buchanan et al., 1998), customer service (McHenry & Schmitt, 1994; Weekley & Jones, 1997), and passenger relations (Jones, 1987).

Hunter (1986) made an analogous argument in the cognitive ability domain. He showed that the more distal construct, cognitive ability, had a relationship with job performance through job knowledge. The interaction between Hunter's (1983) model showing how cognitive ability predicts task performance through the intervening variable of job knowledge, and Motowidlo, Borman, and Schmit's (1997) model showing how personality predicts contextual performance through the intervening variable of

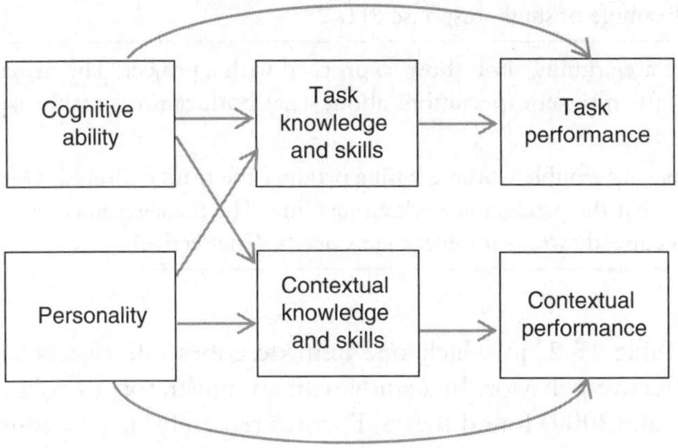

Figure 15.1 Relationships among cognitive ability and personality and performance, with task and contextual knowledge as intervening variables. Adapted from Bergman, Donovan, Drasgow, Overton, and Henning (2008).

contextual knowledge, is shown in Figure 15.1. In sum, prior research suggests that personality is related to job performance as mediated by job knowledge, and this job knowledge (procedural, contextual) can be measured using SJTs.

Lievens and Sackett (2012) provided evidence for this model using four samples (N = 723) of medical students. They used a video-based SJT to assess procedural knowledge of interpersonal behavior at the time of admission to medical school, and then assessed internship performance seven years later and job performance nine years later. They found that the SJT showed incremental validity over cognitive factors. They concluded that there is a conceptual link between procedural knowledge of interpersonal behavior and how that knowledge translates into actual behavior in internships and job performance.

The idea that SJTs measure procedural job knowledge was further corroborated by MacKenzie et al. (2010). They found that across six organizations studied, cognitive ability was a stronger correlate of SJT scores for incumbents than applicants. This led the authors to conclude that incumbents with greater cognitive ability more effectively acquired and used organization-specific knowledge.

Evidence further supporting the model was provided Bergman et al. (2008), who studied support staff working with agents who sell financial and insurance products (N = 148). Using a test battery that included personality (i.e., openness and assertiveness) and an SJT that measured knowledge of customer relations, they found that openness to experience was related to customer service knowledge, as measured with their SJT, which was related to service performance. In a study with human factors professionals (HFPs), Motowidlo, Martin, and Crook (2013) created an SJT that measured contextual knowledge of HFP service encounters. They showed that conscientiousness was significantly related to knowledge about effective and ineffective behavior in simulated service encounters.

Further evidence of the indirect relationship between using SJTs to measure personality and the prediction of job performance are provided using single-response SJTs (Motowidlo, Crook, Kell, & Naemi, 2009). Examples of such items are

Table 15.2 Example of single-response SJTs

Two colleagues are arguing about how to proceed with a project. The manager schedules a meeting with them to set expectations about what both can reasonably expect from each other. (Effective)
A customer is having trouble working with a product the team delivered. One of the team members insists that the product is working just fine. The manager informs the customer that the product already works for everyone's needs. (Ineffective)

provided in Table 15.2, in which one item describes effective behavior and one describes ineffective behavior. In a study with administrators of volunteer agencies, Motowidlo et al. (2009) found that SJT scores representing procedural knowledge about work effort were significantly correlated with ratings of work effort performance, demonstrating the construct validity of the single-item SJT. They further found that conscientiousness was correlated with work effort procedural knowledge, and that this procedural knowledge was significantly correlated with ratings of work effort performance. However, conscientiousness was not directly correlated with work effort performance, thus supporting the indirect relationship of personality with job performance.

Crook et al. (2011) conducted two studies investigating single-response SJTs as measures of job knowledge. In the first study of museum tour guides, they developed an SJT to measure procedural job knowledge and computed effective and ineffective SJT scores. They correlated the SJT scores with a measure of Big Five personality traits and job performance. They found that personality was significantly related to job knowledge as measured by the single-response SJT; however, knowledge did not account for incremental variance after personality was accounted for. In their second study of volunteers, they found that knowledge as measured by the single-response SJTs was significantly correlated with volunteer performance, and that personality traits were related to job knowledge. Unlike the first study, they found that job knowledge was an intervening variable between personality traits and job performance, as knowledge accounted for significant variance in performance after personality traits were accounted for. These results provide support for the notion that job knowledge is an intervening variable in the relationship between personality, as measured by SJTs, and job performance.

In sum, we argue that SJTs provide a better prediction of job performance than traditional personality measures because they measure personality indirectly by assessing procedural job knowledge. This is important because procedural job knowledge should not be fakable. Similar to tests of cognitive ability, either one has the knowledge or one does not.

Recommendations for Future SJT Research

This chapter has offered evidence that SJTs may be a better approach to measuring personality in high-stakes testing situations than traditional personality tests. We do not anticipate that those with commercial and scholarly investments in traditional personality tests will wholeheartedly embrace this position. We offer a few issues best addressed by future research that may help to resolve differences in perspectives on this topic.

A key issue in resolving whether SJTs or traditional personality tests are better at assessing personality in high-stakes testing situations is the need for clear knowledge of a respondent's personality. Self-reports of personality likely include inaccuracies due to impression management and self-deception. The reports of others with respect to a person's personality are also likely to have some inaccuracies. The reporting other may lack full and accurate knowledge of the target's personality and may have motivations to distort the personality of the target.

One approach to sidestep the issue of a true knowledge deficit is to determine whether an SJT or a traditional personality measure best predicts in a high-stakes testing situation. From a prediction perspective, such a horse race is both informative and serves to guide practice. However, the SJT and the traditional personality measure may not be tapping exactly the same personality traits, and the SJT may be better in prediction due to constructs outside of personality (e.g., most SJTs measure, in part, cognitive ability).

Evaluating the relative merit of SJTs and traditional personality tests in high-stakes testing would benefit from greater knowledge of SJTs and their role in prediction. One relevant topic is to better understand the nature of procedural knowledge and skills. For example, procedural knowledge regarding interpersonal interactions are probably different for different audiences (e.g., when dealing with clients vs. co-workers) and different situations (e.g., conflict management vs. teambuilding). One possible method for developing a better understanding of what kind of knowledge is measured by SJTs is to use think-aloud protocol analysis, where respondents are asked to describe aloud what they are thinking as they respond to an SJT item.

Finally, Ployhart (2006) offered a process model for situational judgment measures. The predictor response process (PRPR) model suggests that interpreting and responding to an SJT item requires four distinct processes: comprehension, retrieval, judgment, and response. Individual difference variables, such as cognitive ability and personality, may differentially affect one's responses to SJTs. For example, cognitive ability is likely related to how effectively and how quickly one comprehends and retrieves relevant examples of appropriate behavior from memory. The judgment and responses that one makes could be driven by personality and implicit personality theory (Motowidlo, Hooper, & Jackson, 2006) (e.g., those who are more agreeable are more likely to rate agreeable actions favorably than people who are less agreeable). Decomposing the response process by introducing an interference task and assessing participants' memory may be one method for understanding the psychological processes underlying SJT responses, and may inform the debate over whether SJTs are better assessments of personality than traditional personality tests in high-stakes testing situations.

References

Alliger, G.M., & Dwight, S.A. (2000). A meta-analytic investigation of the susceptibility of integrity tests to faking and coaching. *Educational and Psychological Measurement, 60* (1), 59–72.

Arthur, W., Glaze, R.M., Jarrett, S.M., White, C.D., Schurig, I., & Taylor, J.E. (2014). Comparative evaluation of three situational judgment test response formats in terms of construct-related validity, subgroup differences, and susceptibility to response distortion. *Journal of Applied Psychology, 99* (3), 535–545.

Becker, T.E. (2005). Development and validation of a situational judgment test of employee integrity. *International Journal of Selection and Assessment, 13* (3), 225–232.

Becker, T.E., & Colquitt, A.L. (1992). Potential versus actual faking on a biodata form: An analysis along several dimensions of item type. *Personnel Psychology, 45* (2), 389–406.

Bergman, M.E., Donovan, M.A., Drasgow, F., Overton, R.C., & Henning, J.B. (2008). Test of Motowidlo et al.'s (1997) theory of individual differences in task and contextual performance. *Human Performance, 21* (3), 227–253.

Bledow, R., & Frese, M. (2009). A situational judgment test of personal initiative and its relationship to performance. *Personnel Psychology, 62* (2), 229–258.

Campbell, J.P. (1990). Modeling the performance prediction problem in industrial and organizational psychology. In M.D. Dunnette, & L.M. Hough (Eds.), *Handbook of Industrial and Organizational Psychology* (pp. 687–732). Palo Alto, CA: Consulting Psychologists Press.

Campbell, J.P., McCloy, R.A., Oppler, S.H., & Sager, C.E. (1992). A theory of performance. In N. Schmitt, & W.C. Borman (Eds.), *Personnel Selection in Organizations* (pp. 35–70). San Francisco: Jossey-Bass.

Christian, M.S., Edwards, B.D., & Bradley, J.C. (2010). Situational judgment tests: Constructs assessed and a meta-analysis of their criterion-related validities. *Personnel Psychology, 63* (1), 83–117.

Crook, A.E., Beier, M.E., Cox, C.B., Kell, H.J., Hanks, A.R., & Motowidlo, S.J. (2011). Measuring relationships between personality, knowledge, and performance using single-response situational judgment tests. *International Journal of Selection and Assessment, 19* (4), 363–373.

Digman, J.M. (1990). Personality structure: Emergence of the five-factor model. *Annual Review of Psychology, 41*, 417–440.

Douglas, E.F., McDaniel, M.A., & Snell, E.F. (1996). The validity of non-cognitive measures decays when applicants fake. *Proceedings of the Academy of Management, 1,* 127–131.

Goldberg, L.R. (1999). A broad-bandwidth, public domain, personality inventory measuring the lower-level facets of several five-factor models. In I. Mervielde, I. Deary, F. De Fruyt, & F. Ostendorf (Eds.), *Personality Psychology in Europe*, Vol. *7* (pp. 7–28). The Netherlands: Tilburg University Press.

Graham, K.E., McDaniel, M.A., Douglas, E.F., & Snell, A.F. (2002). Biodata validity decay and score inflation with faking: Do item attributes explain variance across items? *Journal of Business and Psychology, 16* (4), 573–592.

Hooper, A.C., Cullen, M.J., & Sackett, P.R. (2006). Operational threats to the use of SJTs: faking, coaching, and retesting issues. In J.A. Weekley, & R.E. Ployhart (Eds.), *Situational Judgment Tests: Theory, Measurement and Application* (pp. 205–232). Mahwah, NJ: Lawrence Erlbaum Associates.

Huffcutt, A.I., Conway, J.M., Roth, P.L., & Stone, N.J. (2001). Identification and meta-analytic assessment of psychological constructs measured in employment interviews. *Journal of Applied Psychology, 86* (5), 897–913.

Hunter, D.R. (2003). Measuring general aviation pilot judgment using a situational judgment technique. *International Journal of Aviation Psychology, 13* (4), 373–386.

Hunter, J.E. (1983). A causal analysis of cognitive ability, job knowledge, job performance, and supervisory ratings. In F. Landy, S. Zedeck, & J. Cleveland (Eds.), *Performance Measurement and Theory* (pp. 257–266). Hillsdale, NJ: Erlbaum.

Hunter, J.E. (1986). Cognitive ability, cognitive aptitude, job knowledge, and job performance. *Journal of Vocational Behavior, 29* (3), 340–362.
Jones, C. (1987). *Passenger relations video test manual for version 2.0 and 1.0.* Seattle: Casey Jones & Associates.
Juraska, S.E., & Drasgow, F. (2001). *Faking situational judgment: A test of the Conflict Resolution Skills Assessment.* Paper presented at the 16th Annual Conference of the Society for Industrial and Organizational Psychology, San Diego, CA.
Konradt, U., Hertel, G., & Joder, K. (2003). Web-based assessment of call center agents: Development and validation of a computerized instrument. *International Journal of Selection and Assessment, 11* (2/3), 184–193.
Lievens, F., Peeters, H., & Schollaert, E. (2008). Situational judgment tests: A review of recent research. *Personnel Review, 37* (4), 426– 441.
Lievens, F., & Sackett, P.R. (2012). The validity of interpersonal skills assessment via situational judgment tests for predicting academic success and job performance. *Journal of Applied Psychology, 97* (2), 460–468.
MacKenzie, W.I., Ployhart, R.E., Weekley, J.A., & Ehlers, C. (2010). Contextual effects on SJT responses: An examination of construct validity and mean differences across applicant and incumbent contexts. *Human Performance, 23* (1), 1–21.
McClough, A.C., & Rogelberg, S.G. (2003). Selection in teams: An exploration of the teamwork knowledge, skills, and ability test. *International Journal of Selection and Assessment, 11* (1), 56–66.
McDaniel, M.A., Hartman, N.S., Whetzel, D.L., & Grubb, W.L. (2007). Situational judgment tests, response instructions, and validity: A meta-analysis. *Personnel Psychology, 60* (1), 63–91.
McDaniel, M.A., & Whetzel, D.L. (2005). Situational judgment test research: Informing the debate on practical intelligence theory. *Intelligence, 33* (5), 515–525.
McHenry, J.J., & Schmitt, N. (1994). Multimedia testing. In M.J. Rumsey, C.D. Walker, & J. Harris (Eds.) *Personnel Selection and Classification Research* (pp. 183–232). Mahwah, NJ: Erlbaum.
Morgeson, F.P., Reider, M.H., & Campion, M.A. (2005). Selecting individuals in team settings: The importance of social skills, personality characteristics, and teamwork knowledge. *Personnel Psychology, 58* (3), 583–611.
Motowidlo, S.J., Borman, W.C., & Schmit, M.J. (1997). A theory of individual differences in task and contextual performance. *Human Performance, 10* (2), 71–83.
Motowidlo, S.J., Crook, A.E., Kell, H.J., & Naemi, B. (2009). Measuring procedural knowledge more simply with a single response situational judgment test. *Journal of Business and Psychology, 24* (3), 281–287.
Motowidlo, S.J., Hooper, A.C., & Jackson, H.L. (2006). Implicit policies about relations between personality traits and behavioral effectiveness in situational judgment items. *Journal of Applied Psychology, 91* (4), 749–761.
Motowidlo, S.J., Martin, M.P., & Crook, A.E. (2013). Relations between personality, knowledge, and behavior in professional service encounters. *Journal of Applied Social Psychology, 43* (9), 1851–1861.
Mumford, T.V., Van Iddekinge, C.H., Morgeson, M.P., & Campion, M.A. (2008). The team role test: Development and validation of a team role knowledge situational judgment test. *Journal of Applied Psychology, 93* (2), 250–267.
Nguyen, N.T., Biderman, M.D., & McDaniel, M.A. (2005). Effects of response instructions on faking a situational judgment tests. *International Journal of Selection and Assessment, 13* (4), 250–260.

Olson-Buchanan, J.B., Drasgow, F., Moberg, P.J., Mead, A.D., Keenan, P.A., & Donovan, M.A. (1998). An interactive video assessment of conflict resolution skills. *Personnel Psychology, 51* (1), 1–24.

Ones, D.S., Viswesvaran, C., & Reiss, A.D. (1996). Role of social desirability in personality testing for personnel selection: The red herring. *Journal of Applied Psychology, 81* (6), 660–679.

Oswald, F.L., Schmitt, N., Kim, B.H., Ramsay, L.J., & Gillespie, M.A. (2004). Developing a biodata measure and situational judgment inventory as predictors of college student performance. *Journal of Applied Psychology, 89* (2), 187–208.

Peeters, H., & Lievens, F. (2005). Situational judgment tests and their prediction of college students' success: The influence of faking. *Educational and Psychological Measurement, 65* (1), 70–89.

Ployhart, R.E. (2006). The predictor response process model. In J.A. Weekley, & R.E. Ployhart (Eds.), *Situational Judgment Tests: Theory, Measurement, and Application* (pp. 83–105). Mahwah, NJ: Erlbaum.

Ployhart, R.E., Weekley, J.A., Holtz, B.C., & Kemp, C. (2003). Web-based and paper-and-pencil testing of applicants in a proctored setting: Are personality, biodata and situational judgment comparable? *Personnel Psychology, 56* (3), 733–752.

Schmitt, N., & Chan, D. (2006). Situational judgment tests: method or construct? In J.A. Weekley, & R.E. Ployhart (Eds.), *Situational Judgment Tests: Theory, Measurement, and Application* (pp. 135–156). Mahwah, NJ: Erlbaum

Stevens, M.J., & Campion, M.A. (1999). Staffing work teams: Development and validation of a selection test for teamwork. *Journal of Management, 25* (2), 207–228.

Weekley, J.A., & Jones, C. (1997). Video-based situational testing. *Personnel Psychology, 50* (1), 25–49.

16

Alternatives to Self-Reports: Conditional Reasoning Problems and Implicit Association Test (IAT) Based Tasks

Zvonimir Galić
University of Zagreb, Croatia

Andreja Bubić
University of Split, Croatia

Maja Parmač Kovačić
University of Zagreb, Croatia

Most of personality research relies on questionnaires and self-reports as the most dominant assessment method. Within this method, individuals are asked to report their behaviors, thoughts and feelings, and researchers determine their standing on any given trait by arithmetically combining their responses on a set of items intended to measure that trait. However, despite their wide use, the reliance on self-reports in personality assessment might be unwarranted because this method is associated with a number of problems.

First, self-reports rest on the assumption that self-assessments are mostly accurate. However, assessments people give about themselves are "flawed in substantive and systematic ways" (Dunning, Heath, & Suls, 2004, p. 69). For example, people's inclination toward self-deception reflects in overrating on desirable traits and overly confident self-ratings of skills that do not match their actual performance across fields (Dunning et al., 2004) Thus, relying only on self-reports provides a systematically biased assessment of numerous personal characteristics that are often measured in personality research.

Second, even if respondents had an accurate self-insight and were able to report it in personality questionnaires, they might be unwilling to disclose themselves. It is now widely accepted that personality questionnaires are susceptible to impression management or faking (Viswesvaran & Ones, 1999). Faking might particularly be a problem in situations where important outcomes depend on the results of personality testing (e.g., personnel selection).

The Wiley Handbook of Personality Assessment, First Edition. Edited by Updesh Kumar.
© 2016 John Wiley & Sons, Ltd. Published 2016 by John Wiley & Sons, Ltd.

Finally, even if respondents were both able and willing to provide accurate self-assessments, personality questionnaires may only reveal aspects of personality that are accessible to introspection, usually labeled as explicit personality. However, the focus on explicit personality leaves out many important personality processes that happen below the consciousness level (i.e., implicit processes). Although implicit processes, such as implicit motives or defense mechanisms, are extremely important for psychological functioning (Pervin, 1999), they are completely overlooked in the currently dominant trait theory.

In this chapter we will describe two new and promising approaches to implicit personality measurement that circumvent both self-deception and impression management: the conditional reasoning approach to personality measurement (James & LeBreton, 2012), and the Implicit Association Test (IAT) for self-concept measurement (Schnabel, Asendorpf, & Greenwald, 2008). For each approach we will first briefly describe the theoretical arguments for its use in personality assessment and the general implementation procedure, and then proceed with a description of the method's application for measuring one specific trait – aggressiveness.

Conditional Reasoning Approach to Personality Assessment

The conditional reasoning approach to personality measurement (James & LeBreton, 2012) derives from the idea that individuals' reasoning is conditional on their personality, and that specific patterns in reasoning may reflect the underlying psychological motives. In order to collect information regarding respondents' personality, conditional reasoning researchers analyze their performance on a set of inductive reasoning tasks. On these reasoning tasks the respondents are instructed to give the most logical conclusion that follows from the story described in the item stem. However, unlike "ordinary" reasoning tasks that are designed to have only one correct answer, conditional reasoning problems have more than one possible solution. Logically equally plausible, these solutions are chosen to be differently attractive to individuals differing in the assessed personality characteristic. This is possible because conditional reasoning problems are designed as inductive reasoning problems in which the conclusion does not follow with certainty. Instead, the individuals must go beyond the information explicitly provided within the item in order to reach a conclusion that is probable but not certain.[1] According to James and LeBreton (2012), when solving these problems the respondents rely on their typical thinking patterns to reach the required conclusions. Considering that individuals with different personality characteristics usually reason differently, they select different responses within this task.

The conditional reasoning approach has an elaborated theoretical background whose main pillar is the assumption that people always want to hold positive self-regard and are, because of that, inclined to see their behavior as reasonable (James & LeBreton, 2012). In order to be able to accomplish that, they develop unconscious rationalizations whose role is to justify their behavior as rational. Specific rationalizations depend on the behavior in question and its underlying motives.

These rationalizations are stable and bias individuals' everyday reasoning. As such, these biases may be considered a part of implicit personality processes that cannot be measured directly. According to James et al. (2005), an insight into what an individual believes to be the logical analysis of various situations enables us to identify the occurrence of motive-based biases in his/her reasoning.

The conditional reasoning approach to implicit personality measurement has received wide scientific attention. It has been evaluated as "a model for psychometric, conceptual, and theory based implicit association measurement" (Landy, 2008, p. 390), and even labeled as a "ground breaking" approach to implicit personality assessment by the American Psychological Association (2013, p. 4). However, before developing a psychological test based on the conditional reasoning approach, extensive theoretical and empirical work must be done. First, justification mechanisms characteristic for certain psychological motives should be identified. Next, a set of conditional reasoning problems should be developed and pretested. Finally, a subset of well-functioning items should be thoroughly validated. In addition to appreciating the complexity of this process, it is also important to highlight that the development of a conditional reasoning task is very process-specific and that it is very hard to generalize across tasks measuring different traits and behaviors. In this chapter we will describe the Conditional Reasoning Test for Aggression (CRT-A), the most extensively validated of all conditional reasoning tests.

The CRT-A (James et al., 2005) is based on the idea that aggressive individuals use motive-based cognitive biases to see their aggressive acts as completely reasonable and justified reactions. These biases are labeled as justification mechanisms because they help aggressive individuals to justify their behavior and reconcile their motive to hurt others with the need to keep a positive view of themselves.

Justification mechanisms for aggression and their measurement within the CRT-A

Based on an extensive search of scientific and popular literature, James and associates (James et al., 2005; James & LeBreton, 2010, 2012) have identified six justification mechanisms that characterize the reasoning of aggressive individuals. First, aggressive individuals have an unconscious tendency to see hostile and malevolent intention in others' behavior, even in situations when that behavior is neutral or friendly. This *hostile attributions bias* offers them the opportunity to see their aggressive behaviors as justified acts of self-defense. Second, aggressive individuals are inclined to see targets of their aggression as evil, immoral, and untrustworthy. Again, this *derogation of target bias* helps them to see their aggression as justified because the behaviors are seen as reactions to an outside threat. Third, aggressive people have a proclivity to favor revenge and retribution over reconciliation and compromise. This *retribution bias* helps them to see their aggression as a reasonable way of restoring pride and a sense of dignity that is endangered by other people's behavior. Fourth, aggressive individuals are characterized by the *potency bias*, a tendency to see most interactions with other people as contests to establish dominance/submissiveness. In this way, aggressive individuals see their aggression as an act of strength that helps them to gain others' respect, whereas the failure to act would be seen as a sign of weakness. The final two justification mechanisms are the *victimization by powerful others* and the *social discounting biases.* These two biases justify aggressive acts because aggressive individuals see themselves as victims of exploitation by powerful others from their environments in the case of *victimization by powerful others* (e.g., professors, supervisors), or the society whose norms preclude the chances of a free and fulfilling life in the case of the *social discounting bias.* Both biases help aggressive individuals to see the aggressive acts as reasonable deeds that help them to free themselves from oppression.

According to James and LeBreton (2010, 2012), these six biases are stable, operate out of conscious awareness, and influence everyday reasoning through cognitive processes such as selective attention, confirmatory biases, and causal inferences. Considering that they are cognitive in nature, James et al. (2005) proposed that these biases can be measured with conditional reasoning problems that are designed to trigger the activation of described justification mechanisms for aggression.

Each of the items consists of a short story (item stem) followed by four possible choices (one indicating aggressive reasoning, one indicating non-aggressive reasoning, and two illogical responses). The two illogical responses are there only to strengthen the face validity of the test and are rarely selected by respondents. An example of the conditional reasoning problem for aggression measurement is given in Table 16.1. In this example, the respondents are asked to choose the most logical explanation for the information presented in the problem's stem. The answers (a) and (c) are not inductively plausible solutions and represent the "distractor" responses. Both alternatives (b) and (d) are inductively plausible. Answer (d) is expected to be endorsed by individuals who habitually use the *retribution bias* and the *victimization by powerful others bias* in their reasoning, whereas the non-aggressive alternative (b) should appear the most logical to non-aggressive individuals.

The CRT-A is administered as an inductive reasoning test in which the respondents are instructed to identify the most logical response to each of the 25 inductive reasoning problems it comprises. Among these, the 22 conditional reasoning problems similar to that reported in the example are interspersed with three "classical" inductive reasoning tasks (i.e., those with only one correct solution) whose role is to further improve the face validity of the test. Thus, the occurrence of motive-based cognitive biases in this test is measured indirectly due to the fact that the respondents are not informed about the purpose of the test, and believe that they are solving an ordinary reasoning test.

Table 16.1 A sample item for the CRT-A

The old saying, "an eye for an eye," means that if someone hurts you, then you should hurt that person back. If you are hit, then you should hit back. If someone burns your house, then you should burn that person's house.

Which of the following is the biggest problem with the "eye for an eye" plan?

(a) It tells people to "turn the other cheek."
(b) It offers no way to settle a conflict in a friendly manner.
(c) It can only be used at certain times of the year.
(d) People have to wait until they are attacked before they can strike.

Validation of the CRT-A

The research studies that have thus far employed the CRT-A have indicated this method to have sound basic psychometric characteristics. Specifically, based on the data collected on a large sample of participants (N = 5,238) James and LeBreton (2012) report an internal consistency coefficient of 0.76. The CRT-A scores also seem relatively stable: the correlation between the two forms of the test over a two-month period was 0.82. Additionally, exploratory factor analyses of the CRT-A problems revealed the factor structure that was coherent with the theoretical foundations of this test, as the problems that were intended for the measurement of similar justification mechanisms clustered together into moderately correlated latent factors (James et al., 2005; James & LeBreton, 2012).

Furthermore, the CRT-A showed moderate to high validities in predicting aggressive behavior both in laboratory and field studies, across university, sports, and work settings. The criteria James and LeBreton (2012) reported in their overview of the CRT-A validity studies ranged from class absenteeism, lying and cheating in internet-based simulations, lying about extra credits, traffic and conduct violations (university setting), over hard fouls and fights in basketball games (sport setting), to various work outcomes such as absenteeism, attrition, work unreliability, and theft, to job performance (work setting). In their overview, validity coefficients ranged from 0.11 to 0.64 with an unweighted mean of 0.41. This value largely surpasses the ones usually reported for personality measures in predicting various outcomes (e.g., Barrick, Mount, & Judge, 2001; Roberts, Kuncel, Shiner, Caspi, & Goldberg, 2007). Later meta-analyses were not so favorable for the CRT-A (e.g., Berry, Sackett, & Tobares, 2010), but still indicated that this method is useful in predicting important criteria.

Finally, it has been demonstrated that the CRT-A is unrelated either to general mental ability or self-reported aggression. A large number of US studies repeatedly found that scores on the CRT-A are uncorrelated with various measures of cognitive ability (James & LeBreton, 2010, 2012; LeBreton, Barksdale, Robin, & James, 2007). Similarly, it has been shown that the CRT-A is uncorrelated or weakly correlated with self-reported aggression (James et al., 2005; James & LeBreton, 2012), which is consistent with the notion that the CRT-A score reflects aspects of implicit, unconscious personality.

Prospects for conditional reasoning in personality assessment

Research on the CRT-A indicates that the conditional reasoning task represents a promising approach to personality assessment. Yet, many questions still remain to be answered in future studies. Among these, we believe that personality assessment would profit most from following three avenues of research: development of conditional reasoning measures of other constructs, measurement in other contexts, and the research on (un)susceptibility to response distortion.

First, the conditional reasoning approach requires extensive theoretical and empirical work before the test of a construct is developed. This is the most likely explanation for why only a few conditional reasoning tests have thus far been reported in peer-reviewed literature, among which the CRT-A represents the most extensively validated test. Smaller but still well developed was the research program on the conditional reasoning approach to achievement motive measurement (Bing, LeBreton, Davison, Migetz, & James, 2007; James, 1998; James & LeBreton, 2012). Preliminary validation data have also been reported for the tests measuring the power motive (James et al., 2013), addiction proneness (Bowler, Bowler, & Cope, 2013; Bowler, Bowler, & James, 2011), and integrity at work (Fine & Gottlieb-Litvin, 2013). Future research should first identify the constructs for which conditional reasoning represents an appropriate assessment approach, and then conduct extensive validation, such as the one we reported for the CRT-A.

Current research on the validity of the conditional reasoning approach to personality assessment in contexts other than the US is scarce. To the best of our knowledge, the only systematic evidence of the validity of the conditional reasoning assumptions in a context largely outside the US was recently published for the Croatian validation of the CRT-A (Galić, Scherer, & LeBreton, 2014). The dearth of international research on conditional reasoning could be traced to the problems related to the adaptation of the measures constructed in the US to other cultures (i.e., difficulties with preserving the subtle meaning of the conditional reasoning problems).

Third, current research on conditional reasoning dominantly shows that this approach to personality assessment circumvents the faking problem. This fact might represent a significant comparative advantage of conditional reasoning over self-reports, especially in high-stakes situations. For example, in a series of studies LeBreton et al. (2007) showed that the CRT-A is resistant to faking as long as the respondents are unaware of its true measurement object. In one of the studies a sample of undergraduates completed the CRT-A and a set of self-report personality questionnaires twice, under honesty instruction and in a simulated personnel selection. While personality questionnaires expectedly were responsive to situational demands, mean CRT-A score did not change between the conditions. Recently, Bowler et al. (2013) reported that the conditional reasoning test of addiction proneness was also unaffected by response distortion in a simulated personnel selection context. However, the test measuring justifications for counterproductive behavior at work (i.e., workplace integrity) was shown to be susceptible and less valid in "fake good" conditions (Fine & Gottlieb-Litvin, 2013). Future research should explore the reasons for these discrepant findings and test the boundary conditions for (un)susceptibility of conditional reasoning tests to response distortion.

The Implicit Association Test and Personality Assessment

The Implicit Association Test (IAT; Greenwald & Farnham, 2000; Greenwald, McGhee, & Schwartz, 1998) represents a procedure that has been developed for measuring implicit associations with the hypothesis that these provide access to mental processes existing outside our control and awareness. Specifically, the IAT is based on the idea that individuals form associations between concepts based on everyday experiences, and that these relationships can be measured with a response latency task. In doing so, it is not of relevance whether the person is aware of those associations or not, or whether he or she believes them to be true or not. Instead, the crucial characteristic of the associations of interest is their strength measured with a sorting task within which the participants are required to respond to concepts based on two categorization criteria and using the same types of responses. The premise underlying this procedure is that it will be easier for participants to provide equivalent responses to two types of mutually associated stimuli or concepts than to those that are unrelated. For instance, it will be easier for most women to respond in the same manner to words such as "female" or "girl" and those related to the self (e.g., "me" or "I"), than it will be to use the same motor response for "male" or "boy" and the same "self" words (i.e., "me" or "I"). Such ease of responding is then captured in the measured response latencies within the sorting task, with the assumption that faster response latencies reveal stronger associations between concepts and attributes.

While the initial applications of the IAT were focused on measuring implicit attitudes (Greenwald et al., 1998), the IAT was later also used for assessing the self-concept and personality traits (e.g., Asendorpf, Banse, & Mücke, 2002; Greenwald & Farnham, 2000; Perkins & Forehand, 2006; Spalding & Hardin, 1999). The fundamental idea behind the IAT procedure for personality assessment is that the implicit self-concept consists of clusters of associations between the concept of self and various psychological attributes, and that the strength of these associations can be measured with the IAT. For instance, we have previously described how men and women differ in the ease of associating words related to their respective genders and those referring to self or others. This reflects one example of assessing a specific aspect of self-concept, namely individuals' gender identity using the IAT. In other investigations of the gender self-concept, instead of words that explicitly describe members of each gender, it is possible to use those associated with more psychological aspects of gender identity reflected in masculinity–femininity or instrumentality–expressiveness personality traits (e.g., warm and sensitive versus strong and competitive) (Greenwald & Farnham, 2000; Nosek, Banaji, & Greenwald, 2002). In using these approaches, it is assumed that women will associate words relating to the self more strongly with feminine or expressive attributes when compared to more masculine or instrumental attributes, while men will do the opposite. The same logic can be applied with respect to other personality traits such as the Big Five dimensions of personality, dominance or aggression (Banse, Messer, & Fischer, 2015; Grumm & von Collani, 2007; Haines, 1999). In order to better understand the application, procedural specificity and the findings that may be obtained using this measure, a specific example of the IAT for aggressiveness will be described.

The case of the Implicit Association Test for Aggressiveness (IAT-A)

The IAT for aggressiveness (IAT-A) is a double discrimination task in which the participants need to sort stimuli from two contrasted target categories (*self* vs. *others*) and two contrasted aggression-related attribute categories (*aggressive* vs. *peaceful*), using two response keys. In line with the logic behind the IAT described above, an

Table 16.2 An example of the block sequence in the IAT-A

Block	*No. of trials*	*Task*	*Response key 1*	*Response key 2*
1	20	Sorting of target stimuli	Self	Others
2	20	Sorting of attribute stimuli	Aggressive	Peaceful
3	20 + 40	Simultaneous sorting of target and attribute stimuli	Self + aggressive	Others + peaceful
4	20	Sorting of attribute stimuli	Peaceful	Aggressive
5	20 + 40	Simultaneous sorting of target and attribute stimuli	Self + peaceful	Others + aggressive

aggressive individual will have faster reactions and fewer errors when answering to *self* and *aggressive* stimuli with one response key and to *others* and *peaceful* stimuli with the other response key, than when answering to *self* and *peaceful* stimuli with one and *others* and *aggressive* stimuli with the other response key. For a non-aggressive individual the situation will be reversed.

A typical IAT for assessing aggressiveness as a part of the implicit self-concept consists of five blocks, displayed in Table 16.2. Among these five blocks, three are considered as the practice blocks (1, 2, and 4) and two as the critical blocks (3 and 5). In the first block of the IAT-A, the participants are asked to categorize stimuli referring to the target concepts either representative of *self* or *others* by pressing different response keys (for example, "left" for *self* and "right" for *others* stimuli). Usually, stimuli referring to these concepts are generic pronouns such as *I*, *me*, or *my* (for the *self* category) and *they, them*, or *their* (for the *others* category) (Banse et al., 2015; Uhlmann & Swanson, 2004). In the second block, participants need to categorize the stimuli referring to the attribute categories representative of either *aggressive* or *peaceful* (*aggressive, provocative,* or *unfriendly* for the *aggressive* category and *amicable, conciliatory*, or *indulgent* for the *peaceful* category). The third, as the first critical block, involves simultaneous sorting of the stimulus items representing two target and two attribute categories. Stimuli related to *self* and *aggressive* share one response key and stimuli related to *other* and *peaceful* the other response key. In the fourth, practice block participants again categorize only stimuli referring to the attribute categories representative of either *aggressive* or *peaceful.* However, the assignment of the *aggressive* and *peaceful* categories to the response keys is reversed. Finally, the fifth, the second critical block, again involves sorting stimuli from all four categories, using two response keys. However, stimuli related to *self* and *peaceful* now share one response key and stimuli related to *other* and *aggressive* the other response key.

For the calculation of the IAT-A score, only the critical third and fifth blocks are relevant. Specifically, individual IAT-A scores are determined by calculating the difference in the mean response latencies between blocks 5 and 3. Thus, quicker sorting of stimuli related to *self* and *aggressive* with one response key and *other* and *peaceful* with the other response key (block 3), contrasted to the reversed pairing (block 5), will result in a positive IAT-A score. More positive IAT-A scores reflect stronger associations between the concepts *self* and *aggressive*, thus indicating stronger implicit aggressiveness (Banse et al., 2015; Schnabel et al., 2008).

Previous studies have shown satisfactory reliabilities of the IAT-A (Cronbach's Alpha ranged from 0.69 to 0.91; Banse et al., 2015; Richetin, Richardson, & Mason, 2010; Teubel, Asendorpf, Banse, & Schnabel, 2011; Spearman-Brown split-half 0.74, Grumm, Hein, & Fingerle, 2011). It has been shown that the IAT-A predicted different types of aggressive behaviors, at least at the level of self-report measures of aggressiveness (validities ranged between 0.27 and 0.49; Banse & Fischer, 2002; Teubel et al., 2011; Banse et al., 2015). More importantly, it has been shown that the IAT-A is mostly unrelated to aggression and predicts specific aggressive behaviors over and above the corresponding direct questionnaire measures (incremental validities ranged from 5–15% of variance in aggressive behavior: Banse et al., 2015; Grumm et al., 2011; Teubel et al., 2011).

However, it seems that the size of the predictive validity depends on some variations in the IAT-A procedure. For instance, Bluemke and Friese (2012) showed that idiographic stimuli for self and other categories (e.g., *respondent's first name* for the *self* category and *specific other's first name* for the *others* category) led to higher IAT validity coefficients when compared with the typically used generic pronouns. An alternative to the generic pronouns in the *others* category was also offered by Teubel et al. (2011) and Banse et al. (2015). They suggested using the job titles stereotypically occupied by people with low to medium levels of aggressiveness (e.g., *architect*, *book-keeper*, and *educator*). This use of job titles should ensure that participants associate the *others* category with a neutral reference group, and might result in higher predictive validity of the IAT-A. Finally, Banse et al. (2015) have shown that using behavior words denoting aggressive and peaceful activities (e.g., *to attack*, *to punch* vs. *to talk*, *to comply*), instead of only trait adjectives in the attribute categories (i.e., *aggressive* vs. *peaceful*) also resulted in higher validity coefficients. The authors believe that the association between the self and aggressive behavior might better reflect clusters of associations in the self-concept related to implicit aggressions rather than association between the self-concept and trait adjectives.

Procedural specificity and metric characteristics of the IAT

Ever since it was developed, the IAT has been subjected to numerous investigations of its validity and other metric characteristics, some of which have indicated that this method is associated with several extraneous influences. For example, it has been demonstrated that the size of the IAT effect is somewhat dependent on the individual's cognitive skill and response speed (McFarland & Crouch, 2002; but see Cai, Sriram, Greenwald, & McFarland, 2004) as well as the order of measurements used within experiments (Bosson, Swann Jr, & Pennebaker, 2000; but see Hofmann, Gawronski, Gschwendner, Le, & Schmitt, 2005), or some of the design characteristics, such as the choice of categories or stimuli (Lane, Banaji, Nosek, & Greenwald, 2007). Also, it has been shown that individuals attempting to fake their scores on the IAT may be statistically detected and, at least in part, corrected (Cvencek, Greenwald, Brown, Gray, & Snowden, 2010). Despite these limitations, it has been demonstrated that the IAT score remains stable across numerous other procedural variations within experiments that include, for example, the chosen motor response, number of trials, familiarity with the IAT stimulus materials, or interstimuli intervals

(Dasgupta, McGhee, Greenwald, & Banaji, 2000; Greenwald & Farnham, 2000; Greenwald et al., 1998; Nosek, Greenwald, & Banaji, 2005; Rudman, Greenwald, Mellott, & Schwartz, 1999), suggesting a satisfactory internal validity for this measure. Moreover, numerous studies and meta-analyses have shown that the IAT has predictive value that is independent of the corresponding explicit measures (Greenwald, Poehlman, Uhlmann, & Banaji, 2009; Hofmann et al., 2005; Lane et al., 2007; Nosek et al., 2005). Despite the controversies relating to the exact meaning of the IAT score (De Houwer, Teige-Mocigemba, Spruyt, & Moors, 2009) and its procedural complexities, previous experiences have indicated that the IAT has strong potential for basic and applied scientific usage that has thus far resulted in valuable insights into individuals' motives, processes, and behaviors, which would otherwise remain hidden from the eyes of explicit psychological instruments.

Conclusions

In this chapter we have introduced two novel approaches that hold great promise for personality assessment: conditional reasoning and the IAT for self-concept measurement. Both approaches represent psychometrically sound and practically convenient methods of personality assessment. These methods might be especially appropriate when the targeted personality construct lies outside of conscious awareness or when the respondents are motivated to give socially desirable responses (Uhlmann et al., 2012). Additionally, researchers in applied psychology might be particularly interested in them in situations where even the smallest incremental prediction of criteria is critical (e.g., in the case of job performance or violence prediction). Although promising, the two methods do not represent a substitute for the self-report method. Personality questionnaires based on the self-report method remain essential for understanding respondents' perspectives because self-perceptions strongly influence how people interact with the world (Paulhus & Vazire, 2007) and are important in predicting a number of important criteria (Roberts et al., 2007). We hope that the utilization of novel methods of personality assessment described in the present chapter will, in concert with self-reports, improve our understanding of psychological functioning, thus constituting another important step "toward the science of personality psychology" (Winter, 1998, p. 153).

Acknowledgments

This work has been fully supported by the Croatian Science Foundation under project 6719.

Note

[1]Inductive reasoning is a form of reasoning where a general law or principle is inferred from particular instances that have been observed. The problem with this type of reasoning is that the obtained conclusion is never certain but only probable. The opposite case represents

deductive reasoning where a conclusion is derived from a set of premises using rules of inference. Conclusions reached through deductive reasoning are certain (Colman, 2009).

References

American Psychological Association. (2013). APA Books & APA Videos: Spring 2013 [Brochure]. Retrieved from http://www.nxtbook.com/nxtbooks/apa/catalog_2013spring/#/16

Asendorpf, J.B., Banse, R., & Mücke, D. (2002). Double dissociation between implicit and explicit personality self-concept: The case of shy behavior. *Journal of Personality and Social Psychology, 83* (2), 380–393.

Banse, R., & Fischer, I. (2002). *Implicit and explicit aggressiveness and the prediction of aggressive behavior.* Poster presented at the 11th European Conference of Personality by the European Society of Personality Psychology, July 21–25, Jena, Germany.

Banse, R., Messer, M., & Fischer, I. (2015). Predicting aggressive behavior with the Aggressiveness-IAT. *Aggressive Behavior, 41*, 65–83.

Barrick, M.R., Mount, M.K., & Judge, T.A. (2001). Personality and performance at the beginning of the new millennium: What do we know and where do we go next? *International Journal of Selection and Assessment, 9* (1–2), 9–30.

Berry, C.M., Sackett, P.R., & Tobares, V. (2010). A meta-analysis of Conditional Reasoning Test of Aggression. *Personnel Psychology, 63* (2), 361–384.

Bing, M.N., LeBreton, J.M., Davison, H.K., Migetz, D.Z., & James, L.R. (2007). Integrating implicit and explicit social cognitions for enhanced personality assessment: A general framework for choosing measurement and statistical methods. *Organizational Research Methods, 10* (2), 346–389.

Bluemke, M., & Friese, M. (2012). On the validity of idiographic and generic self-concept Implicit Association Tests: A core-concept model. *European Journal of Personality, 26* (5), 515–528.

Bosson, J.K., Swann Jr, W.B., & Pennebaker, J.W. (2000). Stalking the perfect measure of implicit self-esteem: The blind men and the elephant revisited? *Journal of Personality and Social Psychology, 79* (4), 631–643.

Bowler, J.L., Bowler, M.C., & Cope, J.G. (2013). Measurement issues associated with Conditional Reasoning Tests: An examination of faking. *Personality and Individual Differences, 55* (5), 459–464.

Bowler, J.L., Bowler, M.C., & James, L.R. (2011). The cognitive underpinnings of addiction. *Substance Use & Misuse, 46* (8), 1060–1071.

Cai, H., Sriram, N., Greenwald, A.G., & McFarland, S.G. (2004). The Implicit Association Test's D measure can minimize a cognitive skill confound: Comment on McFarland and Crouch (2002). *Social Cognition, 22* (6), 673–684.

Colman, A.M. (2009). *A Dictionary of Psychology.* Oxford: Oxford University Press.

Cvencek, D., Greenwald, A.G., Brown, A.S., Gray, N.S., & Snowden, R.J. (2010). Faking of the Implicit Association Test is statistically detectable and partly correctable. *Basic and Applied Social Psychology, 32* (4), 302–314.

Dasgupta, N., McGhee, D.E., Greenwald, A.G., & Banaji, M.R. (2000). Automatic preference for White Americans: Eliminating the familiarity explanation. *Journal of Experimental Social Psychology, 36* (3), 316–328.

De Houwer, J., Teige-Mocigemba, S., Spruyt, A., & Moors, A. (2009). Implicit measures: A normative analysis and review. *Psychological Bulletin, 135* (3), 347–368.

Dunning, D., Heath, C., & Suls, J.M. (2004). Flawed self-assessment implications for health, education, and the workplace. *Psychological Science in the Public Interest, 5* (3), 69–106.

Fine, S., & Gottlieb-Litvin, Y. (2013). Justifying counterproductive work behaviors and an integrity-based Conditional Reasoning Test: Back to the drawing board? *International Journal of Selection and Assessment, 21* (3), 328–333.

Galić, Z., Scherer, K.T., & LeBreton, J.M. (2014). Validity evidences for Croatian version of the Conditional Reasoning Test for aggression. *International Journal of Selection and Assessment, 22* (4), 343–354.

Greenwald, A.G., & Farnham, S.D. (2000). Using the Implicit Association Test to measure self-esteem and self-concept. *Journal of Personality and Social Psychology, 79* (6), 1022–1038.

Greenwald, A.G., McGhee, D.E., & Schwartz, J.L. (1998). Measuring individual differences in implicit cognition: The Implicit Association Test. *Journal of Personality and Social Psychology, 74* (6), 1464–1480.

Greenwald, A.G., Poehlman, T.A., Uhlmann, E.L., & Banaji, M.R. (2009). Understanding and using the Implicit Association Test: III. Meta-analysis of predictive validity. *Journal of Personality and Social Psychology, 97* (1), 17–41.

Grumm, M., Hein, S., & Fingerle, M. (2011). Predicting aggressive behavior in children with the help of measures of implicit and explicit aggression. *International Journal of Behavioral Development, 35* (4), 352–357.

Grumm, M., & von Collani, G. (2007). Measuring Big-Five personality dimensions with the implicit association test – Implicit personality traits or self-esteem? *Personality and Individual Differences, 43* (8), 2205–2217.

Haines, E.L. (1999). *Elements of a Social Power Schema: Gender Standpoint, Self-concept, and Experience.* New York: University of New York.

Hofmann, W., Gawronski, B., Gschwendner, T., Le, H., & Schmitt, M. (2005). A meta-analysis on the correlation between the Implicit Association Test and explicit self-report measures. *Personality and Social Psychology Bulletin, 31* (10), 1369–1385.

James, L.R. (1998). Measurement of personality via conditional reasoning. *Organizational Research Methods, 1* (2), 131–163.

James, L.R., & LeBreton, J.M. (2010). Assessing aggression using Conditional Reasoning. *Current Directions in Psychological Science, 19* (1), 30–35.

James, L.R., & LeBreton, J.M. (2012). *Assessing the Implicit Personality through Conditional Reasoning* (1st ed.). Washington, DC: American Psychological Association.

James, L.R., LeBreton, J.M., Mitchell, T.R., Smith, D.R., Desimone, J.A., Cookson, R., & Lee, H.J. (2013). Use of Conditional Reasoning to measure the power motive. In J.M. Cortina, & R.S. Landis (Eds.), *Modern Research Methods for the Study of Behavior in Organizations* (pp. 233–261). New York: Brunner-Routledge.

James, L.R., McIntyre, M.D., Glisson, C.A., Green, P.D., Patton, T.W., LeBreton, J.M., & Mitchell, T.R. (2005). A Conditional Reasoning Measure for aggression. *Organizational Research Methods, 8* (1), 69–99.

Landy, F.J. (2008). Stereotypes, bias, and personnel decisions: Strange and stranger. *Industrial and Organizational Psychology, 1* (4), 379–392.

Lane, K.A., Banaji, M.R., Nosek, B.A., & Greenwald, A.G. (2007). Understanding and using the Implicit Association Test: IV. In B. Wittenbrink, & N. Schwarz (Eds.), *Implicit Measures of Attitudes* (pp. 59–102). New York: Guilford Press.

LeBreton, J.M., Barksdale, C.D., Robin, J., & James, L.R. (2007). Measurement issues associated with Conditional Reasoning Tests: Indirect measurement and test faking. *Journal of Applied Psychology, 92* (1), 1–16.

McFarland, S.G., & Crouch, Z. (2002). A cognitive skill confound on the Implicit Association Test. *Social Cognition, 20* (6), 483–510.

Nosek, B.A., Banaji, M.R., & Greenwald, A.G. (2002). Math = male, me = female, therefore math not me. *Journal of Personality and Social Psychology, 83* (1), 44–59.

Nosek, B.A., Greenwald, A.G., & Banaji, M.R. (2005). Understanding and using the Implicit Association Test: II. Method variables and construct validity. *Personality and Social Psychology Bulletin, 31* (2), 166–180.

Paulhus, D.L., & Vazire, S. (2007). The self-report method. In R.W. Robins, R.C. Fraley, and R. Krueger (Eds.), *Handbook of Research Methods in Personality Psychology* (pp. 224–239). New York: Guilford Press.

Perkins, A.W., & Forehand, M.R. (2006). Decomposing the implicit self-concept: The relative influence of semantic meaning and valence on attribute self-association. *Social Cognition, 24* (4), 387–408.

Pervin, L.A. (1999). Epilogue: Constancy and change in personality theory and research. In L.A. Pervin, & O.P. John (Eds.), *Handbook of Personality Psychology* (pp. 689–704). New York: Guilford Press.

Richetin, J., Richardson, D.S., & Mason, G.D. (2010). Predictive validity of IAT aggressiveness in the context of provocation. *Social Psychology, 41* (1), 27–34.

Roberts, B.W., Kuncel, N.R., Shiner, R., Caspi, A., & Goldberg, L.R. (2007). The power of personality: The comparative validity of personality traits, socioeconomic status, and cognitive ability for predicting important life outcomes. *Perspectives on Psychological Science, 2* (4), 313–345.

Rudman, L.A., Greenwald, A.G., Mellott, D.S., & Schwartz, J.L.K. (1999). Measuring the automatic components of prejudice: Flexibility and generality of the Implicit Association Test. *Social Cognition, 17* (4), 437–465.

Schnabel, K., Asendorpf, J.B., & Greenwald, A.G. (2008). Using Implicit Association Tests for the assessment of implicit personality self-concept. In G.J. Boyle, G. Matthews, and D.H. Saklofske (Eds.), *Handbook of Personality Theory and Testing* (pp. 508–528). London: Sage.

Spalding, L.R., & Hardin, C.D. (1999). Unconscious unease and self-handicapping: Behavioral consequences of individual differences in implicit and explicit self-esteem. *Psychological Science, 10* (6), 535–539.

Teubel, T., Asendorpf, J.B., Banse, R., & Schnabel, K. (2011). Implicit but not explicit aggressiveness predicts performance outcome in basketball players. *International Journal of Sport Psychology, 42* (4), 390–400.

Uhlmann, E.L., Leavitt, K., Menges, J.I., Koopman, J., Howe, M., & Johnson, R.E. (2012). Getting explicit about the implicit: A taxonomy of implicit measures and guide for their use in organizational research. *Organizational Research Methods, 15* (4), 553–601.

Uhlmann, E., & Swanson, J. (2004). Exposure to violent video games increases automatic aggressiveness. *Journal of Adolescence, 27* (1), 41–52.

Viswesvaran, C., & Ones, D.S. (1999). Meta-analyses of fakability estimates: Implications for personality measurement. *Educational and Psychological Measurement, 59* (2), 197–210.

Winter, D.G. (1998). Toward a science of personality psychology: David McClelland's development of empirically derived TAT measures. *History of Psychology, 1* (2), 130–153.

17

Therapeutic Assessment in Clinical and Counseling Psychology Practice

Radhika Krishnamurthy
Florida Institute of Technology, Florida, USA

Stephen E. Finn
Center for Therapeutic Assessment, Austin, Texas, USA

Filippo Aschieri
Università Cattolica del Sacro Cuore, Milan, Italy

Psychological assessment has been a core component of clinical and counseling psychology since the formal development of these applied specialties. Spurred on by practical demands for selection and assignment of military recruits during World Wars I and II, the psychological testing movement gained momentum in the first half of the twentieth century. Testing practices of that era were inevitably shaped by the necessities and constraints of that time. Testing large numbers of individuals required expeditious methods, giving rise to the use of fixed test batteries as opposed to individually tailored assessments, and group testing approaches were developed to meet the need for rapid, large-scale assessments. Although individual assessments prevailed within mental health treatment settings, they were shaped by the professional zeitgeist wherein the examiner was the dispassionate expert and the examinee was the *subject* of the evaluation. This stance was influenced by advances in statistical methods and psychometric studies in testing laboratories, which accorded the respectability of science to psychological methods. It fostered a test-centered (as opposed to person-centered) approach, and emphasized nomothetic over idiographic portrayals of examinees' functioning. The evaluating psychiatrist or psychologist, armed with knowledge of psychological theories and scientific methods, aspired to conduct an *objective* appraisal of the individual and tended to make diagnostic and dispositional determinations unilaterally.

Modifications to the testing approach came from several fronts, including psychoanalytic, interpersonal, humanistic, and phenomenological traditions, each of which critiqued the detached and superordinate role of the examiner. They offered alternative

The Wiley Handbook of Personality Assessment, First Edition. Edited by Updesh Kumar.
© 2016 John Wiley & Sons, Ltd. Published 2016 by John Wiley & Sons, Ltd.

perspectives on clients' contributions to the assessment and assessor–assessee interaction. Among mid-century expositions of this nature were Schafer's (1954) discourse on the interpersonal dynamics of the testing situation, and Harrower's (1956) explication of a psychotherapeutic assessment technique, followed by Berg's (1984) delineation of a flexible and collaborative assessment process. A particularly strong push for a new direction came from Fischer's (1985/1994) individualized psychological assessment approach that evolved into a collaborative assessment method (e.g., Fischer, 2000), and Finn's (1996) development of an assessment-as-therapeutic-intervention strategy that became formalized into Therapeutic Assessment (TA) (e.g., Finn, 2007). In Fischer's method, assessor and assessee actively collaborate, or "co-labor," to achieve a productive understanding of the examinee (Fischer, 2000, p. 3), using testing and assessment as a means to explore his or her life world. In Finn's (2007) paradigm, assessor and assessee jointly generate questions to be addressed in the assessment, followed by a collaborative dialog about the findings that is designed to be transformative. Through these developments, the assessor's role has altered from that of sole decision-maker to partner, and the assessee's role has evolved from passive recipient to active, informed participant in the assessment process. On these bases, TA today represents an example of effective integration of empirically oriented techniques within a reflexive, post-modern epistemological framework (Aschieri, 2012a).

Principles and Methods

TA relies on humanistic/phenomenological and intersubjective principles. TA is, in humanistic/phenomenological terms, a hermeneutic cycle (Husserl, 1962): a process in which two observers produce a co-constructed understanding by sharing observations (e.g., focusing on problems in the client's life, or on a score or a behavior during a test), frame the observations into different contexts (e.g., the client's life, the experience of the assessor, the client's and the assessor's values, the client's and the assessor's lay or professional theories, the task and processes elicited by the test), and test the adequacy of the conclusions through new observations. Psychological tests are crucial elements of TA as they represent controlled environments to observe and define reality (e.g., by reaching a mutually agreed definition of the problem at hand in the assessment), to understand and contextualize the problem (e.g., by pondering the meaning of the same result across different tests, or the meaning of different behaviors and responses in tests that measure the same construct in different manners), and to intervene with clients' problematic behaviors (e.g., by asking clients to change their approach or to try out new behaviors to a test).

The contribution of the assessor in the assessment process is understood through intersubjective principles. Building on Stolorow (Stolorow, Brandchaft, & Atwood, 1987) and Bromberg's (2012) assumptions about psychotherapeutic processes, in TA assessors see themselves as co-participants in their clients' assessments and use their personal histories, values, and emotions in sessions to promote an authentic encounter with clients.

Steps of a Therapeutic Assessment

There are currently four models of TA tailored to work with adults, families with children (TA-C), families with adolescents (TA-A), and couples. Virtually every TA begins with an initial telephone contact in which the assessor asks clients to think of questions they have about themselves and their problems, which they hope to have answered through the assessment. The assessor then sends clients reading material regarding the main features of the assessment, and provides space in the first session to address doubts about the procedures, the length and the costs of the process, confidentiality, and so on. The main goal of the first session is to establish a collaborative relationship between assessor and client and then co-develop Assessment Questions – individualized questions that capture puzzles, issues, and problems that bother clients or referring professionals (such as: "Why I can't tolerate long-term relationships?" or "How can I get past my laziness and finish my degree?" or "Why is our child so afraid of the dark?"). By asking clients what they want to learn about their problems, assessors elicit curiosity, introspection, and other important psychological processes connected to exploring one's own inner world (Aschieri & Durosini, 2015). Subsequently, in the step of Standardized Test Administration, assessors select and administer psychological tests chosen on the basis of the Assessment Questions. Matching the choice of tests with assessment questions and with specific aspects of a client's situation (see, for example, the use of the consensus Rorschach with couples: Aschieri, 2012b) helps clients to feel the assessment is directed towards reaching their goals; in turn, they tend to provide more open, valid, and reliable test scores.

After the standardized tests are administered, assessors expand the personal meaning of clients' test responses in the Extended Inquiry. The Extended Inquiry can focus on any aspect that clients or assessors find worth discussing, either of the testing experience or of its contents. For example, clients might be asked to elucidate "critical items" they endorsed on self-report measures, or to reflect on the emotions they experienced when telling stories to certain Thematic Apperception Test (TAT) cards, or to discuss and co-interpret particular images they saw on the Rorschach. Then, the assessor integrates information from the interviews, the standardized tests, and the Extended Inquiry into a case formulation that leads to the next step in TA, the Assessment Intervention Session. During Assessment Intervention Sessions assessors use testing materials in non-standardized ways to help clients to discover and grasp important answers to their assessment questions or to help them to explore new behaviors. More information about this unique aspect of TA can be found in Finn (2007).

The TA interactive process culminates in a Summary and Discussion Session in which assessors and clients review the findings of the assessment and use them to reply directly to the initial Assessment Questions. The assessor presents feedback in carefully ordered "levels," proceeding from information congruent with clients' self-perceptions to those that expand and shift their conceptions of themselves. Assessment Questions help clinicians to introduce information that is otherwise potentially difficult for clients to integrate, but which becomes more accessible to clients because it addresses their individualized goals for the assessment. Each finding and each potential answer is discussed, re-shaped, and enriched with new material from the clients' reactions, associations, and real-life examples. All the information is finally summarized in a written Feedback Letter that is sent to clients to provide them with a review of the main findings and recommendations of the assessment. The combination of oral and written feedback has been shown by Lance and Krishnamurthy (2003) to be better than either one alone in helping clients to understand and make use of assessment findings.

A two- to four-month Follow-up Session is the last step of TA. This meeting allows assessors to address possible new questions from clients using the testing, to track the changes in their lives, and to refine treatment recommendations.

Empirical Evidence

Initial evidence for beneficial outcomes associated with therapeutic test feedback came from two controlled studies conducted by Finn and Tonsager (1992) in the US, and Newman and Greenway (1997) in Australia. The first study demonstrated that carefully crafted therapeutic feedback produced significantly decreased symptomatic distress, increased self-esteem, and increased hope about managing problems in an outpatient counseling center client sample, compared with wait-list controls. These gains were achieved regardless of initial level of distress, severity and type of pathology, prior attitudes about mental health providers and services, and time interval between testing, feedback, and follow-up. The outcomes were also shown not to be a function simply of feeling accepted or cared for by the examiner. The second investigation replicated these findings in a similarly designed study, with supplemental evidence that the results were not due to the test administration itself or overall level of client satisfaction. These compelling findings have since received expanded support in a series of empirical investigations with diverse samples, revealing positive process and outcome effects. For example, Allen, Montgomery, Tubman, Frazier, and Escovar (2003) showed that university students who received personalized assessment feedback achieved significantly higher scores on rapport (i.e., positive evaluations of examiner and sessions) and self-enhancement (accurate mirroring, self-esteem, self-competence, and self-understanding) indices than no-feedback controls.

With regards to treatment samples, Ackerman, Hilsenroth, Baity, and Blagys (2000) compared the utility of a TA model and a traditional model of assessment in an outpatient sample. They found significantly fewer dropouts/greater continuance into psychotherapy in the TA group, and facilitative effects of the TA model on therapeutic alliance. Smith, Eichler, Norman, and Smith (2015) found a significant reduction in client-reported symptomatic distress, reflected in a medium effect size of $d = 0.50$, and a significant change in the direction of a downward trajectory of distress, for adult clients who received a collaborative/therapeutic assessment as a mid-therapy consultative intervention. Tharinger et al. (2009) reported effects of TA with children and their caregivers as including significantly higher service satisfaction, higher positive emotions, and lower ratings of child externalizing and internalizing problems by mothers in pre–post assessment comparisons. They also found significantly decreased child symptomatology and improved family functioning as reported by both children and mothers.

Notably, a recent meta-analytic study provided strong support for the effectiveness of therapeutic assessment methods. Poston and Hanson's (2010) meta-analysis of data from 17 published studies involving a total of 1,496 participants showed an overall robust effect of therapeutic assessment ($d = 0.42$). Furthermore, they found significant positive effects for therapy process and outcome variables. The researchers concluded that therapeutically delivered psychological assessment and feedback offers substantial, clinically meaningful benefits.

A recent development in collaborative/therapeutic assessment investigations has involved newer methodologies such as single-case/time-series research designs, which are well suited to efficacy studies. For example, Smith, Wolf, Handler, and Nash (2009) employed a time-series design to evaluate clinical improvements associated with a family TA intervention. Using multiple personality and behavioral measures as dependent variables, the researchers conducted five-phase comparison analyses extending from pretreatment baseline assessment through intervention and follow-up. Results showed significant improvements in parent-rated child behaviors and family distress, and an overall trajectory of positive change as a result of the family TA intervention. Note that use of this design revealed specific change mechanisms at different stages. Aschieri and Smith (2012) similarly utilized a time-series design in a TA demonstration with an adult client, which consisted of daily data collection over a 28-day period extending from pre-TA baseline assessment through TA application. Level-change analyses indicated significant improvements in the client's ability to express affection and a trend toward improvement in anxiety from baseline to TA delivery, with an overall significant improvement on a composite index. Slope-change analyses revealed movement towards positive change over the course of the study period. The researchers commented that case-based daily measure designs of the kind used in this and similar studies are particularly useful as a clinically-oriented, client- and researcher/practitioner-friendly method of documenting TA effectiveness.

Overall, the evidence for collaborative/therapeutic assessment effects is strong in terms of positive change processes and outcomes associated with this method of assessment, even without the introduction of conventional psychotherapy. Numerous other investigations have amplified the data on these effects in a variety of applications, discussed in the next section.

Applications

The literature on collaborative/therapeutic assessment contains illustrations of its applications with various age groups (adult, adolescent, child/family), settings (e.g., clinical inpatient and outpatient, forensic, counseling), and contexts (neuropsychological evaluation, career counseling, healthcare). Case studies have shown its use with clients presenting with various disorders (e.g. adult Attention Deficit Disorder, child Oppositional Defiant Disorder, trauma and dissociation, eating disorders, personality disorders, self-harm, etc.). This literature further shows worldwide, cross-national applications.

Age groups

Among applications of the TA model with adult clients, Finn (2003) provided a case study of a man diagnosed with Attention Deficit Disorder and presenting with disorganization and relationship difficulties. This report illustrated TA's utility in (a) helping clients to "rewrite" problematic or incomplete self-narratives through the use of the assessment tools as "empathy magnifiers" (p. 126), and (b) overcoming treatment impasses by enlisting both client and referring therapist as collaborators. Wygant and Fleming (2008) summarized a TA with a young adult man assessed after receiving crisis stabilization for a suicide attempt. In this case, the assessment and feedback generated useful insight through processes of conceptualizing and discussing underlying personality characteristics. Armstrong (2012) and Overton (2012) discussed TA use with female clients who had traumatic/abusive backgrounds, showing how assessment and feedback can aid such clients to develop cognitive control and emotional strength. Tarocchi, Aschieri, Fantini, and Smith (2013) used a single-case repeated measure design with a severely traumatized woman suffering from complicated trauma; this case highlighted the transformative effect of TA during the intervention and the follow-up. Across the aforementioned studies, the tests used ranged from an intelligence test to self-report personality inventories, a trauma measure, a performance-based personality measure, and a structured diagnostic interview, demonstrating that TA is not limited to the use of specific tests and measures.

TA may be particularly useful as a timely and rapid intervention with adolescent clients so as to prevent difficulties from intensifying or becoming entrenched. In TA-A, the adolescent's parent is involved in generating questions to be addressed in the summary session, while the adolescent's privacy is maintained during the testing. Among recent published reports of TA-A are Ougrin et al.'s (2012) application of a modified TA approach with teenagers engaging in self-harm, revealing a more favorable impact for non-suicidal than suicidal self-harming adolescents. Austin, Krumholz, and Tharinger's (2012) case example of TA with a drug-using adolescent and his parents demonstrated the responsiveness of the method to the developmental status and family context of adolescents. Toivakka (2012) described his collaborative assessment of a teenage girl with psychotic features complicated by self-mutilation, drug overdose, and alcohol misuse, assessed in a psychiatric hospital in Finland. Using a series of measures including an intelligence test, the Rorschach, human figure drawings, and fantasy animal drawings, the case demonstrated the impact of feedback in fostering parents' understanding and empathy as a vehicle for improvement in the adolescent's functioning. Another case example by Frackowiak (2012), involving assessment of attachment and neuropsychological functioning in a poorly functioning adopted teenager, also underscored the importance of developing a relationship with both parent(s) and teenager in the process of conducting therapeutically oriented assessment and feedback.

TA with children requires some further adjustments relative to procedures used with adults and adolescents. It invariably involves parents/legal guardians throughout the process, and is designed to enhance parents' understanding of their child as well as promote change (Tharinger et al., 2009). Handler (2006) provided a detailed description of TA with children and adolescents that includes discussing how to adapt traditional assessment techniques and incorporate storytelling approaches in this paradigm. More recently, Aschieri, Fantini, and Bertrando (2012) gave a detailed overview of TA-C procedures with children in family therapy. Examples of TA-C work are also provided in several case reports. Purves (2002) examined the value of collaborative/therapeutic assessments of children in foster care and mothers seeking return of their children from foster care, showing how their initial resistances dissipate through the method's provision of a sense of agency. Hamilton et al. (2009) demonstrated how maladaptive family processes and interactions come to light and can be addressed through this method. Tharinger et al. (2012) described having parents observe and process their child's assessment through live video feed or a one-way mirror as a means of fostering understanding and change. Fantini, Aschieri, and Bertrando (2013) described performing TA in a series of systematic steps, including family intervention, summary/discussion and feedback segments, in the case of a four-year-old child assessed in Italy; this method was shown to be a useful means of achieving new viewpoints and emotions in the family. These and other published works shed light on a variety of useful strategies and the overall merits of TA with children and families.

Settings and contexts

Collaborative/Therapeutic Assessment has been usefully applied with clients in a broad range of clinical, counseling, and forensic settings. While most of the previously mentioned case reports come from outpatient clinical and counseling settings, one noteworthy example of inpatient application is from Michel (2002) who described TA with adolescents hospitalized for eating disorders. In this account, TA-A was shown to help overcome typical resistances seen in this population through providing teenage clients with a sense of personal control and assisting in identity development. The TA literature spans case examples involving a variety of disorders seen in outpatient and inpatient settings, ranging from child Oppositional Defiant Disorder (e.g., Smith, Handler, & Nash, 2010) to adult personality disorders (e.g., de Saeger et al., 2014). In addition to its use with individuals and families, TA has been usefully applied in the context of couples counseling (e.g., Uhinki, 2001).

TA's reach is certainly not limited to personality assessment, as several previously mentioned examples show its utility in cases where the referral for assessment includes questions of cognitive/intellectual functioning. In fact, Gorske (2008) provided a report of therapeutic neuropsychological assessment of a young woman with a brain tumor to demonstrate how it can enhance the patient's overall sense of wellbeing. Forensic application of TA is discussed by Evans (2013), addressing its use in cases involving termination of parental rights as well as with criminal offenders; this is a relatively new frontier for TA that is likely to expand in the near future.

TA applications are beginning to extend from traditional mental health settings into the broader healthcare arena. Smith and George (2012) described the application of TA in assessing cancer-related trauma in a patient seen in a healthcare setting.

In this example, TA served as a brief intervention that enabled the patient to reduce affective distress, regain a sense of control and move forward with her life, in addition to addressing her unresolved attachment trauma. Miller, Cano, and Wurm (2013) discussed use of a motivational TA approach in alleviating pain and improving well-being in chronic pain patients and their spouses; this was a demonstration of an effective couples assessment and intervention strategy that fostered gains in both partners. Smith, Finn, Swain, and Handler (2010) described a family-centered application in the case of a child presenting in the emergency department of a children's hospital with medically unexplained neurological impairments. This report exemplified a systemic approach wherein the recipients of feedback included the medical professionals. With the recent entry of psychologists into primary and integrated healthcare settings, TA can support systemic goals in cases involving the interface of medical and psychological conditions.

Training in Therapeutic Assessment

TA training has gained momentum in graduate psychology programs, being incorporated into personality assessment coursework (Finn, 1998) and/or offered through advanced seminars (e.g., Martin, 2013) and practica (Hanson, 2013). As a result, many students have some exposure to TA during their professional training. On the other hand, several graduate programs and internships in clinical and counseling psychology are doing less overall training in psychological assessment, with the result that some students/psychologists interested in learning TA have to find private sources of training (e.g., professional workshops). Among these alternative resources are TA institutes established in Austin (Texas), Milan (Italy) and Tokyo (Japan) that offer advanced, in-depth training. TA workshops and research presentations have also featured prominently in the international Society for Personality Assessment's annual convention over the last several years.

Training in Therapeutic Assessment has three aspects: (1) gaining competence in standardized psychological tests and in case conceptualization; (2) learning the structure and techniques of Therapeutic Assessment (e.g., how to do an Extended Inquiry of a standardized test); and (3) developing therapeutic skills such as alliance building and supporting clients as they explore dissociated affect states. The Therapeutic Assessment Institute (TAI) coordinates workshops around the world on the theory and techniques of TA (www.therapeuticassessment.com), and there are now many published teaching resources available (e.g., Finn, 1996, 2007; Finn, Fischer, & Handler, 2012; Levak, Siegel, & Nichols, 2011). TAI faculty members provide consultation to advanced practitioners learning how to use test materials therapeutically with clients. And an intriguing fact frequently reported in the literature is that assessors often grow and change personally in important ways as they learn TA (e.g., Finn, 1998; Haydel, Mercer, & Rosenblatt, 2011; Krishnamurthy, 2012). Finn (2005) attributes this effect to the expanded empathy assessors must develop in order to understand and help clients whom other professionals find confusing, disturbing, or off-putting.

Future Directions

Current research on TA is focused on identifying moderator variables – those client, assessor, or contextual factors that influence how useful TA is for a particular client. Also, although much has been written about why TA works, very little research has been done to test and identify specific therapeutic mechanisms. A recent study by Jourdan and Krishnamurthy (2015) represents a first step in investigating whether active note-taking by the client during the feedback session will strengthen his/her recollection and use of the oral feedback in subsequent therapy sessions. Also, some research is being directed towards evaluating how effective certain TA techniques are in isolation. For example, Tharinger and Pilgrim (2012) studied the use of child feedback fables in a standard neuropsychology practice and found that they greatly impacted children and parents.

Currently, the Therapeutic Assessment Institute is working to develop distance learning methods, such as supervision groups, webinars, and training videotapes, for practitioners interesting in learning TA in their localities. The TAI is also developing teaching materials, reading lists, and sample syllabi for graduate instructors who wish to include TA in their courses. In recent years, the TAI has established a certification program in TA, for those practitioners who want a guarantee that they are practicing TA at an advanced level.

As described above, TA was developed for use in clinical and counseling practice, but some practitioners are exploring its use in new settings, such as parenting plan evaluations (Evans, 2013), mandatory treatment of violent offenders (Chudzik & Aschieri, 2013), career counseling (Essig & Kelly, 2013), and executive coaching (Del Giudice, Yanovsky, & Finn, 2014).

Conclusions

The future of psychological assessment in clinical and counseling practice lies in value-laden, meaningful assessment practices. This is essential when current time demands promote quick screenings that may result in unsatisfying assessment experiences for clients. Collaborative/Therapeutic Assessment models, particularly TA, represent an evidence-based approach that has proven effectiveness in a broad range of applications. Further research, demonstrations, and training should solidify its use in assessment practice.

References

Ackerman, S.J., Hilsenroth, M.J., Baity, M.R., & Blagys, M.D. (2000). Interaction of therapeutic process and alliance during psychological assessment. *Journal of Personality Assessment, 75* (1), 82–109.

Allen, A., Montgomery, M., Tubman, J., Frazier, L., & Escovar, L. (2003). The effects of assessment feedback on rapport-building and self-enhancement processes. *Journal of Mental Health Counseling, 25* (3), 165–182.

Armstrong, J. (2012). Therapeutic assessment of a dissociating client: Learning internal navigation. In S.E. Finn, C.T. Fischer, & L. Handler (Eds.), *Collaborative/Therapeutic Assessment: A Casebook and Guide* (pp. 27–46). Hoboken, NJ: John Wiley & Sons, Ltd.

Aschieri, F. (2012a). Epistemological and ethical challenges in standardized testing and collaborative assessment. *Journal of Humanistic Psychology, 52* (3), 350–368.

Aschieri, F. (2012b). The conjoint Rorschach comprehensive system: Reliability and validity in clinical and non-clinical couples. *Journal of Personality Assessment, 95* (1), 46–53.

Aschieri, F., & Durosini, I. (2015). Development of a new measure of curiosity about self: The Self-Curiosity Attitude-Interest Scale. *Testing, Psychometrics, Methodology in Applied Psychology, 22* (3), 326–346.

Aschieri, F., Fantini, F., & Bertrando, P. (2012). Therapeutic Assessment with children in family therapy. *Australian and New Zealand Journal of Family Therapy, 33* (4), 285–298.

Aschieri, F., & Smith, J.D. (2012). The effectiveness of an adult Therapeutic Assessment: A single-case time-series experiment. *Journal of Personality Assessment, 94* (1), 1–11.

Austin, C.A., Krumholz, L.S., & Tharinger, D.J. (2012). Therapeutic Assessment with an adolescent: Choosing connections over substances. *Journal of Personality Assessment, 94* (6), 571–585.

Berg, M.R. (1984). Expanding the parameters of psychological testing. *Bulletin of the Menninger Clinic, 48* (1), 10–24.

Bromberg, P.M. (2012). *The Shadow of the Tsunami and the Growth of the Relational Mind.* New York: Routledge.

Chudzik, L., & Aschieri, F. (2013). Clinical relationships with forensic clients: A three-dimensional model. *Aggression and Violent Behavior, 18* (6), 722–731.

Del Giudice, M.J., Yanovsky, B., & Finn, S.E. (2014). Personality assessment and feedback practices among executive coaches: In search of a paradigm. *Consulting Psychology Journal: Practice and Research, 66* (3), 155–172.

de Saeger, H., Kamphuis, J.H., Finn, S.E., Smith, J.D., Verheul, R., van Busschbach, J.J., ... Horn, E.K. (2014). Therapeutic Assessment promotes treatment readiness but does not affect symptom change in patients with personality disorders: Findings from a randomized clinical trial. *Psychological Assessment, 26* (2), 474–483.

Essig, G.N., & Kelly, K.R. (2013). Comparison of the effectiveness of two assessment feedback models in reducing career indecision. *Journal of Career Assessment, 21* (4), 519–536.

Evans, B. (2013). The forensic corner. *The TA Connection, 1* (1), 18–21.

Fantini, F., Aschieri, F., & Bertrando, P. (2013). "Is our daughter crazy or bad?" A case study of Therapeutic Assessment with children. *Contemporary Family Therapy: An International Journal, 35* (4), 731–744.

Finn, S.E. (1996). *Manual for Using the MMPI-2 as a Therapeutic Intervention.* Minneapolis: University of Minnesota Press.

Finn, S.E. (1998). Teaching Therapeutic Assessment in a required graduate course. In L. Handler, & M.J. Hilsenroth (Eds.), *Teaching and Learning Personality Assessment* (pp. 359–376). Mahwah, NJ: Erlbaum.

Finn, S.E. (2003). Therapeutic Assessment of a man with "ADD". *Journal of Personality Assessment, 80* (2), 115–129.

Finn, S.E. (2005). How psychological assessment taught me compassion and firmness. *Journal of Personality Assessment, 84* (1), 27–30.

Finn, S.E. (2007). *In Our Clients' Shoes: Theory and Techniques of Therapeutic Assessment.* Mahwah, NJ: Erlbaum.

Finn, S.E., Fischer, C.T., & Handler, L. (Eds.) (2012). *Collaborative/Therapeutic Assessment: A Casebook and Guide.* Hoboken, NJ: Wiley.

Finn, S.E., & Tonsager, M.E. (1992). Therapeutic effects of providing MMPI-2 test feedback to college students awaiting therapy. *Psychological Assessment, 4* (3), 278–287.

Fischer, C.T. (1985/1994). *Individualizing Psychological Assessment.* Hillsdale, NJ: Erlbaum.

Fischer, C.T. (2000). Collaborative, individualized assessment. *Journal of Personality Assessment, 74* (1), 2–14.

Frackowiak, M. (2012). Therapeutic Assessment with an adolescent: An adopted teenager comes to feel understood. In S.E. Finn, C.T. Fischer, and L. Handler (Eds.), *Collaborative/Therapeutic Assessment: A Casebook and Guide* (pp. 225–242). Hoboken, NJ: Wiley.

Gorske, T.T. (2008). Therapeutic neuropsychological assessment: A humanistic model and case example. *Journal of Humanistic Psychology, 48* (3), 320–339.

Hamilton, A.M., Fowler, J.L., Hersh, B., Austin, C.A., Finn, S.E., Tharinger, D.J., ... Arora, P. (2009). "Why won't my parents help me?": Therapeutic Assessment of a child and her family. *Journal of Personality Assessment, 91* (2), 108–120.

Handler, L. (2006). The use of therapeutic assessment with children and adolescents. In S.R. Smith, & L. Handler (Eds.), *The Clinical Assessment of Children and Adolescents: A Practitioner's Handbook* (pp. 53–72). Mahwah, NJ: Erlbaum.

Hanson, W. (2013). Teaching Therapeutic Assessment practica. *The TA Connection, 1* (2), 7–13.

Harrower, M. (1956). Projective counseling: A psychotherapeutic technique. *American Journal of Psychotherapy, 10* (1), 74–86.

Haydel, M.E., Mercer, B.L., & Rosenblatt, E. (2011). Training assessors in Therapeutic Assessment. *Journal of Personality Assessment, 93* (1), 16–22.

Husserl, E. (1962). *Ideas: General Introduction to Pure Phenomenology.* London: Collier (originally published 1913).

Jourdan, B., & Krishnamurthy, R. (2015). *Increasing the recall and use of psychological test feedback through client note-taking activity.* Paper submitted for presentation at the 2016 Annual Convention of the Society for Personality Assessment, Chicago, IL.

Krishnamurthy, R. (2012). *Introduction to teaching and learning therapeutic assessment.* In R. Krishnamurthy (Chair), "Self-discovery and reflective learning through therapeutic assessment". Integrated paper session presented at the Annual Meeting of the Society for Personality Assessment, Chicago, IL.

Lance, B.R., & Krishnamurthy, R. (2003). *A comparison of the effectiveness of three modes of MMPI-2 test feedback.* In A. Caldwell (Chair), "MMPI-2/MMPI-A". Paper presented at the Annual Meeting of the Society for Personality Assessment, San Francisco, CA.

Levak, R.W., Siegel, L., & Nichols, D.S. (2011). *Therapeutic Feedback with the MMPI-2: A Positive Psychology Approach.* New York: Routledge.

Martin, H. (2013). Teaching Therapeutic Assessment. *The TA Connection, 1* (1), 7–12.

Michel, D.M. (2002). Psychological assessment as a therapeutic intervention in patients hospitalized with eating disorders. *Professional Psychology: Research and Practice, 33* (5), 470–477.

Miller, L.R., Cano, A., & Wurm, L.H. (2013). A motivational therapeutic assessment improves pain, mood, and relationship satisfaction in couples with chronic pain. *Journal of Pain, 14* (5), 525–537.

Newman, M.L., & Greenway, P. (1997). Therapeutic effects of providing MMPI-2 test feedback to clients at a university counseling service: A collaborative approach. *Psychological Assessment, 9* (2), 122–131.

Ougrin, D., Zundel, T., Kyriakopoulos, M., Banarsee, R., Stahl, D., & Taylor, E. (2012). Adolescents with suicidal and nonsuicidal self-harm: Clinical characteristics and response to therapeutic assessment. *Psychological Assessment, 24* (1), 11–20.

Overton, C.G. (2012). Therapeutic assessment of severe abuse: A woman living with her past. In S.E. Finn, C.T. Fischer, & L. Handler (Eds.), *Collaborative/Therapeutic Assessment: A Casebook and Guide* (pp. 199–222). Hoboken, NJ: John Wiley & Sons, Ltd.

Poston, J.M., & Hanson, W.E. (2010). Meta-analysis of psychological assessment as a therapeutic intervention. *Psychological Assessment, 22* (2), 203–212.

Purves, C. (2002). Collaborative assessment with involuntary populations: Foster children and their mothers. *The Humanistic Psychologist, 30* (1–2), 164–174.

Schafer, R. (1954). *Psychoanalytic interpretation in Rorschach testing.* New York: Grune & Stratton.

Smith, J.D., Eichler, W.C., Norman, K.R., & Smith, S.R. (2015). The effectiveness of collaborative/therapeutic assessment for psychotherapy consultation: A pragmatic replicated single-case study. *Journal of Personality Assessment, 97* (3), 261–270.

Smith, J.D., Finn, S.E., Swain, N.F., & Handler, L. (2010). Therapeutic Assessment of families in healthcare settings: A case presentation of the model's application. *Families, Systems, & Health, 28* (4), 369–386.

Smith, J.D., & George, C. (2012). Therapeutic Assessment case study: Treatment of a woman diagnosed with metastatic cancer and attachment trauma. *Journal of Personality Assessment, 94* (4), 331–344.

Smith, J.D., Handler, L., & Nash, M.R. (2010). Therapeutic Assessment for preadolescent boys with oppositional defiant disorder: A replicated single-case time-series design. *Psychological Assessment, 22* (3), 593–602.

Smith, J.D., Wolf, N.J., Handler, L., & Nash, M.R. (2009). Testing the effectiveness of family Therapeutic Assessment: A case study using a time-series design. *Journal of Personality Assessment, 91* (6), 518–536.

Stolorow, R.D., Brandchaft, B., & Atwood, G.E. (1987) *Psychoanalytic Treatment: An Intersubjective Approach.* Hillsdale, NJ: Analytic Press.

Tarocchi, A., Aschieri, F., Fantini, F., & Smith, J.D. (2013). Therapeutic Assessment of complex trauma: A single-case time-series study. *Clinical Case Studies, 12* (3), 228–245.

Tharinger, D.J., Finn, S.E., Arora, P., Judd-Glossy, L., Ihorn, S.M., & Wan, J.T. (2012). Therapeutic Assessment with children: Intervening with parents "behind the mirror". *Journal of Personality Assessment, 94* (2), 111–123.

Tharinger, D.J., Finn, S.E., Gentry, L., Hamilton, A., Fowler, J., Matson, M., Krumholz, L., & Walkowiak, J. (2009). Therapeutic Assessment with children: A pilot study of treatment acceptability and outcome. *Journal of Personality Assessment, 91* (3), 238–244.

Tharinger, D.J., & Pilgrim, S. (2012). Child and parent experiences of neuropsychological assessment as a function of child feedback by individualized fable. *Child Neuropsychology, 18* (3), 228–241.

Toivakka, H. (2012). Collaborative assessment on an adolescent psychiatric teenage girl. In S.E. Finn, C.T. Fischer, & L. Handler (Eds.), *Collaborative/Therapeutic Assessment: A Casebook and Guide* (pp. 335–354). Hoboken, NJ: John Wiley & Sons, Ltd.

Uhinki, A. (2001). Experiences of the therapeutic assessment with couples. *Journal of Projective Psychology & Mental Health, 8* (1), 15–18.

Wygant, D.B., & Fleming, K.P. (2008). Clinical utility of MMPI-2 Restructured Clinical (RC) scales in therapeutic assessment: A case study. *Journal of Personality Assessment, 90* (2), 110–118.

18

Personality Assessment in Ecological Settings by Means of Virtual Reality

Pietro Cipresso
Istituto Auxologico Italiano, Milan, Italy

Giuseppe Riva
Istituto Auxologico Italiano, and Università Cattolica del Sacro Cuore, Milan, Italy

Personality has traditionally been assessed by means of questionnaires (Cattell & Eber, 1950; Eysenck, 1968; Francis, Brown, & Philipchalk, 1992; Gosling, Rentfrow, & Swann Jr, 2003; Hough, 1992; Hurtz & Donovan, 2000; Rammstedt & John, 2007; Tellegen & Waller, 2008; Wiggins & Trapnell, 1997). Unfortunately, the use of self-reported measures is vulnerable to a variety of biases related to the self-judgment and self-consciousness of the subjects in front of the investigator (Albright, Kenny, & Malloy, 1988; Dweck, 1991; Kolar, Funder, & Colvin, 1996; Trapnell & Campbell, 1999). To cope with these issues, many psychometric methods have been used to identify and delete possible instances of lying and deceitfulness to eradicate any deceiving biases (Bond Jr & DePaulo, 2008; Bond Jr & Uysal, 2007; Farrow et al., 2003); however, personality is so "personal" that biases are never easy to statistically control (Ambady & Rosenthal, 1992; O'Sullivan, 2007).

A possible solution to these problems is to build tests with a higher rate of ecological validity (Bem & Lord, 1979; Burgess, Alderman, Evans, Emslie, & Wilson, 1998; Chaytor & Schmitter-Edgecombe, 2003; Ready, Stierman, & Paulsen, 2001). The ideal situation is to assess behaviors in specific tasks in daily situations (Burgess et al., 1998; Chaytor & Schmitter-Edgecombe, 2003; Mischel & Shoda, 1995). Unfortunately, there are many problems that prevent researchers from doing so. First, there are many ethical issues that would arise from conducting invasive experiments in participants' real-life situations, so it is preferable to create prototypical situations under the control of a researcher (Baumrind, 1985). Unfortunately, though, this is difficult. For example, to evaluate specific personality traits in real-life contexts, a researcher would have to bring participants

The Wiley Handbook of Personality Assessment, First Edition. Edited by Updesh Kumar.
© 2016 John Wiley & Sons, Ltd. Published 2016 by John Wiley & Sons, Ltd.

into a supermarket and observe their behaviors gradually during the assigned task performance. This is very complex and – above all – prohibitively expensive.

Virtual Reality for Psychological Research

Virtual reality (VR) offers a great opportunity to create prototypical situations that can help researchers to understand personality traits (Heim, 1993; Ryan, 2001; Sherman & Craig, 2002). Unfortunately, VR is generally complex to manage, and many researchers are discouraged from adopting it due to technological barriers such as the need for programming skills that are generally missing among psychological researchers (Brooks Jr, 1999; Riva, Davide, & IJsselsteijn, 2003; Riva & Waterworth, 2014).

Even if the cost of technology has dropped consistently over the last decade, the cost of creating virtual environments is still high, as it requires programmers and 3D graphics experts. To address this problem, Riva and colleagues created some years ago a platform that enables psychologists to create and distribute virtual environments and situations that replicate real-life prototypical situations for the creation of personality assessment tests in ecological settings.

Until the late 1990s, virtual therapy was considered nothing more than a promising field of research (Lamson, 1994; North, North, & Coble, 1996; Rothbaum, Hodges, & Kooper, 1997). At that time, the main limitations were the lack of controlled studies demonstrating the clinical efficacy of this approach, and the high cost of the hardware. Typically, a complete system of immersive virtual reality was estimated to cost around $100,000 per unit (including head-mounted display of medium quality, graphics workstations, sensors, and devices for interaction). Moreover, the cost for the development (or the purchase) of the therapeutic virtual environments had to be added to these expenses.

In recent years, however, some of these barriers have been partially overcome. First of all, the definition of clinical protocols for several diseases has led to the execution of controlled trials demonstrating the efficacy of cybertherapy (Holden, 2005; Malloy & Milling, 2010; McCann et al., 2014; Riva, 2003, 2005). Also, the hardware costs have dramatically decreased. Due to the incredible expansion of the 3D gaming industry and LCD displays, the cost of an immersive VR system consisting of a laptop with a graphics card of good quality and wearable head-mounted display with motion-tracking sensors is approximately 1,500 Euros.

The obstacle of software development cost, however, still remains a problem limiting the expansion of the market. Despite this barrier, cybertherapy is an extremely vital and rapidly developing research community.

In recent decades, the number of scientific events devoted to this topic has rapidly grown. Each year, there are three major international conferences on cybertherapy: Medicine Meets Virtual Reality, Virtual Rehabilitation, and CyberTherapy. These conferences attract a broad range of scholars and clinicians from around the world. There are also several other conferences dealing with directly related topics, such as SIGGRAPH, Human–Computer Interaction, and Presence.

The number of scientific publications in the field of virtual therapy has increased considerably in volume and reputation. The cybertherapy community has several scientific journals of international level (the most important of which is *CyberPsychology, Behavior, and Social Networking*, with a readership of 18,000 and an impact factor of more than 2). Papers from this community are published in journals of significant scientific importance, including *Science*, *Nature* and *Scientific American*. The community garners impressive media coverage, including documentaries and special services on virtual therapy that have appeared on major television networks (e.g., ABC, CNN, RAI, BBC).

The potential growth of this scientific sector is also highlighted by the increasing investments in R&D by the public sector. In the US, a military research program for the development of therapeutic solutions based on VR for veterans of Iraq has been funded by a recent governmental program with $10 million. At the European level, within the Fifth and Sixth Framework Programme, the research field of VR has been funded by the IST/ICT Programme with over 80 million Euros; the Seventh Framework Programme (up to 2013) also provided significant investment in this field, with particular reference to Future Emerging Technologies Program (http://cordis.europa.eu/fp7/ict/programme/fet_en.html).

Personality Assessment in Ecological Settings (Environments and their Creation Process)

Generally, personality assessment tests evaluate five dimensions: extraversion, agreeableness, conscientiousness, emotional stability, and openness to experiences. One of the most commonly used questionnaires for investigating these dimensions is the Big Five (Gosling et al., 2003; Hough, 1992; Hurtz & Donovan, 2000) and its reduced version (ten items) (Rammstedt & John, 2007), which can be synthesized as follows, where (R) indicates reverse-scored items.

- **Extraversion**: Extraverted/enthusiastic vs. Reserved/quiet (R)
- **Agreeableness**: Critical/quarrelsome (R) vs. Sympathetic/warm
- **Conscientiousness**: Dependable/self-disciplined vs. Disorganized/careless
- **Emotional Stability**: Anxious/easily upset (R) vs. Calm/emotionally stable
- **Openness to Experiences**: Open to new experiences/complex vs. Conventional/uncreative (R)

To assess personality within these five dimensions, it is possible to think of different situations where one component and its antagonist are posed either in multiple situations with a single choice, or in only one situation with multiple choice.

This means that if researchers want to create a virtual environment that encodes one specific dimension (e.g., Openness to Experiences), they will have two possibilities:

1 We could create seven situations, like a path in the forest with a crossroads, where the participant through a narrative in the virtual environment must choose a visible street (lowest openness to experiences) on one side or a dark street (highest openness to experiences) on the other side.

2 Alternatively, we could create a path in the forest with a crossroads that contains seven possible paths from the most conventional lighted and clear street (lowest openness to experiences) to the darkest one (highest openness to experiences).

In each case, we will obtain a score from one to seven for the Openness to Experiences dimension of personality.

This method can be used for each dimension of personality using virtual environments and narrative situations using audio, video, and virtual objects. To create these ecological tests, researchers can use different kinds of software available on the market, ranging from video games to complex 3D engines. Unfortunately psychologists, who are the experts in personality assessment, generally are not engineers, and thus need to build a strong team in order to build each experiment.

To solve this problem, we propose to use Neuro Virtual 3D (Cipresso, Serino, Pallavicini, Gaggioli, & Riva, 2014b), a powerful platform that enables psychologists with low technical skills to build complex environments and narratives and thus create very effective personality tests. Neuro Virtual 3D has been built thanks to the experience in developing Neuro VR software in all its versions (Riva et al., 2007, 2008, 2009, 2010).

Neuro Virtual 3D (http://neurovirtual.eu/) is a free platform composed of two modules: (1) an editor which enables researchers to create virtual environments with videos, pictures, and other 3D virtual objects; and (2) a player which is used to play the environment and the tasks prepared by the researchers. The software also incorporates external low-cost motion-tracking systems (Cipresso et al., 2014a). Once the scene has been created, it can be launched with the preferred options (Figure 18.1).

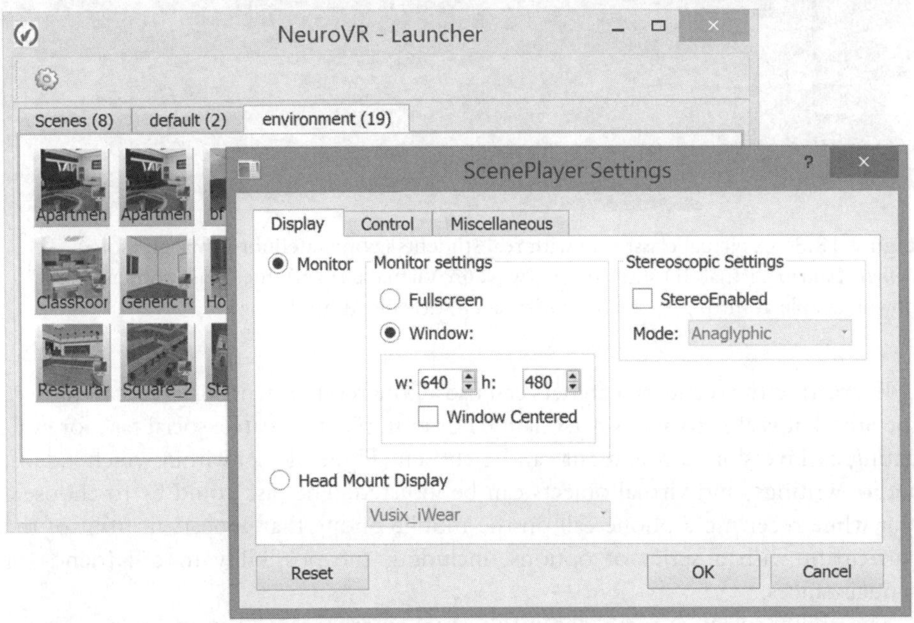

Figure 18.1 Through the launcher, the researcher is able to choose the environment and the conditions for the participants (e.g., the use of a monitor or head-mounted display). *Source*: Neuro Virtual 3D software (www.NeuroVirtual.eu).

Figure 18.2 A virtual environment (restaurant) within which to execute the task.
Source: Neuro Virtual 3D software (www.NeuroVirtual.eu) with "Restaurant" environment downloadable at: http://www.neurovirtual.eu/download.html.

Figure 18.3 A virtual classroom with real students (obfuscated for privacy reasons).
Source: Neuro Virtual 3D software (www.NeuroVirtual.eu) with the "Base contents pack" downloadable at: http://www.neurovirtual.eu/download.html.

In creating the scene, researchers can use all the requirements of a real task, where they think it is able to assess personality. For example, to create a social task for evaluating extraversion, a restaurant can be chosen (Figure 18.2) within which videos, audio, writings, and virtual objects can be inserted. The task could be to choose a seat while receiving a phone call on the mobile phone that appears in front of the participant with a series of options, including the possibility to call friends or acquaintances.

The ability to insert real video into virtual environments also makes the Neuro Virtual 3D platform very suitable for the creation of personality assessment tests. Also, video images of real people can be inserted (Figure 18.3).

Discussions and Conclusion

Although these data reveal that the market for VR has great potential for developing personality assessment tests, few companies are operating in this market with solutions focused on assessment; in fact, the core business of these companies is not software development for the assessment but rather VR treatment services.

With regard to expertise, new rehabilitative VR-based therapies in the field are fundamentally different from the traditional therapies (Castelnuovo, Gaggioli, Mantovani, & Riva, 2003; Grenier et al., 2014; Riva & Repetto, 2014; Shin, Ryu, & Jang, 2014; Wiederhold & Riva, 2014; Wiederhold & Wiederhold, 2004, 2014). Their integration with the use of immersive VR is now well established thanks to the great therapeutic potential of this technology. In this field of research, know-how is certainly not comprehensive because many studies are still underway. However, it could surely be increased by platforms similar to Neuro Virtual 3D, which include the innovative design of rehabilitation protocols and the ability to apply them through the use of immersive VR, and this would also benefit the personality assessment field with more validated measures.

In terms of technological impact, we believe that some features of the Neuro Virtual 3D platform can have an impact in the personality assessment field. This innovative therapeutic engine allows researchers to download different scenarios from an internet repository customizable on the basis of the different assessment strategies and psychological approaches, and it provides an effective interface that makes the experience truly immersive, thus amplifying the usability effect.

Acknowledgments

This study was partially supported by the research project "Neuro Virtual 3D", funded by Regione Piemonte (Grant No. FA 211-432C- 2012).

References

Albright, L., Kenny, D.A., & Malloy, T.E. (1988). Consensus in personality judgments at zero acquaintance. *Journal of Personality and Social Psychology, 55* (3), 387–395.

Ambady, N., & Rosenthal, R. (1992). Thin slices of expressive behavior as predictors of interpersonal consequences: A meta-analysis. *Psychological Bulletin, 111* (2), 256–274.

Baumrind, D. (1985). Research using intentional deception: ethical issues revisited. *American Psychologist, 40* (2), 165–174.

Bem, D.J., & Lord, C.G. (1979). Template matching: A proposal for probing the ecological validity of experimental settings in social psychology. *Journal of Personality and Social Psychology, 37* (6), 833–846.

Bond Jr, C.F., & DePaulo, B.M. (2008). Individual differences in judging deception: accuracy and bias. *Psychological Bulletin, 134* (4), 477–492.

Bond Jr, C.F., & Uysal, A. (2007). On lie detection "wizards". *Law and Human Behavior, 31* (1), 109–115.

Brooks Jr, F.P. (1999). What's real about virtual reality? *Computer Graphics and Applications, IEEE, 19* (6), 16–27.

Burgess, P.W., Alderman, N., Evans, J., Emslie, H., & Wilson, B.A. (1998). The ecological validity of tests of executive function. *Journal of the International Neuropsychological Society, 4* (6), 547–558.

Castelnuovo, G., Gaggioli, A., Mantovani, F., & Riva, G. (2003). New and old tools in psychotherapy: The use of technology for the integration of the traditional clinical treatments. *Psychotherapy: Theory, Research, Practice, Training, 40* (1–2), 33–44.

Cattell, R.B., & Eber, H. (1950). *The 16 Personality Factor Questionnaire.* Raymond, Illinois: Institute for Personality and Ability Testing.

Chaytor, N., & Schmitter-Edgecombe, M. (2003). The ecological validity of neuropsychological tests: A review of the literature on everyday cognitive skills. *Neuropsychology Review, 13* (4), 181–197.

Cipresso, P., Serino, S., Giglioli, I.A.C., Giuliano, I., Borra, D., Farina, A., & Riva, G. (2014a). Low-cost motion-tracking for computational psychometrics based on virtual reality. *Augmented and Virtual Reality, 8853,* 137–148.

Cipresso, P., Serino, S., Pallavicini, F., Gaggioli, A., & Riva, G. (2014b). NeuroVirtual 3D: A multiplatform 3D simulation system for application in psychology and neuro-rehabilitation. *Virtual, Augmented Reality and Serious Games for Healthcare, 68,* 275–286.

Dweck, C.S. (1991). *Self-theories and goals: Their role in motivation, personality, and development.* Paper presented at the Nebraska Symposium on Motivation.

Eysenck, H.J. (1968). *Eysenck Personality Inventory.* San Diego, CA: Educational and Industrial Testing Service.

Farrow, T.F., Reilly, R., Rahman, T.A., Herford, A.E., Woodruff, P.W., & Spence, S.A. (2003). Sex and personality traits influence the difference between time taken to tell the truth or lie. *Perceptual and Motor Skills, 97* (2), 451–460.

Francis, L.J., Brown, L.B., & Philipchalk, R. (1992). The development of an abbreviated form of the Revised Eysenck Personality Questionnaire (EPQR-A): Its use among students in England, Canada, the USA and Australia. *Personality and Individual Differences, 13* (4), 443–449.

Gosling, S.D., Rentfrow, P.J., & Swann Jr, W.B. (2003). A very brief measure of the Big-Five personality domains. *Journal of Research in Personality, 37* (6), 504–528.

Grenier, S., Forget, H., Bouchard, S., Isere, S., Belleville, S., Potvin, O., … Talbot, M. (2014). Using virtual reality to improve the efficacy of cognitive-behavioral therapy (CBT) in the treatment of late-life anxiety: preliminary recommendations for future research. *International Psychogeriatrics, 10,* 1–9.

Heim, M. (1993). *The Metaphysics of Virtual Reality*: New York: Oxford University Press.

Holden, M.K. (2005). Virtual environments for motor rehabilitation: review. *Cyberpsychology & Behavior, 8* (3), 187–211.

Hough, L.M. (1992). The 'Big Five' personality variables – construct confusion: Description versus prediction. *Human Performance, 5* (1–2), 139–155.

Hurtz, G.M., & Donovan, J.J. (2000). Personality and job performance: the Big Five revisited. *Journal of Applied Psychology, 85* (6), 869–879.

Kolar, D.W., Funder, D.C., & Colvin, C.R. (1996). Comparing the accuracy of personality judgments by the self and knowledgeable others. *Journal of Personality, 64* (2), 311–337.

Lamson, R. (1994). Virtual therapy of anxiety disorders. *CyberEdge Journal, 4* (2), 1–28.

Malloy, K.M., & Milling, L.S. (2010). The effectiveness of virtual reality distraction for pain reduction: a systematic review. *Clinical Psychology Review, 30* (8), 1011–1018.

McCann, R.A., Armstrong, C.M., Skopp, N.A., Edwards-Stewart, A., Smolenski, D.J., June, J.D., … Reger, G.M. (2014). Virtual reality exposure therapy for the treatment of anxiety disorders: An evaluation of research quality. *Journal of Anxiety Disorders, 28* (6), 625–631.

Mischel, W., & Shoda, Y. (1995). A cognitive-affective system theory of personality: reconceptualizing situations, dispositions, dynamics, and invariance in personality structure. *Psychological Review, 102* (2), 246–268.

North, M.M., North, S., & Coble, J. (1996). *Virtual Reality Therapy.* Ann Arbor, Michigan: IPI Press.

O'Sullivan, M. (2007). Unicorns or Tiger Woods: Are lie detection experts myths or rarities? A response to "On lie detection Wizards" by Bond and Uysal. *Law and Human Behaviour, 31* (1), 117–123.

Rammstedt, B., & John, O.P. (2007). Measuring personality in one minute or less: A 10-item short version of the Big Five Inventory in English and German. *Journal of Research in Personality, 41* (1), 203–212.

Ready, R.E., Stierman, L., & Paulsen, J.S. (2001). Ecological validity of neuropsychological and personality measures of executive functions. *The Clinical Neuropsychologist, 15* (3), 314–323.

Riva, G. (2003). Applications of virtual environments in medicine. *Methods of Information in Medicine, 42* (5), 524–534.

Riva, G. (2005). Virtual reality in psychotherapy: review. *Cyberpsychology & Behavior, 8* (3), 220–230.

Riva, G., Carelli, L., Gaggioli, A., Gorini, A., Vigna, C., Algeri, D., ... Faletti, G. (2008). NeuroVR 1.5 in practice: Actual clinical applications of the open source VR system. *Studies in Health Technology and Informatics, 144*, 57–60.

Riva, G., Carelli, L., Gaggioli, A., Gorini, A., Vigna, C., Corsi, R., ... Vezzadini, L. (2009). NeuroVR 1.5 – a free virtual reality platform for the assessment and treatment in clinical psychology and neuroscience. *Studies in Health Technology and Informatics, 142*, 268–270.

Riva, G., Davide, F., & IJsselsteijn, W.A. (2003). *Being There: Concepts, Effects and Measurements of User Presence in Synthetic Environments.* IOS Press.

Riva, G., Gaggioli, A., Grassi, A., Raspelli, S., Cipresso, P., Pallavicini, F., ... Donvito, G. (2010). NeuroVR 2 – a free virtual reality platform for the assessment and treatment in behavioral health care. *Studies in Health Technology and Informatics, 163*, 493–495.

Riva, G., Gaggioli, A., Villani, D., Preziosa, A., Morganti, F., Corsi, R., ... Vezzadini, L. (2007). NeuroVR: an open source virtual reality platform for clinical psychology and behavioral neurosciences. *Studies in Health Technology and Informatics, 125*, 394–399.

Riva, G., & Repetto, C. (2014). Conclusions: The present and the future of virtual reality in the treatment of anxiety disorders. In B.K. Wiederhold, & S. Bouchard (Eds.), *Advances in Virtual Reality and Anxiety Disorders* (pp. 265–283). New York: Springer.

Riva, G., & Waterworth, J. (2014). Being present in a virtual world. In M. Grimshaw (Ed.), *The Oxford Handbook of Virtuality* (pp. 205–221). New York: Oxford University Press.

Rothbaum, B.O., Hodges, L., & Kooper, R. (1997). Virtual reality exposure therapy. *Journal of Psychotherapy Practice & Research, 6*, 219–226.

Ryan, M.-L. (2001). *Narrative as Virtual Reality.* London: Parallax.

Sherman, W.R., & Craig, A.B. (2002). *Understanding Virtual Reality: Interface, Application, and Design*: Amsterdam: Elsevier.

Shin, J.-H., Ryu, H., & Jang, S.H. (2014). A task-specific interactive game-based virtual reality rehabilitation system for patients with stroke: a usability test and two clinical experiments. *Journal of Neuroengineering and Rehabilitation, 11* (1), 1–10.

Tellegen, A., & Waller, N.G. (2008). Exploring personality through test construction: Development of the Multidimensional Personality Questionnaire. *The SAGE Handbook of Personality Theory and Assessment, 2*, 261–292.

Trapnell, P.D., & Campbell, J.D. (1999). Private self-consciousness and the five-factor model of personality: distinguishing rumination from reflection. *Journal of Personality and Social Psychology, 76* (2), 284–304.

Wiederhold, B.K., & Riva, G. (2014). *Annual Review of Cybertherapy and Telemedicine 2014: Positive Change: Connecting the Virtual and the Real* (Vol. *199*). IOS Press.

Wiederhold, B.K., & Wiederhold, M.D. (2004). The future of cybertherapy: Improved options with advanced technologies. *Studies in Health Technology and Informatics, 99*, 263–270.

Wiederhold, B.K., & Wiederhold, M.D. (2014). Virtual reality for posttraumatic stress disorder. In B.K. Wiederhold, & S. Bouchard (Eds.), *Advances in Virtual Reality and Anxiety Disorders* (pp. 211–233). New York: Springer.

Wiggins, J.S., & Trapnell, P.D. (1997). Personality structure: The return of the big five. In S.R. Briggs, R. Hogan, & W.H. Jones (Eds.), *Handbook of Personality Psychology* (pp. 737–765). San Diego, CA: Academic Press.

19

The Use of the Hare Psychopathy Checklist (PCL-R) and Rorschach Inkblot Method (RIM) in Forensic Psychological Assessment

Carl B. Gacono
Licensed Psychologist, Austin, Texas, USA

Aaron J. Kivisto
University of Indianapolis, Indiana, USA

Jason M. Smith
FCC Hazelton, Bruceton Mills, West Virginia, USA

Ted B. Cunliffe
Licensed Psychologist, Lake Worth, Florida, USA

Paradoxically, psychological assessment and psychological testing have been de-emphasized during a time when their usefulness has been clearly articulated (Meyer et al., 1998; Gacono & Evans, 2008; Gacono, 2015). In clinical work, this de-emphasis is often rationalized for two general reasons: psychological assessment is (1) "too costly," and/or (2) "too time-intensive." Minimal attention is given to the relative costs, financial and otherwise, when needed assessments are neglected, and the role of the clinician's skill level in determining the time it takes to administer, score, and interpret data is frequently overlooked. Partially in response to these concerns regarding cost and time, the practice of utilizing easily administered paper and pencil tests, which require minimal contact with the patient, have gained popularity, despite the fact that there may be little if any relationship between the test and referral question. Of no surprise, these poorly conceived "window dressing" assessment protocols result in findings of little value and, tautologically, this is used to further justify the de-emphasis of formal psychological assessment (Gacono, 2002a, 2002b).

Forensic psychologists have also faced a third argument, unique to forensic practice. In this argument, critics assert, psychological tests are "irrelevant" to helping

The Wiley Handbook of Personality Assessment, First Edition. Edited by Updesh Kumar.
© 2016 John Wiley & Sons, Ltd. Published 2016 by John Wiley & Sons, Ltd.

courts decide legal issues, such as whether a defendant is "insane," which parent should have primary custody, or the amount of damages that should be awarded to a civil litigant (see Ziskin & Faust, 1989, for review). While it is accurate to say that psychological tests generally do not assess specific legal criteria (Otto, 2002), the leap to conclude that psychological tests are therefore irrelevant to the legal process and should be excluded is clearly problematic, as will be discussed below.

In order to justify the use of psychological *assessment* in clinical and forensic practice, it is first important to be able to articulate the differences between psychological testing and psychological assessment. Viewing the two as synonymous detracts from psychologists' unique contributions to assessment based upon their knowledge, training, and experience. Further, by conflating assessment with the relatively more simplistic process of testing, this misunderstanding encourages a de-emphasis of well-balanced and in-depth clinical training in graduate psychology programs (Gacono, 2002a, 2002b; Gacono & Bodholdt, 2001; Gacono, Loving, & Bodholdt, 2001a). Distinguishing testing from assessment:

> Psychological testing is a relatively straightforward process wherein a particular scale is administered to obtain a specific score. Subsequently, a descriptive meaning can be applied to the score on the basis of normative, nomothetic findings. In contrast, psychological assessment is concerned with the clinician who takes a variety of test scores, generally obtained from multiple test methods, and considers the data in the context of history, referral information, and observed behavior to understand the person being evaluated, to answer the referral questions, and then to communicate findings to the patient, his or her significant others, and referral sources. (Meyer et al., 1998, p. 143).

Highlighting the disciplined mindset required for forensic psychological assessment, Gacono (2000) wrote:

> Assessment is a process of deduction, selective inquiry, and also inference … rooted in a knowledge of developmental psychology, personality and individual differences, statistics and measurement, with knowledge of limits (e.g., in prediction), in cognitive science, ethics, abnormal psychology including dynamics and defenses … Assessment forms the cornerstone of the "forensic mind-set" – one that is data based, utilizing test data, observation, interviewing, and multi-sources of substantiated historical information in *forming, testing, and modifying hypotheses* … Assessment is a multifaceted, ongoing, interactive process. (pp. 194–195)

With this distinction in mind, in order to justify psychological assessment, clinicians focus primarily on the accuracy and utility of their assessments. Does their assessment (a) capture something salient that would not have been recognized with a less intensive process, and (b) does this information translate into something that can be useful to the evaluee or referral source? In short, the literature provides strong support for the accuracy and utility of psychological assessment for clinical practice: the validity of commonly used psychological tests is generally on a par with commonly used medical tests (Meyer et al., 1998; Viglione & Meyer, 2008); psychological tests contribute incrementally above and beyond clinical interviews (Samuel et al., 2013); and data consistently indicate that the integration of multiple methods – for example, self-report with performance-based measures – contributes additional incremental validity beyond single method assessment approaches (Blais, Hilsenroth, Castlebury, Fowler, & Baity, 2001; Mihura, 2012). Campbell and Fiske's (1959) now half-century old observation that multimethod assessment can illuminate otherwise unrecognized complexity, largely conjecture at that point, now has convincing empirical support.

The accuracy and utility of psychological assessment is a necessary but insufficient justification for psychological assessment in forensic settings. In addition to considerations regarding accuracy, assessment clinicians practicing in forensic settings must also consider: (a) the relevance of the assessment to the psycho-legal question; (b) the legal standards regarding the admissibility of scientific evidence; and (c) the influence of response style, given the competing motivations for examinees to be entirely forthright. Psychologists are also always aware that psychological testing is only one component of psychological assessment, and that no single data source can accurately assess the complexity inherent in a given case. Using standardized methods, forensic psychologists obtain data from three sources: collateral information, interview, and psychological testing (Meloy & Gacono, 2000). To form opinions without data generated from multiple sources can be problematic if not unethical. It seems that even Sherlock Holmes understood this principle: "I have no data yet. It is a capital mistake to theorize before one has data. Insensibly one begins to twist facts to suit theories, instead of theories, to suit facts" (Conan Doyle, 1905, p. 163).

Due to our training and areas of expertise, our focus in this chapter is on forensic personality assessment. The same principles offered here, however, apply to clinical contexts. Additionally, while practitioners have multiple assessment instruments in their arsenal, we have chosen to emphasize the Rorschach and PCL-R as we have found them to uniquely add to the assessment process (Gacono, Jumes, & Gray, 2008a, 2015).

Forensic Assessment

The role of the forensic evaluator differs from that of the clinical evaluator or psychotherapist. Opposed to the traditional therapeutic role of a "collaborative helper," operating in the best interests of the patient, the forensic evaluator maintains a neutral and skeptical stance to preserve objectivity (Greenberg & Shuman, 1997). From this neutral stance, the forensic evaluator shifts from testing diagnostic hypotheses for the purpose of treatment planning to diagnostic hypothesis testing aimed at understanding whether and how examinees' mental health might impact their functional psycho-legal abilities – the specific knowledge and reasoning required by law for a particular legal finding (Greenberg & Shuman, 1997; Grisso, 2003). Beneath this fundamental role difference between the clinical and forensic evaluator are additional considerations unique to forensic psychological evaluators that directly influence test selection and interpretation.

Whether criminal or civil, the forensic evaluation is always conducted within a legal context and is intended to assist the trier of fact to resolve litigation. The *relevance* of forensic psychological assessment – which Heilbrun (1992) suggests should be the guiding principle for forensic evaluators – therefore depends on whether it makes the existence of a given fact more or less likely, such that the trier of fact receives additional information relevant to the ultimate legal determination. With a few exceptions, a diagnostic assessment is only sometimes necessary and very rarely sufficient, on its own, to help answer the legal issue (Otto, 2002). That is, a diagnostic evaluation based upon a comprehensive psychological assessment will generally be legally irrelevant. Instead, and unique to forensic evaluations, clinicians must have a working knowledge of the guiding legal standard(s) and relevant case law in order to understand what functional capacities are relevant to the psycho-legal issue (Grisso, 2003).

Psychological test data can serve different functions depending on the nature of the forensic psychological evaluation, and is not always necessary. For example, when assessing a defendant's understanding of their current legal situation and their ability to cooperate with counsel in an evaluation of competency to stand trial (Gray & Acklin, 2008), a structured interview designed to ascertain the evaluee's knowledge may suffice. However, if the evaluation involves an identified psychopath (PCL-R $\geq$ 30) suspected of malingering schizophrenia, the evaluation of malingering may necessitate administration of the Structured Interview of Reported Symptoms-2nd Edition (SIRS-2; Rogers, Sewell, & Gillard, 2010), observation of ward behavior, and assessment of thought disorder with the Rorschach.

Some psycho-legal questions, such as competency to be executed (Kaser-Boyd, 2008; *Panetti v. Quarterman,* 2007) or criminal responsibility (Acklin, 2008; *M'Naghten's Case*, 1843), require the presence of a severe psychiatric illness as a predicate condition prior to considering how litigants' symptoms might impair their understanding as required by law. Psychological assessment provides a direct link to establishing the presence or absence of a major mental disorder. Once established, the way in which the disorder's symptoms impact the evaluee's understanding of the relevant psycho-legal issue can be assessed. In other psycho-legal contexts, such as those involved in child custody determinations, psychological test data bear even more directly on the legally relevant functional abilities specific to parenting, such as the capacity for emotional reciprocity, empathy, aggression, and adequate affective controls (Evans & Schutz, 2008). In yet other situations, psychological testing can help the court to understand the underlying cause of any already observed functional deficits (Medoff, 2003).

Having clarified the psycho-legal issue and considered the relevance of various assessment methods, the evaluator must choose their assessment tools. In the US, several legal standards – including *Frye v. United States* (1923), *Daubert v. Merrell Dow Pharamceuticals* (1995), *Kumho Tire Co. v. Carmichael* (1999), and/or the *Federal Rules of Evidence* (1992) – help to determine the admissibility of "scientific," "technical," or "other specialized knowledge" provided by expert witnesses. These legal standards, although different, each reflect efforts to filter junk science out of the courtroom. These principles apply to the use of psychological testing.

Under *Daubert*, forensic evaluators must consider the following threshold questions when selecting their assessment instruments:

(a) Is the theory or technique testable or falsifiable?
(b) Has the theory or technique been subject to peer review and publication?
(c) Is there a known error rate and standards for controlling the technique's operation?
(d) Is the technique or methodology generally accepted in the scientific community?

Related to our focus on the Rorschach and the Hare Psychopathy Checklist (PCL-R), an abundance of research suggests that these measures – assuming use of the Rorschach Comprehensive System (CS) opposed to the Rorschach Performance Assessment (R-PAS) System (Kivisto, Gacono, & Medoff, 2013) – meet the legal standards for admissibility in jurisdictions throughout the US (McCann & Evans, 2008; Walsh & Walsh, 2006). Further, reviews of state, federal, and military appellate court decisions over a 60-year period clearly indicate that forensic evaluators face very little challenge to the admissibility of the Rorschach (Meloy, 2008; Meloy, Hansen, & Weiner, 1997). Similarly, a 13-year review of US court cases revealed widespread use and acceptance of the PCL-R (DeMatteo & Edens, 2006).

Having understood the distinct role of the forensic evaluator, given due consideration to the standards of admissibility for scientific evidence necessary for selecting psychological tests, and established the importance of multiple sources of information (collateral information, interview, and psychological testing), the forensic evaluator must also consider the impact of response style (Gacono & Gacono, 2008; Heilbrun, 1992; Melton, Petrila, Poythress, & Slobogin, 2007; Rogers, 2008). Response style considers the contribution of the assessment context (legal proceedings, out-patient clinical) and individual's personality style to the assessment results. By comparing and contrasting information gleaned from collaterals, interviews, and psychological testing, the forensic evaluator is able to cross-validate the information received and to follow up on any inconsistencies from the forensic interview. This process of triangulating multiple sources of information is essential to considering examinee's response styles (Otto, 2008).

Once all tests are appropriately selected for a forensic evaluation, it is important that evaluators have a framework for deciding relevant assessment issues and selecting methods for obtaining the information (Gacono & Evans, 2008). In conducting forensic examinations, we have found Monahan and Steadman's (1994) risk assessment model useful as a guide for directing specific assessment methods (Gacono, 2002a, 2002b, 2002c).[1] Monahan et al. (2001) emphasized the need for gathering data using multiple methods from multiple domains, including:

1 dispositional factors (including anger, impulsivity, psychopathy, and personality disorders);

[1]Monahan et al.'s (2001) model for risk assessment has been adapted for forensic treatment evaluations (Gacono, 2002a, 2002b; Gacono & Evans, 2008).

2 clinical or psychopathological factors (including diagnosis of mental disorder, alcohol or substance misuse, and the presence of delusions, hallucinations, or violent fantasies);
3 historical or case history variables (including previous violence, arrest history, treatment history, history of self-harm, as well as social, work, and family history);
4 contextual factors (including perceived stress, social support, and means for violence).

After the psychologist's role in assessing the relevant clinical or psycho-legal issue is clearly defined, the psychologist must determine which, if any, of the above domains provide information needed to address the referral questions (psycho-legal issue). Next, the forensic psychologist chooses reliable, valid, and legally admissible methods and instruments for obtaining and organizing the data from the relevant domains. Finally, valid results from the assessment methods are integrated into opinions that aid the court in addressing the psycho-legal issue (Gacono & Evans, 2008). This process can be summarized as follows:

1 Establish referral questions/psycho-legal issue.
2 Determine domains of information relevant to 1.
3 Choose assessment methods for addressing domains identified in 2.
4 Valid data are integrated into forensic opinions.

Some assessment methods, such as the Hare Psychopathy Checklist-Revised (PCL-R) (Hare, 2003) and other semi-structured interviews, are useful for collecting and quantifying certain dispositional and historical variables, while other methods such as the RIM, MMPI-2, and PAI add to understanding certain clinical and dispositional variables.

The PCL-R and Rorschach Inkblot Method

A combination of assessment instruments is best suited to understanding individual differences, as multiple methods assess different but complementary aspects of personality functioning (Erdberg, 2008). Considering administration time and the type of information obtained, we have found the PCL-R and Rorschach Inkblot Method (RIM) to form an efficient tandem in forensic treatment settings as they provide a comprehensive picture of a forensic patient's psychology. What should never be overlooked is the fact that both necessitate invaluable face-to-face interactions between examiner and examinee. Other personality testing helps to better understand individual differences and dimensional aspects of personality necessary for formulating treatment interventions.

The PCL-R provides a method for quantifying attitudes and behaviors (patient's history) that aids in assessing violence risk, formulating diagnostic impressions, and treatability (Gacono, 1998; Gacono, Jumes, & Gray, 2008, 2015). The PCL-R is a 20-item protocol based on interview findings anchored in a thorough record review and substantiation through related corroborative sources. High psychopathy scores have consistently been related to findings of criminal recidivism, including violent recidivism, and are viewed as a particularly intractable dispositional factor that should never be ignored (Bodholdt, Richards, & Gacono, 2000; Gacono, 2000). High PCL or PCL-R scores have been associated with a higher frequency and wider variety of offenses committed (Hare, 1991), higher frequency of violent offenses (Hare, 1991), higher re-offense rates (Hare, 1991), poor treatment response (Hughes, Hogue, Hollin, & Champion, 1997; Ogloff, Wong, & Greenwood, 1990; Rice, Harris, & Cormier, 1992), and more serious and persistent institutional misbehavior (Gacono, Meloy, Sheppard, Speth, & Roske, 1995; Gacono, Meloy, Speth, & Roske, 1997; Heilbrun et al., 1998). PCL-R high-scorers are also less likely to benefit from treatment, and, when in treatment, are likely to disrupt the milieu and/or terminate (drop out or get dismissed) prematurely. Through analysis of individual items and item clusters, PCL-R data are also useful in pinpointing issues in need of treatment (Gacono, 2000, 2005). Since the majority of patients assessed are not psychopathic, the cost-benefit ratio for using the PCL-R swings heavily in favor of benefits when the clinician understands that its use is greater than simply determining risk and/or the presence of psychopathy.

The Rorschach Inkblot Method (RIM) provides an open, structured, performance-based cognitive perceptual problem-solving task that is quite different from self-report measures. As research has demonstrated (Ganellen, 1994, 1996; Hartmann & Hartmann, 2014), it is difficult to manipulate by conscious effort, whether to underreport or overreport psychological difficulties. Research has further found that Rorschach measures of aggression appear to be more strongly associated with actual aggression than self-reports of one's aggressive tendencies (Kivisto & Swan, 2013). These abilities to more successfully bypass conscious manipulation while predicting actual behavior reflect two unique elements that add to the RIM's value in forensic assessment (Gacono, Evans, & Viglione, 2002; Ganellen, 1994, 1996; Ganellen, Wasyliw, Haywood, & Grossman, 1996; Grossman et al., 2002). Most readily apparent, the Rorschach's capacity to bypass volitional processes helps clarify test-taking approaches that may support, or alternatively discount, the validity of other assessment methods (Gacono & Gacono, 2008). That is, the relationship between validity configurations for self-report personality inventories and Rorschach variables help to establish degrees of defensiveness (Lambda, R, Sequence of Scores), stress (D, Adjusted D), qualities of inner tension (C′, V, m), and together provide a more complete description of motivations for change. Assessment data that include self-report data suggesting a stable current mental state, but alternatively, includes Rorschach data suggesting rigid defensiveness, is immediately suspect.

The RIM adds to and refines hypotheses generated from history, behavioral observations, and the PCL-R (Gacono, 2002a, 2002b; Gacono & Meloy, 1991, 1994). It provides information concerning problem-solving and response style (Lambda, introversive, extratensive), processing (Zd), reality testing (X-%), perceptual accuracy (F+, X+), controls and current stress levels (D/AdjD), levels of emotionality and how the patient deals with them (FC:CF+C, Afr; i.e., avoidance), self-perceptions (W:M, Fr+rF, MOR), coping resources (EA, CDI), desire for affectional relatedness

(T), and interpersonal interest, maturity, and expectations (H, (H), COP, AG). The PCL-R *quantifies* observable attitudes and behaviors, while Rorschach data *correlates* with them.

The RIM Comprehensive Systems (Exner, 1993/2001) clusters and constellations are readily organized within the organizational framework described earlier (Monahan et al., 2001). **Mediation variables** assess the extent to which an individual is oriented toward making conventional or acceptable responses. These relate behavioral and personality data consistent with *Dispositional* or *Characterological factors.* **Ideation variables** address how inputs become conceptualized and used, and elucidate *Clinical Factors* associated with florid and subtle thought disorder symptoms. **Processing** reveals processing effort, motivation and processing efficiency, and corresponds to elements of *Clinical and Dispositional factors.* The **Affect cluster** examines the role of emotion in psychology and functioning, and may likewise relate to *Clinical and Dispositional factors*, and assist with identifying the degree of controls and coping strategies employed to contend with stress. The **Self-perception cluster** provides a picture of self-image and self-esteem, and considered with **Interpersonal variables** reveal how an individual perceives and relates to others (Exner, 1993/2001), elucidating aspects of the intersection between the *Individual and Contextual factors.* The growing forensic Rorschach database (Cunliffe & Gacono, 2008; Gacono, Gacono, & Evans, 2008b; Gacono, Meloy, & Bridges, 2008c; Gacono & Gacono, 2008; Singer, Hoppe, Lee, Olesen, & Walters, 2008; Young, Erdberg & Justice, 2008) has ensured its adaptability to forensic patients.

Other work has examined RIM treatment outcome correlates. Weiner and Exner (1991) compared treatment outcomes for groups of patients in short vs. long-term psychodynamic therapy. Comprehensive System (CS) variables included markers of acute and chronic distress (D, AdjD, respectively), organized coping resources and problem-solving approaches (EA, CDI, Ambitent, Lambda, Zd), reality testing (X+%, X-%), affect regulation and controls (SumShad:FM+m, DEPI, Afr, CF:FC+C), formal thought process and organization (Sum6, M-), defensive operations and self-inspecting (Intellect, Reflections, Pairs, FD), rigidity (a:p), and attachments and interpersonal qualities (T, H:Hd+(H)+(Hd)). For both groups, more than half of these variables marked clinical improvement after the first year, and roughly 75% of the selected variables measured gains after four years. With respect to forensic treatment, Gacono (1998) found that certain non-psychopathic antisocial personality disorder (ASPD) individuals in forensic settings, who were willing to engage in ambiguous, emotionally salient situations (low Lambda), and who tended to be introversive (M>WsumC) while maintaining potential for attachment (T=1), appeared reasonably amenable to therapeutic change.

Through a series of studies (Gacono, 1990; Gacono, Meloy, & Heaven, 1990; Gacono & Meloy, 1991, 1992, 1994; Meloy & Gacono, 1992), the Rorschach has proven to be a sensitive instrument to discriminate between psychopathic and non-psychopathic subjects. Psychodynamic differences include more pathological narcissism and sadism (Gacono, Meloy & Heaven, 1990), less anxiety, and less capacity for attachment (Gacono & Meloy, 1991). Personality organization (Kernberg, 1984) is predominately at the borderline level (Gacono, 1990).

Commonly used defenses include devaluation, massive denial, projective identification, omnipotence, and splitting. Idealization and higher-level neurotic defenses are virtually absent. Psychopathic criminals produce significantly more narcissistic mirroring, boundary disturbance, and total primitive object relations than non-psychopathic criminals (Gacono & Meloy, 1992). While we have found female psychopaths to share a similar borderline personality organization with males, their predominantly hysterical style differs from the malignant narcissism found in males, leading to some unique differences relevant to scoring the PCL-R (see Cunliffe et al., 2015; Smith, 2013; Smith, Gacono, Cunliffe, Kivisto, & Taylor, 2014).

The prototypical Rorschach protocol of a male or female psychopath will evidence certain abnormal structural characteristics (see Table 19.1).

The numbers represent mean scores or frequencies of the majority of the subjects in a sample of 33 male antisocial personality disordered psychopaths (PCL-R ≥ 30)

Table 19.1 Select Comprehensive System variables for a prototypical psychopath

	*Male**	*Female***
Responses	21	20
Core characteristics		
Lambda	>0.99	0.71
D	0	−1
Adj D	0	−0.5
Affects		
FC:CF+C	1:4	1:3
Afr	<0.50	<0.55
Pure C	>0	>0
T	0 (9% T=1)	0 (29% T = 1; 14% T ≥ 2)
Y	0	>0
Space	>2	>2
Interpersonal relations		
Pure H	2	2.4
(H)+Hd+(Hd)	2.5	3.8
COP	0	1
Ag	0	0
Sx	1	0.6
Self-perception		
Rf	1	0
PER	>2	2
W:M	>3:1	>2:1
Cognitions		
X+%	54	51
F+%	56	41
X-%	22	25
M-	1	<1
WSum6SpecSc	17	24

*Gacono & Meloy (1994).
**Cunliffe (2002).

in prison (Gacono & Meloy, 1994) and a sample of 27 ASPD psychopathic (PCL-R ≥ 30) females in prison (Cunliffe & Gacono, 2008).

Deviations from these typical findings do not necessarily rule out a psychopathic disturbance (the PCL-R does this), but should deepen understanding of the individual differences within any one patient. The examiner should be familiar with the growing body of empirical research pointing to several subtypes of psychopathy (Hicks, Markon, Patrick, Krueger, & Newman, 2004). From a Rorschach perspective, a male psychopathic patient might also show histrionic features, structurally evident in some idealizing defenses; a color projection (CP) response; a low lambda (L); and an elevated affective ratio (Afr). On the other hand, a paranoid psychopath might produce a constricted protocol; elevated Dd responses; a low H+A:Hd+Ad ratio; and a positive hypervigilance index (HVI). A psychopathic subject scoring 36 on the PCL-R might also have schizophrenia, evident on the Rorschach in a positive schizophrenia index (SCZI). What begins as a determination of the degree of psychopathic disturbance using the PCL-R is further refined through the Rorschach to measure the internal structure and dynamics of the particular patient.

Assessment: Assessing Historical, Dispositional, Clinical, and Contextual Factors

The following provides an approach for assessing violence risk. A first step in risk assessment involves a thorough review of historical and collateral information, including documentation relating to history of violence (including sexual assault), previous offenses, weapon use, and other factors relevant to specific risk concerns. These data provide historical and contextual information essential to forming an opinion. Next, the forensic psychologist assesses clinical and dispositional factors, including contemporary data on critical mental status markers, acute paranoid ideation, and delusions, which require third-party corroboration from a review of treatment records, staff interviews, and other pertinent sources. Also, the evaluator reviews specific antecedents and consequents surrounding previous violent acts (contextual and dispositional) as well as the mode or type of violence (affective versus predatory). The evaluee's violence history is further clarified through interviewing concerning cognitive, affective, and behavioral patterns prior to, during, and consequent to violent episodes, as well as any current situational or dynamic factors that could be influenced by immediate intervention.[2] In addition to relevant historical, dispositional, clinical, and contextual factors, victim characteristics should also be assessed, such as age, gender, and the circumstances under which predation occurred.

Subsequent to assessing history and mental status through a review of records and other documentation, and conducting forensic and collateral interviews, the forensic

[2] Record review and clinical interview allow identification of specific person-context factors (e.g., medication non-compliance, alcohol or drug use, level of supervision or custody) expected to mitigate or amplify more immediate risk of re-offense, including violent re-offense.

psychologist's opinions can be further enhanced by using an established actuarial risk assessment instrument such as the Violence Risk Appraisal Guide (VRAG), the Sex Offender Risk Appraisal Guide (SORAG; Quinsey, Harris, Rice, & Cormier, 1998), and/or the HCR-20 (Webster, Douglas, Eaves, & Hart, 1997). Historical, clinical, dispositional, and contextual variables are quantified through the completion of such assessment procedures. Although these actuarial data establish an essential basis for forming opinions, the forensic psychologist must consider the limitations of primarily static, unchangeable data that are acquired through these methods (see Zamble & Quinsey, 1997).

Forensic evaluation using the above assessment domains provides a sound basis for case conceptualization. In addition, personality testing refines our understanding of dispositional or clinical factors such as impulsivity, levels of anger and hostility, presence of thought disorder, problems with affect regulation, and methods of coping with emotions (Gacono & Meloy, 1994, 2002; Gacono et al., 2001a). Standardized psychological testing adds to our understanding of important similarities and differences among individuals to an extent not possible using only risk assessment guides and PCL-R scores, which provide primarily nomothetic comparisons (Gacono, 1998). Combining historical information, risk assessment guide scores, PCL-R scores, and personality testing data allow the forensic psychologist to provide opinions emphasizing *specific, individualized context-person dynamics*; that is, under what circumstances a given patient is more likely to perpetrate a certain type of violence toward a particular type of victim. Such specificity allows the rigor of scientific knowledge to blend with the art of clinical insight to provide a uniquely comprehensive and human view of the individual being assessed. The forensic psychologist operates from the assumption that assessment is a multifaceted, ongoing, interactive process involving a continuous process of *forming, testing, and modifying hypotheses.*

The choice of actuarial tools and evaluation format is dictated by setting, referral question, clinical presentation, resource availability such as treatment, and the purposes served by the evaluation. Probabilities and other correlations determined from actuarially derived methods require a consideration of their clinical application. The following case example (previously reported in Gacono & Bodholdt, 2001) illustrates the use of historical, dispositional, clinical, and contextual factors in evaluating risk in a previously violent and potentially dangerous individual.

Case Example

Mr Jones was a married, Caucasian male in his mid-twenties, who was referred for a psychological evaluation to determine risk of future offending and to better understand offense and substance misuse history. At the time of the examination, Mr Jones was serving a three-year sentence for assault with a deadly weapon.

Mr. Jones' background revealed a sporadic work history, a lengthy history of substance and alcohol misuse, and the absence of a major mental disorder. He met criteria for multiple substance dependencies, dysthymia, and antisocial personality disorder (historical, clinical, dispositional; *from records, forensic and PCL-R interview*). His violence had never been predatory; rather, it had always been impulsive, unplanned, driven by intense affect, and associated with intoxication (dispositional, contextual factors; *from records, forensic and PCL-R interview*).

PCL-R (28) and VRAG (+23, category 8) scores, both static variables based primarily on historical data, placed him at a high risk for violent re-offense within the next 7–10 years. Rorschach and MMPI-2 findings highlighted dispositional and clinical factors suggesting problems managing emotions, high levels of hostility, difficulties handling complexity, and associated problems with perception and judgment. Legal factors were also of consequence. Mr Jones had two remaining years of probation. If discharged to the community at the end of his parole, Mr. Jones presented a fairly substantial risk of re-offense. There were also no institutionally based resources (substance misuse, anger management, or similar treatment) to target the somewhat more malleable (dynamic) but difficult dispositional and clinical risk factors. Thus, any treatment impact on those risk factors highlighted through psychological assessment would have to come from a community setting, preferably offered under parole supervision.

The parole board decision to release or retain became more straightforward when presented with evaluation findings. They could have: (1) incarcerated Mr Jones until his time is completed and subsequently release him unsupervised to the community with all the "static" actuarial risk unmitigated or; (2) use his remaining supervision period in an attempt to impact any dynamic (changeable) factors relevant to re-offense rates. The first author (CBG) recommended the latter, including recommendations that the parole board consider a 9–12 month residential substance misuse treatment program with transition to a halfway house.

In any setting, assessing potentially dangerous and violent patients quite frequently becomes an exercise in harm reduction based on an entire assessment protocol rather than reliance on a single score derived from one method. Had our case example involved a highly predatory individual, with or without substance misuse problems or a supportive family, available data concerning amenability to treatment would very likely have resulted in a harm-reduction strategy involving no parole, thus minimizing exposure to the public for a year or two, but not impacting subsequent risk (Gacono, Nieberding, Owen, Rubel, & Bodholdt, 2001).

Conclusion

Advances in the actuarial prediction of violence have been impressive, and continue to be more fully elaborated and refined. In assessing individuals, actuarial protocols, including use of the PCL-R, VRAG, SORAG, and others, can inform, but not replace, clinical judgment. A comprehensive forensic evaluation begins with historical and actuarial formulations, but it also assesses dynamic factors addressing risk reduction, setting, available resources, as well as ethical and legal constraints. Not only should the assessment consider the probability of violence within a given setting, but it must also consider the capacity of the setting to control or contain the potential violence to staff or other patients. A harm reduction approach allows the evaluator to organize his or her data into a cogent conceptual model.

The PCL-R is one important method for quantifying certain dispositional and historical risk factors. As with any other standardized assessment method, ethical guidelines must guide implementation and use (Gacono, 2000). In all cases, sensitivity to the issue of using the PCL-R score for designating an individual as a "psychopath" is always relevant and a process that has been assiduously argued against (Bodholdt et al., 2000). We have emphasized using PCL-R scores as one organizing point within a much larger body of data brought to bear on clinical decisions or recommendations for the particular individual referred, in all their individuality, and relative to the particular setting, circumstances, and other relevant environmental factors at hand. Inappropriate use of the PCL-R, such as using a single cutoff score as the sole data point for denying patients treatment or access to lower security levels, can discredit the instrument and undermine progress in the important field of risk assessment.

As clinicians, we provide informed assessment of a person's risk level based on any number of factors, such as treatment follow-up, abstinence, and so on. Courts and social forces at large determine the degree of risk that is acceptable, and researchers and clinicians map these considerations onto balancing an instrument's positive and negative predictive values at different cut scores. Historically, and in most conventional practice, we recognize and are sympathetic to what typically involves greater scrutiny, recommendation for treatment, and certainly no "substantive harm," in borderline cases (where the potential for violence is not overwhelmingly convincing, but the consequences of mistakenly underestimating risk could be catastrophic). The PCL-R is one reliable and valid method for gathering data relevant to future risk that must be *considered* in all, and *included* in most, risk assessment evaluations. It is, however, only one component of the risk assessment process.

The RIM provides a rich idiographic counterpoint to the nomothetic applications of the PCL-R, and provides evaluating clinicians with the opportunity to "say more" about their forensic evaluees (Bram, 2013). Returning to the distinction between psychological testing and psychological assessment, the exclusive reliance on actuarial prediction models is a quintessential example of testing. It is straightforward, simplistic, and has some degree of empirical support. And while it is free of bias, assuming that it is accurately scored (see Murrie et al., 2009, for challenges to this assumption), it is also free of disciplined clinical judgment informed by multiple sources of information. The RIM's ability to indirectly assess a range of dispositional characteristics, which makes it less susceptible to intentional distortion (Hartmann & Hartmann, 2014), allows the clinician to generate informed "if–then" contingency statements (Mischel & Shoda, 2008) about risk for future violence and captures a degree of complexity lost in straightforward actuarial prediction. More importantly, the integration of the RIM with the PCL-R provides clinical utility in linking forensic evaluees' idiosyncratic strengths and vulnerabilities to clearer approaches to risk management, as specific situations and contexts will be found to be more or less risky depending on each offender's idiographic geography.

Note

The assertions and opinions contained herein are the private views of the authors and should not be construed as official or as reflecting the views of the Federal Bureau of Prisons or the US Department of Justice.

References

Acklin, M.A. (2008). The Rorschach Test and forensic psychological evaluation: Psychosis and the insanity defense. In C.B. Gacono, F.B. Evans, N. Kaser-Boyd, & L.A. Gacono (Eds.), *The Handbook of Forensic Rorschach Assessment* (pp. 157–174). New York: Routledge.

Bodholdt, R.H., Richards, H.R., & Gacono, C.B. (2000). Assessing psychopathy in adults: The Psychopathy Checklist—Revised and Screening Version. In C. B. Gacono (Ed.), *The clinical and forensic assessment of psychopathy: A practitioner's guide* (pp. 55–86). Mahwah, NJ US: Lawrence Erlbaum Associates Publishers.

Blais, M.A., Hilsenroth, M.J., Castlebury, F., Fowler, J.C., & Baity, M.R. (2001). Predicting cluster B personality disorder criteria from MMPI-2 and Rorschach data: A test of incremental validity. *Journal of Personality Assessment, 76* (1), 150–168.

Bram, A.D. (2013). Psychological testing and treatment implications: We can say more. *Journal of Personality Assessment, 95* (4), 319–331.

Campbell, D., & Fiske, D. (1959). Convergent and discriminant validation by the multitrait-multimethod matrix. *Psychological Bulletin, 56* (2), 81–105.

Conan Doyle, A. (1905). *The Complete Works of Sherlock Holmes.* New York: Doubleday.

Cunliffe, T. (2002). *A Rorschach investigation of incarcerated female psychopaths.* (Unpublished doctoral dissertation.) Pacific Graduate School of Psychology, Palo Alto, CA.

Cunliffe, T.B., & Gacono, C.B. (2008). A Rorschach understanding of antisocial women high in psychopathy. In C.B. Gacono, F.B. Evans, N. Kaser-Boyd, & L.A. Gacono (Eds.), *The Handbook of Forensic Rorschach Assessment* (pp. 361–378). New York: Routledge.

Cunliffe, T.B., Gacono, C.B., Smith, J.M., Kivisto, A., Meloy, J.R., & Taylor, E.E. (2015). Assessing psychopathy in women. In C.B. Gacono (Ed.), *The Clinical and Forensic Assessment of Psychopathy: A Practitioner's Guide* (2nd ed.) (pp. 167–190). New York: Routledge/Taylor & Francis.

DeMatteo, D., & Edens, J.F. (2006). The role and relevance of the psychopathy checklist-revised in court: A case law survey of U.S. courts (1991–2004). *Psychology, Public Policy, and Law, 12* (2), 214–241.

Daubert v. Merrell Dow Pharmaceuticals. (1995). 516 US 869.

Erdberg, P.S. (2008). Multimethod assessment as a forensic standard. In C.B. Gacono, & F.B. Evans (Eds.), *The Handbook of Forensic Rorschach Assessment* (pp. 561–566). New York: Routledge.

Evans, F.B., & Schutz, B.M. (2008). The Rorschach in child custody and parenting plan evaluations: A new conceptualization. In C.B. Gacono, & F.B. Evans (Eds.), *The Handbook of Forensic Rorschach Assessment* (pp. 233–254). New York: Routledge.

Exner, J.E. (1993/2001). *The Rorschach: A Comprehensive System: Basic Foundations and Principles of Interpretation* (4th ed.). Hoboken, New Jersey: John Wiley & Sons, Ltd.

Federal Rules of Evidence. (1992). Boston, MA: Little, Brown.

Frye v. United States. (1923). 293 F. 1013 (D.C. Cir. 1923).

Gacono, C.B. (1990). An empirical study of object relations and defensive operations in antisocial personality disorder. *Journal of Personality Assessment, 54* (3–4), 589–600.

Gacono, C.B. (1998). The use of the Psychopathy Checklist-Revised (PCL-R) and Rorschach in treatment planning with Antisocial Personality Disordered patients. *International Journal of Offender Therapy and Comparative Criminology, 42* (1), 49–64.

Gacono, C.B. (2000). Suggestions for the implementation and use of the Psychopathy Checklists in forensic and clinical practice. In C.B. Gacono (Ed.), *The Clinical and Forensic Assessment of Psychopathy: a Practitioner's Guide* (pp. 175–202). Mahwah, New Jersey: Lawrence Erlbaum.

Gacono, C.B. (2002a). Guest editorial: Why there is a need for the personality assessment of offenders. *International Journal of Offender Therapy and Comparative Criminology, 46* (3), 271–273.

Gacono, C.B. (2002b). Introduction to a special series: Psychological testing in forensic settings. *International Journal of Offender Therapy and Comparative Criminology, 46* (3), 274–280.

Gacono, C.B. (2002c). Introduction to a special series: Forensic psychodiagnostic testing. *Journal of Forensic Psychology Practice, 2* (3), 1–10.

Gacono, C. (2005). *A Clinical and Forensic Interview Schedule for the Hare Psychopathy Checklist-Revised and Screening Version.* Mahwah, NJ: Erlbaum.

Gacono, C.B. (2015). *The Clinical and Forensic Assessment of Psychopathy: A Practitioner's Guide* (2nd ed.). New York: Routledge/Taylor & Francis.

Gacono, C.B., & Bodholdt, R. (2001). The role of the Psychopathy Checklist-Revised (PCL-R) in violence risk and threat assessment. *Journal of Threat Assessment, 1* (4), 65–79.

Gacono, C.B., & Evans, B. (2008). Preface. In C.B. Gacono, & F.B. Evans (Eds.), *The Handbook of Forensic Rorschach Assessment* (pp. 11–20). New York: Routledge.

Gacono, C.B., Evans, B., & Viglione, D. (2002). The Rorschach in forensic practice. *Journal of Forensic Psychology Practice, 2* (3), 33–53.

Gacono, C.B., Gacono, L.A., & Evans, F. (2008a). The Rorschach and antisocial personality disorder. In C.B. Gacono, F. Evans, N. Kaser-Boyd, & L. Gacono (Eds.), *The Handbook of Forensic Rorschach Assessment* (pp. 323–359). New York: Routledge/Taylor & Francis Group.

Gacono, C.B., Jumes, M., & Gray, T. (2008b). Use of the Rorschach in forensic treatment planning. In C.B. Gacono, F.B. Evans, N. Kaser-Boyd, & L.A. Gacono (Eds.), *The Handbook of Forensic Rorschach Assessment* (pp. 211–232). New York: Routledge.

Gacono, C.B, Jumes, M., & Gray, T. (2015). Use of the PCL-R and Rorschach in forensic treatment planning. In C.B. Gacono (Ed.), *The Clinical and Forensic Assessment of Psychopathy: A Practitioner's Guide* (2nd ed.) (pp. 311–331). New York: Routledge/Taylor & Francis Group.

Gacono, C., Loving, J., & Bodholdt, R. (2001a). The Rorschach and psychopathy: Toward a more accurate understanding of the research findings. *Journal of Personality Assessment, 77* (1), 16–38.

Gacono, C.B., & Meloy, J.R. (1991). A Rorschach investigation of attachment and anxiety in antisocial personality disorder. *Journal of Nervous and Mental Disease, 179* (9), 546–552.

Gacono, C.B. & Meloy, J.R. (1992). The Rorschach and the DSM-III-R antisocial personality: A tribute to Robert Lindner. *Journal of Clinical Psychology, 48* (3), 393–405.

Gacono, C.B., & Meloy, J.R. (1994). *The Rorschach Assessment of Aggressive and Psychopathic Personalities.* Hillsdale, NJ: Lawrence Erlbaum.

Gacono, C.B., & Meloy, J.R. (2002). Assessing antisocial and psychopathic personalities. In J. Butcher (Ed.), *Clinical Foundations of Personality Assessment* (2nd ed.) (pp. 361–375). New York: Oxford University Press.

Gacono, C.B., Meloy, J.R., & Bridges, M.R. (2008c). A Rorschach understanding of psychopaths, sexual homicide perpetrators, and nonviolent pedophiles. In C. Gacono, B. Evans, N. Kaser-Boyd, & L. Gacono (Eds.), *The Handbook of Forensic Rorschach Assessment* (pp. 379–402). Mahwah, NJ: Lawrence Erlbaum.

Gacono, C.B., Meloy, J.R., & Heaven, T.R. (1990). A Rorschach investigation of narcissism and hysteria in antisocial personality. *Journal of Personality Assessment, 55* (1–2), 270–279.

Gacono, C.B., Meloy, J.R., Sheppard, K., Speth, E., & Roske, A. (1995). A clinical investigation of malingering and psychopathy in hospitalized insanity acquittees. *Bulletin of the American Academy of Psychiatry and the Law, 23* (3), 387–397.

Gacono, C.B., Meloy, J.R., Speth, E., & Roske, A. (1997). Above the law: Escapes from a maximum security forensic hospital and psychopathy. *Journal of the American Academy of Psychiatry and the Law, 25* (4), 547–550.

Gacono, C.B., Nieberding, R.J., Owen, A., Rubel, J., & Bodholdt, R. (2001b). Treating conduct disorder, antisocial, and psychopathic personalities. In J.B. Ashford, B. Sales, W.H. Reid, J.B. Ashford, B. Sales, & W.H. Reid (Eds.), *Treating Adult and Juvenile Offenders with Special Needs* (pp. 99–129). Washington, DC: American Psychological Association.

Gacono, L.A., & Gacono, C.B. (2008). Some considerations for the Rorschach assessment of forensic psychiatric outpatients. In C.B. Gacono, F. Evans, N. Kaser-Boyd, & L. Gacono (Eds.), *The Handbook of Forensic Rorschach Assessment* (pp. 421–444). New York: Routledge/Taylor & Francis Group.

Ganellen, R.J. (1994). Attempting to conceal psychological disturbance: MMPI defensive response sets and the Rorschach. *Journal of Personality Assessment, 63* (3), 423–437.

Ganellen, R.J. (1996). Exploring MMPI-Rorschach relationships. *Journal of Personality Assessment, 67* (3), 529–542.

Ganellen, R.J., Wasyliw, O.E., Haywood, T.W., & Grossman, L.S. (1996). Can psychosis be malingered on the Rorschach: An empirical study. *Journal of Personality Assessment, 66* (1), 65–80.

Gray, B.T., & Acklin, M.W. (2008). The Use of the Rorschach Inkblot Method in Trial Competency Evaluations. In C.B. Gacono, F.B. Evans, N. Kaser-Boyd, & L.A. Gacono (Eds.). *The Handbook of Forensic Rorschach Assessment* (pp. 141–156). New York: Routledge.

Greenberg, S.A., & Shuman, D.W. (1997). Irreconcilable conflict between therapeutic and forensic roles. *Professional Psychology, Research and Practice, 28* (1), 50–57.

Grisso, T. (2003). *Evaluating Competencies: Forensic Assessments and Instruments* (2nd ed.). Kluwer Academic/Plenum Publishers.

Grossman, L.S., Wasyliw, O.E., Benn, A.F., & Gyoerkoe, K.L. (2002). Can sex offenders who minimize on the MMPI conceal psychopathology on the Rorschach. *Journal of Personality Assessment, 78* (3), 484–501.

Hare, R. (1991). *Hare Psychopathy Checklist Revised (PCL-R) Technical Manual.* North Tonawanda, NY: Multi-Health Systems, Inc.

Hare, R. (2003). *Hare Psychopathy Checklist Revised (PCL-R) Technical Manual* (2nd ed.). North Tonawanda, NY: Multi-Health Systems, Inc.

Hartmann, E., & Hartmann, T. (2014). The impact of exposure to internet-based information about the Rorschach and the MMPI-2 on psychiatric outpatients ability to simulate mentally healthy test performance. *Journal of Personality Assessment, 96* (4), 432–444.

Heilbrun, K. (1992). The role of psychological testing in forensic assessment. *Law and Human Behavior, 16* (3), 257–272.

Heilbrun, K., Hart, S.D., Hare, R.D., Gustafson, D., Nunez, C., & White, A.J. (1998). Inpatient and postdischarge aggression in mentally disordered offenders. *Journal of Interpersonal Violence, 13* (4), 514–527.

Hicks, B.M., Markon, K.E., Patrick, C.J., Krueger, R., & Newman, J.P. (2004). Identifying psychopathy subtypes on the basis of personality structure. *Psychological Assessment, 16* (3), 276–288.

Hughes, G., Hogue, T., Hollin, C., & Champion, H. (1997). First-stage evaluation of a treatment programme for personality disordered offenders. *Journal of Forensic Psychiatry, 8* (3), 515–527.

Kaser-Boyd, N. (2008). Battered woman syndrome: Assessment-based expert testimony. In C.B. Gacono, F. Evans, N. Kaser-Boyd, & L. Gacono (Eds.), *The Handbook of Forensic Rorschach Assessment* (pp. 467–487). New York: Routledge/Taylor & Francis Group.

Kernberg, O. (1984). *Severe Personality Disorders: Psychotherapeutic Strategies.* London: Yale University Press.

Kivisto, A.J., Gacono, C.B., & Medoff, D. (2013). Does the R-PAS meet standards for forensic use? Considerations with introducing a new Rorschach coding system. *Journal of Forensic Psychology Practice, 13* (5), 389–410.

Kivisto, A.J., & Swan, S.A. (2013). Rorschach measures of aggression: A laboratory-based validity study. *Journal of Personality Assessment, 95* (1), 38–45.

Kumho Tire Co. v. Carmichael. (1999). 526 US 137.

McCann, J., & Evans, F.B. (2008). Rorschach admissibility. In C.B. Gacono, F. Barton Evans, & N. Kaser-Boyd (Eds.), *The Handbook of Forensic Rorschach Psychology*, (pp. 55–78). New York: Routledge.

Medoff, D. (2003). The scientific basis of psychological testing: Considerations following Daubert, Kumho, and Joiner. *Family Court Review, 41* (2), 199–213.

Meloy, J.R. (2008). The authority of the Rorschach: An update. In C.B. Gacono, & F.B. Evans, (Eds.), *Handbook of Forensic Rorschach Assessment* (pp. 79–88). New York: Routledge.

Meloy, J.R., & Gacono, C.B. (1992). The aggression response and the Rorschach. *Journal of Clinical Psychology, 48* (1), 104–114.

Meloy, J.R., & Gacono, C.B. (2000). Assessing psychopathy: Psychological testing and report writing. In C.B. Gacono (Ed.), *The Clinical and Forensic Assessment of Psychopathy: A Practitioner's Guide* (pp. 231–250). New York: Routledge.

Meloy, J.R., Hansen, T.L., & Weiner, I.B. (1997). Authority of the Rorschach: Legal citations during the past 50 years. *Journal of Personality Assessment, 69* (1), 53–62.

Melton, G., Petrila, J., Poythress, N., & Slobogin, C. (2007). *Psychological Evaluations for the Courts: A Handbook for Mental Health Professionals and Lawyers* (3rd ed.). New York: Guilford.

Meyer, G., Finn, S., Eyde, L., Kay, G., Kubiszyn, R., Moreland, K., … & Dies, R. (1998). *Benefits and costs of psychological assessment in healthcare delivery: Report of the Board of Professional Affairs Psychological Assessment Work Group, Part I.* Washington, DC: American Psychological Association Practice Directorate.

Mihura, J.L. (2012). The necessity of multiple methods in conducting assessments: The role of the Rorschach and self-report. *Psychological Injury and the Law, 5* (2), 97–106.

Mischel, W., & Shoda, Y. (2008). Toward a unified theory of personality: Integrating dispositions and processing dynamics within the Cognitive-Affective Processing System (CAPS). In O.P. John, R.W. Robins, & L.A. Pervin (Eds.), *Handbook of Personality* (3rd ed.) (pp. 208–241). New York: Guilford.

M'Naghten's Case. (1843). All ER Rep 229.

Monahan, J., & Steadman, H. (1994). Toward a rejuvenation of risk assessment research. In J. Monahan, & H. Steadman (Eds.) *Violence and Mental Disorder: Developments in Risk Assessment* (pp. 1–17). Chicago: University of Chicago Press.

Monahan, J., Steadman, H., Silver, E., Appelbaum, P., Robbins, P., Mulvey, E., ... & Banks, S. (2001). *Rethinking Risk Assessment: The MacArthur Study of Mental Disorder and Violence*. New York: Oxford.

Murrie, D.C., Boccaccini, M.T., Turner, D.B., Meeks, M., Woods, C., & Tussey, C. (2009). Rater (dis)agreement on risk assessment measures in sexually violent predator proceedings: Evidence of adversarial allegiance in forensic evaluation? *Psychology, Public Policy, and the Law, 15* (1), 19–53.

Ogloff, J., Wong, S., & Greenwood, A. (1990). Treating criminal psychopaths in a therapeutic community program. *Behavioral Sciences and the Law, 8* (2), 181–190.

Otto, R. (2002). Use of the MMPI-2 in forensic settings. *Journal of Forensic Psychology Practice, 2* (3), 71–91.

Otto, R.K. (2008). Challenges and advances in the assessment of response styles in forensic examination contexts. In R. Rogers (Ed.), *Clinical Assessment of Malingering and Deception* (3rd ed.) (pp. 365–375). New York: Guilford Press.

Panetti v. Quarterman. (2007). 127 S. Ct. 2842.

Quinsey, V., Harris, G., Rice, M., & Cormier, C. (1998). *Violent Offenders: Appraising and Managing Risk*. Washington, DC: American Psychological Association.

Rice, M.E., Harris, G.T., & Cormier, C.A. (1992). An evaluation of a maximum security therapeutic community for psychopaths and other mentally disordered offenders. *Law & Human Behavior, 16* (4), 399–412.

Rogers, R. (2008). *Clinical Assessment of Malingering and Deception*. New York: Guilford Press.

Rogers, R., Sewell, K.W., & Gillard, N.D. (2010). *Structured Interview of Reported Symptoms (SIRS), 2nd Edition, Professional Manual*. Lutz, FL: Psychological Assessment Resources, Inc.

Samuel, D.B., Sanislow, C.A., Hopwood, C.J., Shea, M.T., Skodol, A.E., Morey, L.C., ... & Grilo, C.M. (2013). Convergent and incremental predictive validity of clinician, self-report, and structured interview diagnoses for personality disorders over 5 years. *Journal of Consulting and Clinical Psychology, 81* (4), 650–659.

Singer, J., Hoppe, C.F., Lee, S., Olesen, N.W., & Walters, M.G. (2008). Child custody litigants: Rorschach data from a large sample. In C.B. Gacono, & F. Evans (Eds.), *The Handbook of Forensic Rorschach Assessment* (pp. 445–464). New York: Routledge/Taylor & Francis Group.

Smith, J.M. (2013). *Female psychopathy: A Rorschach investigation of personality structure*. (Unpublished doctoral project.) Carlos Albizu University, Miami, FL.

Smith, J.M., Gacono, C.B., Cunliffe, T.B., Kivisto, A., & Taylor, E.E. (2014). Psychodynamics in the female psychopath: A PCL-R/Rorschach investigation. *Violence and Gender, 1* (4), 176–187.

Viglione, D.J, & Meyer, G.J. (2008). An overview of psychometrics for forensic practice. In C.B. Gacono, F.B. Evans, N. Kaser-Boyd, & L.A. Gacono (Eds.). *The Handbook of Forensic Rorschach Assessment* (pp. 21–54). New York: Routledge.

Walsh, T., & Walsh, Z. (2006). The evidentiary introduction of Psychopathy Checklist-Revised assessed psychopathy in U.S. courts: Extent and appropriateness. *Law and Human Behavior, 30* (4), 493–507.

Webster, C.D., Douglas, K.S., Eaves, D., & Hart, S.D. (1997). *HCR-20 Assessing Risk for Violence Version 2.* British Columbia Mental Health Law and Policy Institute, Simon Fraser University.

Weiner, I.B., & Exner, J.E. (1991). Rorschach changes in long-term and short-term psychotherapy. *Journal of Personality Assessment, 56* (3), 453–465.

Young, M.H., Erdberg, P.S., & Justice, J. (2008). Inmates in prison psychiatric treatment: A multimethod description. In C.B. Gacono, & F. Evans (Eds.), *The Handbook of Forensic Rorschach Assessment* (pp. 403–421). New York: Routledge/Taylor & Francis Group.

Zamble, E., & Quinsey, V. (1997). *The Criminal Recidivism Process.* New York: Cambridge University Press.

Ziskin, J., & Faust, D. (1989). Psychiatric and psychological evidence in child custody cases. *Trial, 25* (8), 44–46.

20

Holtzman Inkblot Technique and Personality Assessment

C.R. Darolia

Kurukshetra University, Kurukshetra, India

Inkblot techniques are considered to have an edge over other personality assessment devices in the sense that they provide rich and qualitative information about unconscious aspects of behavior. The Rorschach inkblot technique (Rorschach, 1921) was a landmark in the history of personality assessment. By 1945, the Rorschach technique became a leading clinical instrument for psychodiagnosis and overall personality assessment. But by the 1950s numerous studies piled a wave of criticism from which the Rorschach movement could never fully recover. The Rorschach was criticized for its "culturist character" and lack of scientific vigor. It was attributed chiefly to having low reliability, a lack of objectivity in scoring, poor differential diagnosis, less efficient prognosis, and being insensitive to differences between extreme groups (Zubin, 1954). In spite of negative findings of the Rorschach inkblot technique, Wayne H. Holtzman was fascinated by the rich qualitative essence of the inkblot technique. He believed that despite these negative findings with the Rorschach, the fundamental ideas underlying the technique were still intuitively attractive and could not easily be set aside. It seemed apparent to Holtzman that the major limitations in the Rorschach could be overcome by developing a new technique using more inkblots with simplified procedures (Holtzman, Thorpe, Swartz, & Herron, 1961).

The new inkblot technique became a reality in 1956 after strenuous work spanning over seven years in diverse fields of test development. The final version of the Holtzman Inkblot Technique (HIT) and the detailed write-up on the technique *Inkblot Perception and Personality* were published in 1961 (Holtzman, 1961; Holtzman et al., 1961). The HIT consists of two parallel sets of inkblots, each containing 45 test blots and two trial blots, X and Y, that are identical in both Form A and Form B. The order of inkblots in each form is arranged so that most of the best inkblots appear early in the series. After the two trial inkblots, two achromatic blots appear, followed by an inkblot that is predominantly black but has a splotch of

The Wiley Handbook of Personality Assessment, First Edition. Edited by Updesh Kumar.
© 2016 John Wiley & Sons, Ltd. Published 2016 by John Wiley & Sons, Ltd.

bright red. Thereafter, the order of achromatic and chromatic blots is sufficiently random to minimize undesirable sequential effects (Holtzman, 1975). Overall A and B are truly equivalent forms that can be considered interchangeable for most purposes.

The HIT demonstrated several psychometric advantages over the Rorschach. First, the number of responses per individual could be held constant at one per inkblot. Second, it was convenient for quantitative treatment of inkblot responses. Third, the new inkblot technique resulted in a richer variety of stimuli with 45 inkblots, which can elicit more information than 10 Rorschach inkblots. Fourth, two parallel forms of the inkblots add to the reliability and other psychometric properties of the technique. Unlike the Rorschach, the subject is asked to give only one response per card, and a simple standardized inquiry immediately follows in order to ascertain where the percept is seen (query about location, Q_L), what qualities of the blot it suggested (query about characteristics, Q_C), and anything else one cares to tell about the percept (query about elaboration, Q_E). The examiner records the response, reaction time of the response, location of the percept, and direction of each card on the Record Form so that responses can be scored for all the 22 variables.

While developing scoring for the 22 HIT variables, the system of Rorschach scoring was carefully taken into account so that most of the relevant scores could be easily derived from the basic element in the protocols. Holtzman et al. (1961) considered four criteria in the formulation of variables for the scoring of the HIT. First, the variable could be one, which is scored for any legitimate response with a score ranging from 0 to 45. Second, the variable had to be sufficiently objective to permit high scoring agreement among trained scorers. Third, the variable had to show *a priori* its pertinence to the study of personality through perception. And fourth, each variable had to be logically independent of others whenever possible in order to code the maximum amount of information. These criteria resulted in objective scoring of 22 quantitative variables. A brief definition and scoring weight for each of these variables is necessary to understand their basic nature:

Reaction Time (RT): The reaction time is the average time in seconds from the presentation of the inkblot to the beginning of the primary response.

Rejection (R): Score 1 when subject returns inkblot to examiner without giving a scorable response; otherwise, score 0.

Location (L): Tendency to break down blot into smaller fragments. Score 0 for use of whole blot, 1 for large area, and 2 for smaller area.

Space (S): Score 1 for true figure-ground reversals; otherwise, score 0.

Form Definiteness (FD): The definiteness of the form of the concept reported, regardless of the goodness-of-fit to the inkblot. A 5-point scale with 0 for very vague and 4 for highly specific form.

Form Appropriateness (FA): The goodness of fit of the form of the percept to the form of the inkblot. Score 0 for poor, 1 for fair, and 2 for good.

Color (C): The apparent primacy of color (including black, gray, or white) as a response-determinant. Score 0 for no use of color, 1 for use secondary to form, 2 when used as primary determinant but some form present, and 3 when used as primary determinant with no form present.

Shading (Sh): The apparent primacy of shading as response-determinant (texture, depth, or vista). Score 0 for no use of shading, 1 when used in secondary manner, and 2 when used as primary determinant with little or no form present.

Movement (M): The energy level of movement or potential movement ascribed to the percept, regardless of content. Score 0 for none, 1 for static potential, 2 for casual, 3 for dynamic, and 4 for violent movement.

Pathognomic Verbalization (V): Degree of autistic, bizarre thinking evident in the response as rated on a 5-point scale. Score 0 where no pathology is present. The nine categories of *V* and the range of scoring weights for each is as follows: Fabulation 1; Fabulized Combination 2, 3, 4; Queer Response 1, 2, 3; Incoherence 4; Autistic Logic 1, 2, 3, 4; Contamination 2, 3, 4; Self Reference 2, 3, 4; Deterioration Co1or, 2, 3, 4; and Absurd Response 3.

Integration (I): Score 1 for the organization of two or more adequately perceived blot elements into a larger whole; otherwise score 0.

Human (H): Degree of human quality in the content of response. Score 0 for none, 1 for parts for humans, distortions, cartoons, and 2 for whole human beings or elaborated human faces.

Animal (A): Degree of animal quality in the content. Score 0 for none (including animal objects and microscopic life), 1 for animal parts, bugs, or insects, and 2 for whole animals.

Anatomy (At): Degree of "gutlike" quality in the content. Score 0 for none, 1 for bones, X-rays, or medical drawings, and 2 for visceral and crude anatomy.

Sex (Sx): Degree of sexual quality in the content. Score 0 for no sexual reference, 1 for socially accepted sexual activity or expressions (buttocks, bust, kissing), and 2 for blatant sexual content (penis, vagina).

Abstract (Ab): Degree of abstract quality in the content. Score 0 for none, 1 for abstract elements along with other elements having form, and 2 for purely abstract content ("bright colors remind me of gaiety").

Anxiety (Ax): Signs of anxiety in the fantasy content as indicated by emotions and attitudes, expressive behaviour, symbolism, or cultural stereotypes of fear. Score 0 for none, 1 for questionable or indirect signs, and 2 for overt or clear-cut evidence.

Hostility (Hs): Signs of hostility in the fantasy content. Scored on a 4-point scale ranging from 0 for none to 3 for direct, violent, interpersonal destruction.

Barrier (Br): Score 1 for reference to any protective covering, membrane, shell, or skin that might be symbolically related to the perception of body-image boundaries; otherwise, score 0.

Penetration (Pn): Score 1 for concept which might be symbolic of an individual's feeling that his body exterior is of little protective value and can be easily penetrated; otherwise, score 0.

Balance (B): Score 1 where there is overt concern for the symmetry–asymmetry feature of the inkblot; otherwise, score 0.

Popular (P): Each form contains 25 inkblots in which one or more popular percepts occur. "Popular" in the standardization studies means that a percept had to occur at least 14% of the time among normal subjects. Score 1 for popular core concepts (or their precision alternatives) as listed in the scoring manual; otherwise, score 0.

Dimensions Underlying HIT Variables

Factor analytic studies of the 22 HIT variables have repeatedly yielded five or six common dimensions underlying inkblot perception, regardless of culture, age group, or psychiatric classification (e.g., Darolia & Joshi, 2004b; Holtzman, 1975; Holtzman et al., 1961; Holtzman & Swartz, 2003). The most outstanding dimensions explored through a series of developmental and other studies are described here.

I. Perceptual maturity and ideational activity. This dimension of inkblot perception is characterized most by Movement, Integration, Human, Barrier, and modestly by other two markers, Form Definiteness and Popular. Clustering of all these variables in one factor implies that it deals mainly with perceptual maturity, integrated ideational activity, good imaginative capacity, and awareness of conventional percepts (Holtzman, 1975; Holtzman et al., 1961). This dimension has been found to be consistently associated with cognitive ability, creativity potential (Swartz, Reinehr, & Holtzman, 1983), and reading comprehension among children (Laird, Laosa, & Swartz, 1973).

Perception of Movement in inkblots has been found to be strongly associated with cognitive component among young children when measured by the Verbal subtests from the Wechsler Intelligence Scale for Children (WISC). The variable Movement taps the verbal ability characterized by a lively, active imagination and the ability to project outward from one's fantasies (Holtzman & Swartz, 2003). High score on Human is indicative of a greater degree of social interest, whereas lack of Human content suggests the opposite (Fernald & Linden, 1966). High loading of Barrier on this factor, which is symbolically related to the body image boundaries, is indicative of a strong ego identity, being influential and independent (Cleveland & Morton, 1962), and being able to tolerate pain and stress (Nichols & Tursky, 1967).

II. Perceptual sensitivity. Factor II is generally defined by high loading of Color, Shading, and Form Definiteness (reversed) in every sample. Like Rorschach, in the scoring of HIT, when greater weight is given to the use of Color or Shading, the form of the percept plays a subordinate role. That is why Form Definiteness is inversely loaded on this factor. These three variables (Color, Shading, and Form Definiteness) represent in combination the major determinants with direct stimulus correlates in the inkblot. Occasional negative loading of Location on this factor is consistent with findings that high use of color and shading is coupled with use of the whole inkblot rather than small areas. Significant negative loadings of Animal in the samples of younger children suggest that children tend to use color and shading as stimulus determinants only when they cannot find a familiar animal form (Holtzman, 1975).

The positive pole of this factor would indicate overreactivity to color or shading, while the negative pole would indicate primary concern for form alone as a determinant. Certain studies have demonstrated that greater reference of

Color has been found associated with increased expression of affect (Mayfield, 1968), to impulsivity (Holtzman, 1950), and the quality of Color responses may be of help in making interpretations about the lability of affect in clinical cases (Hill, 1972).

III. Psychopathology of thought. The third factor is generally defined by Pathognomic Verbalization, Anxiety, Hostility, and modestly by Movement. Holtzman et al. (1961) believed that the structure of this factor is suggestive of disordered thought process, bizarre perception, and fantasy life of an emotionally disturbing nature. The best single measure of this dimension is Pathognomic Verbalization, even though the loadings of Anxiety and Hostility are generally high. Among adults, the bizarre perception and autistic logic underlying high scores on this variable are indicative of either schizophrenia or a high degree of artistic content in inkblot responses. In the case of normal children, moderately high scores on Pathognomic Verbalization may simply indicate immature thought process coupled with uncontrolled fantasies and loose imagination, rather than serious psychopathology. However, very high scores would be evidence of psychopathology and uncontrolled bizarreness (e.g., Conners, 1965; Hill, 1972).

IV. Good-form differentiation. In general, factor IV is not sharply defined because of a poor fit of the hypothesized marker variables across samples and the factor pattern being not as consistent as in the first three factors. It predominantly loads for two variables, Location and Form Appropriateness. A high score on Location indicates the tendency to focus on smaller areas of the inkblot while making a response. This kind of perceptual style is more likely when the form of the blot is highly appropriate for the reported percept. Holtzman et al. (1961) believed that fragmentation of the inkblot into smaller parts generally tends to be associated with more accurate form, and a greater variety of concepts with good form are possible only when smaller areas of the inkblot are used. In certain studies (e.g., Holtzman, 1975), Anatomy, Barrier, and Penetration also tend to have substantial but negative loadings on this factor, suggesting it to be bipolar in nature. The positive pole tends to indicate perceptual differentiation coupled with a critical sense of good form, while the negative pole appears more indicative of immaturity, diffuse bodily preoccupation, and possibly some degree of psychopathology.

V. Perceptual inability. It is a relatively narrower factor, with Reaction Time, Rejection, and Animal (reversed) as the defining variables. Reaction Time and Rejection tend to be closely related for obvious reasons. It is most likely that an inability to see anything meaningful in the inkblot leads to longer reaction time and finally rejection of the card. Hence, Reaction Time and Rejection are both indicative of some degree of inhibition or outright perceptual inability (Holtzman & Swartz, 2003). Negative loading of Animal on this factor of perceptual inability is suggestive of the fact that the greater the possibility of Animal response, the faster the reaction time with fewer rejections. Factor V generally stands orthogonal to the first four factors, indicating that there exists little or no commonality between perceptual inability and other latent components of inkblot perception.

VI. Disturbed bodily preoccupations. In most studies factor VI is usually defined by Anatomy, Sex, Abstract, and Penetration. All of these variables predominantly deal with bodily preoccupation and are occasionally clustered together in one factor (Holtzman & Swartz, 2003). Moreover, no prior hypotheses were offered in defining marker variables for factor VI as only five factors were extracted in some of the samples (Holtzman et al., 1961). In this sense, it is understood to be a residual factor tapping only those common components of inkblot perception that cannot be covered by the other five factors.

Technical Extensions and Versions of the HIT

The HIT has been widely accepted as the preferred method in clinical and research studies for the assessment of personality characteristics that are not readily measured by other tests. In addition, the availability of parallel forms and a standardized set of projective variables provides clinicians and researchers with a powerful tool for personality assessment. In view of its popularity, certain, more convenient variations of the HIT have also been published.

Group methods

The HIT, unlike the Rorschach, is well suited for group administration as it involves one response and a brief standardized inquiry. Several standardized group methods of the HIT have come into existence. Swartz and Holtzman (1963) recommended the use of colored slides and a special booklet for group administration. This group method can be substituted for the individual method in cases where subjects are competent to write their own responses, although some of the qualitative richness and several of the variables are lost (Holtzman, 1988). Swartz and Reinehr (1983) have also proposed a quick version of the standard group method with slides presented at a rapid rate (i.e., presenting all 45 inkblots in 50 minutes).

Gorham's (1967) group method uses the same colored slides but utilizes a streamlined record form on which the subject merely writes a brief response and checks the amount of the blot used for the percept. Studies have indicated that split-half reliability and test–retest stability with a one-week interval for the group method essentially are as high as for the individual method (Holtzman, 1975). Another standardized group version of a short form was developed by Herron (1963). It comprises only 30 inkblots of the test and is very effective for a college population. Herron has shown that a short form of the group-administered HIT produces means and standard deviations for most variables that are highly similar to those observed on the 45-inkblot test. Most of the variables attaining the 0.70 criterion of internal stability can be used to detect differences between criterion groups.

Short version HIT 25

Holtzman (1988) realized that some clinicians who are accustomed to using only 10 inkblots in the Rorschach find 45 inkblots to be burdensome. Also, the sequential qualitative analysis of multiple responses to a single inkblot is not possible when only one response per card is recorded. Therefore, Holtzman decided to use two responses per card with a shorter series of 25 inkblots (HIT 25) than the standard 45-inkblot HIT. A pilot study on the groups of normal and schizophrenic subjects revealed that HIT 25 is as good as the standard HIT in differential diagnoses of normals and schizophrenics (Holtzman, 1988).

Computer scored HIT

Gorham and his associates (Gorham, 1967; Moseley, Gorham, & Hill 1963) provided a system for scoring 17 of the HIT variables through a computer program. Computerized scoring had a surprisingly high agreement with hand scoring of the same protocols. Intercorrelations between the two methods of scoring were over 0.80 for seven variables: Rejection, Location, Movement, Human, Colour, Form Definiteness, and Animal. Cross-method correlations for Hostility, Popular, Anxiety, Anatomy, Shading, Penetration, Abstract, Sex, Barrier, and Integration ranged from 0.50 to 0.75.

Psychometric Characteristics

Reliability

The various forms of reliabilities of HIT variables have been reported in great detail elsewhere (Darolia & Joshi, 2004a; Holtzman et al., 1961; Holtzman, Diaz-Guerroro, & Swartz, 1975; Holtzman & Swartz, 2003; Shukla, 1976). Reliability coefficients for various HIT variables are exceedingly high, which is very uncommon in projective tests. Spilt-half reliabilities (odd-even) have been found to range from a low of 0.31 to a high of 0.96, with most falling between 0.70 to 0.90. The four scores with highest internal consistency (generally about 0.90) regardless of population sampled are Reaction Time, Rejection, Location, and Form Definiteness. Eight additional scores that have internal consistency reliability generally higher than 0.80 are Form Appropriateness, Color, Shading, Movement, Pathognomic Verbalization, Human, Animal, and Anatomy. Odd-even reliability coefficients for the content scores for Anxiety, Hostility, Barrier, and Penetration are only slightly lower and are more variable. Internal consistency coefficients of HIT scores among preschool children are equally high, ranging from 0.53 for Penetration to 0.97 for Reaction Time. The median reliability for all variables among the 5-year-olds was 0.86 (Holtzman & Swartz, 2003).

The test–retest reliability coefficients were determined in a series of studies using parallel forms of the HIT (Holtzman et al., 1961, 1975). The most stable scores are for Reaction Time, Location, Movement, and Human. Test–retest correlations between the forms for these variables are around 0.60–0.80, even after a one-year interval. The most unstable scores for normals over a one-year interval, usually with coefficients around 0.20–0.40, are for Popular, Anatomy, Space, Sex, Balance, and Pathognomic Verbalization. The remaining 11 variables yield scores that are moderately stable over a year, with test–retest coefficients from 0.40 to 0.60.

Highly trained scorers agree to an exceptionally high degree of interscorer correlation on nearly all the 22 variables. On a sample of schizophrenics, interscorer coefficients ranged between 0.89 and 0.99 with a median value of 0.98 (Holtzman et al., 1961). In a study involving four examiners with varied experience, the interscorer correlations ranged from 0.73 to 0.89 with a median value of 0.84. However, intrascorer consistency ranged from 0.89 to 0.97.

Validity

The validity of the HIT for personality assessment is of special interest. Several hundred studies have been published demonstrating distinct lines of evidence for the validity of HIT variables. Extensive reviews by Gamble (1972), Hill (1972), Holtzman et al. (1975), and Holtzman and Swartz (1983) have dealt with the findings of these studies. One of the important lines of evidence for validity of the HIT variables is sensitivity to developmental changes throughout the life span. In summarizing the data from several of these studies, Gamble (1972) concluded that "ignoring slight ambiguities in the interpretations of minor aspects of the data, the consistency of findings with respect to theoretically relevant and developmentally meaningful conceptions is noteworthy." Thorpe (1960) derived 29 basic pattern scores using elements of the HIT scoring system, and highly significant age trends were found for eight of ten individual variables. Thorpe and Swartz (1965) and Costa and McCrae (1986) noticed marked age-related changes in personality scores as measured by HIT.

The HIT has been commended for its ability in differentiating among groups of normals, psychiatric patients, and the intellectually disabled (e.g. Hill, 1972; Holtzman, 1988; Holtzman et al., 1961). Findings of numerous studies in this respect appear elsewhere in the chapter. Studies on the relationship with behavioral measures of personality and related variables offer modest support to the validity of HIT variables (Gamble, 1972; Holtzman & Swartz, 1983). Most of the conventional psychometric measures of personality have been studied for possible HIT correlates, but without much success, as projective and self-report measures seem to be tapping different levels of personality attributes. Detailed review of such research appears in the next section.

Personality Correlates of HIT Variables

Several hundred studies have been conducted to examine possible personality correlates of HIT variables. Extensive reviews of such studies have already appeared elsewhere (e.g., Darolia & Panghal, 2010; Gamble, 1972; Holtzman, 1981;

Holtzman & Swartz, 1983, 2003; Holtzman et al., 1975; Swartz, Reinehr, & Holtzman, 1999). Such studies provide modest support to the external validity of inkblot measures of Anxiety and Hostility. Megargee and Swartz (1968) observed that high scores on HIT factor III, tapping Pathognomic Verbalization, Anxiety, and Hostility, were significantly associated with high scores on MPI Neuroticism. In another study, Currie, Holtzman, and Swartz (1974) found that HIT factor III variables are useful in predicting maladjustment in young children at a later stage. Cook, Iacino, Murray, and Auerbach (1973) noted that STAI A-state, but not the A-trait, is significantly correlated with HIT *Ax* in a sample of college students. However, in a later study (Iacino & Cook, 1974), STAI A-Trait was also found to be correlated significantly with HIT *Ax*.

Both Anxiety and Hostility inkblot variables demonstrated a considerable degree of construct validity by showing a correlation coefficient of 0.35 with the IPAT Anxiety Scale Questionnaire and 0.43 with the Manifest Hostility Scale, respectively (Fehr, 1976). Further analysis of Anxiety and Hostility variables in an Argentine sample (Sacchi, 1977) revealed that the Animal response causes more anxiety and hostility, while aggression feelings predominate over injury in the Hostility variable. Some other HIT variables (Form Appropriateness, Movement, Anxiety, Barrier, and Affect Arousal) differentiated successfully between low- and high-anxiety children matched for grade, sex, and IQ (Swartz, 1965). On a similar pattern, Swartz and Swartz (1968) found that high-anxiety children scored significantly higher on Anatomy, Penetration, and Affect Arousal, but lower on Movement than the low-anxiety group. Hypertensive subjects were found to be more interpunitive, dependent, anxious, and had a lower Human score on the HIT (Lucas, 1976).

However, certain studies have shown a weak association between inkblot measures and objective self-report measures of anxiety and hostility. The multitrait–multimethod matrix yielded slim support for the validity of Anxiety and Affect Arousal in relation to comparable measures from the MMPI and peer ratings (Berger & Sechrest, 1961). No significant correlations were found between Trait Anxiety and Human Movement (Prokop, 1977), and none of the HIT measures shared its variance with a factor of anxiety defined by psychometric measures (Vats, 1997). These findings may be understood in the light of Holtzman's (1975) assertion that fantasy expressions of anxiety or hostility do not have a simple and direct relationship to observed anxiety in one's behavior or self-admission of such traits in personality inventories (p. 254).

The most remarkable support for the validity of HIT variables comes from experimental studies. Rosenstiel (1966) reported that persons particularly impressed by a gruesome passage from a poem showed numerous anxiety and hostility responses in the subsequently administered HIT. Five Holtzman variables – Hostility, Barrier, Human, Movement, and Popular – successfully discriminated between control and experimental groups after having viewed a stress-producing film. Results showed a significant correlation between the STAI A-State scale and Hostility, Barrier, Popular, Movement, and Human variables (Kamen, 1969). Individuals with high Anxiety have been found to be less tolerant of pain (Nichols & Tursky, 1967) and more rapidly acquire the conditioned eyelid response (Herron, 1965). Feldstein (1973) observed a significant increase in Pathognomic Verbalization and Movement scores following three consecutive REM-deprived nights. Herron (1969) observed significant differences between research-oriented and mental-illness instructional sets on HIT Anxiety and Hostility. Mental-illness instructions yielded significant correlations between HIT Anxiety and Manifest Anxiety ($r = 0.26$) and between HIT Hostility and Manifest Hostility ($r = 0.37$).

Holtzman Hostility (*Hs*) has consistently shown at least modest associations with self-report or behavioral indices of aggression. Hostility correlated 0.24 ($p < 0.05$) with total physical aggression and 0.25 ($p < 0.05$) with a global rating of aggression (Megargee & Cook, 1967), HIT Hostility and Anatomy correlated with psychometric hostility (Rishi, 1995), and HIT Space with aggression (Sanders, 1976). Rosensteil (1973) observed that *Hs* responses after a frustrating stimulus correlated significantly with the Buss-Durkee hostility scale. Adding to the validity of inkblot Hostility and Anxiety scores, Shalit (1970) found that hostile content in fantasy (HIT Hostility) is reduced by vicarious participation in overt hostility. The testing of prisoners in conditions of either verbal or non-verbal reinforcement yielded more Movement responses under non-verbal conditions (Guarnaccia & Curry, 1990).

The results of more conventional measures of personality are not that encouraging; only a few personality scales have yielded a considerable degree of association with HIT variables. While analyzing data from 15 HIT variables, Cattell's Junior Personality Quiz, McCandelss' Anxiety Scale, and scores from the personal problem and attitude scales, McGuire, Hindsman, King, and Jennings (1961) found that only Cattell's Neuroticism correlated significantly with Human (–0.25, $p < 0.001$); a lower score on Human is also an indicator of hypertension (Swartz et al., 1983). Though Megargee and Swartz (1968) did not find significant correlation between MPI Extraversion and HIT *C*, *M*, or *H*, HIT Psychopathology Factor III was significantly associated with MPI Neuroticism. Color response found to be related to impulsivity (Holtzman, Santos, Bouquet, & Barth, 1966), while Abstract tends to relate positively with Endurance and Sentience but negatively with Harm avoidance and Order in males, and positively with Dominance, Nurturance, and Exhibition but negatively with Abasement and Affiliation in females (Sanders, 1977).

Hill (1971) reported a number of 16 PF scales having significant relationships with HIT scores. Warmth has shown a significant relationship with Form Definiteness, Abstract, Balance, Popular, Movement (–) and Human (–); Liveliness with Form Appropriate and Animal; Social boldness with Sex, Anxiety, and Animal; and Vigilance with Human and Abstract. Significant associations between HIT variables and their corresponding psychometric measures have also been reported by Panghal (2005). Pathognomic Verbalization response correlated significantly with Schizophrenia, Paranoia, Depression, Impulsivity, and Psychopathic deviance; Anxiety response with A-trait, A-state, and Depression; Hostility response with A-trait, A-state, Aggression, and Impulsiveness; Penetration response with Psychopathic deviance and Anxiety; Human with Order, Feelings, and Fear (–); Animal response with A-state and Impulsivity; and Color response with A-trait. Social interest scores tend to relate significantly with Human response on the HIT (Fernald & Linden, 1966).

Nevertheless, Rimoldi, Insua, and Erdmann (1975) did not find any significant relationship between HIT scores and self-report measures of personality.

Empathy and HIT scores

Results of certain studies are suggestive of relationships between HIT responses and questionnaire measures of empathy. Perceived or projected movement tends to correlate significantly with the accuracy with which others perceive the subject's behavior – an unusual component of Empathy (Mueller & Abeles, 1964). It seems that high M scorers are likely to make more information available for appraisal by others. Rosensteil's (1969) findings show that, for anxious subjects, inkblot Human responses (interpreted as a need for contact) are related negatively to capacity for empathy. Human responses were measured with the Holtzman technique, capacity for empathy by interview, and anxiety by the second factor of the 16 PF test. Not high anxiety scores, but deviations from the norm were shown to be appropriate measures of anxiety, at least in questionnaires subject to dissemblance. Four content scales of HIT were found to relate significantly with projective distance, but only Anxiety and Hostility correlated significantly with interpersonal distance behavior (Greenberg, Aronow, & Rauchway, 1977). The projective measure of interpersonal distance correlated significantly with the live measure of distance.

In an attempt to test the hypothesis that the HIT variable Human is positively related to social isolation and functional pathology, Fernald and Linden (1966) employed a group sociometric technique for assessing social isolation and empathy. Their results indicated that social isolation and empathy have no relationship to Human response. However, social interest scores on the Strong Vocational Interest Test were significantly related to HIT. The relationship between personality factors, social isolation, and confinement was further examined by Taylor, Altman, Wheeler, and Kushner (1969). The participants were pairs of men who were confined to small rooms without recreational materials of any kind and a minimal work schedule for eight days. Eight HIT variables showed significant changes from before to after confinement. Most of these changes were among variables included in Holtzman's factors I and II – Movement, Color, Penetration, and Barrier changes were associated with varying conditions of confinement.

Relationship with body image

Barrier and Penetration have been studied extensively because of their direct relevance to body image and personality. Support was found for the view that the more definite an individual's boundaries, the more likely s/he is to manifest relatively higher physiological reactivity in body exterior in contrast with body interior sectors (Fisher, 1963). Barrier scores successfully differentiated exterior eczematiod dermatitis and interior duodenal ulcer symptom patients, but the Penetration score is a considerably weaker predictor (Shultz, 1966). Cleveland and Fisher (1960) reported significantly higher Barrier scores in arthritics as opposed to ulcer patients, while the reverse trend was found on Penetration scores. Low Barrier subjects performed more adequately under low stress, and conversely high Barrier subjects perform more adequately under high stress. Further, a significant positive correlation was found between pain tolerance (electric shock) and definiteness of body boundaries (Nichols & Tursky, 1967). Megargee (1965) found that a delinquent sample had a mean Barrier score significantly lower than the non-delinquent sample.

High Barrier subjects were found to receive significantly more descriptions as influential, active, independent and goal-striving in the group situation, and they were less influenced by group opinion than low Barrier subjects (Cleveland & Morton, 1962). Comparison of 7th grade underachievers in a residential school with average boys lent support to the hypothesis that underachievers have lower barrier scores. The findings support the variations in body image as a function of achievement level in school performance (Hawkins & Horowitz, 1971). There was a significant decrease in Penetration score after body awareness training of the intellectually disabled (Chasey, Swartz, & Chasey, 1974). Roger (1982) investigated the effects of a self-esteem manipulation on measures of body image and personal space. Significant interaction effects were obtained for penetration, body-cathexis, and stimulated interaction distance, and the results confirmed the prediction that subjects whose self-esteem had been enhanced would obtain significantly higher body-cathexis and significantly lower penetration.

Diagnostic assessment and HIT

Since its development, the most extensive use of Holtzman Inkblot Technique can be seen in providing important information for differential diagnosis. Holtzman et al. (1961) have provided the standardization data on 15 different populations in percentile norms for eight major reference groups. Five of the groups represent different developmental levels ranging from five-year-olds to superior adults, and three of which deal with psychiatric classes of chronic paranoid schizophrenics, depressed neurotics and psychotics, and the intellectually disabled. Separate norms have been published for male juvenile delinquents and forensic patients (Mullen, Reinehr, & Swartz, 1983), emotionally disturbed adolescents, adult neurotics, and adult alcoholics (Hill, 1972), and normal reference population (Darolia & Joshi, 2004a). Hill (1972) has provided elaborate guidelines on how to interpret HIT variables and the qualitative aspects of content scores in respect of cognitive functioning, affective functioning, and self-identity. She believed that accumulating evidence justifies the clinical use of the HIT in the everyday assessment of clients. Later, Hill (1980) reported on the use of the HIT in a battery of psychological tests in assessing change in a patient over a period of eight years.

In the standardization sample of the HIT (Holtzman et al., 1961) compared with normal reference groups, the chronic schizophrenics got significantly higher scores on Rejection, Pathognomic Verbalization, Penetration, Anatomy, and Sex, and significantly lower scores on Location, Form Definiteness, Form Appropriateness, Shading, Movement, Integration, Human, Barrier, and Popular. Emotionally disturbed children (neurosis and conduct disorders) received markedly higher scores than normal children on HIT Rejection and Anatomy, and lower on all other variables except Pathognomic Verbalization, Sex, Abstract, Hostility, Penetration, and Balance (Conners, 1965). HIT factor scores indicated that the neurotic group showed more perceptual differentiation (Form Appropriateness and Location) and more inhibition (Reaction Time, Rejection, and Animal reverse). Hartung and Skorke (1980) found that psychedelic drug users scored significantly higher on HIT Pathognomic Verbalization, Hostility, Sex, Color, Movement, and Abstract than non-drug users matched for age, sex, and level of education.

Moseley (1963) developed an objective approach to differential diagnosis through a linear combination of 16 HIT variables. He was able to classify successfully 82% of the normals from schizophrenics, 71% of the normals from depressed patients, and 78% of the depressives from the schizophrenics. Addition of Pathognomic Verbalization to the model further improved the efficiency of the differential diagnosis. Cross-validation of the criterion was impressive, suggesting that it can be used with some confidence in the diagnosis of schizophrenia. HIT scores differentiated between brain-damaged and normal individuals with about 80% accuracy (Barnes, 1963), with successful differential diagnosis of organics, neurotics, and schizophrenics (Shukla, 1976). HIT scores were able to separate 30 hospitalized borderline and 30 hospitalized neurotic patients by the more severe degrees of deviant thinking with relatively high values for sensitivity and specificity (Leichsenring, 1990), and successful classification of acute schizophrenics, chronic schizophrenics and borderline patients, and neurotic versus normal individuals, on the basis of HIT deviant verbalizations (Leichsenring, 1991).

Correlational studies also indicate considerable degree of association between inkblot responses and various kinds of psychopathology. Moseley, Duffey, and Sherman (1963) found that HIT variables have significant relationships with clinical ratings of overt behavior (IMPS) in samples of diagnosed neurotic depressive and psychotic depressive patients. Factor analysis indicated significant communality (>0.40) between HIT Pathognomic Verbalization and Sex, and IMPS Disorientation and Grandiose Expansiveness. HIT Form Definiteness (reverse), Color, and Shading were found to be related to IMPS variables Paranoid Projection and Perceptual Distortion. In the hospitalized group, seven HIT scores were significantly correlated with MMPI-rated depression, including Location, Anatomy, Rejection, and Color. In the out-patient group HIT L (0.55) was significantly related to rated depression (Endicott & Jortner, 1967). The Q factor analysis on the 19 HIT scores (Smith & Barclay, 1975) of normal, delinquent, and intellectually disabled groups provided four factors. Definable subfactors appeared within the delinquent and intellectually disabled groups, but loadings for normal subjects were primarily on one factor. The splitting of the delinquent and intellectually disabled populations into two factors appeared to indicate the existence of subgroups within their general classification.

References

Barnes, C. (1963). *Prediction of brain damage using the Holtzman Inkblot Technique and other selected variables.* (Unpublished doctoral dissertation.) University of Iowa.

Berger, P.M., & Sechrest, L. (1961). Convergent and discriminant validity for four Holtzman Inkblot Test variables. *Psychological Studies, 12* (6), 227–236.

Chasey, W.C., Swartz, J.D., & Chasey, C.G. (1974). Effect of motor development on body image scores for institutionalized mentally retarded children. *American Journal of Mental Deficiency, 78* (4), 440–445.

Cleveland, S.E., & Fisher, S. (1960). A comparison of psychological characteristics and physiological reactivity in ulcer and rheumatoid arthritis groups. *Psychosomatic Medicine, 22*, 283–289.

Cleveland, S.E., & Morton, R.B. (1962). Group behavior and body image: a follow-up study. *Human Relations, 15* (1), 77–85.

Conners, C.K. (1965). Effects of brief psychotherapy, drugs, and type of disturbance on Human Inkblot scores in children. *Proceedings of the 73rd Annual Convention of the American Psychological Association, 1*, 201–202.

Cook, P.E., Iacino, L.W., Murray, J., & Auerbach, S.M. (1973). Holtzman inkblot anxiety and shading scores related to state and trait anxiety. *Journal of Personality Assessment, 37* (4), 337–339.

Costa, P.T. Jr., & McCrae, R.R. (1986). Major contributions to personality psychology. In S. Modgil, & C. Modgil (Eds.) *Hans Eysenck: Consensus and Controversy* (pp. 63–72). Barcombe, Lewes, UK: Flamer.

Currie, S.F., Holtzman, W.H., & Swartz, J.D. (1974). Early indicators of personality traits viewed retrospectively. *Journal of School Psychology, 12* (1), 51–59.

Darolia, C.R., & Joshi, H.L. (2004a). Standardization of Holtzman Inkblot Technique on Indian high school students. *Psychological Studies, 49* (1), 52–58.

Darolia, C.R., & Joshi, H.L. (2004b). Psychometric evaluation of a short form of Holtzman Inkblot Technique. *Journal of Projective Psychology and Mental Health, 11* (2), 124–132.

Darolia, C.R., & Panghal, U. (2010). *Personality assessment through Holtzman Inkblot Technique*. Invited Address in CEP Workshop on Psychological Assessment, Defence Institute of Psychological Research, DRDO, New Delhi.

Endicott, N.A., & Jortner, S. (1967). Correlates of somatic concern derived from psychological tests. *Journal of Nervous and Mental Disease, 144* (2), 133–138.

Fehr, L.A. (1976). Construct validity of the Holtzman Inkblot anxiety and hostility scores. *Journal of Personality Assessment, 40* (5), 483–486.

Feldstein, S. (1973). REM deprivation: The effects of inkblot perception and fantasy processes. *Dissertation Abstracts International, 33*, 3934B–3935B.

Fernald, P.S., & Linden, J.D. (1966). The human content response in the Holtzman Inkblot Technique. *Journal of Projective Techniques and Personality Assessment, 30* (5), 441–446.

Fisher, S. (1963). A further appraisal of the body boundary concept. *Journal of Consulting Psychology, 27* (1), 62–74.

Gamble, K.R. (1972). The Holtzman Inkblot Technique: A review. *Psychological Bulletin, 77* (3), 172–194.

Gorham, D.R. (1967). Validity and reliability studies of a computer-based scoring system of inkblot responses. *Journal of Consulting Psychology, 31* (1), 67–70.

Greenberg, E., Aronow, E., & Rauchway, A. (1977). Inkblot content and interpersonal distance. *Journal of Clinical Psychology, 33* (3), 882–887.

Guarnaccia, V., & Curry, K. (1990). Contingent reinforcement effects on movement responses of prison inmates to the Holtzman Inkblot Technique. *Journal of Personality Assessment, 55* (1–2), 263–269.

Hartung, J.R., & Skorke, D. (1980). The HIT clinical profile of psychedelic drug users. *Journal of Personality Assessment, 44* (3), 237–245.

Hawkins, D.B., & Horowitz, H. (1971). Variations in body image as a function of achievement level in school performance. *Perceptual and Motor Skills, 33* (3), 1299–1302.

Herron, E.W. (1963). Psychometric characteristics of a thirty-item version of the group method of the Holtzman Inkblot Technique. *Journal of Clinical Psychology, 19* (4), 450–453.

Herron, E.W. (1965). Personality factors associated with the acquisition of the conditioned eyelid response. *Journal of Personality and Social Psychology, 2* (5), 775–777.

Herron, E.W. (1969). Value of experimental manipulation in multivariate studies of personality. *Proceedings of the 77th Annual Convention of the American Psychological Association, 4,* 131–132.

Hill, D.O. (1971). Extraversion-introversion: An investigation of typological theory. (Doctoral dissertation.) Texas Tech. University. *Dissertation Abstracts.*

Hill, E.F. (1972). *The Holtzman Inkblot Technique: A Handbook for Clinical Application.* San Francisco: Jossey-Bass.

Hill, E.F. (1980). A comparison of three psychological testings of trans-sexual. *Journal of Personality Assessment, 44* (1), 52–100.

Holtzman, W.H. (1950). *The Rorschach test in the assessment of the normal superior adult.* (Unpublished doctoral dissertation.) Stanford University.

Holtzman, W.H. (1961). *Holtzman Inkblot Technique.* New York: The Psychological Corporation.

Holtzman, W.H. (1975). New developments in Holtzman Inkblot Technique. In P. McReynolds (Ed.), *Advances in Psychological Assessment* (Vol. *3*) (pp. 243–274). San Francisco: Jossey-Bass.

Holtzman, W.H. (1981). Holtzman Inkblot Technique (HIT). In A.I. Rabin (Ed.), *Assessment with Projective Techniques: A Concise Introduction* (pp. 47–83). New York: Springer.

Holtzman, W.H. (1988). Beyond the Rorschach. *Journal of Personality Assessment, 52* (4), 578–609.

Holtzman, W.H., Diaz-Guerroro, R., & Swartz, J.D. (1975). *Personality Development in Two Cultures: A Cross-Cultural Longitudinal Study of School Children in Mexico and United States.* Austin, TX: University of Texas Press.

Holtzman, W.H., Santos, J.F., Bouquet, S., & Barth, P. (1966). *The Peace Corps in Brazil.* Austin, TX: University of Texas Press.

Holtzman, W.H., & Swartz, J.D. (1983). The Holtzman Inkblot Technique: A review of 25 years of research. *Zeitschrift fur Differentielle und Diagnostische Psychologie, 4* (3), 241–259.

Holtzman, W.H., & Swartz, J.D., (2003). Use of the Holtzman Inkblot Technique with children. In CR. Reynolds, & R.W. Kamphaus (Eds.), *Handbook of Psychological and Educational Assessment of Children: Personality, Behaviour, and Context* (2nd ed.) (pp. 198–215). New York: Guilford Press.

Holtzman, W.H., Thorpe, J.S., Swartz, J.D., & Herron, E.W. (1961). *Inkblot Perception and Personality: Holtzman Inkblot Technique.* Austin, TX: University of Texas Press.

Iacino, L.W., & Cook, P.E. (1974). Threat of shock, state anxiety and the HIT. *Journal of Personality Assessment, 38* (5), 450–458.

Kamen, G.B. (1969). The effects of a stress-producing film on the test performance of adults. *Journal of Projective Techniques and Personality Assessment, 33* (3), 281–285.

Laird, D.R., Laosa, L.M., & Swartz, J.D. (1973). Inkblot perception and reading achievement in children: A developmental analysis. *British Journal of Projective Psychology and Personality Study, 18* (2), 25–31.

Leichsenring, F. (1990). Discriminating borderline from neurotic patients. A study with the Holtzman Inkblot Technique. *Psychopathology, 23* (1), 21–26.

Leichsenring, F. (1991). Discriminating schizophrenics from borderline patients: Study with the Holtzman Inkblot Technique. *Psychopathology, 24* (4), 225–231.

Lucas, J.D. (1976). *A study of personality factors which characterize essential hypertensives.* (Doctoral dissertation.) George Washington University.

Mayfield, D.G. (1968). Holtzman Inkblot Technique in acute experimental alcohol intoxication. *Journal of Projective Techniques and Personality Assessment, 32* (5), 491–494.

McGuire, C., Hindsman, E., King, F.J., & Jennings (1961). Dimensions of talent behaviour. *Educational Psychology Bulletin, 21,* 2–38.

Megargee, E.I. (1965). The performance of juvenile delinquents on the Holtzman Inkblot Technique: A normative study. *Journal of Projective Techniques and Personality Assessment, 29* (4), 504–512.

Megargee, E.I., & Cook, P.E. (1967). The relation of TAT and inkblot aggressive content scales with each other and with criteria of overt aggressiveness in juvenile delinquents. *Journal of Projective Techniques and Personality Assessment, 31* (1), 48–60.

Megargee, E.I., & Swartz, J.D. (1968). Extraversion, neuroticism and scores on the Holtzman Inkblot Technique. *Journal of Projective Techniques and Personality Assessment, 32* (3), 262–265.

Moseley, E.C. (1963). Psychodiagnosis on the basis of the Holtzman Inkblot Technique. *Journal of Projective Techniques and Personality Assessment, 27,* 86–91.

Moseley, E.C., Gorham, D.R., & Hill, K. (1963a). Computer scoring of inkblot perceptions. *Perceptual and Motor Skills, 17* (2), 498.

Moseley, E.C., Duffey, R.F., & Sherman, L.J. (1963b). An extension of the construct validity of the Holtzman Inkblot Technique. *Journal of Clinical Psychology, 19* (2), 186–192.

Mueller, W.J., & Abeles, N. (1964). The components of empathy and their relationship to the projection of human movement responses. *Journal of Projective Techniques and Personality Assessment, 28* (3), 322–330.

Mullen, J.M., Reinehr, R.C., & Swartz, J.D. (1983). Holtzman Inkblot Technique scores of delinquent adolescents: a replication and extension. *Journal of Personality Assessment, 47* (2), 158–160.

Nichols, D.C., & Tursky, B. (1967). Body image, anxiety and tolerance for experimental pain. *Psychosomatic Medicine, 29* (2), 103–110.

Panghal, U. (2005). *A study of some indices of Holtzman Inkblot Technique in relation to their psychometric measures.* (Unpublished doctoral dissertation.) Kurukshetra University, India.

Prokop, C. (1977). The experience balance as a predictor of state anxiety and response latency in differing stimulated group interactions. *Dissertation Abstracts International, 38* (8-B), 3902.

Rimoldi, H.J.A., Insua, A.M., & Erdmann, J.B. (1975). Personality dimensions as assessed by projective and verbal instruments. *Journal of Clinical Psychology, 31* (3), 529–539.

Rishi, N. (1995). *A study of hostility in relation to personality and motivation of girl students.* (Unpublished MPhil dissertation.) Kurukshetra University, India.

Roger, D.B. (1982). Body-image, personal space, and self-esteem: preliminary evidence of 'focusing' effects. *Journal of Personality Assessment, 46* (5), 468–478.

Rorschach, H. (1921). *Psychodiagnostics* (Hans Huber Verlag Trans.). Bern: Bircher.

Rosenstiel, L.V. (1966). Zur frage der angst-und feindseligkei-tsinhalte in formdeutverfahren. *Zeitschrift fur Experimentelle und Angewandte Psychologie, 8,* 611–631.

Rosenstiel, L.V. (1969). Capacity of empathy: A function of anxiety in the production of H-responses. *Journal of Projective Techniques and Personality Assessment, 33* (4), 336–342.

Rosenstiel, L.V. (1973). Increase in hostility responses in the HIT after frustration. *Journal of Personality Assessment, 37* (1), 22–24.

Sacchi, J.C. (1977). Variables de ansiedad y hostilidad en el test de Holtzman. *Revista Latinoamericana de Psicologia, 9* (2), 271–276.

Sanders, J.L. (1976). Aggression and autonomy as correlates of the space response on Holtzman Inkblot Technique. *Perceptual and Motor Skills, 42* (3c), 1049–1050.

Sanders, J.L. (1977). Personality correlates of the abstract response on the Holtzman inkblot technique. *Journal of Personality Assessment, 41* (4), 349–350.

Shalit, B. (1970). Environmental hostility and hostility in fantasy. *Journal of Personality and Social Psychology, 15* (2), 171–174.

Shukla, T.R. (1976). Psychodiagnostic efficiency of the HIT under Indian conditions: A normative study. *Indian Journal of Clinical Psychology, 3* (2), 189–198.

Shultz, T.D. (1966). A comparison of the reactions and attitudes toward stress of two psychosomatic symptom groups. *Dissertation Abstracts, 27*, 6168–6178.

Smith, P.M., & Barclay, A.G. (1975). Q analysis of the Holtzman Inkblot Technique. *Journal of Clinical Psychology, 31* (1), 131–134.

Swartz, J.D. (1965). Performance of high and low-anxious children on the Holtzman Inkblot Technique. *Child Development, 36* (2), 569–575.

Swartz, J.D., & Holtzman, W.H. (1963). Group method of administration for the Holtzman Inkblot Technique. *Journal of Clinical Psychology, 19* (4), 433–441.

Swartz, J.D., & Reinehr, R.C. (1983). A quick version of administration for the group Holtzman Inkblot Technique. *Perceptual and Motor Skills, 56* (3), 813–814.

Swartz, J.D., Reinehr, R.C., & Holtzman, W.H. (1983). *Holtzman Inkblot Technique, 1956–1982: An Annotated Bibliography.* Austin, TX: Hogg Foundation for Mental Health.

Swartz, J.D., Reinehr, R.C., & Holtzman, W.H. (1999). *Holtzman Inkblot Technique, Research Guide and Bibliography.* Austin, TX: Hogg Foundation for Mental Health.

Swartz, J.D., & Swartz, C.J. (1968). Test anxiety and performance on the Holtzman Inkblot Technique. *Journal of Clinical Psychology, 24* (4), 463–467.

Taylor, D.A., Altman, I., Wheeler, L., & Kushner, E.N. (1969). Personality factors related to response to social isolation and confinement. *Journal of Consulting and Clinical Psychology, 33* (4), 411–419.

Thorpe, J.S. (1960). *Level of perceptual development as reflected in responses to the Holtzman Inkblot Technique.* (Doctoral dissertation.) University of Texas.

Thorpe, J.S., & Swartz, J.D. (1965). Level of perceptual development as reflected in responses to the Holtzman Inkblot Technique. *Journal of Projective Techniques and Personality Assessment, 29* (3), 380–386.

Vats, S. (1997). *A study of projective and psychometric personality correlates of anxiety.* (Unpublished MPhil dissertation.) Kurukshetra University, India.

Zubin, J. (1954). Failures of the Rorschach Technique. *Journal of Projective Techniques, 18* (3), 303–315.

21

Integrative Treatments Come of Age: Systematic Treatment Selection (STS)

Christopher J. Edwards, Lori Holleran, and Larry E. Beutler

Palo Alto University, California, USA

The Evolution of Integrative Treatment

Psychotherapy as a profession is relatively young, its history extending slightly more than 100 years (Gold & Stricker, 2006). Throughout this time, the field of psychotherapy has drawn heavily from many other fields, including scientific and social disciplines. However, within the discipline, psychotherapists remained religiously divided amongst various psychotherapy theories and models for much of this history. Gold and Stricker (2006) describe how practitioners were reluctant to recognize strengths and promise in theories and procedures outside of their own, and were dismissive of any potential benefits that might be attached to these unfamiliar procedures. Integration within the field of psychotherapy has come to refer to the combination of two or more theories or models, either through finding common theoretical ground or by mixing and blending the use of distinguishing techniques. The latter method of integration has traditionally been referred to as "eclecticism," but has gravitated to the more general term "integration" over time (Gold & Stricker, 2006). Thus, integration is the term that we will use throughout this chapter to refer to the amalgamation or blending either of techniques or theories across theories/models/interventions.

In the mid-1970s the rigid belief in a single model or view of psychotherapy began to change toward some form of integration as many psychotherapists became disaffected with the ideas proposed by any single theory, but most particularly by psychoanalytic formulations. These practitioners found fault with the shallow evidentiary base of theoretical approaches, and as they became educated about the various other approaches available, they came to see that an integration of ideas and

The Wiley Handbook of Personality Assessment, First Edition. Edited by Updesh Kumar.
© 2016 John Wiley & Sons, Ltd. Published 2016 by John Wiley & Sons, Ltd.

practices may be a better avenue to help their patients (Nguyen, Bertoni, Charvat, Gheytanchi, & Beutler, 2007). While this transition promoted integration in the field, the early attempts were not necessarily ideal, as these amalgamations, like the approaches they hoped to replace, were long on theory and short on solid evidence. They were all based largely on personal experiences and preferences of their founder. In more contemporary times, many traditional treatment approaches have demonstrated efficacy, but there has yet to be a single one of these theory-based approaches that emerged as singularly effective. In comparative studies, the dodo bird reigns supreme (Wampold, 2001).

As a result, increasingly systematized approaches began to appear in the early 1980s (Gold & Stricker, 2006; Nguyen et al., 2007). As this trend evolved, many psychotherapists contributed to the evolution of an empirically based integration of theoretical and treatment modalities (Gold & Stricker, 2006). Some practitioner/scientists (e.g., Garfield, 1980) leaned towards identifying factors that were common to different approaches, and developed treatment models that optimized these approaches. These common-factors theorists relied heavily on empirical data to describe and identify these factors, as well as on training therapists to provide these common qualities. Partially because of this reliance on empirical data, common-factors approaches continue to be dominant forces in contemporary psychotherapy thought (e.g.,Wampold, 2001).

Others who sought to develop integrative approaches relied more heavily on blending the distinctive techniques developed by different theories into a common framework. These approaches are referred to as technically or systematically eclectic, recognizing an emphasis on combining techniques or strategies based on a patient's individual assessment (Gold & Stricker, 2006; Nguyen et al., 2007). For example, Dr Arnold Lazarus (1981), a pioneer in the field of eclectic integration, earned his fame for systematically incorporating the techniques derived from diverse models and theories into his Multimodal Therapy (MMT; Nguyen et al., 2007). His work emphasized the importance of matching symptoms drawn from different theories to various patient personality and symptom traits in order to optimize their combined effects (Lazarus, 1981).

A somewhat different approach to developing integrative models sought to identify the strategies or principles that contributed to optimal change among different patient groups. Prochaska (1979), for example, identified various stages of the patient's readiness for making change and then linked various classes of interventions to these stages. His approach generated a good deal of research, particularly on habit disorders (e.g., smoking, chemical misuse, etc.) and confirmed the importance of such matching (Norcross, Krebs, & Prochaska, 2011).

The transition of the integrated movement over time is exemplified in the development of Systematic Eclectic Psychotherapy (Beutler, 1983). This model sought to activate the potential for increasing effectiveness by selecting specific appropriate techniques from various approaches to provide optimal treatment for different patients, similar to the method proposed by Lazarus (1981). However, it gradually morphed by integrating with other models (e.g., differential therapeutics by Frances, Clarkin, & Perry, 1984; common factors eclecticism, Garfield, 1980) to eventually derive an approach that is much more similar to that proposed by Prochaska (1979) than to the original Systematic Eclectic Psychotherapy of Beutler (1983). The evolved approach was dubbed Systematic Treatment Selection (STS: Beutler & Clarkin, 1990; Beutler, Clarkin, & Bongar, 2000a). The transition of this approach to one that is formulated around the application of principles that can be applied across theories (e.g., common principles) to optimize both mediating and moderating (matching) variables in the service of change culminated in efforts to extend the role of principles to patients with wide-ranging symptoms and to therapists with wide-ranging theoretical leanings (Castonguay & Beutler, 2006; Castonguay, Constantino, & Beutler, in press).

Many newer therapeutic models including short-term and symptom-focused treatments have been created, many still relying on single theories to justify their assumptions. But, just as treatment approaches have expanded, so too has the willingness of clinicians to collaborate and explore various treatment approaches, resulting in more and more integrative efforts and an environment where integrative treatment models can flourish.

Yet unsaid is the importance of this movement to empirically based personality assessment. Integrative methods require the use of integrative and empirically derived assessments of patients and of therapeutic processes. In these approaches, non-diagnostic patient factors are central to fitting the treatment to the patient; whether these factors are evolving states, like Prochaska's (1979) assessment of readiness for change, or more traditional, such as Beutler et al.'s (2011a, 2011b) reliance on patient coping styles and resistant traits, measurement is imperative.

The formation of reliable and systematic integrative treatment approaches, most notably the STS approach, have provided a road map for using effective tools by clinicians that closely align with the more modern desires of the field (Beutler & Berren, 1995; Harwood, Beutler, & Groth-Marnat, 2011a). These methods are imperative as the majority of psychotherapists gravitate to identifying their preferred treatment modality as integrative in nature (Santoro, Kister, Karpiak, & Norcross, 2004). This overwhelming preference within the field for integrative methods may be related to numerous treatment-related factors (Norcross & Newman, 2003) and it calls for the development and use of measures that focus less on psychopathology than on dispositions to change and the conditions that optimize these changes. In pursuit of this ideal, the remainder of this chapter will illustrate the nature of measurement in these integrative approaches through the example of contemporary Systematic Treatment Selection (STS).

Development of Systematic Treatment Selection

As outlined earlier, STS is not a traditional integrative therapeutic approach, as it does not promote a therapeutic technique or set of techniques based on the merging of theories (Beutler, Harwood, Bertoni, & Thomann, 2006; Harwood et al., 2011a). Rather it endorses principle-driven amalgamation in which techniques from various theories and approaches are used in so far as they are consistent with the empirically established principles of effective practice. Applying these principles, however, requires a comprehensive assessment of both individual factors and therapy applications in order to determine how to fit interventions that are appropriate for the client (Beutler et al., 2006). In this way, STS is a "contemporary, empirically based, conceptualization of the treatment of psychological problems" (Nguyen et al., 2007, p. 14).

STS was initially created as a "cross-cutting or cross-theory model" for assessing patient behaviors as they relate to treatment decisions. The assessments were designed to address "the major questions typically encountered by psychological consultants" when patients are referred (Harwood et al., 2011a, p. 6). The STS model, including the underlying principles that guide its applications, was informed through a multistep process (Beutler et al., 2000a, 2006; Nguyen et al., 2007). Initially, a comprehensive literature search was completed to identify factors and conditions that correlated with improvement, providing a list of predictors, mediators, and moderators of improvement. This was followed by clustering these change-related qualities into groups reflecting patient and treatment qualities, with a special focus on qualities that suggested the presence of compatible relationships among patient attributes and treatment factors that reliably correlated with change.

Finally, based on predictions extending from the initial literature reviews, an examination of treatment factors contributing to the greatest therapeutic change were considered (Beutler et al., 2000a, 2006). Some of the many influential moderating factors identified include a patient's level of resistance, as well as their individual coping style (Beutler et al., 1991). Indeed, up to 90% of outcome variations can potentially be attributed to factors indicating the fit of treatment and patient examined by STS (Beutler, Moleiro, & Malik, 2000b). Ultimately, these procedures and revisions "resulted in the identification of a relatively small number of constructs and patient variables that can be assessed reliably and used in treatment decision making" (Harwood et al., 2011a, p.6). Once the importance of these relational clusters had been identified, it was integral to establish a method and means for measuring these patient-related qualities and treatment techniques.

Disposition-Centered Assessment: Systematic Treatment Selection

The range of problems that lead people to seek psychological treatment and assistance is manifold and seems to increase with every new edition of the *Diagnostic and Statistical Manual.* These problems include transitory distress to struggles with the environment in which one lives, to diagnosed "illnesses" of feelings, thoughts, and social discourse. Even more extensive than these lists of treatable conditions, however, is the range and wealth of the theoretical models and approaches that vie for the clinician's attention as a means of addressing these problems. Assessment clinicians are often faced with a dilemma of what theoretical stance to recommend to use with specific patients (Beutler, Rosner, Groth-Marnat, & Harwood, 2011b), but alas, there is little correspondence between the assessment of the problem and the treatment selected. In spite of being touted as specific treatments for depression, anxiety, marital problems, and many others, there is little empirical data to suggest that the literally hundreds of treatments existing produce effects that are specific to the problems presented (Beutler, 1991, 2009; Beutler & Malik, 2002; Budd & Hughes, 2009; Wampold, 2001). Even the procedures that are most frequently used to diagnose conditions and problems are rarely conceptualized as providing specific treatment suggestions. As a result, treatment planning processes between and among clinicians is often sporadic and unreliable. In contrast, Systematic Treatment Selection (STS) has been specifically designed to provide an empirically based framework that identifies and uses patient response dispositions in the process of treatment planning (Nguyen et al., 2007). The specific factors used to predict response to treatment cut across disorders, circumstances, and conditions.

The STS is, first of all, a conceptual framework of how treatment interacts with the problems, personalities, and preferences of patients (Beutler & Clarkin, 1990; Beutler et al., 2000a). Accompanying this framework are both descriptions of the principles that guide the selection of optimal treatment (Beutler et al., 2000a; Castonguay & Beutler, 2006), illustrations of how these principles can be applied to various patient problems (Beutler & Harwood, 2000; Castonguay et al., in press; Housley & Beutler, 2007), and a formal, cloud-based instrument that is designed to measure the treatment-relevant parameters that optimize change (Fisher, Beutler, & Williams, 1999; Beutler, Williams, & Norcross, 2008).

STS is based on the premise that neither a single brand of treatment nor a specific set of techniques are equally effective for all patients. Using a systematic approach that is specifically designed to predict and recommend procedures that optimize treatment change to the process of individual treatment planning is more effective than the usual method of diagnosis-focused assessment (Beutler & Harwood, 2000). To identify which patient will benefit from which brand of empirically based treatment, or more importantly, from what collection of cross-cutting strategies, the patient is assessed within four specific Decisional Domains in order to guide decisions of clinical treatment (Beutler & Harwood, 2000). The domains in which treatment decisions are made include: (1) patient predisposing factors; (2) the contexts of optimal treatment, (3) variations among relationship qualities that encourage the processes of treatment; and (4) the fit of the therapeutic strategies used to the patient (Beutler et al., 2000a).

The implementation of STS begins with evaluation on a list of specific traits and states. This evaluation can be based either on a selection of established assessment procedures that include scales which approximate the constructs found useful in STS evaluation, or by using a specifically developed procedure, the STS/Innerlife. In the first case, measures such as the Global Assessment of Functioning (GAF), the Minnesota Multiphasic Personality Inventory II (MMPI-II), the Dowd Therapeutic Reactance Scale (DOWD-TRS), the Millon Clinical Multiaxial Inventory (MCMI), and others (Harwood et al., 2011a), contain information and scales that are similar to the Functional Impairment, Resistance, Coping Style, and other variables identified in STS. Alternatively, assessment of the same relevant contributors to change can be done by using the STS/Innerlife, which is composed of scales that are specifically designed as a focused means of assessing the most powerful qualities and characteristics that contribute to optimizing change (Harwood, Beutler, Williams, & Stegman, 2011b). Once the patient has been assessed in this manner and the predisposing treatment factors have been identified, decisions about the context of optimal therapy can be established and the likely value of a particular setting, format, frequency, and duration of treatment can be determined. Next, optimizing the relationship quality for work with this patient and therapist can be determined, as can the types of intervention that are most likely to evoke change. Lastly, the means by which either an established type of treatment can be applied, or more often, the nature of the strategies that will encourage optimal change is selected based upon the optimal compatibility of the patient and intervention (Beutler & Clarkin, 1990). Favorable outcomes in treatment is a direct function of the fit of the patient to the treatment domains and the principles of intervention (Beutler et al., 2000a). The following subsections will break down each of the decisional domains to further illustrate how STS is implemented.

Patient predisposing factors

The predisposing factors of the patient are state and trait characteristics that have been empirically demonstrated to relate to optimized change. A diagnosis-based approach implicitly assumes that all patients with the same diagnosis can be treated identically, thus overshadowing important differences that exist among patients (Beutler & Clarkin, 1990). In this approach, personality characteristics are seen as assisting in the determination of the client's diagnosis and are based on the client's initial presentation. In contrast, the STS's theoretical approach takes a broader conceptualization of the patient to create a more holistic image for the clinician by labeling personality characteristics as important moderators and mediators to therapeutic change, more important than diagnosis *per se*. The clinical diagnosis is seen as only one of several components in the decisional domain (Beutler & Clarkin, 1990).

Beutler and Clarkin (1990) and Castonguay and Beutler (2006) emphasized the importance of socio-demographic background factors, patient preferences, and the patient's relationship to the clinician as significant mediators in the process of change. Identifying socio-demographic characteristics (e.g., gender, age, ethnicity, and socioeconomic status) as well as determining how the patient and clinician are connecting in therapy, is important in assessing the length, motivation, and effectiveness of treatment. These moderators have also been found to indicate what class of interventions will be effective with a particular patient (Beutler & Clarkin, 1990).

Whereas socio-demographic characteristics and patient–clinician connection work as mediators in therapeutic change, the patient's level of functional impairment, coping style, resistance, and subjective distress are considered to be moderates in determining the outcome of therapy (Beutler, Forrester, Gallagher-Thompson, Thompson, & Tomlins, 2012; Beutler & Clarkin, 1990; Beutler & Harwood, 2000). The patient's level of functional impairment is assessed on a continuum and can be quantified by assessing a series of factors. Level of social support, complexity of the mental illness, and chronicity of the illness are all factors that have a significant effect on a patient's functional impairment (Harwood, Beutler, & Groth-Marnat, 2011a). The level of social support is defined by the presence, or absence, and intensity of family problems, social isolation, and supportive relationships (Beutler & Clarkin, 1990). The complexity and chronicity of symptomatology are defined by the severity of presenting symptoms and chronicity of the problems (Harwood et al., 2011a). Evaluating these factors can help to determine where the patient falls in the continuum of functional impairment.

Coping style is defined as a patient's pattern of protective mechanisms along the joint dimensions of externalization and internalization (Beutler & Clarkin, 1990; Beutler & Harwood, 2000). An externalized coping style reflects a pattern in which the patient responds to change by moving against or physically away from those who provoke the problem. The predominance of this coping style signals the probable efficacy of a symptom-oriented approach (Beutler, Harwood, Kimpara, Verdirame, & Blau, 2011).

In contrast, an internalized coping style is indicative of patients who confront change or threat by emotional withdrawal and self-focus or blame (Beutler & Clarkin, 1990). An insight oriented approach proves to be more effective than those that seek direct change among those who prefer this coping style (Beutler, Harwood, Kimpara, Verdirame, & Blau, 2011a). Though all patients display some aspects both of externalizing and internalizing coping styles, it is important for the clinician to recognize both the preferred methods across situations and the unique responses drawn from the contexts in which coping styles emerge. For example, a patient may primarily utilize an internalizing coping style, unless faced with an overwhelming threatening experience. The patient may utilize a more externalizing coping style in this latter case. It would be appropriate for the clinician to select interventions that address both styles, externalization in the short run and internalization in the long run, in order to effectively address the problems (Beutler & Clarkin, 1990; Beutler & Harwood, 2000; Harwood et al., 2011a).

Clinical resistance is defined as the patient's lack of trust in the therapist or therapeutic process to the extent that they resist change. The level of resistance in a patient is also assigned on a continuum based on the patient's inclination, at one extreme, to respond in an oppositional manner or, at the other extreme, to respond with a cooperative stance (Beutler & Harwood, 2000). A resistant patient will display interpersonal reactance (i.e., oppositional resistance) or, if less oppositional, with rigid adherence to ineffective behaviors when faced with the threatened loss of power or control. Non-resistant or cooperative patients find it less threatening to give up control (Beutler & Harwood, 2000). The context of therapy requires that a resistant patient must involve themselves in the process of letting go of control. Determining the level of resistance helps the clinician to select either therapist-direct or client-direct treatment approaches so that they may best work with the patient (Beutler & Harwood, 2000).

Subjective distress refers to the amount of psychological pain the patient is experiencing: "how bad the patient is feeling" (Beutler & Harwood, 2000). The level of subjective distress is measured by assessing the range and intensity of the emotions that a patient endorses. The patient will usually present for treatment when negatively perceived emotions become too distressing to manage (Beutler & Harwood, 2000). The ability to recognize the emotion and its intensity and then to alleviate this distress by providing a place of safety and a direction for intended change are essential elements in most therapeutic practices. Persistently high levels of distress are indicative of a poor treatment prognosis and suggest the need for emphasizing the safe environment. Acute emotional reactions are associated with a stronger, more positive treatment prognosis because they are often easily relieved. Understanding the emotional reactions of the patient and determining whether emotional intensity should be raised or lowered is a key factor in the choice of an intervention (Beutler & Clarkin, 1990).

The level of subjective distress a client experiences is also highly interconnected with how motivated the client will be to make a therapeutic change. Prochaska (1979) explained that any individual undergoing a behavioral change will go through a series of stages, in which the client will become more motivated and committed to the change as they progress through the various stages. With regard to STS, identifying the client's "readiness to change" is therefore key in determining the treatment context and goals (Castonguay & Beutler, 2006).

Treatment context

Understanding the predisposing qualities that characterize the presenting patient enables the clinician to determine the optimal context and format for treatment. Treatment context is defined in STS as the "setting" of treatment, which includes the mode/format of therapy as well as the frequency/duration of therapy (Beutler & Clarkin, 1990). A treatment setting and context is designed by the sensitive therapist to reflect the level of safety that is called for by the level of subjective distress experienced by the patient (Beutler & Clarkin, 1990). Patients in a significant crisis may require in-patient treatment to establish the constancy needed, the alternative being frequent and ongoing out-patient treatment. The type of intervention, beyond that dictated by reinforcing safety needs, may vary in both in-patient and out-patient settings. If an out-patient setting is determined to be most suitable, then the mode of treatment becomes the next decision facing the effective clinician (Beutler & Clarkin, 1990). In this case, the clinician is called upon to choose to use one or more psychosocial formats (individual, group, family, couple intervention) and/or a regimen of medical/somatic treatment.

The expected frequency of sessions and duration of treatment is reliant on judgments that take into account the treatment mode and setting selected. From this knowledge, one has the information to select among a crisis intervention, short-term or long-term intervention, and the use of multiple modes and formats (Beutler & Clarkin, 1990). Decisions about the length of treatment should include addressing the question of whether a treatment of any type should be considered. Treatment should not be done if treatment is not necessary, would not be useful, could worsen the client's condition, or if there are cheaper or more convenient treatments available that are effective. Once the context of treatment has been established the actual therapeutic process can be considered, starting with the building of a therapeutic alliance (Beutler & Clarkin, 1990).

Relationship variables

The therapeutic relationship between the patient and the clinician is a powerfully significant mediating variable for the effectiveness of therapy (Beutler et al., 2012; Wampold, 2001). The therapeutic relationship is based on mutual understanding for the context and goals of therapy (Norcross, 2002). Building and maintaining a strong therapeutic relationship is crucial in any therapeutic intervention. A collaborative, supportive, trusting, respectful, and caring relationship between clinician and patient will maximize the patient's motivation to participate fully in the therapeutic process (Beutler & Clarkin, 1990; Beutler & Harwood, 2000; Norcross, 2002).

Variables relevant to the successful therapeutic relationship fall into two categories: matching compatibility criteria, and relationship enhancement skills (Beutler & Clarkin, 1990). Compatibility criteria consist of how well the patient and clinician demographic characteristics and interpersonal response patterns match. Similarities in age, gender, ethnicity, and social economic status have been shown to improve the positive perceptions of the patient in the early stages of treatment (Beutler & Clarkin, 1990). Acknowledging such similarities facilitates the patient's building of trust when starting therapy. The patient is more likely to feel they will be understood by the clinician. Ethnic similarities are particularly important for patients of a minority group, increasing their commitment to therapy (Beutler & Clarkin, 1990).

Various similarities and differences in the interpersonal response patterns between the patient and the clinician have been shown to provoke change in the patient's behaviors and beliefs (Beutler & Clarkin, 1990). In terms of similarities, conceptualizations of beliefs, goals, and attributions should be shared with the patient for a positive therapeutic relationship. Change in therapy is more likely when the patient and the clinician have opposite patterns of interpersonal behavior, in that a dependent patient would benefit more from a clinician who promotes autonomy. The role of clinician is to recognize the patient's interpersonal patterns and to be ready to adapt to the patient when appropriate (Beutler & Clarkin, 1990).

Relationship enhancement skills help to enrich and maintain the therapeutic relationship. In order to develop a strong alliance between patient and clinician, the clinician must remain sensitive to problems that emerge throughout the course of therapy. "Role induction" and "in-therapy environment management" are two processes discussed as specific examples in the STS approach to fortify the therapeutic relationship (Beutler & Clarkin, 1990). Role induction refers to efforts by the clinician to prepare the patient for the therapeutic process by educating them about what to expect as a result of treatment and the roles of both the clinician and therapist. As therapy progresses, a wide range of factors such as verbal and non-verbal behaviors, situational stimuli, and other external influences can impact the therapeutic relationship (Beutler & Clarkin, 1990). A patient undergoing therapy is inherently put in an emotionally vulnerable situation, thus the patient can be increasingly defensive in therapy. The propensity for the patient to perceive the various factors as a negative characteristic of therapy is a frequent threat in session. In-therapy environment management entails remaining aware of the factors that can influence the alliance, while being proactive in addressing therapeutic ruptures as they occur (Beutler & Clarkin, 1990; Beutler & Harwood, 2000). By constantly being aware of the therapeutic relationship as a whole throughout therapy, the therapist can maintain an effective environment (Beutler & Clarkin, 1990).

Intervention selection

The STS system assumes that each therapeutic intervention has its own specific weaknesses and strengths. Rather than focusing on specific techniques, the STS approach clusters interventions together based on the demand characteristics that accompany their implementation (e.g., the insight or symptomatic focus of the intervention, the level of control used by the therapist, the method of emotional management implied in their use, etc.) Selecting an intervention through STS is based both on knowing what procedures are effective and the level of therapist skill in applying different procedures. The procedures selected, therefore, are the responsibility of the clinician. That responsibility includes ensuring that these procedures embody the designated demand characteristics identified by STS as appropriate to establish a "fit" between a patient's dispositions and the demand characteristics of the treatment method recommended.

This latter decisional domain is the fourth in the STS system and entails the application of the interventions selected to fit the patient. Effective selection and application of interventions relies on knowing and observing interactions that occur among the three domains discussed previously. Matching a specific therapeutic intervention to a patient is a complex process and involves measuring a number of distinguished variables. Beutler and Clarkin (1990) have highlighted five areas to consider in selecting effective interventions: (1) choosing focal targets of change; (2) deciding on levels of intervention; (3) determining mediating goals; (4) building the intra-therapy structure required for initiating productive work; and (5) implementing maintenance/relapse prevention.

The initial step with regard to treatment selection is to decide the focus and goals of therapy, based both on the level of impairment and the patient's coping style. Within this context, selecting the focal targets of change must be a collaborative effort between the patient and clinician, so as to create mutual understanding about how treatment will progress and to what point (Harwood et al., 2011a). Treatment can be focused on symptomatic and/or conflictual foci. If a patient presents with a unidimensional issue, a situation-specific problem, or exhibits a preference for an externalizing coping style, then treatment can be focused on directly addressing the symptoms related to the issue. On the other hand, patients with presenting issues that are greater in their complexity, are more severe, or around which the patient exhibits an internalizing coping style, are optimally served by adopting a focus on a core conflict or theme that binds the symptoms and problems together. But there is also a pattern of change in even internalizing and complex patients that requires an initial emphasis on direct symptom change to help build the patient's confidence in the therapeutic process, before addressing the more complex/overarching thematic issues (Beutler & Clarkin, 1990).

The clinician will also have to determine the mediating goals of intervention with the patient, in order to define the sequence of anticipated change. Here the clinician needs to be aware of the patient's current "readiness for change" within the "change process" (Beutler & Harwood, 2000; Miller & Rollnick, 2012; Norcross, Krebs, & Prochaska, 2011). Effectiveness of therapy is directly contingent upon where the patient is on the dimension of readiness for change. The clinician must remain aware of the client's readiness for change as well as highlight the goals the patient has met to help drive the client through the therapeutic process (Beutler & Clarkin, 1990).

Conducting the actual therapeutic work also consists of a constant awareness of how therapy is unfolding. It is to be expected that the patient's emotional state will vary throughout therapy as a direct result of the therapeutic process. The clinician should remain attentive to the changes inherent in the process and to employ techniques that are designed to maintain the integrity of the treatment (i.e., indirect/direct observations, self-disclosure, etc.). As treatment goals are met, maintenance and relapse prevention should be given adequate attention near the terminating stages of therapy so that patients will be able to optimize the benefits of therapy well after the conclusion of treatment (Beutler & Clarkin, 1990).

The STS model represents a dispositional assessment, designed to provide systematically applied integrative care based on how a patient presents, to guide the clinician's decision-making process. Use of STS challenges the clinician to conceptualize a more effective form of therapeutic intervention based on the patient's personality. Further, the clinician is also challenged to remain mindful of the ever-changing dynamics that occur within the context of therapy (Beutler & Clarkin, 1990; Beutler & Harwood, 2000). The following section introduces "Innerlife", an assessment tool designed to be a practical and generalized form of STS.

Integrating STS into Clinical Practice/Innerlife

The concepts of STS help to outline a model that can be utilized for tailoring a treatment plan for an individual patient (Beutler & Clarkin, 1990). Utilizing the dimensions of STS helps the clinician identify important patient principles, as well as therapeutic strategies that can act as catalyst for change. Developers of STS have worked to advance this prescriptive approach to therapy into a practical program that clinicians and patients can both access and use (Beutler et al., 2008). "Innerlife" is a STS-based treatment guidance program that was designed as a web-based, patient-driven assessment tool (Beutler et al., 2008).

In order to provide the consumers of Innerlife with highly specified and sensitive measures of treatment selection, the theoretical elements of STS have been organized into a broad set of applications that is applicable to a wide variety of clinical settings (Beutler et al., 2008). STS and its extraction, STS/Innerlife assessment, both work on the assumption that the selection of effective treatment techniques and strategies is best done through the application of basic principles of change

(Beutler et al., 2000a; Harwood et al., 2011a, 2011b). Beutler and Harwood (2000) and Beutler et al. (2000a) introduced 18 guiding principles based on the empirically supported theories of STS. This list was later extended by a consolidated, APA Divisional Task Force to 61 (Castonguay & Beutler, 2006), and then consolidated to a smaller number to reduce overlap and to emphasize those with the most empirical grounding (Constantino et al., in press).

The number and articulation of the principles that act as cross-cutting guides to selecting intervention strategies have undergone many refinements throughout the development of STS. In this process, it is apparent that one of the attractive features of the STS system, when applied, is that one need not apply the entire array of principles to enhance the effectiveness of their own treatments. For example, recently in our own research, we have focused on eight of the most well established principles both to determine variations in treatment and to provide basic psychotherapy training (Holt et al., 2015). These eight principles are used as a framework in interpreting the computerized results of administering Innerlife as an aid to a student's learning how to fit available interventions to a given patient's treatment, as well as to help these students adopt a cross-cutting, empirically grounded view of psychotherapy.

These principles are categorized into five main groups (Beutler et al., 2008; Table 21.1). Adhering to the eight principles during assessment as well as throughout intervention increases the likelihood and magnitude of effecting positive change (Beutler et al., 2014).

As a means to achieve an accurate and valid prescription for treatment, Innerlife decisional criteria were written into a cloud-based system that yields treatment and self-help recommendations as well as a means for monitoring change (www.innerlife.com). The goals of this system are to: (1) identify patient responses that are reliably indicative of treatment-relevant traits and states; (2) accurately assess the level in which these indicators occur; and (3) provide narrative descriptions and recommendations of interventions whose demand characteristics fit the patient's levels of each indicator (Harwood et al., 2011a, 2011b). To accomplish their goals, the designers of Innerlife expanded the application of the STS and prescriptive therapy approaches by developing a series of patient assessments. Innerlife.com retains the theoretical context of the original STS but in a patient-reported (rather than clinician-rated) format. The design of Innerlife thus allows the patient to provide direct input into the process that will ultimately yield recommendations of treatment based on empirically founded research (Beutler et al., 2008). The results provided by the Innerlife assessments offer clinicians and patients a wealth of information that can be applied to making specific and crucial decisions in therapy (as indicated in Table 21.2). Use of Innerlife thereby facilitates the work of the clinician by directing the typically generalized decision of determining the best intervention into a series of more precise decisional domains (Harwood et al., 2011a, 2011b).

The predictive dimensions measured by the STS/Innerlife assessment system include: (1) level of functional impairment, (2) level of social support, (3) problem complexity, (4) coping style, (5) level of trait-like resistance, (6) level of subjective distress, (7) treatment preferences, (8) readiness for change, (9) demographic status

Table 21.1 Innerlife principles of therapeutic change

Impairment Principle

1. For all patients with moderate to severe impairment, the clinician should identify social service or medical care needs and arrange for attention to these needs. Those with low social support systems, in particular, need assistance from the clinician to develop social support and support services. This may mean the use of adjunctive group or multiperson interventions.

Relationship Principles

2. Therapy is likely to be beneficial if a strong working alliance is established and maintained during the course of treatment.
3. The qualities of a good working alliance are likely to be facilitated if the clinician relates to patients in an empathic way, adopts an attitude of caring, warmth, and acceptance, and an attitude of congruence or authenticity.
4. Clinicians are likely to resolve alliance ruptures when addressing such ruptures in an empathetic and flexible way.

Resistance Principle

5. In dealing with the resistant client, the clinician's use of directive therapeutic interventions should be planned to inversely correspond with the patient's manifested level of resistant traits and states. Non-confrontational strategies are most helpful in working with such patients.

Coping Style Principles

6. Patients whose personalities are characterized by relatively high "externalizing" styles (e.g., impulsivity, social gregariousness, emotional lability, and external blame for problems) benefit more from direct behavioral change and symptom reduction efforts, including building new skills and managing impulses, than they do from procedures that are designed to facilitate insight and self-awareness.
7. Patients whose personalities are characterized by relatively high "internalizing" styles (e.g., low levels of impulsivity, indecisiveness, self-introspection, and overcontrol) tend to benefit more from procedures that foster self-inspection, self-understanding, insight, interpersonal attachments, and self-esteem that they do from procedures that aim at directly altering symptoms and building new social skills.

Readiness Principle

8. Patients who are in more advanced stages of readiness for change (e.g., preparation, action, maintenance) are more likely to improve in psychotherapy than those in lower stages of readiness (pre-contemplation, contemplation).

relative to resource support, (10) diversity implications for change, and (11) risk status (Beutler et al., 2008). The various domains assessed serve as indicators for predicting the patient's most likely response to treatments, as established by contemporary research evidence. Knowing how a patient scores on the measured qualities can give the clinician an early conceptualization of the expectations of therapy based on a large normative sample of patients, as well as guide the best course for treatment (Harwood et al., 2011a, 2011b).

The Innerlife assessment also includes items that measure the presence of 22 major symptom groupings (e.g., anxiety and distress, depression and hopelessness,

Table 21.2 Decisional levels assessed through the utilization of Innerlife

- Assessment of six patient predisposing dimensions.
- Determination of whether the patient's presenting issues could be effectively treated by psychotherapy.
- Identification of certain treatment types that would not be beneficial to the patient.
- Specification of compatible clinicians that are likely to be highly effective in working with the patient to meet his/her therapeutic goals.
- Identification of tailored self-help resources for the patient.
- Assignment of the appropriate level of care and treatment context for the patient by determining the patient's: level of subjective distress, availability of social support, and the presenting issue's complexity/chronicity.
- Guidelines for the therapeutic relationship as well as determining the level of family intervention.
- Matching different types of interventions to the patient's particular needs.

disturbances of thought process or content, addiction, thoughts of harming self), as well as more a specified list of secondary symptoms that may also require clinical attention (e.g., attention and concentration issues, avoidance of eating, family conflict, etc.) to complete the holistic conceptualization of the patient's case (Beutler et al., 2008). Recently, the designers of Innerlife have incorporated the use of a minority stress scale. The scale is used as a measure of subjective stress experienced by the patient as a direct result of being a racial, sexual, or other type of minority (Chu et al., 2013).

The Innerlife program consists of both patient self-report and clinician response versions. The items are response-prompted and offered in both English and Spanish. Results are indicated by a T score and compared with a normative sample. Symptom scores outside the normal distribution are indicated as needing clinical attention. Completing the measures on Innerlife provides the clinician and patient with graphical representations of the results, making the data easier to read and more accessible to various members of the patient's treatment team (Beutler et al., 2008).

The completed measures are designed to provide both clinicians and patients with the most efficacious treatment options (Harwood et al., 2011a, 2011b). Clinicians can use the Innerlife program to plot a treatment plan while tracking the patient's trajectory throughout treatment, while patients can use Innerlife either independently or within the context of therapy to advocate for their own treatment options. Patients who use Innerlife as a tool to initiate the process of seeking intervention can be connected with therapists that would be most effective in treating the patient. They are also given a personalized list of relevant self-help resources (Harwood et al., 2011a, 2011b). Specifically for clinicians, Innerlife can be used to assess the patient's treatment progression, which includes the patient's tracked progression throughout treatment as well as the projected trajectories of future progress based on a regression analysis of similar patient populations (Harwood et al., 2011a, 2011b). Altogether, Innerlife is a powerful therapeutic tool designed to inspire therapeutic change in a patient by focusing on the best-founded related principles (Beutler et al., 2008).

Summary

STS is the hallmark of the prescriptive approach to therapeutic intervention. Unlike traditional approaches to psychotherapy, the developers of STS and Innerlife understood that each differently styled therapeutic approach has its own inherent strengths and weaknesses. The efficacy of each approach is thereby dependent on the individual to which it is being applied. The clinician can attend to the principles that promote change in a patient by focusing on four distinct decisional domains: (1) the patient's predisposing factors; (2) the contexts of the treatment; (3) relationship qualities within treatment; and (4) connecting the therapeutic approach to the patient.

Innerlife embodies the spirit of STS by offering clinicians and patients a structure for intervention based on empirically based evidence. The validity of Innerlife has been shown in various clinical settings and its application towards clinical treatment continues to grow. Structuring therapy based on the patient's personality, presenting issues, and personal goals creates a form of treatment based on the aforementioned principles of change. Innerlife is an assessment designed to measure all such principles of the patient throughout treatment. The web-based assessment is a clinical tool with unmatched ability to support patients and clinicians.

References

Beutler, L.E. (1983). *Eclectic Psychotherapy: A Systematic Approach.* New York: Pergamon Press.

Beutler, L.E. (1991). Have all won and must all have prizes? Revisiting Luborsky et al.'s verdict. *Journal of Consulting and Clinical Psychology, 59* (2), 226–232.

Beutler, L.E. (2009). Making science matter in clinical practice: Redefining psychotherapy. *Clinical Psychology: Science & Practice, 16* (3), 301–317.

Beutler, L.E., & Berren, M.R. (1995). *Integrative Assessment of Adult Personality.* New York: Guilford Press.

Beutler, L.E., & Clarkin, J.F. (1990). *Systematic Treatment Selection: Toward Targeted Therapeutic Interventions.* New York: Brunner/Mazel, Inc.

Beutler, L.E., Clarkin, J.F., & Bongar, B. (2000a). *Guidelines for the Systematic Treatment of the Depressed Patient.* New York: Oxford University Press.

Beutler, L.E., Engle, D., Mohr, D., Daldrup, R.J., Bergan, J., Meredith, K., & Merry, W. (1991). Predictors of differential response to cognitive, experiential and self-directed psychotherapeutic procedures. *Journal of Consulting and Clinical Psychology, 59* (2), 333–340.

Beutler, L.E., Forrester, B., Gallagher-Thompson, D., Thompson, L., & Tomlins, J.B. (2012). Common, specific, and treatment fit variables in psychotherapy outcome. *Journal of Psychotherapy Integration, 22* (3), 255–281.

Beutler, L.E., & Harwood, T.M. (2000). *Prescriptive Psychotherapy: A Practical Guide to Systematic Treatment Selection.* New York: Oxford University Press.

Beutler, L.E., Harwood, T.M., Bertoni, M., & Thomann, J. (2006). Systematic Treatment Selection and Prescriptive Therapy. In G. Stricker, & J. Gold (Eds.), *A Casebook of Psychotherapy Integration* (pp. 29–41). Washington, DC: American Psychological Association.

Beutler, L.E., Harwood, T.M., Kimpara, S., Verdirame, D., & Blau, K. (2011a). Coping style. *Journal of Clinical Psychology, 67* (2), 176–183.

Beutler, L.E., Haug, N.A., Kimpara, S., Macias, S., Shiloff, N., Goldblum, P.B., ... Temkin, R.S. (2014) *Systematic treatment selection: How to implement eight evidenced-based principles into supervision.* Poster session presented at the 122nd Annual Convention of the American Psychological Association, Washington, DC.

Beutler, L.E., & Malik, M.L. (2002). *Rethinking the DSM: A Psychological Perspective.* Washington, DC: American Psychological Association.

Beutler, L.E., Moleiro, C., & Malik, M. (2000b). *The UC Santa Barbara Study of therapy to patients: First results.* Paper presented at the annual meeting of the Society for Psychotherapy Research (International), Chicago, IL.

Beutler, L.E., Rosner, R., Groth-Marnat, G., & Harwood, T.M. (2011b). Introduction to integrative assessment of adult personality. In T.M. Harwood, L.E. Beutler, & G. Groth-Marnat (Eds.), *Integrative Assessment of Adult Personality* (3rd ed.) (pp. 1–31). New York: Guilford Press.

Beutler, L.E., Williams, O.B., & Norcross, J.N. (2008). *Innerlife.com. A copyrighted software package for treatment planning.* Available at www.innerlife.com

Budd, R., & Hughes, I. (2009). The dodo bird verdict – controversial, inevitable and important: A commentary on 30 years of meta-analyses. *Clinical Psychology and Psychotherapy, 16* (6), 510–522.

Castonguay, L.G., & Beutler, L.E. (2006). *Principles of Therapeutic Change that Work.* New York: Oxford University.

Castonguay, L.G., Constantino, M., & Beutler, L.E. (Eds) (in press). *Principles of Psychotherapy that Work: Applications, Vol. II.* New York: Oxford University Press.

Chu, J., Floyd, R., Diep, H., Pardo, S., Goldblum, P., & Bongar, B. (2013). A tool for the culturally competent assessment of suicide: The Cultural Assessment of Risk for Suicide (CARS) Measure. *Psychological Assessment, 25* (2), 424–434.

Fisher, D., Beutler, L.E., & Williams, O.B. (1999). Making assessment relevant to treatment planning: The STS clinician rating form. *Journal of Clinical Psychology, 55* (7), 825–842.

Frances, A., Clarkin, J.F., & Perry, S. (1984). *Differential Therapeutics in Psychiatry: The Art and Science of Treatment Selection.* New York: Brunner/Mazel.

Garfield, S.L. (1980). *Psychotherapy: An Eclectic Approach.* New York: John Wiley & Sons, Ltd.

Gold, J., & Stricker, G. (2006). Introduction: An overview of psychotherapy integration. In G. Stricker, & J. Gold (Eds.), *A Casebook of Psychotherapy Integration* (pp. 3–16). Washington, DC: American Psychological Association.

Harwood, T.M., Beutler, L.E., & Groth-Marnat, G. (2011a). *Integrative Assessment of Adult Personality* (3rd ed.). New York: Guilford Press.

Harwood, T.M., Beutler, L.E., Williams, O.B., & Stegman, R.S. (2011b). Identifying treatment-relevant assessment: Systematic Treatment Selection/InnerLife. In T.M. Harwood, L.E. Beutler, & G. Groth-Marnat (Eds.), *Integrative Assessment of Adult Personality* (3rd ed.) (pp. 61–79). New York: Guilford Press.

Holt, H., Beutler, L.E., Kimpara, S., Macias, S., Haug, N.A., Shiloff, N., ... Stein, M. (2015). Evidence-based supervision: Tracking outcome and teaching principles of change in clinical supervision to bring science to integrative practice. *Psychotherapy, 52* (2), 185–189.

Housley, J., & Beutler, L.E. (2007). *Treating Victims of Mass Disaster and Terrorism.* Hogrefe & Huber Publishers.

Lazarus, A. (1981). *The Practice of Multimodal Therapy.* New York: McGraw-Hill Book Company.

Miller, W.R., & Rollnick, S. (2012). *Motivational Interviewing: Helping People Change* (3rd ed.). New York: Guilford Press.

Nguyen, T., Bertoni, M., Charvat, M., Gheytanchi, A., & Beutler, L.E. (2007). Systematic Treatment Selection (STS): A review and future directions. *International Journal of Behavioral Consultation and Therapy, 3* (1), 13–29.

Norcross, J. (2002). *Psychotherapy Relationships that Work: Evidence-Based Relationships.* New York: Oxford University Press.

Norcross, J.C., Krebs, P.M., & Prochaska, J.O. (2011). Stages of change. *Journal of Clinical Psychology, 67* (2), 143–154.

Norcross, J.C., & Newman, C.F. (2003). Psychotherapy integration: Setting the context. In J.C. Norcross, & M.R. Goldfried (Eds.), *Handbook of Psychotherapy Integration* (pp. 3–45). New York: Oxford University Press

Prochaska, J.O. (1979). *Systems of Psychotherapy: A Transtheoretical Analysis.* Homewood, IL: Dorsey.

Santoro, S.O., Kister, K.M., Karpiak, C.P., & Norcross, J.C. (2004). *Clinical psychologists in the 2000s: A national study.* Paper presented at the annual meeting of the Eastern Psychological Association, Washington, DC.

Wampold, B.E. (2001). *The Great Psychotherapy Debate: Models, Methods, and Findings.* Mahwah, NJ: Erlbaum.

22

Personality Assessment Paradigms: Issues and Challenges

Vijay Parkash and Updesh Kumar
Defence Institute of Psychological Research, Delhi, India

As social beings, most people continuously try to understand and evaluate the behavior and personality of the others they meet, knowingly or unknowingly. People try to evaluate whether someone is introvert, outgoing, quiet, happy-go-lucky, honest, social, proud, indifferent, anxious, perceptive, critical or introspective. The understanding of such characteristics has an impact on the quality of relationships among different people. According to the tendency of persistence of these characteristics in someone to certain specific degrees across different times and circumstances, one tends to think of them as a specific type of personality. Most interpersonal interactions among different individuals involve some sort of a personality assessment. Indeed, most people are both unaware subjects and unconscious administrators of subjective personality assessments with every interpersonal encounter, and they tend to indentify others or themselves being identified with broad descriptions of personality makeup (Ellis, Abrams, & Abrams, 2009).

Most people are inclined to describe others in certain categories of personal attributes. Since it lies in basic human nature to try to understand other people's enduring traits or dispositions, description of personality in various terminologies and in the form of different models has been at the centre of the field of psychology. There is an abundance of adjective terms in the English language to describe personal attributes or types of human character. Though there are plentiful personality descriptor terms, the question arises of whether these terms only describe some part of overt behavior, or do they represent the enduring personality traits of an individual? The evidence existing in the form of various personality models, theories, and conceptualizations seems to suggest that most personality psychologists appear to agree that certain combinations of these English terms, along some specific dimensions, are undeniably useful in describing human personality. There exist several models that describe personality in terms of different numbers of factors. As one of the widely accepted descriptions, the Five-Factor Model by McCrae and Costa (1997) best describes the dimensions of personality. However, there are other descriptions

The Wiley Handbook of Personality Assessment, First Edition. Edited by Updesh Kumar.
© 2016 John Wiley & Sons, Ltd. Published 2016 by John Wiley & Sons, Ltd.

that describe personality in terms of two factors (Block, 1995, 2001), three factors (Eysenck, 1991, 1992; Eysenck & Eysenck, 1968), six factors (Ashton & Lee, 2002), and even 16 factors (Delhees & Cattell, 1970). All these models have ample research evidence to support them and are followed by various researchers. Contrary to some other areas of study, personality psychology does not yet have universally accepted principles, and research in this domain is still in progress. Different psychologists still subscribe to different schools of personality description (Ellis, Abrams, & Abrams, 2009). Therefore, for a researcher in personality psychology there is a need to look more deeply and examine various theoretical models that explain human personality in varied ways.

Associated with different explanations provided for human personality are the varied methods, paradigms, and measures utilized to assess personality of a person. As it remains a challenge for a researcher as to which model should be subscribed to in order to arrive at the most comprehensive and best understanding of human personality, another big challenge is about adopting the best assessment paradigm and most appropriate methodology for personality assessment. Moreover, what comes prior is the issue of adequate analytic awareness of such challenges for the personality psychologist. In the present chapter we attempt to put together all such issues and challenges related to personality assessment paradigms and methodologies. In the forthcoming sections we try to comment briefly upon the personality assessment realm, and will endeavor to analytically compare various personality assessment paradigms for various advantages and disadvantages linked with the use of each of them.

Personality Testing or Personality Assessment

The term used to define certain operations that are utilized to assess and describe people is generally referred to as measurement by the psychologists (Berdie, Layton, Swanson, & Hagenah, 1963; p. 69). Psychologists are often concerned with objective descriptions of behavior, and according to Berdie and colleagues (1963), the problem before them is to construct an efficient framework in which the behavior of an individual can be described. The same is true in the case of personality psychologists. The procedure used to arrive at the solution of the cited problem is broadly known as testing. In testing, we are often concerned with prediction of future behavior by means of measuring the results of previous learning as they are expressed at the present moment. The characteristics of the individual are inferred by using the individual's responses at a given moment. While inferring the characteristics, it is assumed that the behavioral correlates can be identified with a response (Berdie et al., 1963).

Psychological testing and assessment are most of the time used interchangeably. Although psychological assessment is similar to psychological testing, it usually involves a more comprehensive assessment of the individual that involves the integration of information from multiple sources, such as different kinds of tests, as well as information from personal interviews, observations, family histories, peer ratings, and so forth. A psychological test is one of the sources of data used within the process of assessment; and usually more than one test is used in any psychological assessment as it is a more complex, detailed, in-depth process (Rani & Parkash, 2010). This connotation might be seen by some researchers as too simplistic to include the multitude of activities involved in assessment. Handler and Meyer (1998) made the distinction between testing and assessment more clear:

> Testing is a relatively straightforward process wherein a particular test is administered to obtain a specific score. Subsequently, a descriptive meaning can be applied to the score based on normative, nomothetic findings. … Psychological assessment, however, is a quite different enterprise. The focus … is on taking a variety of test derived pieces of information, obtained from multiple methods of assessment, and placing these data in the context of historical information, referral information, and behavioral observations in order to generate a cohesive and comprehensive understanding of the person being evaluated (Handler & Meyer, 1998, pp. 4–5).

In a broader and more categorical way, assessment in general and personality assessment in particular is more than an isolated sampling of behavior and a distinct observation of a few selected behavioral expressions; rather, it is an elaborative conceptualization of ongoing inner dynamics and dispositions (Rorer, 1990). In other words, personality assessment must be targeted to explore what a person *does* as well as what that person *is like*. This assessment of what a person does and what they are like is important in predicting their behavior (Smith & Archer, 2008). Proponents of different models of personality assert that personality can be best assessed by the tool that they have developed to assess it. And, while making such assumptions, the issues that are unconsciously ignored are those of the limitations associated with every measure and the existence of better methodologies. In the following sections, attempts are made to put forth the advantages and disadvantages associated with different methodologies of personality assessment.

Qualitative, Quantitative, and Mixed Approaches

When a researcher has to plan for a comprehensive personality assessment, one of the first decisions that one has to make is which assessment approach would be the best fit for the targeted assessment. Different scholars use different approaches depending upon their research objectives. These approaches may be qualitative, quantitative, or using mixed methods. The question before the researcher is – which one should be used? Why should one approach be preferred over the other? What are the advantages and disadvantages of each?

Qualitative approach

A qualitative approach to personality assessment uses open-ended descriptive data providing an elaborative picture of the way people feel and act and why they do so in certain particular ways. This approach is based on gathering information in non-numerical form that might include responses to open-ended questions, conversation dialogs, daily diaries, and so on. Like any other approach, the qualitative approach has its own strengths and limitations. Its biggest advantage is the wide latitude of data that it provides about one's behavior by recording attitudes and feelings, which can, in turn, offer significant assessment information about the object of study. There remains the scope of creating openness and encouraging the participant to further explain their responses so that maximum appropriate information can be gathered. The open-ended responses provide an opportunity to let people's individual experiences come out, so as to educe a comprehensive causal sequence for the specific thoughts and behavior of the respondent. Further, while qualitative data is gathered, contextual information is gathered which provides the researcher a basis for his/her conclusions, and this way qualitative data helps to avoid the formation of prejudgement or bias on the part of the researcher. Another advantage of the qualitative approach is that respondents are not constrained to a predetermined set of possible responses – they are free to answer any way they would like.

Many researchers prefer the qualitative approach for its obvious advantages, but simultaneously it carries some negative points. The major limitation of qualitative data analysis concerns the smaller size of the study sample. Since the gathering of qualitative data generally consumes more resources and time, generally fewer participants are studied. This lesser representation of the target population reduces the generalizability of the findings. Further, making systematic comparisons is relatively difficult with qualitative data, as participants are likely to give widely differing and subjective responses. Qualitative data information cannot be interpreted by anyone or everyone like objective tests; rather, it requires experts to interpret it, and still there remains a probability of subjective influence on the results depending on the skills of the researcher, which may in turn influence the reliability of findings with different researchers. Often a qualitative approach consumes a lot of time in collecting data as well as interpreting it. In addition, since time is generally linked with expenditure, qualitative approaches are more costly and may not be affordable by every researcher (Creswell, 2013; Maxwell, 2012).

Quantitative approach

As the qualitative approach has certain limitations, now the question before the researcher is whether a quantitative approach is the answer. Again a dilemma arises about the evaluation of positive and negative points of the quantitative approach. As all of the data collected are quantified or counted or numbered, one advantageous point that can be associated with the use of a quantitative approach is that this approach seems quite an efficient method for gathering information from a large number of participants. Objective tests or multiple choice-type surveys are an example of it (Creswell, 2013). Quantitative data can help to give better comparative analyses, and better psychometric properties of quantitatively oriented tools can help to formulate new theories and/or test existing hypotheses in an error-free way (Ackroyd & Hughes, 1981; Popper, 1959). Since a quantitative approach can provide data from large numbers of participants in less time and with less specialized training required on the part of the researcher, so this approach is also less expensive. And with the introduction of and increasingly frequent use of online data collection and computerized scoring and databases, less monitoring is required from the assessor, which further reduces the cost and time liabilities. Hence, it may be said that the analysis of the information gathered by quantitative methods is relatively more objective, specific, and scientific compared with other assessment methods.

Looking at the limitations of the quantitative approach, the researcher may find that it does not usually provide a detailed explanation of the underlying dynamics of behavior beyond the information sought through specific objective items, and therefore quantitative measures remain insufficient to understand and tap changes in feelings, other emotional states, and behavior; and due to this fact, they tend to have lesser validity in a real sense of understanding of human behavior. As a further disadvantage, in the quantitative methodology adopted in the form of multiple choice-type response options, there is a likelihood of respondents having limited choice of response alternatives, and they may be in a dilemma if they feel that none of the response options best describes their behavior (Creswell, 2013). The issue of socially desirable responding or faking is also a big challenge to quantitative measures. There is no certain way to quantify the exact extent of social desirability, or deceit or truthfulness in a response, even though plenty of attempts have been made to tap the same. Linked with the likelihood of different people reading differently into different items is the likelihood of a component of respondent subjectivity. Furthermore, a researcher's subjectivity is also probable in the form of designing the scoring for different objective responses (Ackroyd & Hughes, 1981; Popper, 1959).

Having insights into the advantages and disadvantages of both qualitative and quantitative approaches, the bigger question before the scientist is to decide which of the two approaches should be preferred and why. Should the priority be the richness of data? Should one ignore the aspects of time, cost, and specialized interpretational training? Is compromising on any of the aspects justified if the target is comprehensive personality assessment? And, can there be a middle path? These challenging questions make a researcher consider a mixed methods approach. So let us discuss the advantages and disadvantages of a mixed methods approach a little.

Mixed approach

In a general sense, a mixed method approach is the one that integrates both qualitative and quantitative aspects in such a way that the information collected through the qualitative and quantitative approaches complements each other. It might be achieved by combining qualitative and quantitative items on the same measure. The qualitative items may provide in-depth information regarding certain more integral behavioral aspects, and the quantitative approach may provide countable or numerical information on certain surface-level behavioral traits. Is it what suits the objective of the researcher? If the answer is yes, then the next issue is to evaluate whether it is all advantageous, or whether there are any limitations linked to the use of this mixed approach. The advantage of using mixed methods may be believed to be inherent in the balance that it can create between efficient, specific data collection and detailed contextual analysis. The quantitative part can quickly capture potentially large amounts of data, and the qualitative part can provide the thorough contextual information and may facilitate better interpretation of the quantitative data and deeper understanding of the domain under study (Smith & Davis, 2012). But will it be time- and cost-effective? Although the costs can be mitigated if qualitative data are taken only from a smaller representative sample, the challenge of a mixed method approach is to ensure that the data from the two approaches provide the complete required information and are not duplicated, because duplication of data will obviously double the costs and efforts (Smith & Davis, 2012).

Keeping all the above in mind, another challenging issue is to decide which approach should be used – qualitative, quantitative, or mixed methods. The biggest hurdle in the mind of the researcher is the fact that none of the three approaches can be termed the best. And while the researcher considers the configuration of each approach with the objective of personality assessment, the aspect of following a specific descriptive model explaining personality again comes to influence the thought of whether the entire gamut of personality will actually be assessed or not. Although the approach that best fits with the specific model is usually the right one, the challenge of the various linkages of the issues explained above will stand firm in front of the psychologist.

Assessment Measures

One important goal of psychological assessment is using measures that accurately represent particular theoretical constructs. Which measure should be used should be decided after weighing the strengths and limitations of assessment methods in terms of methodological feasibility and their potential to accurately measure the personality constructs. The issue of validity of the measures is quite challenging for the researcher, as psychological and personality constructs are "postulated" or inferred characteristics of an individual. There are numerous intangible constructs in psychology; if we cannot physically see personality traits, do they really exist or not (Cronbach & Meehl, 1955)? Social scientists have long been attempting to infer what people are like and trying to measure abstract and hypothetical constructs like conscientiousness, to fully understand the way people behave and why they behave that particular way (Smith, 2005). In order to understand personality dynamics, it is imperative that these abstract traits are measured "in a convincing, valid way" (Smith, 2005, p. 396). Therefore, abstract personality constructs can only be understood properly if the validity of the measure is unquestionable (McDonald, 2008). It is a general notion as well as an existing fact that personality psychologists primarily rely on self-report measures (Robins, Tracy, & Sherman, 2007). However, there exist several different types of measures to assess personality, and it is not sufficient to simply assume the accuracy of any one measure in fully representing the desired personality trait. Every measure has its own advantages and disadvantages. Depending on specific assessment requirements, researchers use projective measures, self-reports, peer or informant ratings, and other behavioral assessment methods. In the following sections we attempt to put forth the issues related to different measures, so that the researcher has a wider range of information to choose a specific measure.

Objective Questionnaires/Self-Report Measures

Using objective self-report measures and getting direct information from people regarding a particular behavioral trait is quite common in personality psychology (Schwarz, 1999). The most preferred method for personality assessment seems to be asking people to respond directly to questions or statements about the way they feel, think, and behave. Citing supporting evidence, an analysis conducted by Vazire (2006) showed that self-report measures were used in 98% of the research related to assessment of personality traits published in the *Journal of Research in Personality* during the year 2003. Moreover, the self-report was the only measure that was used in 70% of these studies (Vazire, 2006). A similar observation was made by Kagan (2007) who found that self-report questionnaires were used in more than 95% of studies reported in the *Journal of Personality* in 2006. A poll conducted among psychologists by Robins et al. (2007) showed that self-reports are "by far" the most frequently used measurement methods for the purpose of personality assessment. By this evidence it is clear that the use of self-report objective personality measures, like questionnaires and inventories, is central to personality assessment. What makes psychologists use them so much? Some important questions in the mind of the researcher regarding the test being used may be: does the test answer his questions? Does the test have adequate psychometric properties? Is the test appropriate for the test-taker? Is the associated time and cost less than the benefit? It appears that the above-cited prevalence of self-report tests suggests an affirmative answer to these questions. Certainly there must be many advantages linked to their use. What are those advantages? And, are there only advantages and no disadvantages? Although some of the advantages and disadvantages may be inferred from those of quantitative measures in the preceding sections, finding more precise answers to these specific questions remains a challenge to the personality researcher.

Advantages and disadvantages of use of self-reports

The researchers favoring the use of self-report measures assert that if one has to know more about someone, he or she should directly approach that particular person. The most revealing and precise information about any personality trait is likely to be provided by the individual possessing that trait (McDonald, 2008). Pioneers like McCrae and Costa (1999) also posit that people can make a large number of revelations about themselves through the expression of certain "relatively enduring patterns of thoughts, feelings, and actions" (p. 140). Some other personality psychologists (e.g., Paulhus & Vazire, 2007) also argue in favor of using self-reports, and assert that the information provided by the individual himself involves motivational and other introspective details about oneself which someone else cannot be aware of, and they further say that "no one else has access to more information" than oneself (Paulhus & Vazire, 2007, p. 227). Paulhus and Vazire (2007) believe that respondents can individually identify with the test questions/items and feel more motivated to talk about themselves compared with others. It is common sense that the information that comes direct from the horse's mouth is the most precise (McDonald, 2008).

On the advantageous side, use of self-report objective measures is more practical; adequately large data can be collected from a larger sample with relatively less cost and time (Kline, 1993; Paulhus & Vazire, 2007); it can be used by anyone without any effect on reliability and/or validity of results; the obtained data are easily and quickly scorable and quantifiable (Kline, 1993); analysis of its findings is relatively more objective and scientific; the obtained data can be suitably used for comparison purposes; and the findings may help propound new theories and conceptualizations. Although there are many positive aspects regarding use of self-report objective measures in personality assessment, they are never free from limitations. Their limitations may begin in the item construction stage itself, and even the structure of the questions may influence whether the response of the subject accurately represents the target personality trait. It is believed that "… minor changes in question wording, question format, or question context can result in major changes in the obtained results" (Schwarz, 1999, p. 93, as cited by McDonald, 2008).

With self-report measures, there remains a probability of errors on the part of the respondent. Response biases (Moskowitz, 1986), socially desirable responding (Paulhus, 1991), acquiescent responding, and extreme responding (Paulhus, 1991) are examples of some of the common erroneous response tendencies of the respondents (Paulhus & Vazire, 2007). Such errors are likely to affect the validity of the measure negatively, and may thereby defeat the very purpose of assessment of any target personality trait, which poses a serious challenge to personality psychologists. Nevertheless, there have been measurement efforts devoted to tapping various types of response biases. However, another associated apprehension concerning credibility of the subject is that socially desirable responding is not necessarily due to the fact that people want to create a specific impression; one school of thought believes that an individual's distorted outlook about oneself is the cause of his/her positive responding (John & Robins, 1994). In this view, it is the unrealistic or faulty self-perceptions about themselves that provoke the biased responding in the individual (Fiske & Taylor, 1991), and such a situation cannot be corrected or tapped by using scales or measures of social desirability. Another potential issue with self-reports is the long time taken to develop a test, keeping in mind the need to establish construct validity of the measure and tap cultural variations in individual response styles (Paulhus & Vazire, 2007).

As another disadvantage, some researchers believe that questionnaires fail to help understand some information related to feelings, emotions, and behavior; the information collected is quite limited in scope and relatively unexplanatory. It is considered that questionnaires have relatively less validity to comprehensively cover the target domain, since the extent of lying and truthfulness in the responses cannot be estimated exactly. The items may be subjectively interpreted by the respondent and may be understood in a different sense than the researcher intended to target. Also, there remains a likelihood of subjectivity involved on the part of the researcher while making certain test-related assumptions, scoring, and interpretation (Ackroyd & Hughes, 1981; Popper, 1959).

Another fascinating question and a probable limitation is about people's knowledge of themselves, in the sense of being able to accurately convey what the self-report measure is intended to determine. Kagan (1988) opines that people do not possess sufficient self-awareness about why they do the things they do. He later reminisced that prior to the emergence and prominence of factor-derived personality traits, projective tests were used to assess personality rather than self-reports, somewhat due to the belief that individuals were not able to provide absolute and precise information about themselves (Kagan, 2007, as cited by McDonald, 2008). Even with the prevailing use of self-report measures, there are many challenging issues linked with their use. One big issue is that even considering the wide use of objective self-report measures, what type of test development, out of classical test theory or item response theory, should be adopted.

Objective test development: classical test theory (CTT) or item response theory (IRT)?

The purpose of a psychological measurement is assessing an individual's traits using valid and adequate theoretical models with respect to reliability and scientific interpretation of the obtained outputs (Erguven, 2013). One of the most salient and challenging phenomena related to the measurements in the social sciences is the unreliability – measuring the same attribute twice often yields two different results (Steyer, 2001). The adequacy of its measurement is the prime basis of science, and if the measures used are scientifically poor, then they will provide a feeble base for research (Foster & Cone, 1995). Tests are essentially required measures in most cases of psychological assessment. Therefore, a serious challenge to the researcher is related to the test development process. As seriously debated in recent times, classical test theory (CTT) or item response theory (IRT) are the two main theoretical test development approaches available to the researcher, and s/he has to decide to choose one. Which one should be used and why? Why not the other? Which one will better suit the purpose of constructing a specific type of test as desired by the researcher? These are a few of the prominent questions which demand answers before beginning to develop a test intended to assess personality. Accordingly, the researcher first needs to have an understanding of both these paradigms and their strengths and weaknesses.

Classical test theory. Having an insight into the conceptualizations and their associated facts, we can start with an understanding of CTT, which has been used for over a century. CTT, which is also regarded as "true-score theory," considers an observed test score as made up of two components, a "true score" and an "error," and both of these components are considered to be independent of each other. The true score on a particular construct and a particular test is considered to remain constant and consistent across parallel test forms and across different testing times, whereas the error is considered to be unique to the specific measurement, and may not be the same on another measurement of the same construct. CTT assumes that it is not possible to observe the true score directly, and it is the extent of consistency of performance from one test score to another that reflects the index of true score (Stage, 2003).

CTT is a simple model that explains the ways in which the observed scores on a psychological test can be influenced by errors of measurement (Marcoulides, 1999). Being the earliest theory of measurement (Gulliksen, 1950), for a long time CTT assumptions have been the basis for examining the psychometric properties of the measures of personality. As reflected in terms of the true score, the main objective of CTT is to estimate the reliability of the computed test scores.

> Under all possible conditions at various times, using all possible similar items, the mean of all these observed scores would be the most unbiased estimate of the subject's ability. Thus, mean is defined as the true score. In any single administration of a test, the observed score is most likely different from the true score. (Suen, 1990, as cited by Erguven, 2013, p. 24)

The difference is caused by the inclusion of a random error score in the total observed score. The goal of CTT while developing psychological tests is to minimize this error score (McBride, 2001). In other words, CTT assigns importance to the reliability of a test and considers it as an attribute of the test data and not the assessment itself (Erguven, 2013). Using the concept of error of true score, a number of useful relationships have been established using the CTT model. A few of these are "the relation between test length and test precision (reliability); estimates of the precision of difference scores and change scores; the estimation of properties of composites of two or more measures; the estimation of the degree to which indices of relationship between different measurements are attenuated by the error of measurement in each" (Stage, 2003).

CTT is a relatively simple model and its prime focus is on the test-level information. Along with the test reliability, item-level statistics including item difficulty and item discrimination are also given importance by CTT. The proportion of participants giving the correct answer is used as the index for the item difficulty (in an inverse sense). Item discrimination index is represented by the correlation coefficient between the individual item score and the total test score (Stage, 2003). Other positive points linked to CTT models include the requirement of smaller sample sizes for the analyses (which is advantageous keeping the field tests in mind), relatively simple mathematical analyses compared with IRT, conceptually simple and straight model parameter estimation, and analyses not requiring strict goodness-of-fit studies (Erguven, 2013; Hambleton & Jones, 1993).

Although the focal points of CTT are adequate as per some of the psychometric requirements in psychological measures, CTT models are considered weak because the assumptions of these models are not considered to be robust as they are easily met by test data. CTT models are criticized for the fact that they are based on "... rather arbitrarily defined test score variables. If these test score variables are not well chosen, any model based on them is not well-founded, either" (Erguven, 2013, p. 27). Stage (2003) has also put forth certain shortcomings of CTT that a researcher should keep in mind while making his measurement decision. One limitation is that item difficulty and item discrimination indices are examinee group-dependent. Another limitation is the dependency of observed and true scores on changes in test difficulty. Further, the assumption of equal errors of measurement for all examinees is also criticized, citing its lesser precision in ability estimates of low-ability and high-ability participants (Stage, 2003). This assumption of measurement precision being constant across the entire trait range is likely to be wrong, as measurement precision may not be constant for different people (Fraley, Waller, & Brennan, 2000). Furthermore, the CTT framework focuses only on reliability and it almost never addresses the issue of model validity (Progar & Sočan, 2008).

Item response theory. Keeping the design, construction and evaluation of tests in mind, during the last few decades item response theory (IRT) has become a vital alternative to CTT. Looking at the limitations of CTT, with IRT it is possible to obtain item characteristics that are *not* group-dependent; ability scores that are *not* test-dependent; and a measure of precision for each ability level (Stage, 2003). Where CTT was considered to be test-based, IRT is considered as item-based. IRT is also known as "latent trait theory," as models of IRT specify how the probability of giving a specific response to a particular item depends on the attribute to be measured or the latent variable (Steyer, 2001). IRT incorporates a scale for the underlying latent variable being measured by a set of items, and reflecting the presence of a linking mechanism, items are calibrated with respect to this same scale (Edelen & Reeve, 2007).

Looking on the positive aspects of IRT, since IRT has test items as its central elements rather than the test as a whole, a better analysis of each item of the test is possible. It creates the possibility of comparing between the latent traits of different individuals administered with questionnaires having common items, and it is also possible to compare individuals from the same population administered with completely different tests. Further, IRT models do not assume measurement precision being constant for all people (Fraley, Waller, & Brennan, 2000). IRT models are considered strong models as their assumptions of unidimensionality (i.e., only one ability being measured by the test items) and local independence (i.e., responses to any pair of test items are statistically independent when the abilities influencing the test are held constant) may be difficult to meet (Hambleton & Jones, 1993). Moreover, the possibility of computer adaptive testing with IRT also adds certain advantages.

On the critical side, in order to achieve possible advantages of IRT it is necessary to have a fit between the model and the test data. A poorly fitting IRT model will not yield invariant parameters (Stage, 2003). Hambleton, Swaminathan and Rogers (1991) cited that "in many IRT applications reported in the literature, model-data fit and the consequences of misfit have not been investigated adequately. As a result, less is known about the appropriateness of particular IRT models for various applications that might be assumed from the voluminous IRT literature" (p. 53). They further warn against placing too much confidence in statistical tests, since these tests are highly sensitive to sample size (Hambleton et al., 1991). Furthermore, a majority of researchers lack expertise for using IRT. As compared with CTT, the IRT models are more complex and difficult to understand and use; computer programs for their use are generally not readily available. The assumptions of IRT are strict to meet and hence might not be applied everywhere. Large samples are usually required in order to arrive at more accurate estimation. And since it is largely based on individual items, IRT does not address domain convergence or construct definition. Keeping all the above in mind, the researcher is again in a dilemma about using IRT or CTT. The challenge in front of him is to choose between the advantages of the two, keeping in view his own abilities and expertise and the associated limitations of both. The researcher also has an issue of analyzing the aspects that remain uncovered by choosing any specific model.

Considering the cumbersome process of test development and the related shortcomings, does the solution lie in using other methods like projective tests, peer/informant ratings, or behavioral observation measures? Is it possible that other methods will be free from limitations? There arises a need to look into other methods in order to search for answers to these questions.

Projective Measures

Projective measures generally use unstructured or ambiguous test stimuli. The term "projective measures" characteristically refers to the instruments in which the ambiguous and unstructured stimulus is presented to the respondent and s/he is required to respond to that stimulus openly in whatever way s/he wants without any restrictions on the nature of that response. The projective element here is the generation of response in the face of ambiguity; and while doing so the elements of an individual's personal characteristics get projected (Meyer & Kurtz, 2006). Researchers using projective tests believe that the responses of people are based on their subjective meaning of stimuli and on the feelings they experience while responding.

Advantages and limitations of projective measures

Projective tests tend to extract a person's internal motives, drives, conflicts, and other highly personal issues. Therefore these measures are often used to detect unconscious thoughts in order to arrive at an in-depth understanding of personality characteristics. Due to this advantage of tapping unconscious impulses and bringing out the complete internal aspects of individuals, projective tests have long been used and continue to be used in clinical settings.

Do projective measures solve the limitations of self-reports or objective measures? Meyer and Kurtz (2006) believe that "the terms objective and projective carry multiple, often unclear, meanings, including some connotations that are very misleading when applied to personality assessment instruments and methods" (p. 223). Many years ago, while comprehensively defining projective tests, Frank (1939) had opined that through projective tests "we elicit a projection of the individual personality's private world" (p. 402). Meyer and Kurtz (2006) assert that "this conceptualization of a projective test implies that stimulus features or task requirements are essentially immaterial; personality characteristics will shine through with force and clarity regardless of the medium. Although desirable, this view is clearly incorrect" (p. 224).

In recent times the use and status of projective techniques is diminishing (Groth-Marnat, 2000; Piotrowski, 1999). Projective tests are being criticized widely for overly complex scoring systems, the element of subjectivity in scoring and interpretation on the part of the researcher, dubious norms, poor predictive utility, and poor psychometric properties (Garb, Wood, Nezworski, Grove, & Stejskal, 2001; Smith & Dumont, 1995). An extensive amount of time is required to learn the use of projective measures effectively. Further criticism of projective techniques centers on their heavy reliance on psychoanalytic theory, and the greater time and cost efficiency of alternative objective tests. These limitations have usually been cited by the academic community, where the use of projective measures for personality assessment related research is getting less and less (Piotrowski, 1999; Piotrowski & Zalewski, 1993). The criticism has also led to a reduction in the use of standard projective tests even in professional practice (Camara, Nathan, & Puente, 2000; Kamphaus, Petoskey, & Rowe, 2000; Piotrowski, 1999).

Rorschach Inkblots and the Thematic Apperception Test are still quite frequently used in clinical settings. It might be due to lack of time for practitioners to learn new techniques (Piotrowski & Zalewski, 1993), a paucity of other practical options, and clinical experience being weighed more heavily than empirical evidence (Beutler, Williams, Wakefield, & Entwistle, 1995). There is hardly any empirical evidence supporting the effectiveness of projective measures in personality assessment. Assessment practices in many professional settings using projective tests appear to have very little association with empirical research studies conducted on a particular assessment measure or its psychometric robustness (Piotrowski & Zalewski, 1993). This discourse makes the researcher more apprehensive when deciding on a preferred objective or projective measure, and the challenge is still to choose the best measure of personality assessment. Hence the need arises to look at whether other types of measures can provide the most comprehensive personality assessment.

Peer Ratings

Considering the limitations of self-report measures, it may be recommended to ask other people what someone is really like (Hofstee, 1994). This may incorporate taking ratings about the individual from a number of peers who get to know their often-observed behavior and actions, based upon which they can judge an individual's personality (Funder, 1989). Peer ratings are often interchangeably called informant reports, and these methods use the belief that others can provide a distinctive perspective on an individual's personality (Hogan, 1998). That is what makes informant ratings a potential tool for personality assessment, and the derived objectivity may be seen as an advantage over self-reports.

Advantages and disadvantages of peer ratings

Kenny (1994) suggested that judgments by peer observers are based more on recent real behaviors, so therefore they provide better information and are better judges of behavior (as cited by McDonald, 2008). Moskowitz (1986) opines that peers observe an individual "engaging in many different behaviors; consequently, the report can include many attributes that are supposed to reflect the characteristic" (p. 305). Adding to the positive points, Hofstee (1994) considered that by getting multiple judgments about one individual, the results are likely to be more reliable and more informative compared with self-reports. However, some other researchers (Rushton, Brainerd, & Pressley, 1983) believe that Hofstee's assertion is paradoxical in nature as the principle of aggregation requires use of multiple methods, which in turn has associated limitations.

However, even if the informants' data carries rich information, peer reports are less used due to many associated costs in terms of time and money (Vazire, 2006). Undoubtedly, it requires more effort to collect data from two or three persons compared with one person. Further, obtaining informant reports is likely to be difficult and might be invalid if appropriate cooperation is not provided by the informant. The issue of agreement among the raters is also quite important to the informant or peer ratings, failing which a situation of personality being in the eyes of the beholder may arise (Kenrick & Funder, 1988). Further, although the social desirability bias would not arise, the probability of response biases like acquiescence and extreme ratings still remains with informant ratings (McCrae & Weiss, 2007). Moreover, there may be additional biases like the fundamental attribution error, which involves the tendency to highlight certain characteristics of others (Ross & Nisbett, 1991). Another major weakness of peer ratings is that other informants do not have access to another person's thoughts, feelings, and motives, which are the primary indicators of his personality makeup. Also, informants are less likely to comment on that individual's probable behavior in a more specific situation (Moskowitz, 1986). Having the criticism of informant reports and self-reports in mind, it becomes a necessary issue for the researcher to look at the other potential avenues for personality assessment that may come with minimum possible limitations and maximum advantages. Can behavioral measures be an alternative?

Behavioral Observation Measures

It is believed that the most apparently understandable and essential means of assessing someone's personality is to "see how they act" (Furr & Funder, 2007, p. 273). The method of behavioral observation is beginning to gain momentum; however, there is a paucity of research studying links between personality and behavior (Furr & Funder, 2007). Obviously, as behavior is central to personality, so observing behavior will be certainly beneficial to assess one's personality. Furr and Funder (2007) assert that although there are numerous associated costs and considerations when conducting research with behavioral observation, considering the prime importance of behavior, observational methods should be used for assessing personality. The alternative of observing behavior in an artificial as well as a natural setting is a major positive aspect of this method. Moreover, this method being based on real-time observations, the problems associated with retrospective behavior assessments such as in peer reports are eliminated (Henry, Moffitt, Caspi, Langley, & Silva, 1994).

Providing a critique of behavioral observation measures, it can be seen that using other methods like self-report is more practical and easy. Constant observation of others' behavior or manipulating various situations may have problematic ethical issues. Further, huge efforts are required to design and develop the behavioral recording procedures and to devise interpretation schemes. And, simultaneous to all this is the fact that relatively large amounts of money and time are required to be invested in this method compared with other methods (Furr & Funder, 2007). If conducted in an artificially controlled situation, the scope of this method to assess the broad spectrum of behavior is limited, as generally only one situation is often observed (Kagan, 2007). Linked with this is the limitation that single-time observational data cannot be relied upon to reveal enduring personality dispositions (Furr & Funder, 2007). On the other hand, conducting behavioral observation in natural settings is likely to be even more expensive and time-consuming. Another drawback of behavioral observation is the conceptual difficulty in tapping a particular dispositional trait by observing a small sample of behavior, since "the link between a specific behaviour and a specific personality characteristic may not be direct" (Furr & Funder, 2007, p. 275). These limitations of behavioral observations call for the examination of mixed approaches.

Multiple Method Approaches

Analysis of the above methods has shown that there are numerous factors that need to be considered when using any measure for personality assessment. This poses the challenge of how to wade between the strengths and limitations of different methods and choose between the measures. Or should several methods be used in combination? Moskowitz (1986) has asserted that, considering the ability to measure global personality traits, none of the above methods stood as the best one to use. He advocated use of different methods for different purposes. Using multiple methods may be better, since utilizing more than one method to measure a concept can help to demonstrate construct validity, and the accuracy of findings is likely to increase with combined application of multiple methods (Campbell & Fiske, 1959). Additionally, use of multiple measures can make it possible to assess certain aspects that might have remained unassessed with a single method. Vazire (2006) posited that the conjunction of self-reports and informant reports or peer ratings "allow researchers to address new questions that cannot be examined with self-reports alone" (p. 8). Paulhus and Vazire (2007) later stated that "as with the use of any method, self-reports should be corroborated with alternative assessment methods" (p. 235). Many other prominent researchers in the area of personality assessment have suggested the necessity of using multiple measures and having good construct validity (e.g. Funder, 1989, 2002; John & Soto, 2007; Pervin, 1999). In other words, when it comes to the measurement of psychological constructs or personality, more is better.

It can be said that the primary advantage of using multiple methods is having more precision in personality assessment, and having better construct validity to support the conceptualizations. Use of multiple methods can provide more comprehensive understanding of the underlying personality disposition by means of providing rich data. However, "research using multiple methods to measure the same construct has not been very frequent" (John & Benet-Martinez, 2000, p. 356). Looking on the adverse side, it is not easily possible to use multiple methods in personality assessment. Firstly, it will be much more time-consuming, quite costly, and will require additional resources and specialized training on the part of the researcher. And secondly, the methods that can be used to assess personality are those suggested by the proponents of the specific personality conceptualization or theoretical models, hence using any or every method will not provide the requisite description of personality. So the dilemma still continues to exist for the personality psychologist.

Assessment of Change in Personality

Although it is believed by the majority of psychologists that personality keeps being shaped over a period of time as it is subject to maturational, developmental, and social changes, only the statistical methods applied to determine change have an ability to predict whether personality is changeable or stable (Heatherton & Nichols, 1994). For example, Heatherton and Nichols (1994) cite that methods such as difference scores or test–retest correlations have been questioned by some researchers for their ability to measure personality change (Alder & Scher, 1994). Assessment of change in personality again poses a challenge to the researcher as different researchers advocate different methods to assess that change. For instance, some researchers assert that use of individual growth curves allows for a more accurate approximation of changes in an individual, and thus they advocate the use of individual growth curves for assessment of personality change (Alder & Scher, 1994; Francis, Fletcher, Stuebing, Davidson, & Thompson, 1991). Other researchers put an emphasis on looking at individual lives in order to understand change (McAdams, 1993; Murray, 1938). Heatherton and Nichols (1994) argue that even if group means show little change in terms of difference scores, and test–retest correlations are very high, suggesting stability, a substantial number of individuals might still be experiencing significant changes in personality; and therefore, a researcher might look at the outliers in longitudinal studies to assess systematic change patterns among the people showing indications of changes in personality.

Looking at all these different approaches, deciding on the method of assessing personality change is an issue with even less supporting data for the use of any single approach, thereby making the analysis of advantages and disadvantages of different approaches quite difficult, leaving the researcher in a fix. Bagozzi (1993) has put forth another challenge regarding the issue of construct validity in personality research. His assertion is that even after choosing a specific approach, determination of convergent and/or discriminant validity remains a challenge for the researcher. Hence, ascertaining the validity of a personality assessment measure has various debatable and critical aspects, which puts the researcher in a dilemma.

Conclusions

Having huge diversity in the conceptual and methodological arena, the field of personality assessment has existed for more than a century. However, some queries still stand tall before the researcher. Every researcher is engaged in different subdomains of personality psychology, but no scientist can objectively answer the question of how to understand personality in its most comprehensive form. The efforts to answer this question posit different models and different assessment methods. And then comes the issue of looking at varied conceptualizations and methodologies from an analytical perspective in order to arrive at the most comprehensive personality assessment. The pros and cons of all approaches and methods need to be analyzed in order to select the best. However, all paradigms come with certain limitations, and the dilemma of the primary question remains open. We have attempted to raise multiple issues and challenges related to comprehensive personality assessment in the form of various questions at various points in this chapter, and have tried to present some major points of concern to the scientists and researchers. Considering the presented issues and many more which could not be covered in this short chapter, the scientific community in the field of personality assessment needs to address the queries, conduct more research, and develop methodologies for providing the most comprehensive, all-inclusive personality assessment for the future.

References

Ackroyd, S., & Hughes, J.A. (1981). *Data Collection in Context.* London: Longman.

Alder, A.G., & Scher, S.J. (1994). Using growth curve analyses to assess personality change and stability in adulthood. In T.F. Heatherton, & J.L. Weinberger (Eds.), *Can Personality Change?* (pp. 149–174). Washington, DC: American Psychological Association.

Ashton, M.C., & Lee, K. (2002). Six independent factors of personality variation: A response to Saucier. *European Journal of Personality, 16* (1), 63–75.

Bagozzi, R.P. (1993). Assessing construct validity in personality research: Applications to measures of self-esteem. *Journal of Research in Personality, 27* (1), 49–87.

Berdie, R.F., Layton, W.L., Swanson, E.O., & Hagenah, T. (1963). *Testing in Guidance and Counseling.* New York: McGraw-Hill.

Beutler, L.E., Williams, R.E., Wakefield, P.J., & Entwistle, S.R. (1995). Bridging scientist and practitioner perspectives in clinical psychology. *American Psychologist, 50* (12), 984–994.

Block, J. (1995). A contrarian view of the five-factor approach to personality description. *Psychological Bulletin, 117* (2), 187–229.

Block, J. (2001). Millenial contrarianism: the five factor approach to personality description 5 years later. *Journal of Research in Personality, 35* (1), 98–107.

Camara, W.J., Nathan, J.S., & Puente, A.E. (2000). Psychological test usage: Implications in professional psychology. *Professional Psychology: Research and Practice, 31* (2), 141–154.

Campbell, D.T., & Fiske, D.W. (1959). Convergent and discriminant validation by the multitrait-multimethod matrix. *Psychological Bulletin, 56* (2), 81–105.

Creswell, J.W. (2013). *Qualitative, Quantitative, and Mixed Methods Approaches* (4th ed.). Thousand Oaks, CA: Sage Publications.

Cronbach, L.J., & Meehl, P.E. (1955). Construct validity in psychological tests. *Psychological Bulletin, 52* (4), 281–301.

Delhees, K.H., & Cattell, R.B. (1970). Obtaining 16 P.F. scores from the MMPI, and MMPI scores from the 16 P.F. *Journal of Projective Techniques and Personality Assessment, 34* (3), 251–255.

Edelen, M.O., & Reeve, B.B. (2007). Applying item response theory (IRT) modeling to questionnaire development, evaluation, and refinement. *Quality of Life Research, 16* (1), 5–18.

Ellis, A., Abrams, M., & Abrams, L.D. (2009). *Personality Theories: Critical Perspectives.* Thousand Oaks, CA: Sage Publications.

Erguven, M. (2013). Two approaches to psychometric process: Classical test theory and item response theory. *Journal of Education, 2* (2), 23–30.

Eysenck, H.J. (1991). Dimensions of personality: 16, 5, or 3? Criteria for a taxonomic paradigm. *Personality and Individual Differences, 12* (8), 773–790.

Eysenck, H.J. (1992). Four ways five factors are not basic. *Personality and Individual Differences, 13* (6), 667–673.

Eysenck, H.J., & Eysenck, S.B.G. (1968). A factorial study of psychoticism as a dimension of personality. *Multivariate Behavioural Research, 3* (Special Issue), 15–31.

Fiske, S.T., & Taylor, S.E. (1991). *Social Cognition* (2nd ed.). New York: McGraw Hill.

Foster, S.L., & Cone, J.D. (1995). Validity issues in clinical assessment. *Psychological Assessment, 7* (3), 248–260.

Fraley, R.C., Waller, N.G., & Brennan, K.A. (2000). An item response theory analysis of self-report measures of adult attachment. *Personality and Social Psychology, 78* (2), 350–365.

Francis, D.J., Fletcher, J.M., Stuebing, K.K., Davidson, K.C., & Thompson, N.M. (1991). Analysis of change: Modeling individual growth. *Journal of Clinical and Consulting Psychology, 59* (1), 27–37.

Frank, L.K. (1939). Projective methods for the study of personality. *Journal of Psychology, 8* (2), 389–413.

Funder, D.C. (1989). Accuracy in personality judgment and the dancing bear. In D.M. Buss, & N. Cantor (Eds.), *Personality Psychology: Recent Trends and Emerging Directions* (pp. 210–223). New York: Springer-Verlag.

Funder, D.C. (2002). Personality psychology: Current status and some issues for the future. *Journal of Research in Personality, 36* (6), 638–639.

Furr, R.M., & Funder, D.C. (2007). Behavioral observation. In R.W. Robins, R.C. Fraley, & R.F. Krueger (Eds.), *Handbook of Research Methods in Personality Psychology* (pp. 273–291). New York: Guilford Press.

Garb, H.N., Wood, J.M., Nezworski, M.T., Grove, W.M., & Stejskal, W.J. (2001). Toward a resolution of the Rorschach controversy. *Psychological Assessment, 13* (4), 433–448.

Groth-Marnat, G. (2000). Visions of clinical assessment: Then, now, and a brief history of the future. *Journal of Clinical Psychology, 56* (3), 349–365.

Gulliksen, H. (1950). *Theory of Mental Tests.* New York: John Wiley & Sons, Ltd.

Hambleton, R.K., & Jones, R.W. (1993). Comparison of classical test theory and item response theory and their applications to test development. *Educational Measurement: Issues and Practice, 12* (3), 253–262.

Hambleton, R.K., Swaminathan, H., & Rogers, H.J. (1991). *Fundamentals of Item Response Theory.* Newbury: Sage Publications.

Handler, L., & Meyer, G.J. (1998). The importance of teaching and learning personality assessment. In L. Handler, & M.J. Hilsenroth (Eds.), *Teaching and Learning Personality Assessment* (pp. 3–30). Mahwah, NJ: Erlbaum.

Heatherton, T.F., & Nichols, P.A. (1994). Conceptual issues in assessing whether personality can change. In T.F. Heatherton, & J.L. Weinberger (Eds.), *Can Personality Change?* (pp. 3–18). Washington, DC: American Psychological Association.

Henry, B., Moffitt, T.E., Caspi, A., Langley, J., & Silva, P. (1994). On the "remembrance of things past": A longitudinal evaluation of the retrospective method. *Psychological Assessment, 6* (2), 92–101.

Hofstee, W.K.B. (1994). Who should own the definition of personality? *European Journal of Personality, 8* (3), 149–162.

Hogan, R. (1998). Reinventing personality. *Journal of Social and Clinical Psychology, 17* (1), 1–10.

John, O.P., & Benet-Martinez, V. (2000). Measurement: Reliability, construct validation, and scale construction. In H.T. Reis, & C.M. Judd (Eds.), *Handbook of Research Methods in Social and Personality Psychology* (pp. 339–369). Cambridge: Cambridge University Press.

John, O.P., & Robins, R.W. (1994). Accuracy and bias in self-perception: Individual differences in self-enhancement and the role of narcissism. *Journal of Personality and Social Psychology, 66* (1), 206–219.

John, O.P., & Soto, C.J. (2007). The importance of being valid: Reliability and the process of construct validation. In R.W. Robins, R.C. Fraley, & R.F. Krueger (Eds.), *Handbook of Research Methods in Personality Psychology* (pp. 461–494). New York: Guilford Press.

Kagan, J. (1988). The meanings of personality predicates. *American Psychologist, 43* (8), 614–620.

Kagan, J. (2007). A trio of concerns. *Perspectives on Psychological Science, 2* (4), 361–376.

Kamphaus, R.W., Petoskey, M.D., & Rowe, E.W. (2000). Current trends in psychological testing of children. *Professional Psychology: Research and Practice, 31* (2), 155–164.

Kenny, D.A. (1994). *Interpersonal Perception: A Social Relations Analysis.* New York: Guilford Press.

Kenrick, D.T., & Funder, D.C. (1988). Profiting from controversy: Lessons from the person-situation debate. *American Psychologist, 43* (1), 23–34.

Kline, P. (1993). *Personality: The Psychometric View.* London: Routledge.

Marcoulides, G. (1999). Generalizability theory: Picking up where the Rasch IRT model leaves off? In S. Embretson, & S. Hershberger (Eds.), *The New Rules of Measurement: What Every Psychologist and Educator Should Know* (pp. 129–130). Mahwah, NJ: Lawrence Erlbaum.

Maxwell, J.A. (2012). *Qualitative Research Design: An Interactive Approach* (3rd ed.). Thousand Oaks, CA: Sage Publications.

McAdams, D. (1993). *The Stories We Live By: Personal Myths and the Making of the Self.* New York: William Morrow.

McBride, N.L. (2001). *An Item Response Theory Analysis of the Scales from the International Personality Item Pool and the NEO Personality Inventory-Revised.* (Master of Science thesis.) Virginia Polytechnic Institute and State University, Blacksburg, Virginia, USA. Retrieved from http://scholar.lib.vt.edu/theses/available/etd-08092001-142211/unrestricted/thesis.pdf

McCrae, R.R., & Costa, P.T., Jr. (1997). Personality trait structure as a human universal. *American Psychologist, 52* (5), 509–516.

McCrae, R.R., & Costa, P.T. Jr. (1999). A five-factor theory of personality. In L.A. Pervin, & O.P. John (Eds.), *Handbook of Personality: Theory and Research* (2nd ed.) (pp. 139–153). New York: Guilford Press.

McCrae, R.R., & Weiss, A. (2007). Observer ratings of personality. In R.W. Robins, R.C. Fraley, & R.F. Krueger (Eds.), *Handbook of Research Methods in Personality Psychology* (pp. 259–272). New York: Guilford Press.

McDonald, J.D. (2008). Measuring personality constructs: The advantages and disadvantages of self-reports, informant reports and behavioural assessments. *Enquire, 1* (1), 1–18.

Meyer, G.J., & Kurtz, J.E. (2006). Advancing personality assessment terminology: Time to retire "objective" and "projective" as personality test descriptors. *Journal of Personality Assessment, 87* (3), 223–225.

Moskowitz, D.S. (1986). Comparison of self-reports, reports by knowledgeable informants, and behavioral observation data. *Journal of Personality, 54* (1), 294–317.

Murray, H.A. (1938). *Explorations in Personality.* New York: Oxford University Press.

Paulhus, D.L., & Vazire, S. (2007). The self-report method. In R.W. Robins, R.C. Fraley, & R.F. Krueger (Eds.), *Handbook of Research Methods in Personality Psychology* (pp. 224–239). New York: Guilford Press.

Paulhus, D.P. (1991). Measurement and control of response bias. In J.P. Robinson, P.R. Shaver, & L.S. Wrightsman (Eds.), *Measures of Personality and Social Psychological Attitudes* (pp. 17–59). San Diego: Academic Press.

Pervin, L.A. (1999). Epilogue: Constancy and change in personality theory and research. In L.A. Pervin, & O.P. John (Eds.), *Handbook of Personality: Theory and Research* (2nd ed.) (pp. 689–704). London: Guilford Press.

Piotrowski, C. (1999). Assessment practices in the era of managed care: Current status and future directions. *Journal of Clinical Psychology, 55* (7), 787–796.

Piotrowski, C., & Zalewski, C. (1993). Training in psychodiagnostic testing in APA approved PsyD and PhD clinical training programs. *Journal of Personality Assessment, 61* (2), 394–405.

Popper, K. (1959). *The Logic of Scientific Discovery.* London: Hutchinson & Co.

Progar, Š., & Sočan, G. (2008). An empirical comparison of Item Response Theory and Classical Test Theory. *Horizons of Psychology, 17* (3), 5–24.

Rani, A., & Parkash, V. (2010). Psychological testing in counseling. In U. Kumar, N. Misra, & V. Parkash (Eds.), *Counseling: A Practical Approach* (pp. 57–74). New Delhi: Academic Excellence.

Robins, R.W., Tracy, J.L., & Sherman, J.W. (2007). What kinds of methods do personality psychologists use? A survey of journal editors and editorial board members. In R.W. Robins, R.C. Fraley, & R.F. Krueger (Eds.), *Handbook of Research Methods in Personality Psychology* (pp. 673–678). New York: Guilford Press.

Rorer, L.G. (1990). Personality assessment: A conceptual survey. In L.A. Pervin (Ed.), *Handbook of Personality: Theory and Research* (pp. 693–720). New York: Guilford Press.

Ross, L., & Nisbett, R.E. (1991). *The Person and the Situation: Perspectives of Social Psychology.* Philadelphia: Temple University Press.

Rushton, J.P., Brainerd, C.J., & Pressley, M. (1983). Behavioral development and construct validity: The principle of aggregation. *Psychological Bulletin, 94* (1), 18–38.

Schwarz, N. (1999). Self-reports: How the questions shape the answers. *American Psychologist, 54* (2), 93–105.

Smith, D., & Dumont, F. (1995). A cautionary study: Unwarranted interpretations of the Draw-A-Person Test. *Professional Psychology: Research and Practice, 26* (3), 298–303.

Smith, G.T. (2005). On construct validity: Issues of method and measurement. *Psychological Assessment, 17*(4), 396–408.

Smith, R.A., & Davis, S.F. (2012). *The Psychologist as Detective: An Introduction to Conducting Research in Psychology* (6th ed.). London: Pearson.

Smith, S.R., & Archer, R.P. (2008). Introducing personality assessment. In R.P. Archer, & S.R. Smith (Eds.), *Personality Assessment* (pp. 1–35). New York: Routledge.

Stage, C. (2003). *Classical test theory or item response theory: The Swedish experience (Educational Measurement No. 42).* Umeå University, Sweden: Publications in Applied Educational Science. Retrieved from http://www.nmd.umu.se/digitalAssets/59/59524_em-no-42.pdf

Steyer, R. (2001). Classical test theory. In C. Ragin, & T. Cook (Eds.), *International Encyclopedia of the Social and Behavioral Sciences. Logic of Inquiry and Research Design* (pp. 481–520). Oxford: Pergamon.

Suen, H.K. (1990). *Principles of Test Theories.* Hillsdale, NJ: Lawrence Erlbaum

Vazire, S. (2006). Informant reports: A cheap, fast, and easy method for personality assessment. *Journal of Research in Personality, 40*(5), 472–481.

23

Identification and Assessment of the Correlates of Military Suicide

Kasie L. Hummel, James Sottile, Danielle Spangler, and Bruce Bongar

Palo Alto University, California, USA

Since 2001, over two million United States service members have been deployed to Afghanistan and Iraq (Spelman, Hunt, Seal, & Burgo-Black, 2012). Many return home unable to cope with their altered states of physical, social, and mental functioning. This is demonstrated by the troubling increase in suicide-related deaths among military personnel and veterans (Barnes, Walter, & Chard, 2012). Suicide is the "third leading cause of death among those fighting the War on Terror" (Barnes et al., 2012, p. 18). Moreover, research has demonstrated that veterans are twice as likely as civilians to die by suicide (Kaplan, Huguet, McFarland, & Newsom, 2007). The increasing rates of suicide within these populations establish the paramount importance of understanding the correlates of military suicide in an attempt to identify those at increased risk (Barnes et al., 2012). This knowledge may assist practitioners in treating our service members and veterans, while increasing the quality of care to this unique population.

Situational Correlates

Demographic factors

In 2008, the Department of Veteran Affairs (VA) Mental Health Services established a suicide surveillance system to increase their awareness and knowledge about suicidal behavior among veterans (Kemp, 2014). The data obtained from these sources have allowed mental health professionals to have an overall understanding of which military service members have the highest risk for suicide. Service members who are at highest risk are Caucasian males between the ages of 18 to 25 (Smolenski et al., 2013; Kemp, 2014). The Department of Defense (DoD) reported that approximately 75% of military suicides are completed by Caucasians (Luxton et al.,

The Wiley Handbook of Personality Assessment, First Edition. Edited by Updesh Kumar.
© 2016 John Wiley & Sons, Ltd. Published 2016 by John Wiley & Sons, Ltd.

2012). African-American service members account for 12% of suicides, while Asian and American Indian individuals represent 5.65% and 1.99% respectively (Luxton et al., 2012). The findings demonstrate that Caucasian service members have a disproportionately higher risk of suicide compared with any other race. It is also clear that male service members are much more likely than female service members to commit suicide, as female service members account for less than 8% of all military suicides (Luxton et al., 2010; Smolenski et al., 2013).

Since 2001 there has been a significant increase in suicide rates for military service members, particularly those under the age of 25 (Griffith, 2012; Kemp, 2014). The DoD reported that service members under the age of 25 represent over 35% of all military suicides (Luxton et al., 2010). These results do not appear to be unique to the US. A recent study examining correlates of suicide among service members in the UK discovered that service members under the age of 24 represented the highest number of suicides (Kapur, While, Blatchley, Bray, & Harrison, 2009).

Other correlates of military suicide include level of education and military rank. Kaplan and colleagues (2007) found that the highest level of education obtained by most veterans who completed suicide was high school. Furthermore, the DoD reported that less than 10% of military suicides occurred by service members with a bachelor's degree or higher (Luxton et al., 2012). Moreover, military suicide has also been found to correlate with military rank. Military rankings (E-1 through E-4) have an inverse correlation with suicide rates, indicating that those who have a lower rank are at increased risk for suicide (Griffith, 2012; Ritchie, Keppler, & Rothberg, 2003; Smolenski et al., 2013).

Combat events

The suicide rates among US service members have steadily increased from 9.6 for every 100,000 deaths in 2001, to 22.7 in 2012 (DoD, 2011; Luxton et al., 2012; Smolenski et al., 2013). During this time, the US launched Operation Enduring Freedom (OEF), Operation Iraqi Freedom (OIF), and Operation New Dawn (OND), which consisted of an all-volunteer force. This marked the first time that military suicide rates had surpassed the civilian rate of 19.2 since the military began recording all suicide events (Centers for Disease Control, 2009; DoD, 2011).

Suicide rates across each military branch increased among OIF/OEF/OND veterans between 2008 and 2012 (Smolenski et al., 2013). The Department of Veterans Affairs Suicide Data Reports (Kemp & Bossarte, 2012) allow for a simple comparison of suicide rates over the years and across the branches. The rate of suicide for the Army increased from 18.5 (per 100,000) in 2008 to 29.7 in 2010. The Marine Corps also had a significant increase of completed suicides from 19.5 in 2008 to 24.3 in 2010. Additionally, the Navy and Air Force had a slight increase between 2008 and 2010. The Navy increased from 11.6 to 17.8 suicides, while the Air Force had the smallest change from 12.5 to 15 suicides. One possible explanation for the dramatic increase of suicide rates among military service members is the unique nature of combat experienced within the OEF/OIF/OND conflicts. Furthermore, service members are experiencing multiple deployments and having shorter dwell-time

(Gilman et al., 2014). Another explanation might relate to the all-volunteer force, which may have impacted the overall nature of the force.

Military sexual trauma

Military sexual trauma (MST) has become a particular area of interest with regard to suicide, particularly with female service members. The Department of Veteran Affairs (2010) reported that nearly one in five women reported having a history of MST when screened at the Veterans Health Administration (VHA). Female veterans who reported having a history of MST revealed that approximately half of the incidents involved sexual harassment, and the remainder involved sexual assault (Department of Veteran Affairs, 2010). MST is associated with an increased risk for suicidal behavior among female OEF/OIF veterans (Lemaire & Graham, 2011). In a study by Kelly, Skelton, Patel, and Bradley (2011), 43% of female veterans who reported MST endorsed having suicidal ideation in the past month. Additionally, 6.7% had attempted suicide in the previous four months. While women are often targeted for MST, male service members are also at risk of experiencing MST. Males who have been targets of MST ranged between 0.7%–5.8%, though this statistic may be an underrepresentation due to the shame associated with males who have experienced sexual trauma (Kimerling et al., 2010; Suris & Lind, 2008). Practitioners should screen all patients for MST, as this will have an influence on suicide risk, case conceptualization, and treatment.

Social connectedness

Readjustment following discharge has a definitive impact on suicidality in service members. A study conducted by Kapur and colleagues (2009) found that veterans are at exceptional risk for suicide during the first two years following their discharge from the military. In addition, the study determined that among veterans who commit suicide, the median time to commit suicide after discharge is 31 months (with a range between 16–57 months).

Social connectedness has a major influence on suicidality among service members and veterans. Unit cohesion and veteran readjustment following discharge are two main factors that impact suicidality in service members. Unit cohesion is the term given to describe the group process by which service members provide social support to one another based on advocacy, cooperation, and dependability (Mitchell, Gallaway, Millikan, & Bell, 2012). Mitchell and colleagues (2012) found that unit cohesion correlated with suicidal behavior for soldiers who were exposed to combat. Moreover, the results indicated that unit cohesion acts as a protective factor against suicidal ideation. Marital status is another form of social connection that was found to be a protective factor against suicide for service members (Ritchie et al., 2003; Mitchell et al., 2012). Unmarried veterans are most at risk for committing suicide, when compared with veterans with other marital statuses (Griffith, 2012). Additionally, married soldiers were significantly less likely to report suicidal ideation (Mitchell et al., 2012). In regards to assessing social connectedness and community reintegration, the Military to Civilian Questionnaire (M2C-Q) has demonstrated exceptional validity among military and VA populations (Sayer et al., 2011). It examines levels of functioning at work, home, in relationships, and the community.

Physiological Correlates

Traumatic brain injury (TBI)

"Traumatic brain injury (TBI) is the disruption of normal brain functioning that occurs secondary to any number of traumas including a bump, blow, or jolt to the head or a penetrating head injury" (Breshears, Brenner, Harwood, & Gutierrez, 2010, p. 349). An estimated 15–23% of service members obtain a deployment-related TBI, and it has been labeled as the "signature wound" of the OEF/OIF/OND wars (Barnes et al., 2012; Breshears et al., 2010). Over the last ten years it has become evident that those who acquire such injuries and survive are at an increased risk for suicidal ideation and attempts, as well as death by suicide (Antsey et al., 2004; Simpson & Tate, 2005; Mainio et al., 2007). Teasdale and Engberg (2001) demonstrated that rates of suicide among those with TBI were 2.7 to 4.1 times higher than those without brain injuries.

With regard to assessment, projective measures such as the Rorschach have demonstrated efficacy in assessing those with TBI for symptoms of suicide; however, projective measures of personality tend to be time-consuming and subjective in nature (Breshears et al., 2010). Two objective measures of personality that have demonstrated validity in assessing for suicide risk among those with brain injuries are the Minnesota Multiphasic Personality Inventory-2 (MMPI-2) and the Personality Assessment Inventory (PAI). Although the MMPI-2 has been considered the gold standard of psychological assessment, the PAI has the ability to directly assess and predict suicidal behavior over at least a two-year period (Breshears et al., 2010). It is important that practitioners utilize measures such as the examples listed above in order to thoroughly assess for suicide risk among our veterans and service members.

Chronic pain

Issues with chronic pain are extremely prevalent among service members and veterans. In fact, roughly 47% of veterans endorse mild levels of pain, while 28% endorse moderate to severe intensities (Gironda, Clark, Messengale, & Walker, 2006). In a literature review conducted by Tang and Crane (2006), individuals with chronic pain were twice as likely to die by suicide, with a 14% prevalence of suicide attempts and a 20% prevalence of suicidal ideation. Furthermore, in a study focusing on veterans, "self-reported severe pain was predictive of subsequent suicide, even after controlling for physician-diagnosed psychiatric comorbidities" (Magruder, Yeager, & Brawman-Mintzer, 2012, p. 118).

With regard to assessing chronic pain in an attempt to identify those at risk for suicide, practitioners working within pain clinics should routinely assess for suicide, as well as pain-related functioning limitations, as these are correlated with an increased risk for suicide (Magruder et al., 2012). Furthermore, the National Veteran's Affairs Pain Outcomes Working Group has developed a VHA Pain Outcomes Toolkit, which provides guidelines for assessing pain and all its facets (Department of Veterans Affairs, 2014). In addition, the VA has developed a Pain Numeric Rating Scale (NRS) that is often used to assess current, usual, least, and worst pain (Department of Veterans Affairs, 2014).

Personality and Psychological Correlates

Substance use disorders

Substance use disorder (SUD) increases the risk of suicidal behavior among service members and veterans. Ilgen and colleagues (2010a) found that female veterans with a diagnosis of SUD had a greater risk of suicide than female veterans diagnosed with any other psychiatric disorder. Roughly 70% of all suicides among veterans diagnosed with SUDs treated by the VA are committed with a violent method (e.g., firearm) compared with 30% by non-violent means (e.g., poisoning) (Ilgen, Conner, Valenstein, Austin, & Blow, 2010b). Additionally, opiate use was associated with an increased risk of non-violent suicide, while cocaine use and poly-substance use/dependence was associated with a lower risk of violent suicide (Ilgen et al., 2010b). These findings suggest that substance use disorders affect veterans and service members' risk for suicide differentially depending on other demographic factors.

Moreover, substance use disorders affect the procedure for suicide risk assessment among service members and veterans. VHA SUD treatment providers expressed concerns that current suicide risk assessment procedures at their agencies were too standardized and did not leave enough room for clinical judgment (Webster, Eisenberg, Bohnert, Kleinberg, & Ilgen, 2012). These routine risk assessments allow some veterans, who are not suicidal, to take advantage of the system in order to meet their own needs (Webster et al., 2012). Treatment providers suggested that suicide risk assessment procedures could be improved by training all agency staff members who have contact with patients in suicide risk assessment, instead of relying on the judgment of one practitioner (Webster et al., 2012). Male veterans diagnosed with SUD who committed suicide were frequently seen in a general medical or specialty mental health treatment setting shortly before their deaths (Ilgen et al., 2012). This finding suggests that current suicide risk assessment procedures for military personnel with SUD are failing to identify many individuals at risk for suicide.

Post-traumatic stress disorder

Post-traumatic stress disorder (PTSD) is associated with an increased risk for suicidal behaviors among veterans and service members. Jakupcak and colleagues (2009) found that OEF/OIF veterans diagnosed with PTSD were significantly more likely to report suicidal ideation after controlling for substance use and depression. Veterans with two or more comorbid diagnoses in addition to PTSD were also at greater risk for suicidal ideation (Jakupcak et al., 2009). In addition, Ramsawh et al. (2014) found that the presence of PTSD increases the risk for suicidal ideation and attempts among soldiers in the US Army after controlling for depression and other demographic variables.

With regard to assessment, a diagnosis of PTSD may affect the suicide risk assessment procedures among veterans and service members. Ganzini and colleagues (2013) interviewed a sample of OEF/OIF veterans diagnosed with PTSD or depression and identified several factors that affect the willingness of veterans to disclose suicidal thoughts during risk assessment procedures. Some veterans were hesitant to disclose suicidal thoughts for fear of involuntary hospitalization (Ganzini et al., 2013). Others thought that suicidal thoughts were disgraceful and should be kept private, or saw current automated risk assessment procedures as cursory and impersonal (Ganzini et al., 2013). Ganzini and colleagues (2013) found that veterans were most likely to disclose suicidal thoughts in the context of a supportive, ongoing therapeutic relationship.

The Collaborative Assessment and Management of Suicidality (CAMS) is one of the only evidenced-based assessment and treatment tools currently in use by the military for treating patients who endorse suicidal thoughts (Jobes, Lento, & Brazaitis, 2012). The CAMS is an integrative approach to suicide risk assessment and treatment planning which involves a collaborative effort by both the clinician and the patient to identify and comprehend the function of suicidal thoughts in the context of an ongoing therapeutic relationship (Jobes et al., 2012). By integrating suicide risk assessment into the context of a relationship with a trusted treatment provider, the CAMS may address several of Ganzini and colleagues' (2013) concerns about suicide risk assessment among veterans and service members with PTSD.

Major depressive disorder

Major depressive disorder (MDD) is associated with an increased risk for suicide among military service members. Moreover, MDD is one of the strongest risk factors in predicting suicidal ideation among older male veterans (Fanning & Pietrzak, 2013). The presence of depression increases the risk for suicidal ideation and attempts among soldiers in the US Army after controlling for PTSD and other demographic variables (Ramsawh et al., 2014). Veterans and service members with MDD should be regularly assessed for suicidality as part of regular mental health screening and treatment.

A MDD diagnosis may affect the suicide risk assessment procedure among military and veteran populations. Pfeiffer and colleagues (2014) found that somatic–affective symptoms of depression significantly predicted active suicidal ideation at baseline among a sample of veterans in a VHA clinical trial. This finding suggests that clinicians conducting suicide risk assessments with depressed veterans should specifically address somatic–affective symptoms of depression with their patients. With regard to self-report measures, the Beck Depression Inventory-II (BDI-II) and the Beck Scale for Suicide Ideation (BSS) have demonstrated substantial efficacy in assessing for depression severity, somatic symptomatology, and suicidality (Healy, Barry, Blow, Welsch, & Milner, 2006; Pfeiffer et al., 2014).

Feelings of burdensomeness and hopelessness

Recent research has identified perceived burdensomeness and feelings of hopelessness as two of the most significant interpersonal risk factors for suicide. Pfeiffer and colleagues (2014) found that burdensomeness and hopelessness were significantly associated with an increased risk for passive suicidal ideation among a sample of depressed veterans. In addition, Cox et al. (2011) identified perceived burdensomeness and hopelessness among US Air Force service members as contributing factors for suicide that were not frequently verbalized prior to death, and were most often communicated through suicide notes alone. This finding suggests that perceived burdensomeness and hopelessness are often concealed risk factors for suicide among military service members, which must be directly inquired about by treatment providers during suicide risk assessment. The Beck Hopelessness Scale (BHS) is one self-report measure that may be utilized which has demonstrated efficacy in assessing these constructs among veterans and service members (Pfeiffer et al., 2014).

Personality disorders

Recent research has found that personality disorders may increase the risk for suicidal behavior among military service members. Lundin, Lundberg, Allebeck, and Hemmingsson (2011) found that a personality disorder diagnosis was significantly associated with an increased risk for suicide among a sample of Swedish men enlisted for mandatory military service. Furthermore, personality disorders were the only psychiatric diagnoses that continued to predict an increased risk of suicide 19–36 years following military conscription due to the chronic and relatively unremitting nature of these disorders (Lundin et al., 2011). However, Kochanski-Ruscio, Carreno-Ponce, DeYoung, Grammer, and Ghahramanlou-Holloway (2014) found that personality disorders were not significantly associated with an increased risk for multiple suicide attempts after controlling for mood disorders among a sample of inpatient Army soldiers. This finding may be attributed to the relative rarity of personality disorder diagnoses in the military due to the stigma that comes with such a diagnosis (Kochanski-Ruscio et al., 2014). With regard to assessing for personality disorders, the previously discussed MMPI-2 and PAI are the most frequently used measures of personality assessment and can be useful when assessing for personality disorders (Weiner & Greene, 2008).

Conclusion

As indicated previously, many service members discharge from the service with transformed states of physical, social, and mental functioning. Many of these individuals experience numerous changes to these areas concurrently, which can be overwhelming and disconcerting. Coping can be difficult, and with the increase in deaths by suicide it is evident that these service members are not receiving the assistance that they need. Therefore, it is imperative that practitioners assess and identify those at increased risk for suicide before they take their own lives.

A large component of this inability to cope adaptively is a service member's perceived burdensomeness and feelings of hopelessness, both of which are significant interpersonal risk factors for suicide (Pfeiffer et al., 2014). In addition, themes in the literature have indicated that Caucasian males aged 18–24 are at the highest risk for suicide (Kemp, 2014; Smolenski et al., 2013). Furthermore, with regard to physiological correlates, those who have acquired a TBI and/or experience chronic pain are also more likely to attempt and/or commit suicide (Barnes et al., 2012; Magruder et al., 2012). Lastly, research on the psychological correlates of military and veteran suicide indicates that PTSD, MDD, and personality disorders significantly impact the likelihood that an individual will attempt and/or commit suicide (Fanning & Pietrzak, 2013; Jakupcak et al., 2009; Lundin et al., 2011). Each of these factors (i.e., situational, physiological, and psychological) should be comprehensively addressed in order to ensure the highest quality treatment for our veterans and service members, all of whom deserve and have earned such care.

References

Antsey, K.J., Butterworth, P., Jorm, A.F., Christensen, H., Rodgers, B., & Windsor, T.D. (2004). A population survey found an association between self-reports of traumatic brain injury and increased psychiatric symptoms. *Journal of Clinical Epidemiology*, *57* (7), 1201–1209.

Barnes, S.M., Walter, K.H., & Chard, K.M. (2012). Does a history of mild traumatic brain injury increase suicide risk in veterans with PTSD? *Rehabilitation Psychology*, *57*(1), 18–26.

Breshears, R.E., Brenner, L.A., Harwood, J.E.F., & Gutierrez, P.M. (2010). Predicting suicidal behavior in veterans with traumatic brain injury: The utility of the personality assessment inventory. *Journal of Personality Assessment*, *92* (4), 349–355.

Centers for Disease Control. (2009). *United States suicide injury deaths and rates per 100,000.* Retrieved from http://webappa.cdc.gov/sasweb/ncipc/mortrate10_us.html

Cox, D.W., Ghahramanlou-Holloway, M., Greene, F.N., Bakalar, J.L., Schendel, C.L., Nademin, M.E., … Kindt, M. (2011). Suicide in the United States Air Force: Risk factors communicated before and at death. *Journal of Affective Disorders*, *133* (3), 398–405.

Department of Defense. (2011). *Active duty military death rates per 100,000 serving.* Retrieved from https://www.dmdc.osd.mil/dcas/pages/report_number_serve.xhtml

Department of Veterans Affairs. (2010). *Military sexual trauma.* Retrieved from http://www.lebanon.va.gov/Services/MilitarySexualTrauma/MSTGeneralFactSheet.pdf

Department of Veterans Affairs. (2014). *Veterans Health Administration (VHA) pain management.* Retrieved from http://www.va.gov/painmanagement/clinical_resources.asp

Fanning, J.R., & Pietrzak, R.H. (2013). Suicidality among older male veterans in the United States: Results from the National Health and Resilience in Veterans study. *Journal of Psychiatric Research*, *47* (11), 1766–1775.

Ganzini, L., Denneson, L.M., Press, N., Bair, M.J., Helmer, D.A., Poat, J., & Dobscha, S.K. (2013). Trust is the basis for effective suicide risk screening and assessment in veterans. *Journal of General Internal Medicine*, *28* (9), 1215–1221.

Gilman, S.E., Bromet, E.J., Cox, K.L., Colpe, L.J., Fullerton, C.S., Gruber, M.J., … Kessler, R.C. (2014). Sociodemographic and career history predictors of suicide mortality in the United States Army 2004–2009. *Psychological Medicine*, *44* (12), 2579–2592

Gironda, R.J., Clark, M.E., Messengale, J.P., & Walker, R.L. (2006). Pain among veterans of operations enduring freedom and Iraqi freedom. *Pain Medicine*, *7* (4), 339–343.

Griffith, J. (2012). Suicide in the Army National Guard: An empirical inquiry. *Suicide and Life-Threatening Behavior*, *42* (1), 104–119.

Healy, M.D., Barry, K., Blow, F., Welsch, D., & Milner, K.K. (2006). Routine use of the Beck scale for suicide ideation in a psychiatric emergency department. *General Hospital Psychiatry*, *28* (4), 323–329.

Ilgen, M.A., Bohnert, A.B., Ignacio, R.V., Mccarthy, J.F., Valenstein, M.M., Kim, M., & Blow, F.C. (2010a). Psychiatric diagnoses and risk of suicide in veterans. *Archives of General Psychiatry*, *67* (11), 1152–1158.

Ilgen, M.A., Conner, K.R., Valenstein, M., Austin, K., & Blow, F.C. (2010b). Violent and nonviolent suicide in veterans with substance-use disorders. *Journal of Studies on Alcohol and Drugs*, *71* (4), 473–476.

Ilgen, M.A., Conner, K.R., Roeder, K.M., Blow, F.C., Austin, K., & Valenstein, M. (2012). Patterns of treatment utilization before suicide among male veterans with substance use disorders. *American Journal of Public Health*, *102* (S1), S88–S92.

Jakupcak, M., Cook, J., Imel, Z., Fontana, A., Rosenheck, R., & McFall, M. (2009). Posttraumatic stress disorder as a risk factor for suicidal ideation in Iraq and Afghanistan war veterans. *Journal of Traumatic Stress*, *22* (4), 303–306.

Jobes, D.A., Lento, R., & Brazaitis, K. (2012). An evidence-based clinical approach to suicide prevention in the Department of Defense: The Collaborative Assessment and Management of Suicidality (CAMS). *Military Psychology*, *24* (6), 604–623.

Kaplan, M.S., Huguet, N., McFarland, B.H., & Newsom, J.T. (2007). Suicide among male veterans: A prospective population-based study. *Journal of Epidemiology & Community Health*, *61* (7), 619–624.

Kapur, N., While, D., Blatchley, N., Bray, I., & Harrison, K. (2009). Suicide after leaving the UK Armed Forces: A cohort study. *PLos Medicine*, *6* (3), 269–277.

Kelly, U.A., Skelton, K., Patel, M., & Bradley, B. (2011). More than military sexual trauma: Interpersonal violence, PTSD, and mental health in women veterans. *Research in Nursing & Health*, *34* (6), 457–467.

Kemp, J.E. (2014). *Suicide rates in VHA patients through 2011 with comparisons with other Americans and other veterans through 2010.* Retrieved from http://www.mentalhealth.va.gov/docs/suicide_data_report_update_january_2014.pdf

Kemp, J., & Bossarte, R. (2012). *Suicide Data Report, 2013.* Retrieved from http://www.va.gov/opa/docs/suicide-data-report-2012-final.pdf

Kimerling, R., Street, A.E., Pavao, J., Smith, M.W., Cronkite, R.C., Holmes, T.H., & Frayne, S.M. (2010). Military-related sexual trauma among veterans health administration patients returning from Afghanistan and Iraq. *American Journal of Public Health*, *100* (8), 1409–1412.

Kochanski-Ruscio, K.M., Carreno-Ponce, J.T., DeYoung, K., Grammer, G., & Ghahramanlou-Holloway, M. (2014). Diagnostic and psychosocial differences in psychiatrically hospitalized military service members with single versus multiple suicide attempts. *Comprehensive Psychiatry*, *55* (3), 450–456.

Lemaire, C.M., & Graham, D.P. (2011). Factors associated with suicidal ideation in OEF/OIF veterans. *Journal of Affective Disorders*, *130* (1–2), 231–238.

Lundin, A., Lundberg, I., Allebeck, P., & Hemmingsson, T. (2011). Psychiatric diagnosis in late adolescence and long-term risk of suicide and suicide attempt. *Acta Psychiatrica Scandinavica*, *124* (6), 454–461.

Luxton, D.D., Osenbach, J.E., Reger, M.A., Smolenski, D.J., Skopp, N.A., Bush, N.E., & Gahm, G.A. (2012). *Department of Defense suicide event report (DoDSER) calendar year 2011 annual report.* Retrieved from http://www.t2.health.mil/sites/default/files/dodser/DoDSER_2011_Annual_Report.pdf

Luxton, D.D., Skopp, N.A., Kinn, J.T., Bush, N.E., Reger, M.A., & Gahm, G.A. (2010). *Department of Defense suicide event report (DoDSER) calendar year 2009 annual report.* Retrieved from http://www.t2.health.mil/sites/default/files/dodser/DoDSER_2009_Annual_Report.pf

Magruder, K.M., Yeager, D., & Brawman-Mintzer, O. (2012). The role of pain, functioning, and mental health in suicidality among veterans affairs primary care patients. *American Journal of Public Health, 102* (1), 118–124.

Mainio, A., Kyllonen, T., Viilo, K., Hakko, H., Sarkioja, T., & Rassanen, P. (2007). Traumatic brain injury, psychiatric disorders and suicide: A population-based study of suicide victims during the years 1988–2004 in Northern Finland. *Brain Injury, 21* (8), 851–855.

Mitchell, M.M., Gallaway, M.S., Millikan, A.M., & Bell, M. (2012). Interaction of combat exposure and unit cohesion in predicting suicide-related ideation among post-deployment soldiers. *Suicide and Life-Threatening Behavior, 42* (5), 486–494.

Pfeiffer, P.N., Brandfon, S., Garcia, E., Duffy, S., Ganoczy, D., Kim, H.M., & Valenstein, M. (2014). Predictors of suicidal ideation among depressed veterans and the interpersonal theory of suicide. *Journal of Affective Disorders, 152–154,* 277–281.

Ramsawh, H.J., Fullerton, C.S., Mash, H.H., Ng, T.H., Kessler, R.C., Stein, M.B., & Ursano, R.J. (2014). Risk for suicidal behaviors associated with PTSD, depression, and their comorbidity in the U.S. Army. *Journal of Affective Disorders, 161,* 116–122.

Ritchie, E.C., Keppler, W.C., & Rothberg, J.M. (2003). Suicidal admissions in the United States military. *Military Medicine, 168* (3), 177–181.

Sayer, N.A., Frazier, P., Orazem, R.J., Murdoch, M., Gravely, A., Carlson, K.F., … Noorbaloochi, S. (2011). Military to civilian questionnaire: A measure of postdeployment community reintegration difficulty among veterans using Department of Veterans Affairs medical care. *Journal of Traumatic Stress, 24* (6), 660–670.

Simpson, G., & Tate, R. (2005). Clinical features of suicide attempts after traumatic brain injury. *Journal of Nervous and Mental Disease, 193* (10), 680–685.

Smolenski, D.J., Reger, M.A., Alexander, C.L., Skopp, N.A., Bush, N.E., Luxton, D.D., & Gahm, G.A. (2013). *Department of Defense suicide event report (DoDSER) calendar year 2012 annual report.* Retrieved from http://www.suicideoutreach.org/Docs/Reports/2012_DoDSER_Annual_Report.pdf

Spelman, J.F., Hunt, S.C., Seal, K.H., & Burgo-Black, A.L. (2012). Post deployment care for returning combat veterans. *Journal of General Internal Medicine, 27* (9), 1200–1209.

Suris, A., & Lind, L. (2008). Military sexual trauma: A review of prevalence and associated health consequences in veterans. *Trauma, Violence, & Abuse, 9* (4), 250–269.

Tang, N.K., & Crane, C. (2006). Suicidality in chronic pain: A review of the prevalence, risk factors, and psychological links. *Psychological Medicine, 36* (5), 575–586.

Teasdale, T.W., & Engberg, A.W. (2001). Suicide after traumatic brain injury: A population study. *Journal of Neurology, Neurosurgery, and Psychiatry, 71* (4), 436–440.

Webster, L., Eisenberg, A., Bohnert, A.B., Kleinberg, F., & Ilgen, M.A. (2012). Qualitative evaluation of suicide and overdose risk assessment procedures among veterans in substance use disorder treatment clinics. *Archives of Suicide Research, 16* (3), 250–262.

Weiner, I.B., & Greene, R.L. (2008). *Handbook of Personality Assessment.* Hoboken, NJ: John Wiley & Sons, Inc.

24

Integrative Clinical Assessment of Sexual and Gender Minority Clients

Whitney Bliss, Samantha Pflum, Matthew Skinta, Rylan J. Testa, Rebecca Floyd, and Peter Goldblum

Palo Alto University, California, USA

Lesbian, gay, bisexual, transgender, and queer/questioning (LGBTQ) individuals are becoming increasingly visible, with greater public acceptance and, in some places, improved legal status. As a substantial minority, which can be divided further into sexual (LGBQ) and gender (TQ) minority groups, mental health providers should be aware of the specific cultural influences that shape these populations. This includes harassment, discrimination, pervasive negative portrayals in media, and violence. Of crucial importance to the ethical and competent treatment of gender and sexual minorities is a thorough and culturally informed assessment process. Moreover, this assessment process should be integrative in nature, combining information from several different sources such as the clinical interview and thoughtfully chosen assessment tools that reflect an understanding of the psychosocial context of these populations. The integrative process guards against a fragmented, test-oriented description of the client, and promotes a holistic understanding of individual (Beutler, Groth-Marnat, & Rosner, 2003). This chapter will introduce mental health disparities in the LGBTQ population and an explanatory model for these disparities. This will be followed by an overview of the assessment process, which accounts for chronic and acute stressors related to gender and sexual minority status, as well as psychological co-morbidities that may or may not be related to these stress processes.

Integrative Assessment

The assessment process for gender and sexual minorities consists of both LGBTQ-specific and non-specific components. Upon initial interview, clinicians working with LGBTQ-identified clients should obtain a general impression of overall

The Wiley Handbook of Personality Assessment, First Edition. Edited by Updesh Kumar.
© 2016 John Wiley & Sons, Ltd. Published 2016 by John Wiley & Sons, Ltd.

psychological distress, strengths and life satisfaction, and minority stress. This information can be obtained using clinical interview and psychometrically validated screeners. Using this preliminary information, the therapist can then progress to more in-depth exploration of identity development, general and minority stressors, and other significant psychological issues. All of this is done in the context of other intersecting, salient cultural identities such as race, ethnicity, religion, and cohort. We include an overview of tools and models that clinicians can use throughout the course of therapy to ensure a thorough, evidence-based, and clinically relevant assessment process.

Establishing Assessment Relationship and Rapport

Building rapport is a crucial step in creating a working alliance. In addition to principles such as empathy, warmth, and positive regard, additional rapport-building considerations may apply to LGBTQ clients. The approach a therapist may take in establishing rapport depends on a number of factors, including whether or not the patient openly identifies as LGBTQ. There are several ways in which therapists can obtain data on a client's sexual orientation and gender identity. One method is to inquire about sexual and gender identities on intake paperwork, offering a broad range of choices including "I don't know" and space for clients to write in a chosen identity that is not listed (Bradford, Cahill, Grasso, & Makadon, 2012). Although answers on this intake paperwork can aid the clinician in identifying LGBTQ clients from the onset of therapy, the identity selected on the intake paperwork may not be a true reflection of the client's actual sexual orientation or feeling of gender. Because of this, it is important to maintain an open, inquisitive stance when following up with questions related to relationships. This may include questions such as "Do you have a significant other?" rather than asking sex-specific questions based on initial patient identification (e.g., "do you have a girlfriend or wife?") (Bradford et al., 2012).

LGBTQ clients may also have expectations of rejection and therefore may be highly sensitive to therapists' verbal and non-verbal cues when discussing related topics. In order to gauge the therapist's openness to these topics, and indeed, to gauge the safety of the therapeutic relationship, the client may comment on aspects of their identity or behavior and observe therapist responses. This may be thought of as a "test" that a therapist can "pass" by demonstrating empathy, gentle curiosity, and knowledge about LGBTQ issues. An openly affirmative and welcoming stance can positively affect the therapeutic relationship by reducing tension and creating an environment where clients can express themselves openly. This may make the difference between a valid, accurate assessment and an assessment biased by self-protective non-disclosure.

Mental health organizations such as the American Psychological Association (APA) advocate for affirmative treatment approaches when working with gender and sexual minorities (APA, 2008, 2009). An affirmative stance is constructed on the premise that variations in sexual orientation and gender identity are normal and should not be pathologized. Affirmative therapy and assessment may focus on issues specific to gender or sexual identity (e.g., minority stress, coming out, identity development), or may serve as a backdrop for work on psychological concerns not specifically related to being a gender or sexual minority (Perez, DeBord, & Bieschke, 2000). Affirmative stances may be exploratory or goal-oriented; exploratory stances are more appropriate for clients in the early stages of investigation of their sexual or gender identity. An exploratory stance is more neutral and does not assume (a) a client's clarity of sexual orientation or (b) comfort with identifying as a sexual or gender minority. Active stances help clients move forward from confusion to taking active steps to meet the challenges of their lives (Goldblum, Balsam, Skinta, Pflum, & Evans, in press). Work with LGBTQ populations also ideally involves the same competencies inherent in work with other culturally different groups, such as knowledge about common issues facing gender and sexual minorities, development of skills that reflect an understanding of these populations, and an awareness of attitudes toward LGBTQ populations in general and toward the client specifically (APA, 2002).

Minority Stress and Resilience

Compared with non-LGBTQ individuals, gender and sexual minority people are at an increased risk for psychological distress and mental disorders. Lesbian, gay, and bisexual individuals are more likely than their heterosexual counterparts to experience mental health issues such as depression, anxiety, and substance misuse (King et al., 2008). Transgender individuals are also at increased risk for mood disorders and anxiety (Bockting, Miner, Swinburne Romine, Hamilton, & Coleman, 2013). In addition, both gender and sexual minorities are at increased risk for fatal and nonfatal suicidal behavior (see Haas et al., 2010, for a review).

The minority stress theory has consistently shown to have explanatory benefit for the observed mental health disparity between LGBTQ and non-LGBTQ individuals (Meyer, 1995, 2003). This model was originally developed to explain why gay men have higher levels of psychological distress compared with straight men (Meyer, 1995). The model was later expanded to account for the differences in distress observed in individuals who identify as lesbian or bisexual (Meyer, 2003). Meyer's minority stress model (1995, 2003) posits that LGB individuals experience unusually high rates of discrimination and victimization because of their sexual orientation, which leads to stress-related problems. Minority stressors, both acute and chronic, include experiencing harassment, discrimination, and negative societal attitudes. In response to this, individuals may: (a) expect rejection and demonstrate hypervigilance and sensitivity; (b) internalize society's negative attitudes, often called internalized homophobia or stigma; and (c) make efforts to conceal their sexual minority status.

While certain aspects identified by the minority stress model for sexual minorities likely hold for transgender and gender-nonconforming (TGNC) people, there are also differences in the minority stressors experienced between them (Hendricks & Testa, 2012). In terms of distal minority stressors, TGNC people may experience additional forms of discrimination, including being refused medical care and being unable to access safe restrooms in public places (Grant et al., 2010). In addition, TGNC individuals may experience an additional distal stressor of non-affirmation, which occurs when others do not affirm one's internal sense of gender. An example of this is a trans woman being addressed as "sir" when making a purchase or answering the phone. TGNC individuals who identify as neither male nor female may also experience a sense of non-affirmation, as people in their life may not refer to them in gender-neutral ways. Non-affirmation of one's gender identity may occur more or less often for any TGNC individual, based on how their gender expression is interpreted by their social context at that particular time (Beemyn & Rankin, 2011; Bockting & Coleman, 2007; Nuttbrock, Rosenblum, & Blumenstein, 2002).

Additionally, there are some differences in how identity concealment may be experienced by LGB and TGNC people. First, gender is often primarily conveyed by physical cues, such as body size, shape, and hair patterns, instead of behavior or verbalized identity. Thus, decisions regarding identity disclosure are in part guided by genetics, access to medical care, stage of transition, and age at time of transition. Second, in many languages, gender is a primary identifier specifying genderized word usage. Therefore, in some ways there is no option for "don't ask, don't tell" regarding gender. Finally, for TGNC people who do go through a social and physical transition, the issue of disclosure changes drastically over the course of their transition.

Given the widespread prevalence of discrimination, harassment, and violence against sexual and gender minorities (Grant et al., 2010; Herek, 2009), Meyer's minority stress model plays a significant role in the integrative psychological assessment and treatment of LGBTQ clients.

LGBTQ resilience factors

LGBTQ individuals are frequently exposed to threat, trauma, stress, and adversity, experiences that can impair overall functioning, lead to negative mental health consequences, and detrimentally impact physical health (Meyer, 2003). However, not all individuals exposed to trauma or maltreatment suffer such costs (Cicchetti & Rogosch, 2009). Resilience, a dynamic process encompassing positive adaptation within the context of significant adversity, can enable individuals to function competently and cope successfully despite experiencing extreme stress or difficulty (Cicchetti & Rogosch, 2009; Luthar, Cicchetti, & Becker, 2000). Two critical conditions are necessary for resilience to develop: (1) exposure to significant threat, extreme stress, or severe adversity; and (2) the attainment of positive adaptation despite major attacks on one's development. Often described as the ability to "bounce back" from adversity, resilience is a multidimensional construct that contributes to the absence of mental health problems in the face of extreme stress or hardship (Luthar et al., 2000).

Assessment of resilience factors

The assessment of resilience among LGBTQ individuals can facilitate culturally competent, strengths-based treatment that emphasizes protective and health-promoting factors. Social support is perhaps the most-studied protective factor contributing to resilience in the LGBTQ community (Kwon, 2013). Social support can catalyze healthy, facilitative coping mechanisms (e.g., use of humor, educating others, participating in hobbies, spirituality, seeking psychotherapy), can buffer against the health consequences of stressful experiences, and can reduce psychological distress related to homophobia and discrimination. The resilience-bolstering nature of social support is particularly salient when it specifically addresses an individual's sexual orientation and is consistent with their developmental needs across the lifespan. Additional resilience-promoting factors include the ability to tolerate and process emotions and to maintain hope and optimism when faced with prejudice (Kwon, 2013). For TGNC individuals, social support also has a significant positive impact on mental health and resilience. Higher self-esteem, personal mastery, pride in one's gender, hope for the future, and access to competent healthcare are frequently cited as resilience-bolstering factors within the TGNC community (Grossman, D'Augelli, & Frank, 2011; Singh & McKleroy, 2011). Supportive psychotherapy can aid in the assessment and reinforcement of these protective factors, ultimately contributing to greater psychosocial resilience.

Minority Stress Assessment

Despite extensive population-based research linking sexual and gender minority stress to elevations in psychopathology among LGBTQ clients, the translational research linking these findings with the identification of measures for clinical use is still in its infancy. This research gap has limited the capacity of clinicians to reliably assess minority stress among LGBTQ persons. The establishment of clinical measures of minority stress is necessary to understand the relationship between sexual and gender minority stress and symptom presentation. Further, it is only through tracking the outcomes of both LGBTQ and non-LGBTQ-focused therapies that the impact of psychotherapy on LGBTQ-related concerns can be assessed.

Screening for minority stress

Near the outset of therapy with an LGBTQ-identified client, the clinician may conduct a screening of the impact of minority stressors. The Cultural Minority Stress Scale (CMSS) originated as a subscale of the Cultural Assessment of Risk for Suicide (CARS), a measure designed to be culturally sensitive to factors affecting suicide behavior risk assessment. Owing to the perceived need for a brief screener to assess clients for the presence of clinically significant minority stress, the CMSS was extracted from the CARS and its validity as a clinical screener was tested. The CMSS was designed to be used with sexual, gender, ethnic, and immigrant minority clients. At 12 items, endorsed on a 6-point Likert scale, the CMSS is an appropriate screening device for the prevalence and effects of minority stress within a diverse population. Validation studies of the measure found that minority stress was better able to classify individuals on four indicators of psychological distress (hopelessness, depression, current suicide ideation, recent suicide attempt) than minority status alone. Cut scores, occurring between 1 and 2 standard units of deviation and in excess of 2 standard units of deviation, provide the clinician with indications of levels of minority stress that meet clinical significance. Odds ratios associated with these cut scores on the four indicators of psychological distress and risk for suicide behavior provide support for the measure's validity and add to its clinical utility.

Although any item on the CMSS may be responded to with either one's ethnic, sexual, or gender identity in mind, and the items relate to a variety of essential, theoretical constructs of minority stress (i.e., stigma events, internalized negativity, perceived negativity, acculturative stress, and identity concealment), factor analysis supports that the CMSS can be additionally divided into three subscales (Chu et al., 2013). These three subscales are conceptualized as Sexual Minority Stress, Immigrant Stress, and Nonspecific Minority Stress. The subscales of the CMSS were statistically determined to be non-duplicative in their association with the four indicators of psychological distress and suicide behavior risk. Along with odds ratios tied to specific items on the CMSS, this information further refines the CMSS's ability to assist clinicians in specifying unique challenges facing the individual assessed. This degree of guidance, informed by statistical analyses, provided to clinicians to facilitate interpretation of sources and impact of minority stress, is absent from other measures of minority stress.

Amplifying the assessment of gender and sexual minority stress

Based on the results of the initial minority stress screening, the goals of treatment, or the content of therapy sessions, the clinician may wish to obtain more information about specific domains of minority stress, including internalized homophobia, rejection expectation, discrimination events, concealment, or minority stressors specific to TGNC clients. Measures can be given once or be repeated over time to assess for therapeutic progress in these domains.

Internalized homophobia. The Internalized Homophobia Scale is a nine-item measure developed by Martin and Dean (1992) to determine the extent to which individuals reject their same-sex attractions (Meyer, 1995). Items include "I would like to get professional help in order to change my sexual orientation from gay to straight." Using a 5-point Likert scale, clients indicate their level of agreement or disagreement with these statements.

Perceived stigma and rejection expectation. The assessment of the expectation of rejection has largely been influenced by Link's (1987) pioneering work, which was originally generalized for use with mental illness (Link, 1987; Kessler, Mickelson, & Williams, 1999). Expectations of stigma were quantified in Meyer's (1995) minority stress research using six items ($\alpha = 0.88$) from Link's (1987) scale. Items include agreement with statements such as "Most people look down on people like you."

Discriminatory events. Experiences of discrimination have been measured in a wide variety of ways, both specific and non-specific to minority stress research.

Acute events were measured in Meyer's research on minority stress using eight items ($\alpha = 0.84$) from Williams, Yu, Jackson, and Anderson's (1997) scale. Meyer has also measured general stressors according to Turner, Wheaton, and Lloyd's (1995) procedure, using a 28-item ($\alpha = 0.73$) scale.

Outness. Measures assessing this domain may address "outness" or concealment of sexual identity. The literature ranges from the self-report of outness to attempts to systematically assess the degree of concealment (e.g., Self-Concealment Scale: Larson & Chastain, 1990), to the life domains and types of relationships in which one is "out" (Outness Inventory: Mohr & Fassinger, 2000). Outness has been found to have either positive or negative effects, depending on the stage of identity development (Feldman & Wright, 2013). Additional questions related to the satisfaction with level of outness may be useful for clinical assessment.

Gender minority stress. The Gender Minority Stress and Resilience (GMSR) measure was developed to assess minority stress in TGNC populations. The GMSR includes scales assessing nine constructs: gender-related discrimination, gender-related rejection, gender-related victimization, non-affirmation of gender identity, internalized transphobia, negative expectations for future events, non-disclosure, community connectedness, and pride. Based on data from 844 TGNC participants, reliability and validity of the measure is supported (Testa, Habarth, Peta, Balsam, & Bockting, 2015). Specifically, results indicated a good model fit, criterion validity, convergent validity, and discriminant validity for the nine hypothesized scales.

Assessment of Sexual and Gender Identity Formation

Following initial assessment for minority stress, general psychological distress, strengths, and life satisfaction, it is important to have an understanding of the roles that gender and sexuality play in the client's life. One model to guide clinical inquiry and inform treatment is the Five-Phase Model (Goldblum et al., in press). This model accounts for the phases that sexual and gender minority individuals may go through as they identify, explore, accept, express, and integrate their gender identity and sexual orientation/identity into daily life. The primary method of assessing the client's current location in the model is the clinical interview. The initial assessment process may take place over several sessions, depending on the focus and skill of the therapist, as well as client openness, insight, and ability to articulate their thoughts and feelings related to gender identity and sexual orientation/identity. This initial assessment can also be used to jointly determine therapeutic goals (e.g., coming out to co-workers, entering the dating scene). Periodic re-assessment of the client's place in the model can be helpful in guiding further exploration and altering of the goals of therapy, if necessary. The following is an overview of each phase, including major characteristics and targets for assessment:

Phase 1 – Awareness, conflict, and confusion

Sexual minorities. The client may be confused or conflicted by their same-sex attractions ("not sure which label fits"). The assessment is focused on inquiry about client's certainty and comfort with same- and other-sex attractions, as well as their understanding of these attractions. A careful review of attractions to men, women, or both is combined with eliciting associated affect and values. An affirmative, exploratory clinical stance is required to allow the client the fullest range of autonomy for decision-making.

Gender minorities. An initial awareness of a "mismatch" between one's assigned sex and differently experienced gender can lead to conflict and uncertainty regarding gender identity. Clients may be confused and conflicted as to whether to identify with their gender assigned at birth, accepting their gender variance, or begin to consider the process of gender transition. Thus, clinicians must check their biases as to the "right" way for clients to proceed with gender identity formation. A sense of gender difference often occurs during childhood, when gender-variant youth recognize the sharp societal distinctions between girls and boys. Upon first recognizing that they are different from others of their assigned gender, TGNC individuals may feel angry, fearful, confused, shameful, marginalized, and suicidal. In contrast, some may feel comfortable, confident, and at peace after becoming aware of their true gender identity (Beemyn & Rankin, 2011).

Phase 2 – Questioning and experimentation

Sexual minorities. As clients become clearer as to their attractions and values, they may also be ready to begin experimenting with alternative sexual/intimate behavior, relationships, or self-labeling as lesbian, gay, bisexual, or queer or questioning. Assessment is focused on ascertaining the client's knowledge of sexual orientation (attractions), the LGBQ community, sexual relationships, and so on, and the degree to which they have or are willing to experiment with expressing their sexuality in ways consistent with their sexual attractions and values. A focus on value clarification is often needed to reduce internalized homophobia for clients plagued with religious conflicts or strong family expectations. Gender-variant clients may need to sort through their negative experiences and comfort with their gender and its expression. For example, some gender-conflicted female clients who initially identify as "butch lesbians" may become less comfortable with this identity if they perceive that their lesbian peers do not share their inner sense of being male. Again, clients are best served by an affirmative, exploratory stance that allows time to explore all possible variants of sexual orientation, knowing that this is not a linear process.

Gender minorities. For individuals on the trans spectrum, time is often required to settle on a commitment to transition. Once the client chooses to accept a trans identity, careful review of implications and strategies can further solidify plans to transition or re-open doubts. Patience by the clinician is needed to provide a safe place to vacillate, experiment, and consider. For those on the trans female spectrum (i.e., MTF, assigned male at birth), cross-dressing may serve as a useful intermediary stage for discovering one's female identity. For those on the male spectrum (i.e., FTM, assigned female at birth), involvement in the lesbian community sometimes provides an environment to explore gender expression during an intermediary stage. For both female and male spectrum individuals, becoming educated about gender variance and meeting other trans individuals can be a powerful experience to assist clients to understand and explore the range of options open to them (Beemyn & Rankin, 2011).

Phase 3 – Acceptance, labeling, and disclosure

Sexual minorities. The client is increasingly confident with self-labeling and with "coming out" to family, friends, co-workers, and other important individuals. Assessment is focused on the client's satisfaction with level of outness, self-labeling as LGBQ, and comfort with their self-disclosing to others. Clients may be well served by a more active gay affirmative stance by clinicians, as clients begin to navigate the world as an "out" person. This active stance may require alteration if a client's ambivalence returns, requiring a return to an affirmative, exploratory stance.

Gender minorities. Acceptance and labeling of one's gender identity is often aided by social support (from both trans and cisgender peers), self-exploration, and political activism. Social support can encourage the use of healthy, facilitative coping mechanisms (e.g., use of humor, educating others, participating in hobbies, spirituality, seeking gender-affirming psychotherapy), and can reduce psychological distress related to trans phobia and discrimination (Budge et al., 2013). Greater acceptance of one's identity often precedes disclosure to others. In contrast to the coming-out experiences of sexual minorities, gender minorities may have "no choice about disclosure" when they transition to a gender different from the one assigned to them at birth (Beemyn & Rankin, 2011, p. 66). Some trans individuals may attempt to "pass" as a member of their experienced gender (i.e., a trans man who desires to be recognized solely as a man, indistinguishable from those born male), while others are more comfortable with a more androgynous or gender-fluid appearance.

Phase 4 – Living out, meeting life goals

Sexual minorities. The client is largely "out" and may be encountering latent minority stress processes (e.g., internalized homophobia, concealment) interfering with the attainment of valued goals (e.g., development of relationships or improvement in sense of self-agency). Assessment is focused on the client's experience of minority stress processes and perceived barriers to meeting life goals. Clients may need to specifically focus on reducing covert and overt forms of negative self-esteem that are associated with "shame events" related to being a sexual minority.

Gender minorities. For gender minorities, "living out" often involves social or biological transition to align their bodies with their self-image. Trans and gender-variant individuals may maintain a personal style (e.g., clothing, hairstyle, makeup) consistent with their gender identity, take cross-sex hormones, and/or have gender-confirming surgery (e.g., "top" and "bottom" surgery). However, it is important to recognize that trans and gender-variant people do not always feel the need to physically transition. Such individuals may not have access to hormones, may lack financial resources, or may feel that physical transition is unnecessary to live as their desired gender (Nadal, 2013). When living in a manner consistent with their affirmed gender – regardless of whether biological transition is sought – trans individuals often feel an increased sense of comfort, confidence, happiness, relief and fulfillment (Beemyn & Rankin, 2011).

Phase 5 – Synthesis and re-examination of previous adaptation

Sexual minorities. The client has integrated sexual orientation into their other valued identities, where it may or may not maintain the salience it had in previous phases. Assessment is focused on the importance the client places on sexual orientation and identity relative to other identities, and whether this identity integration remains adaptive. It is important to note that clients may not progress through the phases of the model in a linear fashion. For example, a negative coming-out experience may move a client from Phase 3 back to Phase 2. This possibility highlights the importance of periodic re-assessment to ensure that the focus of treatment is aligned with the client's current stage of identity development.

Gender minorities. During and after transitioning socially and/or medically, trans individuals often experience a "sense of wholeness" as "real" men, women, or something else (Beemyn & Rankin, 2011, p. 126). For many, this stage involves a re-examination of previous developmental milestones and a clarification of values to determine the salience of gender identity in one's constellation of identities (i.e., gender, work, family, religion, etc.). This stage may also encompass educating others about trans-related health disparities and societal inequality, greater recognition of the possibility for personal fulfillment and happiness, and a celebration of the inherent fluidity and creativity of gender identity.

Identifying Clinical Focus and Treatment Planning

Gender and sexual minority clients may or may not initiate therapy to address issues related to these identities. For clients who have chosen gender or sexuality as a focus of treatment, the assessments described herein can assist with homing in on specific areas of clinical importance, which can thereby inform treatment planning and goals. For those clients who have identified other areas of clinical focus, such as depression, relationship issues, or trauma, the clinician should take care to avoid over-attributing these problems to sexual or gender identity. However, since minority stressors such as internalized stigma may not be readily evident to the client, the clinician should keep the minority stress model in mind as the client-identified issues are explored. Given the relationship between minority stressors and psychological distress, measures assessing psychological distress should also continue throughout the course of therapy. These measures can serve as an indication of therapeutic progress and inform therapists of a need for a new therapeutic approach or treatment.

As with all stages of assessment and treatment of sexual and gender minorities, an open, inquisitive, and empathic approach will go far in sustaining the therapeutic alliance through the challenges and pain of addressing effects of systemic and personal discrimination. In this sense, the therapeutic relationship can serve as the bedrock upon which the client can construct a more congruent and fulfilling life, an outcome aided greatly by culturally informed assessment and treatment practices.

References

American Psychological Association. (2002). *Guidelines on Multicultural Education, Training, Research, Practice, and Organizational Change for Psychologists.* Washington, DC: American Psychological Association.

American Psychological Association. (2008). *Resolution on transgender and gender identity and gender expression non-discrimination.* Retrieved from http://www.apa.org/about/policy/chapter-12b.aspx#transgender

American Psychological Association (2009). *Report of the American Psychological Association Task Force on Appropriate Responses to Sexual Orientation.* Washington, DC: American Psychological Association.

Beemyn, G., & Rankin, S. (2011). *The Lives of Transgender People.* New York: Columbia.

Beutler, L.E.B., Groth-Marnat, G., & Rosner, R. (2003). Introduction to integrative assessment and adult personality. In L.E. Beutler, & G. Groth-Marnat (Eds.), *Integrative Assessment of Adult Personality* (2nd ed.) (pp. 1–36). New York: Guilford Press

Bockting, W.O., & Coleman, E. (2007). Developmental stages of the transgender coming out process: Toward an integrated identity. In R. Ettner, S. Monstrey, & A.E. Eyler (Eds.), *Principles of Transgender Medicine and Surgery* (pp. 185–208). Binghamton, NY: Haworth Press.

Bockting, W.O., Miner, M.H., Swinburne Romine, R.E., Hamilton, A., & Coleman, E. (2013). Stigma, mental health, and resilience in an online sample of the US transgender population. *American Journal of Public Health, 103* (5), 943–951.

Bradford, J.B., Cahill, S., Grasso, C., & Makadon, H.J. (2012). *How to gather data on sexual orientation and gender identity in clinical settings.* Retrieved from http://thefenwayinstitute.org/documents/Policy_Brief_HowtoGather..._v3_01.09.12.pdf

Budge, S.L., Katz-Wise, S.L., Tebbe, E.N., Howard, K.A.S., Schneider, C.L., & Rodriguez, A. (2013). Transgender emotional and coping processes: Facilitative and avoidant coping throughout gender transitioning. *The Counseling Psychologist, 41* (4), 601–647.

Cicchetti, D., & Rogosch, F.A. (2009). Adaptive coping under conditions of extreme stress: Multilevel influences on the determinants of resilience in maltreated children. *New Directions for Child and Adolescent Development, 124,* 47–59.

Chu, J., Floyd, R., Diep, H., Pardo, S., Goldblum, P., & Bongar, B. (2013). A tool for the culturally competent assessment of suicide: The Cultural Assessment of Risk for Suicide (CARS) Measure. *Psychological Assessment, 25* (2), 424–434.

Feldman, S.E., & Wright, A.J. (2013). Dual impact: Outness and LGB identity formation on mental health. *Journal of Gay & Lesbian Social Services, 25* (4), 443–464.

Goldblum, P.B., Balsam, K.F, Skinta, M., Pflum, S., & Evans, R.W. (in press). Psychotherapy with lesbian, gay, and bisexual clients. In L.E. Beutler, A.J. Consoli, & B. Bongar (Eds.), *Comprehensive Textbook of Psychotherapy: Theory and Practice.* New York: Oxford University Press.

Grant, J.M., Mottet, L.A., Tanis, J., Herman, J.L., Harrison, J., & Keisling, M. (2010). *National Transgender Discrimination Survey. Report on Health and Health Care.* Washington, DC: National Center for Transgender Equality and National Gay and Lesbian Task Force.

Grossman, A.H., D'Augelli, A.R., & Frank, J.A. (2011) Aspects of psychological resilience among transgender youth. *Journal of LGBT Youth, 8* (2), 103–115.

Haas, A.P., Eliason, M., Mays, V.M., Mathy, R.M., Cochran, S.D., D'Augelli, A.R., … Clayton, P.J. (2010). Suicide and suicide risk in lesbian, gay, bisexual, and transgender populations: review and recommendations. *Journal of Homosexuality, 58* (1), 10–51.

Hendricks, M., & Testa, R.J. (2012). Model for understanding risk and resiliency in transgender and gender-nonconforming individuals. *Professional Psychology: Research and Practice, 43* (5), 460–467.

Herek, G. (2009). Sexual stigma and sexual prejudice in the United States: A conceptual framework. In D.A. Hope (Ed.), *Contemporary Perspectives on Lesbian, Gay, Bisexual Identities* (pp. 65–111). New York: Springer.

Kessler, R.C., Mickelson, K.D., & Williams, D.R. (1999). The prevalence, distribution, and mental health correlates of perceived discrimination in the united states. *Journal of Health and Social Behavior, 40* (3), 208–230.

King, M., Semlyen, J., Tai, S.S., Killaspy, H., Osborn, D., Popelyuk, D., & Nazareth, I. (2008). A systematic review of mental disorder, suicide, and deliberate self harm in lesbian, gay and bisexual people. *BMC Psychiatry, 8* (70), 1–17.

Kwon, P. (2013). Resilience in lesbian, gay, and bisexual individuals. *Personality and Social Psychology Review, 17* (4), 371–383.

Larson, D.G., & Chastain, R.L. (1990). Self-concealment: Conceptualization, measurement, and health implications. *Journal of Social and Clinical psychology, 9* (4), 439–455.

Link, B.G. (1987). Understanding labeling effects in the area of mental disorders: An assessment of the effects of expectations of rejection. *American Sociological Review, 52* (1), 96–112.

Luthar, S.S., Cicchetti, D., & Becker, B. (2000). The construct of resilience: A critical evaluation and guidelines for future work. *Child Development, 71* (3), 543–562.

Martin, J.L., & Dean, L. (1992). *Summary of measures: Mental health effects of AIDS on at-risk homosexual men.* Unpublished manuscript. Columbia, Mailman School of Public Health.

Meyer, I.H. (1995). Minority stress and mental health in gay men. *Journal of Health and Social Behavior, 36* (1), 38–56.

Meyer, I.H. (2003). Prejudice, social stress, and mental health in lesbian, gay, and bisexual populations: Conceptual issues and research evidence. *Psychological Bulletin, 129* (5), 674–697.

Mohr, J., & Fassinger, R. (2000). Measuring dimensions of lesbian and gay male experience. *Measurement & Evaluation in Counseling & Development, 33* (2), 66–90.

Nadal, K.L. (2013). *That's So Gay! Micro Aggressions and the Lesbian, Gay, Bisexual, and Transgender Community.* Washington, DC: American Psychological Association.

Nuttbrock, L., Rosenblum, A., & Blumenstein, R. (2002). Transgender identity affirmation and mental health. *International Journal of Transgenderism, 6* (4), 97–103.

Perez, R.M., DeBord, K.A., & Bieschke, K.J. (2000). *Handbook of Counseling and Psychotherapy with Lesbian, Gay, and Bisexual Clients.* Washington, DC: American Psychological Association

Singh, A.A., & McKleroy, V.S. (2011). "Just getting out of bed is a revolutionary act": The resilience of transgender people of color who have survived traumatic life events. *Traumatology, 17* (2), 34–44.

Testa, R.J., Habarth, J., Peta, J., & Balsam, K., & Bockting, W. (2015). Development of the Gender Minority Stress and Resilience Measure. *Psychology of Sexual Orientation and Gender Diversity, 2* (1), 65–77.

Turner, R.J., Wheaton, B., & Lloyd, D.A. (1995). The epidemiology of social stress. *American Sociological Review, 60* (1), 104–125

Williams, D.R., Yu, Y., Jackson, J.S., & Anderson, N.B. (1997). Racial differences in physical and mental health: Socioeconomic status, stress and discrimination. *Journal of Health Psychology, 2* (3), 335–351.

25

Using the Johnson-Neyman Procedure to Detect Item Bias in Personality Tests: A Proposed New Method and Practical Guidelines for Data Analysis

Burak Tunca

University of Agder, Norway

Personality researchers are often interested in examining trait differences between groups. For instance, are men more assertive than women? Or, are the Americans more impulsive than the Chinese? The common practice in answering such questions is first to administer the same personality scale to members of each group, and then to compare groups' scores on the scale. Validity of such comparisons, however, rests on the assumption that the scale items are not biased: respondents with different group memberships understand and interpret the scale items in a similar manner. If this assumption is violated, the validity of the results becomes questionable. Personality researchers have long been warned against this potential problem in between-group comparisons (e.g., Smith, 2002; Thissen, Steinberg, & Gerrard, 1986).

The significance of this problem has also led to development of various statistical techniques to detect biased items (for reviews, see Reynolds, 2000; Zumbo, 2007). In the current chapter, I first review one of these techniques known as the analysis of variance (ANOVA) procedure (van de Vijver & Leung, 1997), which has been widely used in personality research (e.g., Caprara, Barbaranelli, Bermúdez, Maslach, & Ruch, 2000; Ramírez-Esparza, Gosling, Benet-Martínez, Potter, & Pennebaker, 2006; Vecchione, Alessandri, & Barbaranelli, 2012). Next, I propose an alternative to the ANOVA method. The alternative method, which is based on the Johnson-Neyman procedure (Johnson & Neyman, 1936), has the potential to overcome

The Wiley Handbook of Personality Assessment, First Edition. Edited by Updesh Kumar.
© 2016 John Wiley & Sons, Ltd. Published 2016 by John Wiley & Sons, Ltd.

some of the major weaknesses of the ANOVA procedure. I introduce the proposed method in a non-technical manner and I present practical guidelines for data analysis using an add-on for mainstream statistical software packages (PROCESS Macro; Hayes, 2013), so that researchers who are inexperienced in item bias analysis can easily apply the Johnson-Neyman procedure to their research.

What is Item Bias?

Item bias, also known as *differential item functioning* (DIF), refers to item-level anomalies within an instrument that can threaten the validity of group comparisons. In psychology research, an item is considered to be biased when respondents with different group memberships score differently on a survey item, while being at the same level of the latent trait (Smith, 2002; van de Vijver & Leung, 2011). To illustrate, Santor, Ramsay, and Zuroff (1994) examined gender-level item bias in the Beck Depression Inventory (Beck, Ward, Mendelson, Mock, & Erbaugh, 1961) and found that men and women, who were equally depressed, responded differently to an item related to their perceived body image distortion. At all levels of depression, women were more likely than men to report concerns about looking unattractive. The authors concluded that the item was endorsed differently across gender groups, thus it was biased, and scores for this item would lead to misleading results when comparing the degree of depression between men and women.

Item bias exists in two forms: *uniform* and *non-uniform* (van de Vijver & Leung, 1997). Uniform bias manifests itself when there is a systematic difference between groups for an item score across all score levels (see Figure 25.1A). This indicates that one group endorses the item differently than the other group (either at a higher or lower level), regardless of their total score on the latent trait. Non-uniform bias, on the other hand, is a less common form, and it occurs when the item score differences between groups are not systematic across all score levels (see Figure 25.1B). For example, an item may be more discriminating for one group at lower score levels and more discriminating for the other group at higher score levels, which implies an interaction effect of group membership and total score on the latent trait. Various statistical techniques have been proposed to test for evidence of uniform and non-uniform item bias. While item response theory (IRT) and logistic regression methods are commonly used to detect item bias in dichotomous scores, the ANOVA procedure (van de Vijver & Leung, 1997) has been a popular technique for examining item bias in numerical scores.

The ANOVA Procedure

To test for evidence of item bias in unidimensional scales, van de Vijver and Leung (1997) introduced a procedure based on conditional analysis of variance (ANOVA). To illustrate how the ANOVA procedure functions, consider a test instrument with ten items (*item 1* to *item 10*) measured with a seven-point Likert-type scale (1 = strongly disagree to 7 = strongly agree), which was administered to members of two groups

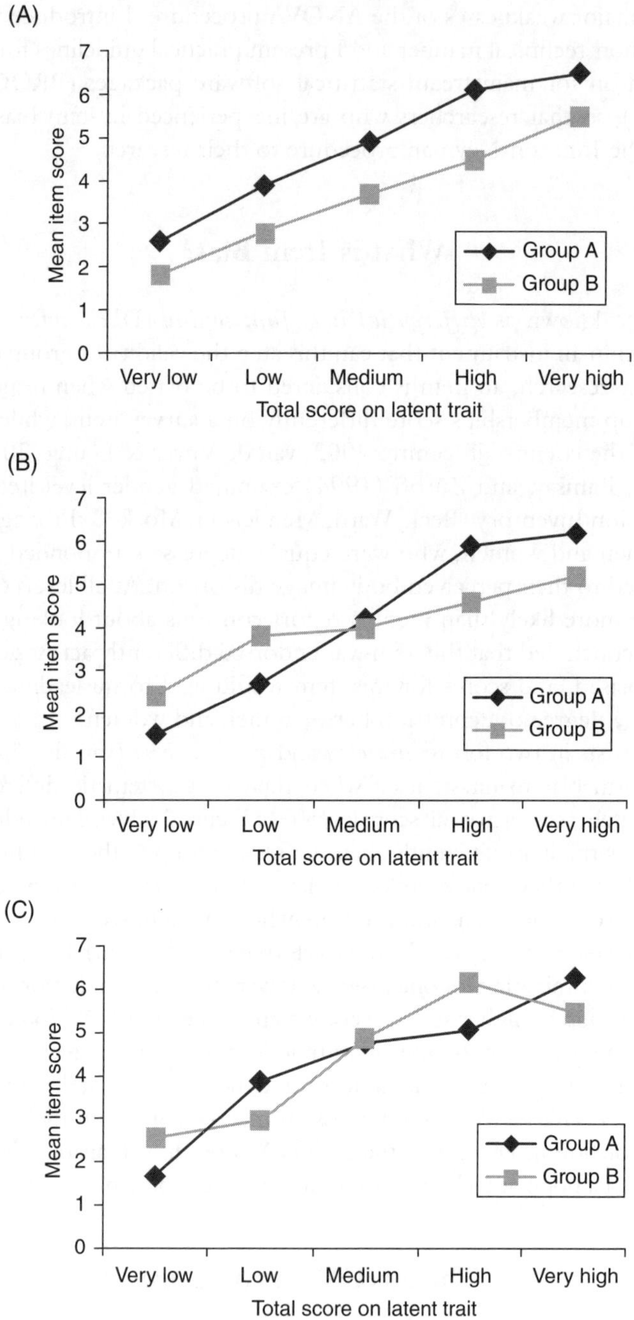

Figure 25.1 Hypothetical examples of an item with (A) uniform bias, (B) non-uniform bias, and (C) no bias (adapted from van de Vijver & Leung, 2011).

(*group A* and *group B*) to examine between-group differences. The ANOVA procedure is centered on three variables (i.e., *item*, *group*, and *score level*): *Group* and *score level* are categorical independent variables and *item* is a continuous dependent variable.

Item is the dependent variable in the ANOVA procedure, and it refers to the item we would like to examine for evidence of bias in the research instrument. In our hypothetical example there are ten items (*item 1* to *item 10*), and in the ANOVA procedure each item is examined independently for evidence of bias. *Group* and *score level* are the independent variables. *Group* refers to the groups that are compared in the study (e.g., gender or culture; in our example *group A* and *group B*). The *group* variable is dummy coded in the dataset (e.g., *group A* = 0 and *group B* = 1).

Unlike *item* and *group*, which are already present in the dataset, *score level* is a new variable that must be calculated by the researcher. This is done by first computing a *total score* variable, which is simply the sum of all item scores (i.e., *item 1* + *item 2* + ··· + *item 10*) for each respondent. Recall that the test instrument had ten items measured by a seven-point scale. If a respondent selects 1 (strongly disagree) for all items, she will have the lowest possible total score (i.e., 10 × 1 = 10). On the other hand, if she selects 7 (strongly agree) for all items, her total score will be the maximum possible score (i.e., 10 × 7 = 70). Thus, each respondent's total score on the test instrument is a value between 10 and 70. Next, the *total score* variable is transformed into the *score level* variable. *Score level* is a categorical variable that is created by splitting the continuous *total score* variable into groups based on predetermined cut-points. The aim of this procedure is to group respondents with similar total scores, so that groups are ranging from "low total scores" to "high total scores". According to van de Vijver and Leung (1997), the cut-points should be determined in a way that each score level contains at least 50 respondents. If the sample size is 500, for instance, there are eight or nine groups in the *score level* variable (for a more detailed explanation of this procedure, see van de Vijver & Leung, 1997). It should be noted that these cut-points, which designate score levels, are arbitrary.

Once the three variables (i.e., *item*, *group*, and *score level*) are ready, a conditional two-way ANOVA is conducted to test for item bias. Conceptually, the ANOVA procedure tests the null hypothesis that "item scores are not different between groups" across different score levels. The ANOVA identifies three effects on the dependent variable *item*: the main effects of *score level* and *group*, and the *group* × *score level* interaction effect. The main effect of *score level* is of little interest to the researcher; respondents at higher score levels usually have a higher score on the item than respondents at lower score levels do, thus this main effect will often be significant. The significance levels of the remaining two effects are, however, essential to the ANOVA procedure.

When both the main effect of *group* and the *group* × *score level* interaction effect are non-significant, the item under scrutiny is unbiased (van de Vijver & Leung, 1997). On the other hand, a significant main effect of *group* and *group* × *score level* interaction effect indicate the presence of uniform and non-uniform bias, respectively (van de Vijver & Leung, 1997). Given our example, if respondents in *Group A* score higher (or lower) than respondents in *Group B* for *item 1* at all score levels, this uniform bias for *item 1* will be evident as a significant main effect of the *group* variable. Finally, if the differences between groups are not equivalent across all score levels, this non-uniform bias will be evident as a significant *group* × *score level* interaction effect.

The ANOVA procedure is easy to apply and interpret using mainstream statistical software packages. It also enables visual examination of item bias with graphical displays. Despite such advantages, the ANOVA procedure has two interrelated shortcomings: the need to discretize a continuous variable (i.e., transforming the continuous *total score* variable into the categorical *score level* variable) and the need for large sample sizes. Given that the higher the number of score levels, the more sensitive the analysis of item bias (van de Vijver & Leung, 1997, 2011), large sample sizes become necessary for the ANOVA procedure to achieve the "minimum 50 respondents per score level" rule of thumb and to retain the statistical power reduced as a result of the discretization procedure. Large sample sizes may, however, inflate significance levels, thereby making statistical significance testing less informative. Recognizing this issue, van de Vijver and Leung (2011) suggest using effect sizes instead of significance values to detect biased items with the ANOVA procedure.

There is compelling evidence in the literature concerning the limitations of discretizing a continuous variable based on arbitrary groups (e.g., Fitzsimons, 2008; Irwin & McClelland, 2003; MacCallum, Zhang, Preacher, & Rucker, 2002; Maxwell & Delaney, 1993). Taken together, these studies conclude that the discretization procedure should be avoided for it may result in reduced statistical power, loss of information, and misleading results. We can therefore conclude that the main shortcoming of the ANOVA procedure stems from discretizing a continuous variable to create a categorical alternative. Nonetheless, there are alternative methods such as the Johnson-Neyman procedure (Johnson & Neyman, 1936), which allows the conduct of similar analyses without discretizing continuous variables.

The Johnson-Neyman Procedure

The Johnson-Neyman procedure, introduced by Johnson and Neyman (1936) and extended to multiple regression models by Preacher, Curran, and Bauer (2006), has been proposed as an alternative to analysis of covariance techniques (D'Alonzo, 2004; Miyazaki & Maier, 2005). Analogous to the ANOVA method, the Johnson-Neyman procedure is used for examining the conditional effect of an independent variable on a dependent variable at different values of another independent variable (i.e., a moderator). Unlike the ANOVA method, the Johnson-Neyman procedure does not require any transformation of the continuous variables. Instead of discretizing a continuous variable into groups, it tests the same null hypothesis that "item scores are not different between groups" at all levels of the continuous variable and returns a "region of significance" within which the scores between groups differ at a specified significance level (e.g., $p < 0.05$). The region of significance can then be plotted for a visual inspection of the results.

Based on its similarities with the ANOVA method, the Johnson-Neyman procedure can easily be adopted to item bias analysis. In the item bias analysis context, the Johnson-Neyman procedure is also based on three main variables (i.e., *item*, *group*, and *total score)*, as explained in the previous section. Note that the categorical *score level* variable is redundant for the Johnson-Neyman procedure, as the continuous *total score* variable can be used without any transformation. These three variables can be entered into a moderated multiple regression analysis as follows: *item* is the dependent variable, whereas *group*, *total score*, and *group* × *total score* interaction are the independent variables. The multiple regression analysis then provides an output with two main effects (*group* and *total score*) and one interaction effect (*group* × *total score*). As for the ANOVA method, the significant main effect of *group* indicates uniform bias and the significant *group* × *total score* interaction effect indicates non-uniform bias. At this point, the region of significance can also assist the researcher in determining biased items such that high proportions of the sample within the significance region provide further evidence of item bias.

The biggest advantage of the Johnson-Neyman procedure over the ANOVA method in detecting item bias is that it accommodates the *total score* variable in the analysis as a continuous variable and tests the conditional effect of *group* on *item* at all levels of the *total score* variable. Testing all levels of the *total score* variable is more informative to the researcher, because respondents' total item scores are arbitrary and there are no meaningful values that can be selected and analyzed independently (see also floodlight analysis by Spiller, Fitzsimons, Lynch, & McClelland, 2013). For example, when conducting the Johnson-Neyman analysis with the body-mass index (BMI) as the moderator (e.g., Spiller et al., 2013), researchers may choose to examine the moderator at specific meaningful values (e.g., overweight respondents; BMI > 25). The *total score* variable in the item bias analysis, however, does not have such focal meaningful values; it therefore needs to be analyzed at all levels. Treating the *total score* variable as continuous rather than discretizing it with arbitrary cut-points also avoids loss of statistical power and the possibility of spurious effects (West, Aiken, & Krull, 1996), which may be of concern when the ANOVA method is used.

Although the Johnson-Neyman procedure is not a new development, its complexity and lack of availability in statistical analysis programs has impeded its implementation. Today, however, add-ons like PROCESS Macro (Hayes, 2013) enable researchers to conduct the Johnson-Neyman analysis with ease using mainstream statistical packages (e.g., SPSS and SAS).

An Illustrative Example Using Conscientiousness

An illustration of the Johnson-Neyman procedure is presented here using a dataset that was collected from a university student sample in Norway. 230 students (120 females and 110 males) responded to a brief conscientiousness measure (8 items; Saucier, 1994) using a 7-point Likert-type scale (1 = strongly disagree to

Table 25.1 Descriptive statistics and independent sample *t*-test results between gender groups for a conscientiousness scale

	Gender				
	Females (N=120)	*Males (N=110)*	*t*	*p*	*Cohen's d*
Organized	5.23 (1.28)	4.55 (1.41)	3.83	<0.001	0.51
Efficient	5.05 (0.96)	4.86 (1.26)	1.26	0.206	0.17
Systematic	5.29 (1.16)	4.51 (1.39)	4.65	<0.001	0.62
Practical	5.02 (1.14)	4.79 (1.26)	1.42	0.157	0.19
Disorganized (R)	5.59 (1.14)	4.90 (1.38)	4.14	<0.001	0.55
Sloppy (R)	5.55 (1.08)	5.31 (1.10)	1.68	0.094	0.22
Inefficient (R)	5.62 (1.22)	5.31 (1.19)	1.93	0.055	0.26
Careless (R)	5.51 (1.28)	5.54 (1.23)	−0.17	0.866	0.02
Conscientiousness (scale)	5.36 (0.78)	4.97 (0.87)	3.54	<0.001	0.47
Alpha coefficient	α = 0.83	α = 0.83			

Note: (R) denotes reverse-coded item.

7 = strongly agree) as part of a battery of survey questions. Our objective in this example is to examine item bias across gender groups. The scale had satisfactory alpha levels ($\alpha_{total} = 0.84$, $\alpha_{male} = 0.83$, $\alpha_{female} = 0.83$). Because the purpose here is to illustrate the procedure, advanced unidimensionality tests were not conducted and the scale was assumed to be unidimensional. Researchers are recommended to ensure their instruments' unidimensionality prior to conducting item bias analysis.

The results of an independent samples *t*-test analysis showed significant differences for various individual item scores and total scale mean score, such that females scored higher on trait conscientiousness than males did (see Table 25.1). An examination of effect sizes (Cohen's *d*) in Table 25.1 shows that the magnitudes of gender differences across items vary from small to medium (Cohen, 1992). It is important to take note of this variation in the effect sizes, as it may signal the presence of item bias in the scale (Smith, 2002).

To conduct the main item bias analysis, first the total score variable (i.e., *total*) was created. Recall that this variable is the sum of all item scores for each respondent. Hayes' PROCESS Macro for SPSS (Hayes, 2013) was used for data analysis (information regarding the installation of the macro is available online at http://www.processmacro.org). Separate analyses were conducted for each of the eight items in the scale. In the main PROCESS Macro dialogue box, first the scale item of interest (e.g., *careless*) was entered into the outcome variable (*Y*) box. Next, the dummy coded group variable (i.e., *gender*) was entered into the independent variable (*X*) box. Finally, the total score variable (i.e., *total*) was entered into the moderator variables (*M*) box. Model number 1 (the moderated regression model)

Table 25.2 Moderated regression analysis results and the Johnson-Neyman significance regions ($N = 230$)

Items	*B*	*SE (B)*	*t*	*p*	*Sample within the significance region (%)*
Organized					
Gender	−0.20	0.12	−1.67	0.096	–
Gender × Total score	0.01	0.02	0.80	0.422	
Efficient					
Gender	0.12	0.12	0.93	0.351	–
Gender × Total score	0.01	0.02	0.34	0.736	
Systematic					
Gender	−0.31	0.11	−2.85	0.005	64.3%
Gender × Total score	0.03	0.01	2.18	0.030	
Practical					
Gender	0.03	0.15	0.19	0.851	–
Gender × Total score	−0.01	0.02	−0.27	0.789	
Disorganized (R)					
Gender	−0.27	0.13	−2.09	0.038	27%
Gender × Total score	0.01	0.02	0.74	0.462	
Sloppy (R)					
Gender	0.12	0.11	1.09	0.278	–
Gender × Total score	0.01	0.02	0.14	0.891	
Inefficient (R)					
Gender	0.09	0.12	0.71	0.478	–
Gender × Total score	−0.03	0.02	−1.81	0.071	
Careless (R)					
Gender	0.43	0.12	3.47	0.001	76.5%
Gender × Total score	−0.03	0.02	−1.48	0.141	

Note: (R) denotes reverse-coded item.

was also selected in the main screen menu. In the "options" menu, "mean center for products" option was selected. This option mean centers the independent variables (*X* and *M*; *gender* and *total*) prior to computation of the interaction variable (*X* × *M*; *gender* × *total*). Mean centering renders the regression coefficients of the independent variables more meaningful (Hayes, 2013); given that our main interest lies in interpreting the main effect of the group variable (in our case *gender*), mean centering must be employed. Graphical representations of the results are useful in item bias analysis; hence, the "generate data for plotting" option in the "options" menu was also selected. The final step was to select the "Johnson-Neyman" option from the menu titled "conditioning". Pressing the "OK" button in the main dialogue box ran the regression model and generated the output.

The results of the item bias analyses are presented in Table 25.2 and an example of PROCESS Macro output is presented in Table 25.3. Similar to the ANOVA

Table 25.3 Example PROCESS Macro output for the Johnson-Neyman analysis of the item "careless"

```
************ PROCESS Procedure for SPSS Release 2.13 *************
Written by Andrew F. Hayes, Ph.D.          www.afhayes.com
Documentation available in Hayes (2013). www.guilford.com/p/hayes3
******************************************************************
Model = 1
    Y = CARELESS
    X = GENDER
    M = TOTAL
Sample size
        230
******************************************************************
Outcome: CARELESS

Model Summary
R         R-sq      MSE       F         df1       df2       p
,6889     ,4746     ,8401     58,1149   3,0000    226,0000  ,0000
Model
          Coeff     se        t         p         LLCI      ULCI
constant  5,4973    ,0625     87,9862   ,0000     5,3741    5,6204
TOTAL      ,1319    ,0107     12,3828   ,0000      ,1109     ,1529
GENDER     ,4308    ,1241      3,4724   ,0006      ,1863     ,6753
int_1     -,0318    ,0215     -1,4764   ,1412     -,0742     ,0106

Interactions:
int_1     GENDER    X         TOTAL
********************* JOHNSON-NEYMAN TECHNIQUE ****************
Moderator value(s) defining Johnson-Neyman significance region(s):
    Value  % below  % above
   5,4176  76,5217  23,4783

Conditional effect of X on Y at values of the moderator (M)
      TOTAL   Effect        se         t         p      LLCI      ULCI
   -21,3826   1,1107     ,5234    2,1220     ,0349     ,0793    2,1421
   -19,5826   1,0535     ,4856    2,1692     ,0311     ,0965    2,0104
   -17,7826    ,9962     ,4480    2,2235     ,0272     ,1134    1,8791
   -15,9826    ,9390     ,4107    2,2866     ,0231     ,1298    1,7482
   -14,1826    ,8818     ,3736    2,3605     ,0191     ,1457    1,6179
   -12,3826    ,8245     ,3368    2,4480     ,0151     ,1608    1,4882
   -10,5826    ,7673     ,3006    2,5526     ,0114     ,1750    1,3596
    -8,7826    ,7101     ,2651    2,6785     ,0079     ,1877    1,2324
    -6,9826    ,6528     ,2306    2,8304     ,0051     ,1983    1,1073
    -5,1826    ,5956     ,1978    3,0111     ,0029     ,2058     ,9854
    -3,3826    ,5384     ,1675    3,2139     ,0015     ,2083     ,8685
    -1,5826    ,4811     ,1414    3,4023     ,0008     ,2025     ,7598
      ,2174    ,4239     ,1222    3,4679     ,0006     ,1830     ,6648
```

(Continued)

Table 25.3 (Continued)

```
   2,0174      ,3667      ,1135    3,2295      ,0014      ,1429      ,5904
   3,8174      ,3094      ,1177    2,6298      ,0091      ,0776      ,5413
   5,4176      ,2586      ,1312    1,9705      ,0500      ,0000      ,5171
   5,6174      ,2522      ,1334    1,8901      ,0600    -,0107      ,5151
   7,4174      ,1950      ,1574    1,2389      ,2167    -,1152      ,5051
   9,2174      ,1377      ,1864      ,7390      ,4607    -,2295      ,5050
  11,0174      ,0805      ,2184      ,3686      ,7128    -,3499      ,5109
  12,8174      ,0233      ,2524      ,0922      ,9266    -,4740      ,5206
  14,6174    -,0340      ,2875    -,1181      ,9061    -,6006      ,5327
****************************************************************
Data for visualizing conditional effect of X on Y
Paste text below into a SPSS syntax window and execute to produce
plot.

DATA LIST FREE/GENDER TOTAL CARELESS.
BEGIN DATA.
   -,4783   -6,7721     4,2949
    ,5217   -6,7721     4,9410
   -,4783     ,0000     5,2912
    ,5217     ,0000     5,7220
   -,4783    6,7721     6,2876
    ,5217    6,7721     6,5031

END DATA.
GRAPH/SCATTERPLOT=GENDER WITH CARELESS BY TOTAL.
***************** ANALYSIS NOTES AND WARNINGS *****************
```

procedure, we are interested in the main effect of the group (*gender*) and the interaction effect (*gender* × *total*) to examine uniform and non-uniform bias, respectively. The "model summary" section of the output (see Table 25.3) displays these effects. For the item "*careless*," for example, we observe a significant main effect of gender group ($B = 0.43$, $t(226) = 3.47$, $p < 0.001$) and a non-significant interaction effect ($B = -0.03$, $t(226) = -1.48$, $p = 0.141$). These results indicate the presence of uniform bias for the item "*careless*."

In the Johnson-Neyman procedure, conclusions regarding biased items do not have to be based solely on the statistical significance levels. As discussed previously, an advantage of the Johnson-Neyman procedure is that it provides a "region of significance", which informs us about the amount of sample within the region where the conditional effect of *group* on *item* is significant. The "Johnson-Neyman Technique" section of the output in Table 25.3 provides us the Johnson-Neyman point for the moderator (i.e., 5.42). An examination of the regression results in this section reveals that gender group had a significant effect on item score for all cases with a mean centered total score below 5.42. Of particular importance here is not only the Johnson-Neyman point, but also the amount of sample present within the region of significance. For example, if there are hardly any respondents who have scores

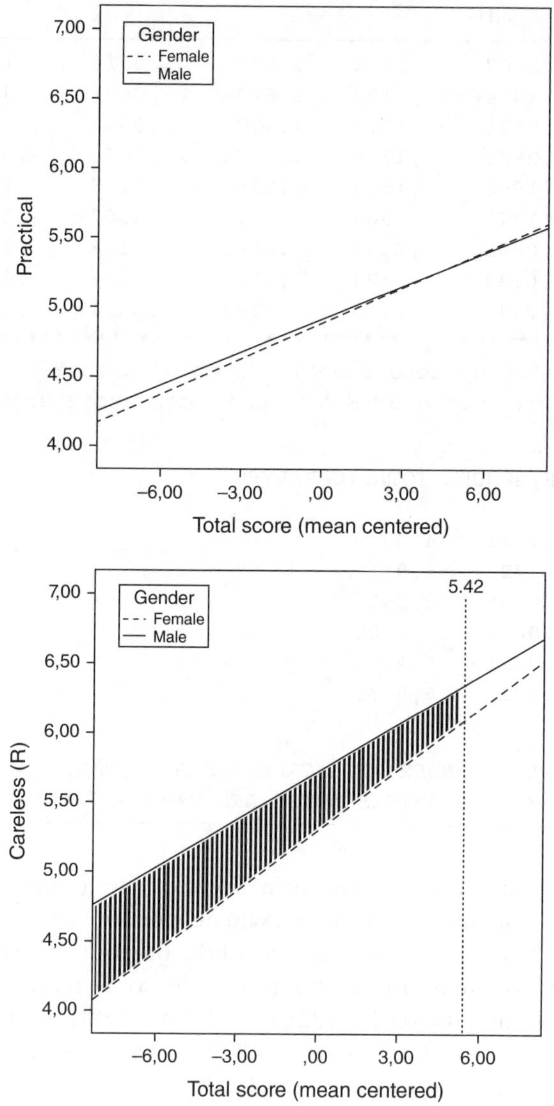

Figure 25.2 Example graphical displays of the moderated regression analysis results (unbiased item to the top and biased item to the bottom). The Johnson-Neyman region of significance is shaded in gray. (R) denotes a reverse-coded item.

below the Johnson-Neyman point, we should be cautious in making item bias claims. The PROCESS Macro output provides this necessary information. As seen on the "Johnson-Neyman Technique" section of the output in Table 25.3, about 76.5% of the cases in the dataset had values below the Johnson-Neyman point when the item "*careless*" was analyzed. On the other hand, when the item "*disorganized*" was taken into consideration, there was again a significant effect of gender group, indicating presence of uniform bias, but only 27% of the cases were within the significance region (see Table 25.2). Researchers should be cautious in making conclusions about item bias in such cases where there are insufficient cases within the region of significance. Although there are no rules of thumb, it is reasonable to expect more than half of the sample to be within the region of significance to have substantial evidence of item bias.

The Johnson-Neyman region of significance can also be plotted graphically for visual inspection of the results. The last section of the output in Table 25.3 provides the syntax codes to produce plots in SPSS. These codes can be executed using the SPSS syntax window. Examples of plots for an unbiased item (*practical*) and an item with uniform bias (*careless*) are presented in Figure 25.2. Note that the regression lines for groups have a substantial overlap when the item is unbiased (top), but there is a large gap between the regression lines when uniform bias is present (bottom).

To test whether the results were stable in a smaller sample, item bias analyses were repeated in a random subsample from the dataset (N = 100, 43 females, 57 males). The results were nearly identical (see Table 25.4): the significant effect

Table 25.4 Moderated regression analysis results and the Johnson-Neyman significance regions using a randon subsample (N = 100)

Items	*B*	*SE (B)*	*t*	*p*	*Sample within the significance region (%)*
Organized					
Gender	−0.17	0.17	−1.03	0.308	–
Gender × Total score	0.03	0.03	1.05	0.296	
Efficient					
Gender	0.29	0.19	1.57	0.119	–
Gender × Total score	0.01	0.03	0.14	0.889	
Systematic					
Gender	−0.43	0.16	−2.67	0.009	69%
Gender × Total score	0.02	0.02	1.03	0.304	
Practical					
Gender	−0.18	0.20	−0.88	0.382	–
Gender × Total score	−0.01	0.03	−0.55	0.580	
Disorganized (R)					
Gender	−0.21	0.19	−1.11	0.271	–
Gender × Total score	0.01	0.02	0.47	0.641	
Sloppy (R)					
Gender	0.16	0.17	0.92	0.360	–
Gender × Total score	−0.01	0.02	−0.11	0.910	
Inefficient (R)					
Gender	0.02	0.18	0.11	0.909	–
Gender × Total score	−0.02	0.02	−0.89	0.382	
Careless (R)					
Gender	0.52	0.18	2.86	0.005	68%
Gender × Total score	−0.03	0.03	−1.01	0.312	

Note: (R) denotes reverse-coded item.

of gender group was again evident for items "*systematic*" and "*careless*". The only difference was that the significant *gender* × *total score* interaction effect on item "*systematic*" did not emerge in the subsample analysis. This finding was anticipated, given that detecting interactions in multiple regression analysis generally require large sample sizes (McClelland & Judd, 1993). Therefore, the Johnson-Neyman procedure may not be reliable to detect non-uniform bias when the sample size is small. Small sample sizes (e.g., $N = 100$) are not ideal for item bias analysis in general.

Concluding Remarks

Methods are indispensable to theory development (Greenwald, 2012). Advancing item bias methods and making them available to a wider audience will not only yield more valid group comparisons and better-refined measurement instruments, but also enhance theory development through understanding of why specific items are biased across groups. Therefore, as suggested by Zumbo (2007), new generation item bias methods should be made accessible to researchers who are not measurement specialists. The current chapter is an attempt in this direction.

The present research has introduced the Johnson-Neyman procedure as an item bias analysis tool. Future research can advance the ideas presented here through simulation studies where the ANOVA and the Johnson-Neyman procedures are compared with respect to their sensitivity to detect biased items across different sample sizes. This will be a welcome contribution to the literature on item bias analysis.

Acknowledgments

I am grateful to Professor Sigurd V. Troye for his valuable comments on an earlier draft of this chapter.

References

Beck, A.T., Ward, C.H., Mendelson, M., Mock, J., & Erbaugh, J. (1961). An inventory for measuring depression. *Archives of General Psychiatry, 4* (6), 561–571.

Caprara, G.V., Barbaranelli, C., Bermúdez, J., Maslach, C., & Ruch, W. (2000). Multivariate methods for the comparison of factor structures in cross-cultural research: An illustration with the Big Five questionnaire. *Journal of Cross-Cultural Psychology, 31* (4), 437–464.

Cohen, J. (1992). A power primer. *Psychological Bulletin, 112* (1), 155–159.

D'Alonzo, K.T. (2004). The Johnson-Neyman Procedure as an alternative to ANCOVA. *Western Journal of Nursing Research, 26* (7), 804–812.

Fitzsimons, G.J. (2008). Editorial: Death to dichotomizing. *Journal of Consumer Research, 35* (1), 5–8.

Greenwald, A.G. (2012). There is nothing so theoretical as a good method. *Perspectives on Psychological Science, 7* (2), 99–108.

Hayes, A.F. (2013). *Introduction to Mediation, Moderation, and Conditional Process Analysis: A Regression-Based Approach*. New York: Guilford Press.

Irwin, J.R., & McClelland, G.H. (2003). Negative consequences of dichotomizing continuous predictor variables. *Journal of Marketing Research, 40* (3), 366–371.

Johnson, P.O., & Neyman, J. (1936). Tests of certain linear hypotheses and their application to some educational problems. *Statistical Research Memoirs, 1*, 57–93.

MacCallum, R.C., Zhang, S., Preacher, K.J., & Rucker, D.D. (2002). On the practice of dichotomization of quantitative variables. *Psychological Methods, 7* (1), 19–40.

Maxwell, S.E., & Delaney, H.D. (1993). Bivariate median splits and spurious statistical significance. *Psychological Bulletin, 113* (1), 181–190.

McClelland, G.H., & Judd, C.M. (1993). Statistical difficulties of detecting interactions and moderator effects. *Psychological Bulletin, 114* (2), 376–390.

Miyazaki, Y., & Maier, K.S. (2005). Johnson-Neyman type technique in hierarchical linear models. *Journal of Educational and Behavioral Statistics, 30* (3), 233–259.

Preacher, K.J., Curran, P.J., & Bauer, D.J. (2006). Computational tools for probing interactions in multiple linear regression, multilevel modeling, and latent curve analysis. *Journal of Educational and Behavioral Statistics, 31* (4), 437–448.

Ramírez-Esparza, N., Gosling, S.D., Benet-Martínez, V., Potter, J.P., & Pennebaker, J.W. (2006). Do bilinguals have two personalities? A special case of cultural frame switching. *Journal of Research in Personality, 40* (2), 99–120.

Reynolds, C.R. (2000). Methods for detecting and evaluating cultural bias in neuropsychological tests. In E. Fletcher-Janzen, T. Strickland, & C.R. Reynolds (Eds.), *Handbook of Cross-Cultural Neuropsychology* (pp. 249–285). New York: Kluwer Academic/Plenum Publishers.

Santor, D.A., Ramsay, J., & Zuroff, D.C. (1994). Nonparametric item analyses of the Beck Depression Inventory: Evaluating gender item bias and response option weights. *Psychological Assessment, 6* (3), 255–270.

Saucier, G. (1994). Mini-markers: A brief version of Goldberg's unipolar Big-Five markers. *Journal of Personality Assessment, 63* (3), 506–516.

Smith, L.L. (2002). On the usefulness of item bias analysis to personality psychology. *Personality and Social Psychology Bulletin, 28* (6), 754–763.

Spiller, S.A., Fitzsimons, G.J., Lynch, J.G., & McClelland, G.H. (2013). Spotlights, floodlights, and the magic number zero: Simple effects tests in moderated regression. *Journal of Marketing Research, 50* (2), 277–288.

Thissen, D., Steinberg, L., & Gerrard, M. (1986). Beyond group-mean differences: The concept of item bias. *Psychological Bulletin, 99* (1), 118–128.

van de Vijver, F., & Leung, K. (1997). *Methods and Data Analysis for Cross-Cultural Research*. Thousand Oaks, CA: Sage.

van de Vijver, F., & Leung, K. (2011). Equivalence and bias: A review of concepts, models, and data analytic procedures. In D. Matsumoto, & F. van de Vijver (Eds.), *Cross-Cultural Research Methods in Psychology* (pp. 17–45). New York: Cambridge University Press.

Vecchione, M., Alessandri, G., & Barbaranelli, C. (2012). The Five Factor Model in personnel selection: Measurement equivalence between applicant and non-applicant groups. *Personality and Individual Differences, 52* (4), 503–508.

West, S.G., Aiken, L.S., & Krull, J.L. (1996). Experimental personality designs: Analyzing categorical by continuous variable interactions. *Journal of Personality, 64* (1), 1–48.

Zumbo, B.D. (2007). Three generations of DIF analyses: Considering where it has been, where it is now, and where it is going. *Language Assessment Quarterly, 4* (2), 223–233.

26

User Reactions to Personality Assessment: Implications for Assessment Credibility, Utility, and Practicality

Chris D. Fluckinger

Bowling Green State University, Bowling Green, Ohio, USA

Andrea F. Snell

University of Akron, Akron, Ohio, USA

The perceived credibility or favorability of personality tests has become an area of research interest only recently. A major reason is perhaps because reactions do not figure into most models of test utility, practicality or quality (Morgeson et al., 2007; Ryan & Huth, 2008). The majority of research investigating personality measures, particularly in applied settings, has reflected this paradigm, as great effort has been spent in boosting personality test criterion-related validity with little mention of assessment reactions.

Researchers and practitioners have occasionally voiced concern about the reactions that traditional personality tests may generate (Podsakoff & Organ, 1986), though only recently have specific calls been made to understand the process behind unfavorable reactions, and to investigate boundary conditions and remedies for the situation (Hough & Oswald, 2008). Morgeson et al. (2007) emphasized the potential detrimental effects of negative reactions by stating that "we cannot ignore the potential for personality inventories to offend" (p. 1040). Indeed, even though perceptions and reactions do not enter into most models of test utility, we argue that negative reactions could be expected to affect a number of important organizational outcomes, although this hypothesis has not yet been tested empirically (Ployhart, 2006).

Recent models aid in further specifying the importance of assessment reactions in organizations. One framework views the assessment context as a *communication exchange process* (Potosky, 2008), which contrasts with the traditional goal of testing, which focuses largely on how to probe individuals to elicit the most useful information. Potosky (2008) noted that assessments should be considered in a larger

The Wiley Handbook of Personality Assessment, First Edition. Edited by Updesh Kumar.
© 2016 John Wiley & Sons, Ltd. Published 2016 by John Wiley & Sons, Ltd.

context than strictly psychometric concerns such as equivalence, construct validity, and criterion-related validity (although those remain as important as ever). These concerns map onto larger, macro-level models such as organizational justice. From this perspective, organizations and clients/applicants/employees are engaged in a dialog, with information flowing bidirectionally throughout the process. Personality tests, which can be an important part of the process, communicate information to test-takers and can factor into more holistic justice appraisals (Gilliland, 1993). More research and theory are needed to explicate the kinds of information that are communicated in the personality assessment dialog.

Current Understanding of Reactions to Personality Assessment

Of the signals for the recent interest in personality test reactions, Hausknecht, Day, and Thomas' (2004) meta-analytic review of reactions to assessment procedures (in this case, employee selection methods) may be the most influential. Upon aggregating results of the perceived favorability of various common psychometric assessments, the results indicated that personality tests are viewed less favorably than interviews, references, work samples, and even cognitive ability tests. This basic pattern has generally been supported internationally in Vietnamese, Dutch, French, Spanish, Portuguese, and Singaporean samples (Anderson & Witvliet, 2008; Hoang, Truxillo, Erdogan, & Bauer, 2012). These results may be counterintuitive to beliefs held by many personality vendors and researchers. Non-cognitive measures often were thought to produce more favorable reactions because they are not ability-based, and personality tests could be useful complements to cognitive tests (McFarland & Ryan, 2000).

The Hausknecht et al. (2004) results are also qualified by a number of limitations. First, the reactions used in the primary studies were grouped together into an overall favorability index, prohibiting investigation of different results by various components of favorability. Second, these findings were largely based on an insufficient paradigm by Steiner and Gilliland (1996). In this paradigm, participants were given a list of approximately 10 different selection instruments, each with a brief description of the content of the measure. For example, the definition for personality tests was "paper-and-pencil tests that ask you questions about your opinions and past experiences to assess your personality traits" (p. 136). Participants then provided various reactions to the tests *without actually experiencing the full tests*, and researchers have advised caution in generalizing results based on this paradigm to applied settings (Berry, Sackett, & Weimann, 2007).

The effect of measurement method on test favorability would be impossible to assess given the above paradigm, as there is no mention of features such as test interactivity (i.e., monotonous responding to potentially repetitive items) or how the items are to be approached (i.e., absolute ratings or prioritizing items relative to other items). Marcus (2003) provided an important test of the viability of the Steiner and Gilliland (1996) paradigm by obtaining reactions measures both after exposure to the test definitions and after completion of actual cognitive ability and personality tests. Marcus (2003) observed a significant drop in favorability after completion of the personality test (but not the cognitive ability test), indicating that estimates of personality test favorability based on the Steiner and Gilliland (1996) paradigm actually *overestimated* the perceived favorability of personality tests in applied settings. This should be a sobering finding for personality test vendors, developers, and researchers alike.

One conclusion that can be drawn from this line of research is that personality tests are viewed unfavorably and should not be used (Morgeson et al., 2007). Conversely, one may conclude that more research should be devoted to understanding whether personality itself in applied contexts is objectionable or if changes to test content, method of assessment, or other factors could negate these negative reactions. This review is based on the belief that personality assessment is important to the goals and functions of many organizations, as well as related issues such as organizational fit and human capital (Ployhart, 2006), and that efforts to improve reactions to personality testing are worthwhile.

Relevant Theory for Reactions to Personality Assessment

Before presenting specific aspects of reactions and implications discussed in this review, it is helpful to address key models and perspectives. One important point involves differentiating between organizational justice perspectives and reactions to tests and/or measures. Organizational justice has received much attention since Gilliland's (1993) model, which presents a macro-level perspective that takes a holistic approach to the recruitment, assessment, selection and placement process. Emphasis is placed on procedural components (i.e., timeliness of feedback, consistency of test administration across applicants, and the presence/application of structural procedures) and interpersonal components (friendliness of assessment administrators, genuineness of recruiters, and attentiveness of interviewers). By focusing on these aspects of the overall procedure, Gilliland's model does not directly account for numerous micro-level factors about the effects that various methods of assessment could have on personality assessment reactions.

Narrative reviews conducted by Ryan and Ployhart (2000) and Ryan and Huth (2008) note the presence of a related stream of research that focuses on assessment reactions largely outside of the organizational justice framework. Much of this work has focused on individual differences such as test-taking motivation, test self-efficacy, test experience, and the effects of negative feedback on general test reactions (Ryan & Ployhart, 2000). This has led to calls for assessment reactions research to also consider structural test factors, including extent of computerization, response formats, and different levels of interactivity, to help guide test developers in creating tests that also generate favorable test-taker reactions (Hausknecht et al., 2004; Ryan & Huth, 2008).

When combining these perspectives, it is clear that a holistic understanding of the dialog between organizations and clients/applicants/test-takers involves both the macro- and micro-level features. Organizations have strategic goals, some of which

Table 26.1 Key stages and variables for reactions to personality assessments

Stage of assessment	*Relevant variables/constructs*
Assessment context	Assessment purpose/instructions
	Cultural considerations
Assessment features	Response choice/format
	Customization/fidelity to context
	Aesthetic qualities
Direct test perceptions	Enjoyability
	Interactivity
	Fakability/perceived accuracy
Reactions/behavior	Organizational attraction
	Recommendation intentions
Organizational consequences	Size of applicant/client pool
	Reputation within industry/region

are translated into the design and implementation of critical assessments, often involving some aspect, either directly or indirectly, of personality assessment. Test-takers enter into the interaction with expectations, organizational impressions, and/or strategies that affect the test-taking experience (Bell, Wiechmann, & Ryan, 2006). These variables then influence perceptions about the assessment itself, as well as reactions to the organization that implemented the assessment. Expanding back out to the macro-level, when patterns are observed over large samples of test-takers, these could reasonably be translated into important organizational considerations and outcomes.

Our current understanding of many of these aspects of the organization/test-taker dialog is likely insufficient to piece together into a strong, testable model. However, there are a number of important general stages within the process, which Table 26.1 presents. The form and results of each stage in the process is loosely expected to cause, or at least influence, the stage below it, as can be seen in the left-hand column. Key variables to each stage can be found in the right-hand column. Each stage and characteristic variables/constructs are presented in detail below.

Stages of Personality Assessment

Personality assessment context

Given that personality assessment could be useful across a broad spectrum of situations, it is important to consider contextual factors that could be relevant to test-takers. Numerous variables could be included here, but we choose to focus on two in particular that have often been discussed directly in relation to personality assessment: the purpose of the assessment and cultural considerations.

Assessment purpose/instructions. Personality assessments may vary considerably in terms of what kinds of instructions are provided to test-takers, particularly in high-stakes settings. For example, a substantial amount of research has focused on whether a warning to test-takers not to attempt to fake, or dishonestly present themselves, has a positive impact on the criterion-related validity of the assessment results. If it is assumed that a large number of test-takers will engage in faking behavior, then this strategy might be suitable to deal with criterion-related validity concerns. However, it is unclear what effects this strategy may have on test-taker reactions to the assessment, such as leading test-takers to feel threatened or challenged, and these concerns have been voiced (Hough & Oswald, 2008). Warnings not to fake represent just one type of assessment instruction that may negatively affect reactions.

Although an important consideration, specific instructions represent only a portion of pre-assessment information to which test-takers might be attentive. Another key factor involves the stated purpose of the personality assessment, whether presented explicitly or implied. The test could be used primarily, or often exclusively, to measure relevant personality attributes that the organization will use to guide future judgments and decisions. However, personality assessments can also be presented as ways for test-takers to learn about or discover internal qualities and patterns. In the applicant selection context, test batteries are increasingly presented to applicants as means for them to learn about the position for which they are applying, and by extension, to use this information to decide both the extent to which the job in question represents a strong fit and whether to self-select out of the process.

Cultural considerations. Although research continues to cross-culturally replicate the general place of personality assessment in the psychometric assessment hierarchy with respect to test-taker reactions, a number of additional research possibilities remain. Given that cultures typically differ in terms of the individualism/collectivism dimensions (Nisbett & Miyamoto, 2005), it would be helpful to understand how these dimensions translate into different attitudes about the value and use of personality assessment. For example, if a general definition of personality involves consistency of behavior and thought patterns across situations, then expression of personality as an enduring personal characteristic is simply more a function of an individualist mindset. By extension, the use of personality measures – particularly in high-stakes settings – would be less useful for those with a collectivist mindset. If there is a mismatch between the organizational goals for the use of a personality assessment and cultural differences in the value of the assessment, this mismatch could be reflected in test-taker perceptions and reactions.

Personality assessment features

Personality assessments come in all shapes and sizes, and one of the advantages to the enormous corpus of personality research is that there are ample data to compare the various item lists and response formats of different personality assessments across a variety of criteria. Of course, a notable exception is test-taker reaction differences across various personality assessment features. As with the assessment context, there are numerous features we could include to understand personality assessment features, but here we focus on three that have been clearly mentioned in the literature: response choice/format, customization/fidelity to context, and aesthetic qualities.

Response choice/format. We find it interesting that much of the impetus for designing, validating, and implementing different personality assessment methods has originated from general goals of understanding the orthogonality of personality dimensions and to improve criterion-related validity, but has almost completely overlooked the impact on test-taker reactions that these structural test features might have. A wide variety of research options exist to compare many different personality assessment formats with relation to test-taker reactions.

These investigations can take the form of relatively straightforward experimental designs. For example, using a within-subjects design, Fluckinger and Brodke (2013) had participants complete a 50-item Big Five personality assessment in both Q-sort and Likert formats. Even though the measures were largely equivalent from a psychometric standpoint (Fluckinger, 2014), test-takers showed a preference for the Q-sort across a variety of dimensions, including perceiving the Q-sort as less limiting in expression of personality. Although Likert-based personality assessments are often viewed as the "gold-standard," it is also possible that negative reactions to personality assessment are driven more by negative reactions to the method rather than the general concept of personality assessment.

Customization/fidelity to context. As described above with respect to response formats, personality assessments also show a great deal of variability across contexts in terms of the extent of customization for a specific organization. Even if the items on the assessment are taken from a well-known inventory, a number of features may be customized toward a particular context. Some of these, such as organizational branding within the assessment and specialized instructions/information about how and why the test is being used, have been discussed above. In addition, some measurement formats are intrinsically more customized than others. For example, situational judgment tests are often thought to measure, at least partially, personality traits. Unlike global personality inventories, however, situational judgment tests are designed with respect to certain contexts, and have been shown to be viewed more favorably by test-takers than standard personality assessments (Patterson, Zibarras, Carr, Irish & Gregory, 2011). Moving toward increasingly customized tests, whether developed in-house or altered from "off-the-shelf" varieties, will likely be more expensive, and it is currently unclear whether the expense for such assessments would be recovered through more favorable test-taker reactions.

Aesthetic qualities. As personality assessments are increasingly customized, automated, and delivered online (Bartram & Brown, 2004), it is also more feasible to consider aesthetic qualities of the assessment, such as visual appearance. Strategies to improve assessment appearance can range from complex, holistic approaches to relatively simple solutions, such as adding color where possible. The question is how much do test-takers appreciate, or even demand, aesthetically pleasing assessments? Aside from Fluckinger and Brodke's (2013) study, in which participants viewed a Q-sort with identical Big Five items (compared with a Likert measure, both delivered online) as substantially more visually appealing, there is little research directly investigating the effects of personality assessment design on test-taker reactions, and this represents another potentially fruitful avenue for future research.

Direct perceptions of personality assessment features

Interactivity. Qualitative reviews have expressed surprise that more research has not investigated the effects that test properties such as interactivity, functionality, and "slickness" may have on test-taker perceptions and reactions (Ryan & Huth, 2008; Ryan & Ployhart, 2000). Increased interactivity is particularly important in applied contexts, where psychometric tests must convey a modicum of credibility to test-takers (Schleicher, Venkataramani, Morgeson, & Campion, 2006). Interactivity is also noted as an important feature of the communication exchange process between organizations and applicants (Potosky, 2008), and of the recruiting process via engaging online material (Cober, Brown, Levy, Cober & Keeping, 2003).

One factor affecting interactivity – test computerization – generally improves test-taker perceptions (Potosky & Bobko, 2004); however, the positive effect of computerization on test favorability is likely not specific to personality tests. Just as traditional personality instruments are often deployed in online and computerized formats in both research and applied settings, a number of different personality assessment programs have been put forth.

Research indicates that adding interactive features to computerized measures can increase perceptions such as perceived predictive validity (Richman-Hirsch, Olson-Buchanan, & Drasgow, 2000) and general perceptions of face validity (Shotland, Alliger, & Sales, 1998). Interactive test content can also reduce test boredom and off-task cognition (Kluger & Rothstein, 1993). Although there appears to be some disagreement in the literature as to the precise specifications of interactivity, it is operationalized here as retaining test-taker attention through being perceived as less repetitive and more engaging.

Fakability/perceived accuracy. As noted by Ryan and Huth (2008), much applied personality research has been devoted to developing tests that are less fakable, potentially at the expense of investigating test-taker perceptions of fakability. One reason for this lies with the different perspectives of test administrators and test-takers – test-takers, particularly honest ones, may view high test fakability as a serious threat to general test credibility, but test administrators can endure some level of fakability as long as the test can predict important criteria. However, Likert-based personality tests are intuitively fakable, researchers and practitioners believe they are fakable (Morgeson et al., 2007), and qualitative evidence indirectly supports these beliefs (Robie, Brown & Beaty, 2007; Schleicher et al., 2006).

Enjoyability. Psychometric tests and assessments are typically not evaluated with regard to their perceived enjoyability, particularly in employment selection contexts. When test enjoyability is studied, personality measures are viewed unfavorably, as Kluger and Rothstein (1993) found that non-cognitive tests were viewed as less enjoyable than cognitive ability or work sample tests. Affective appraisals and reactions throughout the assessment process can have large effects on key variables such as organizational attraction and fairness perceptions (Gilliland, 1993; Ryan & Ployhart, 2000). This variable certainly represents an opportunity for future research, as the concept of exploring, understanding and expressing one's personality should be at least somewhat affirming and enjoyable. Perhaps this is lessened in high-stakes contexts by structural test features and contextual factors.

Reactions/behavior to use of personality assessment

Predictive validity. It is somewhat surprising that there is not much research involving perceptions of predictive validity of different personality measures. Many studies have only included a single item measure and aggregated overall favorability ratings across different kinds of reactions (Hausknecht et al., 2004). By extension, there is little evidence specifically comparing the perceived predictive validity of personality measures with other common selection tools. Available evidence suggests that personality and related non-cognitive measures (i.e., personality-oriented biographical data) demonstrate lower perceived predictive validity than most selection tools, particularly intuitively job-related measures such as interviews, résumés and work samples (Smither et al., 1993). Some have posited that the perceived predictive validity of a non-cognitive test used for selection may be heavily influenced by how fakable the measure is perceived to be (McFarland & Ryan, 2000; Ryan & Huth, 2008). Basically, if test-takers perceive that a test is easy to fake and that others are likely to fake, then test-takers may have lowered expectations regarding the ability of the test to actually predict whatever criteria the assessment is purportedly intended to predict.

Organizational attraction. There is strong support for the effects of procedural justice perceptions, including the extent of interpersonal treatment and consistency of test administration as well as test characteristics (Gilliland, 1993). In fact, perceptions of procedural justice are some of the most powerful bivariate predictors of organizational attraction, along with perceptions of organizational fit and characteristics of the actual work environment (Bauer et al., 2006; Chapman, Uggerslev, Carroll, Piasentin & Jones, 2005). Given these findings, it is reasonable to believe that different testing methods may influence organizational attraction, but it is unclear which direct test perceptions may drive this effect. A frequent finding is that macro-level perceptions such as organizational attraction are directly caused by affective heuristic judgments about the selection procedure (Ployhart, 2006; Ryan & Ployhart, 2000).

Ployhart (2006) suggested that perceptions of organizational attraction may be heavily influenced by emotional judgments regarding the process, such as the extent to which the test experience was enjoyable. For example, Smither et al. (1993) found that affectively-driven process enjoyment was a substantial predictor of organizational attraction compared with variables such as perceived predictive validity. Such a process also supports the recent emphasis on consideration of the testing and assessment process as part of a dialogue with recruits and applicants that can be used for purposes of organizational branding (Ployhart, 2006; Potosky, 2008).

Recommendation intentions. The traditional separation between recruitment and applicant assessment is changing, particularly due to the effect of web-based application and selection tools (Ployhart, 2006; Chapman et al., 2005). Job-seekers may currently hunt for numerous jobs online, often having the option of submitting a profile that includes a non-cognitive (i.e., personality) test. Test features such as usability, interactivity, and aesthetic appearance may influence a number of user outcomes, such as willingness to take the test, level of diligence applied while taking the test, and recommending the procedure to others (Cober, Brown, Blumenthal, Doverspike, & Levy, 2000). The traditional view – that "soft" test features such as aesthetics and interactivity are unimportant because responsible, and therefore desirable, applicants will complete them regardless – may not be accurate (Potosky, 2008). Current job-seekers may search many organizations online, and assessment materials must be usable and interactive to keep applicants engaged in completing the process.

Perhaps more importantly, job-seekers often collaborate and support the job search efforts of friends and colleagues, indicating that word-of-mouth, or "viral," forms of communication are crucial considerations (Ployhart, 2006). Online selection material can either help or hinder this process for organizations seeking to develop a large base of applicants from which to choose. Job-seekers are unlikely to recommend a job application process that includes a test that is boring or uninteresting. Conversely, interactive testing procedures communicate to applicants that the organization is concerned about the applicant's perspective and not just profitability.

Organizational consequences

Here lies the component of the personality assessment process that will ultimately determine the importance of research directed toward understanding reactions to personality assessment. Unlike many evaluations of assessment value, in which different test instructions or contextual features could be expected to affect the criterion-related validity of the test, test reactions are generally not expected to have substantial, if any, effects on the criterion-related validity of personality assessments. Instead, the negative consequences of unfavorable reactions would be anticipated to reveal themselves over time and to affect macro-level organizational outcomes. We freely acknowledge that this represents a proposition that will be difficult to support, as the types of research designs involving personality assessment rarely feature both the multilevel and longitudinal qualities required.

Given the relative lack of research involving potential organizational consequences of negative test reactions, we refrain from presenting each in detail. Instead, we briefly discuss two potential organizational consequences: size (and quality) of applicant/client pool, and reputation within industry/region. To the extent that negative word-of-mouth resulting from personality assessment causes people – whether they be applicants, clients or other interested parties – to either consider or actively search out competing entities that offer similar services, organizations should be mindful of these reactions. This process could impact the size, quality, and/or diversity of applicant or client pools. Conversely, positive word-of-mouth generated through the implementation of personality assessments viewed more favorably than competitors could result in a number of desirable outcomes, ranging from a better client/applicant base to increased marketing opportunities. However, the primary challenge with regard to this macro-level stage is twofold: (1) empirical demonstration of these proposed effects, and (2) proper placement of the personality reactions issue with relation to numerous other organizational considerations.

Conclusion

Although there has been increased attention to the importance of test-taker reactions to psychometric assessment tools – particularly in high-stakes and applied contexts (Ryan & Ployhart, 2014) – we believe that there are a number of issues that must be considered specifically with regard to personality assessment. We have identified a number of themes that can guide future research and implementation issues with regard to personality assessment reactions presented in Table 26.2, which we organized into three general clusters: general findings/conclusions, future challenges, and recommendations. We view this summary less as a comprehensive understanding of the current state of the issue, and more as a general starting point for future applications involving reactions to personality assessment.

The foundation for much of this chapter involves the general finding that personality is rated less favorably – again, particularly in applied settings – than other traditional psychometric assessments, such as cognitive ability tests (Anderson & Witvliet, 2008; Hausknecht et al., 2004; Hoang et al., 2012; Steiner & Gilliland, 1996). We believe that the consistency of this finding may be somewhat unknown outside of applied (i.e., employee selection) circles. However, the fact that this finding is often replicated in applied contexts suggests the need to explore boundary conditions for this pattern outside of traditional employment selection contexts. At the very least, this pattern represents a potential concern for many applications of personality assessment.

Table 26.2 Summary of reactions to personality assessment status

General findings/conclusions
• Personality is viewed less favorably than many psychological assessments
• High-fidelity and/or customized assessments are viewed more favorably
• Little research specifically addressing unfavorable reactions to personality assessment
Future challenges
• Placement of the importance of reactions relative to other assessment considerations
• Establishing measurement equivalence of favorable assessments to traditional measures
• Difficulty of applying experimental designs to high-stakes/applied/clinical samples
Recommendations
• Need for direct links from personality assessment reactions to behavior
• Consider assessment reactions in terms of organizational branding/marketing
• Consideration of cultural differences relating to personality assessment reactions

The primary issue regarding future exploration of test-taker reactions to personality assessment involves the current difficulty of weighting the importance of this issue relative to other notable – and generally more traditional – challenges characteristic of personality assessment, such as attention to the criterion-related validity and structural integrity (i.e., reliability, factor structure, etc.) of a given test (Ryan & Huth, 2008). Given that attempts to improve test-taker reactions will involve modifications to standard test properties, response formats and/or instructions, it will be crucial to demonstrate that an assessment that generates more favorable reactions also results in equivalent structural properties when compared with the traditional assessment. In addition, addressing these kinds of questions often requires experimental designs, which can be more difficult, time-intensive, and costly to implement in applied contexts (Ryan & Ployhart, 2014).

Finally, as discussed earlier, a crucial point is that criterion-related validity is likely to be largely unaffected by test-taker reactions, and that the importance of test-taker reactions will become evident upon consideration of the larger organizational context, including implications for the quality/size of the client base and organizational reputation/branding. This will require more complex research designs, including multilevel and longitudinal approaches, but the ultimate importance of test-taker reactions to personality assessment cannot be established without such research (Ryan & Ployhart, 2014). As personality measurement, theory, and application continues to improve, we believe that efforts to improve test-taker perceptions of personality assessments will also grow increasingly important. As the basic discussion of personality represents a means for individuals to learn both about themselves and others, at least in a very general manner, consideration of the personality assessment process as a dialogue represents a good place to start in the exploration of reactions to personality assessments.

References

Anderson, N., & Witvliet, C. (2008). Fairness reactions to personnel selection methods: An international comparison between the Netherlands, the United States, France, Spain, Portugal and Singapore. *International Journal of Selection and Assessment, 16* (1), 1–13.

Bartram, D., & Brown, A. (2004). Online testing: Mode of administration and the stability of OPQ 32i scores. *International Journal of Selection and Assessment, 12* (3), 278–284.

Bauer, T.N., Truxillo, D.M., Tucker, J.S., Weathers, V., Bertolino, M., Erdogan, B., & Campion, M.A. (2006). Selection in the information age: The impact of privacy concerns and computer experience on applicant reactions. *Journal of Management, 32* (5), 601–621.

Bell, B.S., Wiechmann, D., & Ryan, A.M. (2006). Consequences of organizational justice expectations in a selection system. *Journal of Applied Psychology, 91* (2), 455–466.

Berry, C.M., Sackett, P.R., & Weimann, S. (2007). A review of recent developments in integrity test research. *Personnel Psychology, 60* (2), 271–301.

Chapman, D.S., Uggerslev, K.L., Carroll, S.A., Piasentin, K.A., & Jones, D.A. (2005). Applicant attraction to organizations and job choice. *Journal of Applied Psychology, 90* (5), 928–944.

Cober, R.T., Brown, D.J., Blumenthal, A.J., Doverspike, D., & Levy, P. (2000). The quest for the qualified job-seeker: It's time the public sector catches the wave. *Public Personnel Management, 29* (4), 479–492.

Cober, R.T., Brown, D.J., Levy, P.L., Cober, A.B., & Keeping, L.M. (2003). Organizational web sites: Web site content and style as determinants of organization attraction. *International Journal of Selection and Assessment, 11* (2/3), 158–169.

Fluckinger, C.D. (2014). Big Five measurement via Q-sort: An alternative method for constraining socially desirable responding. *SAGE Open, 4* (3), 1–8.

Fluckinger, C.D., & Brodke, M.R.H. (2013). Positive reactions to Q-sort in a job applicant setting. *Operant Subjectivity: The International Journal of Q Methodology, 36* (4), 335–341.

Gilliland, S.W. (1993). The perceived fairness of selection systems: An organizational justice perspective. *Academy of Management Review, 18* (4), 694–734.

Hausknecht, J.P., Day, D.V., & Thomas, S.C. (2004). Applicant reactions to selection procedures: An updated model and meta-analysis. *Personnel Psychology, 57* (3), 639–683.

Hoang, T.G., Truxillo, D.M., Erdogan, B., & Bauer, T.N. (2012). Cross-cultural examination of applicant reactions to selection methods: United States and Vietnam. *International Journal of Selection and Assessment, 20* (2), 209–219.

Hough, L.M., & Oswald, F.L. (2008). Personality testing and industrial-organizational psychology: Reflections, progress and prospects. *Industrial and Organizational Psychology, 1* (3), 272–290.

Kluger, A.N., & Rothstein, H.R. (1993). The influence of selection test type on applicant reactions to employment testing. *Journal of Business and Psychology, 8* (1), 3–25.

Marcus, B. (2003). Attitudes towards personnel selection methods: A partial replication and extension in a German sample. *Applied Psychology: An International Review, 52* (4), 515–532.

McFarland, L.A., & Ryan, A.M. (2000). Variance in faking across non-cognitive measures. *Journal of Applied Psychology, 85* (5), 812–821.

Morgeson, F.P., Campion, M.A., Dipboye, R.L., Hollenbeck, J.R., Murphy, K., & Schmitt, N. (2007). Are we getting fooled again? Coming to terms with limitations in the use of personality tests for personnel selection. *Personnel Psychology, 60* (4), 1029–1049.

Nisbett, R.E., & Miyamoto, Y. (2005). The influence of culture: Holistic versus analytic perception. *Trends in Cognitive Sciences, 9* (10), 467–473.

Patterson, F., Zibarras, L., Carr, V., Irish, B., & Gregory, S. (2011). Evaluating candidate reactions to selection practices using organizational justice theory. *Medical Education, 45* (3), 289–297.

Ployhart, R.E. (2006). Staffing in the 21st century: New challenges and strategic opportunities. *Journal of Management, 32* (6), 868–897.

Podsakoff, P.M., & Organ, D.W. (1986). Self-reports in organizational research: Problems and prospects. *Journal of Management, 12* (4), 531–544.

Potosky, D. (2008). A conceptual framework for the role of the administration medium in the personnel assessment process. *Academy of Management Review, 33* (3), 629–648.

Potosky, D., & Bobko, P. (2004). Selection testing via the internet: Practical considerations and exploratory empirical findings. *Personnel Psychology, 57* (4), 1003–1034.

Richman-Hirsch, W.L., Olson-Buchanan, J.B., & Drasgow, F. (2000). Examining the impact of administration medium on examinee perceptions and attitudes. *Journal of Applied Psychology, 85* (6), 880–887.

Robie, C., Brown, D.J., & Beaty, J.C. (2007). Do people fake on personality inventories? A verbal protocol analysis. *Journal of Business and Psychology, 21* (4), 489–508.

Ryan, A.M., & Huth, M. (2008). Not much more than platitudes? A critical look at the utility of applicant reactions research. *Human Resource Management Review, 18* (3), 119–132.

Ryan, A.M., & Ployhart, R.E. (2000). Applicants' perceptions of selection procedures and decisions: A critical review and agenda for the future. *Journal of Management, 26* (3), 565–606.

Ryan, A.M., & Ployhart, R.E. (2014). A century of selection. *Annual Review of Psychology, 65*, 693–717.

Schleicher, D.J., Venkataramani, V., Morgeson, F.P., & Campion, M.A. (2006). So you didn't get the job … *now* what do you think? Examining opportunity-to-perform fairness perceptions. *Personnel Psychology, 59* (3), 559–590.

Shotland, A., Alliger, G.M., & Sales, T. (1998). Face validity in the context of personnel selection: A multimedia approach. *International Journal of Selection and Assessment, 6* (2), 124–130.

Smither, J.W., Reilly, R.R., Millsap, R.E., Pearlman, K., & Stoffey, R.W. (1993). Applicant reactions to selection procedures. *Personnel Psychology, 46* (1), 49–76.

Steiner, D.D., & Gilliland, S.W. (1996). Fairness reactions to personnel selection techniques in France and the United States. *Journal of Applied Psychology, 81* (2), 134–141.

27

Novel Approaches to Adjusting for Positive Response Distortion with the Personality Assessment Inventory

John E. Kurtz
Villanova University, Pennsylvania, USA

Lindsey L. Bupp
Wichita State University, USA

Corinne M. Henk
University of North Carolina at Chapel Hill, USA

There are many reasons why self-report questionnaires are the most commonly used methods of personality assessment by practitioners and researchers. The highly structured nature of questionnaires imparts many advantages, including ease of administration and scoring, and the possibility of gathering data remotely via the internet or conventional mail. However, these advantages are offset by the problem of positive response distortion (PRD), a response style inferred from observed scores that indicate better psychological functioning and/or less psychopathology than is objectively the case. The potential for PRD in self-report questionnaires was recognized by some of the earliest test developers. Several strategies for identifying and adjusting for PRD have been developed with somewhat mixed results. This chapter reviews the history of PRD assessment, offers an elaboration of the concept of PRD, and evaluates two novel approaches to dealing with PRD that have been recently introduced for use with the Personality Assessment Inventory (PAI: Morey, 1991, 2007).

The development of the Minnesota Multiphasic Personality Inventory (MMPI: Hathaway & McKinley, 1940) produced one of the earliest systematic attempts at PRD assessment. The original collection of MMPI scales included two indicators of PRD: the L scale and the K scale. The L scale is a rationally derived scale of 15 false-keyed items that describe common faults. In contrast, the items of the K scale were

The Wiley Handbook of Personality Assessment, First Edition. Edited by Updesh Kumar.
© 2016 John Wiley & Sons, Ltd. Published 2016 by John Wiley & Sons, Ltd.

selected empirically by contrasting the responses of known psychiatric patients who produced normal MMPI score profiles with the responses of non-patients. The K scale is proposed to offer a more subtle indication of defensiveness than the L scale (Graham, 2000). Moreover, the K scale is used as a "correction factor" in standard MMPI interpretation (McKinley, Hathaway, & Meehl, 1948); points are added to increase scores on five of the basic scales based on the degree of K-score elevation. Despite the research that has accumulated suggesting that the K correction procedure does not enhance the predictive validity (e.g., Sellbom, Fischler, & Ben-Porath, 2007), this procedure for dealing with PRD was retained when the test was revised and re-normed (MMPI-2: Butcher, Dahlstrom, Graham, Tellegen, & Kaemmer, 1989).

Scales designed to detect PRD are included in many major personality inventories such as the California Psychological Inventory (Gough, 1987); the Personality Research Form (Jackson, 1984); and the Millon Clinical Multiaxial Personality Inventory (Millon, Millon, Davis, & Grossman, 2006). Most PRD scales utilize some combination of items that present common faults and unlikely virtues; denial of faults and endorsement of virtues are keyed responses that indicate the presence of PRD. The PAI (Morey, 1991) assesses PRD with the Positive Impression Management (PIM) scale. The nine items that comprise the PIM scale include eight that relate to common faults and one that relates to an unlikely virtue.

Empirical research demonstrates that these measures of PRD can discriminate groups of respondents who are instructed to create a good impression from groups of respondents who are instructed to respond honestly. A meta-analysis by Baer and Miller (2002) found large effect size differences between instructional groups on L, K, and several other indicators of PRD developed subsequently with the MMPI and MMPI-2 item pools. Several analog studies of the PIM scale from the PAI converge on a *T*-score of 57 as the optimal cut-point for making this discrimination (Cashel, Rogers, Sewell, & Martin-Cannici, 1995; Fals-Stewart, 1996; Morey, 1991; Morey & Lanier, 1998; Peebles & Moore, 1998). The proximity of this cut score to the normative mean of 50 demonstrates how challenging it is for self-report questionnaires to distinguish between PRD and *bona fide* good adjustment. Naturalistic studies of respondents with real motivation to conceal problems and appear healthy provide additional support for the validity of PRD indicators (Detrick, Chibnall, & Call, 2010). Elevations on L and K have been observed among individuals completing the MMPI-2 in child custody proceedings (Bagby, Nicholson, Buis, Radovanovic, & Fidler, 1999), parenting capacity evaluations (Carr, Moretti, & Cue, 2005), and pre-employment screening for airline pilots (Butcher, 1994). Elevations on PIM are common among respondents completing the PAI in pre-employment screening of police officers (Lowmaster & Morey, 2012) and in psychological evaluations of egg donor and gestational carrier candidates (Sims, Thomas, Hopwood, Chen, & Pascale, 2013). Thus, the context of the assessment scenario likely has a potent effect on PRD independent of the characteristics of the respondent or the measure employed.

Standard procedures for interpretation equate elevated scores on measures of PRD with dishonest respondents and invalid test results. However, this conclusion runs the risk of committing the logical fallacy of affirming the consequent (McCrae et al., 1989); the fact that instructions to fake good raise scores on PRD scales does not confirm that all elevated scores are the result of faking good. Elevated K scores on the MMPI have been associated with higher educational levels (Graham, 2000) and interviewer ratings of good adjustment (Block, 1965). Other studies demonstrate that high scores on the Marlowe-Crowne Social Desirability scale (Crowne & Marlowe, 1960), a measure of PRD commonly used in psychological research, are associated with higher levels of extraversion, agreeableness, and conscientiousness as rated by knowledgeable informants (Kurtz, Tarquini, & Iobst, 2008; McCrae & Costa, 1983). These findings are cited in support of a "substantive" interpretation of PRD scales wherein the distinction between simulated and actual psychological adjustment becomes one of the more vexing problems of personality assessment. Indeed, the debate over whether positive illusions about the self are associated with better mental and physical health has amplified concerns about the validity of self-report methods for some psychologists (Colvin & Block, 1994).

Following the accumulation of questionnaire scales to measure PRD, it eventually became clear that it is not a unidimensional construct (e.g., Wiggins, 1964). Sackheim and Gur (1979) proposed an important distinction between conscious deception of others to appear healthy (or virtuous), and unconscious deception of the self in an otherwise sincere attempt to describe one's traits. Accordingly, Paulhus (1984) proposed a two-component model of socially desirable responding, and introduced a pair of scales called Impression Management and Self-deceptive Enhancement. It was anticipated that much of the confusion between substance and style in responding to personality questionnaires could be resolved by this model and measure. If conscious efforts at impression management could be isolated from self-deceptive responding that putatively formed the substantive element of social desirability, then effective corrections for PRD could be applied in the selection context. Although the two components of conscious and unconscious responding in PRD remain conceptually appealing, attempts to completely discriminate the two types of responding using questionnaire items have been largely unsuccessful (Paulhus, 2002).

Recent developments have produced two novel approaches to adjusting for PRD in the interpretation of the PAI. The first approach employs PIM-predicted profiles, which can be obtained by using the overlay feature in the software program (Morey, 2000). The PIM prediction strategy takes advantage of the medium to large negative correlations that are observed between PIM and the substantive scales of the PAI. Each full scale and subscale score can be predicted on the basis of the PIM score alone, generating PIM-predicted profiles for both sets of scales. The score profile obtained from a respondent is compared with this PIM-predicted profile, and the deviations between the observed and PIM-predicted scores are computed for each scale. When the observed score on a given scale exceeds the PIM-predicted score by at least one standard error of measurement (SEM), then the examiner infers that the scale in question may have particular salience for the respondent (Morey, 2003; Morey & Hopwood, 2007). In other words, the respondent is endorsing the items on that scale to a greater degree than is expected given the degree of defensiveness indicated by the PIM score.

Kurtz, Henk, Bupp, and Dresler (2015) validated this PIM-predicted profiling approach in a large sample of undergraduate students who completed the PAI on two occasions separated by a 10- to 21-day interval. On one occasion, participants completed the PAI under standard instructions to provide "honest" responses. On the other occasion, they were asked to role-play the experience of completing the PAI in the process of applying for a highly desirable job. Order of administration was alternated across two otherwise comparable subsamples. Deviations between the PAI full scale and subscale scores and the PIM-predicted scores were computed from the PAI results obtained during role-play. These PIM-predicted deviation scores were correlated with the corresponding scores obtained during the standard administration. All of the full scales and most of the subscales demonstrated convergent and discriminant validity to detect elevations observed in the "honest" administration where respondents presumably exerted no conscious effort to suppress symptoms or problems. Kurtz et al. (2015) found that PIM-predicted deviation scores of two SEM or greater were reliably associated with score elevations in the standard condition of one or more standard deviations higher than the normative mean. Anomalous findings were obtained for a few scales; the role-play condition increased scores on the Mania (MAN), Treatment Rejection (RXR), Dominance (DOM), and Warmth (WRM) full scales. Scores also increased between standard and role-play conditions on the Obsessive-Compulsive (ARD-O) and Grandiosity (MAN-G) subscales. This resulted in a high rate of significantly discrepant PIM-predicted deviation scores for these scales, because many respondents chose to exaggerate rather than conceal these features in the role-play condition. This finding was consistent with previous "fake good" studies of the PAI (e.g., Cashel et al., 1995); accordingly, Kurtz et al. cautioned users against using PIM-predicted deviation scores for these scales.

The second approach to adjust for PRD is called PIM-specific scoring. When PIM is elevated at 57*T* or higher, the PAI scales and subscales are re-normed using one of two samples of respondents with similar levels of PIM elevation drawn from the community adult standardization sample. One group has PIM scores between 57*T* and 67*T*, and the second has PIM scores at 68*T* or higher. PIM-specific scores are expressed in the form of *z*-scores. The method differs from PIM-predicted profiling, but the interpretation of significant (i.e., >1.0) PIM-specific scores is consistent in that it is inferred that the symptoms or problems measured by that scale are being endorsed more readily than is expected given the level of suppression predicted on the basis of PIM. In this chapter, the PIM-specific scoring approach will be applied to the data reported in Kurtz et al. (2015) and the results will be compared with those from the PIM-predicted profile approach. Morey and Hopwood (2007) suggested that PIM-specific scores may show better validity than PIM-predicted deviation scores, as the latter show greater restriction of range in the standardization sample. The convergent and discriminant validity of PIM-specific scores obtained during role-play of a selection scenario will be evaluated using the corresponding scores from the standard administration of the PAI. The mean *T*-scores on corresponding PAI full scales and subscales from the standard administration will be compared between groups of cases with elevated (>1.0) versus non-elevated PIM-specific scores observed in role-play.

Method

Participants

The current sample of respondents was drawn from a larger sample of 334 undergraduate students described in Kurtz et al. (2015); these 195 cases met an additional requirement of obtaining a *T*-score of 57 or higher on PIM during the role-play administration. The mean age was 19.4 years and ranged from 18 to 22 years. The sample was 71.8% female, 80.5% White, 2.6% Black, 2.6% Hispanic, 8.2% Asian, and 6.1% of mixed or other ethnicity. The majority of the sample were first-year students (53.8%), with smaller proportions of student in the second year (30.3%), third year (12.3%), and fourth year (3.6%).

Measure

The Personality Assessment Inventory (PAI: Morey, 1991, 2007) is a 344-item questionnaire designed to assess psychological disorders and personality features. The PAI has 22 full scales with non-overlapping items: 11 clinical scales, five treatment considerations scales, two interpersonal scales, and four validity scales, including PIM. Additionally, ten full scales contain subscales, for a total of 31 subscales. Information about the reliability and validity of this instrument is reported in the second edition of the test manual and elsewhere (Morey, 2007; see also Blais, Baity, & Hopwood, 2010).

Procedure

Participants completed the PAI in groups of one to four in a laboratory setting on two different occasions. The interval between assessment sessions ranged from 10 to 21 days ($M = 13.5$ days, $SD = 1.4$) and involved two instruction sets. In the standard condition, participants were read the instructions printed in the PAI item booklet, which ask them to respond honestly to all test items. In the role-play condition, participants were read aloud the following script:

> Imagine that you are already a college senior, about to graduate, who is applying for a job that offers a yearly salary which is $20,000 more than the next highest offer you have considered. You really want to be hired. However, the employers want to be sure you do not have any mental or emotional problems. You need to answer the following questions in such a way that describes you in the best possible manner. But remember, you also want them to believe you. So, answer the following questions believably, but in a way that makes you look like the best possible candidate.

This script is similar to those used by Cashel et al. (1995) and Morey (1996), with a few modifications to make it more relevant to a younger college student population. To increase incentive in the role-play condition, three cash prizes ($75, $50, and $50) were given to the best job candidates at the end of each of the four semesters during which data collection took place. Winners were selected based on an algorithm that examined various indicators of defensiveness and the total score profile. The order of the instruction conditions was alternated; of the 195 participants studied here, 126 students (64.6%) completed the standard condition first, and 69 students (36.4%) completed the role-play condition first.

Exclusion criteria were utilized to ensure that standard administration profiles accurately represented the "true" psychological status of respondents (i.e., not flagged for any validity issues). To ensure that students were responding carefully and honestly, cases were excluded if the standard administration protocol produced Inconsistency (ICN) or Infrequency (INF) *T*-scores of 70 or higher, Negative Impression Management (NIM) *T*-scores of 77+, or PIM *T*-scores of 57+. In order to ensure sufficient effort in the role-play condition, the ICN and INF scales were utilized to detect random or careless responding.

Results

The mean *T*-score on PIM significantly increased during role-play ($M = 62.6$, $SD = 5.0$) compared with the PIM score observed from the same respondent under instructions to answer honestly ($M = 44.8$, $SD = 8.4$; $t(194) = 25.85$; $p < 0.001$; $d = 2.57$). Thus, the role-play instructions were highly effective in simulating the presence of PRD commonly associated with selection scenarios. The role-play manipulation significantly reduced PAI full scale scores relative to the standard condition for 14 of the 18 full scales of interest (not including validity scales). These significant differences were associated with medium to large effect sizes, ranging from $d = -0.58$ for Drug Problems (DRG) to $d = -1.57$ for Borderline Features (BOR).

The exceptions were the Mania (MAN) scale, which demonstrated a non-significant increase from standard to role-play conditions, and the Treatment Rejection (RXR), Dominance (DOM), and Warmth (WRM) scales, which significantly increased from standard to role-play. These latter three scales are less problematic for the validity of PIM-specific scoring, because RXR assesses attitudes about changing the self and accepting help from others, and DOM and WRM assess two basic dimensions of normal personality. As such, these scales do not assess symptoms or problems that psychologists are looking for in the context of a screening evaluation. The MAN scale, however, does assess clinically important phenomena, but some respondents in this study construed items that inquire about high energy, lack of the need for sleep, self-confidence, and important plans as attributes to be emphasized rather than concealed. This reverse interpretation of the MAN scale has been observed in other studies simulating PRD with the PAI (e.g., Cashel et al., 1995; Morey & Lanier, 1998). Most of the effect for MAN was accounted for by the significant increase in its Grandiosity (MAN-G) subscale during role-play. The only other PAI subscale to show an increase from standard to role-play was the Obsessive–Compulsive (ARD-O) subscale; some respondents construed questions about perfectionism and rigidity as virtues to be shared with a prospective employer. The difference for ARD-O was not statistically significant and the effect size was negligible ($d = 0.13$), so there was no evidence of a preferred strategy for answering these items during role-play.

The effects of the role-play instructions can also be observed with respect to the elevation rates for the clinical scales and for selected treatment consideration scales (i.e., excluding RXR, DOM, and WRM). Thirty-nine percent of respondents obtained elevations of 70*T* or higher and 71.6% obtained elevations of 60*T* or higher on one or more of these scales when responding honestly to the PAI. Thus, there was a considerable amount of psychopathology to be concealed in the role-play in order to make a positive impression on the prospective employer. Respondents were successful in their efforts to suppress symptoms and problems; only 14 cases (7.2%) demonstrated elevations of 70*T* in role-play, and all of these elevations occurred on the MAN scale. Aside from the problematic MAN scale, all other full-scale means from the role-play were below 50*T*, and the majority of role-play profiles (90.3%) produced no elevations higher than 59*T*.

Descriptive statistics of the PIM-specific scores for each full scale and subscale of the PAI are presented in Table 27.1. Distributional properties revealed substantial positive skew for all of the PIM-specific scores; therefore, Table 27.1 reports the median, first quartile, and third quartile values for these scores in place of means and standard deviations. It is noteworthy that the majority of these PIM-specific scores are less than zero. Students role-playing a selection scenario suppress their PAI scores to a greater extent than similarly defensive community adults who are responding under anonymous research conditions. The exceptions include those scales listed above (MAN, RXR, DOM, WRM, MAN-G, ARD-O), which had median scores nearing or exceeding the suggested cut score of 1.0. Again, these anomalies are accounted for by the increase in scores on these scales during role-play, effects which are contrary to the logic of evaluating the degree of suppression due to defensiveness that is central to the PIM-specific scoring technique. For those scales with negative median values in Table 27.1, the PIM-specific scoring strategy will be somewhat conservative for identifying likely elevations in the standard condition.

Table 27.1 also reports the convergent and discriminant correlations between PIM-specific scores obtained from the role-play condition and the "honest" scores obtained from the standard administration condition. PIM-specific role-play scores correlated positively and significantly with scores from the corresponding standard scores, with mostly medium to large effect sizes. Small convergent correlations were observed for DRG and Suicidal Ideation (SUI), and a non-significant *rho* value was observed for the Conversion symptoms (SOM-C) subscale. The mean discriminant *rho* values for the full scales in Table 27.1 represent the average of the PIM-specific score correlations with the 17 non-corresponding full scales from the standard administration. The mean discriminant *rho* values for the PIM-specific subscales were computed based on correlations with the 30 non-corresponding subscales. The pattern of convergent and discriminant *rho* coefficients supports the PIM-specific scoring approach to PRD; higher PIM-specific scores are related specifically to higher scores on that scale under conditions of honest responding.

Table 27.1 further includes the percentages of cases producing elevated (>1.0) and non-elevated PIM-specific scores in the role-play condition. Frequencies of elevation varied widely across the PAI full scales and subscales. Across the full scales, PIM-specific elevation rates were correlated with rates of elevation (70*T* or higher)

Table 27.1 Psychometric characteristics of PIM-specific scores for PAI full scales and subscales

Scale	*Median*	*1st q*	*3rd q*	*Conv rho*	*M disc rho*	*Elevated*		*Non-elevated*	
						%	*M*	*%*	*M*
Somatic complaints (SOM)	−0.71	−0.97	−0.44	0.43	0.10	1.0	60.5	99.0	48.5
Conversion (SOM-C)	−0.66	−0.66	−0.66	0.12†	0.00	1.0	54.5	99.0	47.6
Somatization (SOM-S)	−0.79	−1.16	−0.54	0.34	0.13	3.1	62.2	96.9	48.3
Health Concerns (SOM-H)	−0.46	−0.98	−0.09	0.47	0.09	0.5	71.0	99.5	49.4
Anxiety (ANX)	−0.22	−0.65	0.23	0.53	0.08	6.7	64.5	93.3	53.0
Cognitive (ANX-C)	0.04	−0.36	0.67	0.44	0.13	10.8	67.6	89.2	53.6
Affective (ANX-A)	−0.52	−0.90	0.11	0.53	0.13	7.2	64.3	92.8	52.0
Physiological (ANX-P)	−0.38	−0.82	0.07	0.44	0.12	6.2	59.1	93.8	51.4
Anxiety-Related Disorders (ARD)	−0.11	−0.52	0.35	0.52	0.08	14.9	64.6	85.1	51.0
Obsessive-Compulsive (ARD-O)	0.75	0.15	1.32	0.57	0.12	46.2	59.4	53.8	47.8
Phobias (ARD-P)	−0.81	−1.21	−0.30	0.48	0.03	3.1	69.7	96.9	50.5
Traumatic Stress (ARD-T)	−0.51	−0.87	0.07	0.48	0.15	5.1	69.1	94.9	51.3
Depression (DEP)	−0.85	−1.25	−0.49	0.52	0.13	0.5	62.0	99.5	49.4
Cognitive (DEP-C)	−0.90	−1.29	−0.51	0.37	0.05	3.1	59.3	96.9	51.0
Affective (DEP-A)	−0.66	−1.16	−0.33	0.30	0.12	1.5	62.0	98.5	49.7
Physiological (DEP-P)	−0.75	−1.08	−0.30	0.58	0.18	3.1	63.3	96.9	47.2
Mania (MAN)	1.11	0.42	1.79	0.59	0.11	50.8	58.4	49.2	49.3
Activity Level (MAN-A)	0.16	−0.18	0.84	0.49	0.09	20.0	58.4	80.0	50.1
Grandiosity (MAN-G)	1.25	0.65	2.18	0.51	0.04	65.6	56.2	34.4	47.5
Irritability (MAN-I)	0.63	−0.24	1.24	0.57	0.16	30.8	60.5	69.2	51.2
Paranoia (PAR)	−0.22	−0.78	0.45	0.53	0.17	6.7	57.4	93.3	50.8
Hypervigilance (PAR-H)	0.26	−0.21	1.04	0.50	0.17	26.2	60.0	73.8	51.4
Persecution (PAR-P)	−0.31	−0.83	0.20	0.48	0.20	11.3	54.6	88.7	47.5
Resentment (PAR-R)	−0.36	−0.97	−0.04	0.41	0.18	3.1	68.3	96.9	50.5
Schizophrenia (SCZ)	−0.80	−1.19	−0.46	0.38	0.09	1.0	67.0	99.0	47.6
Psychotic Experiences (SCZ-P)	−0.46	−0.83	0.14	0.48	0.11	6.2	59.1	93.8	47.2

Social Detachment (SCZ-S)	−0.91	−1.20	−0.53	0.51	0.12	0.5	64.0	99.5	46.3
Thought Disorder (SCZ-T)	−0.35	−1.07	0.05	0.29	0.09	4.6	59.7	95.4	50.5
Borderline Features (BOR)	−0.36	−0.79	0.08	0.32	0.09	2.1	65.0	97.9	53.5
Affective Instability (BOR-A)	−0.42	−0.86	0.03	0.30	0.15	1.5	52.0	98.5	49.9
Identity Problems (BOR-I)	−0.14	−0.60	0.78	0.37	0.10	16.4	62.3	83.6	56.7
Negative Relationships (BOR-N)	−0.39	−0.77	0.21	0.39	0.11	10.8	62.0	89.2	52.3
Self-Harm (BOR-S)	−0.69	−1.23	−0.15	0.40	0.00	2.1	70.0	97.9	49.7
Antisocial Features (ANT)	0.01	−0.55	0.72	0.61	0.09	17.9	64.3	82.1	52.7
Antisocial Behaviors (ANT-A)	−0.76	−1.00	−0.41	0.40	0.02	4.6	65.1	95.4	50.7
Egocentricity (ANT-E)	0.57	−0.37	0.97	0.59	0.08	21.5	63.5	78.5	53.2
Stimulus-Seeking (ANT-S)	0.17	−0.32	1.13	0.50	0.02	26.7	65.1	73.3	52.5
Alcohol Problems (ALC)	−0.66	−0.89	−0.13	0.57	0.09	1.5	69.3	98.5	51.6
Drug Problems (DRG)	−0.92	−0.92	−0.40	0.17	0.00	1.5	52.7	98.5	48.9
Aggression (AGG)	−0.48	−1.02	−0.17	0.55	0.16	3.6	57.4	96.4	47.3
Aggressive Attitude (AGG-A)	−1.00	−1.03	−0.56	0.35	0.14	1.5	60.7	98.5	45.9
Verbal Aggression (AGG-V)	0.07	−0.61	0.76	0.57	0.12	8.7	56.7	91.3	49.0
Physical Aggression (AGG-P)	−0.65	−0.65	−0.58	0.29	0.06	1.0	59.0	99.0	48.3
Suicidal Ideation (SUI)	−0.62	−0.62	−0.53	0.17	0.08	2.1	51.5	97.9	49.8
Stress (STR)	−0.27	−0.69	0.29	0.47	0.11	4.6	53.0	95.4	49.1
Non-support (NON)	−1.00	−1.23	−0.45	0.45	0.05	1.5	61.0	98.5	46.0
Treatment Rejection (RXR)	0.48	0.17	0.95	0.45	0.13	25.1	56.9	74.9	50.5
Dominance (DOM)	0.97	0.30	1.31	0.55	0.04	41.5	56.7	58.5	46.3
Warmth (WRM)	0.98	0.35	1.38	0.53	0.00	44.1	56.8	55.9	49.4

Notes: $N = 195$; 1st q = score at first quartile; 3rd q = score at third quartile; Conv rho = rho correlation between PIM-specific score obtained from role-play condition and corresponding scale score from standard condition; M disc rho = mean discriminant correlation between PIM-specific score obtained from role-play condition and all non-corresponding full or subscale scores from standard condition; Elevated % = percentage of cases with PIM-specific score of 1.0 or higher and elevated M = mean of scale scores in standard condition for elevated group; Non-Elevated % = percentage of cases with PIM-specific score of less than 1.0 and Non-Elevated M = mean of scale scores in standard condition for non-elevated group.

† conv rho has $p > 0.05$ (n.s.).

in the standard condition on the corresponding scale (*rho* = 0.49). Rates of PIM-specific elevation from role-play were generally lower than rates of honest elevation in the standard condition, especially if the threshold for honest elevation is reduced to 65T. The mean *T*-scores for respondents in the elevated and non-elevated groups are compared in Table 27.1. For eight of the 11 clinical scales, the means for these groups differ by 10 *T*-score points or more and the mean associated with elevated PIM-specific scores is greater than 60*T*. Exceptions to this pattern are seen with the Paranoia (PAR), DRG, and MAN scales. The mean differences on the treatment considerations and interpersonal scales are less encouraging of the PIM-specific scoring technique. It is noteworthy that at least half of the respondents obtained elevated PIM-specific scores on MAN, MAN-G, and ARD-O. This result underscores the point made above; namely, that these scales tend to be elevated rather than suppressed under conditions of PRD. Thus, the use of PIM-specific scoring is not recommended for these particular scales.

Finally, the psychometric characteristics of the PIM-specific scores were compared with the PIM-predicted deviation scores obtained from the same cases. The two approaches produce largely congruent results; the correlations between PIM-specific and PIM-predicted deviation scores for the full scales ranged from 0.88 to 0.99. The convergent correlations were higher for the PIM-predicted deviation scores for 14 of the 18 full scales, but none of the differences exceeded 0.04. Morey and Hopwood (2007) suggested that PIM-predicted deviations that exceed one standard error of measurement (SEM) for that scale (in *T*-score units) indicate the potentially significant issues. For all 18 full scales, the number of cases with PIM-predicted deviation scores exceeding one SEM was higher than the number of cases with elevated PIM-specific scores. The correspondence between elevation rates is much closer when the threshold for PIM-predicted deviation scores is increased to two SEM. Overall, the PIM-specific scoring approach tends to be somewhat more conservative than the PIM-predicted deviation score approach, in that fewer cases are identified as deviant.

Discussion

The current study examined the validity of the PIM-specific scoring approach to adjusting for PRD introduced by Morey and Hopwood (2007). PIM-specific scores obtained from students completing the PAI in a job applicant role-play condition were significantly correlated with scores on the corresponding scales obtained from those students completing the PAI honestly. Moreover, elevated PIM-specific scores (>1.0) were frequently associated with standard administration scores of 60*T* or higher. These findings supplement the previous validity study of PIM-predicted deviation scores (Kurtz et al., 2015). Although the PIM-specific and PIM-predicted approaches will frequently point to the same scales as matters of concern, the current data suggest that PIM-specific scoring is the more conservative approach of the two. As such, PIM-specific scores may serve as means of cross-validating hypotheses based on elevated PIM-predicted deviation scores.

Validation of both novel approaches to adjusting for PRD have significant implications for applied clinical assessment, especially in selection scenarios or other contexts where there are strong incentives to conceal psychopathology. It is clear from simulation studies (e.g., Cashel et al., 1995; Morey & Lanier 1998) and from naturalistic studies (e.g., Lowmaster & Morey, 2012; Sims et al., 2013) that the selection context yields a very high rate of PAI protocols invalidated by indications of PRD. But it is less clear whether an elevated PIM score indicates denial of real problems or just a response to the demands of the selection context. In the current study, the mean PIM scores produced during role-play were equally elevated for a subsample of respondents (n = 76) with at least one full scale elevated at or above 70*T* versus a subsample (n = 58) with no full scales elevated higher than 59*T*. The mean PIM scores from role-play were 62.9 and 62.2 for these "concealing" and "clean" subsamples, respectively. Thus, excluding respondents in a selection scenario on the basis of PIM alone will lead the examiner to overlook many psychologically healthy candidates, a result quite contrary to the purpose of the evaluation process. The novel approaches of PIM-specific scoring and PIM-predicted deviation scoring of the PAI offer the opportunity to give further consideration to defensive candidates. If respondents with elevated PIM scores do not "leak" (i.e., produce elevated PIM-specific score or PIM-predicted deviation scores), then the examiner can infer that the defensiveness of the candidate was unwarranted and honest responding would have produced an acceptable profile. Moreover, the specificity of these scoring adjustments provides the examiner with good clues about which particular scales would be elevated if the candidate were responding under conditions that promote candid disclosure.

These novel approaches to adjusting for PRD are effective because the selection context mostly affects the elevation of the score profile and leaves the shape of the profile relatively preserved (Kurtz et al., 2015). However, the validity of PIM-specific scoring varies widely across the scales and subscales of the PAI. PIM-specific scoring works best for scales like Anxiety (ANX), Anxiety-Related Disorders (ARD), Antisocial Features (ANT), and Alcohol Problems (ALC), probably because these traits and behaviors have a higher natural base rate in the college student population. The validity evidence for PIM-specific scores appears weaker for scales that assess lower base rate phenomena, like Paranoia (PAR), Suicidal Ideation (SUI), and Stress (STR), and for content that respondents do not construe as symptoms or problems to be concealed from a prospective employer. Accordingly, the current study serves to caution PAI users about using PIM-specific scoring for four full scales (MAN, RXR, DOM, and WRM) and two subscales (MAN-G and ARD-O). Because scores on these full scales and subscales are amplified rather than suppressed by PRD, the use of PIM-specific scores to infer true elevations on these scales is not recommended.

There are several limitations of the current study that should be addressed in future research on the validity of these approaches. Although college students are likely to be involved in job application scenarios in the real world, the current sample is still not entirely representative of the population of persons tasked with completing the PAI in a selection or screening context. The repeated assessments design of the current study also limits its generalizability to actual assessment situations in which the instrument is typically completed only once. Future studies could avoid this limitation by asking patients with known diagnoses to complete the PAI in a role-play scenario simulating a screening situation. Finally, the ecological validity of the role-play method to represent pre-employment selection in the real world can be questioned. Although reward incentives were used in the current study and the resulting profiles were similar to those obtained from respondents operating in actual selection contexts (e.g., Sims et al., 2013), future research should evaluate the power of PIM-specific scores observed in real screening situations to predict subsequent work outcomes and performance on the job. In the meantime, the current findings encourage use of these novel approaches by professionals who regularly conduct personality assessment in situations where PRD is prevalent.

References

Baer, R.A., & Miller, J. (2002). Underreporting of psychopathology on the MMPI-2: A meta-analytic review. *Psychological Assessment, 14* (1), 16–26.

Bagby, R.M., Nicholson, R.A., Buis, T., Radovanovic, H., & Fidler, B.J. (1999). Defensive responding on the MMPI-2 in family custody and access evaluations. *Psychological Assessment, 11* (1), 24–28.

Blais, M.A., Baity, M.R., & Hopwood, C.J. (Eds.) (2010). *Clinical Applications of the Personality Assessment Inventory.* Philadelphia, PA: Routledge.

Block, J. (1965). *The Challenge of Response Sets.* New York: Appleton-Century-Crofts.

Butcher, J.N. (1994). Psychological assessment of airline pilot applicants with the MMPI-2. *Journal of Personality Assessment, 62* (1), 31–44.

Butcher, J.N., Dahlstrom, W.G., Graham, J.R., Tellegen, A., & Kaemmer, B. (1989). *Minnesota Multiphasic Personality Inventory (MMPI-2): Manual for Administration and Scoring.* Minneapolis, MN: University of Minnesota Press.

Carr, G.D., Moretti, M.M., & Cue, B.J.H. (2005). Evaluating parenting capacity: Validity problems with the MMPI-2, PAI, CAPI, and ratings of child adjustment. *Professional Psychology: Research and Practice, 36* (2), 188–196.

Cashel, M.L., Rogers, R., Sewell, K., & Martin-Cannici, C. (1995). The Personality Assessment Inventory (PAI) and the detection of defensiveness. *Assessment, 2* (4), 333–342.

Colvin, C.R., & Block, J. (1994). Do positive illusions foster mental health? An examination of the Taylor and Brown formulation. *Psychological Bulletin, 116* (1), 3–20.

Crowne, D.P., & Marlowe, D. (1960). A new scale of social desirability independent of psychopathology. *Journal of Consulting Psychology, 24* (4), 349–354.

Detrick, P., Chibnall, J.T., & Call, C. (2010). Demand effects on positive response distortion by police officer applicants on the Revised NEO Personality Inventory. *Journal of Personality Assessment, 92* (5), 410–415.

Fals-Stewart, W. (1996). The ability of individuals with psychoactive substance use disorders to escape detection by the Personality Assessment Inventory. *Psychological Assessment, 8* (1), 60–68.

Gough, H.G. (1987). *The California Psychological Inventory: Administrator's Guide.* Palo Alto, CA: Consulting Psychologists Press.

Graham, J.R. (2000). *MMPI-2: Assessing Personality and Psychopathology* (3rd ed.). New York: Oxford University Press.

Hathaway, S.R., & McKinley, J.C. (1940). A multiphasic personality schedule (Minnesota): I. Construction of the schedule. *Journal of Psychology, 10* (2), 249–254.

Jackson, D.N. (1984). *Personality Research Form Manual* (3rd ed.). Port Huron, MI: Research Psychologists Press.

Kurtz, J.E., Henk, C.M., Bupp, L.L., & Dresler, C.M. (2015). The validity of a regression-based procedure for detecting concealed psychopathology in structured personality assessment. *Psychological Assessment, 27* (2), 392–402.

Kurtz, J.E., Tarquini, S.J., & Iobst, E.A. (2008). Socially desirable responding in personality assessment: Still more substance than style. *Personality and Individual Differences, 45* (1), 22–27.

Lowmaster, S.E., & Morey, L.C. (2012). Predicting law enforcement officer job performance with the Personality Assessment Inventory. *Journal of Personality Assessment, 94* (3), 254–261.

McCrae, R.R., & Costa, P.T. (1983). Social desirability scales: More substance than style. *Journal of Consulting and Clinical Psychology, 51* (6), 882–888.

McCrae, R.R., Costa, P.T., Jr., Dahlstrom, W.G., Barefoot, J.C., Siegler, I.C., & Williams, R.B., Jr. (1989). A caution on the use of the MMPI K-correction in research in psychosomatic medicine. *Psychosomatic Medicine, 51* (1), 58–65.

McKinley, J.C., Hathaway, S.R., & Meehl, P.E. (1948). The Minnesota Multiphasic Personality Inventory: VI. The K scale. *Journal of Consulting Psychology, 12* (1), 20–31.

Millon, T., Millon, C., Davis, R., & Grossman, S. (2006). *MCMI-III Manual* (3rd ed.). Minneapolis, MN: Pearson.

Morey, L.C. (1991). *Personality Assessment Inventory Professional Manual.* Odessa, FL: Psychological Assessment Resources.

Morey, L.C. (1996). *An Interpretive Guide to the Personality Assessment Inventory (PAI).* Odessa, FL: Psychological Assessment Resources.

Morey, L.C. (2000). *PAI Software Portfolio.* Lutz, FL: Psychological Assessment Resources.

Morey, L.C. (2003). *Essentials of PAI Assessment.* Hoboken, NJ: John Wiley & Sons, Ltd.

Morey, L.C. (2007). *Personality Assessment Inventory Professional Manual* (2nd ed.). Lutz, FL: Psychological Assessment Resources.

Morey, L.C., & Hopwood, C.J. (2007). *Casebook for the Personality Assessment Inventory: A Structural Summary Approach.* Lutz, FL: Psychological Assessment Resources.

Morey, L.C., & Lanier, V.W. (1998). Operating characteristics of six response distortion indicators for the personality assessment inventory. *Assessment, 5* (3), 203–214.

Paulhus, D.L. (1984). Two-component models of socially desirable responding. *Journal of Personality and Social Psychology, 46* (3), 598–609.

Paulhus, D.L. (2002). Socially desirable responding: The evolution of a construct. In H.I. Braun, D.L. Jackson, & D.E. Wiley (Eds.), *The Role of Psychological Constructs in Psychological and Educational Measurement* (pp. 49–69). Mahwah, NJ: Lawrence Erlbaum.

Peebles, J., & Moore, R.J. (1998). Detecting socially desirable responding with the Personality Assessment Inventory: The Positive Impression Management scale and the Defensiveness Index. *Journal of Clinical Psychology, 54* (5), 621–628.

Sackheim, H.A., & Gur, R.C. (1979). Self-deception, other-deception, and self-reported psychopathology. *Journal of Consulting and Clinical Psychology, 47* (1), 213–215.

Sellbom, M., Fischler, G.L., & Ben-Porath, Y.S. (2007). Identifying MMPI-2 predictors of police officer integrity and misconduct. *Criminal Justice and Behavior, 34* (8), 985–1004.

Sims, J.A., Thomas, K.M., Hopwood, C.J., Chen, S.H., & Pascale, C. (2013). Psychometric properties and norms for the Personality Assessment Inventory in egg donors and gestational carriers. *Journal of Personality Assessment, 95* (5), 495–499.

Wiggins, J.S. (1964). Convergences among stylistic response measures from objective personality tests. *Educational and Psychological Measurement, 24* (3), 551–562.

28

Applicant Faking Behavior: The Elephant in the Room

Richard L. Griffith, Patrick D. Converse and Yumiko Mochinushi

Florida Institute of Technology, USA

Matthias Ziegler

Humboldt-Universität zu Berlin, Germany

The story of the blind men and the elephant is a long-told tale of Indian origin that illustrates the disconnect between observation and reality. At the beginning of the story, a group of blind men stumble upon an elephant. Unable to see the totality of the animal, each man begins to feel part of the elephant closest to him. One man begins to feel the tusks, and describes his interpretation of the animal. Another feels the tail, and begins to describe the animal in quite different terms. As each description differs more from the previous one, a heated argument ensues until a sighted man passes by and clarifies the situation.

The progress of science often follows a similar pattern. What we know about a phenomenon stems from systematic observations. But these observations are often collected one at a time using different methodologies and studying different aspects of the phenomenon. In addition, a phenomenon can be studied at many different levels of analysis, or different levels of granularity. Thus, the observations may capture only a portion of the phenomenon, or they are bounded by a particular point of reference. If the description of the results of our observations makes that clear, then little harm is done. But all too often scientists overstate their findings and try to generalize their observations to the entirety of the phenomenon. Inevitably arguments ensue. Unfortunately, it often takes a very long time before the "sighted man" comes along to provide a resolution to these arguments. Heisenberg once stated "We have to remember that what we observe is not nature in itself, but nature exposed to our method of questioning" (Heisenberg, 1958).

The history of science is replete with examples where seemingly incompatible descriptions of phenomena are no more than another case of blind men and elephants. Luckily, scientific communication has improved, and scattered disparate results have been made more available. It is rare that one program of research can

The Wiley Handbook of Personality Assessment, First Edition. Edited by Updesh Kumar.
© 2016 John Wiley & Sons, Ltd. Published 2016 by John Wiley & Sons, Ltd.

gain a complete picture of the elephant, but we have become much better at stitching together a complete picture by aggregating observations and reconciling different levels of analysis. While the stitched-together picture is still far from reality, we gain a more complete perspective when these diverse observations are combined.

Often, the act of reconciling data from different levels of analysis leads to a new understanding of the phenomena. On occasion, different levels of analysis align perfectly and observations at any level yield similar results. Such is the case with fractal patterns found across many natural phenomena, suggesting that a single elegant explanation is enough to describe the phenomenon at all levels of observation (Peitgen, Jürgens, & Saupe, 2004). But even when different levels provide dissimilar answers, science can learn and grow by asking why the two levels of analysis are incongruent. Perhaps the best-known example of incongruent observations at different levels of analysis is the varied tenets of Newtonian physics and quantum physics. While seemingly irreconcilable, these varied viewpoints led to string theory, which may unify our understanding of the universe (Greene, 1999).

In this chapter, we will discuss the phenomenon of applicant faking behavior and provide some insight regarding the findings at different levels of analysis. While much has been learned about the phenomenon over the past 20 years, behavioral researchers may still be feeling different parts of the elephant, and may not be taking the whole animal into account when testing theories. We will first describe the phenomenon of applicant faking behavior in general. We will then provide an explanation for why researchers have primarily focused on one level of analysis, namely scale-level observations. We will then discuss two other levels that may provide fruitful observations and complete our understanding of applicant faking behavior. Finally, we will propose a number of research questions that could be addressed at these levels of analysis, and discuss the implications of this research for our understanding of personality measurement.

Applicant Faking

Personality measurement is currently a major focus of research and practice in personnel selection (e.g., Hough & Oswald, 2008; Oswald & Hough, 2011). While not without criticisms, personality measurements are widely used because they provide useful levels of predictive validity (Oswald & Hough, 2011), have low levels of adverse impact (Hough & Oswald, 2008), and can be administered efficiently and cheaply using online testing platforms (Tippins, 2009). However, a potential but persistent weakness of many personality measures, applicant faking behavior, remains.

Applicant faking is commonly defined as conscious response distortion on a non-cognitive measure in order to obtain more favorable results in an applicant situation (e.g., McFarland & Ryan, 2006). Definitions of faking have differed somewhat in previous research, but there is general consensus across these varied definitions. Sackett (2011, 2012) has provided a useful discussion of faking definitions, arguing that an observed score on a personality item (or scale) has multiple variance components, including: (a) mean true score across situations;

(b) situationally specific true departure from grand mean; (c) cross-domain erroneous self-perception; (d) situationally specific erroneous self-perception; (e) cross-domain consistent impression management; and (f) situationally specific intentional distortion. In this framework, the final component of variance – situationally specific intentional distortion – reflects faking. Faking is thus seen as intentional rather than reflecting inaccurate self-perception, and situation-specific rather than reflecting consistent impression management.

Intuitively, it is fairly easy to see why faking would be a concern for personality measures in selection contexts. If an individual is interested in a job, applies for it, and is asked to complete a self-report personality measure during the application process, he/she might overstate positive qualities and underreport negative qualities to increase the likelihood of receiving a job offer. However, the antecedents, nature, and implications of this faking behavior are much less straightforward. Substantial research has been devoted to these issues and many important questions remain unanswered. We explore some of these in the next section, but first review some major findings that have been established.

First, there seems to be a general consensus that individuals can fake (Viswesvaran & Ones, 1999). Second, the preponderance of evidence suggests that individuals do fake in applicant settings (Griffith & Converse, 2011). Third, it appears that faking can affect the construct and criterion-related validity of personality measures (although these effects may not always be large; e.g., see Komar, Brown, Komar, & Robie, 2008). Fourth, there is also evidence that faking varies across individuals and thus the presence of faking can influence the rank ordering of individuals (Peterson, Griffith, & Converse, 2009). This can then affect hiring decisions. In combination, these findings suggest faking is a legitimate concern and therefore continued work in this area may have both theoretical and practical benefits.

Given the need to further examine applicant faking, where should researchers focus their efforts? What level of analysis might yield the most useful information?

Applicant Faking and Levels of Analysis

The choice of starting point for a program of research has a great deal of influence on the endpoint. Just as faking research designs have an impact on the questions that can be answered (Mesmer-Magnus & Viswesvaran, 2006), so too does the level at which the data are analyzed. Just as an elephant may feel different depending on whether you started at the tusk or the tail, the dynamics of applicant faking may differ depending on the level of analysis the researcher chooses. At a minimum, researchers have three choices of level of analysis: item level, scale level, or composite or battery level. Overwhelmingly, the choice of level of analysis in previous research has been at the scale level. Thus, what we know about applicant faking behavior has largely been shaped by this perspective. We will first discuss why we believe the scale-level analysis of faking behavior has dominated the literature. Then we will discuss item and composite level approaches to faking research, and touch upon the important research questions that may be informed by this research.

Applicant faking at the scale level

While there are exceptions, the vast majority of faking research has focused on the scale level. Using this approach, individual items are aggregated into internally consistent scales. The degree of faking and the antecedents and consequences of that faking are demonstrated and discussed in the aggregate. There are several reasons why this perspective is the dominant paradigm in the applicant faking literature.

First, for many years the phenomenon of faking was considered synonymous with the concept of social desirability (Griffith & Peterson, 2008). Often, measures of social desirability were embedded in personality measures and served as validity scales. If applicants scored too highly on these validity scales, they were assumed to have faked the remainder of the personality measure. Thus, for perhaps 50 years faking was communicated via the results of a scale, and the notion of faking at the scale level may have become an implicit assumption.

Second, personality measures are ultimately used to make a hiring decision. Although managers may use items in an idiosyncratic manner (Christiansen, personal communication, 2015), the appropriate use of the measures would require the aggregation of items into scale scores or item averages. Organizations could then set a threshold score, and screen out applicants who do not meet this threshold. Thus, hiring decisions are often made using scale-level data.

Third, our current models of validity rely heavily on scale-level assumptions. In the case of an internal examination of measurement properties, we examine items within a scale to determine whether they share content or statistically co-vary (AERA et al., 2014). When we examine the relationship of personality measures to outside variables such as performance appraisals, these correlation analyses are almost exclusively conducted at the scale level.

Fourth, the application of personality questionnaires is usually the result of an extensive requirement analysis. The aim of such analyses is the specification of particular traits relevant for successful job completion. Consequently, the aim of the assessment is to operationalize the whole construct and measure inter-individual differences. This automatically means that the whole scale is evaluated.

Finally, reliability is a powerful concept. Many practitioners have learned during their studies that reliability sets the upper limit for validity. Moreover, it is often argued that aggregation maximizes content and minimizes error variance. This should then lead to a more reliable and hence more valid score.

While the examination of applicant faking behavior at the scale level has been the dominant method of investigation, other levels of analysis may yield useful insights.

Applicant faking at the item level

When considering the phenomenon of applicant faking, it is surprising that more research has not been conducted at the item level. Ultimately, applicants do not complete scales, they complete items. While some theories of applicant faking behavior propose that applicants strategically respond to items, and thus do not endorse them independently, applicants can only complete one item at a time. In fact, based on qualitative and quantitative analyses it can be demonstrated that the item response process entails individual decisions that are made for each item (Robie, Brown, & Beaty, 2007; Ziegler, 2011). One model even assumed that only those items that a test-taker perceives to contain job-relevant information are faked (Ziegler, 2011). Thus, examining the item instead of the scale might reveal a more comprehensive picture of the elephant. We will first review the literature that has chosen the item as the level of analysis, and then propose other research questions that may be best examined using this approach.

One line of item-level research examines item characteristics that facilitate or suppress applicant faking behavior. Doll (1971) examined whether items that were verifiable through independent means (objective) were less susceptible to applicant faking than items that were less verifiable (subjective). Doll found that subjective items were indeed more easily faked, and this result has been replicated by other researchers (e.g., Cascio, 1975; Harold, McFarland, & Weekley, 2006). Graham, McDaniel, Douglas, and Snell (2002) conducted a study in which the attributes of biodata items (as measured by Mael's (1991) taxonomy) were examined in terms of the degree to which the items could be faked. The authors found that continuous items (rather than dichotomous) were most likely to be faked, as well as items that could only be verified through friends, or items querying hypothetical situations.

The work of Kuncel and Borneman (2007) examined the perception of social desirability of personality items in an effort to create scales that might detect applicant faking. Perhaps this work more than any to date illustrates how item-level examinations of data may lead to additional insights. Building on previous work, the authors identified items that produced idiosyncratic response patterns. Intuitively, applicants choosing to fake should maximally endorse an item they view as being job-related so that they can improve their chance of being selected. However, Kuncel and Borneman reported that, depending on item characteristics, some applicants chose less than optimal faking responses, believing that midpoint responding may be more desirable to an employer. A similar finding was presented in Kuncel and Tellegen (2009).

An approach to faking that directly addresses the item pattern of each individual is item response theory (IRT). Here the work by Zickar (Zickar, Gibby, & Robie, 2004; Zickar & Robie, 1999) has contributed fundamentally to the current notion of faking. Using mixed Rasch models (MRMs), those authors tested for person homogeneity. MRMs are a mixture of latent class analysis and the Rasch model. Thus, this approach looks for distinct latent classes (i.e., test-takers with similar item patterns). Moreover, in each of those classes the Rasch model holds true, which means the same latent trait is measured for each test-taker in one class. Based on an interpretation of the thresholds and parameters within each class (Rost, Carstensen, & Von Davier, 1997), it is then possible to determine whether the classes represent response bias like faking (Eid & Zickar, 2007). Zickar and colleagues used this method to suggest the existence of slight and extreme fakers as distinct latent classes. Recently, the contribution of such qualitatively distinct response bias classes to faking variance within items has been questioned (Ziegler & Kemper, 2013; Ziegler, Maaß, Griffith, & Gammon, 2015).

The IRT approach comes with a potentially severe limitation with respect to the item-level information. The main factor for this limitation is the Rasch model component within the MRM. Within the Rasch model, it is assumed that item homogeneity holds for all items or, in other words, it is required that item difficulties are constant for all persons (Rost, 1990). Applied to faking, this means that for each slight faker or extreme faker the item difficulty of a specific item is the same. Thus, if two test-takers are both slight fakers and have the same standing on the latent trait (e.g., Conscientiousness), the MRM approach would suggest that they give the same rating. Consequently, there are no inter-individual differences in faking behavior for test-takers within the same class. Considering that the larger amount of faking variance is due to such inter-individual differences (Ziegler et al., 2015), such a notion seems highly unlikely. Moreover, looking at previous attempts to model the emergence of a faked answer (e.g., Mueller-Hanson, Heggestad, & Thornton, 2006; Ziegler, 2011), a multitude of specific mechanisms have been proposed. For example, Ellingson (Ellingson, 2011; Ellingson & McFarland, 2011) suggested that faking is determined through valence, instrumentality, expectancy (VIE), or ability to fake. Clearly, for a specific item, these attributes and estimates are likely to differ even for test-takers with the same standing on the measured trait. Other factors such as knowledge of the job or the company, employability, or the appraisal of the job market may also influence these VIE components. Therefore, the notion that all slight fakers are equal in terms of their faking intention seems untenable. It would be like assuming that all elephants in Asia have exactly the same ear. It is known that elephants' ears differ depending on the origin of the elephant (i.e., Asia or Africa). However, even within each kind of elephant, ear shapes differ.

Analyses at the item level are surely a very promising approach to unravel some of the remaining mysteries surrounding faking behavior (see also Helmes, Holden, & Ziegler, 2014). However, it is vital to keep in mind that inter-individual differences in faking at the item level need to be modeled. Thus, the approach needs to have a tremendous amount of flexibility. Ultimately, an item-level examination of different ideas of how faking emerges and why there are so many inter-individual differences should be possible. Therefore, a promising approach might be to start by modeling faking on each item separately. This minimizes the risk of losing information due to aggregation or due to assumptions that need to hold for all items. One such approach might be found in diffusion models (see Helmes et al., 2014).

Unanswered item-level questions

The extant literature examining faking at the item level has shed some light on the phenomenon, but there is considerable room for continued research at the item level. A few promising item-level research paths may emerge with the examination of the following questions. Can patterns of item-level responding be interpreted to reflect differing "types" of faking behavior? For instance, Griffith, Lee, Peterson, & Zickar (2011) suggested four distinct categories of faking. Can researchers accurately identify these types of fakers based on a qualitative or quantitative pattern recognition scheme? What item properties serve as cues for fakers? Kuncel and

Borneman (2007) determined that fakers are inconsistent in their choices of items to fake. How are fakers making these decisions and what information are they including in their thought process?

Applicant faking at the composite level

Another alternative for studying applicant faking behavior is to focus on the composite or battery level. Rather than examining faking on individual items or individual scales, this approach involves examining faking across multiple scales. Shifting to this level of analysis may be useful for at least two reasons. First, organizations may often use multiple scales in making hiring decisions based on job analysis results indicating several personality characteristics are important for job performance. For instance, organizations may average applicant scores across multiple scales to create an overall composite used in hiring, or they may develop an ideal personality profile and make hiring decisions in part based on applicant similarity to that profile (see Kulas, 2013). Thus, applicant contexts may often involve multiple scales, and therefore faking research at this level has direct relevance to these contexts.

Second, focusing on this level of analysis might reveal aspects of the faking phenomenon that would not be apparent from research at other levels. This is discussed in more detail below in terms of potentially fruitful research questions that could be examined using this approach.

Research at the multiple scales level of analysis is quite limited. In one of the few studies to report relevant results, Hogan, Barrett, and Hogan (2007) examined applicant score changes on a five-factor model personality measure. The sample consisted of 5,266 individuals who applied for a customer service job (Time 1), were rejected, and reapplied for the same job and completed the same measures after at least six months (Time 2). Score changes from Time 1 to Time 2 were examined under the assumption that failing during the first testing created an incentive to improve scores during the second testing. In terms of faking across multiple scales, results indicated that only three applicants changed scores across all five scales and 22 changed scores for any combination of four scales beyond 95% confidence intervals. In addition, score changes across the five scales were summed and results demonstrated the mean of this total change score was –0.20, indicating that on average applicants lowered their scores from Time 1 to Time 2. Overall, this suggests that substantial score changes across multiple scales was infrequent (if one can surmise no one faked at Time 1).

Other research has demonstrated that would-be fakers do not always make optimal choices, and can engage in maladaptive faking patterns that lower scores (Griffith, Peterson, Quist, Benda, & Evans, 2008). Griffith et al. (2008) hypothesized that this pattern of maladaptive faking, when extended across a composite measure, would result in a low number of applicants successfully faking the full profile. Their hypotheses were supported. When coupled with a non-compensatory scoring scheme, the pattern of maladaptive faking eventually tripped up would-be fakers. Of the more than 10,000 participants in the study, not a single one successfully faked the composite measure composed of eight constructs. Thus, depending on the scoring method, composite measures may prove to be a method to tame the elephant, and substantially reduce the prevalence of successful faking behavior.

A few studies have also examined how individuals may fake across scales when targeting different jobs. Furnham (1990), for example, had participants complete four questionnaires with instructions to respond as ideal candidates for the job of librarian, advertising executive, or banker, or to respond honestly. Results suggested that participants were able to fake different profiles for different jobs (e.g., the advertising executive had the highest artistic and lowest masculinity score, whereas the banker had the lowest artistic and highest masculinity score). However, Furnham also noted: (a) participants likely responded based on occupational stereotypes, but these stereotypes may not be entirely accurate, meaning these responses could decrease the likelihood of selection; (b) there appeared to be substantial disagreement across participants regarding the ideal profiles; and (c) additional evidence is needed to determine the extent to which participants are able to produce the specific profile they intended. Mahar, Cologon, and Duck (1995) examined similar issues in a study in which participants completed the Myers-Briggs Type Indicator under four instructions: standard (control); maximize chances of getting a psychiatric nurse job (fake-job); give the best possible general impression (fake-good); and respond as a typical psychiatric nurse would (stereotype). Scores on the four scales were then compared across these conditions as well as against scores from a sample of actual psychiatric nurses (psychiatric nurse). Results indicated that fake-job profiles were closer to stereotype profiles than to control profiles, fake-good profiles, or psychiatric nurse profiles. This suggests that score profiles are affected by differing instructions, that respondents appear to rely on occupational stereotypes when faking for a particular job, but that faking attempts may not be particularly effective given that the fake-job profiles did not match the psychiatric nurse profiles. In a similar study, Martin, Bowen, and Hunt (2002) had student participants complete both a normative and ipsative version of a personality measure with instructions to answer honestly or to try to look good for a junior manager position. These participants and a separate sample of business managers/human resource professionals also indicated their perceptions of the ideal personality profile for the junior manager job. Findings indicated that, for the student participants, the agreement between their ideal ratings and their actual ratings across the 30 scales did not differ significantly between the honest and faking group for the ipsative measure, whereas the ideal–actual distance was significantly smaller in the faking group than in the honest group for the normative measure. In addition, there was substantial agreement between the students and the business managers regarding the ideal personality profile for the focal job. This suggests that participants were able to fake responses on the normative measure toward their perceptions of the ideal personality profile, and that this ideal profile matched the perceptions of business managers. In combination, these studies suggest that (a) individuals can produce different patterns of scores across multiple scales based on different instructions, (b) these score patterns likely reflect occupational stereotypes, but (c) it is less clear whether these faked patterns will be accurate or effective in a given selection context.

Unanswered composite-level questions

The limited amount of research specifically focusing on this level of analysis – combined with the potential to gain new insights with practical and theoretical implications – suggests this may be a useful area for future research. In fact, a number of basic questions regarding the nature, antecedents, and consequences of faking may need to be revisited at this level, as findings from the scale level may not fully generalize to the multiple-scale level. For example, as noted previously, research at the scale level (e.g., Viswesvaran & Ones, 1999) suggests individuals can fake. However, available (albeit limited) evidence at the multiple-scale level suggests that effective faking across several scales may be more difficult (e.g., Griffith et al., 2008; Hogan et al., 2007). If this is the case, then the antecedents of faking may be somewhat different at this level of analysis. In particular, cognitive ability and job-related experience may be stronger predictors of faking at this level than many of the non-cognitive factors that have been theorized to be influential. The consequences of faking attempts may also differ. For example, validity decrements may be smaller at this level and there may be fewer false positives in selection as applicants struggle to effectively fake the appropriate profile. However, this might come at the cost of introducing unwanted variance due to inter-individual differences. Thus, empirically exploring these and related issues may reveal more about how applicants go about faking on personality measures, as well as how some of the negative effects of faking might be reduced.

Conclusions

While research at any level of analysis can shed light on a particular phenomenon, caution must be taken to frame the results of the research within that level of analysis. If researchers generalize the results of a program of research too broadly, the danger is that we miss seeing other parts of the elephant due to the distraction of focusing on the tusk alone.

Our assertion is that a full understanding of applicant faking behavior is best achieved by a thorough examination of the phenomenon across at least three levels of analysis: the item, the scale, and the composite level. In addition, our field is sorely in need of a "sighted" perspective that can begin to build the model of the whole phenomenon from the pieces discovered at the distinct levels of analysis. Regardless of whether the dynamics of faking hold constant across these levels, or we discover vastly different findings, more is gained when we integrate the whole.

More faking research has been conducted in the last decade than in the 80 years prior (Griffith & Robie, 2013). While we have learned much, most of our learning pertains to only one part of the elephant. If we are to develop methods to mitigate the effects of faking, it is likely that we must have a better understanding of the whole beast. Perhaps when we study the phenomenon as a whole we will discover that a simple and relatively small intervention may deter the beast, just as the elephant will run away from a mouse. Or perhaps as the protagonist in Orwell's *Shooting an Elephant*, we will need a more robust solution.

References

American Educational Research Association (AERA), American Psychological Association, & National Council on Measurement in Education. (2014). *Standards for Educational and Psychological Testing*. Washington, DC: AERA.

Cascio, W.F. (1975). Accuracy of verifiable biographical information blank responses. *Journal of Applied Psychology, 60* (6), 767–769.

Doll, R.E. (1971). Item susceptibility to attempted faking as related to item characteristic and adopted fake set. *Journal of Psychology, 77*, 9–16.

Eid, M., & Zickar, M. (2007). Detecting response styles and faking in personality and organizational assessments by mixed Rasch models. In M. von Davier, & C.H. Carstensen (Eds.), *Multivariate and Mixture Distribution Rasch Models* (pp. 255–270). New York: Springer.

Ellingson, J.E. (2011). People fake only when they need to fake. In M. Ziegler, C. MacCann, & R. Roberts (Eds.), *New Perspectives on Faking in Personality Assessment* (pp. 19–33). New York: Oxford University Press.

Ellingson, J.E., & McFarland, L.A. (2011). Understanding faking behavior through the lens of motivation: An application of VIE theory. *Human Performance, 24* (4), 322–337.

Furnham, A. (1990). Faking personality questionnaires: Fabricating different profiles for different purposes. *Current Psychology: Research & Reviews, 9* (1), 46–55.

Graham, K.E., McDaniel, M.A., Douglas, E.F., & Snell, A.F. (2002). Biodata validity decay and score inflation with faking: Do item attributes explain variance across items? *Journal of Business and Psychology, 16* (4), 573–592.

Greene, B. (1999). *The Elegant Universe: Superstrings, Hidden Dimensions, and the Quest for the Ultimate Theory*. New York: Norton.

Griffith, R.L., Lee, L.M., Peterson, M.H., & Zickar, M.J. (2011). First dates and little white lies: A trait contract classification theory of applicant faking behavior. *Human Performance, 24* (4), 338–357.

Griffith, R.L., & Peterson, M.H. (2008). The failure of social desirability measures to capture applicant faking behavior. *Industrial and Organizational Psychology: Perspectives on Science and Practice, 1* (3), 308–311.

Griffith, R.L., Peterson, M.H., Quist, J.S., Benda, A., & Evans, A. (2008). Faking the personality profile: Easier said than done. In R.L. Griffith, & M.H. Peterson (Chairs), *Complex problems, simple solutions: Contemporary research in applicant faking behavior*. Symposium presented at the 23rd Annual Conference for the Society for Industrial and Organizational Psychology, San Francisco, CA, USA.

Griffith, R.L., & Robie, C. (2013). Personality testing and the "F-Word": Revisiting seven questions about faking. In N.D. Christiansen, & R.P. Tett (Eds.), *Handbook of Personality at Work* (pp. 253–280). New York: Routledge.

Harold, C.M., McFarland, L.A., & Weekley, J.A. (2006). The validity of verifiable and non-verifiable biodata items: An examination across applicants and incumbents. *International Journal of Selection and Assessment, 14* (4), 336–346.

Heisenberg, W. (1958). *Physics and Philosophy: The Revolution in Modern Science*. New York: Harper.

Helmes, E., Holden, R.R., & Ziegler, M. (2014). Response bias, malingering, and impression management. In G.J. Boyle, D.H. Saklofske, & G. Matthews (Eds.), *Measures of Personality and Social Psychological Constructs* (pp. 16–46). London: Elsevier.

Hogan, J., Barrett, P., & Hogan, R. (2007). Personality measurement, faking, and employment selection. *Journal of Applied Psychology, 92* (5), 1270–1285.

Hough, L.M., & Oswald, F.L. (2008). Personality testing and industrial-organizational psychology: Reflections, progress, and prospects. *Industrial and Organizational Psychology, 1* (3), 272–290.

Komar, S., Brown, D.J., Komar, J.A., & Robie, C. (2008). Faking and the validity of conscientiousness: A Monte Carlo investigation. *Journal of Applied Psychology, 93* (1), 140.

Kulas, J.T. (2013). Personality-based profile matching in personnel selection: Estimates of method prevalence and criterion-related validity. *Applied Psychology: An International Review, 62* (3), 519–542.

Kuncel, N.R., & Borneman, M.J. (2007). Toward a new method of detecting deliberately faked personality tests: The use of idiosyncratic item responses. *International Journal of Selection and Assessment, 15* (2), 220–231.

Kuncel, N.R., & Tellegen, A. (2009). A conceptual and empirical reexamination of the measurement of the social desirability of items: Implications for detecting desirable response style and scale development. *Personnel Psychology, 62* (2), 201–228.

Mael, F.A. (1991). A conceptual rational for the domain and attributes of biodata items. *Personnel Psychology, 44* (4), 763–792.

Mahar, D., Cologon, J., & Duck, J. (1995). Response strategies when faking personality questionnaires in a vocational selection setting. *Personality and Individual Differences, 18* (5), 605–609.

Martin, B.A., Bowen, C.C., & Hunt, S.T. (2002). How effective are people at faking on personality questionnaires? *Personality and Individual Differences, 32* (2), 247–256.

McFarland, L.A., & Ryan, A.M. (2006). Toward an integrated model of applicant faking behavior. *Journal of Applied Social Psychology, 36* (4), 979–1016.

Mesmer-Magnus, J., & Viswesvaran, C. (2006). Assessing response distortion in personality tests: A review of research designs and analytic strategies. In R.L. Griffith, & M.H. Peterson (Eds.), *A Closer Examination of Applicant Faking Behavior* (pp. 85–114). Greenwich, CT: Information Age.

Mueller-Hanson, R., Heggestad, E.D., & Thornton, G.C. (2006). Individual differences in impression management: an exploration of the psychological processes underlying faking. *Psychology Science, 3*, 288–312.

Oswald, F.L., & Hough, L.M. (2011). Personality and its assessment in organizations: Theoretical and empirical developments. In S. Zedeck (Ed.), *APA Handbook of Industrial and Organizational Psychology: Vol. 2. Selecting and Developing Members for the Organization* (pp. 153–184). Washington, DC: American Psychological Association.

Peitgen, H.O., Jürgens, H., & Saupe, D. (2004). *Chaos and Fractals: New Frontiers of Science.* New York: Springer Science & Business Media.

Peterson, M.H., Griffith, R.L., & Converse, P.D. (2009). Examining the role of applicant faking in hiring decisions: Percentage of fakers hired and hiring discrepancies in single- and multiple-predictor selection. *Journal of Business and Psychology, 24* (4), 373–386.

Robie, C., Brown, D.J., & Beaty, J.C. (2007). Do people fake on personality inventories? A verbal protocol analysis. *Journal of Business and Psychology, 21* (4), 489–509.

Rost, J. (1990). Rasch models in latent classes: An integration of two approaches to item analysis. *Applied Psychological Measurement, 14* (3), 271–282.

Rost, J., Carstensen, C.H., & Von Davier, M. (1997). Applying the mixed Rasch model to personality questionnaires. In J. Rost, & R.E. Langeheine (Eds.), *Applications of Latent Trait and Latent Class Models in the Social Sciences* (pp. 324–332). New York: Waxmann.

Sackett, P.R. (2011). Integrating and prioritizing theoretical perspectives on applicant faking of personality measures. *Human Performance, 24* (4), 379–385.

Sackett, P.R. (2012). Faking in personality assessment: Where do we stand? In M. Ziegler, C. MacCann, & R.D. Roberts (Eds.), *New Perspectives on Faking in Personality Assessment* (pp. 330–344). New York: Oxford University Press.

Tippins, N.T. (2009). Internet alternatives to traditional proctored testing: Where are we now? *Industrial and Organizational Psychology, 2* (1), 2–10.

Viswesvaran, C., & Ones, D.S. (1999). Meta-analyses of fakability estimates: Implications for personality measurement. *Educational and Psychological Measurement, 59* (2), 197–210.

Zickar, M.J., Gibby, R.E., & Robie, C. (2004). Uncovering faking samples in applicant, incumbent, and experimental data sets: An application of mixed-model item response theory. *Organizational Research Methods, 7* (2), 168–190.

Zickar, M.J., & Robie, C. (1999). Modeling faking good on personality items: An item-level analysis. *Journal of Applied Psychology, 84* (4), 551–563.

Ziegler, M. (2011). Applicant faking: A look into the black box. *The Industrial and Organizational Psychologist, 49* (1), 29–36.

Ziegler, M., & Kemper, C. (2013). Extreme response style and faking: Two sides of the same coin? In P. Winker, R. Porst, & N. Menold (Eds.), *Schriften Zur Empirischen Wirtschaftsforschung [Interviewers' Deviations in Surveys: Impact, Reasons, Detection and Prevention]* (pp. 221–237). Frankfurt: Peter Lang Gmbh.

Ziegler, M., Maaß, U., Griffith, R., & Gammon, A. (2015). What is the nature of faking? Modeling distinct response patterns and quantitative differences in faking at the same time. *Organizational Research Methods.* doi:10.1177/1094428115574518

29

Transforming Assessment: New Pedagogies for the Digital Age

Swati Johar and Updesh Kumar

Defence Institute of Psychological Research, Delhi, India

According to Cronbach and Meehl (1955), psychological and personality constructs are "postulated" or inferred characteristics or traits of a person. If we cannot physically see personality traits, measuring these hypothetical constructs becomes necessary to understand the behaviour of people. It becomes important to construct a coherent picture of the individual and his or her major psychological processes. To study how people are unique or alike requires investigation of individual differences and human nature. Personality assessment is the end result of gathering information intended to advance psychological theory and research and to increase the probability that wise decisions will be made.

Personality tests have not traditionally enjoyed the same level of support as cognitive tests, and their use in employment selection is much more controversial. Many experts conclude that personality tests as used in personnel selection lack validity, are easily faked, and are generally unsuitable for pre-employment screening (Blinkhorn & Johnson, 1990). Despite these reviews, recent research efforts have strengthened the imperative role of personality testing in selection (Heneman, Judge, & Heneman, 2000). Researchers have suggested that pairing personality testing with ability testing may be a means of enhancing validity while reducing the adverse impact of the selection system (Hunter & Hunter, 1984). The assumption underlying this argument is that there are factors related to job performance other than cognitive ability, and that using these factors to predict job success produces less adverse impact (Thomas & Scroggins, 2006).

Different jobs require different types of behaviours for successful performance. To achieve competitive advantage through people, organizations must be able to select individuals who have exceptional skills, and whose talents, values, and motives best fit the organization's culture, structure, and reward systems. Security-critical applications, in particular, demand specific attributes in an individual and these need to be tapped carefully. For years, personality assessments have been used to analyze and measure personality traits and styles, but these assessments can also be used to explore the work performance of an individual in an organization. Personality, in

The Wiley Handbook of Personality Assessment, First Edition. Edited by Updesh Kumar.
© 2016 John Wiley & Sons, Ltd. Published 2016 by John Wiley & Sons, Ltd.

part, determines who has a natural inclination for certain jobs and certain work environments. Performance assessment analyzes people's differing personality characteristics and helps to determine whether they will be a good fit for a certain position. The goal of personality assessment in personnel selection is to identify which individuals, in general, will be successful performers and remain on the job. Using the Big Five Factor model, personality assessments can aid in prediction of job performance (Barrick & Mount, 1991). Personality assessments can be implemented into selection procedures as a way to increase predictive validity and reduce the potential for adverse impact. Therefore, it is not surprising that the use of personality assessment for personnel selection is becoming increasingly popular among organizations.

Individuals today are growing up in a world overflowing with high-tech tools, from computers to sophisticated handheld devices. In the past decade, investments in technology have not led to fundamental changes in our approaches to assessment and testing. Technology, however, has the potential to do more than just make our current approach to testing more efficient. The role of technology ranges from the management of the assessment information to a fully automated assessment system. Whether technology improves assessment and learning is not a simple question, and the challenge begins with defining assessment and is compounded by the complexities of people, their personality, and technological implications on assessment infrastructure. The key facets of assessment are collection, analysis, interpretation of information, and its application for the purpose of improvement. Today, technology has the potential to allow the use of dynamic models and representation of domains and data in ways that previously were not possible. The tools of technology are creating new testing environments that need to be assessed carefully, including the type of assistance necessary to incorporate the tools, the changes in organizational infrastructure to effectively run these technologies, and the cognitive and learning consequences of using these new tools. In addition, significant progress has been made since the late 1990s to develop robust and flexible technical infrastructure to respond to these new opportunities. This wave of technology and innovation offers considerable potential to shift the focus on quality assurance by finding effective new and improved assessment methods and emphasizing the need for cost- and time-effectiveness.

Technology in the broadest sense is filtering into assessment and feedback practice, and practitioners working in this domain are demonstrating the value of integrating a wide range of technologies into their practice, enabling individuals to experience diverse and suitable assessment and feedback strategies at all stages of their assessment system. Digital technologies open new possibilities for more personalized, immediate, and engaging assessment experiences. However, technology-enhanced assessment has yet to be "transformative," with current practices manifesting in pockets of innovation that are not extensively prevalent or known. But technology alone cannot transform assessment. Our approach to testing calls for a radical change supported by a clear purpose behind the proposed innovation. Logical and funding challenges that often hinder the attempts to administer and maintain technological infrastructure would have to be overcome. It must be ensured that new assessment models align with standards for professional development and must not erode efforts to promote high expectations, and nor should they disadvantage individuals with limited access to technology. Assessment and feedback take place in increasingly varied, challenging, and time-constrained contexts. As a result, we need to understand as fully as possible how to achieve the most effective outcomes in the most appropriate and resourceful ways to provide valuable insights into the nature of assessment and feedback in a digital age.

Assessment and Feedback in a Technology-Rich Context

In order to accelerate the learning of students, more powerful assessment systems must be developed. Organizations like PARCC (Partnership for Assessment of Readiness for College and Careers) are pressing the need for the inclusion of more complex tasks to assess the types of skills required in a particular environment.

Technology-enhanced or technology-enabled assessments are often called e-assessments. Several developments have taken place as a logical continuation of the progress already made concerning psychological assessment and measurements in the field of individual characteristics; in physiological and neuro-psychological assessments; and in person–situation interaction assessment (Fernández-Ballesteros, 1995). Some promising avenues are interchanges between new technologies and cognitive sciences, computerized assisted assessment, computer-based assessments, and assessment through virtual reality. It should also be noted that technology should enhance assessment practices, rather than replace highly valued strategies such as face-to-face tutorials. Technology has the potential to make both the assessment process itself and the data resulting from that process more transparent and inclusive, and enables broader involvement in providing feedback. Claims of potential value, however, need to be verified by research-based evidence. E-assessment can be justified in a number of ways. Recent JISC reports (JISC, 2010) indicate a number of benefits that might be experienced in the following areas to enhance our present assessment scenario:

- *Authenticity*: The use of e-portfolios, blogs, online simulations, and video tools offers a richer and a more valid assessment experience than paper-based testing. They allow assessors to focus more on conceptual understanding of what needs to be done to solve problems. Assessments built around virtual worlds can remove the tedium associated with traditional examinations for all types and age groups, and support risk-free rehearsal of real-world skills in professional and educational settings.
- *Self-monitoring*: ICT can support the development of higher-order thinking skills such as critiquing, reflection on cognitive processes, and "learning to learn" stimulus using digital portfolios, which might involve critical and creative input from peers and generate an ownership of learning. A social constructivist view focuses on the importance of reflection and self-regulated learning to increase the validity and efficiency of assessments (JISC, 2010).
- *Quality and timeliness of response*: The technical quality of tests may be increased by improving the reliability of scoring and generating more accurate results via

adaptive testing. Closer alignment of assessment with the pedagogic approach (i.e., use of blended and online models) makes the assessment process increasingly appropriate and relevant. For many academic efforts, the free-for-all of the internet would not provide a meaningful assessment of work, but technology can support connections with online communities of individuals who do have the expertise and interest to judge the work.

- *Immediacy and contingency*: The element of personalization in e-assessments facilitates anytime, anywhere assessments, thus eliminating the difficulties due to distance, language, disability or commitments. Interactive online tests on systems and handheld devices make it possible to deliver immediate and diagnostic feedback.
- *Clear communication and dialog*: Interactive elements like forums, blogs, email and multimedia make assessments more valid, accessible, and engaging, and enable clarity of goals and standards, thereby enriching feedback.
- *Additionality*: Technology makes it possible to assess valuable life skills that were previously difficult to measure. Self-evaluation adds a personal aspect to feedback, and efficiencies gained through automatic scoring and anonymity can enable practitioners to make more productive use of their time and builds a bank of reusable resources.

Transition from Paper-and-Pencil Testing to Computer-Based Testing

The use of paper-and-pencil psychological tests in human resource selection has existed since the beginning of the twentieth century. However, paper-and-pencil tests, the landmark of massive assessments of the industrial epoch, become less and less relevant and cost-effective in information societies. The structure of the global economy today looks very different than it did at the beginning of the twentieth century, largely due to advances in information and communications technologies (ICT). The manufacture and delivery of information products and services form the basis of the economy of leading countries, rather than the manufacture of material goods. Due to the availability of ICT, the twenty-first century has witnessed significant drift in the access and use of information and knowledge.

The technological enhancements and the ability and skills required of personnel are being upgraded rapidly. In view of the changing socioeconomic milieu, an increasing number of job applicants, and an increase in the general education level of candidates, it has become imperative to shift from paper-and-pencil based tests to computer-based tests to assess the individual. The motivations to implement computer-based assessment (CBA) are varied, but have often been rooted in a drive for increased efficiency. Can we produce similar or better results with less effort? With e-assessments it is possible to test areas of knowledge, skills, and understanding that would be impossible using paper-and-pencil based testing.

Computers and electronic technology today offer myriad ways to enrich educational assessment both in the classroom and in large-scale testing environments. Computer-based assessment (CBA) is a method of administering tests in which the responses are electronically recorded and assessed with the aid of dynamic visuals, sound, user interactivity, as well as adaptivity to individual test-takers and near real-time score reporting. CBA vastly expands testing possibilities beyond the limitations of traditional paper-and-pencil tests (PPTs). As the digital divide lessens, technology must reach new frontiers for reformation and innovation in assessment, and formulate new assessment tasks and real-time feedback mechanisms (Scalise & Gifford, 2006).

Computer adaptive testing (CAT) is a form of computer-based test that adapts to the examinee's ability. Based on the responses, the computer software adjusts the difficulty of questions throughout the assessment process. This approach represents a significant improvement over traditional testing practices. Adaptive tests can work well in the case of a heterogeneous group when there is a single scale of difficulty. Also, we can develop intelligent assessment systems using a new generation of tests based on item response theory together with computer modeling and other computer-assisted strategies.

Throughout the past decade, computer programs have conquered diverse areas and addressed multifarious applications. Research must examine the validity of computerized tests in general and the issue of the tests' equivalence to paper-and-pencil measures. As noted by Hofer (1985), there are several factors specific to computerized test administration that could yield disparate results. Foremost among these may be some individuals' discomfort with computers and incompetence when dealing with these technological devices. Factors such as the type of equipment used and the nature of the test material also play a significant role. Hofer (1985) asserted that when the content deals with sensitive and personal information, individuals may be more willing to reveal their true feelings to a computer than to a human being, which may lead to atypical results when computerized assessment is used.

Computer-assisted testing technology greatly increases the efficiency and speed of scoring tests, thereby decreasing the turnaround time to provide response and feedback. The *immediate computation* and *availability of test scores* makes it possible for test-takers to plan for their next steps right after taking the exam. General advantages of CBA systems over traditional paper-and-pencil testing have been demonstrated in several comparative works. *Unbiased and accurate scoring* is an important benefit of such testing, as computers score everyone the same way and do not consider factors irrelevant to the score, such as examinee gender or culture. *Efficiency* of computer-based assessment is much higher than for a PPT. Research has shown that a 50-question computerized test takes much less time to administer than a 50-question PPT. *Reduced costs* of data entry, collection, and aggregation makes electronically administered tests more cost-effective. It also provides convenient individualized administration as computerized tests can be administered at times and locations more convenient to the test-taker. Random ordering of questions, adaptive testing, and other innovations make it impossible to copy content and expose questions less often. New performance-based test questions in adaptive testing are difficult to memorize for future test coaching. Test-takers make fewer extraneous errors answering computerized test questions than by filling out the small circles on answer forms for PPTs. It also enables the test publisher to easily include unobtrusive pre-testing items that are experimental and unscored to identify distinguishing traits. Enhanced interactivity and items composed of multimedia stimuli allow for the measurement of skills not easily measurable by traditional tests. CAT provides a more detailed picture of where students excel or need additional support, and adds flexibility to assessment. These tests require fewer questions to accurately determine a student's achievement level, and since students receive a different set of questions based on their responses, test items are more secure and last for a longer period of time. Finally, a computer allows for better test designs with more flexible item selection routines, and the computerized recording of results facilitates the analysis of individual/group responses.

Despite the many advantages of e-assessment, there are also potential problems and challenges. Chief among these is to ensure that all examinees face the same testing conditions and procedures. Software quality, questions of responsibility for defects in the software, preventing access to private information stored in databases, and operating on a reliable network are some of the aspects that need to be taken into account. Impersonation may be perceived as a huge risk in technologically rich environments. The most obvious way to control this issue is to set summative assessments in exam conditions and checking identities. Authentication of remotely sat examinations is likely to remain a problem, as it is with paper-based assessments. Plagiarism should present no greater problem in an electronic environment than in a more traditional context. Any of the delivery modes, whether paper-pencil and/or computer-based, have advantages and challenges which can hardly be compared. However, the use of technology-enhanced assessment includes additional benefits which can be achieved from an organizational, pedagogical and psychological perspective, and the overall added value and advantages of e-assessments in large-scale assessments have been investigated by various experts over the last decade (Scheuermann & Guimarães Pereira, 2008).

In India, the research efforts in investigating the scope of e-assessment have not yet gained momentum and are only at the nascent stage. Little research has been carried out to understand the scope of growth, or the relationship between the computer familiarity of examinees and their performance on computer-based testing.

Assessments in Modern Psychology

Virtual environment as an assessment tool

Assessment is a complex process that provides a representative sample of behavior of the person being assessed. It forms the core of the learning experience, comprising three major courses of action: (1) designing learning tasks; (2) assessing performance on these tasks and; (3) using the feedback to enhance further the ability to progress.

The assessment tools used by clinical and research psychologists in the modern era date back a half-century or more (Tallent, 1992). Today's psychological assessors are concerned with new and developing concepts of testing and technology and their implications. In this sense, the future practices must be flexible and open-ended, considering the opportunities offered by unexpected situations.

An effective assessment must be as authentic as possible in the desired context, and should accommodate real-world problems and transfer the assessee to the world beyond the unit (Boud, 1998). Many tools are available to support this fidelity and connectedness, and allow the assessment to be seamlessly integrated with the activity. Virtual environments (VEs) offer a new human–computer interaction paradigm in which users are not only present but also interact within a computer-generated three-dimensional virtual world, and have provided a breakthrough in the techniques of learning and assessment. They are advocated as promising tools in psychological research and assessment, to bridge the gap between field experiments with low internal validity and those performed under controlled settings with low external validity, providing a unique combination of both mundane realism and experimental control (Blasçovich et al., 2002). In many applications, VEs are used in order to simulate the real world and to give the researcher full control of all the involved parameters.

The traditional dimensions of time, place, and space have been replaced by three further dimensions – technology, interaction, and control – transforming the individualized learning experience to an open system of communication between the learner and the assessor. In contrast to computer-based learning environments where various technologies are used as tools for learning, VE is a much broader concept which is no longer an individual endeavor. In virtual learning environments (VLEs) technology is used to deliver information and facilitate communication among participants. VLEs can be considered as highly sophisticated forms of adaptive testing that rely on information and communication technology to build higher degree of learner control than traditional assessment settings. Both the synthetic environment itself and the manner in which this environment is modified by the user's responses can be modified to the needs of each client and/or therapeutic application (Glantz, Durlach, Barnett, & Aviles, 1997). VLEs have been built on the constructivist model, wherein reality is constructed either socially or by individuals (Jonassen, 1993). They work at their own pace with additional assessment, support and tracking functionalities, thus providing an environment of personalized learning. It can potentially eliminate geographical barriers while providing increased convenience, flexibility, immediate feedback and interpretation, and also relevance and accessibility of the assessment.

VLEs offer a number of advantages over traditional assessment and learning systems in terms of convenience and flexibility, but their effectiveness remains an open question (Kiser, 1999). VLEs require the participants to interact extensively with computers, and individuals who are comfortable with technology are better able to exploit the unique characteristics of technology-mediated learning, whereas those who are unable to cope with the high degree of learner control report lower levels of satisfaction.

It could be argued that individuals in the VLE spend most of the time interacting with the computer, and the lack of familiarity of communication and learning techniques may be conducive to feelings of isolation, anxiety, and confusion (Brown, 1996; Hara & Kling, 2000).

Riva (1997) and Riva & Gamberini (2000) explore three important aspects of virtual reality systems offering new possibilities for assessment and treatment:

- *How they are controlled*: Most computer interfaces today accept only a single discrete input at a time and fail to monitor bodily movements and communicative gestures. VR systems offer the possibility of multimodal inputs to process actions and translate these actions into meaningful signals.
- *Feedback*: Vision is the primary feedback channel of present-day computers. Multimodal feedback from VR systems provides a larger perspective of the overall environment and provides a means to present information in alternate ways. As a result, it is possible to interpret feedback and response into alternate senses of users with sensory impairments.
- *What is controlled*: The last decade used computers to control numbers and text through the keyboard until recently, when direct manipulation interfaces have permitted exploitation of objects in the real world. Virtual environments provide the opportunity to use multisensory representations of entire environments by natural actions and gestures.

Big Data: decision-making tool

Data are fundamental to information, and the more meaningful the data, the better we can understand the issues and anticipate the future. The unprecedented rise in mobile technologies, sensory devices, social and transactional media, cloud computing, web applications, and so on, together with their interactions have generated a massive repository of data for mining information. These large and complex data-sets are difficult to process using traditional data processing applications and software techniques. *Big Data* is an evolving term that describes technologies and initiatives that involve voluminous and diverse data that may be analyzed computationally to reveal trends and patterns, and aids in decision-making. It no longer matters whether data-sets are structured, semi-structured or unstructured, as new possibilities for data acquisition and processing are thriving at the same time. Big Data is a revolution that will enable scientific breakthroughs, societal transformations, and new business models. Today few doubt that, if data analytic methods are properly planned and executed, organizations will be able to make more effective decisions. For example, Brynjolfsson, Hitt, and Kim (2011), in their study on publicly traded firms, concluded that firms that adopted a data-driven decision-making approach enjoyed 5–6% higher output and productivity than would be expected given their other investments and level of information technology usage.

Three important factors that define the very nature of Big Data are *Volume*, *Variety*, and *Velocity*, popularly known as “the 3Vs,” which influence one another in the flow of data. Many applications require relevant information that is easily possible through Big Data analytics. Some of these are the prediction of behaviour of students at a college or university, employees in an organization, hiring decisions by HR, and so on. Each of these scenarios involves decisions that are central to an organization’s affairs and are made frequently by experts, and in corporate quantifiable information that is readily available (Guszcza & Richardson, 2014). Decision-making is central to all these aspects, and in virtually any domain predictive models built using statistical analysis and innovation can be used to drive better expert decisions.

The use of this concept of Big Data for prediction and analyses of human behavior is still in its nascent stage. Since past behavior often predicts future behavior, the paramount issue is gathering the relevant behavioral content from the data sources. The increasing availability of computational social science tools and methods suggests the practical possibility of harnessing behavioral data to create more effective teams, and systematically reward beneficial behaviors and personality traits that are currently recognized only sporadically (Guszcza & Richardson, 2014).

Alex Pentland (Edge, 2012), the computational social scientist, forcefully articulates this point:

> I believe that the power of big data is that it is information about people's behavior instead of information about their beliefs. It's about the behavior of customers, employees, and prospects for your new business. It's not about the things you post on Facebook, and it's not about your searches on Google, which is what most people think about, and it's not data from internal company processes and RFIDs. This sort of big data comes from things like location data off of your cell phone or credit card: it's the little data breadcrumbs that you leave behind you as you move around in the world.

The power of these "digital breadcrumbs" can be exploited to extract information on such latent psychological traits as intelligence, openness, extraversion, and emotional stability. The non-verbal aspects of communication like voice tones, body language, and gestures can be captured using wearable sensing devices, and these sociometric data can be used to study human behaviour and social relationships.

As the cost of IT solutions continues to drop and software processing power is increasing, mastering Big Data is not necessary to exhaustively tap the benefits of this revolution. Looking at the progress in the maturity of modern data-flow softwares, it will be possible to monitor real-time complex associations more efficiently than using traditional statistical and analytical methods. Big Data is currently the domain of interest and is slowing gaining momentum, but to utilize the potential of this technology, organizations must be appropriately trained and employees must be equipped to translate that information and knowledge into practice, with a view to enhancing organization effectiveness and productivity, and the quality of the people.

Pervasive computing: embedded assessment

Pervasive computing is an emerging application of ICT that is integrated into the everyday world. It is an approach for ubiquitous, invisible, and seamless information and communication that uses sensors, communication, processing, and actuator technologies, and adjusts their behavior accordingly, thus providing context awareness. It involves a large number of smart devices with sensor-rich technologies that provide seamless services to users. An application area of increasing interest is behavior modeling: analysis and adaptation of individuals by focusing on measuring specific facets of personality. Given the wide availability of smartphones and other smart devices, we can measure certain behavior characteristic variables from these smart data, which can further be used to provide feedback and assistance. One important domain that deserves attention in this direction is improving the wellbeing of individuals by intervening in the behavior of successful people and using this knowledge to help others by prompting them to adopt behaviors identified as likely to enhance their happiness and wellbeing. It could enlighten our general understanding of the association of human behavior variants with success and wellbeing.

More prevalent techniques like digital augmentation tend to focus on technology, but fail to incorporate the contextual information to predict human behavior. Context-aware pervasive computing methods address this shortcoming and have been applied in the areas of social networking, healthcare, assessments, and education. Researchers (dos Santos, Cardoso, Ferreira, Diniz, & Chainho, 2010) have worked on the acquisition of context and on the discrimination of human activity, in particular.

Healthcare is another vital area where embedded assessment can leverage the capability of pervasive computing. Environment–behavior connections can be highlighted by implicit sensing to detect subtle changes in patterns and acquiring contextually sensitive data. Feedback by means of interactive visualizations can be delivered at appropriate moments to the end users directly, and not to clinicians or healthcare professionals. Health technology advances in the areas of monitoring and prevention have been reviewed by Morris, Intille, and Beaudin (2005), and an approach to demonstrate ubiquitous computing tools for behavior inspection in natural settings has been discussed. The practicability, accuracy and acceptability of implementing these embedded assessment systems in organizational settings needs to be further investigated. It has great potential to offer possibilities for monitoring and preventive healthcare innovation; however, significant challenges to its implementation in real-world scenarios need to be resolved. Embedded assessment has great potential as a mechanism to gather ongoing information about the health of individuals aging with disabilities; however, there are significant challenges owing to effective implementation of these practices and techniques (Haque & Ahamed, 2006).

Social networks: personality predictor

Social media on the web has grown dramatically over the past decade. In social networking, users interact with unknown individuals and present themselves to the world. The coherent patterning of affect and behavior in a personality may be revealed by analyzing what users share and how they express themselves online. Social networking sites like Facebook are becoming popular tools for public and private interaction and information exchange. Social network profiling is an emerging and potential technique to bridge the gap between personality research and social media. In last few years, studies have explored the relationship between personality traits and profile information provided by social networks.

Ryan and Xenos (2011) suggested that individual differences influence online behavior. The Big Five personality domains of openness, conscientiousness, extraversion, agreeableness, and neuroticism have been shown to correlate with social aspects of behavior and internet usage (Orchard & Fullwood, 2010). Celli (2012) has worked on automatic recognition of personality traits through machine learning in the domain of social networks. Despite more and more individuals using internet and social networks, research concerning the social networking environment has been restricted. Personality tests make it impractical to use personality analysis in the realm of social media. Various methods may be proposed to accurately predict a user's personality through publicly available profile information like status updates, photos, comments, and so on. Differing user profiles (personality, age, sex) may interact differently with different social networks. This information on personality thus obtained may then be used to tailor websites and e-commerce retailers to reflect the particular user's traits and present the most receptive information according to the user. An alternate use of personality is in recommender systems to select and give preference to users who share similar personality traits. Development of such algorithms and techniques may be considered as an open space for future work. Research on personalizing interfaces for business and marketing is one area to be pursued. Understanding how personality or age, for example, integrates with social networking sites in terms of trust and wellbeing remains an important topic of concern (Golbeck, 2005).

Ethical and Legal Issues

Globalization and technological changes that have accelerated over the past few years have transformed life and economy in powerful ways. The emergence of this new global economy has resulted in exponential growth of information access mechanisms, and applied immense pressure to constantly acquire new skills and knowledge. Information and communication technologies have brought change and reform to the traditional assessment processes and systems, strengthened the relevance of education and assessment to the increasingly digital work milieu, and raised quality by providing interactive and engaging environments that replicate real-life scenarios. While appreciating the achievements and prospects of technology-enhanced assessments, the various pitfalls they entail should not be ignored. We must be both hopeful as well as cautious about the technologies and techniques we adopt and use. Concerns over the relevance and quality of e-assessments co-exist with the imperative of effective integration of not just technology, but also incorporation and understanding of institutional readiness, assessor competencies, financing, pedagogy, and ensuring equal access, among others. On the social plane, various ethical and legal aspects guide the use of computer technologies in assessment and feedback. The idea should not be to adopt a technology simply because it exists, but rather we should also learn and understand the implications that can arise by the use of these ICTs. Various issues may arise as these technologically rich assessment tools shift the trend towards an open and distance-independent assessment center approach.

Digital plagiarism, privacy and confidentiality breaches, hacking, net-etiquette, equal accessibility of ICT by the information-rich and information-poor, cognitive effects due to technology addiction, and the need to formulate professional standards and codes of conduct for computer professionals are some of the points of concern.

The use of digital technologies has led to the proliferation of easily accessible electronic resources, and has exposed the risk of duplication in work and content. As a result, the chances of infringing data confidentiality and integrity increase considerably. The increasing incidences of reproduction and content distribution in this age of the internet can be controlled by the establishment of suitable mechanisms and structures which satisfy the necessary requirements of reliability, efficiency, and effectiveness of any assessment technique. The widespread adoption of electronic detection of plagiarism may be seen as an initial step in this direction (Badge & Scott, 2009; Jones, Reid, & Bartlett, 2008). Due to the unrestricted opportunities provided by the internet today, these detection techniques offer little support in dealing with this so-called *academic hurricane.* Thus the need to promote prevention rather than detection needs to be emphasized, to stop cyber plagiarism from becoming a major threat to organizational quality and enhancement.

A critical aspect of any assessment is trust, and trust is undermined when there is no assurance of privacy for users. The challenges to privacy arise because of the capability of technology to collect and analyze large amounts of data. An effective password protection system, data encryption, authorization using digital signatures and message digests, and privacy filters that limit the access to internet content are some of the means to provide security. Good cyber security measures enforce policies that extend the scope of provably secure systems to larger domains. As the use of the internet in the practice of psychology and assessments is expanding, various ethical and professional issues demand attention to enforce strict data security and privacy laws, to promote reliable and powerful internet testing and e-assessment strategies (Naglieri *et al.*, 2004). Breaches of privacy can cause harm to individuals, and the government should enforce regulations or laws to redress those harms. New sources of big data, cameras, sensors, and mobile technologies are bound to raise new privacy concerns. As discussed before, big data techniques may allow the unintentional disclosure of sensitive data which otherwise remains latent in the content. Policy must focus on intervention at various stages of data collection, analyses, and data usage, to inform the successful application of these technologies.

The availability and ease of use of ICTs pose another threat to society and assessments, in particular the digital access divide. Digital illiteracy as a result of *technology leapfrogging* (Napoli & Obar, 2013) brings inequality in access to information. Research suggests that individuals who are comfortable with technology and are able to adapt will perform better than those with lower levels of technological fluency. To effectively address this concern, adoption of any new technology should be accompanied by a process of learning and acquisition of the relevant skills, so that individuals who were previously excluded are able to acclimatize better and integrate with the technological innovations, consequently lessening this digital gap. The problem of the digital divide is also growing within social groups and between countries at national and international levels.

The growing application of technology in assessment is linked to numerous psychological problems as well. Addiction to computers comes in the way of development of human creativity and affects the cognitive capacities of individuals. Though learning from experience with the aid of real-life scenarios enhances logical thinking, at the same time the psychological effects of using computers in daily life are manifested slowly. Hassing (1987) investigated this phenomenon in many countries and found that social isolation, deformation of emotional sphere, decrease of social and cultural levels, and tendency to computer crimes were some of the common impacts of information technology on human psychology. He also suggests that virtual environments weaken the communicative structure of assessment and learning, and thereby lessen the quality of assessment systems.

Ethical, societal, as well as psychological considerations must be combined with the responsibility to conduct methodical research by the researchers and policy-makers. Nevertheless, technology supports personality development, increasing an individual's potential and widening their intellectual horizon. Much research and critical thinking is needed, within the framework that ethical standards and the principles of effective assessment still remain fundamental.

Psychometrics for the Next Generation: Recommendation

As new technologies emerge, we need to understand how to achieve effective assessment and feedback in the most efficient and resourceful ways. Today, an assessment system does not fit the standard model of a multiple-choice questionnaire, nor does it involve highly constrained parameters and response options. The new genre of assessment process provides a dynamic space that is highly interactive, immersive, and adaptive in nature. Assessments in the twenty-first century are believed to be largely data-driven and embedded in games and virtual reality, employing natural language recognition. The focus is likely to fall on developing a seamless digital environment in which peers become both drivers and assessors of learning, and support self-monitoring and self-assessment. In this light, those involved in designing assessments have a big responsibility to refine their practices further. Until recently, psychometrics dealt mostly with the construction and validation of quantitative questionnaires for the measurement of psychological constructs and personality traits. However, there is now a need to augment and invigorate the procedural foundations of psychometrics. The new digital assessment environment will be a domain-independent representation of relatively unconstrained parameters such as open-ended responses, interactions with physical media, as well as intangible assets like facial expressions and gestures, emotions, and so on (Brave & Hass, 2003; Park, Baek, & Gibson, 2008; Parunak, Bisson, Brueckner, Matthews, & Sauter, 2006). This new assessment space demands features like time and spatial sensitivity, in addition to being "internally consistent" and "reliable over time." Performance assessments based on adaptive testing and with a heavy emphasis on innovative item types and artificial intelligence (AI)-based scoring algorithms will dominate the digital age. It is believed that these assessments can enhance the tradeoff between validity and reliability measures through increased task realism. Digital assessment tasks can dynamically adapt to the test-taker's ability, thus providing a degree of personalization and non-linearities in behaviour. This measure is unexplored by traditional population-based statistical methods. These complex approaches from data-driven science and simulations demand new assessment targets and analysis tools. Statistical packages do not address the new objectives presented by these interactive digital-based assessments. Targets are shifting from basic knowledge and skill measures towards high order, collaborative, and critical thinking (Bennett, Persky, Weiss, & Jenkins, 2010; Koch & DeLuca, 2012). Data-mining techniques, web analytics, and pattern recognition using machine learning are the emerging toolsets for assessing the benefits of technology-enhanced assessments. The key challenges to the postmodern assessment era are likely to be successfully addressed by coupling modern data analytic methods with standardized assessment designs, and including the psychometric community throughout the development of assessment.

Overcoming these challenges will be difficult, but with careful attention from policymakers and deliberate strategies to create change, we can build and implement the types of technology-enhanced assessments discussed in this chapter on a large scale. While considering the innovations and recommendations outlined in this chapter, there is a need to spend resources wisely to support a new vision of assessment and feedback. Accountability goals must be maintained, and progress needs to happen at a greater pace in the coming decade. We should plot a different course, where research efforts are focused on prioritizing the use of technology-enabled assessments, minimizing the time and cost of production, and establishing the validity of scoring systems, not just for automation but for maximizing the quality and reliability of assessment, to create new cultural, cognitive, and professional horizons of assessment and education at both national and global levels.

References

Badge, J.L., & Scott, J. (2009). *Dealing with plagiarism in the digital age*. Retrieved from http://evidencenet.pbworks.com/Dealing-with-plagiarism-in-the-digital-age

Barrick, M.R., & Mount, M.K. (1991). The Big Five personality dimensions and job performance: A meta analysis. *Personnel Psychology, 44* (1), 1–26.

Bennett, R.E., Persky, H., Weiss, A., & Jenkins, F. (2010). Measuring problem solving with technology: A demonstration study for NAEP. *Journal of Technology, Learning, and Assessment, 8*(8).

Blascovich, J., Loomis, J., Beall, A., Swinth, K., Hoyt, C., & Bailenson, J.N. (2002). Immersive virtual environment technology as a methodological tool for social psychology. *Psychological Inquiry, 13* (2), 103–124.

Blinkhorn, S., & Johnson, C. (1990). The insignificance of personality testing. *Nature, 348* (6303), 671–672.

Boud, D. (1998). *Assessment and learning – unlearning bad habits of assessment.* Paper presented at the Effective Assessment at University Conference, University of Queensland. Retrieved from http://damianeducationresearchlinks.wikispaces.com/file/view/unlearningassessment_Boud.pdf

Brave, S., & Hass, C. (2003). Emotion in human–computer interaction. In J. Jacko, & Sears (Eds.), *The Human–Computer Interaction Handbook: Fundamentals, Evolving Technologies and Emerging Applications* (pp. 81–96). Mahwah, NJ: Lawrence Erlbaum Associates, Inc.

Brown, K.M. (1996). The role of internal and external factors in the discontinuation of off-campus students. *Distance Education, 17* (1), 44–71.

Brynjolfsson, E., Hitt, L.M., & Kim, H.H. (2011). *Strength in Numbers: How Does Data-Driven Decision making Affect Firm Performance?* Retrieved from http://ssrn.com/abstract=1819486 or 10.2139/ssrn.1819486 DOI:10.2139/ssrn.1819486

Celli, F. (2012). *Unsupervised Personality Recognition for Social Network Sites.* In Proceedings of International Conference on Digital Society (ICDS), Valencia.

Cronbach, L.J., & Meehl, P.E. (1955). Construct validity in psychological tests. *Psychological Bulletin, 52* (4), 281–302.

dos Santos, A.G., Cardoso, J.A.M., Ferreira, D.R., Diniz, P.C., & Chainho, P. (2010). Providing user context for mobile and social networking applications. *Pervasive and Mobile Computing, 6* (3), 324–341.

Edge. (2012). *Reinventing society in the wake of big data: A conversation with Alex (Sandy) Pentland.* Retrieved from http://www.edge.org/conversation/reinventing-society-in-the-wake-of-big-data

Fernández-Ballesteros, R. (1995). Crucial issues in the field of psychological assessment and evaluation during the next decades. *International Association of Applied Psychology (Newsletter), 7* (2), 13–20.

Glantz, K., Durlach, N.I., Barnett, R.C., & Aviles, W.A. (1997). Virtual reality (VR) and psychotherapy: Opportunities and challenges. *Presence, 6* (1), 87–105.

Golbeck, J. (2005). *Computing and Applying Trust in Web-based Social Networks.* PhD thesis, University of Maryland, College Park, MD, USA.

Guszcza, J., & Richardson, B. (2014). Two dogmas of big data: Understanding the power of analytics for predicting human behavior. *Deloitte Review, 15,* 161–175.

Haque, M., & Ahamed, S.I. (2006). Security in pervasive computing: Current status and open issues. *International Journal of Network Security, 3* (3), 203–214.

Hara, N., & Kling, R. (2000). Students' distress with a web-based distance education course. *Information, Communication & Society, 3* (4), 557–579.

Hassing, G. (1987). Angst vor dem Computer? Die Schweiz angesichts einer mod. *Technologie.* Bern, Stuttgart: Haupt.

Heneman III, H.G., Judge, T.A., & Heneman, R.L. (2000). *Staffing Organizations* (3rd ed.). Burr Ridge, IL: Irwin McGraw-Hill.

Hofer, P.J. (1985). Developing standards for computerized psychological testing. *Computers in Human Behavior, 1* (3–4), 301–315.

Hunter, J.E., & Hunter, R.F. (1984). Validity and utility of alternative predictors of job performance. *Psychological Bulletin, 96* (1), 72–98.

JISC. (2010). *Effective Assessment in a Digital Age. A Guide to Technology-Enhanced Assessment and Feedback.* Bristol: Higher Education Funding Council for England. Retrieved from http://www.jisc.ac.uk/media/documents/programmes/elearning/digiassass_eada.pdf

Jonassen, D.H. (1993). Thinking technology: The trouble with learning environments. *Educational Technology, 33* (1), 35–37.

Jones, K.O., Reid, J., & Bartlett, R. (2008). Cyber cheating in an information technology age. In R. Comas, & J. Sureda (coords.). *Academic Cyberplagiarism* [online dossier]. Digithum. No. 10. UOC. Retrieved from http://www.uoc.edu/digithum/10/dt/eng/jones_reid_bartlett.pdf ISSN 1575-2275

Kiser, K. (1999). 10 things we know so far about online training. *Training, 36* (11), 66–74.

Koch, M.J., & DeLuca, C. (2012). Rethinking validation in complex high-stakes assessment contexts. *Assessment in Education: Principles, Policy & Practice, 19* (1), 99–116.

Morris, M., Intille, S.S., & Beaudin, J.S. (2005). Embedded assessment: Overcoming barriers to early detection with pervasive computing. In H.W. Gellersen, R. Want, & A. Schmidt (Eds.), *Pervasive 2005* (pp. 333–346). Berlin: Springer-Verlag.

Naglieri, J.A., Drasgow, F., Schmit, M., Handler, L., Prifitera, A., Margolis, A., & Velasquez, R. (2004). Psychological testing on the Internet: New problems, old issues. *American Psychologist, 59* (3), 150–162.

Napoli, P.M., & Obar, J.A. (2013). *Mobile Leapfrogging and Digital Divide Policy: Assessing the Limitations of Mobile Internet Access.* New York: New America Foundation.

Orchard, L.J., & Fullwood, C. (2010). Current perspectives on personality and Internet use. *Social Science Computer Review, 28* (2), 155–169.

Park, H., Baek, Y., & Gibson, D. (2008). Design of an adaptive mobile learning management system. In J. Lumsden (Ed.), *Handbook of Research on User Interface Design and Evaluation for Mobile Technology* (Vol. *1*) (pp. 286–301). Hershey, PA: Information Science Reference.

Parunak, H., Bisson, R., Brueckner, S., Matthews, R., & Sauter, J. (2006). A model of emotions for situated agents. In *Proceedings of Autonomous Agents and Multi-Agent Systems, '06* (pp. 993–995). New York: ACM.

Riva, G. (1997). Virtual reality as assessment tool in psychology. In G. Riva (Ed.), *Virtual Reality in Neuro-psycho-physiology* (pp. 71–80). Amsterdam: IOS Press.

Riva, G., & Gamberini, L. (2000). Virtual reality as telemedicine tool: technology, ergonomics and actual applications. *Technology and Health Care, 8* (2), 113–127.

Ryan, T., & Xenos, S. (2011). Who uses Facebook? An investigation into the relationship between the Big Five, shyness, narcissism, loneliness, and Facebook usage. *Computers in Human Behavior, 27* (5), 1658–1664.

Scalise, K., & Gifford, B. (2006). Computer-based assessment in e-learning: A framework for constructing "intermediate constraint" questions and tasks for technology platforms. *Journal of Technology, Learning, and Assessment, 4* (6), 4–43.

Scheuermann, F., & Guimarães Pereira, A. (Eds.) (2008). *Towards a Research Agenda on Computer-based Assessment.* Luxembourg: Office for Official Publications of the European Communities.

Tallent, N. (1992). *The Practice of Psychological Assessment.* Englewood Cliffs, NJ: Prentice Hall.

Thomas, S.L., & Scroggins, W.A. (2006). Psychological testing in personnel selection: Contemporary issues in cognitive ability and personality testing. *Journal of Business Inquiry, 5,* 28–38.

30

Ethical Issues in Personality Assessment

Swati Mukherjee and Updesh Kumar

Defence Institute of Psychological Research, Delhi, India

Assessment of personality often forms the core of psychological assessment for varied purposes. Assessment is a crucial activity undertaken by psychologists in the scientific pursuit of prediction and control of human behavior. Scientific assessment has the capability "to translate human behavior, characteristics, and abilities into numbers or other forms that lend themselves to description and comparison across individuals and groups of people" (Koocher & Rey-Casserly, 2003, p. 165). Apart from research in basic personality theories, assessment of personality is usually undertaken upon request either of the client or of a third party. The kind of assessment required, tools to be used, and scope of assessment are all determined on the basis of the kind of answers being sought by the requesting party. Over the last century the techniques of assessment have been steadily refined and developed by the researchers and practitioners in the field. Today a wide variety of choices are available regarding assessment procedures and tools of personality assessment. Allport (1937) classified two major approaches to assessment of personality: *nomothetic*, which aims to establish general laws and principles that can be applied universally to all individuals, and *idiographic*, which attempts to understand the unique aspects of a particular individual through the intensive study of a single or a small number of individuals as complete, complex, and interacting systems. These two approaches have led to the development of a wide range of personality tests. While most personality tests rely on the trait approach to the study of personality, their degree of objectivity and subjectivity differs, leading to the classification of objective tests and projective tests for personality assessment. The basic assumptions underlying the two types of tests lead to diversion not only of assessment procedures, but also of definition issues as to what constitutes personality.

Objective tests of personality assume that personality is consciously accessible and can be measured with the help of self-report inventories. These tests are usually structured to offer a limited range of possible responses, and their administration and scoring is relatively simple. All self-report inventories, in general, are paper-and-pencil tests consisting of a series of questions that require individuals to describe their feelings, environment, thoughts, and actions. In contrast, the projective tests of personality are

The Wiley Handbook of Personality Assessment, First Edition. Edited by Updesh Kumar.
© 2016 John Wiley & Sons, Ltd. Published 2016 by John Wiley & Sons, Ltd.

based on the assumption that personality is primarily unconscious and is, therefore, not directly accessible. These tests rely on ambiguous stimuli in order to extract information from individuals that will help determine their personality characteristics, and are comparatively less structured or unstructured. Theorists who use projective tests believe that in responding to the unstructured ambiguous stimuli, individuals reveal their unconscious motives, conflicts, fears, needs, feelings, drives, and desires. The responses received from individuals to the presented stimuli can be interpreted in many different ways, thus making the process complex and highly subjective. Apart from the objective and projective varieties of personality assessment tools, there are a multitude of tests and inventories available that combine the two in various proportions.

Assessment of personality is often undertaken for clinical, educational, vocational, organizational, or forensic purposes, its scope and extent varying accordingly. A competent assessment implies that the assessor is conversant with the theory of measurement and methods of test construction, and at the same time has an awareness of the strengths and limitations of the tests being chosen for assessment, and employs proper procedures of administration and interpretation, in order to provide a coherent and relevant report (Society for Personality Assessment, 2006). Psychological assessment is often surrounded by an aura of unchallengeable accuracy and portrayed as a solution to a myriad of applied problems. However, psychological assessment is a complex field, with its obvious strengths and not so obvious limitations, and in their pursuit of providing scientifically valid assessments, psychologists have to deal with multiple ethical issues and dilemmas. In applied contexts, psychological assessment is a potent tool through which a psychologist can affect the assessee's life in both positive and negative ways. Hence it is imperative that full scientific rigor and ethically appropriate procedures are ensured by the assessor. Koocher and Rey-Casserly (2003) defined the core ethical challenge in psychological assessment as "the appropriate use of psychological science to make decisions with full recognition of its limitations and the legal and human rights of the people whose lives are influenced" (p. 165).

Ethics and Ethical Behavior in Professional Contexts

Humanity has always been interested in ethics, and every society has set ethical standards of behavior for its members since man started organized living. The rules framed by a society for regulating the conduct of its members provide a description of expected behavioral standards, prescribe desirable behaviors, and set the norms for evaluating good or bad behavior. Traditionally, as a branch of philosophy, ethics has been concerned with what is morally good and bad, right and wrong. The study of ethics involves analyzing and developing normative criteria for dealing with moral problems. Though, etymologically, the Greek origin of the term ethic (i.e., *ethos*) and the Latin origin of the term moral (i.e., *mores*) both have the same meaning (habits or customs), the term ethics connotes a meaning incorporating something more than mere habits or customs. Ethics are the prescriptive and normative standards of behavior expected to be adhered to by members of a group, organization, or society. This implies that besides descriptive and prescriptive norms, ethics provide an evaluative criterion that actively discriminates the desirable from undesirable. Ethics and morals both offer value-based judgments on the acceptability of behavior, though morals have a wider basis derived from the culture or values of a group or society, and have a general all-pervasive application, whereas ethics, in comparison, are more specific both in terms of origin and range of applicability. Leong, Altmaier, and Johnson (2008) define ethics as "the agreed upon standards of aspirational and mandatory behaviours and practices" (p. 182) by the members of a specific group, in their context the American Psychological Association.

Ethics set an aspirational standard of behavior in a manner that distinguishes the *malum in se* (bad in itself) from *malum prohibitum* (wrong only because law prohibits it). This implies that members of the group are expected to internalize these normative standards as inherent values of the group, and adhere to these under all circumstances, and not only in order to avoid punishment or reprimand. The key attribute that places ethics on a higher level than the law is the freedom of choice – choice that one makes in adhering to good and refraining from bad even in the absence of a binding authority. The core thus lies in voluntarily distinguishing the good from bad and structuring one's behavior accordingly. Given the extent of general acceptability and uncritical approval of the results of psychological assessment done by an appropriately qualified trained person, and considering the extensive manner in which the outcomes of an assessment can impact the life of any given individual, it is absolutely essential for the professional to inculcate and imbibe appropriate professional ethical values in his or her conduct and practice.

Moreover, psychological assessment is an inherently human endeavor, wherein the psychologist actively constructs interpretations. Though test data contribute majorly to the assessment decisions, assessment cannot be made solely relying on test data. Psychological assessment involves drawing inferences and making holistic decisions about individuals by combining data drawn from multiple sources, which might include interviews, observations, and rating scales in addition to psychological tests. Such data combination procedures can be aided by mechanical predictions based on statistical computations, and algorithmic prediction using computer programmes, yet it has been shown that clinical prediction done by a qualified professional proves comparatively efficacious, especially when assessment includes interview data (Grove, Zald, Lebow, Snitz, & Nelson, 2000). It is obvious that psychological assessment can prove to be a complex task even for a qualified and competent professional, fraught with ethical dilemmas and difficult decisions.

Ethical standards of conduct are derived from multiple sources, and it is difficult to provide a straightforward prescription of do's and don'ts.

Sources of ethics

Ethics can be derived from a number of sources. Bond (2000) delineated six sources of ethics:

(i) Personal ethics.
(ii) Ethical principles derived from a particular theoretical model.

(iii) Ethical policies and guidelines of the agency that employs the psychologist.
(iv) Guidelines and norms laid down by professional codes.
(v) Moral philosophy.
(vi) Legal obligations.

Nelson-Jones (2002) described these sources, and how they influence ethical decision-making.

Personal ethics are the ethical principles and values that evolve from personal life experiences of the psychologist. The values learned and internalized by the professional as a part of his or her socialization provide the basis for incorporating the professional ethics. Compassion for the client and professional competence can be said to have a basis in the personal ethics of the professional.

The *theoretical model* subscribed to by the psychologist not only determines the choice of tools and procedure of assessment, but also influences the ethical framework to a large extent. Different theoretical models have differing notions about the autonomy of the client and invasion of privacy by the assessor. The theoretical perspective being followed by the assessor is often the crucial factor based upon which the client makes a choice of going on with the assessment.

The *policy of the agency* within which the assessor functions determines the ethics question in a huge way, especially by requiring mandatory sharing of information, or by prescribing specific formats for assessment. Notwithstanding the overall commitment of the psychologist to the welfare of the client, certain limits might be imposed by the agency policies on the way particular issues are to be resolved.

Codes of ethics for psychological assessment are published by various professional organizations, and function as the regulatory guidelines for the practitioners in the field. Nelson-Jones (2002) asserted the importance of ethical codes by portraying these as the "starting point for a process of ethical decision making since they lay out what is generally considered acceptable behaviour in the profession" (p. 317). He valued professional codes for they provide a formal framework within which ethical practices can be assessed, though he also cautioned against development of apathy, passivity, and self-deceiving rationalizations that may arise due to overly relying on the professional codes, and not developing ethical decision-making skills.

Moral philosophy as a source of ethics establishes principles for defining the "good" and "bad" in a particular time and place. Accepted moral principles underlying ethical codes for psychological practice are: respect for individual autonomy, working for the benefit of the client, not harming the client, providing services for the benefit of all, and honoring promises.

Law and legal rules provide an important source of ethical practice within the area where the assessor practices. It is obligatory for the psychologist to be aware of the prevalent legal norms, rules, and the law pertaining especially to their area of practice. Bond (2000) advised in this regard to have a basic knowledge of law relating to contract, negligence, defamation, confidentiality, protection and disclosure of records, and acting as a witness in the courts of law. As a self-regulating profession, the responsibility of practicing psychologists is not limited to codified law, though the limits defined by law are sacrosanct.

Ethical practice in psychological assessment

Koocher and Rey-Casserly (2003) provided a useful template in considering the pertinent ethical concerns that arise in assessment contexts by classifying these in terms of "before, during, and after assessment issues." It is convenient to consider this classification in order to foresee and describe the probable ethical challenges in a linear fashion. As Koocher and Rey-Casserly (2003) emphasized, the contexts before beginning psychological assessment often appear deceptively simple and uncomplicated, usually beginning with a referral by another professional or with a request for assessment by a client or guardian, followed by setting up an appointment for the same. Yet there are ethical issues involved, requiring conscious decision-making by the practitioner, which if left unresolved might jeopardize the scientific validity and reliability of assessment. Drawing from Koocher and Rey-Casserly (2003), it is pertinent to enlist some such issues that pose ethical dilemmas before beginning actual assessment.

1 Resolving conflicts of interest among the client and the authority or authorities making the referral, determining to whom the psychologist has an obligation to provide answers to questions regarding assessment, who has the right to influence the scope or method of assessment, and who should be provided an access to assessment reports and feedback, and to what extent.
2 Obtaining informed consent well before entering into an agreement to assess the client through an explicit procedure that should "explain the nature of the evaluation, clarify the referral questions, and discuss the goals of the assessment, in language the client can readily understand. It is also important to be aware of the limitations of the assessment procedures and discuss these procedures with the client. To the extent possible, the psychologist also should be mindful of the goals of the client, clarify misunderstandings, and correct unrealistic expectations" (Koocher & Rey-Casserly, 2003, p. 166).
3 Ensuring one's own competence in the specific area of assessment before agreeing to conduct it.
4 Planning the evaluation and clarifying the goals as well as limitations of assessment through an interactive process.
5 Critically evaluating the scientific validity and appropriateness of the psychological test or other tools before deciding to use these for a given assessment.
6 Judging the cultural and linguistic appropriateness of a test or tool for the particular client and using these in a careful and sensitive manner, allowing for linguistic or cultural constraints that might affect the individual's range of responses.
7 Ensuring applicability of the normative bases of the test to the client and using a suitable and updated version of the chosen psychological test.

Ethical issues that arise at the time of conducting of psychological assessment also find a prominent place in the discussion by Koocher and Rey-Casserly (2003). To summarize from their detailed discussion, such issues are:

1 Ensuring a conducive environment by making the test-taker physically and emotionally comfortable, monitoring for motivational issues or attempts at faking good or faking bad, and counterbalancing these by use of additional instruments or by appropriately discussing these limiting circumstances in the assessment report.
2 Considering the issue of allowing a third-party observer to be present during the assessment, gauging the impact this might have on the test performance, and deciding upon the matter in the best interests of the client.
3 Ensuring adherence to standard test administration procedures, especially when technicians or other non-psychologist staff are employed either to assist in the assessment or to conduct a part thereof.
4 Preparing a comprehensive written report based on the assessment, and spelling out the limitations and scope of assessment in a clear manner. Making available a written report to the client contingent upon payment of fee is not considered unethical *per se*, provided that the terms and conditions of payment have been clearly spelt out as a part of the consent process while agreeing to the assessment.
5 Providing a professional interpretation and analysis of the test scores that may have been generated by a computer program, making space for describing the impact of specific environmental and contextual conditions and human factors, and providing a contextualized interpretation for the particular case.

The responsibility of a psychologist, however, does not end with conducting of assessment and preparation of the report. Koocher and Rey-Casserly (2003) emphasized and discussed the pertinent questions that psychologists often have to face in post-assessment scenarios and the ethical concerns involved in resolving these. Such issues include:

1 Providing oral and/or written feedback including a copy of the test report to the client, unless the test context precludes this requirement. Even in the contexts where there are limitations on providing feedback to the client, for example in forensic testing, pre-employment testing or security screening, it is required that such limitations be spelt out to the client at the outset.
2 Dealing with requests for alteration or modification of reports, deciding upon the viability and need for such modifications, and maintaining a balance between protecting the rights of the client, ensuring her welfare, and remaining true to the scientific rigor and essence of assessment.
3 Releasing test data to a third party for re-evaluation after deciding upon the competence and right of the third party to have access to the data. Under accepted ethical norms, psychologists are required to exercise caution and ensure that only competent and qualified individuals are given access to the test data. A related concern is to maintain test security, as psychologists are obliged to take care that standardized tests do not fall into the hands of unauthorized and non-competent people.

APA Code of Ethics: General Principles

An important document that defines ethical standards for psychologists in various fields and ensures compliance is the American Psychological Association (APA) Code of Ethics. The APA published the first code of ethics in the year 1953, the latest code of ethics being published in the year 2002, and has been modified again in 2010. The APA Code features two distinct sections – General Principles and Ethical Standards. The general principles set aspirational standards of ethical behavior for psychologists, and the ethical standards provide specific and enforceable rules of ethical conduct. The code contains five general principles of ethical behavior. It is pertinent to discuss these with reference to the specific context of psychological assessment.

The first principle, that of *Beneficence and Non-maleficence*, asserts that psychologists need to maintain a balance between providing benefits in the best interest of the client, at the same time avoiding harm to the client. Beneficence implies a duty to improve the conditions of others through the use of one's professional knowledge and wisdom. The clause of "non- maleficence" puts the onus on the support professional to avoid or minimize any harm to the client. Originating from the Hippocratic Oath, the principle of non-maleficence calls for avoiding all acts that can potentially harm the client, and directs to minimize the effects in case any harm has been caused inadvertently or under unavoidable circumstances. The APA Code states thus, "Psychologists strive to benefit those with whom they work and take care to do no harm." Put in the context of psychological assessment, the principle of beneficence and non-maleficence translates into a responsibility on the shoulders of the psychologist conducting the assessment, beginning with determining the purpose of assessment, selection of appropriate methods and tools of assessment, obtaining informed consent through an interactive process, through to providing an optimally conducive environment to the client at the time of assessment, and providing a comprehensive assessment report. In this process the psychologist might face quite a few dilemmas. For example, in the cases where the person to be assessed is a minor or has a limited comprehension, making him unable to give informed consent, or where layers of authority are involved, it becomes a difficult question for the psychologist to determine who should be given access to assessment data, or who among the various people involved should be considered as acting in the best interest of the client. The psychologist might also face a conflict if the interests of the institution or organization for whom he/she works and the interests of the client are opposed to each other. The answer lies in an unflinching commitment on the part of the psychologist to scientific rigor of assessment and protecting the rights of the client under all circumstances. As Knapp and VandeCreek (2006) put it, a "remedial approach" to ethical behavior involving a bare minimum compliance with required ethical obligations often proves insufficient. What is required in resolving ethical dilemmas is a pro-active commitment to ethical standards by positively structuring one's professional behavior on ethical guidelines and aspirational standards.

The second ethical principle concerns *Fidelity and Responsibility.* Fidelity implies faithfulness of one human being to another (Ramsey, 2002). This includes keeping one's word, discharge and acceptance of responsibilities, and maintenance of relationships, including scientific, professional and teaching relationships. The APA Code states, "Psychologists establish relationships of trust with those with whom they work. They are aware of their professional and scientific responsibilities to society and to the specific communities in which they work." The fidelity of a psychologist is not only an obligation towards the client, but towards the profession and society too. The ethical principle of responsibility expects a psychologist to fulfill this by devoting his time and skills in the interest of social and non-profit purposes. A psychologist engaged in psychological assessment needs to adhere to ethical fidelity and responsibility by honoring the promises and contracts made with clients and professional colleagues; by consistent and responsible professional conduct and performance of duties; by keeping oneself professionally updated and progressively enhancing one's competence in the chosen field of psychological assessment; by not claiming professional expertise in an area in which one does not have competence and responsibly referring the client to an appropriate professional. Maintaining fidelity and responsibility is an important obligation and has a direct bearing on nurturing a professional relationship with the client. Not maintaining fidelity or engaging in irresponsible behavior not only harms the particular client, but also reflects upon the credibility and reliability of psychological assessment *per se*.

The third ethical principle of the APA Code for psychologists pertains to maintaining *Integrity* in professional matters. The code states "Psychologists seek to promote accuracy, honesty, and truthfulness in the science, teaching, and practice of psychology." Maintaining integrity requires the psychologist to refrain from stealing, cheating, engaging in fraud, subterfuge or intentional misrepresentation of facts, avoiding commitments that one would not be able to maintain, and to minimize use of deceptive techniques. In the context of psychological assessment, maintaining integrity translates into a proactive commitment to ensuring wellbeing of the client by being absolutely honest about one's professional competence and limitations, deciding upon the scope and nature of assessment required on the basis of an interactive process, conducting the assessment in a prescribed standard format, not compromising on the test data, and providing a holistic and comprehensible test interpretation. In the event of any conflict arising regarding assessment procedure or test data, the psychologist is obliged to cooperate with a qualified and competent professional in the overall interest of the client.

The fourth principle concerns ensuring equitable *Justice* to all clients. This means that a psychologist is obliged to treat all individuals with care and consistency, not discriminating on the basis of socioeconomic status, role or religion, and to guard against his/her own inadvertent prejudices in providing care to the clients. The APA Code states the principle thus: "Psychologists recognize that fairness and justice entitle all persons to access to and benefit from the contributions of psychology and to equal quality in the processes, procedures, and services being conducted by psychologists." A psychologist conducting assessment needs to be cognizant of his or her own potential biases and guard against the same. In conducting the testing, while interacting with the client s/he must adhere to the scientific procedures of testing and an unbiased interpretation of results. Commitment to justice also implies that the policies, procedures, and norms for scientific assessment remain consistent and reliable across clients and across time.

The fifth principle of ethical conduct propagated by the APA Code refers to ensuring *Respect for People's Rights and Dignity.* This implies being aware of "cultural, individual, and role differences, including those based on age, gender, gender identity, race, ethnicity, culture, national origin, religion, sexual orientation, disability, language, and socioeconomic status, and consider these factors when working with members of such groups." In the context of psychological assessment, it is absolutely essential for the assessor to be cognizant of these differences right from the beginning, and recognize that certain individuals might be especially vulnerable and would require sensitive handling due to their limitations in independent decision-making. The assessor also needs to actively guard against personal biases based on group identities which could creep into their professional work and affect the validity of assessment. A commitment to the right and dignity of the individual also implies that the client has all the right to know about the procedures and scope of assessment and the extent of personal information-sharing this might entail. Certain techniques of psychological assessment provide access to the unconscious psyche of the client, and the client needs to be informed of the potential of these techniques as part of the process of obtaining informed consent. Similarly, assurance about security of the test data and guarding the privacy of the client must be articulated as part of the ethical commitment of the assessor.

APA Code of Ethics: Ethical Standards of Assessment

Psychological assessment forms the core of psychological services across fields. The APA Code of Ethics recognizes the crucial role played by accurate assessment, and lays down specific and enforceable ethical standards to be followed in assessment practice and research. These are enlisted in APA Code 9 (Sections 9.01 to 9.11), incorporating different aspects of psychological assessment (see Table 30.1). Drawing from the APA Code, these are described briefly below.

Ethical Decision-Making

It is a prerequisite of professional competence for a psychologist to be aware of ethical standards of conduct in the chosen field of practice, yet it is a common understanding that mere awareness cannot and does not ensure ethical behavior. No code or ethical guideline can be comprehensive enough to serve as a ready-reckoner in order to deal with the myriad of decision dilemmas that occur in the course of professional practice. Any situation involving an ethical dilemma is unique in itself and there is hardly ever a ready-to-apply clause available in the professional ethical codes. A practitioner over the years, through dealing with a variety of cases, needs to evolve a method of decision-making that can be suitably modified and applied as per the needs of each unique situation.

Table 30.1 APA ethical standards regarding psychological assessment (adapted from APA, 2010)

Code	*Title*	*Brief description*
9.01	Bases of assessments	Providing opinions based on appropriate and adequate techniques, after conducting an examination of the individual, describing the limitations of their reports or recommendations, and if examination was not conducted, the context or reasons for that.
9.02	Use of assessments	Using assessment techniques in appropriate manner and for appropriate purposes in the light of research evidence. Using a test with appropriate norms, language and cultural sensitivity for the client.
9.03	Informed consent in assessments	Obtaining informed consent including an explanation of the nature and purpose of the assessment, fees, involvement of third parties, and limits of confidentiality, and sufficient opportunity for the client to ask questions and receive answers. Explaining about the issues in an understandable manner and language.
9.04	Release of test data	Releasing test data only to the client or an authorized representative, or as mandated by law in order to prevent any misuse or misrepresentation and to guard against compromising confidentiality.
9.05	Test construction	Using appropriate psychometric procedures and scientific knowledge for test construction, elimination of bias, and recommendations for use.
9.06	Interpreting assessment results	Providing interpretations in the context of assessment purposes, test factors, individual characteristics, factors affecting assessment accuracy, and limitations of assessment.
9.07	Assessment by unqualified persons	Not encouraging use of psychological assessment techniques by unqualified persons, except for training under supervision.
9.08	Obsolete tests and outdated test results	Not basing assessments, interventions, or recommendations on obsolete or outdated data or tests.
9.09	Test scoring and interpretation services	Providing accurate technical specifications of procedures for the services provided, choosing a service on the basis of sound technical information, and accepting personal responsibility for the appropriate application, interpretation and use of assessment tools even when using automated or other services.
9.10	Explaining assessment results	Reasonable efforts to provide explanations of results to the client or designated representative, barring certain specific contexts that preclude provision of an explanation.
9.11	Maintaining test security	Reasonable efforts to maintain security of testing materials (tests, manuals, instruments, protocols) in consistency with law and contractual obligations

Certain decision-making models to resolve ethical dilemmas have been proposed (e.g., Bond, 2000; Corey & Corey, 1998). Bond's ethical problem-solving model and Corey and Corey's ethical decision-making model have much in common and prescribe similar steps for the purpose. To summarize: (i) identifying and describing the problem or dilemma; (ii) considering the ethical guidelines, and their adequacy for dealing with the situation; (iii) determining whether consultation or guidance is needed; (iv) identifying all possible alternatives; (v) deciding upon the best alternatives, evaluating and implementing; (vi) evaluating the outcome. Along similar lines, Fisher (2009) has propagated a model for ethical decision-making, beginning with making a commitment to do what is ethically appropriate even before a dilemma arises, becoming familiar with the APA Code of Ethics and the prevalent law of the land, developing an empathetic understanding of the perspective of the parties involved, consulting with colleagues, generating and evaluating available alternatives, selecting and implementing a course of action that appears most ethically appropriate, and finally, monitoring and evaluating the consequences.

There is an abundance of approaches available to facilitate ethical decision-making that either recommend a thorough knowledge of ethical standards and adherence to them, or a high level of personal commitment to ethical conduct, or some combination of both in order to resolve decision-making dilemmas in situations of ethical conflict. The solution lies at the intersection of the two: the general aspirational principles of ethics, and specific enforceable standards of ethical conduct. It is desirable that while making professional decisions, psychologists remain consciously aware and wary of undesirable influences relying solely on scientific and professional knowledge; ensure that the chosen course of action is fair, just and impartial; are cognizant of the way the chosen course of action relates to the modalities of their roles and responsibilities in their area of competence; and make certain that the decisions are based on current and updated knowledge and data (Jeffrey, 2003).

Concluding Comments

Psychological assessment forms the core of professional practice and research in most fields of psychology. Accuracy and validity of assessment data is a crucial requirement upon which the credibility of varied psychological services rests. A psychologist engaged in assessment has access and holds power over personal and sensitive data of the client. Competence and integrity of the psychologist, or a lack thereof, can impact the client in irreparable ways. It is imperative that a strong commitment to ethical behavior is maintained under all circumstances. Despite the availability of elaborate professional guidelines and legal advisories, each situation needs to be considered on its own merits. Appreciating the specificities of each situation and empathetically understanding the needs of the client, along with a strong commitment to and thorough knowledge of professional ethics, appear to facilitate ethical decision-making under most circumstances.

References

Allport, G.W. (1937). *Personality: A Psychological Interpretation.* New York: Henry Holt & Company.

American Psychological Association. (2010). *Ethical principles of psychologists and code of conduct.* Retrieved from http://www.apa.org/ethics/code/principles.pdf

Bond, T. (2000). *Standards and Ethics for Counseling in Action* (2nd ed.). London: Sage.

Corey, M.S., & Corey, G. (1998). *Becoming a Helper* (3rd ed.). Pacific Grove, CA: Brooks/Cole.

Fisher, C.B. (2009). *Decoding the Ethics Code: A Practical Guide for Psychologists.* London: Sage.

Grove, W.M., Zald, D.H., Lebow, B.S., Snitz, B.E., & Nelson, C. (2000). Clinical versus mechanical prediction: A meta analysis. *Psychological Assessment, 12* (1), 19–30.

Jeffrey, M.A. (2003). *Interpreting Qualifying Modifiers: Implications for Ethical Decision Making.* Paper presented at the 111th Annual Conference of the American Psychological Association, Toronto, ON, Canada, August 7–10. Retrieved from http://0files.eric.ed.gov.opac.msmc.edu/fulltext/ED481013.pdf

Knapp, S., & VandeCreek, L. (2006). *Practical Ethics for Psychologists: A Positive Approach.* Washington, DC: American Psychological Association.

Koocher, G.P., & Rey-Casserly, C.M. (2003). Ethical issues in psychological assessment. In J.R. Graham, & J.A. Naglieri (Eds.), *Handbook of Psychology: Assessment Psychology* (Vol. *10*) (pp. 165–180). Hoboken, NJ: John Wiley & Sons, Inc.

Leong, F.T.L., Altmaier, E.M., & Johnson, B.D. (2008). *Encyclopaedia of Counseling* (Vol. *1*). Thousand Oaks, CA: Sage.

Nelson-Jones, R. (2002). *Essential Counseling and Therapy Skills: The Skilled Client Model.* London: Sage.

Ramsey, P. (2002). *The Patient as Person: Explorations in Medical Ethics* (2nd ed.). New Haven, CT: Yale University Press.

Society for Personality Assessment. (2006). Standards for education and training in psychological assessment: Position of the Society For Personality Assessment. *Journal of Personality Assessment, 87* (3), 355–357.

Index

Page numbers in *italics* refer to illustrations; those in **bold** refer to tables

The Wiley Handbook of Personality Assessment, First Edition. Edited by Updesh Kumar.

© 2016 John Wiley & Sons, Ltd. Published 2016 by John Wiley & Sons, Ltd.